Children's Literature Review

Guide to Gale Literary Criticism Series

When you need to review criticism of literary works, these are the Gale series to use:

If the author's death date is: **You should turn to:**

After Dec. 31, 1959
(or author is still living)

CONTEMPORARY LITERARY CRITICISM

for example: Jorge Luis Borges, Anthony Burgess,
William Faulkner, Mary Gordon,
Ernest Hemingway, Iris Murdoch

1900 through 1959

TWENTIETH-CENTURY LITERARY CRITICISM

for example: Willa Cather, F. Scott Fitzgerald,
Henry James, Mark Twain, Virginia Woolf

1800 through 1899

NINETEENTH-CENTURY LITERATURE CRITICISM

for example: Fedor Dostoevski, Nathaniel Hawthorne,
George Sand, William Wordsworth

1400 through 1799

LITERATURE CRITICISM FROM 1400 TO 1800 (excluding Shakespeare)

for example: Anne Bradstreet, Daniel Defoe,
Alexander Pope, François Rabelais,
Jonathan Swift, Phillis Wheatley

SHAKESPEAREAN CRITICISM

Shakespeare's plays and poetry

Antiquity through 1399

CLASSICAL AND MEDIEVAL LITERATURE CRITICISM

for example: Dante, Homer, Plato, Sophocles, Vergil,
the Beowulf Poet

Gale also publishes related criticism series:

CHILDREN'S LITERATURE REVIEW

This series covers authors of all eras who have written for
the preschool through high school audience.

SHORT STORY CRITICISM

This series covers the major short fiction writers of all nationalities
and periods of literary history.

ISSN 0362-4145

volume 22

Children's Literature Review

Excerpts from Reviews,
Criticism, and Commentary
on Books for Children
and Young People

Gerard J. Senick
Editor

Sharon R. Gunton
Associate Editor

Gale Research Inc. • *DETROIT* • *NEW YORK* • *LONDON*

STAFF

Gerard J. Senick, *Editor*

Sharon R. Gunton, *Associate Editor*

Jeanne A. Gough, *Permissions & Production Manager*
Linda M. Pugliese, *Production Supervisor*
Suzanne Powers, Maureen A. Puhl, Jennifer VanSickle, *Editorial Associates*
Donna Craft, Lorna Mabunda, James J. Wittenbach, *Editorial Assistants*

Victoria B. Cariappa, *Research Manager*
H. Nelson Fields, Judy L. Gale, Maureen Richards, *Editorial Associates*
Paula Cutcher, Alan Hedblad, Robin Lupa, Jill M. Ohorodnik, *Editorial Assistants*

Sandra C. Davis, *Permissions Supervisor (Text)*
Josephine M. Keene, Kimberly F. Smilay, *Permissions Associates*
Maria Franklin, Michele M. Lonoconus, Camille P. Robinson,
Shalice Shah, Denise M. Singleton, Rebecca A. Stanko, *Permissions Assistants*

Patricia A. Seefelt, *Permissions Supervisor (Pictures)*
Margaret A. Chamberlain, *Permissions Associate*
Pamela A. Hayes, Lillian Quickley, *Permissions Assistants*

Mary Beth Trimper, *Production Manager*
Evi Seoud, *Assistant Production Manager*

Arthur Chartow, *Art Director*
C. J. Jonik, *Keyliner*

Laura Bryant, *Production Supervisor*
Louise Gagné, *Internal Production Associate*
Yolanda Y. Latham, *Internal Production Assistant*

The paper used in this publication meets the minimum requirements of American National Standard for Information Sciences—Permanence Paper for Printed Library Materials, ANSI Z39.48-1984. ∞™

Copyright © 1991
Gale Research Inc.
835 Penobscot Bldg.
Detroit, MI 48226-4094

Library of Congress Catalog Card Number 76-643301
ISBN 0-8103-4646-X
ISSN 0362-4145

Printed in the United States of America

Published simultaneously in the United Kingdom
by Gale Research International Limited
(An affiliated company of Gale Research Inc.)

Contents

Preface

As children's literature has evolved into both a respected branch of creative writing and a successful industry, literary criticism has documented and influenced each stage of its growth. Critics have recorded the literary development of individual authors as well as the trends and controversies that resulted from changes in values and attitudes, especially as they concerned children. While defining a philosophy of children's literature, critics developed a scholarship that balances an appreciation of children and an awareness of their needs with standards for literary quality much like those required by critics of adult literature. *Children's Literature Review (CLR)* is designed to provide a permanent, accessible record of this ongoing scholarship. Those responsible for bringing children and books together can now make informed choices when selecting reading materials for the young.

Scope of the Series

Each volume of *CLR* contains excerpts from published criticism on the works of authors and illustrators who create books for children from preschool through high school. The author list for each volume is international in scope and represents the variety of genres covered by children's literature—picture books, fiction, nonfiction, poetry, folklore, and drama. The works of approximately twenty authors of all eras are represented in each volume. Although earlier volumes of *CLR* emphasized critical material published after 1960, successive volumes have expanded their coverage to encompass criticism written before 1960. Since many of the authors included in *CLR* are living and continue to write, it is necessary to update their entries periodically. Thus, future volumes will supplement the entries of selected authors covered in earlier volumes as well as include criticism on the works of authors new to the series.

Organization of the Book

An author section consists of the following elements: author heading, author portrait, author introduction, excerpts of criticism (each followed by a bibliographical citation), and illustrations, when available.

- The **author heading** consists of the author's name followed by birth and death dates. The portion of the name outside the parentheses denotes the form under which the author is most frequently published. If the majority of the author's works for children were written under a pseudonym, the pseudonym will be listed in the author heading and the real name given on the first line of the author introduction. Also located at the beginning of the introduction are any other pseudonyms used by the author in writing for children and any name variations, including transliterated forms for authors whose languages use nonroman alphabets. Uncertainty as to a birth or death date is indicated by question marks.

- An **author portrait** is included when available.

- The **author introduction** contains information designed to introduce an author to *CLR* users by presenting an overview of the author's themes and styles, occasional biographical facts that relate to the author's literary career or critical responses to the author's works, and information about major awards and prizes the author has received. Where applicable, introductions conclude with references to additional entries in biographical and critical reference series published by Gale Research Inc. These sources include past volumes of *CLR* as well as *Authors & Artists for Young Adults, Contemporary Authors, Contemporary Literary Criticism, Dictionary of Literary Biography, Nineteenth-Century Literature Criticism, Short Story Criticism, Something about the Author, Something about the Author Autobiography Series, Twentieth-Century Literary Criticism,* and *Yesterday's Authors of Books for Children.*

- **Criticism** is located in three sections: **author's commentary** and **general commentary** (when available) and within individual **title entries,** which are preceded by **title entry headings.** Criticism is arranged chronologically within each section. Titles by authors being profiled are highlighted in boldface type within the text for easier access by readers.

The **author's commentary** presents background material written by the author or by an interviewer. This commentary may cover a specific work or several works. Author's commentary on more than one work appears after the author introduction, while commentary on an individual book follows the title entry heading.

The **general commentary** consists of critical excerpts that consider more than one work by the author or illustrator being profiled. General commentary is preceded by the critic's name in boldface type or, in the case of unsigned criticism, by the title of the journal. Occasionally, *CLR* features entries that emphasize general criticism on the overall career of an author or illustrator. When appropriate, a selection of reviews is included to supplement the general commentary.

Title entry headings precede the criticism on a title and cite publication information on the work being reviewed. Title headings list the title of the work as it appeared in its first English-language edition. The first English-language publication date of each work is listed in parentheses following the title. Differing U.S. and British titles follow the publication date within the parentheses.

Title entries consist of critical excerpts on the author's individual works, arranged chronologically by publication date. The entries generally contain two to six reviews per title, depending on the stature of the book and the amount of criticism it has generated. The editors select titles that reflect the entire scope of the author's literary contribution, covering each genre and subject. An effort is made to reprint criticism that represents the full range of each title's reception—from the year of its initial publication to current assessments. Thus, the reader is provided with a record of the author's critical history. Publication information (such as publisher names and book prices) and parenthetical numerical references (such as footnotes or page and line references to specific editions of works) have been deleted at the editor's discretion to provide smoother reading of the text.

Entries on authors who are also illustrators will occasionally feature commentary on selected works illustrated but not written by the author being profiled. These works are strongly associated with the illustrator and have received critical acclaim for their art. By including critical comment on works of this type, the editors wish to provide a more complete representation of the author's total career. Criticism on these works has been chosen to stress artistic, rather than literary, contributions. Title entry headings for works illustrated by the author being profiled are arranged chronologically within the entry by date of publication and include notes identifying the author of the illustrated work. In order to provide easier access for users, all titles illustrated by the subject of the entry will be boldfaced.

CLR also includes entries on prominent illustrators who have contributed to the field of children's literature. These entries are designed to represent the development of the illustrator as an artist rather than as a literary stylist. The illustrator's section is organized like that of an author, with two exceptions: the introduction presents an overview of the illustrator's styles and techniques rather than outlining his or her literary background, and the commentary written by the illustrator on his or her works is called illustrator's commentary rather than author's commentary. Title entry headings are followed by explanatory notes identifying the author of the illustrated work. All titles of books containing illustrations by the artist being profiled as well as individual illustrations from these books are highlighted in boldface type.

• Selected excerpts are preceded by **explanatory notes,** which provide information on the critic or work of criticism to enhance the reader's understanding of the excerpt.

• A complete **bibliographical citation** designed to facilitate the location of the original book or article follows each piece of criticism.

• Numerous **illustrations** are featured in *CLR*. For entries on illustrators, an effort has been made to include illustrations that reflect the characteristics discussed in the criticism. Entries on major authors who do not illustrate their own works may also include photographs and other illustrative material pertinent to the authors' careers.

Other Features

• An **acknowledgments,** which immediately follows the preface, lists the sources from which material has been reprinted in the volume. It does not, however, list every book or periodical consulted for the volume.

• The **cumulative index to authors** lists authors who have appeared in *CLR* and includes cross-references to *Authors & Artists for Young Adults, Contemporary Authors, Contemporary Literary Criticism, Dictionary of Literary Biography, Nineteenth-Century Literature Criticism, Short Story Criticism, Something about the Author, Something about the Author Autobiography Series, Twentieth-Century Literary Criticism,* and *Yesterday's Authors of Books for Children.*

- The **cumulative nationality index** lists authors alphabetically under their respective nationalities. Author names are followed by the volume number(s) in which they appear. Authors who have changed citizenship or whose current citizenship is not reflected in biographical sources appear under both their original nationality and that of their current residence.

- The **cumulative title index** lists titles covered in *CLR* followed by the volume and page number where criticism begins.

A Note to the Reader

When writing papers, students who quote directly from any volume in the Literature Criticism Series may use the following general forms to footnote reprinted criticism. The first example pertains to material drawn from periodicals, the second to material reprinted from books.

[1]T. S. Eliot, "John Donne," *The Nation and the Athenaeum,* 33 (9 June 1923), 321-32; excerpted and reprinted in *Literature Criticism from 1400 to 1800,* Vol. 10, ed. James E. Person, Jr. (Detroit: Gale Research, 1989), pp. 28-9.

[1]Henry Brooke, *Leslie Brooke and Johnny Crow* (Frederick Warne, 1982); excerpted and reprinted in *Children's Literature Review,* Vol. 20, ed. Gerard J. Senick (Detroit: Gale Research, 1990), p. 47.

Suggestions Are Welcome

In response to various suggestions, several features have been added to *CLR* since the series began, including author entries on retellers of traditional literature as well as those who have been the first to record oral tales and other folklore; entries on prominent illustrators featuring commentary on their styles and techniques; entries on authors whose works are considered controversial or have been challenged; occasional entries devoted to criticism on a single work by a major author; explanatory notes that provide information on the critic or work of criticism to enhance the usefulness of the excerpt; more extensive illustrative material, such as holographs of manuscript pages and photographs of people and places pertinent to the authors' careers; a cumulative nationality index for easy access to authors by nationality; and occasional guest essays written specifically for *CLR* by prominent critics on subjects of their choice.

Readers who wish to suggest authors to appear in future volumes, or who have other suggestions, are cordially invited to write the editor.

Acknowledgments

The editors wish to thank the copyright holders of the excerpted criticism included in this volume, the permissions managers of many book and magazine publishing companies for assisting us in securing reprint rights, and Anthony Bogucki for assistance with copyright research. We are also grateful to the staffs of the Detroit Public Library, the Library of Congress, the University of Detroit Library, Wayne State University Purdy/Kresge Library Complex, and the University of Michigan Libraries for making their resources available to us. Following is a list of the copyright holders who have granted us permission to reprint material in this volume of *CLR*. Every effort has been made to trace copyright, but if omissions have been made, please let us know.

COPYRIGHTED EXCERPTS IN *CLR*, VOLUME 22, WERE REPRINTED FROM THE FOLLOWING PERIODICALS:

The African Studies Review, v. XIX, September, 1976. Reprinted by permission of the publisher.—*American Artist,* v. 26, May, 1962. Copyright © 1962 by Billboard Publications, Inc. Reprinted by permission of the publisher.—*Appraisal: Children's Science Books,* v. 2, Fall, 1969; v. 4, Winter, 1971; v. 5, Fall, 1972; v. 8, Spring, 1975; v. 15, Fall, 1982; v. 16, Winter, 1983; v. 18, Winter, 1985; v. 20, Spring, 1987; v. 21, Fall, 1988; v. 23, Winter, 1990. Copyright © 1969, 1971, 1972, 1975, 1982, 1983, 1985, 1987, 1988, 1990 by the Children's Science Book Review Committee. All reprinted by permission of the publisher.—*The Atlantic Monthly,* v. 180, December, 1947 for a review of "Little Eddie" by Jane Cobb and Helen Dore Boylston. Copyright 1947 by The Atlantic Monthly Company, Boston, MA. Reprinted by permission of the Literary Estates of Jane Cobb Berry and Helen Dore Boylston.—*Best Sellers,* v. 35, December, 1975. Copyright © 1975 Helen Dwight Reid Educational Foundation. Reprinted by permission of the publisher.—*The Book Report,* v. 4, January-February, 1986; v. 5, September-October, 1986. © copyright 1986 Linworth Publishing Co. Both reprinted by permission of the publisher.—*Book Week—New York Herald Tribune,* November 3, 1963; December 29, 1963. © 1963, *The Washington Post.* Both reprinted by permission of the publisher.—*Book Week,* v. 8, Spring, 1981. © 1981 S.C.B.A. and contributors. Reprinted by permission of the publisher.—*Book World—Chicago Tribune,* May 5, 1968 for a review of "The Endless Steppe: Growing Up in Siberia" by Polly Goodwin. © 1968 Postrib Corp. Reprinted by permission of *The Washington Post* and the author./ May 4, 1969 for "Catching Essences with Pictures and Words" by Virginia Haviland. © 1969 Postrib Corp. Reprinted by permission of *The Washington Post* and the Literary Estate of Virginia Haviland.- *Book World—The Washington Post,* May 19, 1974; March 8, 1981; March 14, 1982; May 8, 1988. © 1974, 1981, 1982, 1988, *The Washington Post.* All reprinted by permission of the publisher.—*Bookbird,* v. VII, March 15, 1969; v. VII, June 15, 1969; v. IX, September 15, 1971; September 15, 1988. All reprinted by permission of the publisher.—*Booklist,* v. 73, December 15, 1976; v. 74, October 1, 1977; v. 75, November 15, 1978; v. 75, December 1, 1978; v. 75, May 15, 1979; v. 76, September 15, 1979; v. 76, December 1, 1979; v. 76, December 15, 1979; v. 77, March 15, 1981; v. 77, May 1, 1981; v. 77, July 15/August 1981; v. 78, September 15, 1981; v. 78, December 15, 1981; v. 78, May 15, 1982; v. 79, March 15, 1983; v. 79, June 15, 1983; v. 80, September 1, 1983; v. 80, March 1, 1984; v. 81, October 15, 1984; v. 81, January 15, 1985; v. 82, January 15, 1986; v. 82, June 1, 1986; v. 82, July, 1986; v. 83, September 15, 1986; v. 83, February 1, 1987; v. 83, June 1, 1987; v. 84, September 15, 1987; v. 84, October 15, 1987; v. 84, December 15, 1987; v. 85, September 1, 1988; v. 85, December 1, 1988; v. 85, March 15, 1989; v. 85, May 15, 1989; v. 86, October 1, 1989; v. 86, October 15, 1989. Copyright © 1976, 1977, 1978, 1979, 1981, 1982, 1983, 1984, 1985, 1986, 1987, 1988, 1989 by the American Library Association. All reprinted by permission of the publisher.—*The Booklist,* v. 66, January 1, 1970; v. 71, April 1, 1975; v. 72, December 15, 1975. Copyright © 1970, 1975 by the American Library Association. All reprinted by permission of the publisher.—*The Booklist and Subscription Books Bulletin,* v. 64, June 1, 1968. Copyright © 1968 by the American Library Association. Reprinted by permission of the publisher.—*Books in Canada,* v. 12, February, 1983 for a review of "Up to Low" by Mary Ainslie Smith. Reprinted by permission of the author.—*Books for Keeps,* n. 46, September, 1987; n. 50, May, 1988; n. 53, November, 1988; n. 59, November, 1989. © School Bookshop Association 1987, 1988, 1989. All reprinted by permission of the publisher.—*Books for Young People,* v. 2, October, 1988 for "'Easy Avenue' Is Vintage Doyle" by Eva Martin. All rights reserved. All reprinted by permission of the publisher and the respective authors.—*Books for Your Children,* v. 13, Autumn, 1978. © *Books for Your Children.* Reprinted by permission of the publisher.—*Bulletin of the Center for Children's Books,* v. XV, January, 1962; v. XVI, September, 1962; v. XVI, November, 1962; v. XVII, November, 1963; v. XVII, January, 1964; v. XVII, March, 1964; v. XVIII, April, 1965; v. 22, October, 1968; v. 22, March, 1969; v. 23, June, 1970; v. 24, November, 1970; v. 26, September, 1972; v. 26, November, 1972; v. 26, February, 1973; v. 27, February, 1974; v. 27, April, 1974; v. 27, June, 1974; v. 27, July-August, 1974; v. 28, September, 1974; v. 29, October, 1975; v. 29, July-August, 1976; v. 30, December, 1976; v. 30, April, 1977; v. 30, July-August, 1977; v. 31, November 3, 1977; v. 33, September, 1979; v. 33, December, 1979; v. 33, February, 1980; v. 34, September, 1980; v. 34, November, 1980; v. 35, September, 1981; v. 35, October, 1981; v. 35, February, 1982; v. 35, April, 1982; v. 36, March, 1983; v. 36, May, 1983; v. 37, October, 1983; v. 38, December, 1984; v. 38, July-August, 1985; v. 39, March, 1986; v. 39, May, 1986; v. 39, June, 1986; v. 40, March, 1987; v. 40, June, 1987; v. 40, July- August, 1987; v. 41,

COPYRIGHTED EXCERPTS IN *CLR,* VOLUME 22, WERE REPRINTED FROM THE FOLLOWING BOOKS:

Children's
Literature
Review

Graeme Base

1958-

English-born Australian author and illustrator of picture books.

Lauded as an gifted and especially inventive artist who is a virtuoso of graphic design, Base is the creator of picture books for older readers which are considered fascinating and exciting both in text and illustration. Regarded as innovative and technically accomplished as both a conceptualist and a painter, he invests his works, characteristically puzzle books which challenge the reader's powers of observation and appeal to his or her delight in wordplay, with warmth, enthusiasm, and humor. Although the difficulty of his books is acknowledged, observers generally concur that the answers Base provides for his riddles are within the scope of most children. He is best known as the author and illustrator of *Animalia* (1986), an oversize book which represents the letters of the alphabet with sophisticated texts which include such elements as alliteration and tongue twisters and detailed, intricate single and double-page illustrations which, in addition to representing the animals which provide their focus, incorporate over 1500 objects such as food, musical instruments, and characters from literature, mythology, and popular culture, all of which have names which begin with the letter being addressed. Intending the book as a game for readers to find as many items as possible, *Animalia* became a best seller in Australia, where a prize was given to the person who could identify the most objects. Other contests were later held in England and Canada, and the book is currently considered a cult classic in Australia.

Base followed *Animalia* with a mystery story in a similar format, *The Eleventh Hour* (1988). In this work, which was published in Britain at eleven minutes after eleven on the eleventh day of the eleventh month, an elephant celebrating his eleventh birthday with ten other animals discovers that his banquet is missing. Base's rhyming text lets readers know that the clues to the identity of the thief are in both the opulent pictures, which incorporate ciphers, puzzles, and hidden objects, and the coded message with which *The Eleventh Hour* concludes. The solution to the mystery is contained in a sealed section in the back of the book which also provides Base's explanations for the clues and puzzles in his illustrations. Base is also the author and illustrator of *My Grandma Lived in Gooligulch* (1983), a humorous tale tale in verse about spirited Grandma, who entertains and travels on a variety of animals from the Australian bush before disappearing into the sea; illustrated in sepia-toned line drawings and colorful double-page spreads, *Grandma* also serves to introduce primary graders to the wildlife of Australia. Praised as a superior illustrator whose work in pencil, watercolor, colored ink, and airbrush is successful in a variety of styles, Base also created a wall frieze based on *Animalia* and has provided the pictures for works by Lewis Carroll and Max Dann. Base received the Australian Children's Book of the Year Award picture book honor in 1987 for *Animalia*. He won the latter award for picture book of the year in 1989 for

The Eleventh Hour, a work which was also highly commended by the Australian Book Publishers' Association in 1988 for their Book Design Awards.

AUTHOR'S COMMENTARY

I never meant to be an author. I never meant to make picture books either. What I always wanted to do was draw and paint and construct things that appealed to my sense of aesthetics and satisfied a strong desire to create. (pp. 8-9)

Out of college, with a Diploma of Art under my arm, I dutifully found myself a job in the whacky world of advertising, something that actually was on my list of things I meant to do. And I hated it. This came as quite a shock after years of telling people I was going to be a commercial artist when I grew up (I thought it sounded good). In fact it turned out to be a most frustrating and creatively inhibiting experience, though I recognise it taught me a lot about deadlines and putting up with the tough slog where necessary. . . .

Most evenings I had been working on paintings for myself after mucking up yet another ad for radial tyres or cheap pine furniture at the advertising agency during the day, and amongst the various illustrations I had in the folio were a couple of half-baked ideas for childrens' books.

There was one idea in particular I was quite enthusiastic about—a Fieldguide to Dragons of the World. Dragons have always held a fascination for me—in fact I suspect they are a symbol of my inclination to invent rather than portray. Back in college I tried to turn every project into a fantasy illustration, and if it could be twisted to include a dragon or two, so much the better. I received a fair bit of flack for this.

Two or three years later, when I presented my Dragon Book to various Melbourne publishers, I found that things had not changed. But I received encouragement from the then childrens' book publisher at Thomas Nelson, Bob Sessions. He didn't much like my dragons either but he told me to go away and do something Australian if I had a mind to. He may have been just trying to get rid of me, but I took him at his word and returned six months later with half a dozen illustrations centred on Australian animals and a complete poem called **"My Grandma lived in Gooligulch"**. I hadn't written a poem since I was in school—don't know what came over me really—but Bob was so surprised to see me back he said he would publish it.

I had had a fairly unhappy experience about a year earlier illustrating a book for another author. I enjoyed the story very much but encountered problems of interpretation (my idea of the characters was nothing like the way the author had envisaged them) resulting eventually in a set of drawings which had been reworked three or four times. No one liked them, least of all me, but they were published anyway. This was what spurred me on to try and write my own texts; *Grandma* was the first.

It sold reasonably well, encouraging the publishers to ask if I would like to do another one, and leading me into a ludicrous project that was to take up three years of my new career; an alphabet book of all things. Who needs another alphabet book? If I had stopped to think about it for fifteen seconds I would never have started but it was what I wanted to do, and that was sufficient.

During the next three years I often came to my senses and told myself to either get the thing finished or just give it away and do something sensible like a book on trucks or dinosaurs or something but I persevered and eventually the book was published under the title of *Animalia.* I thought up the title at the very last minute and it was months later that I discovered it was Latin for "Animal Kingdom". It could hardly have been better.

It was a surprise to everyone involved when *Animalia* began to sell. . . . What had happened? Why was this book finding such a response with the reading public? Naturally I was very keen to find the answers to these questions!

Eventually I came up with a theory. I had followed my creative nose with *Animalia,* disregarding all but the strongest suggestions from the publishers regarding alterations to artwork or text, in pursuit of a result that range absolutely true (or as close as possible) to my initial vision of the pictures. I used sophisticated language, I included obscure visual and literary jokes purely to amuse myself,

I ran amok in a world of my own making where I need only answer to my own creativity. What an extraordinarily self-indulgent work! What a selfish way to create a "children's book". And how very sensible it seems to me.

I am my own audience. If I am happy with a picture, a verse, a concept, that is enough. If other people, regardless of age, find a common thread in my work with their own ideas of fun, aesthetics and style, that is an added bonus. And that is the way I work. I count myself incredibly lucky to be doing exactly what I want, and getting feedback from many other people for my efforts. If the feedback stops, though, it doesn't mean I change my ideas. It just means that the happy coincidence of creative integrity coexisting with popular appeal has, for the time being, finished. It would be a mistake to chase it. (p. 9)

Graeme Base, "Dragons, Draaks and Beasties," in Reading Time, *Vol. 34, No. 1, 1990, pp. 8-9.*

GENERAL COMMENTARY

Toss Gascoigne

[Graeme Base] worked his way into writing and illustrating books obliquely. . . .

Writing for his own illustrations came to him rather by accident. It began with *My Grandma lived in Gooligulch,* an original poem which to his surprise was accepted by publishers, and for which he later did the illustrations.

Does he write easily? "Poetry is a really pleasurable experience. I'm very much into music, and in fact I'd much rather be a musician than an artist. The satisfaction from doing pictures is quite removed—it's a cool satisfaction, whereas with music it's passion and it's immediate and it's fantastically exciting!

"I'm now writing instrumental music which I'd like to think could be used in television or films, quite atmospheric stuff. Music has not been kind to me financially—but I'd love to move into music and out of books." . . .

The poetry follows on easily from his music. "The poetry is very rhythmic and quite strictly structured, as my music is."

His technique is simple—he just sits and writes. Sometimes a project overtakes him, and when he was writing *Animalia,* he found himself dreaming of things which began with particular letters. "It started to fill my mind, because I was working on the damn thing for three years and sometimes it became quite obsessive.

With *The Eleventh Hour* I had a very strong concept of wanting to do a mystery story. I did the rough illustrations first, very small detailed pencil drawings while we were travelling Europe, and always influenced by the things we were seeing—architecturally and artistically.

"It was only when all those were totally finished that I got back to England and spent three weeks sitting on a couch, streaming with hay fever and writing the verse to match the pictures. But always I was able to have the feeling, 'Oh, this is a terrific bit of verse here. I'll change the picture to fit.'

From Animalia, *written and illustrated by Graeme Base.*

"The concept was very strong, and I had already worked out how the mystery was going to unfold, who did it, and how it could be solved. All the codes I would think up as I went along."

The Eleventh Hour took two years. He says he had it incredibly well planned, and the black and white roughs—on a sketch pad bought in Barcelona—are almost identical to the finished art work. Each page can be identified with a European city. (p. 21)

[There] are influences from the Uffizi Gallery in Florence, St Peter's in Rome, and the ballroom comes from Salzburg where Mozart used to play. . . .

Is [Base] a wordsmith, a crossword puzzler, a cryptologist? "I got out a book from the library just to discover different types of codes. If I was confronted with a code I would work very hard to try and solve it. In ***Animalia*** there is a display of interest in words—the alliteration you have to delve into. And at school I did invent a language with a friend. It was called Lorgish, and based very much on *Lord of the Rings.*" . . .

He works in Derwent pencils, water colour, coloured inks, "and a bit of white paint for emergencies." And as well, there is that indispensable air-brush.

The next Base project to come to fruition is to be a calendar called **"Dragons, Draaks and Beasties,"** which he has

illustrated with "twelve of the more popular dragons". . . .

What has he learned from all his books so far? . . .

"Oh, well . . . (long pause) I don't think I've learned anything much. Except that this is a really pleasant job. And that some of my theories about books for kids are right. One thing you should never do is talk down to kids." He insisted on maintaining the complicated language of ***Animalia,*** and argued that if children did not understand the words, they could enjoy the pictures.

What is the appeal of his books? "As a child, I used to like books where you had to look very closely and find things. *Animalia* is familiar, but it's an adventure because there are new things to be found every time." (p. 22)

> *Toss Gascoigne, "Know the Author: Graeme Base," in* Magpies, *Vol. 4, No. 4, September, 1989, pp. 20-2.*

My Grandma Lived in Gooligulch (1983)

An Australian import that celebrates the continent's wildlife with a fantastic tale about Grandma's life "nowhere much near anywhere / That shows up on the map."

In rollicking doggerel well-seasoned with place and animal names, Base details Grandma's house, "a jumbled maze of tin and canvas, / Bits of string and wood," where she entertains the rambunctious beasts till the day she flies via pelican to the sea—and then disappears on her blow-up horse while her friend the wombat sleeps.

Though the verse is forced (and not as funny as it might be) and the detailed sepia drawings accompanying it seem flat and static, the alternating textless double-spreads bring the creatures and their antics—in both natural and unnatural habitats—to three-dimensional life in richly glowing colors. There is a key to 22 of these animals on the endpapers; they're probably worth the price of the book. (pp. 1729-30)

> *A review of "My Grandma Lived in Gooligulch," in* Kirkus Reviews, *Vol. LV, No. 24, December 15, 1987, pp. 1729-30.*

Base provides readers with one of the best introductions to the fauna of the Australian bush. A myriad of exotic animals participate in the frolic of the story alongside the enterprising Grandma. Although his bestselling extravaganza ***Animalia*** won Base a reputation for pictorial skill, this, on the whole, is a better book; there is as much wit and humor in the rhyming text as there is mastery and opulence in the illustrations.

> *A review of "My Grandma Lived in Gooligulch," in* Publishers Weekly, *Vol. 233, No. 10, March 11, 1988, p. 101.*

Tall tales should start from a believable base, and Grandma is sufficiently eccentric and spirited to convince readers that she just might ride a kangaroo around town and dine with emus. Children will be delighted by her many strange adventures, shared with a menagerie of Australian animals, in this beautifully illustrated story-poem. Best known for ***Animalia,*** Base alternates between subdued sepia-toned line drawings and richly colored, very detailed illustrations that burst the boundaries of oversized, double-page layouts. Realism and exaggeration are blended almost perfectly and complement the poem's humor. This is a good choice for group use, as children will enjoy trying to find Grandma in several scenes. Certainly not an essential purchase, but a fun way to meet Australia's unique animals and an exciting new illustrator.

> *Jeanette Larson, in a review of "My Grandma Lived in Gooligulch," in* School Library Journal, *Vol. 35, No. 8, May, 1988, p. 76.*

Animalia (1986)

Animalia is first and foremost a dazzling work of art. In one sense, it could be described as an alphabet book opening with the armadillo and closing with the zebra. But such a simplistic account belies the richly imaginative visual and verbal play of *Animalia.* Take one wonderfully alliterative tongue twister as an example: "Crafty crimson cats carefully catching crusty crayfish" compelling the eye to quickly note, on this very large double-page spread, countless objects beginning with the letter "c". And so the visual game begins, doubly enhanced when the familiar is juxtaposed defying time, space, perspective and all that the rational mind expects.

If it were not difficult enough to spot all the innumerable objects (animals and musical instruments in abundance) in each illustration (and the publishers claim at least 1,500 objects are to be found), there is the additional taunt to spot Graeme Base when young, garbed in distinctive clothes and appearing in each illustration for the twenty-six letters.

So in this one book, both visual and verbal skills are required. The tools to unlocking this intricate puzzle?—a magnifying glass (not essential, but handy for spotting the adventuresome Graeme) and a dictionary to check spelling. Animal and mythological dictionaries would be an added advantage. (pp. 23-4)

Other than more animals imaginable in a single thirty-two page book, and numerous musical instruments, there are appetite teasers: ice cream, cake, donuts, even Australian Minties, and a parade of literary familiars: King Kong, Frankenstein, Superman, Zorro and even Noddy. And these are just the beginning. Watch, too, for the small visual jokes such as the artist's own etching on a column, "GB woz 'ere '85".

There is little to criticise in this sumptuous book. Perhaps one could be less appreciative when a pair of letters (such as "n and o" or "t and u") are illustrated on a single page. Here there is a disappointing lack of detail anticipated from earlier illustrations and the inevitable competition between two visuals vying for attention. These pages pale in comparison to the seven magnificent double-page spreads which allow animals to loom large in the foreground with surroundings lavished with intricate detail, yet still offering a satisfying composition. Single-page illustrations of a single letter occasionally jar when the opposite page dramatically changes colour scheme or setting. The artist most successfully overcomes this problem by using a similar framing device with surrounding white

space to suggest a division while still achieving an harmonious relationship. These are only small points, however, certainly open to differences of opinion.

So sparkling, luminous and clear are the transparent watercolours (undiluted from the tube) that the effect is breathtaking. Each turn of the page is visually exciting. (pp. 24-5)

Animalia is a book for anyone who enjoys artistic virtuosity and countless hours of pleasure. And it is one of those books you simply must share with your friends, both young and old. . . . *Animalia* is one of the best books for 1986 and for the foreseeable future. (p. 25)

> *Belle Alderman, in a review of "Animalia," in* Reading Time, *Vol. 31, No. 1, 1987, pp. 23-5.*

This Australian import makes for a delightful visual feast, though it lacks a clear conceptual coherence or unity of action or meaning on every page. No matter—readers will have a fine time guessing at objects and searching for a small child who hides among the pages; and the meticulous artistry is far-reaching in its innovation, detail and humor. Base's monumental effort will not go unrewarded; if books could be honored for the sheer number of hours readers could pore over crammed pages, and for the inexhaustible supply of extra touches, this one surely would be a winner.

> *A review of "Animalia," in* Publishers Weekly, *Vol. 232, No. 11, September 11, 1987, p. 88.*

Following the pattern of the popular 'Ultimate Alphabet', *Animalia* crams its king-size pages with striking and original colour illustrations, each packed with animals and objects beginning with a letter of the alphabet; huge creatures, some mythical, most real, rub shoulders with tiny artifacts. The aim of the game is not only to revel in the riot of colour and artistry but also to spot as many items as possible. So, for example, a magnificent peacock dominates the P page but tucked away are a pine cone and a periscope, the Parthenon and the Leaning Tower of Pisa, Pegasus and Pan, a piano and a poodle, to name but a few . . . and Graeme Base himself as a boy is hidden away on every page.

A best seller in Australia where it was first published, *Animalia* threatens to become addictive. Three years work by the artist has produced a book which combines beauty with inventiveness, talent with teasing, elegance with entertainment, richness with artistic virtuosity.

> *G. Bott, in a review of "Animalia," in* The Junior Bookshelf, *Vol. 52, No. 1, February, 1988, p. 17.*

I've come a year late to the book I'd most like to give an Infant this Christmas—*Animalia* by Graeme Base—but catching up with it has been a great pleasure. An important attribute for a book in this age group is being big enough for two laps, for sharing: and if the sharing is to be genuine the book has to have something other than reflected pleasure in it for the adult. *Animalia* will be grabbed by both parties—with its alliterative artwork, its pages and double spreads of invention in a variety of styles, and its game of I-Spy leading to what the dreaded SRA people would be tempted to call 'word power boosting potential'. The real point is that after looking through this book the world is seen through new eyes—of the closely observing kind.

Bernard Ashley, in a review of "Animalia," in Books for Keeps, *No. 53, November, 1988, p. 28.*

The Eleventh Hour   (1988)

Like *Animalia, The Eleventh Hour* has much to look at, much to hunt for, and, while it carries a story, it is also a problem to solve. A group of animals attend a party and while they play games the feast disappears. It must be one of the guests and it is up to the reader to discover who it is.

There are clues galore, some are red-herrings, some will lead the reader to the solution. Each picture, within a wealth of detail, hides much. There are codes, ciphers, puzzles, hidden objects—each page uses a different means to protect the hidden information. What is more there are several different means by which readers may find the answer, so if one means is too difficult they can always use another.

The appeal of the book should be very wide. Whereas the younger child would find solving the puzzle too difficult, the story is enjoyable enough on its own, and the animals are a delight, all, as they are, in fancy dress for the party. And there is lots of action in the games they play, and lots of detail in the backgrounds that will absorb for hours.

The codes are probably most appropriate for the child somewhere around the eleven years old mark, although many will solve much of it before that age, but for full appreciation of the manipulation of language the reader needs to be that bit older. But it is certainly one of those age-free books that has appeal to all who pick it up.

While the puzzle is an involved and involving one, the author has made sure that it is not a frustrating one and that it can be solved without giving up in despair as works such a *Masquerade* caused many readers to do and that took such a long time for anyone to succeed with. Of course, *Masquerade* was intended to be very difficult; *The Eleventh Hour* is meant to be solved. For those who have problems in the normal manner there is a means included on the last page by which they may find the solution.

Graeme Base has considered the success of *Animalia* very carefully and analysed this success to discover just what it was that gave it such an appeal: the delight of finding more and more items in illustrations, the fun in language play, the large size enabling such a marvellous amount of detail in the illustrations so that there is always more to look at. I believe he has exceeded the previous book in incorporating all the elements into a very satisfying whole.

The fun of *The Eleventh Hour* does not end at the solution. The reader will find endless pleasure in going back over the illustrations and discovering more and more clues that were previously missed. I was amazed at how much has actually been included; there is far, far more than is needed, but this adds to the fun. And what is more, once the solution is gained, that reveals another diversion to entertain the reader for many more hours. The solution is not the end.

Alf Mappin, in a review of "The Eleventh Hour," in Magpies, *Vol. 3, No. 5, November, 1988, p. 4.*

Graeme Base had his work cut out after *Animalia.* Remember that? It was an alphabet-book—not, perhaps, the most promising of popular ventures for an artistic debut yet the combination of the exuberant Base captions and his highly-detailed, flairful draughtsmanship met with astonishing success. Who could forget H, for instance . . .

> Horribly Hairy Hogs Hurrying
> Homewards on Heavily
> Harnessed Horses

. . . with hogs and horses erupting from the page like illuminations that have taken over the manuscript. . . .

What next, then, for Graeme Base?

Not another *Animalia* that's for sure. 'People said "now you've got to do numbers" ' he's reported as saying. 'But I couldn't work to that sort of formula.' Instead, he's come up with *The Eleventh Hour.* . . . Again, his target is the whole family. He describes *The Eleventh Hour* as 'an Agatha Christie-type mystery in pictures'. But with no murders, let it be said. . . .

[The] illustration is lavish and the Base invention boundless: there are codes and ciphers to be cracked, margins to be explored, red herrings to be identified, hidden objects to be discovered. According to the author, the mystery can be explained in at least four or five quite different ways.

And here we'd better pause a moment. There are those for whom this kind of conundrum normally cuts no ice at all. I know, because I'm one of them. For instance, the national *Masquerade* mania unleashed a few years ago by Kit Williams completely passed me by. I took note of it as a phenomenon—hard to miss it when clever kids at my school spent hours poring over each double-spread—but for me the attraction was nil. If *The Eleventh Hour* struck the same cryptic note, I'd be stonily indifferent.

But it doesn't and, much to my surprise, I'm not. There are two reasons for this, perhaps. Firstly, Graeme Base's approach to illustration—painterly and meticulous though it is—offers much more than a merely technical accomplishment. It's warm, funny, full of enthusiasm and offers a range of sympathy that's extraordinarily broad. At one pole we have his animal characters themselves, genuine picture-book creations with none of the record-sleeve coldness of the book's distinguished predecessor. At the other pole, there's the Base feel for background—almost every spread hints at a famous setting: the Uffizi in Florence, St Peter's in Rome, the ballroom in Salzburg where Mozart used to play . . . if you miss them, no matter. If you don't, a lovely bonus.

Secondly, and just as important, the answer to the riddle really is within the scope of most readers. You're *intended* to share it. When the text says . . .

> But in the end, although the thief
> was someone they all knew,
> They never found out who it was
> that stole the feast—can you?

. . . it's on your side. Why, even I got it eventually! And

a thoroughly satisfactory resolution it is, too—even if I did give up on the further search it provokes. In short, **The Eleventh Hour** looks suspiciously like another Base triumph.

> *Chris Powling, in a review of "The Eleventh Hour," in* Books for Keeps, *No. 59, November, 1989, p. 22.*

Following up the huge-selling **Animalia** Graeme Base now publishes **The Eleventh Hour,** a curious mystery. The art work is rich, the story line attractive. . . .

It is totally consuming and captivating. There is a touch of magic, a dash of thrill, a slice of luck when it comes to finding out just who stole the party food. Very much a collector's item, the vast majority will be youngsters who will doubtless return to the book again, again, and again over the years.

> *Wes Magee, in a review of "The Eleventh Hour," in* The Junior Bookshelf, *Vol. 54, No. 2, April, 1990, p. 70.*

James Berry

1925-

Jamaican poet, author of short stories, and reteller.

Respected as a writer whose works address universal themes while reflecting his Caribbean heritage, Berry is praised for his insight into human nature, especially as it regards young people, and for his lyrical prose and poetic style, which often incorporates island patios. He is also acknowledged as being among the first authors to introduce West Indian folktales and realistic stories of Caribbean life to British and American children. A well known poet for adults who has lived in England since 1948 and divides his time between Jamaica and the United Kingdom, Berry invests his works with his understanding of and affection for his homeland. His first work for children, *A Thief in the Village and Other Stories* (1987), is a collection of nine short stories for middle and upper graders which is set in a rural Jamaican seaside village. Written in simple yet evocative language which includes Creole dialect and cadences, the stories depict both the daily lives and the dreams of the village denizens, who encounter poverty, tragedy, and injustice as well as warmth, humor, and hope as they face a variety of often harsh situations. Berry's next book, *The Girls and Yanga Marshall* (1987), is a collection of stories for adolescent readers which is set in and out of schools in both England and the Caribbean. *Anancy-Spiderman* (1988; U. S. edition as *Spiderman-Anancy*) presents middle and upper graders with twenty traditional and original tales about the cunning trickster hero; written in present tense in Creole-flavored language, the book is noted for its strong imagery and for the rhythmic quality of Berry's prose. With *When I Dance: Poems* (1988), Berry makes the transition from lyrical prose to poetry considered notable for its expressiveness, candor, and sensuality. As with his short stories, *When I Dance* reflects Berry's strong sense of community and use of Creole dialect as he addresses such subjects as friendship, growth and individuality, adolescent frustration, and Caribbean life through varying points of view; written both in standard English and patios, the poems are also noted for their innovative phrasing and for the distinctiveness of their appearance on the page. *A Thief in the Village and Other Stories* was named a Coretta Scott King Award honor book in 1988 and *When I Dance* won the Signal Poetry Award in 1989.

A Thief in the Village and Other Stories (1987)

James Berry, a Jamaican born and bred, has some rich and moving tales to tell of life in the West Indies. Possibly the localised stories may be considered of specialist interest only to racial minorities or to students of the West Indies. However careful reading must impress even the most reticent reader. Each story is tightly written and self contained. They focus on family life, of poverty, of joy and sadness, and all have the atmosphere of Jamaican life, tightly bottled ready to fizz out on opening. A lovely collection, it is aimed at lower/middle secondary age.

Lance A. Salway, in a review of "A Thief in the Village," in The Junior Bookshelf, Vol. 51, No. 5, October, 1987, p. 229.

A collection of short stories from a Jamaican poet, featuring a cast of young, rural island characters who face, heroically and otherwise, a variety of pressures and situations.

Becky wants a bicycle so that she can ride with the "Wheels-and-Brake Boys"; Nenna and Man-Man help capture a thief; a boy reflects on the magic of Sunday (". . . all other days run into Sunday"). Whether the focus is as small as a mouth organ, as dramatic as the battle to save a prized banana tree from a hurricane, as common as casual cruelty to a social outcast, or as quiet and poignant as a young boy's sudden need to see his father for the first time, Berry captures universal themes and behavior in stories that are simply told—yet rich with the humor, tragedy, injustice, and warm feelings of daily life in an impoverished but kindred culture. The author's language evokes the sound of Jamaican English without trying to copy it; the dialect thickens occasionally ("Das true wha' Pappy say . . . The good Lord won' gi' we more than we can bear"), but readers won't find the stories difficult to read, nor the lively characters hard to understand.

As in daily life, some of the incidents here lack resolution; still, this is an imaginative, well-told collection.

A review of "A Thief in the Village," in Kirkus Reviews, *Vol. LVI, No. 6, March 15, 1988, p. 450.*

This collection of short stories for teenagers fills a gap that has existed for years in West Indian writing. When I was growing up in Trinidad in the late 1950's and 60's, in a home where books and reading were treasured, my bookshelves—and those of the local library—were crammed with tales, folk and fairy, of every land. It was a rewarding and enriching experience. But, except for the fantasy of the Anansi tales, there was nothing to reflect us children of the West Indies back to ourselves, to consider and explicate our world. Our daily life, it seemed, was too pedestrian to provide drama between hard covers. Now James Berry, in his sprightly and realistic tales of Jamaican life, proves this to be untrue.

In *A Thief in the Village* we meet a variety of boys and girls living lives that seem decades old in a little seaside village 74 miles from Kingston. Donkeys and horses still provide the main means of transportation, automobiles remain a curiosity and the city bus brings with it the excitement of "a letter or some news or a visitor." Farm animals abound—pigs, goats, chickens, cows—and the children all have their chores to perform, even, in the title story, standing armed guard in the threatening darkness of a coconut plantation.

These are simple lives of restricted possibility, but Mr. Berry delves deep, revealing and examining the dreams and yearnings of the children—for bicycles, shoes, mouth organs—showing the importance simple things can have. In **"The Banana Tree,"** Gustus braves the terrors of a hurricane to protect the bunch of bananas he plans to sell in order to raise money to buy the shoes that will allow him to go on school trips.

Intentional or not, the book has a subtle and satisfying symmetry to it. It begins with a story of desire fulfilled (**"Becky and the Wheels-and-Brake Boys"**) and ends with one of desire defeated (**"The Banana Tree"**). Unfortunately, this structure also provides one of the few weaknesses in the book, in that **"Becky and the Wheels-and-Brake Boys"** is an inauspicious beginning, a story without cohesion that comes to a fairy-tale ending. Becky's yearning for a bicycle is fulfilled, and she learns the unfortunate lesson that she is accepted by her peers not for herself but for her possessions. It is an unusual lapse in an otherwise fine, often moving book.

On the other hand, **"Fanso and Granny-Flo,"** the tale of a boy's need to know the man who fathered him and then abandoned his mother, is the best example of Mr. Berry's talents. A probing and compassionate look at Fanso's yearning, it is a complex, moving work, with no easy answers at the end, related, like all the stories, in simple, accessible language.

This collection is not a merry romp through a tropical tourist-land. Mr. Berry, who was born in Jamaica and now lives both there and in Britain, is much too realistic a writer for that. Fathers are often dead or absent. Danger erupts from nature or rises unexpectedly in the midst of beauty. Senseless cruelty is rife. **"Elias and the Mongoose"**

is an unsparing, brutal but ultimately moving tale of violence perpetrated against a retarded boy. **"Tukku-Tukku and Samson"** tells of the humiliation of a boy by other boys because "he is dwarfed, smaller than all of us, though the same age" and because his "face is seldom washed clean. He sleeps on the floor, is half-starved, and has no shoes."

Every story carries an implicit moral, none of them simple: human nature does not change (**"Elias and the Mongoose"**); not all dreams come true (**"The Banana Tree"**); people are not always what they seem (**"A Thief in the Village"**). But it is **"The Banana Tree"** that provides the lasting message of the book: "The storm's bad, chil'run. Really bad. But it'll blow off. It'll spen' itself out. It'll kill itself." It's not a bad lesson to learn.

The stories are all told in an easy, conversational tone, enough so that they may be best appreciated if read out loud. My one reservation concerns the dialogue, which is rendered convincingly in the Jamaican dialect. . . . Might not the initial obscurity—there were times when even I had to re-read some lines—prove frustrating to a child unfamiliar with the accent and cadences? But this may be quibbling. It is not an insurmountable challenge, and perseverance will prove rewarding. (pp. 30-1)

Neil Bissoondath, "The Importance of Simple Things," in The New York Times Book Review, *May 8, 1988, pp. 30-1.*

Linked by their Jamaican village setting, these stories range across the common hopes and fears of childhood. This is no utopia; the close knit community wears its culture proudly and its poverty lightly, but it is a harsh life in which prejudice gang-baits anyone who is different.

A major theme is desperate longing—for an unknown father, a bike, a mouth organ or a pair of shoes. There are unforgettable descriptions of fighting a hurricane, rescuing a horse and boy swept out to sea, night patrolling a coconut plantation, celebrating Sunday. Happiness can be easily found, but witting and unwitting cruelty is commonplace. Most memorable is the harrowing and unresolved story of children bent on killing a crippled boy's pet mongoose.

The unfamiliar dialect and speech patterns forcibly slow the reader into an appreciation of the writer's evocation of island life. These stories have a poetry, power and intensity that makes for satisfying but not easy reading. Though short, they are richly dense, powerfully told, emotionally intense and poetically descriptive, demanding dedication and ability from 10-14 year old readers.

Ward Saylor, in a review of "A Thief in the Village," in Reading Time, *Vol. 33, No. 4, 1989, p. 30.*

The Girls and Yanga Marshall (1987)

Stories about black school kids are few and far between. That in itself should be enough reason to buy this collection of four short stories in a cheap paperback. I enjoyed it thoroughly, but my comments are guarded because I haven't yet had a chance to discuss it with some black London school students I know.

The title story, the longest and most developed, presents Yanga, who wears a Rasta hat to school unless he is made to remove it, and is not overimpressed by the knowledge and authority of teachers, preferring the message he hears at Speakers Corner. He is at odds with the good girls at school, but makes friends with Madeline, not a good girl in anyone's terms. His perception and compassion are in sharp contrast to the school's view of him. In **"Nat and Paula"** the fierce conflict of a tough traditional father and a tough independent son is lightened by Carnival and by a strong bond between brother and sister. The final story is set in a school in a Caribbean country. The common thread is a search for some resolution or reconciliation, much desired but difficult to achieve. Anancy triumphs over Tiger Man by his peace-provoking tactics.

> *Alex McLeod, in a review of "The Girls and Yanga Marshall," in* The School Librarian, *Vol. 36, No. 2, May, 1988, p. 63.*

Anancy-Spiderman **(1988; U. S. edition as** *Spiderman-Anancy***)**

Anancy, Dennis Scott suggests in his poem "Uncle Time", is a "spider-man, cunning and cool". And there are those chaste moralists, concerned churchmen and severe politicians, who have bewailed the effect of the "Anancy mentality" on, and in, Jamaican culture. But Jamaican children of all ages have thrilled at the tales about this trickster transported from West Africa to the Caribbean during the days of African slavery.

Like many other elements which were brought over from West Africa, Anancy suffered a sea change in the Caribbean. For one thing, in West African tales he was from time to time defeated and whipped when he went just too far. The West Indian Anancy hardly ever gets his "comeuppance": a hero in a slave community has not only to be sly and "cunning and cool", he also has to be able to overcome all difficulties, and to defeat formidable opponents—Tiger, for instance—if he is to offer any comfort to his beleaguered devotees.

It would appear that James Berry's Anancy also suffers a sea change—in his crossing the Atlantic in the other direction, and ending up in England where his European analogue, the Fox (of sour grapes and all that) lives. Perhaps the greatest aspect of this change is the fact that our author tells his tales, old and newly invented, in a form of "Standard English", rather than in Jamaican Creole. Thus no doubt the intended audience in multiethnic, multilingual, Britain will find these interesting tales more available to them. They will be able to enjoy the concerns and story line, the characterizations of Bro Tiger and Old Witch Sister, but not I think their original flavour.

The English used is not without some Jamaican features, but is so far from the Creole in which these tales were usually told, that a native like me finds the readjustment difficult. Some of Berry's tales have wonderful openings: "Going about his business, Anancy hears a sound. Anancy stops. Anancy listens. The sound is heavy breathing . . . "

But sometimes, perhaps in an attempt to reflect and suggest the original lingua and style of the tales, the author gets enmeshed in things like: "I have nowhere, sir, nowhere, to draw anything nice from. All I have is feeling bad-bad from feeling sad. I try and find not one song will start in me . . . "

"Anancy and Storm and the Reverend Man-Cow", from which those few lines are quoted, is one of the most interesting of the tales but it seems to end rather weakly.

This collection would be better for class reading and discussion, than for silent private reading. For one thing the characters can then be acted out, the cunning and "wickedness" of the trickster be discussed together with the various ways in which he tries to fool the other animals. After all it's not such a bad thing to be introduced to a "real old Fox", as long as one learns, as we are told at the end of the tale of **"Monkey, Tiger and the Magic Trials,"** that " . . . spells can be broken. Broken! Broken!".

The illustrations by Joseph Olubo add to the attractiveness of the book, but are not as bright and lively as those in *Anansi Stories* retold by Evan Jones (Ginn 1984). In fact this book might well be used along with Berry's—the styles as well as the presentation and illustrations make an interesting and instructive contrast.

> *John Figueroa, "Travelling Trickster," in* The Times Educational Supplement, *No. 3753, June 3, 1988, p. 48.*

James Berry's tales are lively and full of character, colour and wit. Berry says in his introduction that he has . . . *deepened, clarified and expanded the stories . . .* filling out an oral telling that can sometimes read coldly in print. These stories are as alive read silently as they would be read aloud and succeed where a retelling of an oral tale can fail when the reader/listener does not already know and understand . . . *the ways of characters, their situations, motives, hopes, beliefs . . .* The language is rich and evocative. The characters are good and bad together. Anancy's struggle with Bro Tiger forms a loose but strong theme for the stories.

> *Jane Parkinson, in a review of "Anancy-Spiderman," in* Reading Time, *Vol. 33, No. 2, 1989, p. 30.*

With the same lyrical nuance of dialogue that characterized *A Thief in the Village,* Berry has retold twenty Caribbean folktales of West African origin. Like all tricksters, Anancy ranges from hero to villain to fool in his relationships with the other animal characters, but whatever his role, he becomes so integral to readers by the end of the book that we feel as he does about saying good-bye to his arch enemy: "Bro Anancy is surprised how much he misses Bro Tiger. Anancy decides, to keep the memory of Tiger, he'll tell stories about himself and Bro Tiger. Spider Anancy hides in bedrooms and whispers stories like dreams." The word choices here are irresistibly poetic ("They listen how the Anancy goes on wrapping up his words in tricky traps"), and the prose so rhythmic that sometimes it becomes pure chant. Even the titles have a tongue-rolling sound, as in **"Ratbat and Tacooma's Tree."** The narrative, which is cast in the present tense, addresses the reader directly, with immediate impact ("Listen to the Anancy calling loud-loud"). The stories themselves are often gripping, either in plot—the kidnapping in **"Mrs Dog First-Child and Monkey-Mother,"** for instance, and the final fight scene between Lion and Tiger—or simply in imagery. The dialect becomes accessible through its musical appeal and is easy to incorporate for either independent readers or storytellers. Like Berry's oral style, the pen-and-ink drawings have an energy that contrasts sharply with many current adaptations that seem tidied to death. There's no question that this is a living tradition.

> *Betsy Hearne, in a review of "Spiderman-Anancy," in* Bulletin of the Center for Children's Books, *Vol. 43, No. 4, December, 1989, p. 78.*

When I Dance: Poems   (1988)

[James Berry's] keenly-awaited collection for young people **When I Dance,** a substantial but nowhere near overweight 120 pages, is magnificent. It is, to take a phrase from Berry's introduction, a book of "big giving". Rhythmically live to the tips of their toes, always alert with a strong sense of community and an unsentimental relish for celebration ("Using what time tucked in me, I see / my body pops with dance. / Streets break out in carnival") these poems achieve what one of them calls "leaps of feeling". Many of them are in Caribbean dialect but their verbal invention and imaginative generosity exclude nobody. Sensuous, streetwise, candid in their acute understanding of teenage frustration and the preciousness of private worlds, they jump from the page with rare immediacy. Berry's is the kind of gift that seems constrained by brief quotation, but a random snatch from **"Dreaming Black Boy"** must suffice to offer just a hint of the book's full quality:

> I wish life wouldn't spend me out
> opposing. Wish same way creation
> would have me stand it would have
> me stretch, and hold high, my voice
> Paul Robeson's, my inside eye
> a sun. Nobody wants to say
> hello to nasty answers.

> *John Mole, "Rap, Pap and Poetry," in* The Times Educational Supplement, *No. 3776, November 11, 1988, p. 51.*

Sparkling language born out of specific situations distinguishes James Berry's "special bagful of obsessions and celebrations". Writing mostly in the first person, Berry shifts his point of view, adopting different voices, to explore a variety of interests and preoccupations (friendship, growth, invention, movement, individuality, differences, Caribbean life and nature) which divide the book into eight sections. As "scooped bits of the times I've lived in", the poems are contemporary in their settings, but Berry also probes the private thoughts of children and adolescents, whose perspectives are brilliantly achieved, to produce a collection of work that is by turns descriptive, didactic, mundane and fantastic.

Those poems in Creole surprise, excite and engage by the unfamiliar appearance of the words on the page, which, written more phonetically than standard English, create the immediacy of a particular voice. Although these voices are idiosyncratic, their concerns have a familiarity which is amusing and appealing. A mother scolds her son's adolescent posturings, "A boy dohn have to go all boasify- /

bloated, to mek him look smart guy"; an awestruck brother describes his younger sister, "My sista is own car repairer /and yu nah catch me doin judo with her."

The title poem of the collection celebrates expression through music: "when I dance / I gather up all my senses . . . Telling their poetry in movement / And I celebrate all rhythms". Innovative phrasing, pauses, sudden breaks and enjambment mirror this fluidity. By mixing "a lickle talk / with a sweet lickle walk", Berry gives a rhythmic strength to poetry which explores the energies of youth.

> *Deborah Fenn, "Poems and Perspectives," in* The Times Literary Supplement, *No. 4, March 3-9, 1989, p. 232.*

James Berry comes from Jamaica. He lives now in Britain, but his cultural traditions are implicit in everything he writes. In this collection of his verses . . . he calls upon the Caribbean heritage and upon his experiences of inner-city life alike in poems in which there is more warmth than anger. This does not mean that he is either complacent or sentimental. His is a clear gaze which misses no sign of injustice but is quick to recognise goodness.

Some of the poems in **When I Dance** are in colloquial standard English, others in Creole (the accepted language of the Caribbean Nation). On the whole I find that these latter have greater freshness and spontaneity. At first glance they look very difficult, but a brief study shows that it is the ear, not the eye, that governs the understanding. The poet provides guidance in a penetrating introduction which, like the poems, is relaxed and humorous as well as wise. His poems will obviously be a most welcome addition to the still-limited body of Anglo-Caribbean literature. They have much to say too to those communities which have not yet been enriched with a transfusion of this warm and lively blood. (pp. 78-9)

> *M. Crouch, in a review of "When I Dance," in* The Junior Bookshelf, *Vol. 53, No. 2, April, 1989, pp. 78-9.*

[*The following excerpt is from an essay by Jan Mark, one of the judges for the Signal Poetry Award, a prize given to* When I Dance *in 1988.*]

When I Dance; did ever a collection come more aptly titled? In his introduction to the poems James Berry explains: 'In writing them I shared and learnt something of current youth culture. I discovered. I had fun.' To open this exuberant book anywhere is a guarantee that we too shall discover, have fun. I wondered at first—and still wonder a little—if the introduction is necessary. The book introduces itself, like Berry's own importunate wooer on the doorstep, equipped with ingratiating smile and confident of talking his way into a welcome. . . .

The poems are alive with movement; whether the purposeful rhythm of dance or sport, or the restless undirected energy of adolescence, they vibrate with the urge to be up and doing. . . . However pensive, no one ever stays still for long; but this is not to suggest that many poems are not contemplative, profoundly internal:

> Only one of me
> and nobody can get a second one
> from a photocopy machine.

. . .

Nobody can get into my clothes for me
or feel my fall for me, or do my running.
Nobody hears my music for me, either.

This private celebration of uniqueness epitomizes the sense, expressed over and over, of emergent self-awareness, discovery of occupying own space, territorial—but friendly. Everywhere are invitations to advance and connect; invitations which are not always going to be reciprocated. **'The Dreaming Black Boy'** rehearses the pain of the internal exile inflicted on blacks in Britain. . . .

However, like most of the others speaking through Berry, this boy *can* still wish, still hope. It's a rare bitterness that informs **'Getting Nowhere'**. . . .

This is neither black nor white despair, but the universal howl of the hopelessly alienated. In essence, very little in this collection, except for those poems of overtly Caribbean context, could be identified infallibly as black or white . . . , were it not for the language in which they are written. Basically, they are all written in English; some of it Anglo-Saxon (white?) English, and much in an English transfigured by centuries in the Caribbean and returning to us with a different voice. We already know that it *sounds* different, on the page it looks different, the more so for appearing at a time when the custom of writing English phonetically has become an archaism, rightly, after years of malpractice in which menials were represented by dropped aspirates, Orientals by lallation, Asians by Babu circumlocution and blacks, irrespective of origin, by a kind of Christy Minstrel patois. It looked ugly and sounded embarrassing, largely on account of being attempted by people with no oral experience of the accent or dialect that they were trying to reproduce.

When James Berry refers to the Caribbean Nation Language (Creole) as 'dialect', the quotation marks are his. The word implies exclusiveness, inaccessibility, neither element having any place here, and suggests further that it needs clarification. He himself observes that the knee-jerk reaction is, too often, 'I can't read black poetry', as though it were wilfully obscure. Looking at his poems on the page, all is clarity. This is a language with its own syntax, spelling and vocabulary, but nonetheless rooted in 'white' English, and inextricable from it, to the extent that translations into the latter look woefully diminished—as in the section devoted to Jamaican proverbs. It is useful to know exactly what is being said, but who would want to say it like that? The wit and verve are in the original.

Cos parrot noisy-noisy, dem sey a dam one nyam up banana.
(Because parrots are chatterers people say they are the only ones who eat up the fruits.)
De tick wha flog de black dog wi whip de white.
(The same stick that flogs the black dog will also flog the white one.)

Perhaps the translations are offered mischievously, to show us what we obdurate monoglots are missing. The summation of this is in **'Bye Now'**:

Walk good
Walk good
Noh mek macca go juk yu
Or cow go buck yu.
Noh mek dog bite yu
Or hungry go ketch yu, yah!

Noh mek sunhot turn yu dry.
Noh mek rain soak yu.
Noh mek tief tief yu
Or stone go buck yu foot, yah!
Walk good
Walk good

Which reminded me on the instant of Herrick's 'Night Piece to Julia':

No Will-o'-th'-Wisp mislight thee;
Nor snake, or slow-worm bite thee:
But on, on thy way
Not making a stay,
Since ghost there's none to affright thee.

Then I noticed that **'Goodbye Now'**, the poem printed below **'Bye Now'**, was a literal translation, no more than a helpful footnote, and no hint of Herrick.

'The Nativity Play Plan' would have been immediately recognizable to the fifteenth-century shepherds of Wakefield, and the question-and-answer reiteration of **'Me go a Granny Yard'** surely echoes 'The Maiden in the Moor', from a century before. . . . If Berry did nothing more than give us a voice for our times, his book would be worthy of the award, but it seems to me that he is also offering a lifeline back to a language that most of his readers will never have seen, and all the vigour and frankness that went with it. (pp. 75-9)

Jan Mark, "The Signal Poetry Award," by Jan Mark and Aidan Chambers, in Signal, *No. 59, May, 1989, pp. 75-92. [The excerpts of James Berry's work used here were originally published in his* When I Dance, *Hamilton, 1988.]*

Christina Björk

1938-

Swedish author of nonfiction.

Björk is best known as the creator of three distinctive informational books which use a fictional framework to introduce primary and middle graders to such subjects as botany and the life and work of Impressionist painter Claude Monet. She addresses these topics through the narration and perspective of Linnea, a curious and enthusiastic Swedish girl whose love of flowers serves as the starting point for each volume. In Björk's first work, *Linnea in Monet's Garden* (1987), she tells the story of how Linnea and her elderly friend, the retired gardener Mr. Bloom, journey to Paris and Giverny to see Monet's paintings and his home while explaining the elements which influenced his artistic vision. Praised as a charming and insightful book notable both for its approach and for the nontraditional information it includes on its subject, *Linnea in Monet's Garden* concludes with a bibliography of works about Monet as well as other supplementary information. In addition, the title includes illustrations by Lena Anderson, who has also provided the pictures for Björk's other works, as well as reproductions of Monet's paintings, photographs of Monet and his family, and photographs supposedly taken by Linnea at Monet's home in Giverny. *Linnea's Windowsill Garden* (1988) and *Linnea's Almanac* (1989) continue Björk's format of instruction through entertainment: in *Windowsill Garden,* Mr. Bloom teaches Linnea how to grow plants in small places and answers her questions about plants and their cycles, while in *Almanac* Linnea learns about animals, birds, and plants in a study organized according to the months of the year; the latter also includes recipes, craft projects, and information on keeping nature records as well as gardening advice and other instruction.

Linnea in Monet's Garden (1987)

There are really two books here, both good in their different ways, which somehow never quite settle down together. First there is an informal evaluation of Monet's life and work. Then there is the story of how Linnea and her friend Mr. Bloom went to see Monet's house and the scenes of his paintings. The first is done conscientiously, with plenty of accurate information and some adequate reproductions of the paintings. The other is cheerful and relaxed. Linnea emerges as a sensible and lively little girl, Mr. Bloom not too much of a know-all. The illustrations that Lena Anderson has provided are equally lively and amusing, but they fight desperately with the Monet pictures, so that each tends to cancel out the other. It was quite a good idea, but on the whole I believe that it is better to give children information and ideas straight without recourse to sugared pills like these.

M. Crouch, in a review of "Linnea in Monet's Garden," in The Junior Bookshelf, *Vol. 51, No. 6, December, 1987, p. 272.*

When little Linnea returns to Sweden after her visit to París everyone asks: "How was the Eiffel Tower?" "Listen", she replies with spirit, "we had far more important things to see than that." This charming book tells the story of Linnea's love for flowers and of her touching friendship with her neighbour Mr. Bloom, a retired gardener. Mr. Bloom owns a copy of Claire Joyes's *Claude Monet: Life at Giverny* and the little girl and the old man become fascinated by the painter and by the beautiful water garden he created at Giverny in the 1890s. When they discover that Giverny has been restored and that it is now open to the public they set their hearts on a visit.

Because this story has some fairy-tale elements their dream comes true. But the details of their visit to Paris are wonderfully realistic—the Hotel Esmeralda, the bookshop down the street, the stray dogs, the train trip out to Giverny are all lovingly described. So too is the delicious picnic which Mr. Bloom buys in the village and Linnea's first impressions of the garden itself: "It's funny with things you've thought about a lot and finally get to see. They almost always look different." When at last Mr. Bloom and Linnea stand on the Japanese bridge and look out over the lily garden it is a triumphant moment.

As serious students of Monet, neither Mr. Bloom nor Linnea can resist a second visit to Giverny and they are rewarded by meeting Jean-Marie Toulgouat, Monet's step-great-grandson. He explains what it was like to live with Monet. "He was born a lord" said his kinder and cosier friend Renoir. Jean-Marie gives an unidealized picture of Monet's autocratic ways with his large extended family. The sad story of his younger son Michel who wanted to be an inventor is bound to appeal to young readers, as are the family's skating and picnics and their frog-catching outings.

Back in Paris, Linnea and Mr. Bloom visit the Musée Marmottan where they see "Impression, Sunrise" of 1872, the painting which led the critic Louis Leroy to derisively christen Monet and his friends "impressionists". They manage to get into the Lily Room at the Orangerie, although it is characteristically closed for repairs, and on their final morning they get up early to see the sun rise over the Seine and reflect on the series of paintings on that subject which Monet worked on in the summers of 1896 and 1897.

The book is charmingly illustrated in a scrapbook fashion with watercolour drawings by Lena Anderson, with the photographs supposedly taken by little Linnea in the garden, with a selection of Monet's paintings and with photographs of Monet and his family from the Toulgouat collection at Giverny. Mr. Bloom and Linnea could not be a nicer pair and it would be hard to think of a better introduction to Monet's paintings, to the egotism of great painters and to the lost art of exemplary tourism.

Tanya Harrod, "Exemplary Tourists," in The Times Literary Supplement, *No. 4420, December 18-24, 1987, p. 1413.*

An odd book that is not without its charm, this yields an unexpected amount of information on Monet once it gets to the point. The narrator is a young girl who loves flowers so much that she inspires her neighbor, a retired gardener, to take her for a visit to the garden of Claude Monet, whose art she admires. The text describes their trip, with sidelights about the painter's development and complicated family life. Meanwhile, the illustrator's watercolors sit fairly comfortably alongside reproductions of Monet's work and photographs of him and his family and beloved garden. These are too many elements to incorporate into one short book, but there's a flavor that redeems the shaky structure and an honesty about the subject's eccentric and sometimes autocratic behavior that often does not appear in juvenile biography. Though it's not for a picture book audience, this will be most useful shared by an adult; it will also appeal to the artistically gifted child and find ready use in juvenile art collections.

Betsy Hearne, in a review of "Linnea in Monet's Garden," in Bulletin of the Center for Children's Books, *Vol. 41, No. 6, February, 1988, p. 111.*

Linnea in Monet's Garden, a stunning new book collaboratively conceived by author Christina Björk and illustrator Lena Anderson, explores the outside world—how we learn about history, how we expand our consciousness to include more and more of what exists outside of ourselves, and how we make this knowledge our own. With the extraordinary power of the artist creating art about art, the highly personal nature of that process is recorded

in this journal of a fictional child-hero's exploration of the world of the painter, Claude Monet. . . . The beauty of this book—and it is an exquisitely rendered manuscript—is that it recreates, with the excitement and wonder of the most fantastic fictional journeys, the external journey of the informational narrative as it is internalized into a child's consciousness. Linnea's perceptions are noted all along the way and serve to guide us into the world of 19th century Paris, Impressionism, and Monet's famous paintings of water lilies.

This book reveals the truly subjective nature of learning: how our vision is limited by the ways we have learned to perceive; how we know things in very personal and particular ways; how each of us sifts through, orders, and incorporates new learning, as we hang particles of information on so many little hooks in the mind. Linnea, our child guide, notes the steps of her journey with the emotional and intellectual force of a child, responding appropriately to those things most familiar and relevant to her own sense of reality. For example, when she visits Monet's kitchen, she wonders "How did the children reach up to the table?" and notes, "The children thought the garden was a nuisance, because it was their job to weed and water it every evening." The children—their daily tasks, their interests, the pictures of them—are most prominent in her narrative.

Linnea tries to order her narrative in a linear fashion. She says, "maybe I should begin at the beginning," with what led her to this adventure—her love for flowers. She asserts, "(I'm even named after a flower), and I'm interested in everything that grows. That's just the way I am". Her own nature draws her toward Mr. Bloom, her upstairs neighbor, who shares her interest: "And that's how Mr. Bloom is, too," she further asserts. Mr. Bloom introduces her, like the best of teachers, gently facilitating her learning, to Monet's world of flowers through a book. The movement from learning about Monet in this fashion mirrors the child-reader's experience, the best of these experiences, which begins with an interest or an inclination, and leads to a book, often with an adult guide. The story of Monet and his paintings unfolds like a truly suspenseful story, filling out in detail the contexts and the background of his life with the richness of great narrative. *Linnea in Monet's Garden* creates a synthesis of this specific child's perceptions with Monet's creation, in this story about the connection between one child's love of flowers and the artist whose greatest achievement centered on flowers. It is brought to life through a variety of sources as Linnea and Mr. Bloom journey to Paris to see the paintings and experience the culture of the painter.

This book underscores the idea of history and presentation of information as interpretive and subjective, as accompanied by a particular point of view—and as lively and vital. It reinforces the notion that each individual, like Linnea, has a personal way of experiencing history, and that history is made up of the stories of the lives of individuals. Monet is presented ultimately as a real person, flawed despite his genius, living in a specific era with a specific family. This story explores the various elements which shaped Monet's vision of life and its expression in his paintings. It also asserts the complexity of the creative process. This is a scrapbook, a montage, a person's history seen as a conglomeration of elements experienced, always, through a personal, subjective lens. The book is illustrated with drawings, watercolors, and photographs of Monet's paintings and of the structures and people in his life, as it records the story of Linnea's journey into Monet's world.

The first double-page spread depicts Linnea and Mr. Bloom reading the book on Monet on the left in lovely watercolors, while along with the text on the right is a photograph of Monet. This book, Björk and Anderson suggest, is about the link between the two. And the second double-page spread reinforces this impression. On the lower left, Linnea appears, small and childlike, drawn in color, while on the right filling more than half the page is a photograph of Monet's painting of the Japanese bridge under which his water lilies bloomed. Spreading across the two pages, connecting Linnea with this painting, are the silhouettes of Monet, Alice (his second common-law wife), and the eight children they raised together. As their story unfolds, as they come to life for Linnea, their shadow forms gradually fill out, until they appear as fully delineated in their photographs.

And every aspect of this journey toward knowledge is recorded in the same detail, through the reflections of this particular child, as she travels with Mr. Bloom, closer and closer to the source of knowledge, from Paris to Monet's home at Giverny. In Paris Linnea records all her impressions—about the hotel and its history, even down to the details about the painting of Esmeralda from *The Hunchback of Notre Dame*, after whom the hotel is named. On their first trip, to the Marmottan Museum which houses many of Monet's paintings, Linnea learns a subtle aesthetic and philosophical lesson about perspective. She views a painting of the water lilies first from a distance and then from close up. Observing the startling differences, she notes, "We were standing in front of a painting with two white water lilies. I stepped a little closer to the picture and looked at it. It was then I noticed that the lilies were nothing but blobs and blotches of paint. But when I stepped away again, they turned into real water lilies floating in a pond—magic!"

She leads us, with this paradigm, to a difficult concept for children: that there are many perspectives from which a single thing can be viewed. This is the first of many such insights about perception, about time, and about the subjective nature of reality. In the chapter "The Impressionist," for example, Linnea is taught that Monet "painted his *impression* of sunlight reflected in the water," in the revolutionary painting entitled "Impression—Sunrise," thereafter establishing the Impressionist school of painting which attempted to capture "impressions of the moment". Linnea notes how difficult it must be to capture moments that "disappear so quickly . . . [when] it takes so many of them to paint a picture".

This theme is further explored, picked up almost like a leit-motif, when Linnea visits Monet's home at Giverny and cannot decide whether "we should look or take pictures", whether to live in the moment or try to preserve it in art. And at last, when she arrives at the Japanese Bridge, the moment she has been waiting for, she says, with tears in her eyes, "And now we're really here. . . . It could never be more now than right now". Linnea has understood the essentially fleeting nature of time, and of the promise of art to capture the moment and still its ur-

gency. Linnea begins to understand the philosophical implications of Impressionism, that life is a series of shifting moments and of shifting perspectives of a given moment.

As the lilies of Monet's paintings became more abstract over the years, Monet depicted in his many angles of vision the dynamic relationship between the viewer and the object. In a double-page spread towards the center of the book are four different perspectives of the Japanese bridge painted by Monet over the years. Linnea is inspired to do a series of sketches and take a series of photographs of the lily pond "from lots of different angles". Subtly author and illustrator suggest a variety of perspectives on a continuum that extends from the most subjective, the most personal vision, by degrees, to the most objective—from sketches to photographs. Linnea's caption under one of her photographs, "This is the impression the water lilies made on my camera," suggests a fine distinction between modes of expression: that a photograph is created from the viewer's vision, sifted through the mechanism of the camera, the equipment of the artist, a less personal or more "objective" impression than a sketch or painting.

The narrative continues to move closer and closer to a personal perspective on Monet, as the pair of young and old meet Jean-Marie Toulgouat, Monet's step-great-grandson. And through his memories, personal anecdotes, and pictures of the family, we piece together the story of Monet's life, his struggles and achievements, who supported his work, and how he survived. . . . Linnea begins to connect the biographical elements of Monet's life, to interpret his story as if he were a vivid character in a fictional narrative, while maintaining a sense of him as a real human being. . . . This section ends, quietly, with Linnea reading the names of the Monet family on their gravestones, restoring the past to the past, leaving behind the living historical moment to return to the present and to her life at home.

The section "Home Again" raises some interesting questions about journeys—about reentry, about how to keep the journey alive, about how to synthesize or incorporate new and old knowledge. Linnea discovers quickly the many ways to retain special experiences: through narration, the creation of the stories she tells people about her trip, and by immortalizing it through the photographs, tickets, postcards—the memorabilia from Paris and Giverny—she pins to the bulletin board in her room. Linnea's story ends there, but the child-reader is invited to explore further. The author ends with a list of more museums which contain Monet collections, more wonderful things to do in Paris, and more books about Monet. The last page offers a chronology of significant events in Monet's life and a diagram of the Monet family tree. These structures restore the specific details to their historical context. They are the hooks upon which to hang new ideas and knowledge, and they provide a sense of order, a way of remembering and internalizing new experiences. (pp. 96-100)

Roni Natov, "Internal and External Journeys: The Child Hero in 'The Zabajaba Jungle' and 'Linnea in Monet's Garden'," in Children's literature in education, *Vol. 20, No. 2, June, 1989, pp. 91-101.*

Linnea's Windowsill Garden (1988)

The heroine of *Linnea in Monet's Garden* returns with her own perspective on plantings, and offers an accessible guide to growing greens in small places. From an orange tree that started as a seed to garlic sprouts (from cloves placed in soil) to a silly game with plum pits and a suggestion for dyeing half a rose, Linnea has hints, step-by-step instructions and an occasional lesson in natural science offered by her friend Mr. Bloom. For all her enthusiasm, Linnea is wise enough to have realistic expectations—flowers don't always bloom by the book, and every now and then there may be setbacks. But her zeal is infectious; readers will be looking around the house for seeds they can press into soil or coax into germination. [Lena] Anderson's two-color illustrations explicate the projects cleanly and clearly, giving gardeners an excellent idea of when to look for shoots and when to run for the insecticide.

A review of "Linnea's Windowsill Garden," in Publishers Weekly, *Vol. 234, No. 14, September 30, 1988, p. 64.*

The charming young girl of *Linnea in Monet's Garden* shares her enthusiasm for plants and shows how to grow windowsill varieties in pots, jars, plastic lids, peat pellets, and planters. Linnea plants seeds and pits, bulbs, and cuttings; prunes her avocado; gives advice on watering, fertilizer and bugs; and shares plant games and contests (which grows faster?). Mr. Bloom, an elderly friend, answers the tougher questions: How does the water cycle work, what do plants eat, where do seeds come from, and what to plants need to live? Lively line drawings in black and green enhance the text. An attractive title for urban plant lovers.

A review of "Linnea's Windowsill Garden," in Kirkus Reviews, *Vol. LVII, No. 19, October 1, 1988, p. 1464.*

Linnea's Almanac (1989)

Linnaea borealis is a plant: stems slender, pubescent, creeping, forming a mat; not an altogether inaccurate if fanciful appraisal of Christina Björk's *Almanac.* Its index provides entries such as the following:

March: Horray! the first spring flower.
        What are you allowed to pick?
        Vernal equinox
October: My autumn crown.
        Why do leaves turn yellow?
        This is how city animals live

and a reader might make similar annotations from the text except to enlarge October with pigeons, squirrels, house mouse, bat, fox, badger and brown rat, and so for the rest. The *Almanac* is rather like an old-fashioned Lucky Dip at an old-fashioned fête; whatever you dredged up, larger or smaller, was *always* interesting. Select here any page at random and pertinent information abounds. Go back to 'January' and you find a mini treatise on the feeding of winter birds, a bird restaurant, a monograph on the house sparrow, instructions for building a titmouse bell and a note on the life styles of city birds, ending:

Feed water birds in the water
Don't let them come up on land where they can be
   run over.

'Riders' like this last one pop up everywhere in case you become complacent about your own procedures.

Carlos Linnaeus (Carl von Linné, 1707-1778) was a Swedish botanist who originated the classification of animals and plants, the founder of modern systematic botany. This Linnea is a city girl who brings the countryside into her home and heart. There is no plodding in her painstaking logging of her year's round but some fresh interest or excitement at every turn. Linnea might be considered an old-fashioned child but in using her as a first-person narrator or compère Miss Björk has contrived a natural, intimate style free of any hint of condescension or superciliousness. Linnaea is not herself omniscient; she has two elderly and informed friends, a retired gardener and an enthusiastic amateur.

In this account justice cannot be done to the book's innumerable and varied illustrations. [Lena] Anderson has faithfully reflected her author's old-fashioned hues. Her Linnea is a funny-face but far from daft; her exuberance comes alive with her pictures. The factual paintings on any scale are meticulous. The book amounts to a cornucopia of personal interests and activities, a pleasant guide to changing seasons, a very well-stocked lucky dip.

Questions do remain. Has this busy but happy little girl no friends or collaborators of her own age? parents? relatives? school? church? It surely looks as though she could have little time to spare for them, happy as she is made to appear; but one does wonder. All the same, another inquiring child could hog or hug this book for years. (pp. 21-2)

A. R. Williams, in a review of "Linnea's Almanac," in The Junior Bookshelf, *Vol. 54, No. 1, February, 1990, pp. 21-2.*

Charming Linnea is back from previous appearances in *Linnea in Monet's Garden* and *Linnea's Windowsill Garden*. Here, she and her friends and neighbors study nature month by month. The intent of being simultaneously instructive and entertaining is a tall order, yet Linnea makes learning fun. Altogether, there are more than 30 ideas—from recipes to craft projects to keeping nature records—for readers' delight. Even more impressive is the book's visual appeal. The watercolor and ink pictures are captivating; the well-planned layout and varying lettering styles are sure to appeal to readers. Because the book is a Swedish import, some objects of nature (e.g. the chaffinch) will be unfamiliar to American readers. Still, this beautiful book deserves to be placed within reach of nature-loving and inquistive children.

Amy Adler, in a review of "Linnea's Almanac," in School Library Journal, *Vol. 36, No. 4, April, 1990, p. 102.*

Alden R(ichardson) Carter
1947-

American author of fiction and nonfiction.

Respected as a writer of contemporary realistic fiction for young adults as well as the author of informational books on national and international history and the history of technology for middle graders and young adults, Carter is perhaps best known for creating coming-of-age stories about teenagers dealing with personal problems which are noted for their believability, candor, and refreshing, three-dimensional characters. Carter's books for young adults characteristically focus on the growth and maturation of their adolescent male protagonists, young men who encounter emotional issues in both urban and country settings. For example, in his first novel, *Growing Season* (1984), Carter describes how Rick, a high school senior, learns about responsibility and self-control when his parents move him from the city to a Wisconsin dairy farm. A similar theme of the healing qualities of family, friends, and rural living underscores *Up Country* (1989), in which sixteen-year-old Carl, an electronics whiz who repairs stolen stereos in order to earn money to get into engineering school and to distance himself from his alchoholic, promiscuous mother, is sent to the country to live with an an aunt and uncle.

Sheila's Dying (1987) is considered one of Carter's most outstanding works for the young: the story of how narrator Jerry confronts illness and death when he becomes the caretaker for his girlfriend, a sixteen-year-old with uterine cancer, the novel is praised as a moving, accurate, and insightful work which thoroughly describes the details of Sheila's illness, the procedures followed by the hospital where she is a patient, and the emotions faced by Jerry and Sheila's best friend Bonnie as they nurse Sheila until her death. Although some observers question his use of profanity and the candid nature of some of the situations in his young adult novels, Carter is well regarded for his depiction of relationships and for providing realistic solutions to the problems of his characters. In his nonfiction, Carter addresses such subjects as computer evolution, radio, the electronics field, and the history of Illinois; Carter and his wife Carol also provided the photographs for *Modern China* (1986), a work based both on research and on first-hand observation which discusses the attributes and problems of contemporary China from a historical perspective. He is also the creator of a series of four books on the American Revolution—*Birth of the Republic* (1988), *Colonies in Revolt* (1988), *Darkest Hours* (1988), and *At the Forge of Liberty* (1989)—which cover the period from the crowning of George III through the adoption of the Constitution. In his informational books, Carter draws on such techniques as personal sketches, personalized narrations, historical vignettes, and discussion of political implications to provide young readers with interesting approaches to his subjects. Carter has received many child and adult-selected awards for his works, including several "best book" designations.

AUTHOR'S COMMENTARY

My mother denies ever knowing a song entitled "Beloved Old Percy." Yet, I have a distinct memory of her singing it one school morning as she roused her children from bed. Later that day, I wrote a story with that title. Percy, a retired race horse, pines to race again. His obliging owners allow him to compete in a steeplechase. (At age eight, I knew nothing of horse racing and did not give Percy a rider.) The race begins. Percy runs with all his heart but tires quickly. He attempts to jump a picket fence, doesn't make it, and dies impaled on the sharp stakes. Ouch. A quarter of a century later, I told my wife about my first story. "Good Lord!" she said. "Did they send you to the school psychologist?" "Not as I recall," I replied, "but I do remember that my sister cried when I read it to her. At that moment, I think I knew I had to be a writer." "Well," my wife said, "you sure weren't in any hurry."

That's true. . . .

I taught English and journalism for four years at the high school in Marshfield, Wisconsin. I wrote in the summers, producing a handful of short stories and the first drafts of two novels, one of which would eventually become my first published novel, *Growing Season.* However, teaching was far more demanding than I had imagined. At thirty-three, I knew I had to either quit teaching or quit dreaming of becoming a professional writer. With the support of my wife, I resigned that spring. Most of my family and friends thought I was crazy. In my more lucid moments over the next two and a half years, I could hardly blame them. My hours at the typewriter produced a fair amount of prose but no income. I had enough rejection letters to wallpaper much of my office by the fall of 1982 when Coward-McCann, a member of The Putnam & Grosset Group, offered me a contract for my young adult novel *Growing Season* on the condition that I rewrite it. They did not have to ask me twice. *Growing Season* is narrated by Rick Simons, a contented city boy who deeply resents being uprooted in the middle of his senior year when his country-bred parents buy a dairy farm. In writing the novel, I had to devote considerable time to research. I had no background in farming beyond the casual connection of growing up in an agricultural region. My ignorance proved an advantage in the countless hours I spent visiting farms. No doubt some of my questions were hilarious to the farmers I interviewed, but they were the same questions Rick might have asked.

Revising *Growing Season* with the help of a skilled editor taught me a great deal about developing characters, writing dialogue, and pacing the flow of a novel. In 1984, *Growing Season* made me a published writer. Few moments in my life have been so grand. The novel received good reviews and was selected as an American Library Association Best Book for Young Adults. Particularly gratifying was the praise the book received from people who knew farming intimately.

I began revising my second young adult novel, *Wart, Son of Toad.* As a high school teacher, I had been concerned that many students did poorly not because of a lack of intelligence or ambition but because of incapacitating personal problems. Steve, my narrator and main character, has both his share of problems and a distressing lack of self-esteem. Yet, he also has a stubborn anger and more courage than he realizes.

Sheila's Dying, my third young adult novel, came from my musings on the fact that everyone at one time or another is trapped by circumstances. Sheila's friend Jerry must provide care and comfort for a dying girl he bears only moderate affection. The story he relates is not so much about dying as it is about living on. I hope *Sheila's Dying* says something about the great truth that it is not so much human mortality but the resiliency of the human heart that ultimately matters.

I have chosen to write for and about young adults. I find myself constantly impressed with their courage. Despite all the problems—both traditional and recently invented—that fill the teenage years, the vast majority not only survive, but triumph. Their stories are far more dramatic than the tales I once imagined about pirates, cowboys, and an ill-starred race horse named Percy.

> *Alden Carter, "Alden Carter in His Own Words," in a promotional piece, The Putnam Publishing Group, October, 1987.*

GENERAL COMMENTARY

Phillis Wilson

America declared its independence to the world, but only victory on the battlefield could give truth to this claim. Within these four volumes [*At the Forge of Liberty, Birth of the Republic, Colonies in Revolt,* and *Darkest Hours*], Carter presents a carefully constructed analysis of issues on both sides of the Atlantic that ultimately resulted in the "shot heard round the world." In *Colonies in Revolt,* it becomes evident that the ties that bind America to Britain are fraying. Coverage is from 1760, when George III is crowned, through the battles of Lexington and Concord in April 1775. A summary of these events leads into an account, in *Darkest Hours,* of the early revolutionary war battles, the forming of the Second Continental Congress, and the signing of the Declaration of Independence. A succinct description of British general Burgoyne's surrender at Saratoga opens *Forge of Liberty,* which concludes with Cornwallis beginning his withdrawal from the South. In *Birth of the Republic,* patriots rejoice at final victory, and a new nation is structured through the adoption of the Constitution. Throughout, Carter plays out passionate and volatile events with a sense of immediacy. Copious descriptions of key figures, especially Washington, add a personal dimension to these . . . books on the ideals, blood, and courage that forged a new nation. Valuable as both reference and circulating resources. (pp. 644-45)

> *Phillis Wilson, in a review of "At the Forge of Liberty" and others, in Booklist, Vol. 85, No. 7, December 1, 1988, pp. 644-45.*

Growing Season   **(1984)**

Fulfilling a long-held dream, Rick Simon's parents have sold their house in Milwaukee and bought a dairy farm, moving their six children to a new, demanding life. For Rick, the oldest, it is particularly hard to leave during his senior year in high school. But his sisters and brothers are all pleased, looking forward to the change and to a promised assortment of pets. Not surprisingly, none has been prepared for the long working hours or for the strain of financial worries on Mom and Dad. The twins bicker over boyfriends, one child plunges into violent temper tantrums, another frets that everyone ignores her, and all agonize over the youngest one, who is rapidly losing his eyesight. As financial worries mount, Rick sees his dream of college fading but also finds he is developing skills he didn't dream of and is able to contribute substantially to his family's well-being. Rick's transition to responsible manhood is convincing, as is the matter-of-fact picture of farm life. All six children as well as the hard-working father and overweight, worrisome mother have a rugged vitality. The understated drama of the story lies in the progression of the farming year. The birth of calves is balanced by the death of an uncle, and an uncertain planting followed by an ample harvest. A fine, honest novel in the tradition of Robert Newton Peck's *A Day No Pigs Would Die.* (pp. 473-74)

> *Ethel R. Twichell, in a review of "Growing Season," in The Horn Book Magazine, Vol. LX, No. 4, August, 1984, pp. 473-74.*

Growing Season is a realistic chronicle of agricultural and family life. . . . This is not a rose-colored picture of pastoral romanticism about rural life, but a welcome, truthful rendering of farm life: working with manure, fingers mangled by a grain auger, a market system which demands the slaughter of young calves and the details of a calf being born. Not only are the frustrations of a hard life described but also the very real sense of achievement resulting from work satisfactorily completed. From his experiences during the summer, Rick gradually matures and this character growth of a boy becoming a man is especially well done. A virtue of this novel is that it intertwines closely the narrative about farm life with the theme of family relations. The family has many individual problems: Tommy's near blindness; Pam's shyness; Jim's temper tantrums; Judy's first sexual experience; the mother's emotional tension and the father's financial insecurities. Although the narrative is somewhat over-detailed and occasionally rambling, the novel is an honest and sincere portrait of human growth and change. Occasional graphic language is consistent with an honest portrayal of farm life and adolescent problems. Teenagers in any location will find a great deal with which to identify. Although the plot is closely allied to farm life, the human emotions and situations described are universal.

> *Hope Bridgewater, in a review of "Growing Season," in* School Library Journal, *Vol. 31, No. 1, September, 1984, p. 126.*

The bulk of [this] story is about the changes in Rick's values and future plans which occur because of his loyalty to his family and the responsibilities of farm life. Besides being a very good coming-of-age story in a setting too infrequently used in young adult literature, this is an especially rich story of family relationships. Rick's parents have adopted several hard-to-place children, and the ways in which the natural and adopted kids relate to each other is very well done, as well as the loyalties and aggravations of the solid but troubled parental relationship. In the course of the story, Rick meets Lorie, who becomes friend and confidant, but she is far removed from the two-dimensional female "girlfriends" so often found in YA books. In fact, it is the superior characterizations which readily distinguish the high level of quality in this fine first (and I hope not last) novel. Despite its slower pacing than some equally realistic offerings (expletives such as "cowshit" are frequently and appropriately used), the dilemma of choosing between farm and urban life would seem to make this a "must" purchase in libraries serving adolescents in large Midwest farm states, and the richness of the family life depicted would make it of considerable value elsewhere.

> *Mary K. Chelton, in a review of "Growing Season," in* Voice of Youth Advocates, *Vol. 7, No. 4, October, 1984, p. 195.*

Supercomputers (with Wayne J. LeBlanc, 1985)

The authors of **Supercomputers** have succeeded in placing the past and future development of computers in both a historical and a political context. They clearly describe how computers work and explain how each succeeding generation of computers was created as a response to the limitations of its predecessor. The sections on the super-

fast fourth-generation computers, which are just coming into operation, and the futuristic fifth-generation thinking computers are fascinating. The authors include a synopsis of Japanese history and illustrate how the Japanese drive to create thinking computers is derived from their historical experience. In the concluding sections of the book, the authors speculate on the political implications of one country winning the race for the development of the supercomputers and on the cultural changes that the supercomputers may cause. The illustrations and diagrams clarify the text of the book. Provocative reading for students with some background knowledge of computers.

> *Edwin F. Bokee, in a review of "Supercomputers," in* School Library Journal, *Vol. 31, No. 10, August, 1985, p. 27.*

The importance of this book goes beyond the excellent introduction to the fourth and fifth generations of computers to the rivalry between the United States and Japan over the technological markets. The subtle dangers of prejudice are explored as one of the problems that will hamper the United States in its drive for computers with artificial intelligence. If the business managers and scientists continue to believe that the Japanese are limited to making copies or only improving existing models, they have defeated themselves in advance. If they continue to rely on translations of Japanese technological journals instead of learning to read Japanese technical materials, they are handicapping themselves. All in all, a fascinating mystery story is revealed with the possibility of bringing the old science fiction story of intelligent robots off the printed page into reality.

> *Shirley McFerson, in a review of "Supercomputers," in* Voice of Youth Advocates, *Vol. 8, No. 5, December, 1985, p. 330.*

With great detail and precision in reporting computer evolution, the authors predict the imminent arrival of the "fifth-generation" computers that will have a built-in intelligence. They see that day as the culmination of an important race in which the United States and Japan are the principal contestants. They further predict that the widespread application of this technology will change the nature of employment and the economic welfare of every industry and every nation. This topic is made accessible to many readers by the careful in-text definition of terms, simplified diagrams of basic computer workings, a short glossary, and an index. The subject matter and treatment live up to the [Impact Book] series intent of tackling matters of current worldwide importance. However, this thorough treatment will be needed only where sufficient interest exists, or where it can be used for term papers.

> *Georgann K. Jenkins, "Supercomputers," in* The Book Report, *Vol. 4, No. 4, January-February, 1986, p. 40.*

Wart, Son of Toad (1985)

Since the death of his mother and sister in a car crash, Steve Michaels, 16-years-old, has had a tough life. At school, he is nicknamed "Wart," after his father "Toad" (so named for the warts on his hands), who's a strict, almost universally disliked biology teacher. Steve is also a "dirt" ("On the average, dirts drink more, smoke more, skip more classes, and study less than most kids"); passing only his auto-mechanics class, he must bring up his average in order to be accepted into a special vocational ed. program. Tensions are high on the home front as well. Uptight Mr. Michaels is haunted by the memory of his dead wife and daughter (once knocking their photographs to the floor in a drunken fall), and takes it out on Steve. Michaels sneers at his son's lack of discipline, his "dirt" friends, and his blue-collar aspirations. But a series of fortuitous confrontations and crises conveniently solves all: mother and sister are finally laid to rest, Steve gets a girl-friend and his vocational program, Dad wisely changes jobs, and the two begin to accept each other. "So many things that had once seemed very important now seemed very small."

While some of the scenes between father and son have dramatic power, for the most part this is static, sappy, and relies much too heavily on contrivance. Perhaps this is most outrageous when Steve brings peace between arch-enemy dirts and jocks: after he and the star football player are forced to paint a storeroom as punishment for fighting, they unite to perform emergency CPR on the stricken assistant principal.

In sum, oversentimental and marred by a resolution that's far too pat.

A review of "Wart, Son of Toad," in Kirkus Reviews, *Vol. LIII, No. 21, November 1, 1985, p. 1197.*

Steve Michaels (Wart) is the unhappy son of an unhappy, unpopular science teacher whom the students have christened "Toad." The two live together in great tension three years following the accidental death of the boy's mother and younger sister. . . . Neither father nor son seems able to help the other. As Steve puts it, "We were connected by blood and the past, but no real lines of communication." The resolution of this problem, as well as several connecting story lines including a romantic angle, is nicely done. Carter is strong on characterization—readers can connect with any of his readily recognizable people—and Steve is a refreshing protagonist. Bewildered, afraid and sometimes angry, he comes far closer to reality than some of the overly-wise, sophisticated teenagers of many of today's novels and TV programs. Steve's first-person narrative is sprinkled with profanities; he is an unhappy young man expressing his frustrations realistically and in tune with his character. The father, with his faults uncovered, is nonetheless presented with empathy. In all, a good performance. (pp. 93-4)

Carter at his desk.

Robert Unsworth, in a review of "Wart, Son of Toad," in School Library Journal, *Vol. 32, No. 6, February, 1986, pp. 93-4.*

Modern China (1986)

Although this reads like a textbook, this volume should prove adequate for libraries needing curriculum support on China. Beginning with a brief introduction to the most populous country on Earth, Carter briefly describes China's history, emphasizing the events leading up to the revolution and eventually to the Mao era. Individually discussed are subjects such as family life, schooling, recreation, and daily life, while squared-off inserts in smaller print cover additional topics—medical care, the Taiwan question, and eating habits. Many of the black-and-white photographs [by Alden and Carol. S. Carter] offer interesting insights into life-styles but lack the clarity of a professional's camera.

Ilene Cooper, in a review of "Modern China," in Booklist, *Vol. 82, No. 19, June 1, 1986, p. 1458.*

A look at the problems facing China today from a historic point of view. The physical and geographic aspects of China are discussed as well as the historical development. Family life, education, work and recreation are covered. Black-and-white photos are included. Rau's *People of New China* (Messner, 1978; o.p.) looks at China by comparing life in the major cities. *People's Republic of China* (Childrens, 1984) by Valjean McLenighan contains more information on the government and important places. The Filstrups' *China: from Emperors to Communes* (Dillon Pr, 1983) looks at the culture of China and daily life; there is less emphasis on the history and current problems facing this emerging nation. *Modern China* will help with assignments on current problems and trends in China today.

Rena Brunner, in a review of "Modern China," in School Library Journal, *Vol. 32, No. 10, August, 1986, p. 90.*

The Carters have put together a readable text with an abundance of b&w photos of the Chinese at work and play. True to the title, 90% of the book is devoted to the lifestyles of the Chinese today. Only two chapters are dedicated to the long, complex history of China. Much more is given to explaining 20th-century China, its collision with the western world, and the political and cultural revolutions. The chapters are arranged to help children use this book as a general research tool. Separate chapters are devoted to family life and relationships, daily living, schooling, and work and play. The one shortcoming is the lack of maps. One simple map only shows 16 major cities, two major rivers and the bordering countries and ocean. The varied geography and population densities of this huge country are not shown. With a list of books for further study and an index, this book would be especially relevant for the collection that supports a world geography curriculum.

Connie Gilman, in a review of "Modern China," in The Book Report, *Vol. 5, No. 2, September-October, 1986, p. 50.*

Modern Electronics   (with Wayne J. LeBlanc, 1986)

Modern Electronics is intended for students from about grade six through the first two years of high school. The text presents a brief description of the atom and its constituent particles before moving on to simple electric circuits and its components. Semiconductor devices, detectors, amplifiers, and oscillators are dealt with functionally. Electromagnetic waves and the means of producing, detecting, and amplifying these waves are also presented. Some emphasis is placed on digital circuits and on their applications to computers. One of the book's strengths is the inclusion of a few experiments to support the concepts presented. These experiments range from the simple (marbles in a tube to illustrate electrons in a wire) to the rather complex (building a radio with a germanium diode). Elementary books of this sort often do more harm than good. In simplifying a subject, the authors may introduce incorrect concepts or outright errors. LeBlanc and Carter do better than most authors on this point; they have written a book that will be comprehensible to young people without creating too many wrong ideas. However, they cannot be totally absolved. For example, they state that insulators are those materials in which "all the electron shells of each atom are filled." Nevertheless, this book could be useful to an inquiring youngster who can then seek assistance from a knowledgeable teacher or parent.

R. Bowen Loftin, in a review of "Modern Electronics," in Science Books & Films, *Vol. 22, No. 4, March-April, 1987, p. 231.*

In 95 pages, the authors, one an electrical engineer and the other a highly-respected novelist for young adults, combine their abilities to present an overview of the field of electronics, stressing terminology and description rather than electronic theory and equations.

The text is unified by continual reference throughout to electronic circuits and components described in the opening chapters. These are worked into the latter chapters which stress the application of a wide variety of electronic devices in our lives from TV and radio to computers. Some attempt is made to explain electronic theories but this reviewer was left with the uncomfortable feeling of her own inadequacy in understanding basic questions about electricity. For example, why do we need both AC and DC current? Admittedly, the authors did not intend the book to be a remedial physics course, but appreciation of a subject's precision and elegance is often dependent upon a clearer view of basic principles than on detailed technological description. Fortunately, the book concludes with a reference list for further reading.

The authors maintain the perspective of an overview suitable for the First Book format [the volume is part of the "First Book" series published by Franklin Watts] while explaining just enough to give the young reader a sense of immediacy and substance, if not the actual understanding which ultimately depends on a knowledge of physics and mathematics.

Simple and not-so-simple experiments, a glossary and index, as well as thirty diagrams and photographs crystalize many points of the text which might be characterized as dry, despite a competent, lucid presentation about this pervasive presence in our modern lives. A final chapter speculates about the future of electronics. (pp. 39-40)

Sara Greenleaf, in a review of "Modern Electronics," in Appraisal: Science Books for Young People, *Vol. 20, No. 2, Spring, 1987, pp. 39-40.*

Modern Electronics is a very readable "first book" written at the level of Grade Four and above. It seeks to introduce the science of electricity and the technology of electronics. Each chapter has quite a large amount of information including definitions and the way electronic components, circuits and devices work. The sample experiments at the end of each chapter attempt to illustrate the principles using easily accessible material. A child doing it at home, a parent using it to motivate a child, or a teacher demonstrating it to a class can use these experiments to great advantage.

As much ground is covered here as a college level textbook of electronics, but much more simply, of course. In each chapter, there is a great effort to present ideas clearly and to bring home to the young mind, the spectacular forces, speeds, and capabilities of modern-day electronics in a way that generates enthusiasm. I can well imagine a child or an adult, for that matter continuing to learn from the book for years, absorbing and understanding a little more at each reading.

Pictures and photographs add to the clarity. The book is highly recommended, as a gift for a 9-10 year old with a fascination for electronics; or for a fourth or higher grade class unit on electronics.

Indira Nair, in a review of "Modern Electronics," in Appraisal: Science Books for Young People, *Vol. 20, No. 2, Spring, 1987, p. 40.*

Sheila's Dying (1987)

Sheila's Dying is a deeply moving story of the illness and death of a young girl. Sheila was orphaned as an infant and now, at 16, is dying of uterine cancer. Except for the alcoholic grandmother she lives with and cares for, Sheila is all alone. The story is told by her boyfriend, Jerry, who along with her best friend, Bonnie, assumes the responsibility of caring for Sheila until the end. The outstanding feature of this novel is its realism concerning all aspects of illness, hospital procedures, and the final stages of dying. Sheila as the dying patient is realistically portrayed—not extraordinarily heroic, sometimes demanding and impossible, and at other times serenely waiting for death. Jerry, as the narrator, honestly describes the burden of the caretakers—the grief, the fatigue, the anger and resentment, the guilt. Sure to be popular with those looking for "a sad story."

Janet Bryan, in a review of "Sheila's Dying," in School Library Journal, *Vol. 33, No. 8, May, 1987, p. 108.*

Some sensitive moments highlight this bland tale of chirpy teen-ager Sheila's fatal battle against cancer, and the unlikely partnership in deathbed loyalty of her good-guy, jock boyfriend Jerry and her brainy, misanthrophic "best friend" Bonnie.

When aspiring high-school actress Sheila, a riotously funny, rather empty-headed bon vivant, falls prey to her fatal illness, her sturdy basketball-star beau shelves his previous intention to "split up" with her, and dedicates himself to seeing her through "to the end"—despite the fact that he doesn't really love her—and forms an uncomfortable alliance with Bonnie, his high-school committee nemesis whom he nicknames "the Tiger" for her taunting mockery. Already a hospital volunteer, she also pledges time and caring in her friend's decline; and Bonnie and Jerry try to suspend their hostility, alternating hospital visits, cleaning the girl's home, and looking after her incompetent drunk grandmother. Gradually appreciating Jerry's gentle kindness, the Tiger's prejudice evolves into love and, though surprised by her confession of her feelings, Jerry responds and the two end up together after Sheila's death.

Sheila's empty-headed vivacity, Jerry's plodding goodness, and the Tiger's unprovoked hostility are all unconvincing, the result of standard characterization and plot line and unexceptional dialogue. Some tender moments between a briefly vulnerable Bonnie and a saddened Jerry, bonded in their grief, offer relief from the monotonous wait during Sheila's dying and from the predictability of the budding new love in this routine YA offering.

A review of "Sheila's Dying," in Kirkus Reviews, *Vol. LV, No. 8, May 1, 1987, p. 716.*

Carter demonstrates his versatility in a novel that once again features a male protagonist making difficult sacrifices for others. . . . Carter has written a tough book: the initial bloody outset of Sheila's illness and her deathbed desire to please Jerry by having sex with him will shock some; the story's language is rough, yet the author presents an unflinching view of death and conveys a real sense of Jerry's turmoil as he subjugates his desires to Sheila's needs. What is more, though the romance between Jerry and Bonnie seems foreordained, it won't be hard to accept their growing affection, as they struggle to support one another while watching their friend's pain. (pp. 1514-15)

Stephanie Zvirin, in a review of "Sheila's Dying," in Booklist, *Vol. 83, No. 19, June 1, 1987, pp. 1514-15.*

Radio: From Marconi to the Space Age (1987)

A solid history and explanation of an invention that changed history, this survey begins with Marconi's 1901 transoceanic radio transmission and follows with a retrospective look at earlier radio pioneers. Carter then moves forward in time, examining Marconi's career, the golden age of radio, the transistor revolution, and ends with a discussion of radio in the space age. Much of the information is technical; it will take an interested or informed reader to wade through some of the detailed descriptions. Still, those who want or need to know all about radio will certainly find this complete. Illustrated with black-and-white photographs and diagrams that expand on the more technical aspects of the subject.

Ilene Cooper, in a review of "Radio: From Marconi to the Space Age," in Booklist, *Vol. 84, No. 8, December 15, 1987, p. 703.*

Radio is an outstanding review of the development and application of radio technology. Alden Carter weaves personality sketches, historical vignettes, and accessible explanations of physical phenomena into a seamless narrative. In the first three pages of text, for example, the reader meets Marconi, witnesses the first transatlantic broadcast, and learns about the role of the ionosphere in radio wave propagation. The coverage of the book is also impressive, culminating in a discussion of such current topics as pulse code modulated packet radio. Serious students of either the history or technology of radio will want to dig deeper, of course, but it is hard to imagine a more effective 96-page introduction to the topic. (pp. 53-4)

> *Allan L. Fisher, in a review of "Radio: From Marconi to the Space Age," in* Appraisal: Science Books for Young People, *Vol. 21, No. 4, Fall, 1988, pp. 53-4.*

Illinois (1987)

A competent though superficial addition to a series on the states, ***Illinois*** opens with the author's airplane flight into Chicago, which serves to launch some geographical observations. Most of the text is a historical survey from Indian settlement to white expansion and into present-day problems and prosperity. This contains many relevant facts and is smoothly written, though it lacks human interest stories or vivid detail. With black-and-white photographs and an index, the book will serve its purpose for school assignments.

> *Betsy Hearne, in a review of "Illinois," in* Bulletin of the Center for Children's Books, *Vol. 41, No. 5, January, 1988, p. 84.*

This is a very superficial accounting of the history, geography, government, economy, natural resources, and culture of the state of Illinois. There is at least one error in the book. The Sears Tower has 110 stories not 109. The black and white photos are dull; the black and white state map has some dots indicating cities and some white lines indicating rivers. However, it is useless. The bibliography is meant for adults. There are two sentences on the Black Hawk War of 1832. The Lincoln-Douglas debates are mentioned in passing. Neither the Haymarket Riot, the Race Riots of 1919, nor the Columbian Exposition is mentioned in the index. In fact the index is not very helpful. It does not indicate whether a reference is to a photo or to text. There is an entry for buildings under Chicago. However, on page 71 the reference is to the construction industry. There is no mention of a specific building. Those of you who need material on Illinois might want to search elsewhere.

> *Civia Tuteur, in a review of "Illinois," in* Voice of Youth Advocates, *Vol. 10, No. 6, February, 1988, p. 294.*

[Carter's ***Illinois*** and Mary Virginia Fox's *Ohio*] cover the history, geography, politics, industry, natural resources, economy, and people of each state. The black-and-white photographs don't have the visual impact to invite browsing, and the writing is too dry for casual reading. However, the information is up-to-date and well organized, giving the books some potential use for school reports. For content and visual appeal Stein's *Illinois* (Childrens, 1987) is the best choice.

> *Eunice Weech, in a review of "Illinois," in* School Library Journal, *Vol. 34, No. 7, March, 1988, p. 205.*

Birth of the Republic; Colonies in Revolt (1988)

Useful if uninspired titles from "The American Revolution" series, which provide chronological narratives with italicized guide words, indexes, simplified maps, and many historical illustrations. ***Colonies*** describes the concerns of Loyalists and Patriots in 1770, discusses the familiar Stamp Act, Intolerable Acts, and Boston Tea Party, and concludes with the battles of Lexington and Concord in 1775. ***Birth*** begins in 1781 with the Battle of Yorktown and covers the surrender, peace, Articles of Confederation, the Continental Congress and the ratifying of the Constitution. Occasionally marred by effusive prose or unfortunate word choices, this is, nonetheless, serviceable supplemental material.

> *A review of "Birth of the Republic" and "Colonies in Revolt," in* Kirkus Reviews, *Vol. LVI, No. 19, October 1, 1988, p. 1466.*

Both of these books deal with some aspect of the Revolutionary period. Both are attractive and are clearly organized into short chapters. Period illustrations complement the texts nicely. However, ***Birth of the Republic*** lacks a clear focus. It describes the end of the Revolution, the peace treaty, the failure of the Articles of Confederation government, and the writing and ratification of the Constitution. This is just too much to cover in a 90-page format, and the text lacks good background information and is confusing because it jumps from topic to topic. *The Constitutional Convention* (Watts, 1976; o.p.) by Vaughan covers roughly the same material and does a better job. ***Colonies in Revolt*** covers the years before the Revolution, describing how the changes in British colonial policy led to colonial discontent and eventually revolution. It closes with the battles at Lexington and Concord. This book has a clear topic, and Carter follows a simple chronological arrangement, including a good amount of background and allowing readers to see how events moved steadily toward a breaking point. Libraries needing titles on this subject should consider purchasing it. *Birth of the United States* (Morrow, 1976; o.p.) by Bishop is a slightly better book, but ***Colonies*** will draw more readers due to its more attractive and easy-to-read format.

> *Mary Mueller, in a review of "Birth of the Republic" and "Colonies in Revolt," in* School Library Journal, *Vol. 35, No. 3, November, 1988, p. 135.*

Darkest Hours (1988)

If there is a weakness in this book, it is that the narration is personalized. In relating Artemas Ward's role in Boston, Carter states on two occasions that "Ward knew." In a section about George Washington, he writes that "Washington kept to himself the dismay he felt on first seeing the raw militia." If, indeed, Alden can document this and other such statements from diaries and letters, then it is incumbent upon him to include that information either in the text or notes. Nevertheless, this is a unique volume because it chronicles the various battles and their importance in the course of the Revolutionary War. It should be of great interest to war buffs, who will read it from cover to cover, as well as students looking for report material. Topics are illustrated with pertinent black-and-white maps, reproductions, engravings, and drawings.

> *Janet E. Gelfand, in a review of "Darkest Hours: The American Revolution," in* School Library Journal, *Vol. 35, No. 5, January, 1989, p. 97.*

At the Forge of Liberty   (1988)

Carter opens his account of the War for Independence in July of 1777, as Washington marches the Continental army through Philadelphia on its way to the Battle of the Brandywine. He recalls briefly some of the causes of the war and highlights of the events of 1775-77 through the memory of John Adams as he watches the troops pass. Having thus set the stage, Carter then moves quickly through the remaining years of the war, touching briefly on the major battles and campaigns. Of necessity, much detail is sacrificed, and only military action is described, with the sole exception of a short passage dealing with Franklin's negotiations in Paris. Carter's writing is clear, his material well organized, and his style lively enough to hold readers' interest. Reproductions of well-known paintings of Revolutionary subjects and maps of troop deployments illustrate the text. Information on individual topics covered is too brief to be of real use to report writers, but the book should be useful as a supplemental source, or for readers who just want an overview of the war. Bliven's *The American Revolution* (Random, 1963) is a longer treatment for the same age group, while Alderman's *The War We Could Have Lost* (Four Winds, 1974; o.p.) is a livelier and more complete account for a slightly older group.

> *Elaine Fort Weischedel, in a review of "At the Forge of Liberty," in* School Library Journal, *Vol. 35, No. 9, May, 1989, p. 115.*

Up Country   (1989)

Sixteen-year-old Carl uses his talent with electronics both to shield himself from his mother's alcoholism and promiscuity and to try to make enough money repairing stolen stereos to get into engineering school later. But when his mother is arrested for a drunken hit and run and Carl is packed off to live in the country with an aunt and uncle he barely knows, his escape plan seems doomed. Suddenly plunged into an unfamiliar setting, he's surrounded on all sides by "hicks" determined to break through his thin veneer of urban polish and a much thicker wall of guilt and alienation. Just when he begins to feel

at home with something like a real family, his involvement with the stereo thieves is discovered, and he stands to lose everything that has begun to matter to him. Although the premise of rehabilitating a delinquent kid with fresh air, hard work, and country living isn't original, Carter maintains interest by creating in Carl a strong central character and constructing a well-paced, believable plot. Carl's girlfriend is a refreshing change from many in fiction, and the language used is what you might expect from many contemporary teenagers. Carter avoids the temptations to offer easy solutions to the problems of children with alcoholic parents or to caricature his adult characters. A solid, unpreachy novel.

> *Barbara Hutcheson, in a review of "Up Country," in* School Library Journal, *Vol. 35, No. 10, June, 1989, p. 121.*

When his mother is arrested (again) for assault and remanded to an alcoholic treatment center, Carl is sent "up country" from Milwaukee to his aunt and uncle's farm, where he slowly reveals his vulnerability—a development credibly detailed in the novel—and recognizes how big his problems really are. The suspense of Carl's crime, arrest, and punishment sustain the gradual pace of his inner change, and the secondary characters are well developed both individually and in relationship to the protagonist. There's also a satisfying love story that unfolds between Carl and an appealing farm girl nearby. The C. O. A. (children of alcoholics) explanations are a bit overt at the end, but not enough to detract from the solidly realistic positive ending. This would have been melodramatic had it not been so carefully delineated; Carter has created a character who will involve YA readers and a situation that will make them think about the ways they solve whatever problems loom in their own lives.

> *Betsy Hearne, in a review of "Up Country," in* Bulletin of the Center for Children's Books, *Vol. 42, No. 11, July-August, 1989, p. 270.*

In *Growing Season*, Alden Carter explored the healing power of family, friends, and country life. *Up Country* picks up those same themes and integrates them with the effect of growing up in an alcoholic home. . . .

The children and adult children of alcoholics movements are catching fire in this country. Not surprisingly, these "CA/ACA" themes are beginning to surface in YA fiction. Carter has done a terrific job of bringing out the issues, but all within the framework of a well-told, if somewhat predictable, story. Gripping, satisfying, and heart-wrenching—another winner from a talented writer.

> *Stella Baker, in a review of "Up Country," in* Voice of Youth Advocates, *Vol. 12, No. 3, August, 1989, p. 155.*

Alexandra Day

19??-

American author and illustrator of picture books.

The creator of humorous animal fantasies which are often set in the 1940s or 1950s, Day is best known for writing and illustrating the popular picture books about Carl, a good-natured Rottweiler babysitter who takes his young charge on clandestine adventures, and Frank and Ernest, a bear and elephant who own a service agency specializing in taking care of small businesses for their owners. In *Good Dog, Carl* (1985), Carl and his owner's young daughter wreak havoc on their home when the baby's mother leaves Carl in charge, while in *Carl Goes Shopping* (1989) the pair explore a department store after Carl is again ordered to watch the baby; in both works, Carl is able to emerge successfully from his escapades, thus winning the praise of his oblivious owner. As with the "Carl" books, in which Day's realistic paintings tell most of the stories, *Frank and Ernest* (1988) and *Frank and Ernest Play Ball* (1990) include only a few lines of dialogue on each page. These works, however, focus on the joys of wordplay: in the first book, Frank and Ernest, who are asked to take care of a diner for three days, learn the hashhouse lingo and make up inventive names for each order, while in *Play Ball* the pair learn about baseball terms when they are asked to manage a ballpark and its team. Day also adds a glossary of traditional restaurant terms to *Frank and Ernest* and lists forty-three baseball expressions and their meanings at the end of *Play Ball*. Also the author and illustrator of a picture book fantasy about the activities of a performing Irish terrier on his day off in the Ireland of the early 1940s, Day is credited as an artist whose realistic, detailed watercolor illustrations underscore both the plausibility and the humor of her whimsical tales. Day has also provided the illustrations for the works of other authors such as Cooper Edens and Jimmy Kennedy.

sence. David Lassman of Imagination Station finds that the realism of Day's paintings only heightens the sense of whimsy. "The anatomy of the baby and the dog are incredible. And Day gives enough drawings to let the story have time to unfold."

Teresa Moore, "Area Booksellers Name Their Favorite Titles," in Book World—The Washington Post, *May 8, 1988, p. 16.*

Frank and Ernest (1988)

Frank, a bear, and Ernest, an elephant, specialize in taking care of small businesses while the owner is away. When Mrs. Miller hires them to run her diner for three days, they assure her that they will take good care of it. Then Frank decides they must learn diner lingo before they begin. For an order of a hot dog with ketchup and a dish of Jell-O, Ernest yells, "Paint a bow-wow red, and I need a nervous pudding." And for a vanilla milk shake with an egg in it, to go, Frank calls out for a "white cow—make it cackle and let it walk." As Frank and Ernest take care of the customers, readers will enjoy the funny way in which an order is translated into diner-ese; it's just the kind of wordplay that kids like, and love to imitate. Frank

Good Dog, Carl (1985)

Confused about what books to buy a son or daughter, niece or nephew? In the Washington area many booksellers are happy to help nervous shoppers make the perfect match between a young friend and a good writer. . . .

One book that grown-ups and kids alike never seem to tire of is *Good Dog, Carl* by Alexandra Day. Myra Strauss of the Book Nook calls this story told with only two lines of text, "a quiet book. Teachers have been using it to get kids to develop language and sequence skills by having them tell what's happening to Carl and the baby in each picture."

In *Good Dog, Carl* a mother says to a huge black dog, "Look after the baby, Carl. I'll be back soon." Mom's hardly out of the door when the baby climbs over the railing of her bed onto Carl's back. Carl and the baby entertain themselves by wrecking the house. Fortunately, Carl is that rare babysitter who will cover a kid's tracks and not tell Mom what kind of hooliganism occurred in her ab-

and Ernest, in stodgy colors of brown and gray, form a contrast to the airy lines of the gleaming diner, but look perfectly comfortable in the art of slinging hash.

> *A review of "Frank and Ernest," in* Publishers Weekly, *Vol. 233, No. 25, June 24, 1988, p. 112.*

These two partners take their work seriously, but they clearly enjoy working together and know how to have a good time. The full-color illustrations carry the action, as the two are seen pouring coffee, flipping eggs, and popping toast. Background scenes and fashion perfectly capture the late '40s or early '50s setting, particularly the kitchen equipment and the women's hats. Small details that add humor abound: a British flag decorates a plate of English muffins; a safety pin attaches an onion to a hamburger roll. The text is just a few lines of dialogue per page—"I need a white cow—make it cackle and let it walk" (a vanilla milk shake with an egg in it, to go). An added plus is a glossary of additional restaurant language. Clever and original, this playful romp serves up its message with a smile. It's bound to become standard fare for story hour specials.

> *Trev Jones, in a review of "Frank and Ernest," in* School Library Journal, *Vol. 34, No. 11, August, 1988, p. 80.*

Hash house terminology is the whole point of a story that is more situation than narrative, as customers give orders and the eponymous heroes translate. Frank and Ernest fill

in at a diner when the owner goes away for three days; there's no explanation of why Frank and Ernest are the only animals (bear and elephant) while the owner and all the customers are people. Nor is it clear why the owner apparently had no assistant to share the work as the animals do. Oversize pages have adequate but unimpressive paintings. The chief appeal rests in the restaurant cant; a customer orders apple pie and a glass of milk, relayed by Frank as "Eve with a lid and moo juice." This may entice the audience to its own translations.

> *Zena Sutherland, in a review of "Frank and Ernest," in* Bulletin of the Center for Children's Books, *Vol. 42, No. 1, September, 1988, p. 5.*

Paddy's Payday   (1989)

Paddy, an acrobatic Irish terrier, is travelling the Irish countryside in a show wagon with his mistress. The original *Lassie, Come Home* is playing at the local theater, dating this as 1943 (first-run), or a bit later if this is a backwater town. It is Paddy's day off, and his mistress gives him a bag of coins as his pay. Paddy sets out on his errands: buying goodies at a doughnut shop; visiting the barber; paying a hurdy-gurdy man while his purse is snatched by two boys (who use the proceeds to buy ice-cream cones); buying a ribbon at the milliner's; attending the above mentioned flick; going to a sterotypical Irish pub to have a sterotypical baked potato and ale; buying roses for

"Gentlemen, the place looks beautiful, and I've heard nothing but good things from my friends who ate here in the last few days. You did a fine job, and I'll recommend your services to everyone I know."

From Frank and Ernest, *written and illustrated by Alexandra Day.*

his mistress; giving the remains of his pay to an animal fund (pretty ironic for an exploited show dog!); and finally returning home to bestow the flowers on his mistress and sleep on the floor beside her bed. After such an anthropomorphized day, this ending is a bit jarring. Watercolor illustrations are generally pleasant, although the night scenes are less sucessful due to their muddiness. Dialogue is unduly dull, with "Paddy" being apostrophized on practically every page. Although crowded with incident, there is little of interest in this period-piece manqué.

> *John Philbrook, in a review of "Paddy's Pay Day," in* School Library Journal, *Vol. 35, No. 15, November, 1989, p. 78.*

Carl Goes Shopping   (1989)

The sleek, benevolent Rottweiler who took such good care of the baby at home in *Good Dog, Carl* has another babysitting adventure with his young charge—this time, when Mom leaves them at the bottom of the escalator while she goes to pick up some curtains. Carl gets the baby out of her carriage and onto his back so that they can explore—toys, where baby gets a truck ride; books, where she looks at *Rottweilers I Have Known;* hats, carpets, food, and pets, each with an entertaining activity to offer—before they make it back to the carriage, just as Mom returns. The bright, tactile, beguilingly realistic illustrations in this almost wordless book make it all seem surprisingly plausible. (pp. 1668-69)

> *A review of "Carl Goes Shopping," in* Kirkus Reviews, *Vol. LVII, No. 22, November 15, 1989, pp. 1668-69.*

Wordless except for the first and last pages ("I have to go upstairs to get Aunt Martha's curtains. Take good care of the baby, Carl . . . Good Dog Carl!"), this is an entertaining picture narrative in which a large black dog plays nanny. . . . The plot is clearly revealed by the pantomime, which is not always the case in wordless picture-books. The illustrations are thick paint on gray-blue paper, and the fluid drafting of both human and animal against smoothly textured backgrounds focuses the main

characters with magnetic precision. Straightfaced details and closely portrayed expressions lend humor to a wishful fantasy that will storytell well with small children.

> *Betsy Hearne, in a review of "Carl Goes Shopping," in* Bulletin of the Center for Children's Books, *Vol. 43, No. 5, January, 1990, p. 108.*

The hero of *Good Dog, Carl* is back for another thoroughly enjoyable adventure. . . . Day gives free rein to her imagination, and the resulting romp will provoke gasps and giggles from young people. Even nonreaders will be able to follow each turn of the plot, although the youngest may be confused by seeing Carl in separate vignettes as many as three times on a page. Day's intensely realistic paintings cover every inch of each page, offering the most pinchable baby and pettable dog of the season.

> *Ellen Fader, in a review of "Carl Goes Shopping," in* The Horn Book Magazine, *Vol. LXVI, No. 1, January-February, 1990, p. 50.*

Frank and Ernest Play Ball   (1990)

[Alexandra Day introduces] young children to baseball terms in *Frank and Ernest Play Ball.* Frank, a bear, and Ernest, an elephant, make their living as substitute managers who take over for business owners when they're away. They first appeared in *Frank and Ernest,* where they managed a diner and had to learn the lingo. . . . Now they're managing a ballpark and its team, the Elmville Mudcats. When Mr. Palmer tells them that the Mudcats have many fine fans, Frank and Ernest wonder what the fans are used for. Of course they realize their mistake as soon as they look up *fans* in the *Dictionary of Baseball.* Young readers will have fun with the language, and those who don't know the complete words to "The Star-Spangled Banner" and "Take Me Out to the Ball Game" can learn them here. Included on the front and back endpapers are forty-three baseball terms and their meanings.

> *Susan Stan, "Play Ball!" in* The Five Owls, *Vol. IV, No. 5, May-June, 1990, p. 95.*

Brian Doyle

1935-

Canadian author of fiction.

Celebrated as one of Canada's most distinguished writers for young adults, Doyle is the creator of historical and contemporary realistic fiction which balances the exploration of serious themes with humor and optimism. Called Canada's answer to Judy Blume, he is acclaimed for his insight and sensitivity in depicting the moral dilemmas of the young in works which characteristically use the journey motif to parallel the growth of their protagonists. Doyle is often considered unique among Canadian writers for his concentration on the inner feelings of his characters, for the experimental nature of several of his books, and for his concentration on mature concerns. He is also highly praised as a storyteller and a creator of character as well as a powerful, accomplished literary stylist. Credited for the lyrical and anecdotal quality of his narratives as well as for their successful reflection of a variety of moods, Doyle is considered both an exceptional writer of realistic fiction and a brilliant comic writer whose style ranges from spare to extravagant. Set in and around Ottawa, the city in which Doyle grew up and in which he continues to live, his works are often acknowledged for their evocation of atmosphere and place as well as for their universality despite a regional focus.

Doyle began his career with two works about a contemporary family, *Hey, Dad!* (1978) and *You Can Pick Me Up at Peggy's Cove* (1980). In the first novel, thirteen-year-old Megan travels across Canada by car with her family, a journey which provides her with an opportunity to reevaluate her relationship with them, especially with her father; in the second work, Megan's brother Ryan learns to deal with his feelings after his dad runs away. With *Up to Low* (1982), Doyle introduces young readers to a picturesque community with a mythic flavor: in this book, teenage narrator Tommy returns to Low, a hill town in the Ottawa Valley, for the first time since his mother's death and falls in love with the handicapped daughter of his father's rival, who is dying of cancer. A rollicking tale which includes slapstick humor and larger-than-life portrayals, *Up to Low* is also lauded as a moving story which considers such themes as death, healing, and redemption. Its sequel, *Angel Square* (1984), again combines hilarity with seriousness in a novel which takes place in postwar Lowertown; addressing the issue of racism, Doyle describes Tommy's investigation of the beating of the best friend's father, a Jew. In *Easy Avenue* (1988), a comic novel again set in Ottawa just after the war, an impoverished young man encounters a mysterious benefactor. Depicting the battle between good and evil against a background of both poverty and wealth, Doyle provides his audience with a hopeful story which is often compared to *Great Expectations. Up to Low* received the Canadian Library Association Book of the Year Award in 1983, a prize also won by *Easy Avenue* in 1989.

AUTHOR'S COMMENTARY

[The following excerpt is from an interview by Amy Vanderhoof.]

"In all of my books, I've purposefully included a word so that schools won't use them," says Brian Doyle. . . .

The 47-year-old Doyle. . . . sounds as if he has the makings of a publisher's nemesis. But if he appears on the one hand to be deliberately discouraging sales, he's certainly not keeping young readers away. His first two books made respectable showings for the previously unknown author: *Hey Dad* and *You Can Pick Me Up at Peggy's Cove,* . . . have sold 7,000 copies apiece so far. And when he takes to the road to read to groups of children, Doyle is magnetic. "At the launch of last year's Children's Book Festival at Rideau Hall in Ottawa," says Virginia Davis, director of the Children's Book Centre, "Doyle kept the audience of more than 150 children unanimously absorbed and responding to his humour. My conviction is that he's one of the authors who's going to become enormously popular once more kids find out about him through word of mouth."

Up to Low—Low is a town in the Gatineau Hills where Doyle spent his boyhood summers—will intrigue not-so-young as well as young adults. Doyle's writing is rhythmic and musical, mixing humour and incredible sensitivity, and his characterizations are strong and often hilarious. There's Aunt Dottie, for instance, a germ fanatic who recommends, " . . . always put toilet paper on the seat if you're at somebody else's house. And never touch the toothpaste tube on your toothbrush when you're putting on toothpaste. . . . And don't eat candy unless it's wrapped. And always wipe yourself three times."

"Everyone knows someone like Aunt Dottie," Doyle chuckles. "My mother was quite a cleanliness nut; she'd be in the bathroom for hours. My father would say that she was taking so long because she was washing herself with a Q-tip."

But some, no doubt, will be offended by his story-telling, particularly his humorous portrayal of drinking in the character of Frank. "Well, then, they just shouldn't buy the book," replies Doyle, as frankly as he responds to those who complain about an obscene word. ("You want to talk about one word out of 35,000? Let's talk about every word.") "I don't buy the idea that kids shouldn't read it because they're going to run out and get drunk afterwards. You have to have faith in young people's natural instincts. Kids just think the character is funny."

Hey Dad was written for Doyle's daughter following a family trip to the West Coast. "My daughter was at that age, just pre-puberty," he recalls, "when I so desperately loved her, I felt I knew her as well as I knew myself." After their return, father and daughter were comparing their notes of the trip and Doyle started arranging them into paragraphs. "Some of the neighbour kids were coming over and reading them. I first realized it was a book when they started asking what happened next."

The book was rejected by several publishers until Patsy Aldana at Groundwood recognized its potential. But before publication, Doyle says, it underwent substantial changes. "It had been done in an unintentional way, so I rewrote it and smoothed it out into one tone, one voice."

Doyle, however, is the father of two, and after his success with *Hey Dad,* his son Ryan (now 16) began asking, "What about a book for me?" The result was *You Can Pick Me Up at Peggy's Cove,* whose underlying theme, according to Doyle, is the feeling a boy has for his dad. . . .

Out of kids, and his wife not requesting a book about herself, Doyle turned to his own childhood for *Up to Low* and infused the book with tales of his parents, grandparents and great-grandparents. "My family is alive in my mind mainly because of my father, who was a story-teller," he says. "We'd be in our bunks in the Gatineaus pretending to be asleep but listening to his stories. I think he made up most of them, but that's as good as reality."

It is this same technique that Doyle has incorporated into his own writing. His family, his memories of his adventures as son and as parent, provide the jumping off point for his fiction.

The theme of *Up to Low* is forgiveness, which Doyle believes is one of kids' real concerns. Baby Bridget's father, Mean Hughie, a nasty individual deserving of his name, had slapped her when a runaway binding machine cut off her arm when she was a child. Now Mean Hughie is dying, and Baby Bridget and Young Tommy, the book's narrator, learn about loving and forgiveness, healing and dying.

Although he won't talk about other authors (and maintains he doesn't read much of the competition in any case), Doyle feels that kids' concerns—their *real* concerns—are the same as everyone else's: courage, love, strength, fear. "Hitchhiking, masturbation, menstruation, all those problems in kids' books from adultery to zits, those aren't the real concerns; those are problems that adults see in kids. Their real concerns are the classic concerns, the ones with the capital letters." *Huckleberry Finn,* he reminds me, is not cluttered with contemporary notions of sexuality. And neither are his books. There may be the occasional profanity, anecdotes about farting, and Black Horse Ale consumed by the gallon, but there is no sex beyond an innocent kiss.

Up to Low rolls off the tongue, begs to be read aloud. . . .

"A lot of books for kids have information but they don't have language," Doyle stresses. "But kids have ears; they may not be able to articulate the fact, but they like language: they can hear it. A number of publishers who turned my book down said that kids can't do that. But Patsy Aldana saw that kids can."

> *Ann Vanderhoof, "Prankster, Teacher, Writer: Brian Doyle Is Up to Good," in* Quill and Quire, *Vol. 48, No. 12, December, 1982, p. 27.*

GENERAL COMMENTARY

Wendy R. Katz

"Dying and loving somebody," the thirteen-year-old narrator of Brian Doyle's *Hey, Dad!* muses. "I always end up thinking of those two together. Dying and loving". Indeed, dying and loving are of paramount importance in Megan's narration of her family's summer holiday drive from Ottawa to the Pacific. Like the grieving child of Hopkins' "Spring and Fall," Megan is saddened by a sense of mortality that is yet dimly understood. Slowly she makes the connection between death and love, especially as they affect her relationship with her father. Megan eventually reckons with her own mortality as well as that of her parents and considers, in her green and vulnerable way, the deaths of all those people who have gone before her and all those that will come after. *You Can Pick Me Up at Peggy's Cove* . . . is likewise about love and death, although the design here is less obvious and, consequently, more impressive. In this book, also written in the first person, narrator Ryan (Megan's brother, incidentally) must deal with, among other things, the death of a fisherman friend at Peggy's Cove, a death that follows directly from the great love of this man for another fisherman and one that helps Ryan to understand his own sense of loss: he has been sent to this Atlantic Coast fishing village to live with his aunt while his father, having run away from home because of a mid-life crisis, decides whether or not to return. Both books depend heavily on their setting to define and develop their narrator's comprehension of love and death, grief and loss. The children examine the landscape and seascape with an inward- as well as an outward-looking eye. The result, on balance, is strikingly good.

Doyle's books are, superficially at least, part of the "holiday story" tradition. Their season is summer, when children are customarily free to revel in new and exciting experiences. Doyle's children, however, unlike the wholesome adventurers of, say, the Arthur Ransome holiday stories, are not segregated from the adult world; they do not wander at will. On the contrary, they are in close and occasionally oppressive proximity to adults and adult concerns. In this sense the books are unique, as are their fully-rounded adult characters. . . . The tension between adult and child provides the sustaining conflict for these stories.

Doyle's emphasis is not on the adventures the children have but on their psychological states of being. Megan doesn't want to go on the trip to the west and she spends a good deal of time—but not all of it—being miserable. Ryan is the more compelling character: he must deal with his father's crisis, the fisherman Eddie and his mute fishing partner Wingding, his aunt who runs a tourist shop, and all the tourists who visit Peggy's Cove. In an effort to work out what it means to have a father who has suddenly become "different," Ryan goes about defining for himself the bounds of normality. What with Wingding, who makes smacking sounds instead of speaking, the Widow Weed, who talks to a shark's skull, Mrs. Drummond, who lives in a white and black room, and the assorted tourists who appear and disappear, Ryan finds a generous store of diversity among adults.

Doyle clearly tries to establish a network of relationships for his child characters. They see themselves not only in relation to adults in their families—father, mother, aunt, grandfather, etc.—but in relation to people beyond the family, friends and strangers alike, to nature, and to the universe. In *Hey, Dad!,* history, the land, and our place in it all come together towards the end when Megan, simultaneously tormented and awestruck by the landscape and the sovereignty of time, goes down to the Athabaska River and listen to its voice:

> "Decade is ten years. Century is a hundred years. Millennium is a thousand years. Eons is years and years and ages and ages." . . . I was trying to stretch my mind so that I could think about how long an eon was. It was how long the Athabaska roared his deep roar. I stretched my mind. I grunted and held my breath and forced my mind to wrap around that long, long time. I thought of the summer and how long it was, and how long it was that I was in grade four and how long next year would be and then I thought of myself after Dad and Mum were dead and then after I was an old wrinkled lady and how that wouldn't even be a century yet.

In the *Peggy's Cove* book such pointedly "significant" passages are harder to come by. However, when Ryan's father finally returns, the boy imagines father and son together, caught within the lens of a camera in his head that moves "back, back and up, until you could see the whole of Peggy's Cove with the foam smashing away at the lighthouse and the pretty colours and the boats out at sea and the tiny tourists running around the little white dots that were gulls. And the tiny still figures in the middle of it all. That was Dad and me." The child and the father move

from foreground to background, gradually becoming part of the larger landscape, with the camera focus set at infinity.

With regard to structure, both works are carefully developed. Each child works up to a particular crisis prior to a satisfactory resolution of the problems. For Megan the crisis occurs when she succeeds in running away from her troublesome father and discovers almost immediately how much she loves him. Shortly after rejoining her parents, Megan visits the Miette Hot Springs where she momentarily mistakes a man who has just died at poolside for her father and again feels the strength of her love. Ryan's crisis, less contrived than Megan's, occurs when he befriends "the Drummer," a local boy and petty thief. Ryan helps the Drummer to steal from the Peggy's Cove tourists and they are, predictably, caught by the police. Ryan, sufficiently punished by this experience, is returned to the custody of his aunt. Later, Eddie, Ryan's fisherman friend, loses his thumb to a shark and Wingding, who goes after the shark, is drowned. Because the reader actually cares about these characters (they are not simply dragged onto the set for convenience like the dead man in *Hey, Dad!*), Ryan's crisis is far more moving than his sister's.

Brian Doyle is, fortunately for us, not Canada's answer to Judy Blume. His books do not descend to the sit-com or soap variety of children's literature. However popular and accessible his style, it is also sensitive, intelligent, and witty—love and death are relieved by a great deal of humour. Although his work occasionally verges on pretentiousness and contrivance, and Megan and Ryan will not sit comfortably as first-person narrators alongside Huck Finn, Jim Hawkins, or even Oswald Bastable, Brian Doyle's writing for children must be assessed as accomplished and impressive. (pp. 47-50)

> *Wendy R. Katz, " 'Dying and Loving Somebody'," in* Canadian Children's Literature, *No. 22, 1981, pp. 47-50.*

Hey, Dad! (1978)

Here is a new author with a new approach to realistic writing for young people. Doyle has written a junior novel we have been waiting for—one that is not a trend book or a social documentary; rather a novel that will reinforce young people's tender feelings and gently encourage them to find their own answers to the age old questions.

Megan has reached the difficult age of 13 when conflicting competences confuse her understanding of human relationships. Some days she hates her father, mother and brother in turn—and she does *not* want to travel across Canada by car with them.

But off the family go on a summer holiday trip that takes them from Ottawa to Serpent River, Blind River, Thessalon, Echo Bay and other exotic places on the way to the Pacific coast. Subliminally educational, the text does evoke the geography of regional Canada, and in the end Megan finds that she has learned a lot, and not just about Canadian places.

The book essentially deals with family love relationships. How can you hate your brother and be so scared when he almost falls off a mountain? How can you hate your father's easy approach to life, and then almost freak out when you think he has died in the sulphur baths? How can you identify with a competent, intelligent mother who can yet enjoy her husband's silly antics? And Megan finds out about some of life's contradictions on the family odyssey across the nation that epitomizes her own journey toward maturity.

> *Irma McDonough, in a review of "Hey, Dad!" in* In Review: Canadian Books for Children, *Vol. 12, No. 4, Autumn, 1978, p. 57.*

You Can Pick Me Up at Peggy's Cove (1980)

Brian Doyle has that rare gift of insight which enables him to breathe life into his portrayals of adolescents. *Hey, Dad!* focused on Megan's growing pains, and her relationship with her family, especially her father, as they travelled by car across Canada. This sequel to it is her brother Ryan's story of the summer he spent with his aunt at Peggy's Cove—the summer after their father ran away. . . .

[The] overwhelming desire to have his father come for him becomes the catalyst for much of what Ryan does. Maybe if his dad thinks he has turned to a life of crime, he'll come; maybe when he realizes the danger of being out on the high seas fishing, he'll come. Ryan's actions, real and imagined, go into a long letter which hopefully will prompt his dad to return. And all the while, the reader is treated to a look at the inner workings of his mind—a look which will cause many a jolt of recognition.

Doyle's secondary characters are skillfully drawn and delightfully memorable. He establishes some nice moods throughout the story, and did a better job of pacing than in *Hey, Dad!* Once again, the reader will unconsciously pick up a feeling for a Canadian place and its way of life.

My only negative criticism is in regard to the descriptions of the hordes of tourists who invade Peggy's Cove, and a stampede to get photographs of the sunset, or places to eat, or pictures of the fish gutting. Fewer hyperboles would have made these scenes more effective and less distracting.

> *Mickie McClear, in a review of "You Can Pick Me up at Peggy's Cove," in* In Review: Canadian Books for Children, *Vol. 14, No. 4, August, 1980, p. 45.*

Ryan's dad, caught up in a mid-life crisis, runs away from home. Ryan is sent to Peggy's Cove to stay with Aunt Fay for the summer. While he's there, Eddie and Wingding teach him how to fish, and Drummer teaches him how to rip off tourists. On the outside, Ryan is a thief and then a hero; on the inside, he's happy, sad, worried, and scared. He misses his dad, and he tries to figure out how to make him feel sad, how to make him feel guilty, how to make him come back. . . .

In the promotion material that came with the book, Doyle's publisher hails him as "Canada's Judy Blume". Maybe. But why must Canadians be compared with Americans? This book is sensitive, insightful, funny, sad and true. And it's Canadian. Buy it.

> *Adele Ashby, in a review of "You Can Pick Me*

> *Up at Peggy's Cove," in* Quill and Quire, *Vol. 48, No. 8, August, 1980, p. 30.*

You Can Pick Me Up at Peggy's Cove is a very nice book—in the best sense of the term. Doyle respects both his readers and his characters. He is not a condescending story teller, neither does he try to talk as though he were the same age as his readers. He sensitively explores the strengths and weaknesses of his characters and understands well the need of everyone for love. He is also a superb stylist. The book has many moods ranging from loneliness and guilt to love and respect and the style is subtly modulated to reflect them all.

The main setting, Peggy's Cove, one of the best known landmarks in Canada, is not just realistically portrayed. It becomes a symbol. On the one hand, it is a place through which thousands of curious but insensitive tourists stream each year. On the other hand, it is a fishing village in which the residents live and work together, respecting each other's individuality, but cooperating and sensitively responding to the good times and the bad.

You Can Pick Me Up at Peggy's Cove is not a sensational book as are so many of the stories of social realism. Rather it is a sensitive and compelling story which will continue to find readers for many years to come. (pp. 30-1)

> *Jon C. Stott, "A Second Baker's Dozen: Our Selection of the Best Canadian Books of 1980," in* The World of Children's Books, *Vol. VI, 1981, pp. 27-33.*

Up to Low (1982)

Set in the Gatineau Hills of his own boyhood holidays, Brian Doyle's *Up to Low* has a flavour quite unlike that of his earlier work. There is an almost mythic quality in this story of Mean Hughie, a violent and unpopular man, and his handicapped daughter, Baby Bridget. Years ago, as a mere baby, Bridget lost her arm to the knives of a runaway binder and had been struck by her father for getting in its way. Small wonder if such a man has not a friend in the world.

The hero and narrator, Young Tommy, has returned to the hill town of Low for the first time in years and been bowled over by Bridget's beauty, especially by her green eyes which remind him of trilliums. It is a time of crisis in the young 18-year-old woman's life. Mean Hughie is dying of a cancer that is slowly wasting his once powerful frame, and he has vanished into the wilderness to die, as he has lived, alone. Bridget herself has apparently fallen prey to a "healer", and has an impossible dream that her lost arm might be restored. Tommy dreads the disappointment she must surely suffer, but strangely enough, the healer's advice that Bridget make the dangerous effort to seek out Mean Hughie does indeed lead her to the healing she has longed for; a healing not of the flesh but of the wounded spirit.

This story, alternately magically moving and robustly funny, is a loving picture of no-nonsense people of courage and common sense whose faith is enlivened by a dash of superstition. For a more sophisticated audience than Doyle's earlier titles, *Up to Low* is something special among books for young adults.

*Joan McGrath, "A Clutch of Juvenile Novels
with No-Nonsense Plots," in* Quill and Quire,
Vol. 48, No. 11, November, 1982, p. 26.

Novels for young people, almost by definition, are about
misfits searching for their place in the world—the shared
interior journey of every teenager. *Up to Low* reverses the
usual pattern: its hero and narrator, Young Tommy, is a
sane and loving teenager who helps a slapstick and misfit
world find its feet. . . .

[The plot] all sounds grim. But Doyle has a cartoon way
with character that lets him get away with a plot packed
with excess. It also lets him get away with his big themes
of redemption, forgiveness and love. Young Tommy falls
in love with Baby Bridget, the girl with the green eyes
shaped like trillium petals—and the missing arm. And, in
the end, despite his own fear, he helps her find her terrible
father and achieve a healing that has nothing to do with
physical wounds. (p. 56)

*Anne Collins, "Tales for the Computer Gener-
ation," in* Maclean's Magazine, *Vol. 95, No.
50, December 13, 1982, pp. 56-8.*

Tommy's relatives are all caricatures—he has five aunts
always busy with prescribed household tasks, five uncles
always smoking. To describe most of the novel's many
characters as one-dimensional would be generous. There
is Crazy Mickey, Tommy's 100-year-old great-grand-
father; his father's drunken friend Frank, who keeps driving his new car into trees and buildings; Father Sullivan,
the priest who manhandles Frank into church and makes
him sign the pledge. Dominating the story is Mean Hughie, Tommy's father's old rival.

The book is always funny but Doyle's humour is often
black, to say the least, and sometimes heavy, of the out-
house and open-coffin variety. However, he describes with
great sensitivity Tommy's developing affection for Baby
Bridget. . . . That description, along with the strong evocation of setting and the plot's quick and certain action
make this Doyle's best novel yet. (p. 33)

*Mary Ainslie Smith, in a review of "Up to
Low," in* Books in Canada, *Vol. 12, No. 2,
February, 1983, pp. 32-3.*

Up to Low is told in the rambling, anecdotal, extravagant
style of an indefatigable raconteur. The listeners in this
case are hanging around the doorway hoping that nobody
will notice them and send them to bed. The story—and it
goes on far into the night—tells of Young Tommy, who
drives with his father for a holiday up from Ottawa into
the Gatineau Hills.

In the picaresque novel we are introduced to a wonderful
cast of characters. In broad brush strokes Doyle creates
Auntie Dottie, proponent of manic cleanliness; Frank, the
worst driver along the Gatineau River; and a whole family
of red-headed Hendricks. We get to know a host of people
thriftily identified in such community shorthand as
"Mean Hughie," "The Hummer," or "Crazy Mickey."
This is a world ripe with story—with anecdote and rumor,
scandal and tall tale, sentimental ballads that have passed
down four generations, and a running gag we can see ap-
proaching from a mile away. It is an extravagant world,
larger than life—full of big families, catalogs, and gargan-

tuan meals. And everything is tied together with a mastery
of deadpan comic writing that is as strong as binder twine.
For these qualities alone *Up to Low* deserves a wide audience. But the story is more than a series of small-town vignettes à la Stephen Leacock. Above, below, and through
this romp flows a moving story of death, love, and healing.

Many of the tall tales in the story center around Mean
Hughie—his great strength, his terrible temper, his capacity for revenge, and his sickness. "They say Mean
Hughie's got the cancer" says someone at every truck
stop, every bar, every store on the way up to Low. To
which the invariable reply is "I'll believe it when I see it."
We do not actually meet the legendary Hughie until the
end of the book, but we do meet his wife "Poor Bridget"
and his daughter, now a young woman but still known as
"Baby Bridget." And we hear the worst story about Mean
Hughie: how Baby Bridget had her arm cut off in a binder
accident and how Hughie hit her before he made the tour-
niquet that saved her life.

The golden thread that parallels this dark one is the growing love of Tommy, the narrator, for Baby Bridget. In a
state of heightened awareness Tommy sees Low in a new
way. When Doyle describes Tommy noticing how moonlight makes a cross on the screen door or how a dragonfly
emerges, his writing takes on a spare, lyrical quality. . . .

The two threads of love and death come together in the
final scene in which Tommy and Bridget set out looking
for Mean Hughie and find him in a cabin in the bush, lying
in the coffin he has just completed for himself. Before he
dies he and Bridget are reconciled. This scene combines
gothic, comic, and epic elements with a strain of moving
simplicity.

Up to Low is a book that takes a lot of risks. It very nearly
goes out of control. But the reason it succeeds so well lies
in the first-person voice of Tommy, whose quiet, observant, naïve tone frames the whole rollicking crowded narrative in genuine human feeling. Brian Doyle has created
a fine storyteller. (pp. 101-03)

Sarah Ellis, "News from the North," in The
Horn Book Magazine, *Vol. LX, No. 1, February, 1984, pp. 99-103.*

This book for adolescent readers tells Young Tommy's
own story of how he comes to terms with changes: changes
in his life after the death of his mother; changes in the
world around him as he moves out of childhood into adolescence; changes in his relationships with the adults
around him. As the cover notes state, perhaps a trifle por-
tentously, Young Tommy and his friend Baby Bridget discover that "loving and healing and dying are not always
what they seem."

In the story, Young Tommy journeys with his father up
to Low, where they have a summer cabin. It is a journey
well known to Young Tommy, and one he loves. He rel-
ishes the anticipated pleasures of the things which are familiar to him. He and his father have a strong, affectionate
and deeply respectful relationship, one which is obviously
a keystone in Young Tommy's fluctuating world. This trip
will mark their first return to the cabin since the death of
Young Tommy's mother.

For Young Tommy, life is unpredictable at this stage, and

he values highly what he knows and what he can understand. The simple journey, 40 miles from his home to the Gatineau Hills, becomes, however, not the soothing passage into the known—but an excursion into a world of new perceptions and concerns. In many small, concrete ways, the trip is used to mirror the complicated changes taking place in Tommy's inner world. They travel to Low, for example, not in the familiar train, but in the brand new 1950 Buick Special which belongs to drunken Frank, Tommy's father's friend. . . . Young Tommy is eager to get to Low, to explore and reminisce. Instead, he is taken on an odyssey of meandering, at the mercy of Frank, who "was the worst driver in the whole Gatineau." The trip is punctuated with stops at hotels and bars and gas stations, alternately to fuel the car and to fuel Frank. (pp. 67-8)

The arrival is thus delayed until expectations have faltered in the face of the new information and perceptions Young Tommy gleans along the way. Threaded through their peripatetic excursion is one constant, the rumour of the impending death of Mean Hughie. . . . The men share reminiscences of Mean Hughie's mean doings, the pattern of their telling a call-and-response of anecdotes. And all the while Young Tommy turns over in his mind thoughts of Baby Bridget, and what it will be like to see her again after three years. (p. 68)

The boy who has lost his mother is about to re-encounter the girl who is about to lose her father. (p. 69)

When Young Tommy and his father eventually reach the cabin, they carry with them the news flash from the last drink stop: Mean Hughie has disappeared. Not died, just disappeared. Baby Bridget has already "lost" her father. Between Young Tommy's arrival and the death of Mean Hughie at the end of the book, Young Tommy and Baby Bridget embark on a different journey, which acquaints them with their personal strengths, with the power of a real affection for another person, and with the range of those natural human foibles which are better tolerated with good humour than railed against. And finally, they find Mean Hughie, trying to die. Bridget makes peace with Mean Hughie. Young Tommy makes peace with his anxiety over Baby Bridget's arm. And the flawed and colourful adult world around them glides uninterrupted about its business, just as the men-talk in the bars earlier flowed around Young Tommy, allowing him the liberty to scavenge what he could use for his later participation in the world of men his father so amiably typifies.

A reader might take issue with some of the models presented in the character of drunken Hughie and the bar-hopping trip up to Low, as well as with the very funny, but highly dangerous affair of Frank's driving. These are perhaps examples not best set before the young reader. However, what rises from this novel with far more potency than these is the unshakable affection and forbearance which draws the characters to one another. In the long run, Young Tommy's father and uncles get Frank to "take the pledge," promising to drink no more. As they leave the minister's house, Tommy observes Frank closely studying the paper he has just signed. " 'He's lookin' for loopholes,' Dad said and we helped Frank into the car and drove back to the cabin." Even Mean Hughie is regarded as simply another phenomenon of nature: not mean by intent, or even by malice—just mean by makeup like a mountain

goes up on one side and down on the other. It's something to be dealt with.

The book is written with a great deal of humour which nicely offsets the foundation of more sober themes. The author is satisfyingly particular in attention to details of setting, particularly the emotional charge peculiar to each locale. The characters are sketched with great skill, in simple strong strokes of anecdote, and much of the uniqueness of the individuals is displayed through the colourful crackerbarrel chatter of the others. And there is a lot of attention paid to what people are *doing* as they talk: Tommy's father telling stories about Mean Hughie as he helps Frank to pilot the Buick; Tommy's father making supper; Frank struggling out of his collapsed tent; Aunt Dottie getting ready to sterilise the wild berries she picks. All these actions go on while Young Tommy thinks about, talks about, and finds out about, the changing world he and Baby Bridget are in. And these cameos, concentrations of clear and specific action, sit like brilliant fixed points in the fluid constellation of that world. These are the cherished and sustaining familiars. They are the constants which allow him to steer successfully a course through the confusing mix of fears and sorrows he encounters in Mean Hughie's death.

And overall, the story is told in the manner of a tale of some good ol' boys, with lots of back slapping and high jinks, good home cooking, and the whole family pretty much where they always were. For Young Tommy it "was like a photograph . . . or a painting . . . All the people were there, in their places, all with their faces turned looking at us in our car. Like a big crowded beautiful coloured painting in a museum." In this respect, *Up to Low* draws on a favourite story-telling tradition that suits its subject, its characters and quite probably its readers, very well. (pp. 69-70)

Carol Munro, "Life and Growth and Change: Always a Journey," in Canadian Children's Literature, *No. 37, 1985, pp. 67-70.*

Angel Square (1984)

Doyle has used one of the characters from his earlier book *Up to Low* to tell his new story. This use of first-person narration has become almost ubiquitous in the young-adult genre, partly because the readers seem to prefer it, and partly because it works as a device to restrict the vocabulary and concerns of the book to those comprehensible to the teenage reader. The problem with first-person narrative for a young-adult book lies in the limited sophistication of the narrator's voice and the restricted knowledge of the world the narrator has. The trick in overcoming this—a trick Doyle has mastered in *Angel Square*—is to write through the juvenile voice so that the intelligent reader may see levels of complexity necessarily lost on the narrator.

Doyle's narrator, Tommy, is always convincing as a character and a "voice" but can still transcend his own innocence and simplicity. Sometimes a special beauty is achieved, as when Tommy describes the coming of Christmas: "A feeling of bells and chocolate, hymns and carols, beautiful cold winter and warm rooms. Windows with snow and berries. And laughing and hugging."

Younger readers, perhaps unlikely to be moved by the beauty of the prose, will respond well to the sensitive handling of racism in the book and to the mystery story that keeps the plot spinning. The father of Tommy's best friend, a Jew, is beaten up by an unknown assailant. Tommy first locates witnesses, then assembles clues, and finally comes up with the guilty party. In the course of his investigation, Tommy has to deal with a society in which Irish, Jews, and French Canadians are continually battling with each other outside of school. If there is a flaw in Doyle's novel, it is that this racial strife is too violent and too frequent to ring true. But much of the strength of *Angel Square* lies in the way in which Tommy learns about and fights back against the racial hatred that surrounds him. Doyle's use of first-person narration makes Tommy's triumph over bigotry a compelling story.

Doyle's novel is so solid and so well crafted it might well not receive the attention it deserves. That would be a shame since *Angel Square* is a real triumph of young-adult writing.

> *Paul Kropp, "Growing Up Is Hard to Do: Leaving the Boy Behind," in* Quill and Quire, *Vol. 50, No. 11, November, 1984, p. 18.*

[*Angel Square* is a] hilarious yet serious account of life in Lower town Ottawa just after World War II. . . .

Glowing through the humour is a poignant message of tolerance and love. Through Tommy's eyes we see the absurdity of racism and the hope that at least one child will better understand our differences. This is Brian Doyle's best and guarantees an enjoyable yet sobering read for all.

> *A review of "Angel Square," in* Children's Book News, *Toronto, Vol. 7, No. 3, December, 1984, p. 3.*

A uniquely Canadian voice in [the slapstick] style of humor is that of Brian Doyle. In *Up to Low,* and more recently, in *Angel Square,* he manages to combine a sort of Celtic plangency with Ottawa Valley tall tale, Canadian colloquialism, and working-class deadpan. It's an original mixture that proves particularly rewarding in *Angel Square,* a story of postwar bigotry in Ottawa's Lowertown. Roving packs of "Dogans," "Pea Soups," and Jews (Doyle doesn't quite have the courage to name them "kikes" in the real slang of those days) beat each other up in the ironically named Angel Square, the junction all must cross on their way to their various parochial schools. Tommy is the young hero who, together with his friend Coco Laframboise, confronts anti-Semitism and tracks down the brutal assailant of Sammy Rosenberg's father. (p. 89)

The names are wonderful: Toe-Jam Laframboise, Killer Bodnoff, Fleurette Fetherstone Fitchell. So is the evocation of urban winters a generation ago—Flat Fifties given to Dad for Christmas, the smell of cheap chocolates, perfume, and melting snow on wool mitts in Woolworth's, the muffled approach of streetcars in thick snowdrifts.

There's plenty of Irish blarney, an unfortunate predilection on Doyle's part for comic drunks, and a touch of romanticism beautifully carried off. Tommy's favorite teacher (and there's a wickedly funny spoof of the bad ones) is Mr. Maynard, who moves Tommy's imagination in sci-

ence class one day by talking about the utter eternal lifelessness of the moon. If one leaf falls on earth, he says, it's more change than may occur on the moon in a hundred autumns. The words echo in Tommy's mind as he watches the eclipse of the moon one snowy night, and serve as a guide for individual action on earth, too. (pp. 89-90)

> *Michele Landsberg, "Liberating Laughter," in her* Reading for the Love of It: Best Books for Young Readers, *Prentice Hall Press, 1987, pp. 77-98.*

Easy Avenue (1988)

As mass-market teen paperbacks flowed over the 49th parallel, the Canadian publishing industry struggled to produce quality books for children that reflected what was special about Canadian life and thought. With the publication of Kevin Major's *Hold Fast* in 1978, Canada had its first example of an indigenous young-adult novel, and authors from coast to coast followed Major's lead, portraying young people in unabashedly Canadian settings. Brian Doyle is one of those authors, writing about the world he knows best: Ottawa and its environs.

Easy Avenue, Doyle's fifth novel, is once again set in postwar Ottawa, this time in an impoverished area known as the Uplands Emergency Shelter. Hubbo O'Driscoll and his guardian aunt move to the shelter, situated on an airforce base near Ottawa, when they are forced out of their rented house in Lowertown. Hubbo, an orphan, isn't particularly intellectually inclined, but he is completely empathetic to the people and situations that surround him daily. *Easy Avenue* portrays Hubbo's relationships with his classmates and teachers, his neighbours in the closely packed shelter, and the rich people he rubs elbows with on the bus ride to and from Ottawa. When Hubbo becomes involved with Fleurette Featherstone Fitchell, a resident of the shelter who has brought with her a rather seedy reputation from the Lowertown of Doyle's previous novel *Angel Square, Easy Avenue* turns into a kind of Cinderella story, told in Doyle's familiar tall-tale style: everyone is larger than life; evil is depicted in the slimiest, most despicable terms; and goodness is a struggle in both rich and poor environments, but hope is never extinguished.

Doyle's characters have the universal quality of ancient folk-tale characters. They are not prettified. There are women-haters, racists, fools, and connivers. But there's also the love and warmth of simple, quiet people who may never be noticed by the world, but who are all-important in the lives of those around them. In *Easy Avenue,* Hubbo helps people and tries to understand them, and eventually he's able to see a way out of his poverty thanks to the rewards of his friendship.

Doyle is one of the most daring and experimental writers of young-adult novels. He deals with the most sensitive of issues—racism, violence, anti-social activity of all sorts—with a tongue-in-cheek humour that never denigrates the human spirit. He portrays communities in every novel, and one of the major symbols of community is the meal. In all of his books there are lengthy—and often hilarious—descriptions of meals prepared and shared. *Easy Avenue* is no exception. . . . And there is always an underdog—Sammy, whose father was beaten senseless in *Angel*

Square; Baby Bridget, who lost an arm in a combine accident in *Up to Low;* and, in *Easy Avenue,* Fleurette Featherstone Fitchell—who is raised out of his or her situation by the courage and compassion of the hero.

As with all of Doyle's novels, *Easy Avenue* involves two journeys, one physical, one of self-discovery. Each individual takes a daily trip away from his or her impoverished surroundings, only to discover riches never before suspected after returning home.

Regional yet universal, Doyle's imagination is stimulated not by current social issues or middle-class fantasy worlds but by what the author has to say about himself and his community. Thanks to writers like Doyle, Canada, in spite of the lion to the south, has developed a literature for young adults that is as unique as it is universal. (pp. 12, 18)

> *Eva Martin, " 'Easy Avenue' Is Vintage Doyle," in* Books for Young People, *Vol. 2, No. 5, October, 1988, pp. 12, 18.*

Ottawa's Brian Doyle delivers a delightful mix of comedy, irony and sentiment in a tale about a poor boy who gains a mysterious benefactor. . . . Hubbo's moral dilemmas—whether to forsake his impoverished friends in order to join an exclusive club at school and whether he can overcome his snobbism and introduce his cleaning-lady aunt to his wealthy after-school employer—are sketched with keen insight and sly humor. While Doyle's well-paced plot and eccentric characters pay homage to Charles Dickens's *Great Expectations,* he creates an engaging story of his own. . . . *Easy Avenue* offers ample cause for rejoicing. . . . (p. N6)

> *Pamela Young and others, "Tidings of Fun," in* Maclean's Magazine, *Vol. 101, No. 53, December 26, 1988, pp. 60, N6.*

By nicknaming his hero "Hubbo", and using typenames such as Easy Avenue, where Hubbo keeps Mrs. Collar-Cuff alive by reading *War and peace* in weekly instalments, Mr. Doyle risks turning off the early-teens for whom he presumably writes. He also risks failing to grab them during his opening descriptions of life in Uplands Emergency Shelter, Ottawa, where Hubbo lives with his foster-mother, and his girl-friend Fleurette with her mother.

One hopes that Hubbo's resuscitation of the heart-attack victim for whom he has been caddying will keep them hanging in there, for from the moment that Hubbo heard from his school principal that he was to receive fifty dollars per month from an anonymous benefactor, this reader could not put the book down.

The tale echoes *Great expectations* not only in the surprise of the benefactor's self-disclosure but also in the hero's generous impulses. He funds medical treatment for a schoolfellow and buys a new outfit for Fleurette. Like Pip, he thinks the rich old lady his benefactor, and like Pip experiences worldly temptation, in the form of an invitation from the school cad to join the Hi-Y Club.

Yet Mr. Doyle tells his tale with quite un-Victorian frankness. On a riverside picnic Fleurette bathes in her torn slip, while the hero shrinks from exposing his ragged underwear. Her suspicion that Hubbo has betrayed to the Hi-Y crowd her old nickname "Feel" (a corruption of her former street-name) causes her to fling the new clothes down at his door. As Hubbo gradually realizes on seeing her many "uncles" emerge after single visits, the nickname refers to her mother's trade of prostitution. Not until Hubbo has torn up his application for club membership can he bear to acknowledge his foster-mother as school cleaner, yet he lives too near destitution to become a snob like Pip, nor is Fleurette another Estella.

Frankness apart, young readers should enjoy the naturalness of the boy-and-girl friendship and the hero's laid-back ridicule of fools in office, which recalls *The catcher in the rye.* (p. 71)

Easy Avenue is populated by real people as well as the snobs who turn up their noses at the smell of old clothes on the bus. One hopes that the youth of Middle Canada will not balk at this and other things perhaps recalled from Mr. Doyle's Dickensian childhood, such as the foster-mother's delusion that her dead husband has survived the Second World War and is sending the monthly cheques.

For his sometimes grim, sometimes amusing, but never unwholesome tale, Mr. Doyle deserves handsome royalty cheques in today's dollars. (p. 72)

> *Lionel Adey, "Doyle for the Early Teens," in* Canadian Children's Literature, *No. 54, 1989, pp. 71-2.*

Hardie Gramatky

1907-1969

American author and illustrator of picture books.

Recognized as one of the first contributors to children's literature to build his works around anthropomorphic machines, Gramatky is lauded for presenting preschoolers and primary grade readers with exciting and appealing stories which characteristically focus on how his childlike characters achieve success and maturity. He is best known as the creator of Little Toot, a plucky tugboat who proves himself a hero in a series of six adventures. In the first volume of the series, *Little Toot* (1939), the tugboat rescues a huge ocean liner in the New York harbor after being criticized for his frivolity and mischievousness; in subsequent works, Gramatky takes Little Toot to the Mississippi River and the San Francisco Bay as well as to England, Scotland, and Italy, where he continues to distinguish himself through his bravery and helpfulness. Throughout the series, Gramatky provides young readers with information on the countries visited by Little Toot and on the duties of tugboats while investing his books with humor and charming characterizations. Considered an endearing and quintessentially American figure, Little Toot has become internationally popular as a symbol of courage; the first book about him is often acknowledged as a classic of juvenile literature.

In addition to his books about Little Toot, Gramatky wrote several works which follow a similar formula and feature such protagonists as an airplane, a jeep, and a trolley car. Of these stories, *Hercules: the Story of an Old-Fashioned Fire Engine* (1940), which describes how a horse-drawn engine puts out a huge fire and earns a place in the local museum, is considered an especially worthy successor to *Little Toot*. Several of Gramatky's books depart from personifying inanimate objects, such as *Bolivar* (1961), the story of an Ecuadoran donkey who proves himself worthy of his name by outsmarting a bull, and *Nikos and the Sea God* (1963), a fantasy with realistic elements about a small Greek boy who is aided by Poseidon. Celebrated as both a writer and an artist, Gramatky invests his works with a simple yet active literary style which often includes picturesque words and phrases, and provides illustrations, usually bright watercolors, which are praised for their vibrancy, sense of movement, and superior technique. An award-winning watercolorist, Gramatky was also an animator with Walt Disney Productions, an experience which observers note for its influence on his picture book art; he is credited with developing an original and economical method of producing color-separation drawings in which washes of color are printed over each other to capture the full tonality of the picture. *Little Toot* was rated one of the all-time great books of children's literature by the Library of Congress and received the Lewis Carroll Shelf Award in 1969, while *Hercules* was chosen to represent American children's literature at the Brussels World's Fair in 1958.

(See also *Something about the Author,* Vols. 1, 23, 30; *Contemporary Authors New Revision Series,* Vol. 3; *Contempo-*

rary Authors, Vol. 2, rev. ed.; *Contemporary Authors,* Vols. 85-88 [obituary]; and *Dictionary of Literary Biography,* Vol. 22.)

AUTHOR'S COMMENTARY

[The following excerpt is from an interview by American Artist.*]*

Most artists are fortunate who make a place for themselves in one field, but Hardie Gramatky is identified with several. To a generation of Americans, he is the famous writer-illustrator of the perennial classic, ***Little Toot.*** This juvenile . . . has sold over a quarter-million copies, was made into a movie by Walt Disney, and has been rated by the Library of Congress as one of the "all-time greats in children's literature."

In fine arts, this artist has received more than thirty awards for his watercolors and is represented in several major museums, including the Art Institute of Chicago, Toledo and Brooklyn museums.

As an illustrator, Hardie Gramatky has worked for most

of the top periodicals and his work has appeared in numerous national advertising campaigns. (p. 43)

In each of [his children's books], the illustrations have a special appeal for children. They are full of action, colorful, and a compulsion for reading the lively text. From a production standpoint, they have special interest for all book illustrators. The high cost of full-color reproduction, and at the same time, the desirability of using as much color as possible for juveniles, caused Hardie Gramatky to develop his own method of producing color-separation drawings which effect the necessary economy and at the same time, when separately engraved and printed, retain the full tonality and freedom of a watercolor reproduced by the costly photomechanical process.

We have asked the artist to relate his method; his account follows:

"It required three years of continuous visits to publishers before I was finally able to sell **Little Toot.** I showed editors both the manuscript about a naughty little tug boat and the colorful watercolors which I felt were needed to give the story life and vitality. Although I was not aware of it at the time, probably the cost of reproducing these full-color paintings was an obstacle to acceptance, but to me those illustrations were the lifeblood of the story and as important as the text.

"It was my good fortune that G. P. Putnam's Sons had not yet entered the children's book field and were hardly aware of this problem. After we signed a contract, though, it became evident that the cost of reproducing my illustrations in orthodox full color would be prohibitive. A process of making my own color separation drawings had to be worked out, but how was I to achieve the effect of full color? I could find no proven method. There were other separation techniques, such as working on an overlay of glass with grease crayon or laying in flat tones on acetate, but none of these suited my special need.

"About this time I happened to see an exhibition of watercolors by John Marin. I noticed in particular that around the edges of his paintings there are washes of clear color used one over the other in order to build up the subtle gray tones in the body of his paintings. All of a sudden I realized that this was what I had been looking for. Wouldn't it be possible to do color separation drawings in tones like this, then print them together, one over the other?

"This was my breakthrough, and the publisher's printer encouraged me. First, I made a *key* black and white drawing from my original color sketch. The printer then made three prints of this in a light non-photographic blue on watercolor bristol, one for each color—red, yellow, and blue. On each of these I painted a fluid, transparent *black* wash wherever the design called for that particular color, *i.e.,* on the bristol labeled 'red,' I filled in the areas where a red should be printed, and did the same for the yellow and blue. I soon learned that my headaches had only begun, for I found that I had to approximate the dark and light value of each color while actually making the separations in monochrome. For instance, there is much difference between the value of solid yellow and black, yet a medium black had to be used on the separation drawings to produce a medium tone of yellow in the printing.

"Most of my creative work has been in watercolor because I like its flexibility in recording fleeting impressions. Twenty years ago, I felt compelled to dissect the medium and made a color chart, graduating each hue from its full strength to its lightest tint. Beside this scale, I broke down black on a similar graduating scale. Thus I had a comparatively accurate guide to finding the value in black corresponding to a particular color value. Elementary as this may seem, I learned a great deal from the experiment that I applied to my watercolors. It opened up an entirely new approach, for with these charts I learned to achieve a far greater degree of brilliance by underpainting with pure colors and then graying these with a secondary transparent wash. And, of course, these experiments were invaluable in working out the separation drawings.

"An important goal in children's books is plenty of color. The evidence of children's desire for color is found continually in their own drawings and paintings. This certainly does not mean that the illustrator should use garish colors, such as raw reds and greens directly from the tube. Rather, he should strive for rich, harmonious colors. These are difficult to achieve with the color separation process, but when successful, the results are rewarding.

"In speaking before audiences unaware that I am an artist, I have been told that the best part of my books is the close coordination between picture and story, and that I must work well with my illustrator! I do indeed. Even now I write with a story board of sketches in front of me. Many of these drawings will never be used, but all serve to remind me that the visual aspect of a children's book is as important as its text. My best ideas have come from the inspiration I get from sketching outdoors. Come to think of it, **Little Toot** might never have been born if I had not done a series of independent sketches of tugboats along the East River.

"For all these reasons, the reproduction of drawings takes on added meaning. After twenty years and six more books, I am still striving for that loose, juicy watercolor effect. In my new book, **Bolivar,** I have come close to achieving the goals I have worked for so long. I feel that these color pages are my best.

"**Bolivar** is set in South America. Several years ago I was in Quito, a city high in the Andes mountains of Ecuador. I fell in love with this strange and beautiful country, a natural motif for an unusual children's book. I worked four years writing and rewriting the story—which, incidentally, is based on fact—although the pictures were done almost entirely on the spot. In South America, color is everywhere: vivid pinks, spring green on the hillsides, dark blues against reds.

"The biggest production problem in **Bolivar** was achieving a multicolor effect with only four colors. With the reds, for example, I needed a basic color that could be turned hot or cold by various overprintings with other colors. The plant foreman made a series of tests to find just the right mixture—a red that was neither hot nor cold, too dark nor too light. Diminished in intensity through the manipulation of separation values, it is a beautiful pink, yet printed in full strength over yellow, it is a brilliant vermilion. It is a lovely color in itself and only the foreman knows its exact formula. He calls it Bolivar red!

"With an ink swatch of this red before me, plus others of a rich blue and a bright yellow, I did my final color separa-

From Little Toot, *written and illustrated by Hardie Gramatky.*

tion drawings. As in my previous work, I had to concentrate on correct values. The slightest deviation will produce mud instead of lively color. The key to this type of separation is refinement and great sensitivity in the separation process.

"Approximately one third of the sixty-four pages in *Bolivar* are full color. This alone represented about eighty separations, to say nothing of the drawings for the two-color pages. Such a project is perhaps akin to producing a symphony. Only in its playing can the results be realized, for success is not really evident until the presses begin to roll." (pp. 43-5, 54-5)

> *Hardie Gramatky, "A Technique for Making Color Separations," in* American Artist, *Vol. 26, No. 5, May, 1962, pp. 43-7, 54-5.*

GENERAL COMMENTARY

May Hill Arbuthnot

Hardie Gramatky is a water colorist of distinction. . . . Mr. Gramatky's personifications are extremely funny, and his tales have a breezy, masculine touch that all children enjoy and the boys love.

Certainly Virginia Burton and Hardie Gramatky have taken full advantage of the fact that to this generation a machine is something alive and individual. These two artist-authors have proved beyond doubt not only that machines are one of the modern child's liveliest and most continuous interests but that they can be a thrilling center of a good story. (p. 309)

> *May Hill Arbuthnot, "New Magic," in her* Children and Books, *Scott, Foresman and Company, 1947, pp. 276-315.*

Helen W. Painter

Just twenty-one years ago *Little Toot* was published, and this account of a gay little tugboat has maintained, and perhaps even increased, its popularity through the years. Many a teacher of young children has seen Little Toot dart from the pages of this newer classic and into the lives

of boys and girls with a swiftness and smoothness rivalling a modern jet. This is an action story of tremendous appeal to all and to boys especially, a story not only written but also illustrated by one of America's outstanding artists, Hardie Gramatky. The pictures are as exciting as the words. (p. 363)

What has made *Little Toot* so famous? (p. 364)

Surely in our modern world machines are tremendously important. Mr. Gramatky knows children and their interest in the realistic aspects of their environment. . . . To personify machinery, Mr. Gramatky has added appealing individuality to saucy Little Toot. Mr. Gramatky believes that a page comes alive through animation, that it seems to move and take off into space. Children delight in these personifications. The book provides wonderful entertainment not only for small boys but for the entire family and is an excellent story to read aloud.

Mr. Gramatky's pictures entrance his readers-viewers, for with fresh, vigorous, bold strokes he throws bright, deep colors on paper. To have pictures done by such an outstanding artist would in itself give the book a special claim to fame. (p. 365)

Truly in a Gramatky book the pictures are "part and parcel" of the story. . . . When Little Toot cuts a figure 8 so big there is hardly room for it between the two shores of the river, the picture besides the brief text shows a mischievous Toot at such play, with the 8 hitting each bank and with little smoke balls trailing behind him. When the boats become so annoyed with him and he is so lonesome that his spirits droop, the sketch shows even his smokestack, flag, and whistle bent sadly downward. No child has trouble reading the pictures and thus understanding the story, so graphically does each sketch give all the details. The colors match, too, the feelings denoted by the words, as the deep blues and blacks of the storm or the lavish color of the city dock scenes. Truly the pictures interpret the story.

But what of the story itself? The book has a well developed plot. Pointing out that many people today are doing mood books (pictures to portray a mood but with inaction in the text) Johnson, Sickels, and Sayers say [in their *An-*

thology of Children's Literature] that children respond with enthusiasm to a book that has a story to tell. Surely *Little Toot* has a story with a satisfying theme. A captivating character, often as playful and mischievous as any child (and therefore so understandable to children), is unhappy over the situation in which he finds himself, though it may be of his own making. However, as the climax is reached—and the children grow still and breathless at the suspense—the personified machine earns his right to be a hero. From sympathy at the humanized plot, the child relaxes happily at an ending that is deeply satisfying and rewarding.

Perhaps we should examine also the accuracy of the story materials, for children are interested in and most observant of details. Factual material should be handled skillfully, and it should be presented with truth and a respect for the intelligence of the child. A sincere artist-illustrator will go to great lengths to insure for even the young reader accuracy in a story that is not basically an informational one. The boats themselves in *Little Toot* . . . are drawn directly from those on New York's East River. The duties of the tugboat are explained simply and clearly at the level of the young child.

"You see the world through the child's eyes," Mr. Gramatky says. "Then you must play back that world but not make it sound too sweet or not talk down to the child. It must be an honest effort, delivered as a person-to-person talk."

Just as important as the content of the book is the manner or style in which it is written. Here, too, is revealed the skill of the writer to make a book readable. There is a gay, masculine touch to Mr. Gramatky's words and pictures that makes them breeze through the pages. The story is not awkward or stilted but flows evenly and smoothly. The plot is lively and the characters well drawn. And the prose is good—it reads well. However hard it is to define style, we recognize whether it is there or not. Surely the reader senses it in this book. Much of the charm is due in large part to the picturesque words used, as "candystick smokestack," "skinny boats," and "spit the salt water out of his smokestack." Undoubtedly it is expressive writing. (pp. 365-67)

What is the secret of the charm of *Little Toot* and the other Gramatky books? Maybe it is the childlike, irrepressible character who ceases to be a machine but becomes a human personality which delights us all. Whatever the secret, there is no doubt that the appeal is there for children and adults alike. For those of us who are privileged to know Mr. Gramatky there may be evident another reason. To quote from Annis Duff [in her *Bequest of Wings*]:

> It is not so much the books written expressly for children . . . as it is the books written out of the minds that have not lost their childhood that will form the body of literature which shall be classic for the young.

The great product in children's literature is created, someone has said, by the person who keeps the core of childhood within him while others grow old through and through. It could be, therefore, that the secret lies in the modest but captivating Mr. Gramatky himself. (p. 367)

Helen W. Painter, " 'Little Toot'—Hero," in Elementary English, Vol. XXXVII, No. 6, October, 1960, pp. 363-67.

Barbara Bader

Draw and tell stories for children, and the shadow of Walt Disney hovers near. Long before the name Disney meant Disneyland and children's classics emasculated, it meant Mickey Mouse and Minnie and their cohorts Pluto the Pup, the Goof, Donald Duck (1928+); the Silly Symphonies (1929+) making fun with sound; and the best of them, *The Three Little Pigs* (1933), thumbing its nose at the Depression to the tune of "Who's Afraid of the Big Bad Wolf?" Nineteen thirty-seven brought *Snow White and the Seven Dwarfs*, the first of the feature-length films, followed by *Fantasia, Pinocchio, Dumbo*—ergo Dopey, Jiminy Cricket and a fresh cast of characters. What Disney wrought is immeasurable; how he did it, that alone, is reflected in scores of picturebooks.

Hardie Gramatky was a Disney animator become watercolorist and illustrator. When he watched the tugboats from his New York studio window, they took on personality, and in *Little Toot* they become people. Other animated machines have push or drive in a single direction, they want to break away (*Stop Tim!, Little Old Automobile*), prove that they have power (the redoubtable *Little Engine That Could*) or that they haven't lost their power (*Mary Anne*); Little Toot, like any other person, just wants to be taken seriously.

He is growing up. No more fun and games; no more sulks because the other tugs laugh at his little toot-toot-toot; he'll work, make father Big Toot proud. But he's afraid of rough water—a machine, a tugboat, he's afraid—and out in the ocean rescuing a liner he's terrified. The ship comes free from the rocks and Little Toot, now the harbor hero, escorts it in; withal, his conquest of the Atlantic is a conquest of fear.

As a book, *Little Toot* was a hands-down winner: it was fresh and lively and children would love it, was the consensus. They did and more than thirty years later they still do, with a devotion that makes teenagers refuse to give it up and men marrying take it along with their transistors and records.

Like a Disney character going through his paces, Little Toot is personality in constant motion. When his spirits soar, his bow sweeps up, his visor perks, his flag whips smartly behind; morose, even his smokestack sags; aghast, everything tenses. In animating the inanimate—a leaf, a chair—as in working with animals, a Disney animator, wrote Robert Field in 1942, "must be able to feel exactly how the particular character would behave under all circumstances." This after remarking that "action is demanded every fraction of a second." *Little Toot* catches the action on the wing, the feelings at their apogee, leaving the onlooker to fill in the intervals.

It is also one of the airiest books ever, all white space and transparent washes and sweeps of brush (where Disney is controlled, tight, ultra-finished). The full-color pages have the clear gaiety of sun after rain but the two-color pages that predominate have much of the freest, most limpid drawing. Regardless, one is never far from the artist's hand and his pleasure in the doing, a pleasure sometimes free of purpose: the sparkling frontispiece could be a gallery watercolor were it not for the familiar look of that little tug in the middle.

In subsequent books Gramatky applied the same formula with less success, probably because it was a formula—the likes of Hercules the superannuated fire engine and Loopy the irresponsible airplane are not to be seen from any window. (pp. 203-04)

> *Barbara Bader, "The Storytellers: Hardie Gramatky," in her* American Picturebooks from Noah's Ark to the Beast Within, *Macmillan Publishing Co., Inc., 1976, pp. 203-04.*

Linda Gramatky Smith

It's hard to believe that it's been fifty years since the publication of *Little Toot.* I wish my dad, Hardie Gramatky, were here to be writing this article for *The Horn Book.* His enthusiasm, his ability to see everything so fully, his wit, his genuine modesty, his descriptive powers—all these went together to make him a wonderful storyteller and a much-loved person. (p. 746)

My father wanted to be an artist and a writer from the time he was in fifth grade, when he would go out with a friend at 6 A.M. to sketch. He went for two years to Stanford University, where a perceptive English professor recognized his ability in art and encouraged him not only to keep writing but also to attend the Chouinard School of Art in Los Angeles. While at Chouinard, Dad started working for Walt Disney. Dad was hired to do a Disney comic book in 1929, but he completed six months' worth of drawings in three days and told Disney that he'd like to try animation. The experience he got working under Disney influenced my father's style for the rest of his career; even his fine art watercolor paintings have a sense of movement, life, and animation.

In June of 1936, in the midst of the Depression, my parents decided to try their luck in New York, so they set out with their life savings of three thousand dollars. What they considered a fortune went quickly. They started to get a few illustration jobs, and in my father's 1937 diary he noted that he had located a studio loft down in the Wall Street area with "a grand view and lots of room" for only fifteen dollars a month. To rest his eyes when they grew tired, he liked to look out his studio window and watch the boats on the East River. One little tugboat, never in the right place at the right time, seemed to have a personality of its own. On January 12, 1938, Dad wrote in his diary, "IDEA—do children's book on East River—little boats as characters. Sketch character in them each day—chesty little tugs pulling a big load."

During that year he did watercolors and sketches of tugs and began to write a story of the optimistic tugboat that was always getting into trouble. "I'm just like that little tugboat," my father once said. He started submitting the story to publishers. One rejected it with the line, "Children aren't thinking that way this year."

In August of 1938 Dad was having lunch with Charlie Murphy, a *Fortune* editor with whom he'd gone on assignment. Murphy loved the manuscript for *Little Toot* and said, "Hardie, you should have this published." Murphy turned around to Ken Rawson, an editor at Putnam who

From Hercules: The Story of an Old-Fashioned Fire Engine, *written and illustrated by Hardie Gramatky.*

was sitting at the next table, and said, "Here, Ken, take a look at this." Putnam accepted the manuscript and published *Little Toot* as their first children's book. (pp. 746-47)

My parents later moved to Westport, Connecticut, and my father went on to create thirteen more books for children. To the end of his life, he continued visiting schools and libraries where he found a kinship with those who encourage children to enjoy books. Yes, we miss him, but it feels good to know that, as his much-loved story celebrated its fiftieth birthday, Dad's love and his spirit continue in the hearts of children. And we are all part of that magic. (p. 747)

> *Linda Gramatky Smith, " 'Little Toot' Turns Fifty," in* The Horn Book Magazine, *Vol. LXV, No. 6, November-December, 1989, pp. 746-47.*

Little Toot (1939)

Any one with a grain of imagination who has watched the tugboats bustling about their tasks can scarcely help investing them with a kind of generic personality, but it takes a special deftness of invention to have concocted Little Toot, the playboy who became, in one thrilling episode, the Paul Bunyan of his craft.

Little Toot came of a distinguished family. His father was the biggest and fastest tugboat on the river, a fact which Hardie Gramatky underscores by portraying him with a look of efficient command worthy of an admiral, and *his* father was a weathered old salt who breathed smoke and told mighty tales of the old days. Little Toot, however, despite his trim appearance, was nothing more than a young whipper-snapper with a youthful voice (hence his name), a great capacity for blowing smoke balls and none at all for work. He simply spent the whole day, every day, gliding up and down the river, threading the needle around the piers and cutting fancy figure 8's, which drove the hardworking tugs into frenzies. It was the biggest figure 8 of his career which finally caused him a change of heart, for it led to an embarrassing encounter with the short-tempered J. G. McGillicuddy at which all the other boats turned and hooted at him until he fled in shame. It was then, sulking down river in despair and loneliness, that he saw a big steamer in distress and Little Toot, the silliest and most frivolous of tugs, redeemed himself handsomely in a climax which is just as logical in its own cockeyed fashion as is his whole uproarious story.

Here is as daft a little tale as ever set an imaginative child to chuckling and since the author is primarily an artist he has instilled that same comedy into his pictures, mobile, exciting affairs in nautical blues and greens and stormy blacks, painted in a dashing, off-hand manner which exactly matches the bravado of Little Toot.

> *Ellen Lewis Buell, in a review of "Little Toot," in* The New York Times Book Review, *August 20, 1939, p. 10.*

A gay and lively imagination has created an altogether new character in the little tugboat which tooted irresponsibly around the East River waiting to grow up. . . . Mr. Gramatky tells his story with humor and enjoyment, giving too, a genuine sense of the water front in both pictures and story. For small boys and their fathers who love the bustle and stir of a harbor and for all others who rejoice in fresh ideas in children's books.

> *Alice M. Jordan, in a review of "Little Toot," in* The Horn Book Magazine, *Vol. XV, No. 5, September-October, 1939, p. 296.*

[*Little Toot*] pleases from four and five years on. Indeed, a reader of any age who has ever watched boats on a river cannot fail to be amused by this artist-author's tugs, large and small, his ocean liners and other craft. He shows in this gay little tale and in the light-hearted drawings of Little Toot, who was at first only a fun-loving tug but who awakened to a sense of responsibility, an imaginative enjoyment of the boat characters of his tale that is akin to the child's own pleasure in them. (p. 56)

> *Anne Thaxter Eaton, "Through Magic Doorways," in her* Reading with Children, *The Viking Press, 1940, pp. 41-64.*

During our small boy's second summer on our Georgian Bay island, when he was eighteen months old, the seafaring blood of his ancestors began to beat strongly in his veins. His very first word was "boat," and we heard it from morning till night. The sight and sound of boats sent him into spasms of joy, and when we had come back in the autumn to our land-locked life, something had to be done to satisfy his longing for water-craft. The two books we found then were fortunately exactly what he wanted, for we have never come across anything since that quite comes up to them. The first was Lois Lenski's *The Little Sail Boat.* . . . (p. 47)

The second boat book achieved its success by sheer force of personality. ***Little Toot,*** the New York harbor tug-boat, *is* a person, and this is a most perfect example of transference of human characteristics to an inanimate object. . . . It is probably the degree of affection that a writer has for his subject that determines how successfully he can convey the flavor of a personality, and there is no doubt that Hardie Gramatky loves Little Toot, the bad boy of the river, who gloriously becomes the hero. There is such gusto in the pictures, and such forthrightness in the manner of telling the story that the reader, especially if he is a little boy, is captivated at once. It is all ridiculously funny, especially to a grown-up, but there is scarcely time to laugh because events move at a breathless pace, and before you have quite finished reading the last page the little listener flips the book over and says, "Now, read it again." The other day our young man shared somebody's birthday, and was given a nice square sturdy little tug-boat, just enough like Little Toot to pass muster. That night when we went to tuck him in, we found him sleeping with his boat clutched fast in his arms, and as we gently moved it away, he stirred in his sleep and murmured, "Where's Little Toot?" We felt that Hardie Gramatky was the real giver of the gift. (p. 48)

> *Annis Duff, "'The Man of It'," in her "Bequest of Wings": A Family's Pleasures with Books, The Viking Press, 1944, pp. 39-57.*

This story for the seven-year-old is, in both text and illustrations, of a high standard. . . . In a simple but very well-told story the author has captured the atmosphere of the harbour and has illustrated it with excellent liveliness and humour in coloured lithographs.

> *A review of "Little Toot," in* The Junior Bookshelf, *Vol. 10, No. 2, July, 1946, p. 80.*

Hercules: The Story of an Old-Fashioned Fire Engine (1940)

Nobody who saw "Little Toot" last year forgets that exuberant tugboat. Mr. Gramatky's new tale of an old-fashioned horse-drawn fire engine has all the merits of that work, and more plausibility. Hercules is one of those joys no child remembers, of which every child should be reminded. The fire engine and its buffs once stood for the romantic daring and glory of a small town. Many such were received, on their arrival at the firehouse, by just such a mayor's committee welcome as Hercules had when the tale begins. For a long time the little engine is the town's stay and pride. But the motor era arrives. There comes a day when Hercules does not get there first. The three horses are retired and, though the firemen, Hokey, Pokey and Smokey, stay around, it is only because they can't bear to leave.

One day their own alarm clangs for the first time in months. Hercules bangs the bell. All three horses leave their jobs (one brings a mounted cop along) and the little engine is off to fame. One by one the motorized ones have tire trouble or some of the upsets of motors. Hercules, three horses and three men put out the fire, and that's why he's now in a museum. This is in clanging colors and rushing action, carrying an idea. Life in the long run does more than machinery in the battles of this world. There must be a heart back of the machine. This is a book to read to five-year-olds, but their elders will enjoy doing so.

> *"A review of "Hercules," in* New York Herald Tribune Books, *November 10, 1940, p. 11.*

In his new picture-book the creator of Little Toot has done his vivid best to re-create the clashing excitement of the old days of fire-fighting.

Hercules, for all his handsome looks, can scarcely be accounted a rival to Little Toot. His personality is not so carefully built up as was that light-headed little tugboat, and his adventure, less unexpected, seems to bear the cut of a ready-made. Nevertheless, his story is fun and the exciting pictures portray the glorious pandemonium of a four-alarm fire with such verve that you almost hear the clanging of old brass fire bells.

> *Ellen Lewis Buell, "A Fire Engine Story," in* The New York Times Book Review, *November 10, 1940, p. 34.*

This is a gay little book with a cheeky air and plenty of colourful action in text and picture. . . . There is some little technicality in the text which might be lost on the small child for whom the book is intended but these few minor technical terms give the right air of importance and grandeur to Hercules. The style is colloquial and almost coarse at times but with the pictures has a happy spontaneity that wins applause and invites lively participation.

> *A review of "Hercules: The Story of an Old Fashioned Engine," in* The Junior Bookshelf, *Vol. 24, No. 4, October, 1960, p. 214.*

Loopy (1941)

Patterned after **Little Toot,** but, I am afraid, not nearly as clever. . . . *Little Toot* was so perfect and is so popular that I feel that **Loopy** will have little chance in comparison. The subject is a favorite with little boys, of course, but story and pictures lack the originality we look for in Mr. Gramatky's work. Loopy's fat, round face peers out from all the illustrations with a sameness which dulls the interest. Opinions will vary on this picture book for five- to seven-year-olds.

> *Ruth W. Stewart, in a review of "Loopy," in* Library Journal, *Vol. 66, No. 18, October 15, 1941, p. 908.*

In the first of his happy experiments with machinery Hardie Gramatky made a little tugboat into a modern elf: in the second he made a fire engine into a hero, each time successfully so far as small children were concerned. Having found out how to turn the trick, he turns it for the third time best of all. Loopy is an airplane, tiny, bumptious and full of zip. An airplane stays far enough out of

reach anyway to give it a fantastic quality; Loopy is completely believable to a small child who loves to personalize his toys.

In swooping, brightly colored pictures Loopy the hedge-hopper stands all sorts of bad treatment from student pilots. He never knew what to expect, from tangling with the family wash to making a nose-point landing. But one day a show-off took him up, stunted foolishly, got into a storm and bailed out. Loopy, alone at last, went right on by himself. He had always wanted to do that: now he makes scornful circles around the parachute, loops, dives and at last, gathering all the birds of the air, makes a great parade and comes to earth in the prettiest landing ever seen. And now he is a sky-writer who always dots his i's. Somehow it is easy to believe in Loopy, smile and all. He is a bit of modern mythology.

> *"Fun for Little Folks," in* New York Herald Tribune Books, *November 2, 1941, p. 26.*

Gusto is the quality, of all others, that my boys and I most enjoy in a story read aloud to them. By gusto we mean speed, action, a leaning forward into the breeze. We mean savor and relish in the telling. We mean vigor of line and movement in the illustrations. Gusto is the twinkle in the storyteller's eye infused into his printed words. It is the carrying over into type of a tongue racing to keep pace with a swift story. It is the quick push of the artist's pencil;

From Bolivar, *written and illustrated by Hardie Gramatky.*

dashing strokes caught on paper. It is spontaneity and vim. (p. 412)

[Why did my sons and I] never read *Loopy* but twice, where we had read *Hercules* ten times and *Little Toot,* twenty? This cannot be because of any lack of clarity. Perhaps it is because the humor doesn't quite come off. Tugboats, when we see them, which is not very often, do look foolishly small like Little Toot. Little Toot is O.K. with us. Hercules, the fire engine in Hardie Gramatky's book of that name, is a horse-drawn vehicle, about which two of us know nothing, and we can believe he might do these things. But the airplanes we see are all big fellows made for work and they couldn't act foolish like Loopy. It's probably our hard luck—but we wonder if it isn't Mr. Gramatky's, too. (p. 415)

> *L. Felix Ranlett, "Books and Two Small Boys," in The Horn Book Magazine, Vol. XVIII, No. 6, November-December, 1942, pp. 412-16.*

Creeper's Jeep   (1948)

[Hardie Gramatky] here glorifies the mechanical darling of our age, the jeep. Creepers Perkins, who was a nice boy but not much of a worker, simply because there were so many other interesting things to do, won the jeep at the county fair. Father Perkins, so conservative that he still drove to church in a buggy, was scandalized. Even when the jeep took over the plowing and the milking of the cows, he wasn't reconciled. After one especially unhappy experience on the way to church, Father Perkins laid down the law—no more jeep. Creeper was heartbroken and so was the jeep. How they evaded selling it and how on a night of storm and fire the jeep justified its existence make a brave climax to some hilarious antics.

The jeep, unlike the tugboat Little Toot, doesn't always stay in character. However, it is such a versatile machine that young ones will be all the more delighted to see it in a barber shop or at the soda fountain. Certainly the 4 to 8 year olds will enjoy the swiftly moving prose and the slashing action of the pictures.

> *Ellen Lewis Buell, in a review of "Creeper's Jeep," in The New York Times Book Review, September 5, 1948, p. 11.*

A new picture book from Hardie Gramatky is, ordinarily, an occasion for celebration. *Creeper's Jeep,* however, is less appealing, less convincing than *Little Toot* or *Hercules.* But Creeper's adventures are the subject of some lively pictures, which, though sometimes muddy in color, have the action and vitality that will delight little boys.

> *Helen Masten, in a review of "Creeper's Jeep," in New York Herald Tribune Weekly Book Review, September 26, 1948, p. 6.*

As one of the first to give naturalization papers in the picture book world to Hardie Gramatky's *Little Toot,* I wish I could be more enthusiastic over *Creeper's Jeep.* Children will think it good fun, but neither in conception nor production is it in the class with *Little Toot.* Little Toot has a real character with a natural environment; Creeper's Jeep, a made-up one, contrived rather than created.

> *Anne Carroll Moore, in a review of "Creeper's Jeep" in The Horn Book Magazine, Vol. XXIV, No. 6, November–December, 1948, p. 435*

Hardie Gramatky is in a groove, with his long-suffering, finally triumphant machines, but he has great technical virtuosity and plenty of infectious high spirits. In *Creeper's Jeep* his colour and line are equally good. In spite of the aggressive American atmosphere, this is likely to be enormously popular. (p. 213)

> *A review of "Creeper's Jeep," in The Junior Bookshelf, Vol. 24, No. 4, October, 1960, pp. 212-13.*

Sparky: The Story of a Little Trolley Car   (1952)

Another personable book that bids fair to be a classic like *Little Toot.* . . . This concerns the adventures of a bored and imaginative street car with a desire to be a streamliner. Sparky takes it upon himself to de-rail whenever he feels particularly jubilant. He has many mishaps as he free wheels along, and finally tangles with the Mayor, who is about to convert him into a diner until he heroically saves the life of a small boy. Should appeal to the sense of mischief of pre-readers.

> *A review of "Sparky," in Virginia Kirkus' Bookshop Service, Vol. XX, No. 21, November 1, 1952, p. 700.*

Sparky is a lively little trolley car who is never quite content just whizzing back and forth along his daily route. His vivid imagination plus his love for adventure help make all sorts of exciting things happen. As a result, Sparky gets involved in trouble with the very excitable Mayor. But it is Sparky who comes through in an emergency and so becomes endeared to all the townspeople, including the Mayor himself, who proclaims Sparky a great hero.

In this age of widespread bus service many children have never seen a trolley in operation. Nevertheless, *Sparky* should enjoy much of the same enthusiasm accorded the author's previous *Little Toot,* which has remained a favorite for so long.

Hardie Gramatky's amusing illustrations are more than equal to his charming story of this colorful mechanical personality.

> *Alyce L. Seekamp, "Adventurous Trolley," in The New York Times Book Review, November 16, 1952, p. 40.*

One of *Little Toot'*s earliest and most devoted admirers finds *Sparky* a sad disappointment. Not that Mr. Gramatky has not drawn with spirit and great technical dexterity. The pictures are, in their Disneyesque way, excellent. Two things are fundamentally wrong, at least for English children. The idiom of the pictures is strongly American. This is no criticism of the book, nor would it be censure of the English publisher if the book appealed to children who might be curious about American life. It aims, however, at children who are too young for such mental adjustments and for whom a great many of the terms of reference will be quite baffling. More important, however, is the author's insistence on illustrating Sparky's fantasies. Sparky imagines himself a "diner," a helicopter, and so on, and each time the artist shows what he is imagining. This, I believe, will cause havoc in the child's literal mind.

The story is conventional and slow, but the illustrations are charmingly done with splendid colour. But not, I think, a book for import. (pp. 211-12)

> *A review of "Sparky," in* The Junior Bookshelf, *Vol. 23, No. 4, October, 1959, pp. 211-12.*

Small Boys in particular will enjoy this story of the little trolley-car who daydreams of the processions he will lead and the deeds he will do as he rattles along through the town. The illustrations, which are clear and lively tell the story as much as the text which is not at all outstanding and indeed at times confusing. Certain Americanisms are unfortunate.

> *F. P. Parrott, in a review of "Sparky," in* The School Librarian and School Library Review, *Vol. 9, No. 6, December, 1959, p. 516.*

Homer and the Circus Train   (1957)

To be pulled along at the end of a train, facing back to front, is to have a rather unusual view of the world. For Homer, the little red caboose, the railroad signs read backward and the countryside recedes instead of advancing. The other cars make fun of him, and the embarrassed Homer hides away on a siding. There he makes friends with a company of stranded circus animals and when they are sent home by train Homer is pressed into service. It's a terrifying trip up a curving mountain track, but when a coupling breaks the little caboose, daring and resourceful, saves the day—and his friends.

When he created **Little Toot** Hardie Gramatky created his own keenest competition. Still, **Homer** is a worthy successor, upholding Mr. Gramatky's fine tradition of stories with all the right ingredients, including endearing heroes and delightful illustrations.

> *Margaret Macbean, "Little Red Caboose," in* The New York Times Book Review, *January 12, 1958, p. 26.*

This is the old story of the poor little "thing"—it is usually an engine, sometimes a boat, in this instance a caboose—who hasn't "a friend in the world," and how he redeems himself by an act of unselfish courage. The commonplace story is developed with no more than average ability, except when Homer, travelling backwards at the tail end of the train, reads STOP, LOOK & LISTEN as NETSIL & KOOL, POTS and there are far too many words, but the drawing is in its Disneyesque way quite brilliant. I don't much like inanimate objects with faces, but Homer's expressions are well done and Old Engine "the mightiest locomotive in the yard" has the right blend of smugness and brainless determination. There is great vigour in the drawing, a swift impression of background, and most admirable rendering of colour. Commonplace in theme, sometimes vulgar in detail, this little book is still well worth having. (pp. 214, 217)

> *A review of "Homer and the Circus Train," in* The Junior Bookshelf, *Vol. 24, No. 4, October, 1960, pp. 214, 217.*

Bolivar   (1961)

Despite the deluge of picture books on the juvenile market, there is more than ample room at the top for a book like this! In his inimitable fashion, Hardie Gramatky has created another hero as attractive and appealing as Loopy, Sparky or Little Toot and as certain to win a permanent place among the picture book literati. His name is Bolivar and he is a *burrito* who lives high in the Andes of Ecuador. To the disappointment of his young master Pepito and the disdain of the farmers, Bolivar's *joie de vivre,* his wild little antics, brand him unworthy of his great name. And so to prove himself, Bolivar accepts an enormous burden and heads down the trail with Pepito toward the market place and the fiesta. Two accidental collisions send the poor little donkey scurrying off to hide his failure. How can he know that in moments he will outwit a snorting bull and forevermore hear his name with pride. A delightful text is superseded only by illustrations that bounce with color, atmosphere and style.

> *A review of "Bolivar," in* Virginia Kirkus' Service, *Vol. XXIX, No. 22, November 15, 1961, p. 1006.*

A read-aloud book with lively, bright illustrations of market and fiesta scenes in Ecuador. The story is rather ordinary and patterned: unappreciated animal does a good deed and is praised. . . . Bolivar upsets several apple carts before he makes amends. This he does with a contrived incident, distracting the escaped bull that is frightening the populace; he leads the bull into an enclosure and slams the gate shut after "the thought flashed through his mind that he alone could do any good, but whatever it was had to be done right." Were the dénouement realistic or more exaggeratedly humorous it would be more effective.

> *Zena Sutherland, in a review of "Bolivar," in* Bulletin of the Center for Children's Books, *Vol. XV, No. 5, January, 1962, p. 77.*

It would be unreasonable to expect Mr. Gramatky to retain the high level he reached with **Little Toot,** but in this his latest work much of the same joie de vivre is evident. . . . His delightful escapades are encountered merrily and depicted in the gayest of colours. Definitely a vintage Gramatky.

> *A review of "Bolivar," in* The Junior Bookshelf, *Vol. 26, No. 5, November, 1962, p. 249.*

Nikos and the Sea God   (1963)

The modern fairy tale of a Greek boy who believes ardently in Poseidon, god of the sea, is presented with conviction. . . . Each day Nikos sets out to sea, accompanied by his pet pelican Icarus, and each evening he returns with no fish, to be the eternal laughing stock of the successful fishermen. Poseidon first appears to the boy on an old vase which he hooks from the sea, and again (in actual form) when the boy is caught in a storm while on the way to fetch a doctor. Sun shines again as Nikos is rescued; he is rewarded doubly by his faith in Poseidon when his luck as a fisherman changes abruptly. The water color illustrations are pleasing, but fail to capture the mood of the story; they contribute no vitality to the brief, easy-moving tale.

A review of "Nikos and the Sea God," in Virginia Kirkus' Service, *Vol. XXXI, No. 20, October 15, 1963, p. 1006.*

Nikos lives with his aunt on a small Greek island, and the boy is fascinated by the tales Aunt Mara tells of the old Greek gods. Especially when he visits the local museum, Nikos is aware of the importance of the sea god, Poseidon. He catches no fish, but one day Nikos hauls up an amphora picturing Poseidon and it is considered a Sign. When a storm comes up and Aunt Mara is injured, nobody will risk the angry sea; Nikos, feeling that he has the protection of the sea god, sails out to a big boat to get the ship's doctor. The doctor comes, Aunt Mara is cared for, and after that visitors come to the hitherto isolated island every day to hear Aunt Mara's stories. The device of introducing mythology through Nikos' interest is good, but the story falls flat at the ending: the accident seems contrived, the incident of the amphora leads nowhere, and the fact that the island has no doctor, no means of communication, and no adult who will dare the sail to the ship seems improbable. The illustrations are delightful, a few being quite lovely. The writing style is quite good, but the story is an amalgam of mythology, realistic fiction, and fantasy with resultant detriment to all these elements.

Zena Sutherland, in a review of "Nikos and the Sea God," in Bulletin of the Center for Children's Books, *Vol. XVII, No. 5, January, 1964, p. 78.*

[In **Nikos and the Sea,** Hardie Gramatky] is not at his best. He has plenty of vitality and the technical resourcefulness which comes from his Disney training, but the exaggerations which are necessary in the cartoon designer sit uneasily within the pages of a book. This story of a Greek fisherboy has nevertheless some charm, and the illustrations are richly colourful.

A review of "Nikos and the Sea God," in The Junior Bookshelf, *Vol. 28, No. 5, November, 1964, p. 289.*

Little Toot on the Thames (1964)

Little Toot, the friendly little tug with the cheerful whistle, turned cosmopolitan when he tried to bring in a tramp steamer and instead got towed to London. From the confused harbor, he went for a leisurely float up the Thames, taking in the important sights. He was sent home in disgrace after he blocked the way in a boat race, but demonstrated his heroism by staying up all night protecting ships from a sunken barge. His warning saves a ceremonial flotilla, and as a reward Little Toot was led home in style by

From Nikos and the Sea God, *written and illustrated by Hardie Gramatky.*

the *Queen Elizabeth*. Young children can easily identify with the salty tug and his combined qualities of mischief and responsibility. They will be delighted with the repetition of their friend's heroism, and the adults who read this one aloud may be pleased to have a variant. There are the same blithe, easily recognizable illustrations of the original.

> *A review of "Little Toot on the Thames," in* Virginia Kirkus' Service, *Vol. XXXII, No. 18, September 24, 1964, p. 952.*

Twenty-five years after giving birth to Little Toot, author-illustrator Hardie Gramatky has brought out his first sequel. . . . This time, the fun-loving tug accidentally finds himself in London. Before he can return to New York harbor, he gets involved in a number of adventures, some frivolous and some hair-raising. Mr. Gramatky takes full advantage of his setting with many vignettes of British life. Little Toot himself, however, lacks some of his original appeal. At times, he appears aimless instead of playful. (pp. 58-9)

> *Alberta Eiseman, in a review of "Little Toot on the Thames," in* The New York Times Book Review, *November 1, 1964, pp. 58-9.*

Little Toot first came to England in 1946 as one of the assault troops in the post-war American invasion. It was indeed one of the most American of books, in sharp contrast to the Bemelmans, Duvoisins and Rojankowskys which proclaimed their European origins. *Little Toot on the Thames* is a Yankee view of London, American in its brashness, vulgarity and high spirits, and well worth having. Mr. Gramatky learnt his technique, and perhaps acquired his vulgarity, in the Disney Studios, and there is much of Disney here, sensational colour, cheekiness and sentimentality. English children will certainly welcome this new story of the diminutive, enterprising tugboat, and they will like to see him in the setting of London River.

> *A review of "Little Toot on the Thames," in* The Junior Bookshelf, *Vol. 29, No. 5, October, 1965, p. 276.*

Little Toot on the Grand Canal   (1968)

Little Toot on the waterways of the world? This stopover's a string of picture postcards (the Doge's Palace, St. Mark's, the bronze horses, the pigeons, etc., etc.) until pirates ransack the city; then Little Toot, chased back into the glassblowers' shop, emerges blowing bubbles of vari-colored Venetian glass, which the pirates mistake for jewels, chase through the streets and courtyards, over the Bridge of Sighs, and straight into prison. Routine tourism and rootin', tootin' cartoonin'.

> *"A review of "Little Toot on the Grand Canal," in* Kirkus Service, *Vol. XXXVI, No. 5, March 1, 1968, p. 255.*

Happy's Christmas   (1970)

The farmer and his wife and the two old dogs and puppies Merry, Jolly, Joyful, Gay and Happy have a M****, J****, J*****, G**, H**** Christmas after Happy, given away to old Mr. Grump, is put out for chewing the television wire and returns home to be cheered up by the tinsel angel on the tree—whereupon he and his parents set up a glad howl that summons the other pups and their new owners. Sort of speaks for itself.

> *A review of "Happy's Christmas," in* Kirkus Reviews, *Vol. XXXVIII, No. 16, August 15, 1970, p. 867.*

A contrived but pleasant Christmas fantasy, especially for children who love dogs. Hardie Gramatky's puppies are irresistible. This is one that will be fun to look at and to read out loud during the Christmas season.

> *A review of "Happy's Christmas," in* Publishers Weekly, *Vol. 198, No. 8, August 24, 1970, p. 63.*

[*Happy's Christmas* is] an insipid story of an old farmer and his wife who give away a litter of puppies as Christmas presents. They regret this on Christmas day because they are lonely, but Happy runs back home to them, starts singing and is heard by his siblings who come bringing their new families; the old couple has a Christmas party after all. The story rambles and gets nowhere without emanating any of the energy needed to hold reader's interest. The black-and-white illustrations are all right, but those in full-color are distinctly of the greeting-card school. It's the kind of book you can put down at any point—preferably right after the title page. (pp. 146-47)

> *Marilyn R. Singer, "The Making of a Humbug: Christmas Books for 1970," in* School Library Journal, *Vol. 17, No. 2, October, 1970, pp. 146-50.*

Little Toot on the Mississippi   (1973)

The jaunty little tugboat has now been on the scene for a third of a century; and even with his new coat of paint, some of the freshness has faded. Back from foreign waters, the eager little tug is plying the great Mississippi, vainly searching for the fabled steamboats his grandfather used to tell about. One day a dreadful storm sends the Old River into flood and drives terrified Little Toot into a dismal, overgrown bayou. He finds some of the once-proud river boats lying neglected and forgotten; but spurred on by the intrepid tugboat, they round up and rescue hundreds of frightened animals stranded in the flood. Parents and teachers who grew up with Little Toot will welcome these latter-day adventures; but for sheer, bubbly spontaneity, the original story remains unmatched.

> *Ethel L. Heins, in a review of "Little Toot on the Mississippi," in* The Horn Book Magazine, *Vol. XLIX, No. 5, October, 1973, p. 456.*

Thousands of readers who have grown to parenthood since reading Hardie Gramatky's first Little Toot book will hoot with delight at his return, this time to the turgid waters of the great Mississippi.

Some of the pictures in his latest book are in color and some in a gray wash, but as always the artwork is dramatic and impressive. The story is true to the Little Toot character and the tiny tug wins through again with indomitable, bantam-weight courage.

Guernsey Le Pelley, "Stories to Share with Grandpa," in The Christian Science Monitor, *May 1, 1974, p. F2.*

Hardie Gramatky has a well-earned reputation as an extremely competent children's author and illustrator. His stories are simple, yet not patronising, informative, yet not dryly so and his illustrations possess humour and depth. . . . [In *Little Toot on the Mississippi,* the] story and illustrations convey exactly the majestic quality of the Mississippi, its changing moods and inextricably linked to this, the power of the forces of nature. Its clear large print and the sustentation of a good story make this an ideal book for the younger reader of five to seven years as well as for reading aloud.

Vivian Jennings, in a review of "Little Toot on the Mississippi," in Children's Book Review, *Vol. V, No. 1, Spring, 1975, p. 16.*

Little Toot through the Golden Gate (1975)

Little Toot hasn't grown up a bit or learned a thing from his ocean voyage or his previous adventures. Here he is so enchanted by San Francisco's sailboats, ferries and crab boats that he tries to "be" each one in turn—then sadly considers himself a "nothing" when he fails. Once more however he proves his worth, tugging a big freighter loaded with band instruments to shore, and in the end "Bands played. Sailboats sailed. Ferryboats ferried. Crab boats crabbed. And Little Toot tugged. They all did what each did best." (*Sic.*) And Gramatky kept puffing along on the same old track.

A review of "Little Toot through the Golden Gate," in Kirkus Reviews, *Vol. XLIII, No. 17, September 1, 1975, p. 993.*

Little Toot is a tugboat that certainly manages to get around the world. . . . [*Little Toot Through the Golden Gate*] is another delightful tale in the Little Toot series. As always there are more illustrations than text and yet, having finished the book, one does have a sense of having read a complete story and is left eager for more.

G. L. Hughes, in a review of "Little Toot through the Golden Gate," in The Junior Bookshelf, *Vol. 41, No. 3, June, 1977, p. 154.*

Little Toot the tugboat has been a favourite for many years. Here he sails through the Golden Gate of San Francisco. He discovers that he cannot be a crab boat, a ferry boat or a sailing boat, he must do what he does best, be a tugboat. The moral tone of the story is lightened by the bright, amusing pictures, in which all the boats are given personality.

The print is large but the text is not particularly simple and the story is quite long. However, it is a cheerful tale with an open ending that promises that there are more of Little Toot's adventures still to come.

E. Colwell, in a review of "Little Toot through the Golden Gate," in The Junior Bookshelf, *Vol. 41, No. 5, October, 1977, p. 277.*

Little Toot and the Loch Ness Monster (with Dorothea Cooke Gramatky and Linda Gramatky Smith, 1989)

Gramatky died in 1979; his family has completed this last book for publication on the 50th anniversary of his *Little Toot.* The story follows a familiar pattern: on a quest for the famous monster, Little Toot first encounters a group of suspicious, unfriendly search boats. Evading them, he meets Nessie, who turns out to be as benign as the blown-up water toy she resembles; he helps her hide from her would-be captors. Illustrative style varies here from beautifully evocative watercolors of the lake to preliminary sketches, skillfully colored to blend with the finished art without concealing the vigor of Gramatky's line. An interesting conclusion to a well-loved series.

A review of "Little Toot and the Loch Ness Monster," in Kirkus Reviews, *Vol. LVII, No. 14, August 1, 1989, p. 1157.*

It is not entirely clear which parts of [*Little Toot and the Loch Ness Monster*] are directly attributable to Hardie Gramatky. His daughter explains in an end note that at her father's death in 1979, the book consisted of "drafts, notebooks, sketches, and illustrations." She and her mother added illustrations, colored the sketches, and "worked" on the text. Comparisons of the style exhibited in the earlier "Little Toot" titles shows that a different artist has had a large role in creating the watercolor paintings for this book. That isn't a negative criticism, however, for the illustrations in . . . *the Loch Ness Monster* are frequently vivid and flowing, but some do have a somewhat unfinished, preliminary look to them. Little Toot still captivates small children, and the bright colors of this title should attract them.

Ruth Semrau, in a review of "Little Toot and the Loch Ness Monster," in School Library Journal, *Vol. 35, No. 14, October, 1989, p. 84.*

It was 50 years ago that the original *Little Toot* chugged into print and found a permanent place in children's libraries. Now Gramatky's last book, not quite finished when he died in 1979, can join its fellow boaters on the shelves. . . . Gramatky's illustrations were completed by his wife, an artist in her own right, and the text was refined by his daughter. Though it lacks the sparkling simplicity of the earlier books, this last offering is an endearing remembrance from a fine master.

Barbara Elleman, in a review of "Little Toot and the Loch Ness Monster," in Booklist, *Vol. 86, No. 4, October 15, 1989, p. 457.*

René Guillot

1900-1969

French author of fiction, nonfiction, and short stories, and reteller.

Often regarded as the most distinguished French writer of books for children and young adults, Guillot was a prolific author who is respected both as an exceptional storyteller and a successful philosopher. His works, which are lauded for their insight into the human and animal worlds as well as for their evocative atmospheres and strong characterizations, most often blend fact and fancy in animal tales and adventure stories on exotic subjects which are acknowledged as unusual, poetic, and demanding. Although Guillot set much of his fiction in such locations as France, India, Canada, and Siberia, he wrote the majority of his works about Africa, where he lived for twenty-five years; many of Guillot's books are based on his African experiences, such as his hunting trips for big game, and on the native folktales he heard there; Marlow, a hunter and naturalist who appears in several of Guillot's works, is often thought to be a self-portrait.

Guillot is perhaps best known for his animal stories, which often describe how leaders of the animal kingdom such as the king of cats and the prince of elephants are taken from their kingdoms and plunged into a series of adventures before their kingdoms are restored. In these works, which give voice to the thoughts and emotions of animal characters through stylized dialogue, Guillot develops a mythology which provides young readers with a mystical sense of animal nature, habits, and rites. Combining a sensitivity to these creatures with an awareness of the realities of their lives, he depicts the kinship between animals and humans while exploring the nuances of behavior in both species. Guillot is also well known as the creator of romantic adventure novels about corsairs, the pirates who traveled the Atlantic and the Spanish Main in the seventeenth and eighteenth centuries. His first work of this type, *Companions of Fortune* (1952), the story of a treasure hunt to Africa by the survivors of a shipwreck, is often considered his best book. Although his works contain examples of brutality, cruelty, and violence and address such themes as revenge and the harsh relationship between man and the environment, Guillot underscores these depictions with a lyrical appreciation of the natural world and a belief in the joys of being alive. Besides his animal and adventure stories, Guillot created such works as fantasies for younger children, realistic fiction for middle graders, informational books on such subjects as astronomy and the mechanical age, juvenile encyclopedias, and a volume of retold African folktales. Guillot has received several international awards for his books; among them are the Prix Jeunesse in 1950 for *Sama, prince des éléphants* (U. S. edition as *Sama*), the Prix Fantasia in 1961 for *Le maître des éléphants* (U. S. edition as *Fofana*), the Prix Enfance due Monde in 1958 for *Grichka et son ours* (U. S. edition as *Grishka and the Bear*), the Prix Sobrier-Arnould in 1957 for *Encyclopédie Larousse des enfants* (U. S. edition as *The Illustrated Encyclopedia: Based on an Encyclopedia of the*

Famous Librarie Larousse) and in 1962 for *Mon premier atlas: Voyage autour de monde* (U. K. edition as *Our Colourful World and Its Peoples*), and the Hans Christian Andersen Medal in 1964 for his body of work. *The 397th White Elephant* received the Lewis Carroll Shelf Award in 1958, an honor also given to *Grishka and the Bear* in 1961.

(See also *Something about the Author,* Vol. 7, and *Contemporary Authors,* Vols. 49-52).

AUTHOR'S COMMENTARY

[The following excerpt is from a translation by Janine Despinette of Guillot's foreword to his Il était . . . mille et une fois (It Happened . . . a Thousand and One Times), *a collection of stories, fairy tales, and fables with suggestions on how to present them orally.]*

A writer, for whatever audience he may be writing, has to tell stories, as an apple-tree has to bear apples. The whole secret lies in the graft. What variety of fruit may one expect from a branch of a wild apple-tree, of the earth wherein he grows, of the winds that whisper to it, of the bees, which brought pollen for its blossoms from afar?

In children's books just as in the works intended for adults, the reader searches for the spirit which can exalt and excite him in the plot of the novel, or in the magic of a fairy-tale. Children and adults join in this search for something that captivates them, for meetings with characters who invite them to follow them in their adventures, in courageous attempts to tear down the walls around daily life.

For the child there is even more. It has its élan, its spring-board is new. For the book to have its effect its sails must be live with the wind.

In this story, which is like the barge of adventure where one calls "All aboard" to the pilot, we must not forget that it is the cabin-boy who will take the wheel. Learning to read is all discipline. The adults have their reading education behind them and have learned to submit, to let themselves be guided by the book from beginning to end. In the last resort adults never take part in the action. The child, however, very easily becomes the twin of the hero, the brother of the animal who speaks to him.

The child is innocent. It is trusting, ardent and pure. I see it grow up in my school, like the pupils graduate from shorts to long trousers.

They change their reading matter, too, stories written for them against novels from short-lived series.

I know full well where the difficult age begins where the adolescent gets rid of his childhood as of a dress that has become too tight, the moment where unrest sets in, the small shame which one tries to cover with unconcerned arrogance. The small shame of having believed in Santa Claus.

You understand of course that Santa Claus is merely an image. The merry-go-round of childhood revolves around the lit tree. It is a masked ball with the first friend hidden in the middle, he whom one discovers in a crowd and for whom one will search for a life-time.

Happy childhood where the first abstract word that attained meaning was the word *friendship*. And in a world which was pure *love*. Happy childhood of trusting innocence.

I believe I know what the valuable talent is which those have received as their share who can only write for children. First of all, at the very beginning, there are unusual family circumstances which forced them to isolate themselves from the world of the grown-ups, which an instinctual prudence made them avoid. Shyly they closed themselves in in their childish universe. Were they too frightened of life? Perhaps. I believe that they never really became at home in that life which subsequently unfolded for them, that they would never integrate, find their place and submit. They remained on the spring-board of which I spoke and from which they wanted to take their impetus. The adventure for which they kept searching in every period of their lives has always remained that of their youth. And yet they boarded real ships, they travelled the world, they were turned into soldiers and manned canons. But in their memories they only sailed in the dinghies of the corsairs. And they brought nothing back from their travels or from the war but the bow of the Comanches and boomerangs for kangaroo hunts. In truth they have never left

Montignac, the plateau from where the bush of the Papuas was discovered, Chaumet's Asia, the deserts of Arizona, the rolling planes where the guards set the masts for the fireworks on the 14th July.

They have retained the full power of adventure. There are the adventures about which they write. And they write about them because they believe in them. This is the vital word: *believe in them . . .*

Be assured that children are never deceived. They demand that their author does not cheat and that he believes in his books at least as much as they do. (pp. 32-4)

René Guillot, in "In Memorian René Guillot,"
by Janine Despinette, in Bookbird, *Vol. VII,*
No. 2, June 15, 1969, pp. 32-4.

GENERAL COMMENTARY

The Times Literary Supplement

"L'enfant entre chez les bêtes d'un pas bien plus assuré que chez les grands." In these words René Guillot has expressed a truth that lies deep in all animal literature. From Peter Rabbit to White Fang, all its heroes show that "we and the beasts are kin." But the "we" is the "we" of our childhood, our age of innocence, before we learnt to live by reason and judge right from wrong. The child lives on the fringe of the grown-up world and gazes into it with fear and fascination, but he knows he may not yet venture in. Instinctively he turns to animals who also belong outside; they do not worry about doing and becoming, they are content just to be; the animals are his peers and with them he can feel at home.

M. Guillot is now mathematics master at the Lycée Condorcet but for twenty-five years he taught at Dakar and St. Louis-du-Sénégal. It was then that he came to know all those countries stretching from the rain forests of the Ivory Coast to the desert hills of the Hoggar, from the banks of the Sénégal to beyond the Niger—a region which may well be known one day as "Guillot's Africa." He would spend months on end in the company of black tribesmen. He hunted with them, shared their smoke-dried meat round the camp fire and listened to their endless stories far into the night. He understood their reverence for the animals they killed and learnt to accept the contradictions of nature that he saw in the heart of the hunter—fear and joy, reverence and violence, humility and glory—without trying to rationalize them as civilized man is always doing. By showing them in the context of the bush M. Guillot illumines the very essence of these primal emotions which are common to man and beast. It is round them that the structure of his stories takes form. There is no plot; we simply watch an animal grow up and fulfil its nature under the stress of adversity.

Oworo, for instance, plumbs the depths of devotion in a chimpanzee and, in the manner of a myth, it suggests the source of the monkey's feeling and the humble aspirations that well up in his heart in the presence of men. A child looks up to man with fascination because he sees in him the promise of what is to be; in Oworo also the similarity to man excites something within him—call it imagination, or hope—or is it a memory? According to the legend the chimpanzees were once a race of men. They offended their lord, the crocodile, and thereby forfeited the gift of laughter, for he punished them by depriving them of the laughter-giving water of Koguli, the spring which he alone could find, and they became creatures which were neither man nor animal: monkeys. But they believe that one day one of the monkey couples who wander off each new season in search of Koguli will find that secret spring, and that the baby animal that is born to them there will have laughter in his eyes again.

With M. Guillot there is never any question of having to "humanize" the animals before children can share their feelings in a book. Oworo is always wholly a monkey, Sama always a young elephant. The fact that the animals use human speech to express themselves is not confusing for a child. At one time he himself was dumb, like an animal, and he too expressed his feelings with the whole of his body, not just his mouth; he finds it reassuring when the writer does not underestimate things which cannot normally be spoken. Ernest Thompson Seton makes this point in his introduction to *Raggylug, the Story of a Cottontail Rabbit:*

> . . . rabbits . . . have a way of conveying ideas by a system of sounds, signs, scents, whisker-touches, movement and example that answers the purpose of speech; and it must be remembered that though in telling this story I freely translate from rabbit into English, *I repeat nothing that they did not say.*

Seton eventually dropped the device; he was primarily a naturalist and his development led him along other paths. Kipling followed a different principle. His Mowgli stories are more in the nature of myth and the language expresses human ideas. The wild boy and his animal friends up there in the Jungle, far above the puny little men in the valley, whom they only visit to play tricks on or punish, remind one of the gods of Olympus.

But M. Guillot, in his animal talk, is essentially a "translator," though he carries the method to its farthest limits. He speaks of Kipling as having inspired the deepest admiration in him: he is "le plus grand, mon maître, celui que j'ai lu et relu avec toujours la même passion." Yet, although he is in the Kipling tradition, M. Guillot's approach is quite different. Whereas Kipling conceived his stories in a dramatic manner, using the jungle as an artist uses a palette, with due regard for colour and selection, M. Guillot pours out a spontaneous narrative with little apparent art, as if the jungle, in fact, were "using" him. Kipling, like most storytellers (and M. Guillot, too, in his adventure stories), allows the reader to preserve a certain detachment, to watch and be surprised; but in his animal stories M. Guillot allows his reader no detachment whatever: he is inside the animal looking out, accepting everything as it comes. M. Guillot does not emulate Kipling's accuracy of description; he hardly describes the animals at all, taking them for granted as the animals themselves do. But he evokes the world seen through their eyes. Here, for instance, is what Sama saw as he stood underneath the protective arch of his mother's body:

> Marana's ears flapped very gently in the breeze, and her soft trunk seemed to be sniffing here and there in all directions. A shiver ran through the tips of the high branches. Instinctively, Sama felt his ears move too and his trunk stretch out to the wind.

Where as there something moving? How could you find it in the midst of all this green?

> This must be the thing called fear. All at once it transfigured the bush. The hot green air throbbed no more. The grass and trees grew rigid. And in the silence all nature stood still and you could hear the urgent beating of the blood in your body.

In itself this is just a trick of imaginative writing which might easily be imitated. But the vision it imparts is sustained from beginning to end of the book with an extraordinary intensity.

When M. Guillot read Kipling's *Something of Myself,* he was overwhelmed to find that in spite of many differences between himself and the man he revered as a master they had one remarkable thing in common: they both, when writing, felt that they were merely the vehicle for some force outside themselves which dictated to them and drove them on. Kipling calls this force his *daemon. . . .* Kipling's *daemon* was a literary imp of a rare order but he did not hail from the jungle. M. Guillot's on the other hand is

> almost frankly black. My *daemon* is more concerned to fathom the mysteries of the bush, its taboos and its gods than to dwell on what seems mysterious to the eyes of a white man.

This black *daemon* weaves his tales round the age-old themes of friendship, fate, authority and obedience, mother-love and, above all, courage. Animals accept their world. If fate is unkind to them, they endure patiently: that is their courage. No feeling of rebellion or self-pity aggravates their suffering or inhibits their capacity for wonder. That is why, in spite of the terrors Guillot's animals heroes undergo, we are left with a remembrance not of horror or evil but of the most poignant humility and fortitude.

M. Guillot, in taking up the old epic formula of the lone hero who pits his courage and wits against adversity or the forces of nature, has proved once more that there is no other story half so satisfying.

The lore of the bush is his inspiration. He once quoted a proverb from Senegal to explain his starting point for [*Kpo the Leopard*]: "When the mother dies, the grandmother gives suck." When a woman dies leaving a child, custom decrees that the woman in the nearest hut to hers, even if she be a grandmother, should take it and bring it up as her own. The proverb expresses the simple faith in the force of love to bring milk to the aged breast. From this idea Guillot's *daemon* spun his superb story of a leopard cub adopted by a cheetah. Siho, the indomitable foster-mother, is one of the finest creations of all animal literature.

Yaba, the antelope in *Sirga,* is another unforgettable character, noble in his submissiveness, the chosen prey of the lions. The deep wisdom of animals is implicit in all these books. An animal never apportions blame. Guillot, presenting a problem like authority and obedience, herd *versus* individual, touches chords in a child's moral being of which his mind is too young to be aware. Thus the lessons Sama learns from life impress the child like real experiences of his own. Sama, when still very young sees his father, Owedraogo, who has led the herd for countless years, defeated in single combat by the rogue prince Tarkwada. The old chief drags his wounded body away to die, while the herd sets off again with the new chief at its head. Might is Right, his father had always told him; the Law had spoken and Sama saw how all the herd obeyed. But the little elephant had yet to learn that in some strange way Luck is Right too, or the power to master Luck. Tarkwada is courageous but too self-willed to make a good leader; in the early days of his leadership the herd suffer many misfortunes, culminating in the terrible experience of being hunted by fire. After this Sama looks up to Tarkwada as a hero, for the great bull had saved him by carrying him in his trunk through the flames. He must surely be a great chief . . . to which his mother replies:

> "Yes, Sama, but he lacks something all the same. The real leader, whether of men or elephants, possesses a gift, a supernatural power; he is one who attracts good fortune and whose luck never forsakes him."

Does this not describe exactly the feelings a child needs to have for someone he trusts? The authority he looks up to must be able to inspire confidence and give a sense of security. The concept of guilt never once enters into this scheme of things. By primitive logic alone M. Guillot shows how the luck of the herd is bound up with the leader's observance of the law of the bush.

M. Guillot speaks of the bush, *la vieille brousse,* throughout his work as of something all-seeing, all-knowing, inscrutable, which ultimately decides all things, whose will must be accepted and whose laws must be obeyed. The simple tribes of the bush, men and beasts, know that it has all the forces of the elements at its command to strike and punish, but they also attribute to it the will to look after its own. His books convey a direct sense of belonging to a power or will which embraces all life, which one both fears and trusts. George MacDonald came near to doing this in *At the Back of the North Wind,* but it is something that can only be conveyed through a character which is both perfect and humble and when that character is a boy we find him not quite credible; animals, always true to their own nature, have a perfection we do not question, and M. Guillot's animals compel belief both in themselves and in *la vieille brousse* whose sovereignty they so humbly accept.

Whether Guillot's interpretation of the bush is a true statement of the black man's view is not the issue here. He is presenting to children truths about human nature in general, in language which goes deep into the moral heart of things. His themes are epic and the manner of telling has an epic quality also: his stories read as if they were written from one single impulse from first to last. He embroiders and digresses, it is true, but the tempo of his narrative never flags. The construction of these animal stories is hardly literary at all; they flow with a sense of timing and balance all their own, each making its own pattern like a rhapsody. If he had written in a more self-conscious style and imposed a literary discipline, the inspiration of his black *daemon* would have been obscured. He has chosen rather to tell his stories in essentially the same manner as that in which he heard all the lore and legend of the bush himself: as he had it at the camp-fire from the wandering *griot,* the bard of the African bush, who is not just an entertainer but the repository of the accumulated wis-

dom, law and custom of the tribes as it has been handed down by word of mouth through countless generations. True to the oldest art of all, M. Guillot gives us his tales thrilling with the simple heroism of life as it flows through the centuries and is renewed in every child . . . of man or beast.

> *"Chez Les Betes," in* The Times Literary Supplement," No. 2907, November 15, 1957, p. xx.

Boris Ford

[In *Riders of the Wind, Nicolette and the Mill,* and *The White Shadow*] René Guillot gets his effects by describing a colourful locale with effective authenticity, and then injecting his story with an almost lethal shot of magic. In *Riders of the Wind* this formula is applied quite mechanically, with the result that the story of the seventeenth-century French boy's adventures amid the deserts of Africa, on the banks of the Niger, and in Timbuctoo quickly becomes wearisomely heavy with Fate, while the central legend of the white mare puts in a perfunctory appearance from time to time, laden down with fine writing (Calvi, 'very near to death' from exposure in the desert, 'heard the joyful neigh of the horse who had found his rider and would bear him on his last journey into the land of shadows. The white mare!').

René Guillot's considerable reputation has not, of course, been built up only on this brand of cliché (though . . . *Nicolette and the Mill* is again little but a trifle of pointless 'magic' for younger children). *The White Shadow* is a far more substantial offering. It recounts the story of the two-year stay of a French girl in the hill station of the Lobi in French West Africa and of her 'serene and lovely' friendship with her 'white shadow,' her sister-shadow, the simple native girl Yagbo (as was foretold by the snake-charmer in Marrakesh). For all Guillot's Conrad-like indulgences and the unfailing Gallic polish of his style . . . ; for all that Galaire the doctor is 'a man of visions' and Tournoy the customs officer is 'a poet of a kind' and Bruce is an animal-man who 'gave you insight into the forest's secrets': for all this load of disabilities, the story is unusual and unexpectedly compelling. Guillot is himself an odd amalgam of visionary, poet of a kind and animal-man and he knows the African world in which his stories are set. Moreover, as, in this book at least, he doesn't lean heavily on the element of African magic, and even seems to some extent willing to expose its crudities, he leaves himself free to introduce Frances to a remote jungle-world dominated by the language of tom-toms and the cries of wild animals. Back at school in Bordeaux, one can sympathise with her sense that 'only her body seemed to be present in the classroom' and hear 'the secret thrill in the voice of the girl' as she speaks to the others of 'a land far away on the edge of the world.' (pp. 853-54)

> *Boris Ford, "Plain Things and Coloured," in* The Spectator, *Vol. 204, No. 6885, June 10, 1960, pp. 853-54.*

Margery Fisher

Nowadays a serious animal story will less often use direct speech than did the stories of thirty years ago; but the Kipling type of stylized dialogue used by animals has been used brilliantly by René Guillot in his series of tales about

African animals. Guillot knows Senegal and the Sudan well, and the hunter-naturalist Marlow, who plays some part in all the stories, may be taken to be a self-portrait of the author in his relation of interested patron to jungle animals. Guillot writes as accurately as a naturalist but as vividly as a poet. He deliberately enters into the minds of his characters. In *Oworo,* for instance, he relates the chimpanzee's pattern of thought to that of aboriginal tribes, and the story is haunted by the quest of the monkey for the secret spring, Koguli, famed in monkey tradition:

> Oworo, as a child with the tribe, knew nothing of this at first but soon he began to guess the meaning of their annual migration through the heart of Africa in obedience to a law as old as the world. But it is not the rains that lead the chimpanzee—they go quite at random, rather as black men do who hear the rumours of gold and, trusting to luck, quit their villages and go wandering in search of the wonderful river that flows with nuggets of gold. . . .

Animals talk in Guillot's books, they feel, they reflect. The cheetah in *Kpo the Leopard* thinks about her adoption of the leopard cub; Sama the young elephant thinks about the dangers he may meet in the jungle. They give human expression to their instinctive behaviour. Guillot is a poet, in that he believes in an affinity between man and animals, an affinity better shown in action than in philosophy; symbolized by the friendship of Sirga the lioness and the African boy Ulé. These stories are unique. Some children will find them difficult to read; the style, though verbally simple, is very compressed. A few may be impatient with the way plot and reverie are woven together. For the discriminating child, and the child who likes to send his imagination far and wide, they offer at once a firm statement about man's duty towards animals and a series of imaginative exercises which would be hard to beat in any sphere of children's writing. (pp. 61-2)

> *Margery Fisher, "Mrs Bunny and the Rabbits," in her* Intent Upon Reading: A Critical Appraisal of Modern Fiction for Children, *Franklin Watts, Inc., 1962, pp. 50-68.*

Marcus Crouch

[Before] 1952 few people had heard of René Guillot. The publication of *Companions of Fortune* in that year introduced a major writer. This complex, stormy, disturbing book, brilliantly translated by Geoffrey Trease, was something quite new. The tradition of the French corsairs was unfamiliar to English readers; so, largely, was the African setting. The characters were several sizes larger than life and their motives puzzling. The moral and philosophical ideas latent in the story were difficult to grasp. What made a complicated story deeply interesting was superb storytelling and masterly creation of atmosphere. The book breathed out the steamy heat of the African tropics. In the same year *Sama* showed René Guillot in a different light; the best jungle story since Kipling, it could not have been less like his work. There were, and continue to be, disturbing elements in Guillot's writing, but he stands head and shoulders above most of his contemporaries as narrator, adventurer and philosopher. (p. 129)

> *Marcus Crouch, "Widening Horizons," in his* Treasure Seekers and Borrowers: Children's

Books in Britain 1900-1960, *The Library Association, 1962, pp. 112-38.*

Gwen Marsh

[The following excerpt by the English translator of several of Guillot's works is from a speech delivered at the awards ceremony for the Hans Christian Andersen Medal in 1961.]

The Lycée Condorcet, the famous Paris grammar school, is an impressive building. But this ancient seat of learning shows a different face inside. A brave but battered look, I thought as I walked along the dingy corridor to meet René Guillot that first time, over thirteen years ago. A small, lean, dark-complexioned man with lively eyes, he came out of his mathematics class and warmly shook me by the hand. I felt, as I watched and listened to him talk, that there must be in him some vital process continually sparking off ideas. Indeed, M. Guillot's unflagging inventiveness is the reason for his prolific writing. Nearly forty of his books have been translated into English, and more than twice that number exist in France—all written in the last eighteen years. Ideas bubble up, and he must pour them out.

When René Guillot read Kipling's *Something of Myself,* he was thrilled to discover that the great English writer, whom he revered as a master, had known the same sort of creative experience. Both, when writing, felt that they were merely being used by some force outside themselves, which dictated to them and drove them on. Kipling called the force his daemon.

"I too have known this daemon," says M. Guillot . . .

> from the beginning. He works like a fever in the author he inhabits, giving him no rest. He takes over my story, decides which way it shall go . . . clamors for another story—or just an idea, since it is he who does the rest. Once the idea is born I write quickly, very quickly, typing, as if to dictation.

René Guillot lived in Africa for more than twenty years. He taught at Dakar and at St. Louis du Sénégal, where the boy who has grown up to become the present President of the Republic of Senegal was his most brilliant pupil. During these years he was an indefatigable hunter and explorer. He helped to survey the region in the Ivory Coast between the Volta and Comoé Rivers and to turn it into a nature reserve. (This was the "kingdom" to which Sama's tribe turned their longing steps.)

Wherever René Guillot went, along the Niger or into the desert or through the dense rain forests, he listened to the tales of the *griots* (storytellers) who kept alive the history and cultural heritage of the unlettered tribes. At school he got the boys, who came from widely scattered regions, to tell him the tales they were brought up on at home. This was a diet his daemon loved! There is nothing M. Guillot has written about Africa that has not had its source in the lore and legends of the bush or in his own experiences. He has freely adapted the tales that were told to him, for he is not a scholarly folklorist but a writer, who uses them for his own creative purposes.

At the end of the 1940s he returned to France and began his magnificently productive years as a writer for young people. Previously, he had written adult novels, one of them a prize-winning detective story. But a publisher had told him that in France the writing of detective stories was, over-all, *trop ingrat;* that the public bought them freely, but only if they were by British or American authors. Guillot possessed imagination, he could write a good adventure story, and he was a teacher who understood the mentality of boys. There was a vast field to be cultivated. *"Ecrivez un roman d'aventures pour les jeunes"* was the publisher's advice. It was taken.

He has written adventures that take place at sea, in France, in the Far North; but for me, none of these surpasses his African stories (except that perfect little tale, **The 397th White Elephant,** set in an imaginary Indian jungle kingdom).

Until three years ago, when he retired, he also taught at the Condorcet. He lives in a Paris suburb near the Vincennes zoo. For holidays he likes to go to Spain for the bullfights or to his house in the Saintonge, a region in the west of France where both his and his wife's family have always lived. (pp. 192-94)

We visited the Guillots there one sunny summer day. After he had shown us around, . . . we sat in the living room, the rack with all his hunting guns on the wall above us, and listened to his anecdotes about local characters he remembered from his boyhood or about his grandfather's smuggling escapades. He talked too of "psychic" experiences when he has seemed to have foreknowledge of some event; but he never writes about these strange occurrences. Sometimes his psychic sensitivity means an uncanny understanding with an animal. . . .

René Guillot's power as a storyteller has made him one of the best-known contemporary authors for young people. His books are being published in more and more countries: translations total one hundred and fifty to date. (**Grishka** alone accounts for thirteen!) That he was awarded the Hans Christian Andersen Medal is further proof of the widespread popularity of his books—and of the high regard in which he is held. (p. 194)

> *Gwen Marsh, "René Guillot," in* The Horn Book Magazine, *Vol. XLI, No. 2, April, 1965, pp. 192-94.*

Margaret Blount

The pitfalls of giving animals moralising voices, sad or happy thoughts, when you are trying to imitate nature rather than comment on human affairs, are many. René Guillot steps lightly over them in books that are less memorable than *White Fang* or *Bambi,* but solve all the problems very neatly; he gives his animals voiced thoughts in his naturalist's animal stories that are never obtrusive, never out of place. The leopards, elephants, cheetahs and others speak to each other in simple language that an animal might mean rather than use. (p. 259)

> *Margaret Blount, in an excerpt from her* Animal Land: The Creatures of Children's Fiction, *William Morrow & Company, Inc., 1975, p. 324.*

Margery Fisher

The story of Sirga, and the companion stories of Oworo the chimpanzee, Kpo the leopard and Sama the elephant,

relate animals and man in a unique way. Though the lioness Owara is described, as queen and mother, in terms of human myth-making, she is not humanized. The bond between men and animals is nearer to a kind of totemism; it is the expression of a compact which, as the author explains, was made by men in the days when they first entered the district and sued to the animals for permission to hunt and to dwell in their land. Tribesmen and animals govern their habits by the same necessities. Elephants and nomads move at certain seasons: lion cub and youth alike endure a certain initiation. Through Sirga's story René Guillot expresses indirectly the deep, almost mystical experience of his sojourn in the Sudan, his feeling of kinship with the forest and its inhabitants. (p. 324)

> *Margery Fisher, in an excerpt from* Who's Who in Children's Books: A Treasury of the Familiar Characters of Childhood, *Holt, Rinehart and Winston, 1975, 399p.*

Nancy J. Schmidt

Rene Guillot was a teacher by profession. He had the opportunity to learn about Africa and Africans in [great depth] . . . , for Guillot lived in Africa for over twenty years. Guillot went to Africa in 1925 and remained there until 1962 (except for the years when he fought in Europe during World War II). During his residence in Africa he taught mathematics in St. Louis and Dakar in Senegal, traveled extensively in French West Africa, and went on numerous hunting trips accompanied by African hunters. Apparently the African experiences which made the greatest impression on Guillot were his hunting trips, since these are prominent in the plots of his novels and were the subject of several volumes of non-fiction for adults. Despite the length of his residence in Africa and daily contacts with Africans, Guillot wrote about Africa in stereotyped terms. His characters are familiar African archetypes, including "howling savages," "faithful servants," and white hunters. The African characters (primarily men) are "naked pagan fetish-worshippers" who wear "bizarre" hair styles and do "grotesque" dances while wearing "hideous" masks. They live in a jungle with "incredible" rivers, rich vegetation, and many strange animals—a jungle that is teeming with horrors and dangers. (pp. 71-2)

Rene Guillot achieved acclaim that is rare among children's writers in his receipt of the Hans Christian Andersen Prize. . . . Guillot's primary contribution was his development of the adventure story. Guillot also received awards in France, Belgium, and Germany for several of his works, including **Sama** (the story of an elephant prince who befriends a Lobi boy in the Ivory Coast and is later taken to France in a circus), and **Sirga** (the story of the son of an Ivory Coast chief who befriends a lioness). The theme of man-animal friendships in these two prize-winning novels is common in Guillot's other novels and may account in part for their popularity with children. (p. 72)

Guillot was essentially a writer of animal adventure stories, most of which were set in West Africa. When Guillot wrote, he felt that he was the "vehicle of an outside force" which forced him to explore the depths of the bush, its taboos and gods. While it is evident that Guillot described the "bush" from firsthand acquaintance in some of the details that he included in his novels, it is equally clear that he focused on the exotic aspects of the "bush" (both forest and savanna) and described it in stereotyped terms. References to "the mysterious land of Africa" are common. Night in Africa is variously described as "dangerous and formidable"; the roar of a lion "in the depths of night [is] a gross, sordid, barbarous majesty". Numerous natural hazards of the bush are presented: a tornado kills two people in *Atonement in the Sun,* and elephants (which "trumpet savagely" and follow a man's scent "like a bloodhound") trample fields in *Fonabio and the Lion.*

Guillot also presented the gods of the "bush" in stereotyped terms. Although his descriptions of religious beliefs often included snatches of oral tradition, the vocabulary in which he described religious practices made those of the Senufo in *Atonement in the Sun* indistinguishable from those of the Kanga in *Fonabio and the Lion,* the Kikouyou in *The Fantastic Brother,* and the Lobi in *Sama, Fofana,* and *Tom-toms in Kotokro.* African religious leaders are referred to as "witch doctors" who lead "bloody rites" to "barbaric gods." These "witch doctors" practice "juju" and sometimes are subject to "hallucinations." They keep the "tools of their trade," such as iguana skins and secret plants, in "dark wooden chests" which are symbols of their power. The powers of "witch doctors" are both great and long-lasting; one "witch doctor" "reigned" for "half a century".

Dancing is the essential ingredient in group religious rituals in Guillot's novels. "Tom-toms" beat relentlessly, sometimes throughout the night, as "sweaty," "naked," or masked men execute "wild" dances expressing "pagan joy" or "pagan ecstasy." Equally important in the rituals are blood rites to "idols": "fresh" blood is offered, the blood of a recently killed animal is drunk by men or the sacrifice of a chicken is described in some detail.

Twenty years of living in Africa did not enable Guillot to gain an African perspective of life in the "bush" or of the African taboos and gods about which he felt compelled to write. One critic feels that it is unimportant whether Guillot presented his own or Africans' interpretations, since Guillot presented general truths about human nature to children. These truths are said to concern showing the relationship between men and animals, revealing primal emotions, and demonstrating the force of laws of nature.

It is highly doubtful that children can abstract general truths about human nature from Guillot's novels, in which the majority of the characters are repeatedly downgraded. "Full-blooded" Negroes are depicted as "superstitious"; Negro simplicity is considered an "unknown domain of madness"; Africans are variously described as "passionate," "impulsive," and "inscrutable". If a child reads *Fonabio and the Lion,* in which the African boy Fonabio is such a loyal servant of Marlow the white hunter (a character who appears in several of Guillot's novels) that he risks his own life to save Marlow from an attack by a lion, will he consider Fonabio an exception among the Africans? Or will he merely fit Fonabio into the prevalent stereotypes of blacks as loyal servants?

Do Africans in Guillot's novels represent human nature or do Europeans? The European heroes and heroines of Guillot's novels are no more typical members of their society than are the African characters. The European characters are most often men who are big game hunters or are trying to capture animals for a circus or scientific purpose, or boys or girls who live in West Africa or have become lost there. These characters are portrayed in less derogatory terms than the African characters, although they are not the idealized bearers of European civilization found in [G. A.] Henty's novels. The Europeans in Guillot's novels are portrayed in part through their actions and possession of the accoutrements of western culture, such as electric lights, tinned food, and tractors. However, they are more fully portrayed by the implication of what they are not, for they continually label Africans in ways which relegate the Africans to a lower order of humanity than themselves. For example, the hero and heroine of *Riders of the Wind* observe on various occasions that Africans are "ruffians," "a queer sort," "ragamuffins," "as naked as the day they were born," and have "uncouth names." By implication, Europeans are both different and better.

Animals—which are the main characters in some of Guillot's fiction and figure prominently in most of it—are presented with more empathy than either the European or African human characters. It is the animals which have developed personalities, are thinking beings, and live in a relatively complete, clearly-defined social order. In *Kpo the Leopard,* for example, the various species of animals live in "tribes" with internal subdivisions into families, leaders, and followers. The animal "tribes" have codes of behavior to govern both their own "tribe's" relationships with other "tribes." The daily habits of the animals (such as feeding, child care, and defense) are depicted in more detail than commonplace activities of either Africans or Europeans. The thought processes of animals, especially in *Kpo the Leopard, Sirga,* and *Sama,* are more developed than those of human characters. The animals have opinions of each other and of humans and can compare the relative merits of their lives in the forest and outside the forest in captivity.

The relationships which animals develop with people in Guillot's stories reflect upon the characteristics of the people. Except when animals are kept as pets by children (as in *Pascal and the Lionness*), man-animal relationships are usually those of enmity, for the animals are hunted by men. The Europeans typically hunt animals with guns on large expeditions supported by African porters and often assisted by African guides, as in *Mokokambo, The Lost Land* and *Elephant Road.* In contrast, the Africans usually hunt in small groups by burning the bush, shooting poisoned arrows, or setting traps. Africans sometimes fight animals alone, as in *Kpo the Leopard,* where Tuareg men engage lions in single-handed combat.

The attitudes of Africans and Europeans towards the animals they would or kill differ, as do their hunting methods. For example, in *Fonabio and the Lion,* Fonabio does not think of saving the cub of a wounded lionness, but the European hero points out that a European would take the cub home. Whereas Europeans are able to kill, capture, and tame animals, only Africans are able to know animals intimately and communicate with them on their own terms. This theme is fully developed in *Fodai and the Leopard Man,* in which Fode Koro, the son of an African chief, is the intimate friend of a leopard, as well as of other less dangerous animals. In this novel and others, it is implied that Africans have an instinctual or mystical ability to know and control animals, rather than knowledge and skills comparable to those of Europeans.

The animal life depicted in Guillot's animal adventure stories supports the stereotype of Africa as a jungle populated by large, dangerous animals, for it is lions, leopards, elephants, buffaloes, crocodiles, and hippos which are featured in the novels, along with venomous snakes, monkeys, and chimpanzees. Only occasional mention is made of commonplace savanna animals such as antelope, camels, and donkeys, even though part of the action of many novels takes place in the savanna. The numerous smaller forms of animal life which are commonplace in the forests and savannas of West Africa are largely absent from Guillot's novels. How can Guillot's novels teach truths about human nature to children when he describes only a small segment of nature and depicts relationships between only a few atypical kinds of men and an unrepresentative sample of nature?

Guillot's novels about Africa lack the historical basis of Henty's novels. For the most part, Guillot's stories are set in colonial Africa through implication, for the colonial presence is made known primarily through the presence of white hunters and game parks. The Africans are depicted in a tribal world untouched by either colonial administrators or incipient African nationalism. The merest hint of the realities of African politics enters into **Tom-toms in Kotokro,** in which a Polish atomic scientist and his son are forced to flee from South Africa and take refuge in a game park in the Ivory Coast. The backgrounds of most Europeans are ahistorical. The hunters, circus trainers, filmmakers, children who are French royalty, buccaneers, and travelers belong to no specific historical era—they are stock characters of much children's fiction, and Guillot did nothing to differentiate them from their general types. (pp. 72-4)

> *Nancy J. Schmidt, "The Writer as Teacher: A Comparison of the African Adventure Stories of G. A. Henty, Rene Guillot, and Barbara Kimenye," in The African Studies Review, Vol. XIX, No. 2, September, 1976, pp. 69-80.*

Companions of Fortune (1952)

This is a book of most remarkable quality. It stands above the competence of its contemporaries as an undoubted work of art, written with a delicate and loving sensitivity that plays alike round the actors and their environment. It is, indeed, the work of a poet.

The story is that of the search by the survivors of the crew of the *Belle Aude,* wrecked years before, for a treasure of uncertain nature to be found in Africa. So far, conventional enough! But the *Belle Aude's* crew is like that of no other ship, and the voyage seems to take place in a world quite remote, and so much their own that the necessary contacts with workaday humanity are in the nature of intrusions into the much more real world of birds and animals and gentle savages. Over the whole adventure broods the spirit of their drowned captain, Falahaut, guiding them still, and returned in a sense in his grandson, the boy Jean-Marie. The atmosphere of this strange tale is curiously dream-like and deeply imaginative, as though, almost, the whole thing were felt in the boy's mind of Jean-Marie,

than actually experienced. It is beautifully written, and here it must be presumed that Mr. Geoffrey Trease, its translator, has done his work with rare skill. . . . It is a work which a thoughtful child will love and treasure greatly. (pp. 177-78)

> *A review of "Companions of Fortune," in The Junior Bookshelf, Vol. 16, No. 3, October, 1952, pp. 177-78.*

Although ostensibly no more than another tale of a search for pirate gold, [**Companions of Fortune**] is written with a respect for atmosphere and character which few writers for children attempt. The slow building up of anticipation, the holding of tension, the dream-like quality of the story, the feeling that permeates it make strange and real what has in so many books for children become commonplace and unreal. A book for the fastidious. (pp. 357-58)

> *P. M. Hostler, in a review of "Companions of Fortune," in The School Librarian and School Library Review, Vol. 6, No. 5, July, 1953, pp. 357-58.*

There have always been conflicting views of [Guillot's] achievement, some readers being alienated by his political opinions, others by a style which was sometimes as thick as treacle but less sweet. On one point there is a measure of agreement; despite the underlying complexity of his ideas he was at his best—and he was much too prolific a writer to keep always on the crest—a superb story-teller. Guillot was obsessed with a memory of the corsairs, the 'Knights of Fortune' who dominated the Atlantic and the Spanish Main in the seventeenth and eighteenth centuries, brutal pirates—Guillot was seldom disturbed by brutality—but also brave men and master seamen. Several of his books are concerned with their real and fictional exploits. In the novel which shows him at the height of his powers, **Companions of Fortune,** the corsairs have all been long dead, but their spirit lingers and their treasure-hoards haunt their descendants.

There is just enough of *Treasure Island* in **Companions of Fortune** to underline the enormous differences between the two stories. The opening period of waiting, the preparation for the voyage, the treasure-hunt: these stages of the stories are identical, but the pace and the tone of Guillot's narrative are worlds away from Stevenson's brisk and uncomplicated manner. Guillot builds up his story slowly, savouring the dark atmosphere, a heavy foreboding almost outweighing the hopes of good fortune. Almost half of the book is spent in this way, before *Jean-de-Dieu* sails from La Rochelle with the Companions of Fortune aboard, heading for the hot coasts of Africa from which the source of Don Miguel's wealth, the black slaves, had come.

Africa was always René Guillot's particular passion. His heavy, sultry style matches perfectly the humid atmosphere of the jungle where Don Miguel's dead ivory and living gold lie waiting in the mud. So, through danger and hardship, the Companions of Fortune recover their treasure and are able to pay, in a surprising and highly satisfactory conclusion, the debt of their old captain.

Guillot was never an easy writer, and **Companions of Fortune,** which might be claimed as his best as well as his most characteristic book, is as difficult to read as any. It is partly a matter of style, of the ponderous and portentous sentences which Geoffrey Trease rendered most skilfully in an English version as doom-laden as the original. The ideas too, and the narrative with its slow pace and its many asides, do not make for easy reading. They are all, nevertheless, the essential matter of the book, and out of them Guillot created by main force a powerful and literally unforgettable story. The minority of readers, adult and child, who surrender totally to its forces guarantee for themselves disturbed nights, filled with dreams of the howling sea and the steaming river. It is one sign of a great book that it can haunt the reader for a lifetime, and by this criterion *Companions of Fortune* is a great book, a marvellous tale of adventure and a masterly piece of atmospheric writing.

In a tell-tale phrase Guillot speaks of the headquarters of the Companions as 'that house where everything was unusual'. It is the essence of Guillot's work that nothing is commonplace. In this he is exceptional among French writers, who have often taken particular delight in finding romance and adventure on the corner of the street. (pp. 39-40)

> *Marcus Crouch, "High Adventure," in his* The Nesbit Tradition: The Children's Novel in England 1945-1970, *Ernest Benn Limited, 1972, pp. 26-47.*

Sama (1952)

M. Guillot has plainly an unusual knowledge of the lives of the animals of the African jungle, and all must welcome his desire to hand some of it on to children. The portrait, for instance, of his pet chimpanzee, Oworo, is entrancing; so is the elephant lore, and the stories of the hippo-worshipping tribes; yet I am afraid the book will misfire with many who would have risen with enthusiasm to the stories if they had been told without the confusing atmosphere he has created with his talking animals. It makes them sound like mere shop models. The tone of their talk is so often out of tune with the wild life he describes. For the child who has no one reliable at hand to help to sort out fact from fancy, such confusion of mind can be very baffling, even infuriating. Much I am sure could have been achieved in the translation if Miss [Gwen] Marsh had realised the special considerations required in rendering a story into another language for children. She has left too many strange, blank words to prove mere dead patches to the young, and she has been content too often with mere equivalents. M. Guillot's images don't rise from the English edition which seems sometimes perilously near being another *Dumbo* for Disney instead of a delightful glimpse of real life among the elephants. (pp. 217-18)

> *Eleanor Graham, in a review of "Sama," in* The Junior Bookshelf, *Vol. 16, No. 4, November, 1952, pp. 217-18.*

This is a sensitively-written book by a Frenchman who is author, naturalist and explorer; the translation reads well and is understandable by readers of nine and over. All boys who love the *Jungle Books* and, in fact, any tale of wild life, will appreciate the picture of African game, for not only the ways of the elephant tribe are described here, but also those of hippopotami, panthers, lions and mon-

keys. Children may find some of the talk between the animals confusing and disjointed, but the older readers at least will accept the attempt the author has made to translate animals' thought into speech. It is the atmosphere conjured into being by this book and the author's love of wild things which will make it remembered with pleasure.

> *M. E. E., in a review of "Sama," in* The School Librarian and School Library Review, *Vol. 6, No. 4, March, 1953, p. 277.*

When Rene Guillot attributes language and emotions to his animals, we may still regard his treatment as realistic for his unusual sensitivity to the creatures of the wild makes him a most reliable interpreter. The elephant prince Sama knew the hazards of the bush from birth. . . . His perfect years are spent in specialized captivity with the white man Marlow who could understand the language of animals. His second stint in captivity, poignantly depicted, cruelly sees Sama taken across the seas to the circus of Marseilles; but taming cannot destroy the soul of the wild. Marlow perceptively retrieves Sama from near-tragedy and sends him back to the bush, a free fierce creature. Compelling and convincing elements devoid of sentimentality distinguish this work.

> *A review of "Sama," in* Virginia Kirkus' Service, *Vol. XXIV, No. 4, February 15, 1961, p. 166.*

Sama, prince of elephants, roamed the bush country in Africa along with his mother and learned of life from her. He is captured by a white man and taken to live on his farm with other creatures from the wild, later released to the wild, and, eventually, taken to Marseilles to join a circus. Slow-moving, descriptive, rather than adventurous, animal story which never seems alive; rather it is as though the story were moving behind a thin screen. Not recommended.

> *Viola K. Fitch, in a review of "Sama," in* Junior Libraries, *Vol. 7, No. 8, April, 1961, p. 52.*

So masterful is the telling that the animals' human speech seems less anthropomorphic license than an entirely acceptable literary representation of their great dignity and intelligence. Of the book's ten magnificent chapters only two compress too much action.

> *A review of "Sama," in* Saturday Review, *Vol. XLIV, No. 19, May 13, 1961, p. 50.*

Sirga, Queen of the African Bush (1953)

The movement of this story is a slow and majestic one, following the career of Sirga the young lioness and Ule the son of an African chief, with the dignity and simplicity that belongs to their wild life. Brought up together the cub and the baby boy become almost as brother and sister and when later separated by war in the jungle village, seek each other by a kindred instinct, finally to take their places once more as heads of their village and kingdom. The author reveals an intimate knowledge of the jungle and its ways and translates that knowledge into a unique and impressive story, coloured and warmed by a sympathetic understanding and deep insight. The death of Niora the old lion acts as a prelude and is only one of the many moving pictures that impress themselves upon the senses. The quiet rustle and stealth of the wild African scene is here suddenly broken by trouble that stirs and trembles and finally crashes upon partakers and watchers while the ensuing calm drifts slowly in, breathing a hushed and fervid peace upon man and beast. So is the reader carried, lifted and swayed, throughout the book, by M. Guillot's powerful writing. (pp. 192-93)

A review of "Sirga," in The Junior Bookshelf, *Vol. 17, No. 4, October, 1953, pp. 192-93.*

The best children's books, by comparison, make the merely competent and well-written stories seem distressingly juvenile. Such an effect has **Sirga** on the rest of [the books reviewed] . . . Written with the distinction which we have come to expect of the author, **Sirga** captures the heart, the fine imagination binds the senses, the reader is made to sympathize with the African boy who established his kinship with all animals, and claimed the noblest of them as his friend. This is a book which will give its young readers lasting joy.

P. M. Hostler, in a review of "Sirga," in The School Librarian and School Library Review, *Vol. 7, No. 1 March, 1954, p. 69.*

The affinity between a chieftain's son and a female lion cub born of proud stock on the same day makes up the nucleus of this tender but adventurous story. . . . Richly ornamented with description of life in the bush, this novel of adventure and romance contains a poignant depiction of the nature of a wild and highly intelligent animal in her unique reaction to a human being of stature. Tender without being sentimental, Rene Guillot's characters are at every point as compelling as they are convincing.

A review of "Sirga: Queen of the African Bush," in Virginia Kirkus' Service, *Vol. XXVII, No. 14, July 15, 1959, p. 497.*

The King's Corsair (1954)

This yarn of buccaneering in the time of Louis XIV is the work of an author described as 'the most distinguished writer of children's books in France today', in a translation by [Geoffrey Trease,] an author equally renowned on this side of the Channel for work in the same genre. The result is, on the whole, disappointingly watery. The mysterious figure of the great pirate chief, Caravage, appears unconvincing, especially in its posthumous influence, and in trying for effect the author relies far too much on reiterated assurances rather than on skilful building of atmosphere. The morality and humanity of Luke Whaler, its hero, often appear merely sordid in a way that does not occur to one so strongly in recollecting that in fact Drake and Raleigh and the rest were little better than pirates. Possibly the inevitable if slight vitiation resulting from translation has something to do with upsetting the usually delicate balance between the convincing and the unconvincing, but it is a fact that **The King's Corsair** is not by any means as good as M. Guillot's reputation leads one to hope.

A review of "The King's Corsair," in The Junior Bookshelf, *Vol. 18, No. 3, July, 1954, p. 125.*

I am tempted to call this book a second *Treasure Island*. Now that space ships have replaced galleons and Dan Dare has ousted Long John Silver, it is refreshing to read a children's novel which recaptures the thrill and adventure of a pirate's life, gives it plausibility and yet steers clear of the hackneyed plots of most pirate stories.

Although there are the usual ingredients—buried treasure, mutiny, shipwrecks, and the rest—they are, for once, handled cleverly and imaginatively, and welded into an unusual plot. Suspense is maintained until the very last page. There are no lengthy and lurid descriptions of gory fights, though there is plenty of action, and brutality and cruelty are not disguised.

The leading character, Luke Whaler, a sixteen-year-old corsair, is a distinctive personality; he grows in stature and moral courage. He, and his story, will appeal to any boy over the age of eleven.

G. Bott, in a review of "The King's Corsair," in The School Librarian and School Library Review, *Vol. 7, No. 3, December, 1954, p. 210.*

Oworo (1954)

Rene Guillot's animal stories offer a highly individual recreation on original lines of jungle life as seen by a poet, projecting a world so complete as to baffle criticism. They are not to every taste, for the unusually vivid understanding of some aspects of animal behaviour will not win over those who object on principle to any humanization of animals, and the calm acceptance of reality, and impartial view of native methods will not reconcile others to a certain dwelling on horrors, reminiscent of the morbidity which mars much of Felix Salten's work. But for most readers these books have a fresh and often exciting feeling for animals and for the African scene, and there is some very intriguing mythology which may be the author's invention. In this book there is a reversal of Darwinism, for these monkeys believe they were once men and are always searching for a return to humanity and laughter. The story is therefore somewhat melancholy, and at times a bit precious, (though that may be the fault of [Gwen Marsh's] translation), and the last episodes are almost as rushed as those in **Sama,** nor do the meetings of the chimpanzee and elephant always coincide with those described in the earlier work. But the picture of that strange landscape and its creatures, of the chimpanzee parents searching for laughter in their baby's eyes, of Oworo's father dying in the crocodile's trap—these and other scenes seem to prove the author's authority, though time alone can prove his true strength.

A review of "Oworo," in The Junior Bookshelf, *Vol. 18, No. 5, November, 1954, p. 258.*

The 397th White Elephant (1954)

M. Guillot, even in those of his books which come nearest to naturalism is always the mystic. His ships, his animals, all belong half to this world, half to that of the poetic imagination. This brief and lovely tale is more firmly in the spirit of fantasy than anything of his which has yet come to this country. It is a story of extraordinary quality, told with the utmost economy, never straining after effect; yet it leaves behind an unforgettable impression. I went straight back to the beginning and read it again. The nearest parallel to its gentle mysticism is perhaps *The Cat who went to Heaven,* but the quality of M. Guillot's story is more illusive and intangible.

The publishers assign the book to the age range 7-10. In fact it is a timeless and ageless book which will make its appeal to sensitive readers of all ages, not least to those of so-called mature years.

A review of "The 397th White Elephant," in The Junior Bookshelf, *Vol. 18, No. 5, November, 1954, p. 237.*

A beautiful, deeply moving story of a little Hindu king and his big white elephant, Hong-Mo. Happiness is an elusive and a relative thing. Here, in allegorical form, we find its many and strange effects and results. A book for reading aloud in the family circle, to talk about, and to think about.

Inger Boye, in a review of "The 397th White Elephant," in Junior Libraries, *Vol. 3, No. 8, April, 1957, p. 26.*

Everything about **The 397th White Elephant** is a delight. René Guillot has written a "fabulous history" that captures the very feeling of happiness as a poem might. . . . The story is utterly charming. As simple as the "White Cat" or a Jataka tale, it has no age limits. Nine-year-olds can read it, ninety-year-olds too, and all in between. While it is frankly a fable to show that happiness cannot be chained, "not even with chains of gold," nor can it be bought, one enjoys it for the narrative alone.

In a distant province in India there lived a ten-year-old king, Light of the Morning. When his last white elephant died, the 396th, he was indeed sad. Then Hong-Mo, the magnificent, a "pearl white animal, gleaming and sparkling like a rough marble in the sunshine," was found in the course of a mighty hunt, Hong-Mo who may have been an animal or may have been—who knows? What marvels he performed and what trouble came when he departed! Toh, the head keeper, secretly stole the "piece of happiness he left as a present when he went away"—a great ivory tusk—and had it carved into 396 small ivory elephants to sell for luck. Hong-Mo outwitted the wily keeper, and when Light of the Morning found his *second* 397th white elephant, we skip for joy with him.

A review of "The 397th White Elephant," in New York Herald Tribune Book Review, *May 12, 1957, p. 18.*

The Wind of Chance (1955)

Another fine strong adventure tale by the author of **Companions of Fortune** and other books. . . . The steamship in which young Michel Santanrea stows away in Marseilles and the automobile at the timber-lord's headquarters on the Ivory Coast indicate a 20th century setting, but the story might be set in any period, concerning as it does the reaction of men to each other, to nature and to chance. Some of the characters and situations are familiar, in a cruder form, in formula-made boys' popular fiction, but

aside from a few passages when the author seems overimpressed with his own profundity his vision and skill transform the old ingredients into a most absorbing story of one boy's gamble with fate. The gamble is won because he goes on to play a man's part in the gruelling timber trade of the rain-forests; it is very much a man's world, but girls as well as boys can enjoy the book and it seems likely to mean many things to many readers, both as a story and as an exciting reading experience.

There is a special atmosphere in all M. Guillot's books which seems particularly strong in this little volume, combining the dream-like aspects—in this case Michel's double, the old Spanish dreamer, the legendary adventurer Fabregasse, the nightmarish forest—with the reality of hard work, the fight for existence and the pleasures of being alive. One such pleasure might well be to be a boy of Michel's age and to hear with him the old Spaniard's answer to his question of what lies ahead—the unknown. Is there anything better in the world? (pp. 224-25)

A review of "The Wind of Chance," in The Junior Bookshelf, *Vol. 19, No. 4, October, 1955, pp. 224-25.*

The Wind of Chance . . . , though written with the sense of beauty and emotion that we have come to identify as belonging peculiarly to this author, lacks nothing of excitement and movement. The young fifteen-year-old hero bears us with him to the African coasts where he finds his future in the great rain-forest, and once again we are permitted to look into the heart of the wild and the wild creatures who dwell there.

Phyllis Hostler, in a review of "The Wind of Chance," in The School Librarian and School Library Review, *Vol. 7, No. 6, December, 1955, p. 433.*

Kpo, the Leopard (1955)

KPO is an orphaned leopard cub adopted by cheetah parents, subsequently leading a partly hybrid life in the forests and plains of Africa. Just when the leopard strain is asserting itself, KPO is captured by a Tuareg chieftain and trained as a companion of the hunt. It is not long, however, before the call of the wild reasserts itself once more and for all time, and KPO returns to the life for which the leopard was born. The tale, though in translation [by Gwen Marsh], achieves an extraordinary intimacy with the wild creatures which form its principal characters, even to the little birds which combine to act as a sort of guardian angel to the young leopard until he is really able to look after himself. The more violent encounters between man and beast or between beast and beast are well handled and the harsh landscape under the beating sun is definite and alive. There is no doubt the author has a feeling for the subject. . . .

A review of "KPO the Leopard," in The Junior Bookshelf, *Vol. 20, No. 2, March, 1956, p. 77.*

Like others by this writer, **Kpo** is a fine book. Through the experiences of a young leopard cub, Guillot evokes the spirit of the vast African forests and translates their wild life into a vivid and swiftly-moving story. He tells of Kpo's early life, the loss of his parents after a forest fire, his adoption by cheetahs, capture by a young chieftain and final return to the forest of his birth. The stark realities of wild life and a wealth of knowledge and understanding of animal lore lie behind this imaginary theme and make it a powerful story for older primary-school children.

Betty Brazier, in a review of "Kpo the Leopard," in The School Librarian and School Library Review, *Vol. 8, No. 1 March, 1956, p. 77.*

The Elephants of Sargabal   (1956)

In the most lively of M. Guillot's adventure stories, mysticism is always breaking through. He can tell a good tale, few better, but he is primarily a philosopher. *The Elephants of Sargabal* has something of that strange little fantasy *The 397th White Elephant* in it, but it is a bigger work, with greater variety, range and more immediate appeal. It is his best work for some time and, in its different way, as good as *Companions of Fortune.*

It is the story of a little slave boy in India who escapes to the jungle and joins a band of children led by a strange Mowgli-like boy. He becomes involved in a rising against the local prince and is finally instrumental in restoring the princess to the throne. This is the surface theme, and it gives opportunities for much stirring action, vigorous and extremely bloody. The book offers much more than this. It deals with animals and the mysterious communion between animals and men. It deals with the nature of truth and the truth of the imagination.

Like all M. Guillot's books, this is difficult. It makes great demands on the reader and few children will understand intellectually the meaning of the book. The thoughtful child, however, will be stirred by the beauty of its vision and will understand emotionally a great deal of its message. He will know, even if he cannot express the knowledge, that he has been in the presence of a master of story-telling and a master poet. (pp. 346-47)

A review of "The Elephants of Sargabal," in The Junior Bookshelf, *Vol. 20, No. 6, December, 1956, pp. 346-47.*

René Guillot is a master of his art and the fact that his mastery of words and phrases remains so powerful in a translation reflects great credit on his translator [Gwen Marsh]. His is indeed the poetry of prose and the field of children's literature is greatly enriched by his writing. *The Elephants of Sargabal* possesses a mystic quality, a dreaminess of legend which depends largely on the author's sincere belief in the dream life, yet, closely bound to this, he combines a great knowledge of the raw, wild life of the Indian jungle.

The story tells how Ajmil, a boy slave, is left for dead by his masters, a group of elephant hunters. He grows up in the jungle with a supernatural instinct for the lore of the wild and with a spirit stirring within him which leads him on to the city of Rajpur where he saves the Princess Narayana from rebels after the fierce storming of the City, and restores her to her peoples. It has become a legend of India, though it was not Ajmil who finally gave his life for his princess.

The combination of the dream-like quality with the strong, ruthless spirit of adventure makes this an unusual book which will probably be enjoyed by a selective few rather than a wide range of readers.

Betty Brazier, in a review of "The Elephants of Sargabal," in The School Librarian and School Library Review, *Vol. 8, No. 4, March, 1957, p. 307.*

Although *The Elephants of Sargabal* has its source in Indian legend, a legend, the author tells us, that "really happened," it is a book (unlike his enchanting *397th White Elephant* . . .) to be enjoyed by adventure-story enthusiasts. The format is not nearly as lovely as that of the earlier story. The black and white sketches [by Felix Hoffmann], barely suggesting some of the elements of the tale, miss the mood of fear and beauty. We hope, however, that their suggestions of jungle life and fighting will be sufficient to lure boys and girls over eleven, for once started, we feel sure it will be read to the very last page. . . .

We are grateful to Gwen Marsh for her excellent translation of a thrilling adventure in a strange and compelling environment told poetically and excitingly. It's a young people's book that adults would enjoy.

A review of "The Elephants of Sargabal," in New York Herald Tribune Book Review, *November 17, 1957, p. 16.*

The Sea Rover   (1956)

The Sea Rover is Shrimp, a boy who finds manhood and a vocation among the pirates on their relentless quest for vengeance and the vindication of the honour of their leader, the Malamok.

This, like M. Guillot's other corsair tales, is very strong meat. Not only is it full of violent and savage action, but over it broods the gloomy relentless spirit of revenge. It is an ugly theme, made unforgettable and even beautiful by the author's poetic vision and his pervading love of the sea.

M. René Guillot is in the front rank of living writers for children; some might reasonably say that he leads that rank. He is a great story-teller, a master of atmosphere, learned in the mysteries of human behaviour, haunted by the beauties of sea and jungle. He is also perhaps the most difficult writer for English children who have been reared in a simpler tradition. It is hoped that they will make the effort to enter his enchanted kingdom.

A review of "The Sea Rover," in The Junior Bookshelf, *Vol. 20, No. 6, December, 1956, p. 338.*

The Animal Kingdom   (1957)

The most recent translation of M. Guillot's stories ranks him as a creator of animal mythology which cannot be matched so far as one can recollect, in native English. He goes far beyond Kipling in establishing a sense of animal personality which is not just a projection of human values. Often he slides imperceptibly into fantasy, as in **"The**

Kingdom under the Water," or into nursery story as in "Cornseed's Wonderful Ride." Sometimes there appears a relationship between man and animal which is nearly animal on the human side and human on the animal, as in "The Two Chimpanzees," but, however one may attempt to label the treatment, one is always conscious of inadequacy in such classification. The work has just that elusive quality which defies formal comparisons and remains peculiarly the author's own. Aside from, or rather about events, there is always, too, an atmosphere which belongs more to the animals than to mere physical environment, and the book cannot fail to give satisfaction to young readers of more than average sensibility.

> *A review of "The Animal Kingdom," in* The Junior Bookshelf, *Vol. 21, No. 3, July, 1957, p. 119.*

A Boy and Five Huskies (1957)

This is a new setting for René Guillot, in the sub-arctic of North Canada, and once again the author makes one realise just how important atmosphere is to a book. The poetry is there, the mastery of words is there, bringing vividly to the reader's imagination the solemn beauty of the snows.

Again the characterisation is all that one is led to expect of Guillot, tough men of the North with lives and wills conditioned by environment, the perceptive portrayal of the philosophy of a half-breed Eskimo-Indian, the independence of Uncle Como, the hero of the book's hero, fifteen year-old Eric.

Eric is ready for adventure and the book is about his journey North acting as a decoy for his uncle who is being hunted by a Mountie. Eric nearly takes on too much, but the finish sees him safe, with an understanding between Uncle Como and Joe Kling, the Mountie. How deep can one go when reading Guillot's books? What prompts such strong powerful writing? Is it symbolical in any way? There is so much to explore and extract from such books that it is difficult for a young reader and will only appeal to those who have the intelligence and imagination to draw on the treasures of a visionary's work. It is not easy but like all such things worth the reward. (pp. 138-39)

> *A review of "A Boy and Five Huskies," in* The Junior Bookshelf, *Vol. 21, No. 3, July, 1957, pp. 138-39.*

Perhaps not since Jack London has there been a writer of adventure stories about the frozen North as convincing as René Guillot. Written for older boys—who should at the outset realize that Como's jubilant Robin Hood attitude toward established law and order is a romantic tangent—this story of the Canadian Arctic crackles with the excitement and derring do that a real Arctic tale must have.

> *George H. Eavre, ". . . And Older Brothers," in* The Christian Science Monitor, *November 7, 1957, p. 16.*

The story makes tense, exciting reading. Some readers will question the author's knowledge of huskies when he has one barking, since huskies howl rather than bark. The really serious weakness of the book, however, lies in the author's attitude that it is all right for a man to take the law into his own hands and even to force a Mountie to let a criminal go just because he feels confident of his own ability to frighten the man into leading an honest life. The book also suffers from a condescending attitude toward Eskimos and Indians.

> *Zena Sutherland, in a review of "A Boy and Five Huskies," in* Bulletin of the Children's Book Center, *Vol. XI, No. 9, May, 1958, p. 95.*

Tom-Toms in Kotokro (1957)

Is it, perhaps, a sign of the publishing times that here M. Guillot combines his unmatched gift for animal studies with a breeze of "adventure" which activates some of his other books? Certainly it takes some time for Janek and his father to flee from Poland under the Nazi threat and reach the African game paradise which is to be the father's haven for the time. Even there, beside the panther Baoo, and Niki the chimpanzee, international intrigue intrudes and distracts Janek and the African outcast boy Yago, from their hunting brotherhood, and complicates their tuition of Tio, their captured elephant pet. Yet despite the dilution of the animal and tribal lore with spies and politics, M. Guillot captures the reader's interest as completely as ever, the more so perhaps as he includes also elements of tribal magic, superstitious obstacles to progress and the handicap of the sleeping sickness. It is Janek, Yago and the animal associates who keep the real centre of the stage and the writing and the translation [by Brian Rhys] are of the standard one has come to expect. It is something of a pity, however, that the fabulous Marlow, who rules Kotokro as an enlightened despot, is not more fully drawn. Conrad, one feels, would have taken him to his heart.

> *A review of "Tom-Toms in Kotokro," in* The Junior Bookshelf, *Vol. 21, No. 6, December, 1957, p. 314.*

Another remarkable book by perhaps the most gifted and versatile of living writers for children. This story starts, surprisingly, in Poland, from which the hero flees with his father, a great scientist, just before the outbreak of war. After a breathless escape, they take refuge deep in the African jungle with an extraordinary white chief in a household which includes a chimpanzee and a full-grown panther. Here Janek grows up learning the ways of the wild and developing his own kind of wisdom.

This fantastic stuff would be perilously explosive material in other hands. M. Guillot is a master story-teller, however, as well as a philosopher, and he takes the reader with him right into the heart of the jungle and expounds its meaning. He accepts the wild on its own terms, and children brought up in a more conventional school of adventure will be tempted to ask some difficult questions about the functions of witch doctors and the like. The story is a useful corrective to normal views on the differences between civilization and savagery and on the partnership of beast and man. Children who enjoy it as an exciting story of adventure will be richer and wiser for reading it. (pp. 68, 71)

> *M. S. Crouch, in a review of "Tom-Toms in Kotokro," in* The School Librarian and School

Library Review, *Vol. 9, No. 1, March, 1958, pp. 68, 71.*

The Blue Day　(1958)

This is the first of René Guillot's books written for younger children, and although well-told, I don't think it will have the general success that his books for older boys and girls have. A little Dutch doll, left in an attic, is told by the fairies that for one whole day, one blue day, she can have anything she wishes for. The day comes at last and off goes Mia. The book will appeal to little girls chiefly but not to all little girls. Although written with distinction, . . . it somehow fails to hit the jackpot.

G. Taylor, in a review of "The Blue Day," in The School Librarian and School Library Review, *Vol. 9, No. 2, June, 1958, p. 167.*

This is pure enchantment, a little story composed of the most delicate sentiment and informed with true observation. Only a writer of M. Guillot's quality could have done it without smudging the fine lines.

It is a story for very small children. The end is quite unexpected, completely characteristic, and with a touch of the master's bitter-sweet. A lovely book. (pp. 122-23)

A review of "The Blue Day," in The Junior Bookshelf, *Vol. 22, No. 3, July, 1958, pp. 122-23.*

The author begins and ends the tale in first person, injecting a quasi-allegorical note into his remarks. This, plus the fairly difficult vocabulary, will tend to limit the audience for the book; it is already limited in its appeal because of the feminine subject and the fanciful writing.

A review of "The Blue Day," in Bulletin of the Center for Children's Books, *Vol. XIII, No. 10, June, 1960, p. 162.*

Prince of the Jungle　(1958)

One has only to think of Kipling and Beatrix Potter on the one hand, and their all too numerous and frightful imitators on the other, to realise how animals bring out the best and the worst in juvenile fiction. I don't know exactly where René Guillot's jungle is, though it purports to be in India. I suspect that it has as much reality as Blake's forests of the night: which is to say, the more-than-geographical reality of the world of imagination. Certainly it is very satisfying. So authentic is the tribal scene, so intense the half-savage life that goes on there, that no reader, least of all a boy of 11 or so, would stop to question the accuracy of M. Guillot's vision. He is perhaps the nearest equivalent we have today to Rider Haggard, with perhaps a touch of Kipling. He has an astonishing sense of animal life, bringing elephants, tigers, horses and dogs within range of our five senses. His latest story, *Prince of the Jungle,* has not quite the attraction of *The Elephants of Sargabal,* and is to my mind disfigured by rather too much blood and cruelty. This is a pity, for he is one of the very best living boys' authors. It is to be hoped that he is not losing the humanity, and even humour, which illuminate some of his earlier books. (p. 686)

James Reeves, "Wild and Tame," in New Statesman, *Vol. LVI, No. 1444, November 15, 1958, pp. 686, 688.*

From *Sirga* and *Sama* onwards [Guillot's] stories of jungle life have always been exceptionally vivid, with a certain emphasis on savagery and cruelty. The same emphasis has been marked in some of this author's books more concerned with human beings than with animals. M. Guillot seems particularly to enjoy developing his undoubted aptitude for describing this side of animal and human life, until in the latest of his books to be published here, *Prince of the Jungle,* the reader is regaled in detail with the carnage of animal and human conflict. . . .

The setting for these gory scenes is the rivalry of two young Indian tribesmen to secure the vacant chieftainship. After preliminary tests in the initiation ceremonies they and their companions enter the jungle for a "retreat," in which each becomes associated with one or other of the wild animals. Their vigils are most vividly described, and no one is more skilled than M. Guillot in suggesting the eeriness of the jungle, in evoking a certain animal mysticism, and in building up the tension before the sudden battle to the death between beast and beast, man and man, or between the two. But the young hero has qualities which may not appeal to all readers. Will they accept his deliberate stabbing to death of his favourite horse in a fruitless attempt to galvanize it forward a few more yards in a race? Will they approve his nonchalance at seeing his rival being mauled by a python? After some 200 pages in which blood and butchery are never far away even the adult reader may feel rather battered; on the teenager the bestiality of humans and animals alike may not leave a very welcome impression.

"Tooth and Claw," in The Times Literary Supplement," *No. 2960, November 21, 1958, p. xix.*

In the most tensely exciting story for older boys that René Guillot has yet written, we are taken into the jungle near the Ganga River in India, a land the Kiang tribe had settled and partially cleared a thousand years before, after making some kind of mysterious compact with Sharka, the tiger lord of the jungle animals. Fifteen-year-old Raani, after the murder of his father, the Khan, a murder that appeared to be caused by their enemies the Kalanays but which was arranged by traitors of his own tribe, must submit to the jungle ordeal with the twelve other young boys eligible to become the next prince of khan.

For three moons they must wander alone in the jungle until one of them is able to share the life of Sharka and hunt with him. That boy will be the true jungle prince. Among the twelve is one boy, Yasim, a particularly bitter rival of Raani, a ruthless enemy who will stop at nothing to win the chieftainship. The terrible rivalry leads both boys to savagely cruel deeds. Each in turn narrowly escapes death. The tale is a rapid succession of crises, of desperate struggles against panther, python, red ants, Kalanay tribesmen and assassins. These are as frequent as a lover of ordinary "thrillers" could wish, but there is more than melodrama, an abiding sense of the power and beauty of the jungle and the influence on men's lives of the animals. As the story reaches its climax the elephants led by Raani play a part in saving the Kiang tribe (a part similar to that of the elephants in the same author's ***The Elephants of Sargarbal***), and Sharka, the tiger, shows unmistakably who should be the next khan. Primitive, terrible and sometimes repulsively brutal, this story is nevertheless exciting and filled with the fascination of the interrelationships of men and animals which Mr. Guillot can show so skillfully.

> *Margaret Sherwood Libby, in a review of "Prince of the Jungle," in* New York Herald Tribune Book Review, *May 31, 1959, p. 10.*

Elephant Road   (1959)

M. Guillot, incomparable master of atmosphere, is at his weakest in constructing a plot. It is not always easy to follow the narrative of ***Elephant Road,*** although the handling of individual episodes is superb, and the plot when finally unravelled turns out to be highly unconvincing. When that is said all that follows is praise. M. Guillot knows Africa. He also knows the strange, complicated people who inhabit his story, and he has very great skill in releasing just enough information about them while allowing them to retain their essential mystery. It is with animals that he is at his best. These are, in this book, seen from the outside, but seen with the eyes of a zoologist and a poet. They are seen too without sentiment. Life is a savage business, and the author takes no pains to soften it.

It is, as always, in atmospheric writing that M. Guillot excels. A brooding atmosphere, half threatening, wholly fascinating, pervades the book, and gives it unity. However untidy the story-telling, however unconvincing the motives, however great the anti-climax, the reader is held continuously by the wonder and the terror of this dark land, so beautifully conveyed in M. Guillot's subtle evocative writing. (p. 219)

> *A review of "Elephant Road," in* The Junior Bookshelf, *Vol. 23, No. 4, October, 1959, pp. 219-20.*

Fifteen-year-old Serge, a French boy and child of the carnival, is endowed with flawless coordination and an extraordinary sympathy for animals. When a movie producer decides to use him for an elaborate film set in the African elephant territory, he is called upon to use all his circus skills in the broader arena of the jungle. While on location he becomes involved with a boy whose life is curiously similar to the life he portrays on the screen, a boy who is tormented by a secret. As the boy's identity is revealed he and Serge become friends and together they form the foundation of an adventurous and meaningful life in the elephant country. Rene Guillot has the Gallic knack of describing the exotic with an almost cinematographic realism. The result of this is that his stories for teen-agers maintain the flavor of adventure and at the same time preserve a mature and believable climate. Here is one of the few writers addressing the teen-age reader who is able to introduce a wide range of characters and situations, without at any time condescending to his audience. [This] novel should have an immediate appeal to those interested in African adventure and continental sleuthing.

> *A review of "Elephant Road," in* Virginia

Kirkus' Service, *Vol. XXVIII, No. 18, September 15, 1960, p. 819.*

The intense mystery and excitement of the African jungle are always described by René Guillot in a moving fashion. Even in this book which is more hastily constructed and less powerful than his ***Tom-Toms in Kotokre*** or ***Winds of Chance,*** there are passages that are superb. Any boy would be spellbound by the tense excitement of watching the newborn baby elephant and its mother, and the fight between the great males as well as the danger the cameramen were in when they dared to approach a great herd of elephants too closely. Perhaps the reason this seems one of his minor books is because there is less about the theme he handles so well, the kinship of man and beast. This plot centers on a French circus boy who is taken to Africa to act in a documentary film. . . . The most interesting scenes are the glimpses Serge has of an African village during the feast of the "men of the moon" and the encounters with elephants and buffalo.

> *Margaret Sherwood Libby, in a review of "Elephant Road," in* New York Herald Tribune Book Review, *February 26, 1961, p. 35.*

Grishka and the Bear   (1959)

The tale of Grishka, the Siberian boy, and Djidi, the bear cub, is as charming as a legend and has that aura of reality and impossibility that so frequently characterises myth and fable. It develops the theme of friendship between human being and animal convincingly and depicts young Grishka faced with problems that involve not only his courage but also his emotions.

Grishka's father, Orsok, is banished from the tribe for killing a bear before the proper season. The boy befriends a motherless cub and rears him in the village for a year. Then, following a barbarous tribal custom, the cub, Djidi, is condemned to be ritually killed and consigned to the waiting cauldrons. Grishka has saved the bear's life once and he does so again by escaping with Djidi. Later, in the final chapters, the bear saves Grishka's life.

This story could so easily have dwindled into sentimental gush over cuddly bears; but it never shows the remotest sign of doing this. It is firmly embedded in the atmosphere of primitive life among a northern tribe and the whole framework of plot and character is held together by a neat, balanced design; bears are shown as killers as well as pets; cruel tribal customs are set against the happy play of children; ominous figures like the sorcerer are matched by kindly Li Tsou, the travelling Chinese trader, or Yaku, Grishka's playmate; Grishka's fight to the death against a white panther is followed by his inner conflict over the sacrifice of Djidi.

Add to all this the crisp, evocative prose of Rene Guillot . . . , and ***Grishka and the Bear*** deserves to be called a fine book.

> *A review of "Grishka and the Bear," in* The Junior Bookshelf, *Vol. 23, No. 6, December, 1959, p. 349.*

Mutual devotion of child and animal is an old theme, yet this story of a Yakut boy and his friendship with a black bear has a delightful freshness. René Guillot communicates the life and atmosphere of the people of the tundra beautifully, handling the unlikely theme of a boy accepted among wild bears with entire conviction. The book has been well translated [by Gwen Marsh]. The language has a delicate clarity suited admirably to the story which, if slightly precious to the older reader, possesses the timeless simplicity of the legend and fairy tale.

I read it at a sitting and many young readers will wish to do the same.

> *D. Sharples, in a review of "Grishka and the Bear," in* The School Librarian and School Library Review, *Vol. 10, No. 1, March, 1960, p. 88.*

In his preface the author tells how he got this story from a friend who heard in Siberia about the boy Grishka and his life among the black bears in the mountains there long ago. As retold here the tale is simpler, briefer, and less thickly atmospheric than the author's jungle books, but it has just as remarkable a background and episodes of equal dramatic effect. Over and above the incidents in which Grishka contends with the wild and enjoys the friendship of the girl Yaku, hangs the question of his father's eviction from the village of Murkvo because of the shaman's false accusation. When will he return? The folkways picture becomes fascinating: the bear festival, the reverent attentions to Grishka's bear cub who is given a splendid yurt of his own, the rituals of shamanism.

> *Virginia Haviland, in a review of "Grishka and the Bear," in* The Horn Book Magazine, *Vol. XXXVI, No. 2, April, 1960, p. 132.*

The White Shadow   (1959)

[*The following review discusses a translation of* Maraouna du Bambassou *by Brian Rhys.* Maraouna du Bambassou *was also translated by Gwen Marsh and published as* Beyond the Bambassu *in 1961.*]

It has taken eleven years for René Guillot's **Maraouna du Bambassou** to reach this country. The delay is not surprising; it must have taken courage to undertake an English edition of a story which is so entirely original, so far from the cliché-stories which are our daily fare. **The White Shadow** will not be widely popular. It makes demands beyond the average reader's capacity to give. For the right reader, however, it will be a haunting experience.

Frances, whose mother is in a Swiss sanatorium, is going to Africa with her father, a Game Warden. On the way, in Marrakesh, she meets Dominic, a nice ordinary boy, and wishes to bind herself to him with the snake-bond of friendship. The old snake-charmer refuses; Frances is already accompanied by the white shadow, an unknown and as yet unseen friend. At last she reaches Togbiéto, and the jungle tom-tom announces "Three travellers are coming." The third traveller, Frances' shadow, at last appears. This is Yagbo, a little negro girl who is destined to be her friend and more-than-friend. This mysterious friendship is bound up with two other mysteries, that of Bruce, the Breton hunter who has found in this remote country his kingdom, and Yann the savage who is—or is he?—half-

panther. Out of this complex material M. Guillot weaves his bitter-sweet story.

There is much here that will puzzle the child and most adult readers, for this author is wise enough to know that he has not solved all the mysteries of Africa. What is left will still delight the sensitive reader. There are some lovely pictures of life in a wild country, the beauty mixed with that cruelty which M. Guillot so well knows. The animals are irresistible, Saada the lioness and the delightful baby elephant. The humans are full of interest, too, and characteristically complicated. This author writes like a poet. Here is the snake-charmer's music:

> The pipe began sounding, with full notes that seemed to float and sail through the air like soap-bubbles. Louder and louder they swelled, till they broke into shrill squeals which pierced the ear painfully, and just as they died away, the pipe seemed to gather the squealing in, weave it into a flowing, waving air which coiled and uncoiled, just as the little python snake was now doing.

What a lovely book! (pp. 348-49)

> *A review of "The White Shadow," in* The Junior Bookshelf, *Vol. 23, No. 6, December, 1959, pp. 348-49.*

Riders of the Wind   (1960)

At first sight, René Guillot's **Riders of the Wind** looked like *Treasure Island* with a dash of sex. But a closer examination revealed an identity and a splendid vitality of its own. Calvar (or Calvary, his name taken from the wayside cross where he had been found abandoned) is a fifteen-year old ship's boy with heron legs, mouth too wide and eyes too blue. Apprenticed to Cap'n Le Hour, a soot voiced old foam-scraper grounded in the wooden quarter of seventeenth-century Nantes, Calvar is soon lost as a human stake in a card game to the Captain of the frigate *Gabrielle-Anne* and sails for the African coast. **Riders of the Wind** is the beautifully controlled parable of the boy's emergence to manhood. There is a dynamic and hauntingly imaginative strength in the bone and muscles of René Guillot's writing . . . that recalls the best of Roy Campbell.

> *Charles Causley, "With Zest and Feeling," in* New Statesman, *Vol. LIX, No. 1521, May 7, 1960, p. 678.*

Every one of René Guillot's books is an experience, for this is a creative writer whose slightest work bears the fingerprints of genius. **Riders of the Wind** belongs to the group of sea-roving stories of which the prototype, and the finest achievement, was **Companions of Fortune.** In the new book there are some fine scenes at sea and in Africa and some baroque portraits in his characteristic manner, but the brooding, dream-like atmosphere which in his best work pervades every nook and cranny of the story is here little more than a mannerism. Not among the finest of M. Guillot's work, **Riders of the Wind** nevertheless, in its fierce colour, and the powerful, confused sweep of its narrative, makes the books of most of his contemporaries look pale and trivial.

"Exotic Scenes," in The Times Literary Supplement, *No. 3038, May 20, 1960, p. iv.*

This is one of René Guillot's "sea-rover" stories of the seventeenth century. Although it is the tale of a seaman, much of the action, characteristically, takes place in Africa. In it, in fact, are most of the ingredients of a story by this remarkable master.

The hero is Calvar, also known as Calvi, Gorgol, Oulé, and finally Holvegeur. He is a boy of Nantes who goes to sea, visits Africa, becomes, unwillingly, one of the "Riders of the Wind," finally returns home to his sweetheart and to a fortune. Four aliases suggest some complexity, and indeed this is a story which readers may find real difficulty in following. M. Guillot often seems reluctant to admit intruders into his kingdom. He bars the way with esoteric knowledge, a forbidding atmosphere, sudden and unpredictable violence. However, he is not a writer susceptible of criticism. One accepts his books with all their difficulty and aggressive oddness—for the sake of what? Their wisdom, the strange convincing characters, the unforgettable episodes, the strength. One never forgets, when reading M. Guillot, that this is not only a great writer but a great man.

A review of "Riders of the Wind," in The Junior Bookshelf, *Vol. 24, No. 3, July, 1960, p. 151.*

Nicolette and the Mill   (1960)

Third- and fourth-grade readers will enjoy this delightful fantasy of the French countryside. One's interest is caught immediately when Nicolette, the miller's little daughter, is given a magic ring by a sorcerer which enables her to understand the language of the old mill wheel. The mill wheel wants a change and so everyone, even Sauvette, sets out to find the loveliest valley in the world. Easy vocabulary, convincing style. Recommended.

Edith Dodds, in a review of "Nicolette and the Mill," in Junior Libraries, *Vol. 7, No. 5, January, 1961, p. 61.*

The story is translated [by Gwen Marsh] from the French, a fact which is not detectable in the charmingly told, very unusual fairy story of a water-mill and its stream who wanted a change of scenery. The atmosphere again is definitely and enchantingly foreign but the situations are a mixture of the ordinary everyday and the gaily fantastic.

Constance Ball, in a review of "Nicolette and the Mill," in The School Librarian and School Library Review, *Vol. 10, No. 4, March, 1961, p. 375.*

Mokokambo, the Lost Land   (1961)

[For] the hard-headed mysticism of [Guillot's] feeling for animal life there is no English equivalent. In **Mokokambo** young Thiéry asks a friendly air-pilot to drop his tortoise, Aglaia, by parachute into the Sudan. As a result Thiéry is invited to Africa, and there is witness of a strange dance of the animals in a lost part of the forest. There is no one like M. Guillot for maintaining a busy air of practical story-telling while, in fact, seducing the young reader into a belief in the secret powers and complicities of the animal kingdom.

"Imported Adventures: A Fruitful Traffic in Literatures," in The Times Literary Supplement, *No. 3090, May 19, 1961, p. vi.*

Who would guess a turtle could lead the way to high adventure? That's what happened to Thiery Barjaval, 13, the hero of Rene Guillot's beautifully written tale of the African jungles. How Thiery leaves his miniature zoo in his Paris apartment, to follow his turtle, Aglaia, to Africa, and subsequently to the lost land of Mokokambo, is as absorbing a tale as any lover of animals is apt to come across.

One hopes that adults will discover this book—it is entirely too well written, too exciting, to be confined to junior readers (8 to 12). It is obviously no imaginary account of the African savannas—Guillot's familiarity with the terrain and its inhabitants glows from every paragraph.

M. M. R., "Artful Tales Showing Ways of Life in Other Lands," in Chicago Tribune, *November 12, 1961, p. 40.*

Both story line and motivation that get a young French boy into and out of a jungle in Africa just in time to witness a legendary gathering of wild animals are involved and contrived. That the boy, who is especially sensitive toward animals and who easily wins their confidence, can cheerfully go out with his bow and arrow to shoot game seems inconsistent with the final episode. His skill and leadership on the trek through the jungle with a young friend are also hard to believe. The descriptions are smoothly, almost poetically written, but the story as a whole seems confused. Not recommended.

Agnes Krarup, in a review of "Mokokambo: The Lost Land," in Library Journal, *Vol. 87, January 15, 1962, p. 331.*

Beyond the Bambassu   (1961)

The author's reminiscences of Marlow the white hunter gone native, who had for so long refused to kill the creatures of the wild except for meat, have that disconnected aspect which has become increasingly characteristic of M. Guillot in his tales of the African bush. Some of the tales, naturally, are of animals, but they are principally animals which form Marlow's menage (or should it be menagerie?) or play some part in the affairs of Marlow and his Lobi friends. Despite disconnectedness a strong element of suspense invests many of the incidents. Guillot in his own way is a master of the technique of interrupted activity which holds the reader's interest and also doubles it by the time his theme is renewed. At all times the details and novelties of the environment, and of Marlow's eccentric mode of existence are sketched with a raciness that refuses to be bogged down or solemnified by insistence on photographic finickiness. Guillot's method has before been described in these pages as cinematic, but for the modern viewer of lengthy, painstaking films the expression is no longer fully apt. Perhaps kaleidoscopic would be better.

A review of "Beyond the Bambassu," in The

Junior Bookshelf, *Vol. 25, No. 4, October, 1961, p. 221.*

René Guillot's two books, **Beyond the Bambassu** and **Master of the Elephants,** it is perhaps hardly necessary to say, fall squarely into the class of the re-readable. It is not easy to choose between them. **Beyond the Bambassu** consists of a number of short stories and, if only because good short stories are rare, it is perhaps to be preferred. M. Guillot's Africa has something of the quality of Kipling's India, but without any implication of racialism. It is a world in which child is at one with man, and both with animals. This author never writes of an elephant or an antelope without bringing these animals into the orbit of the child's senses—sight, hearing, and above all touch. Just how this is done is M. Guillot's secret, though it was known also to D. H. Lawrence. The story of the lion-cubs suckled by an African girl whose baby has died is deeply moving—a difficult theme, it might appear, for a children's story, but managed with tender and sensuous realism and without mawkishness. Perhaps because of his virtues, especially the absence of sensationalism, some children find it difficult to get into René Guillot's longer books. But there are few authors now writing for children who are more worth the effort. The ten stories in **Beyond the Bambassu** would be an admirable introduction.

"Exotic Settings and the Need for Something More," in The Times Literary Supplement, *No. 3118, December 1, 1961, p. vi.*

The Fantastic Brother   (1961)

A mixture of the romantic and the faery is always a hazardous undertaking. It is more acceptable and more easily manageable in the mysterious jungle where things may happen which no man may explain; it is less manageable and less credible in the cold light of the France and the adventures of the time of Louis XIV. M. Guillot's story of a deception practised on an old French nobleman in the pretence that his son's wife has borne twins whereas the truth is that she has borne a girl only, so that the girl must all her life "double" for the boy, is of the best romantic genre and acceptably maintained, but the idea that a fine wild boar with a jewel in his nose may be—*may* be—a spellbound human being strikes a more than faintly false note. When Lucas Gaud, a common boy, takes the place of the boy "twin" at sea and loses himself among the ancestors of the Kikouyou, the legend of the unicorn and its relationship to the respect paid by these people to the rhinoceros is again vague and disturbing without being in the best sense significant to the story as a whole. Though both aspects, the romantic and the faery, are the subject of fine writing one feels the elements have not been successfully fused. The acceptance of a strange white man as a promised god is old stuff, though M. Guillot handles it well, yet it may well be that the taint of delirium which the second strange interlude suggests will not appeal to the average young reader and may even spoil, to a certain extent, the excitement and exhilaration of the main theme. (pp. 221-22)

A review of "The Fantastic Brother," in The Junior Bookshelf, *Vol. 25, No. 4, October, 1961, pp. 221-22.*

The master French story teller again demonstrates his ability to create a mystifying, poetic tale of adventure and romance. . . . It is a rich, deep tale which belongs to a fading genre; the characters are meticulously developed as the reader is held captive—having willingly suspended disbelief—from first page to last.

A review of "The Fantastic Brother," in Virginia Kirkus' Service, *Vol. XXXI, No. 13, July 1, 1963, p. 609.*

Master of the Elephants   (1961; U.S. edition as *Fofana*)

There is something of the pre-war documentary film in M. Guillot's latest story of the African bush. It is not so much a continuous narrative as a set of sequences which highlight the personalities he hopes to transmit to his readers. Nevertheless, it succeeds where some of M. Guillot's other books have shown a tendency to tediousness in their more faithful continuity. The Lobi-boyman, Fofana, emerges as a being whose ethnos and personal magnetism are something beyond the European ken, yet that point is never laboured though demonstrated through telling instances of his achievements as intermediary between his tribe and the lordly creatures of forest and scrub. Although he and the French Jean Luc accomplish a friendship which would seem to satisfy the basic requirements of a relationship entitled to that name, Fofana remains in part unapproachable and different despite the growth of loyalty and dependence on both sides. Fofana is one upon whom the eventual burden of leadership falls by virtue of atavistic factors which the Western mind can no longer fully comprehend. This the author has amply conveyed. As always, his portrayal of wild creatures has unique personal strokes which add charm to the excitements of undeveloped lands. As usual a note of sadness underlies all. (pp. 222-23)

A review of "Master of the Elephants," in The Junior Bookshelf, *Vol. 25, No. 4, October, 1961, pp. 222-23.*

Rene Guillot, master of the African Bush, conducts another thrilling safari through his mysterious domain with the aid of Jean-Luc, a French boy who joins his father in the remote timber lands of Bakali. From his first day at the native school, Jean-Luc is fascinated by the clay effigy of Fofana, a noble young hunter in bondage to the iron-workers. Oddly, it is Jean-Luc who helps free Fofana and learns of his awesome power to communicate with animals. Fofana repays his debt to Jean-Luc in many ways—mainly by offering him a profound and passionate friendship. A Guillot jungle tale without elephants? Never. Here the magnificent beast Adjinakou understands Fofana's order to obey Jean-Luc, and when he rejoins his herd, the elephant saves the French boy during a stampede. Jean-Luc's relationship with the native boy bridges the gap of time and culture and allows readers the vicarious pleasure of knowing the strange and wonderful Fofana. It is a beautiful story—poetic and simple—another reflection of this dark and primitive world.

A review of "Fofana," in Virginia Kirkus' Service, *Vol. XXX, No. 5, March 1, 1962, p. 238.*

Not often in books for young people does one come across such beautiful writing—such strange tales told with such breathtaking style. But always, it would seem, one finds these elements in the books of Rene Guillot.

Now he takes us to Africa. We watch the wonderful and moving friendship which builds between Jean-Luc, . . . and Fofana. . . . We share Jean-Luc's awe of Fofana, who manages to combine the ancient, superstitious heritage of his jungle people with a modern day classroom skill and flawless French. The adventures these two boys share will take the reader far, far away from the "L," the "Y" pool, and the Oak street beach, into a land mysterious to many but intimately and lovingly known by Guillot.

> *Maurine H. Remenih, in a review of "Fofana,"*
> *in* Chicago Tribune—Books, *May 13, 1962, p.*
> *17.*

The Wild White Stallion   (1961)

[*A revised edition of* The Wild White Stallion *appeared in 1963.*]

This is a "horse story" that may live. It is set in the Camargue, that part of France where wild horses and black bulls roam on the marshes, and concerns the young fisher-boy Folco and his love for the foal which he christens White Crest. It is a sad story, but its effect is uplifting rather than depressing—the boy and the horse are both true to themselves and to each other right to the end, and the grasping ranchers are outwitted. The atmosphere of the wide plains, where rivers wind to the sea and flamingoes unfurl rose-coloured wings against the setting sun, the life of the ranchmen and fisherfolk and their gay carnivals at festival time are presented with the deft touch of one who knows the people and the district and can enter into a boy's world, his dreams and ambitions.

> *A review of "The Wild White Stallion," in* The
> Junior Bookshelf, *Vol. 25, No. 4, October,*
> *1961, p. 223.*

The Wild White Stallion celebrates a close, intense relationship between a boy and a foal growing up in one of the herds in the Camargue. Published in France as long ago as 1959, the book has an increased relevance now that there is renewed concern for the area and its animals. Folco has a directly personal interest in the beautiful animal which he has first seen as a newly born foal, deserted in the marshes when its mother is captured by gypsies, and he achieves what amounts to friendship with the horse he calls White Crest, because he does not threaten its freedom. Indeed, his determination that the stallion shall not fall victim to a greedy rancher and his cowboys leads to the boy's death, as he and White Crest swim out to sea together to escape [cruelty]. . . . Terse, full of controlled feeling, this is a fine story with a marked sense of time and place in it.

> *Margery Fisher, in a review of "The Wild*
> *White Stallion," in* Growing Point, *Vol. 17,*
> *No. 2, July, 1978, p. 3361.*

This is about the stallions of the Camargue, who have little in common with the geldings that normally inhabit the stables of pony books. In this story, Folco—the boy hero—is the only one able to tame the magnificent, fearsome stallion White Crest, through the quality of his de-

voted love. Young readers, in reality usually rather frightened by large, untamed animals, may find this idea both appealing and, to an extent, consoling. Within the story, they can identify with the super-competent child hero, and also with the wild animal; like various untamed human characters in children's fiction, always a sympathetic symbol for the young who themselves have now been more or less broken in by the adult world, but who sometimes regret the loss of personal freedom as they approach the responsibilities and cares of adulthood. (pp. 162-63)

> *Nicholas Tucker, in a review of "The Wild*
> *White Stallion," in his* The Child and the
> Book: A Psychological and Literary Explora-
> tion, *Cambridge University Press, 1982, pp.*
> *162-63.*

Three Girls and a Secret   (1961)

[This is] a story that is as subtle as any of Guillot's other adventures, though the theme is unusual for him. This is a tale of Paris, of two schoolgirls who housekeep secretly (and efficiently) in part of a building due for demolition, and who hide here a baby they find abandoned in a block of flats. If the baby's history is partly a concession to the author's love of mystification, little Laurence has a more important rôle in the story too, for Michele and Manuela, and their older friend Caroline, all treat him differently and feel differently about him. The translator [Joan Selby-Lowndes] has brought out the ease and grace of Guillot's prose and especially of his dialogue. With its sharply defined locality and its human interest, this is a very good domestic story.

Improbable though it might seem that three girls could keep a baby hidden for a month and more, Guillot persuades us that on this occasion it could have been done. (pp. 162-63)

> *Margery Fisher, in a review of "Three Girls*
> *and a Secret," in* Growing Point, *Vol. 2, No.*
> *1, May, 1963, pp. 162-63.*

It must be the dream of all young girls who play 'mothers and fathers' with their dolls to have a real baby to look after. This is an imaginative story telling how three young girls find and successfully look after a lost baby in a derelict flat which they make into their 'home'.

The writing of Rene Guillot varies from book to book and he does not always maintain the standard which he achieved with his earlier animal stories. In this book, however, he portrays with gentleness the tender love and care which these children lavish on their charge. How they manage to keep their secret for some months is perhaps more convenient than probable, but emotionally, the story is outstanding and it is to be strongly recommended for girls between ten and fourteen years of age.

> *Betty Brazier, in a review of "Three Girls and*
> *a Secret," in* The School Librarian and School
> Library Review, *Vol. 11, No. 5, July, 1963, p.*
> *530.*

First published in France in 1960, the story of three young girls in Paris who find and keep an abandoned infant; the conversation in the book is lively and colloquial save for the occasional evidence that the translator is English: "I say . . . ", "Thanks awfully . . . " etcetera. . . . [The] author succeeds in making the story completely credible and the girls are misguided but never criminal. Good style, good characters, and a plot that is tight-knit and suspenseful.

> *Zena Sutherland, in a review of "Three Girls and a Secret," in* Bulletin of the Center for Children's Books, *Vol. XVII, No. 3, November, 1963, p. 43.*

The King of the Cats   (1962)

One wonders often how far the demands imposed on writers by their publishers or by the necessity of keeping a "name" in front of the public affects the quality of successive works from authors who have "caught on"!! The recent taint of staleness in the stories of Simenon, for example, as well as of Guillot tempt one to the belief that, however prolific, favoured authors should be encouraged to "lie fallow" for a year or two now and then. This story of a wild cat who finds himself drawn to domestication with the daughter of a circus owner is still competent, still lit with flashes of creature-drama that survive even in [John Marshall's] translation, but both animal and human figures have a suggestion of puppetry rather than breathing life. The cat is not quite a nursery-tale cat: he is not quite adult either. As for the rest of the animals who occupy the canvas, they give a strong impression of having been borrowed from some other and more mature nature tale of the true wild in which M. Guillot has previously shown himself so gifted. One misses here, as one misses after having read the earlier Maigret stories, the firm impression of sympathy with created characters without which no novelist survives, however competently he goes through the motions of composition and analysis. This is just not vintage Guillot.

> *A review of "The King of the Cats," in* The Junior Bookshelf, *Vol. 26, No. 2, March, 1962, p. 67.*

What makes Jack London the most convincing of all writers about animals is that, somehow, he suspends us while we read in a midway position between human and animal consciousness. . . . We become intensely aware of the gulf between the two kinds of consciousness, while we are made sharply sensitive to the entwined destinies of human and animal. Of course, to claim that few other writers come near to giving us the same sense as Jack London does of what it must be like to be an animal is only to say that few writers in this field have had anything like his extraordinary endowment. Nevertheless, he gives us a measuring stick: he is, one would think, an exemplar whom every successor must study closely.

Today one of the best known of his successors is, of course, René Guillot. M. Guillot's basic feeling about animals is different from London's: he believes in an animal wisdom, in animal rites and magic, that are, as it were, the equivalent of human religion. Some readers (young and old) find this mysticism an irritant: but one must argue, against this, that it never swamps his stories—it is always contained in a sturdy frame of narrative –and that, in any case, M. Guillot's guess about the way the animal consciousness is organized is as good as anyone else's. Perhaps elephants do have their ceremonies. The age of David Attenborough's marvellous films, oddly enough, seems to increase rather than weaken possibilities of this sort—certainly, turning from the television set, one sometimes feels that no explanation of the strange ways of animals could be too improbable.

The King of the Cats, M. Guillot's latest story, has its usual strong narrative. Maou is a wild cat living in woods in the south of France—the king of his tribe. Driven off by a conspiracy among his followers he attaches himself to a girl who belongs to a circus. For her he has a deep, intelligent love: it sustains him even through his harrowing contacts with tiger and chimp and performing squirrel. But always he has a sense of the indignity of being a pet and a performer: he is drawn, and in the end decisively, by the fierce life of the woods and his need to reassert his kingship.

This is all splendidly told, but one must say that this time M. Guillot does, in small ways, make belief more difficult than usual. Jack London's Buck was drawn to the wild, but in him it was an urge, a powerful hunger, a matter of *instinct*. Where, it might be said, M. Guillot goes too far is in giving his wild cat much more than instinct. Maou plots and plans as if he were a highly articulate banished duke out of Shakespeare. One has to take it that wild cats have names among themselves which they recognize when spoken by humans. Maou himself has a mate, a frail farmcat called Mina, and their longing for each other belongs to human consciousness—when Mina coughs in their nest in the woods one almost feels that her true name must be Mimi. They converse in a thoroughly human manner—"You will get to know her", Maou tells Mina, having described to her his human mistress. There is an uneasy mixture of probable animal behaviour and conduct that is unlikely because it closely resembles certain clichés of human activity. The story will hold many of its young readers by its sheer vigour—but others may shy away from it, given too many opportunities for disbelief.

> *"Call of the Wild," in* The Times Literary Supplement, *No. 3144, June 1, 1962, p. 406.*

The longest, most detailed cat book of the season, a book for readers from 11 to 13, has a great feeling for life in the wild, as do the finest of Rene Guillot's books. Here it is not the throbbing jungle that he writes about but simply of wild cats in a forest, their enmity with foxes and their jealous juggling for the position of leadership in their own group.

Mr. Guillot's greatest skill always seems reserved for descriptions of animals—ranging free, unchecked by men. The most exciting parts of this book are the battles in the woods, between the fox and Maou and Patoche, his faithful follower, and the fight that occurs when the whole pack of cats led by the jealous One Ear attacks Maou. The rest of the story often seems contrived and unconvincing after the exciting beginning.

> *Margaret Sherwood Libby, "Three Small Gems Repolished," in* Book Week—New York Herald Tribune, *December 29, 1963, p. 13.*

Mountain with a Secret (1963)

For those who think of an adventure by René Guillot as either maritime or African, there is a surprise in the setting of this new one—New Guinea. In mountain and plain and jungle scenery a story is enacted by characters typical of this writer—lonely men in lonely places, old men trying to make up for mistakes or missed chances earlier in their lives, young men pitting their strength against Nature. As always, the theme is integral to the story, and it is while the reader is thinking of what happens next that he absorbs, perhaps without realising it, lessons about what people are capable of and what drives them on. In his treatment of character Guillot goes deep, and his African stories in particular can stand re-reading by children at different stages in their development. But perhaps what stays mainly in the mind, and especially after this new story, is an almost mystical sense of the power of the wild, a sense of the mystery in lonely places that holds men to them. This is perhaps stated most clearly in a comment dropped by the narrator in the course of this story:

> There remain on earth only a few primeval oases, miraculously preserved, where nature casts her age-old spell; on islands, in the heart of jungles or beneath hanging clouds on lofty, inviolate peaks such as the Himalayas where even now the Snowman may still walk. If one discovers them by some miracle they can never be forgotten.

Such an oasis has been found in New Guinea by Hendrik Dekker, son of an estate-owner, Hendrik who was lost as a boy on the tangled mountain where his father met his death, and who was accepted as a god by the Waoudis, since oral tradition recorded that such beings had first hollowed out their secret dwellings in the mountains. Hendrik, now a young man, has become a notorious outlaw to the settlers on the plain, but to young Johan van der Landen, living with his sea-captain uncle on what was formerly Dekker's land, Hendrik reveals his ambition and, at last, the secret plateau where he has established his kingdom. Gold, danger, romance, antiquity—many of the elements of classic adventure are here, and presented in the classic manner; for though Peter and his uncle are looking eagerly for gold, it is the quest that satisfies them, not the successful end of it.

Guillot's narrative technique reminds me of Masefield's idea of a story as a river with beautiful tributaries and backwaters. This is a complex tale and the mystery depends on several sub-plots, carefully linked. As the story lengthens and gathers in intensity, as the feeling of place becomes more and more dominant, still everything is held together by the character of Hendrik, a younger version of the settler Marlow in the African tales, a man of courage, mystery and power. The crisp yet winding style comes over well in [John Marshall's] translation, and there are evocative black and white illustrations [by B. L. Driscoll] which point to various episodes in the story but which are far more concerned with carrying on the strange atmosphere of a fine tale.

> *Margery Fisher, in a review of "Mountain with a Secret," in* Growing Point, *Vol. 2, No. 1, May, 1963, p. 161.*

To say that this is M. Guillot at his best is sufficient recommendation. The story is set in New Guinea and is concerned with the mysterious disappearance of Hendrik Dekker after an accident in the mountains in which his father is killed. The building up of the tension and the timing of the final revelation, the colourful and strongly-etched character-drawing and the wild and often violent beauty of the Pacific island setting are all handled with the skill and artistry of which the author is such a master.

> *Robert Bell, in a review of "Mountain with a Secret," in* The School Librarian and School Library Review, *Vol. 11, No. 5, June, 1963, p. 529.*

Our Colourful World and Its Peoples (1963)

The most striking aspect of this encyclopedia is also the most obvious—that it comes from France. English children will be startled into new awareness by finding that, for instance, Morocco and the Sudan are treated in more detail than Kenya. This is not to say that the book is overweighted with a French point of view but rather that it has a sharp, academic point of view that makes a valuable contrast to the imperialist note still sounded in similar books written here. The text is exciting, pictorial and vigorous, the pictures numerous and varied, and the maps, pretty to look at and brilliantly informative, are often on unusual projections. A book that will impart a generous measure of knowledge and delight.

> *Margery Fisher, in a review of "Our Colourful World and Its Peoples," in* Growing Point, *Vol. 2, No. 1, May, 1963, p. 172.*

Balloon Journey (1964)

For readers who do not take technical matters too seriously this is a lively and exciting story of a boy's adventures in his grandfather's balloon fitted with an invention with which the old gentleman hopes to confound a crabby rival in the same field. Really, it is the interruptions to the flight and the incidental shifts to which the boy and his grandfather's faithful chauffeur and handyman, Antoine, are put to complete the demonstration so dear to all their hearts which provide most of the interest. The tour of France which is incidental to the voyage provides an additional interest for the British reader but there are several things—particularly the attempt to rescue the lone aviator by parachutists—which will not go down well with knowledgeable boys and girls. Perhaps, on the other hand, the offhand treatment of detail, which even Jules Verne would not have countenanced, lends an old-fashioned air to the story which adds to its charm. One still wonders rather why M. Guillot allows himself to be tempted into a field which is obviously not his metier when he does other things so well.

> *A review of "Balloon Journey," in* The Junior Bookshelf, *Vol. 28, No. 3, July, 1964, p. 165.*

René Guillot is a superb story-teller and his latest title will further enhance his reputation. . . .

The book is full of humorous touches and little pictures of French provincial life, the atmosphere of which is delightfully caught in the many fine drawings by David Knight.

M. Guillot's loyal readers will not be disappointed by this lively, exciting story, and **Balloon Journey** will win him many new followers.

> *Norman F. Goodman, in a review of "Balloon Journey," in* The School Librarian and School Library Review, *Vol. 12, No. 3, December, 1964, p. 331.*

Here is a well-plotted adventure that doesn't quite come off, because the characters remain flat and two-dimensional, and the writing is stiff. Only Antoine, Grandfather's right-hand man, brightens the scene as he races after the balloon in various rescue attempts. Perhaps some of the flavor has been lost in [Anne Carter's] translation. The illustrations are a bonus.

> *Amy Kellman, in a review of "Balloon Journey," in* School Library Journal, *Vol. 13, No. 6, February, 1967, p. 65.*

The Children of the Wind　(1964; U. S. edition as Guillot's African Folk Tales)

This is a splendid book. Collected by the author during the twenty years he lived in West Africa, these twenty-three tales vary enormously in mood. There is a happy version of the Creation, when the god Aziza of the miraculous hands made all kinds of creature from the red clay of the bush and the horns, claws, teeth, and feathers which came from his inexhaustible bag. The story of the wind's marriage with Aminata, a beautiful daughter of men, is happy-sad, and the four nonsense tales at the end of the book finish it on a merry note, especially in the story with a familiar title—**"A Small Boy with Big Ideas."**

> *A review of "The Children of the Wind," in* The Junior Bookshelf, *Vol. 28, No. 5, November, 1964, p. 314.*

Taken from three volumes of tales which Guillot collected during twenty years in Africa, these pieces are shot with humour and sharp excitement; they are very varied in subject but all rest in that totemism which Guillot has made especially his own. [Gwen Marsh's] translation catches [Guillot's] typical story-telling voice, now exclamatory, now reflective. . . .

> *Margery Fisher, in a review of "The Children of the Wind," in* Growing Point, *Vol. 3, No. 6, December, 1964, p. 430.*

There has been considerable interest lately in the African Folk tale and a number of collections have recently been published for younger readers as varied in content as the African tribes themselves. Guillot is at his best when writing about Africa, and these tales are told in some of his finest prose. They are varied and have their roots deep in folk-lore and include a version of the creation, stories of the wind and humorous fables.

> *Betty Brazier, in a review of "The Children of the Wind," in* The School Librarian and School Library Review, *Vol. 13, No. 1, March, 1965, p. 119.*

From three sources and from his years spent in West Africa, the author brings these tales of the supernatural, of

man and beast, magic cults, trickery and deception, man's relationship to nature, fables with subtle meanings. Rather fluid and detailed, the style is sophisticated, lacking, at times, the simplicity associated with tales from this region. Occasional arresting passages, using picturesque words and expressions, give depth. More suitable for reading aloud than for telling, these versions show literary rather than oral artistry.

> *Spencer G. Shaw, in a review of "Guillot's African Folk Tales," in* Library Journal, *Vol. 90, No. 18, October 15, 1965, p. 4615.*

The stories are selected from three collections made by René Guillot during twenty years in West Africa. (Guillot's own stories of African jungle animals bear some relationship to the animal folklore here.) The telling is often more descriptive than is usual for folk stories, though the opening tales, relating how the world was "begun," how animals owned the land and leased it to the tribes of men, have a spare, cadenced style. Variety in form includes the fable, the "how" story, the tall tale, and the legend, while an extraordinary range of characters introduces, in addition to animals, herdsmen, and hunters, such otherworldly beings as genies and the Devil. The trickery and exaggerations in shorter tales will appeal to a wide range of ages, but the tales having to do with the supernatural and with folkways pertaining to the arranging of marriages are for an older audience. A good collection for libraries and storytellers.

> *Virgina Haviland, in a review of "Guillot's African Folk Tales," in* The Horn Book Magazine, *Vol. XLII, No. 1, February, 1966, p. 53.*

Pascal and the Lioness　(1965)

> [Pascal and the Lioness *was translated and abridged by Christina Holyoak.*]

This is a beautifully written story of a little boy's search for his pet lioness who has left him to become Queen of the Jungle, and it has much of the quality of a folk-tale or fable. One hesitates to carp at such a charming story by so distinguished an author, but, because it is so delightful, it will form many children's mental picture of Africa, and this picture will, unfortunately, be an inaccurate one. The French use the word *forêt* to indicate the more open woodlands of the savannah, not the high forest or jungle—a word unknown in Africa—and I might have thought the fact that this story is set in the forest was a translator's error, but too many details of text and illustration suggest that it is the fault of the author. Yet, with his wide experience of Africa, M. Guillot must know that neither lions nor other large mammals inhabit the forest, that it would not be suitable terrain for riding even if horses could live there, and that it is never dry enough for forest fires. Were this story set in the kind of country where it belongs it would be a wholly admirable book; that it is not is a great pity.

> *A review of "Pascal and the Lioness," in* The Junior Bookshelf, *Vol. 29, No. 3, June, 1965, p. 146.*

The alliance of man and beast, almost totemistic in depth, is a theme running through all Guillot's work, no less in this brief tale for younger children about the lioness Diara, who has to leave her well-loved small master when messengers summon her to rule the tribe in place of the dead King. This is a situation rather than a story, described in a style elegantly simple and with a hint of the mystery of the jungle behind it. Children should like it because in these middle years they are, most of them, convinced of the nobility of animals and of the power of humans to convey affection to them.

Margery Fisher, in a review of "Pascal and the Lioness," in Growing Point, *Vol. 4, No. 2, July, 1965, p. 546.*

The idea that love and loyalty can exist between men and animals is very appealing to younger children. This was the theme the author handled with distinction in his **Grishka and the Bear.** Nevertheless, in this attractive novel for the early grades . . . , it has been sentimentalized to an illogical, even unnatural conclusion, although the children may be willing to suspend their disbelief and revel in the happiness of the ending. (p. 1226)

A review of "Pascal and the Lioness," in Virginia Kirkus' Service, *Vol. XXXIII, No. 24, December 15, 1965, pp. 1225-26.*

The Troubadour   (1965)

Let it be said at once, at the risk of sounding smug, that here M. Guillot is very much less off key than he has been with earlier excursions into historical fiction unconnected with nature and animals. He begins intriguingly with an orphan girl child doomed to spend her life performing at fairs, and a troubadour who is obviously something better, and joins their fortunes in the happiest way. Aubrey the singer's mission to restore his former, presumed dead, lord, to his rightful estate is perhaps a trifle old hat, but the plotting and the scheming and the fighting which are entailed in the process are skilfully done. M. Guillot's sense of period is much firmer and his main characters are sympathetically drawn.

A review of "The Troubadour," in The Junior Bookshelf, *Vol. 29, No. 3, June, 1965, p. 156.*

Translation does not obscure the confidence and command of material shown by René Guillot in this story of fourteenth-century France. Aubrey, squire and friend of Oliver of Ornac, learns that his brave prince will be in mortal danger if, on leaving the Crusade, he returns to his castle. The Baron de Mortaille has taken advantage of the King's enmity towards the Knights Templars to seize Oliver's lands. Dressed as a troubadour, Aubrey sets out first to discover the true position and then to warn his friend. Marjolaine, the pretty girl dancer, finds herself involved in the dangers and excitement which eventually lead to the reinstatement of Oliver and a surprising discovery concerning her own identity.

The pace and vitality of the writing—notably an unbearably tense description of Marjolaine's pet fox, Mirka, being chased to an almost certain death by the Baron's hounds in front of her eyes—quite compensate for a plot perhaps a little too mechanically manipulated by coincidence.

Gordon Parsons, in a review of "The Troubadour," in The School Librarian and School Library Review, *Vol. 13, No. 3, December, 1965, p. 353.*

The book contains many of the conventional elements of the chivalric romance—loyalty, friendship, honor, the punishment of cowards and traitors—and includes nicely detailed scenes of a bloody medieval siege. But the author is an expert storyteller and his characters—particularly Marjolaine—have vitality and appeal.

Ethel L. Heins, in a review of "The Troubadour," in The Horn Book Magazine, *Vol. XLIV, No. 1, February, 1968, p. 70.*

Fonabio and the Lion   (1966)

Unlike the Adamsons with Elsa and other true-life instances of Europeans rearing wild animals, the little West African boy, Fonabio, presented with the problem of rearing a lion, leaves him in his lair in the bush and takes food to him. He also teaches him to hunt and to fend for himself, so that there is no problem of returning the full-grown animal to his native habitat. Whether this could have been done quite so easily in practice I doubt. Unfortunately the grown lion turns man-eater, mauls the European planter whom Fonabio idolizes and has to be shot—by the heartbroken Fonabio himself. Fonabio is an interesting and unusual character with a much greater feeling for the life of the wild than is generally found among Africans. This book is to be commended for its sympathetic development of his relationship with the three beings who mean most to him—the lion, the planter and the old witch doctor with whom he has lived since his parents died.

A review of "Fonabio and the Lion," in The Junior Bookshelf, *Vol. 30, No. 2, April, 1966, p. 122.*

René Guillot's white hunter, Marlow, has of course long ago escaped civilisation in the African jungle. In **Fonabio and the Lion** he is only one of a number of characters who affect the life of the young African Fonabio. . . . Like all Guillot's African tales, there is a mixture here of close, detailed realism and poetic fancy, in that rapid, often explosive narrative style, which lures the reader on with the feeling always that there is something still more telling to come. (pp. 719-20)

Margery Fisher, in a review of "Fonabio and the Lion," in Growing Point, *Vol. 5, No. 1, May, 1966, pp. 719-20.*

This story does absolutely nothing to further Guillot's international reputation. . . . The plot is labored and the various elements are never welded into a whole. The native child's adulation of the white hunter makes one feel Guillot is romanticizing some long past relationship of his own. The outstanding feature of Guillot's works—the sensitive portrayal of unusual human-animal relationships—is missing. . . .

Dallas Y. Shaffer, in a review of "Fonabio and the Lion," in School Library Journal, *Vol. 13, No. 1, September, 1966, p. 182.*

The Stranger from the Sea   (1967)

Boys and boats and the influence of a forceful personality—this useful formula gives shape to [this story]. . . . René Guillot has a special fondness for the solitary, the mystery man, and a knack of suggesting how such a person can change the even tenor of other people's lives. Young Mario, son of a Genoese fisherman, has been helping family finances by plying his old *Sardinella* as a ferry. A lonely boy, he comes to rely on the seaman who vouchsafes neither name nor history but who night after night, as he keeps watch on the quay, gives friendly advice—and a ship in a bottle which indirectly brings the boy first a new boat, then a perilous voyage, finally a permanent friend. Like all Guillot's tales, this one has a plot worked out by hints and evasions and a crisp, exclamatory style admirably rendered in [Gwen Marsh's] translation. Not vintage Guillot but, as always, attractive and readable.

> *Margery Fisher, in a review of "The Stranger from the Sea," in* Growing Point, *Vol. 6, No. 3, September, 1967, p. 958.*

This story of a poor fisherman's son in Genoa does not have the same grip on the reader as René Guillot's **Animal Stories.** Mario tries to make a meagre living from his dilapidated boat and his greatest wish is to have a luxury craft like those he has seen. His wish comes true but it is short lived, and although it is doubtless very good for his character to learn that one only really keeps what one earns, children's stories should be more satisfactory. He was a good boy who worked hard and it would have been nice for him to have had some unearned benefits.

> *A review of "The Stranger from the Sea," in* The Junior Bookshelf, *Vol. 31, No. 5, October, 1967, p. 321.*

Friendship between a older man and a teenaged boy handled with care. . . . Eventually, of course, the stranger must move on and Mario finds a new friend his own age. Reliance on coincidence and luck undermines the effectiveness of the plot but the changes of fortune—in the boy's life especially and also in the lives of those around him—are told by inference, sometimes successfully, sometimes not.

> *A review of "Stranger from the Sea," in* Kirkus Service, *Vol. XXXV, No. 22, November 15, 1967, p. 1369.*

King of the Reindeer and Other Animal Stories   (1967)

"Adapted from John Orpen's translation"—it would be interesting to know how much adapted for there is nothing of the Guillot touch here and the large format and flashy illustrations suggest the whole affair was contrived to sell fast on purely superficial appeal. The pictures [by Paul Durand] show some observation of animals and use pretty colours but are somehow all *for* show; the stories are possibly written round them and are mainly very trivial, a surprising number featuring animals who exist primarily for human exploitation and love it—even the alligator takes round a wooden bowl for coins in preference to returning to the wild. Eagles, beaver, penguin, Spanish bull—it looks varied at a glance but has nothing valid to offer.

> *A review of "King of the Reindeer and Other Animal Stories," in* The Junior Bookshelf, *Vol. 31, No. 5, October, 1967, p. 314.*

This collection of short anecdotes takes us on a world tour. Here are an eagle on the Mongolian steppes, a chimpanzee on the Ivory Coast, a reindeer in Lapland, an alligator in the Everglades, a bull in Andalusia and many others. There is a certain monotony in the tales, which often describe an unlikely friendship between man and beast after a dramatic rescue. For readers around eight or nine this would be a pleasant book to dip into. . . .

> *Margery Fisher, in a review of "King of the Reindeer," in* Growing Point, *Vol. 6, No. 5, November, 1967, pp. 1011-12.*

The Champion of Olympia, an Adventure   (1968)

The **Champion** is a Celt chieftain's son who escapes from servitude and wins the Greek Olympic chariot race through contrivance and false sentiment. Donar-Kong takes off from Dromo's galley, rescues fair Pherenice from an almost runaway horse, pals around with her athletic brother Calippes, then discovers the two are Dromo's grandchildren. Not only do they uphold his superiority, they want him in the Olympics, and Mahoe, the local medium and healer, says D-K is a winner. Despite some overemotional obstruction from mulish Mulio, Donar wins his laurel and makes the great escape with the help of a faithful servant via a divide-and-confuse chase. His chances in the chariot race were slim; odds on the book are doubly dubious. Greek squeak in an old set of wheels.

> *A review of "The Champion of Olympia," in* Kirkus Service, *Vol. XXXVI, No. 21, November 1, 1968, p. 1218.*

Good characterizations mark this fast-paced adventure that will please boys who admire unusual physical prowess and girls who like horses and heroic youth. A regional map of Greece is included. . . . (pp. 76-7)

> *Frances Kelly, in a review of "The Champion of Olympia," in* School Library Journal, *Vol. 15, No. 6, February, 1969, pp. 76-7.*

The Castle of the Crested Bird   (1968)

The castle of the crested bird is a curious mixture of fancy and high drama. . . . This is the story of orphaned Mariela who finds she can talk to the blue bird in the forest and half believes that he really is an enchanted prince; the illusion is fostered by the lonely Queen who is mourning her long-lost son. There is a happy ending which again depends more on human imaginings than on magic, but the point of the story is veiled by Guillot's characteristic riddling style and by the decorative embellishments with which he supports a slight neo-fairy-tale.

> *Margery Fisher, in a review of "The Castle of the Crested Bird," in* Growing Point, *Vol. 7, No. 6, December, 1968, p. 1239.*

A fairy-tale in the powerful and poetic tradition of Grimm and Perrault. . . .

Readers may be familiar with M. Guillot's modern stories of adventure. This poignant tale of long ago has the same masterful style; deft characterization and gripping drama, with a pervading mood of haunting magic. A first-class contribution to a genre surfeited by the tenth-rate, for it achieves that rare ingredient, originality.

> *J. Davis, in a review of "Castle of the Crested Bird," in* Children's Book News, *London, Vol. 4, No. 1, January-February, 1969, p. 28.*

Rene Guillot is a master of oblique story-telling. His new book is a strange, sad fantasy, apparently conventional in narrative but full of odd twists and unexplained mysteries. It is told with great tenderness and with a haunting melancholy. The illustrations by Paul Durand have much of the same qualities. They are technically most brilliant, and they manage to be at once atmospheric and remarkably precise. It is a perilous undertaking to turn this frail thread of fancy into line and colour, but he manages it with quite extraordinary success. Not a book for all readers. . . .

> *A review of "The Castle of the Crested Bird," in* The Junior Bookshelf, *Vol. 33, No. 2, April, 1969, p. 108.*

Little Dog Lost   (1968)

Relaxed, descriptive drawings [by Jacques Poirier], a few pictures in colour, add much to a story oddly lacking in variety but with a certain charm. A dachshund pup, lost in the woods, is adopted by a vixen and learns to live as a fox, till he is found by hunters and taken to a human habitation again. As Rusty, as Tiny or as Domino the little animal exhibits a happy mixture of courage and curiosity which makes him a worthy centre of a slight tale—in which, incidentally, the translator [Joan Selby-Lowndes] seems to have curbed Guillot's typical staccato prose.

> *Margery Fisher, in a review of "Little Dog Lost," in* Growing Point, *Vol. 8, No. 3, September, 1969, p. 1380.*

[*A revised edition of* Little Dog Lost *appeared in 1970.*]

[A] short story about a little Welsh corgi found in the forest and adopted by a female fox whose cubs have just been lost to a prowling wildcat. . . . After various adventures—e.g., the fox is caught in a trap—there is an ultra happy ending (both dog and fox live happily with the humans) which children who like animal stories will, of course, thoroughly enjoy. Good third-grade readers will be able to handle the book independently, while second graders will relish hearing the teacher read it aloud.

> *Marian L. Strickland, in a review of "Little Dog Lost," in* School Library Journal, *Vol. 17, No. 1, September 1, 1970, p. 102.*

Fondai and the Leopard-Men   (1969)

M. Guillot ranks among the finest children's novelists, and here he returns to an area he has made particularly his own: the savage land of central Africa. This story of young Fodai Koro, a native boy torn between his loyalties to his white friends of the game reserve and his own tribesmen,

and caught up in the cult of the leopard-men, is told with all the excitement, sensitivity and command that we have come to expect.

> *C. E. J. Smith, in a review of "Fodai and the Leopard Men," in* The School Librarian, *Vol. 18, No. 1, March, 1970, p. 79.*

Adventure with a theme of friendship characterizes this fair story about the son of an African chief, whose loyalties are divided between his own people and the white governor who took him in after his father's death. . . . Though similar to the Willard Price books about Africa—*Lion Adventure* (John Day, 1957), *African Adventure* (John Day, 1963), *Safari Adventure* (John Day, 1966)—this less exciting book features little heightening of suspense or character development.

> *Rose Mary Pace, in a review of "Fodai and the Leopard-Men," in* Library Journal, *Vol. 95, No. 13, July, 1970, p. 2533.*

Castle in Spain   (1970)

This is a good example of how a simple story for young children can have drama and characterisation in the hands of a skilful and imaginative author. It is the story of a few days in the life of a group of poor children in Spain and the central figure round whom the plot revolves is a white mouse, Pepita. The interest of the young reader will be held by what is happening and the large print will make the book seem less daunting than is often the case for this age group.

> *A review of "Castle in Spain," in* The Junior Bookshelf, *Vol. 34, No. 3, June, 1970, p. 151.*

In **Castle in Spain** René Guillot strung together a series of familiar situations which the charm of his writing converted into a mildly attractive whole. Here is that poor but clean and honest family we meet so often in story-books— managing mother, invalid father who makes plaster figures to sell on the beach, helpful small son; here is the boy-with-pet theme, for Pedro's life is complicated by the white mouse Pepita he has rescued from bullies; here is the familiar success story, for Pedro wins a prize for his sandcastle—and narrowly escapes losing Pepita. That compulsive story-teller René Guillot has hardly extended himself in this tale.

> *Margery Fisher, in a review of "Castle in Spain," in* Growing Point, *Vol. 9, No. 2, July, 1970, p. 1549.*

The Great Land of the Elephants   (1971)

This is the late Rene Guillot's reminiscences of the Africa he loved and his big-game hunting expeditions, the raw material of the novels. It shares with them the luminous word-painting of the sights and sounds of the Senegalese bush, and the observation of animals and men. There is no continuous story. One incident may remind him of another connected only by a slender thread (like the delightful anecdote of how he recited La Fontaine all night to a pack of angry monkeys). It is a panorama of bush life, punctuated by frequent and bloody killings (chiefly for meat, ivory or skins), and meals of strong-tasting big game. There is a vivid interlude at a lumber camp, frequent tragedies and narrow escapes, an odd practical joke, fascinating information (on elephants in particular), a character-study of a leper rifle-bearer, and much on the tribal rituals connected with hunting. It is a far more revealing book than the novels: the reader sees the nature of the fascination felt by Guillot for the wild beauty of the countryside, his sense of brotherhood with its people, primitive and silent, free from modern civilisation. Like the many meals described, however, it is strong meat and may not please more sensitive children. (pp. 45-6)

> *M. Hobbs, in a review of "The Great Land of the Elephants," in* The Junior Bookshelf, *Vol. 36, No. 1, February, 1972, pp. 45-6.*

René Guillot evidently moved into the African jungle with every sense keyed up; his awareness of the actualities of animal life was enriched by an almost mystical feeling of kinship with the beasts of forest and plain, especially those which in his stories are often called Kings—lion and elephant. The present book, published as long ago as 1963 in France, is a hunter's apologia; he kills his "friends" the elephants in order to "let the hunt free you from yourself". His paternalistic attitude to native servants and trackers and the ambiguous nature of his sport are hardly current in the present day, nor is his occasional rhetoric ("Ah . . . the reeds so eager to run with the wind, the bare plain straining to be off " . . .) but when he forgets himself he can draw magnificent pictures—of elephants charging, marching and retreating, of water and light.

> *Margery Fisher, in a review of "The Great Land of the Elephants," in* Growing Point, *Vol. 10, No. 8, March, 1972, p. 1889.*

Although the late René Guillot loved animals, at one time he hunted animals for sport in French West Africa. In this book about his experiences on safari, the atmosphere is vividly brought to life for the European reader: one feels the ugly realities and the almost mystic beauty. (p. 70)

It could be asked: are not the roles of big-game hunter and animal lover psychologically incompatible? Those who are familiar with Guillot's sensitive children's books will not doubt his sincerity. In this recounting of some of the French writer's experiences I trace a parallel between his approach to animals and the Spanish attitude towards bullfighting.

I would highly recommend this book to older children. In addition to its literary value, points are raised which need to be discussed. What motivates those who set out to kill animals for sport? How does this conflict with the current realization that we must now conserve wild life if it is not to become extinct?

I believe thoughtful readers will find in this book that Guillot had his own moments of doubt. (pp. 70-1)

> *Doreen Norman, in a review of "The Great Land of the Elephants," in* The School Librarian, *Vol. 20, No. 1, March, 1972, pp. 70-1.*

Martin Handford

1956-

English author and illustrator of picture books.

The creator of popular game books which feature Wally (or Waldo in their U. S. editions), a bespectacled young traveler in a stocking cap and striped sweater, Handford challenges elementary graders to find the character in a series of highly detailed, brightly-colored double-page spreads in watercolor and line which have been praised for stimulating their audience's powers of observation. Often compared to the works of Mitsumasa Anno and Richard Scarry, the books are characterized by their oversize formats, humor, and entertainment, rather than informational, value; at the back of each book, Handford provides checklists of additional items to be found besides those initially noted. In his first book, *Where's Wally?* (1987; U. S. edition as *Where's Waldo?*), Handford takes the character around the world, where he stops at twelve different locales such as a beach and a ski slope. Wally drops a piece of hiking equipment in each place, and readers are encouraged to discover Wally and his lost provisions in the dense yet active pictures. With *Where's Wally Now?* (1988; U. S. edition as *Find Waldo Now*), Handford takes Wally from the stone age to the future, accompanying the twelve different spreads which depict his adventures with tongue-in-cheek narratives describing each time period. *The Great Waldo Search* (1989) asks readers to find both the character and the twelve scrolls he must locate in twelve panels in which he encounters such figures as mermaids, monsters, witches, and vampires; although this title has been criticized as racist and overly violent, most observers note that, as with Handford's other works, it is both inventive and appealing. In 1987, Handford was runner-up for the Mother Goose Award, a prize given to "the most exciting newcomer to British children's book illustration."

Where's Wally? (1987; U. S. edition as **Where's Waldo?**)

Heavily laden with hiking equipment, Waldo strolls his way around the world, stopping in 12 different places—a city, a beach, a ski slope, etc. Each locale is a two-page spread packed with people, animals, and vehicles engaged in every possible kind of activity (and a few impossible ones as well). Readers are challenged not only to find Waldo amid the hundreds of other figures, but to find each piece of hiking equipment as he loses it. "Post cards" from Waldo narrate each scene. Frantic activity (somewhat reminiscent of Richard Scarry) is packed into the line and watercolor illustrations, and finding Waldo in all that chaos is no easy task. This is a book which could keep children busy for hours, not just with finding Waldo but with observing all of the goings-on. Checklists at the back of the book provide even more things to look for. It's a sure bet for amusing older children on long trips, in waiting rooms, or any quiet time. Younger ones will still prefer Hilary Knight's *Where's Wallace?* (HBJ, 1964).

Kathleen Brachman, in a review of "Where's

Waldo?" in School Library Journal, *Vol. 34, No. 2, October, 1987, p. 112.*

Waldo writes postcards on his worldwide tour and readers are expected to locate Waldo in each crowded picture. Waldo's briefly-worded postcard observations tickle the funny bone. Definitely a book for sharing between parent and child as either reader is sure to grab the book away in order to find Waldo among the hordes of tourists. This is heady fun for the serious picture gazer.

Jeannette Cohen, in a review of "Where's Waldo?" in Children's Book Review Service, *Vol. 16, No. 6, Winter, 1988, p. 60.*

The general feeling of the Panel [who chose the recipient of the Mother Goose Award] was that 1987 had been a good year, offering us not only a splendid winner—Emma Chichester Clark—but also four runners-up whose progress in their new field we shall watch with interest: Martin Handford, Jean Christian Knaff, Corinne Pearlman and Carol Thompson. . . .

Martin Handford represents the Hergé, Dupasquier school of busy and engaging cartoons. . . .

No-one present doubted for a moment the hours of amusement and pleasure that Martin Handford's **Where's Wally?** would give to children. And we all applauded the way he, like Anno before him, has ensured that children really look long and hard at each opening (searching for Wally) instead of flicking through the book with the impatience characteristic of our age. We goggled at Martin Handford's sheer industry and inventiveness—but some of us were not too sure that all this added up to children's book illustration in our terms.

Elaine Moss, "Mother Goose 1988," in Books for Keeps, *No. 50, May, 1988, p. 25.*

Where's Wally Now? (1988; U. S. edition as *Find Waldo Now*)

Like Handford's **Where's Waldo?,** this game book challenges children to locate Waldo among the myriad of figures and objects in each picture. They are further challenged to go back to the beginning to find the book that Waldo has lost in each picture, as well as to look for the items listed in checklists at the back of the book. On each of the 12 spreads, Waldo is traveling through time, and the narration consists of a description of each time period. The feeling and tone of this book, like the first, is frantic and frenzied in each of the cartoon-style line and watercolor illustrations. The tongue-in-cheek narrative and the slapstick depiction of characters and actions offer little, if any, historical value but provide abundant amusement. While Anno's books offer subtle, artistic contributions of

both literary and historical substance, **Find Waldo Now** will find a ready audience in the game/puzzle book crowd. Handford's fans will be captivated by and attentive to Waldo's new adventure.

Janie Schomberg, in a review of "Find Waldo Now," in School Library Journal, *Vol. 35, No. 1, September, 1988, p. 160.*

The object of this game book is to find the tiny figure of Waldo, a sort of Jughead Jones in a stocking cap, in the enormously populated double-page spreads of various historical periods. Unlike Anno's books, of which this seems almost a parody, Waldo's journey has zero historical value, peopled as it is with a milk-lapping Sphinx, a gold-rushing cactus, and an ocean full of forever bumbling pirates ("Once there were lots of pirates, but they died out in the end because too many of them were men.") To call the pictures busy would be a drastic understatement, but this large-format picture book is just the sort of thing to keep a table of middle-schoolers (relatively) quiet and looking for at least fifteen minutes. (p. 38)

Robert Strong, in a review of "Find Waldo Now," in Bulletin of the Center for Children's Books, *Vol. 42, No. 2, October, 1988, pp. 37-8.*

In this new-style history lesson the small man with his red and white bobble hat pursued in an earlier picture-book is now concealed in twelve crowded scenes depicting people from cavemen to roisterers in the Gay Paree of the 1920's; among Crusaders, Aztecs, gold prospectors, Greek

From Where's Waldo? *written and illustrated by Martin Handford.*

warriors and medieval traders Wally makes his imperturbable way, while at the end of the book there are lists of 'Hundreds more things for time travellers to look for'. Sharp colour and precise shapes are arranged in an orderly confusion in a book guaranteed to command attention from the most blasé child from eight onwards; perhaps the 'olden days' will take a slightly more definite shape as a result of the entertainment Martin Handford has offered so generously.

> *Margery Fisher, in a review of "Where's Wally Now?" in* Growing Point, *Vol. 27, No. 4, November, 1988, p. 5074.*

The Great Waldo Search   (1989)

Following *Where's Waldo?* and *Find Waldo Now,* the search for Waldo continues. Here, in 12 large, amazingly busy panels Waldo, in hallmark hat and red-striped sweater, travels through a diverse series of land- and seascapes. The reader is set the tasks of finding Waldo and helping him locate 12 scrolls. Over volcanic terrain, Waldo traipses past scores of battling monks; he visits "the Castle of the Nasty Nasties" populated by vampires and witches; and he meets deepsea divers (wearing striped Waldo-colored trunks), and mermaids and monsters of the deep. In the final and most challenging panel, Waldo is in a land of Waldos—hundreds of them, and readers must identify the *real* Waldo. Checklists at the end offer hundreds of other things to look for in the book's minutely detailed drawings. Patient readers are guaranteed hours of enjoyment from this adventure book. All ages.

> *A review of "The Great Waldo Search," in* Publishers Weekly, *Vol. 236, No. 20, November, 1989, p. 69.*

Waldo's many fans will find little fault with this newest offering, but the book has several disturbing elements. As in the previous books, readers are challenged to find Waldo in each busy two-page spread. There are literally hundreds of figures in each picture, most of them attired in similar colors. To add to the challenge, readers are also asked to locate a miniscule scroll, the object sought in the Great Waldo Search. The plot is superficial, a mere excuse to search each page. Children will spend many enjoyable hours pouring over the humorous details as they look for Waldo in vampire castles, amid flying carpets, and in monster-filled mazes. The back pages provide checklists of even more details to find. Unfortunately, a group described as the "many-colored spearmen" is, in fact, all yellow-skinned. While this may be not be objectionable in a book in which there are also green women and blue soldiers, the yellow spearmen are all depicted in coolie hats. Furthermore, it seems unfortunate that Waldo must often be sought amidst scenes of conflict and cruelty. It is a shame that such an entertaining concept should be executed with racial stereotypes and pervasive violence. (pp. 82-3)

> *Lori A. Janick, in a review of "The Great Waldo Search," in* School Library Journal, *Vol. 36, No. 1, January, 1990, pp. 82-3.*

Esther (Rudomin) Hautzig

1930-

(Also writes as Esther Rudomin) Polish-born American author of nonfiction and fiction.

Hautzig is best known as the creator of *The Endless Steppe: Growing Up in Siberia* (1968), an autobiographical account of her childhood and early youth for young adults which is often considered a powerful and moving tribute to the triumph of the human spirit. The book describes Hautzig's life from the ages of ten to fifteen, the years she spent in exile after the Russians transported her and her family from Vilna in eastern Poland to Rubtsovsk, Siberia, in 1941 because, as Polish Jews of wealth and prestige, they were considered capitalists. Although Hautzig represents the dangers and privations which she and her family were forced to endure, such as heat, rats, hard work, crowded living conditions, and near-starvation, she also celebrates the positive aspects of her life, such as discovering the Russian classics and learning to appreciate the beauty of the Siberian landscape. When she returns to Poland at fifteen to find that most of her relatives have been murdered by the Nazis, she finds that Siberia had truly become her home. Hautzig is often acknowledged for her precise attention to detail and focus on the emotional life of her characters as well as for investing her book with optimism, humor, and affection. As with *The Endless Steppe,* her work of fiction for middle graders, *A Gift for Mama* (1981), draws on the memories of Hautzig's Polish childhood and expresses the close relationships shared by her characters. Set in Hautzig's birthplace of Vilna in the 1930s, the story describes how Sara, an enterprising and loving young girl, does mending to buy her mother a pair of black satin slippers for Mother's Day. Hautzig is also recognized as the author of several informational books which provide clear advice and economical suggestions on cooking and crafts for middle and upper graders. In addition, she is the creator of a series of works for younger readers which describe universal childhood experiences—going to the park and to school and being at home—in four languages: English, French, Russian, and Spanish. *The Endless Steppe* won the Lewis Carroll Shelf Award in 1971, the Association of Jewish Libraries Award in 1978, and the Jane Addams Award in 1979; it was also named a *Boston Globe-Horn Book* honor book in 1968 and was a finalist for the National Book Award in 1969.

(See also *Something about the Author,* Vol. 4; *Contemporary Authors New Revision Series,* Vols. 5, 20; and *Contemporary Authors,* Vol. 2, rev. ed.)

Let's Cook without Cooking (as Esther Rudomin, 1955)

Fine dishes and menus for the younger set to concoct are appetizingly outlined in a collection of recipes that never once involve the use of a stove. You can guess what they are—salads, cold soups, sandwiches, drinks, icebox desserts and so forth—but within these limits the author has managed to squeeze a long list of dishes that could keep

anyone from gastronomical boredom. Recipes are divided into categories corresponding to the parts of a full meal from appetizer to sweet, and the instructions [are] clearly written. . . .

A review of "Let's Cook without Cooking," in Virginia Kirkus' Service, *Vol. XXIII, No. 13, July 1, 1955, p. 419.*

All little girls like to cook, and this clever, unusual cook book was designed especially for them, though it may be used to advantage by older girls and mothers, too. There are fifty-five tested recipes. . . . The recipes do not require cooking, so experimentation is safe, and the directions for appetizing, economical recipes are concise and easy to follow.

As a special feature there is an index, and the black-and-white pictures [by Lisl Weil] are humorous and cleverly adapted to subject matter. In fact, no detail has been spared in making this cook book a useful tool. (pp. 73-4)

A review of "Let's Cook without Cooking," in The Saturday Review, *New York, Vol. XXXVIII, No. 46, September 12, 1955, pp. 73-4.*

Let's Make Presents: 100 Gifts for Less than $1.00 (1962)

Gifts for children to make from inexpensive, readily available materials are described here. The directions are easy to follow and amply illustrated, and the gifts are grouped for women, for men, for the family, and good things to eat. Care is taken to show how sewing stitches are made, to include alphabets for tracing, and to encourage the saving of odds and ends of materials, boxes, jars, colorful papers, etc. Attractive book for children to use by themselves or for adults looking for ideas for entertaining children. Care is urged in the use of scissors, knives, and razor blades. The ideas are not new, but they are attractively presented, and it is useful to have a book devoted completely to gifts. A section on foods is unusual in a book primarily about crafts, and the suggested items would make delightful gifts! (pp. 47-8)

> *Eleanor P. Hawley, in a review of "Let's Make Presents: 100 Gifts for Less than $1.00," in* School Library Journal, *Vol. 8, No. 8, April, 1962, pp. 47-8.*

An around-the-year book (with special holiday uses) for club leaders, teachers and parents, and those girls and boys who like to do things on their own, who may be inspired to believe with the author that the fun of presents, both the giving and the receiving, is "greatest of all if the presents are things you have made yourself." A prelude entitled "Before You Begin," addressed to children, introduces the idea of thinking carefully about those for whom gifts are to be made, of collecting useful odds and ends systematically, following directions well, and using ingenuity and imagination. "Sewing Hints and Stitches," three alphabets to trace for decoration, and clear sketches are helpful. The range of suggestions is wide, involving sewing, pasting, cardboard weaving, and cooking—for gifts to men, women, children, and teen-agers, and Christmas cards and decor for the whole family.

> *Virginia Haviland, in a review of "Let's Make Presents: 100 Gifts for Less than $1.00," in* The Horn Book Magazine, *Vol. XXXVIII, No. 3, June, 1962, p. 294.*

Redecorating Your Room for Practically Nothing (1967)

Talking in categories ("tailored or feminine") that no longer exist of projects that sustained *The American Home* for thirty years, the author does a creditable job of presenting information that no wised-up teenager will want. Mostly it's a matter of repainting old furniture or making new curtains or bedspreads via instructions that can be found in commercial pamphlets, with the addition of such decorative details as Pennsylvania Dutch motifs to the wooden pieces, daisies and snowflakes to the fabrics. A section on accessories resembles Mrs. Hautzig's *Let's Make Presents*; one on closets and bureaus features hangers and holders that can be bought ready-made in the five-and-ten. All of this is so far from the poster-and-Pop style of most teenage sanctuaries as to be unusable even when some of it might be useful.

> *A review of "Redecorating Your Room for Practically Nothing," in* Kirkus Service, *Vol. XXXV, No. 20, October 15, 1967, p. 1289.*

Not all of the suggestions or materials would fit into a limited budget, and some of the handyman projects seem over-ambitious for accomplishment by most young teenagers, and some are either downright unaesthetic or impractical. The diagrams and drawings [by illustrator Sidonie Coryn] and step-by-step directions are often not precise enough for a beginner: e.g., no allowance for matching patterns in fabrics, the instructions for making a self-valance would result in the body of the curtain being wrong-side out. This book attempts too much; separate how-to books for individual skills would be more helpful to the beginner, and *The Seventeen Book of Decorating* has better general decorating advice for the same age-group.

> *Nancy Young Orr, in a review of "Redecorating Your Room for Practically Nothing," in* School Library Journal, *Vol. 14, No. 4, December, 1967, p. 80.*

After a stimulating preliminary, but not an overdose, of general ideas about color, furniture arrangement, and treatment of walls and floors, the author of the earlier *Let's Make Presents* offers a bounty of simple and inexpensive suggestions. Her outlines of materials needed and clearly diagramed procedures should seem convincing, ingenious, and enticing; as also are fresh ideas for room dividers, dresser-desk, decorative screen, storage bench, fabric window shades, bed covers and headboards, and a variety of accessories for room and closet. Teen-agers avid to blazen their rooms with posters and psychedelic colors will find these ideas basic and practical for supplying the necessary background.

> *Virginia Haviland, in a review of "Redecorating Your Room for Practically Nothing," in* The Horn Book Magazine, *Vol. XLIV, April, 1968, p. 196.*

The Endless Steppe: Growing Up in Siberia (1968)

AUTHOR'S COMMENTARY

[The following excerpt is from a speech delivered on 8 April 1970.]

When we begin to write a book—and I use the word "we" not in the royal or presidential manner, but merely as a reference to a group of people who spend their lives, or good parts of their lives, struggling with the typewriter—we do not, for the most part, say "I am writing a book for children." Some of us write with one person in mind only. Maia Wojciechowska said in one of her speeches—I think it was the Newbery acceptance speech—that she wrote *Shadow of a Bull* for a girl she did not know but had seen on a bus one day. She just kept that girl in mind while she was writing her story. Ezra Jack Keats saved a picture of a little boy from a magazine for over twenty years and wrote *The Snowy Day* with that particular child in mind. I have a dear friend who is writing a story, and she tells me that as she works on it she keeps my daughter Debbie in mind. Still another friend of mine says that you do not even have to know, or like, children to do books that will appeal to them or make them happy. All you have to do is write the book for yourself—thinking of yourself as the child you once were, and perhaps wish you were again, or still are. I personally cannot accept the notion that you do not have to like children to write books which they will read, but that is my problem, if problem it be. It seems to me that if one does not like children, one does not like people (for can one separate the two?), and then there is not any point in doing anything.

I personally could no more write a book with a particular child in mind than I could climb Mount Everest; I would find it terribly intimidating. Nor do I think about "writing a book for children" as if children were different from adults, adolescents, octogenarians, or whatever. (I must exclude the writing of texts for picture books when making this statement.)

When I started writing *The Endless Steppe* milleniums ago, I did not think of it as a book for children. . . . (p. 461)

Neither did my agent think of it as a children's book; he sent the manuscript in its early stages to adult-trade editors. It did not sell to that audience, although I have a perfectly gorgeous collection of rejection letters. (p. 462)

Well, *The Endless Steppe: Growing Up in Siberia,* begun in 1959, was finally published in 1968 by a children's book department, but not one word in it was changed because it was published as a children's book instead of as an adult book. There were no parts to the story which would have been suitable for adults but not suitable for children. The cuts that were made, and over which I fought long and bitter battles, had nothing whatever to do with the fact that the book was being published for children and not for adults. (In England it is on both the adult and the juvenile list of the same publisher.) For instance, one cut which was made, though not without long discussion and many memorandums, concerned a piece of jewelry, a pendant. This pendant belonged to my mother's natural mother, not to the Grandmother Sara in the story. I did not know that Grandmother Sara (the one I took the kitchen box full of jewelry to at the beginning of the book) was not my mother's natural mother. Neither is the Grandmother Anna in the book, now living in Israel, the natural mother of my father. At any rate, I brought all the jewelry to Grandmother Sara's house. As we were leaving on the truck for the station, Grandmother Sara was standing in the crowd of people on the street below, and she threw up to my mother a small black silk change purse with the pendant wrapped in cotton in an old handkerchief. That it was not confiscated right on the truck, that it survived the train trip to Siberia, that we had it sewn into a pillow on which we slept, that my mother would no more sell it than she would sell me, that it was a terribly important link for all of us with the past, that it was both a sacrifice and an insane revenge on all those idiot officials who did not know that we possessed this lovely pendant—all of this was deemed unbelievable for the American reader. Not for a child, mind you, for the reader in general. I thought, and still do, that it was an important indication of how people can become attached to a physical possession even in the face of hunger—those who seemed in most other ways to be fairly sensible, rational, normally functioning people. Come to think of it, children, so devoted to physical possessions, might be truly able to understand.

Another incident which was to be cut but which remained because I finally won my point was the incident with the shoes. As some of you may recall, I felt that I had lost the declamation contest because I came to it barefoot, not having any shoes to wear, and then for weeks afterwards proceeded to pester the man we considered a "spy" until he gave me a pair of shoes. The last editor of the book, in all other ways a splendid girl (the book has had a number of editors—four to be exact), felt that the incident with the spy was "obscure." I am using her word. I kept saying over and over again to her, "But listen, I will have failed utterly in storytelling, as well as in telling the truth, if I did not show that I did get shoes after that. Won't the reader care enough to want to know whether I ever did get shoes?" (By the way, I bought a pair of brand-new shoes, which hurt, to insure the success of this talk!)

One of the other editors wanted me to cut out references to Miss Rachel in the story, along with a whole incident relating to her. I went along with cutting the incident, but I rebelled against cutting the references to her out of the story completely. In a reiterating memorandum I said:

> Rachel was much too important an influence on my life, and dearer to me more than I can say here in this memorandum, in a book, or anywhere for that matter, to leave her completely out of the book. And I did remember her brushing my hair, reading to me, BEING WITH ME UTTERLY AND COMPLETELY, all through Siberia. She was an anchor, or one of them, in my thoughts, something I could hold on to, something I could go back to, over and over again. I was a very lucky child to have had a governess with the qualities that this woman possessed. She loved me not because she was my mother and had to love me, but because she obviously wanted to. And I loved her, and still do, not because she was my mother and I had to love her, but because I wanted to love her. It is a very complicated, emotional subject for me, and I would feel a traitor, ingrate and what have you, not to have her in my book. In fact as soon as this book is published and makes money I am getting on a plane to Israel where both Rachel and my grandmother now live and with whom I hope to share the joy that the publication of this book will bring to all of us, I hope.

I wonder what battles I would have had to fight with the editors had the book been taken as an adult book. Are quiet books not satisfactory for adults but satisfactory for children? Are children more apt to pick up a book about Siberia of twenty-five years ago than adults are? What is a good book for children as opposed to a good book for adults? Need there be a dichotomy? (I. B. Singer's National Book Award-winner, *A Day of Pleasure: Stories of a Boy Growing Up in Warsaw* is composed of exactly the same material, with the exception of one or two stories, which appeared in his adult book, *In My Father's Court.*)

It seems to me that some books we adults think are marvelous for children, the children themselves often reject. I really do not have statistics to back up this thought, just a kind of smell for things and the benefit of talks with my daughter and her friends. To me *Onion John* is a spectacularly good book published for children. I have yet to meet a child, or even hear of one, who loves it as I do. But surely there are children who love it, even though I do not know of them, and therefore it was important to have written the book and published it. The numbers of children who read a book are somehow immaterial in the long scheme of things. It is the effect that a book has even on the smallest number of children—even on one child—that counts. (pp. 464-66)

I often prefer reading children's books—*About the B'nai Bagels* is a recent favorite—to reading the adult books published nowadays. Aside from the fact that I really do enjoy reading these books, they give me a most marvelous sense of sharing a special world with my children. It seems a pity to me that so many parents miss the pleasure of reading their children's books once they are past the picture-book age. Now when Debbie describes to me her classmate, Polly, and the classmate's mother, Mrs. Smith, all she has to say is "Well, Polly is just a female Sidney and her mother is just another Mrs. Polsky." No further descriptions are necessary, and we both have a good laugh and know exactly what is meant. Perhaps I have a case of arrested development. . . . Or perhaps *for me* some children's books are better than some adult books. *For me* is, of course, a crucial point in discussing books. Books are like people, like friends, and one's chemical reactions to them cannot be really duplicated by anyone else's—much like fingerprints. A book may be universally liked but liked by a thousand people for a thousand different reasons and understood, or read, on a thousand different levels. (pp. 466-67)

Of course, you may say, and very rightly so, that I have strayed afield from *The Endless Steppe.* But I would much rather bandy about other people's books, children and their reactions to books, my children, libraries, the weather, the state of our country, ecology, economics, taxes, almost anything but *The Endless Steppe.* That book was like a heavy load on my shoulders for years, and then I was rid of it—only to be confronted by it time and time again. The only time when I am really, truly happy that I have written it is when letters come from young people, and old people, and middle-aged people, to tell me how much it has meant to them. The letters prove to me that the book has meant different things to different people, and the same things to all the people, too, and I take great pleasure and time in answering them. I am always amused, perhaps maliciously, when I get letters from adults—and I do, many—from the very people the adult-trade editors thought would not be interested in the book. But I am happiest when the letters and comments come from children. (pp. 467-68)

> *Esther Hautzig, " 'The Endless Steppe'—For Children Only?" in* The Horn Book Magazine, *Vol. XLVI, No. 5, October, 1970, pp. 461-68.*

"You are capitalists and therefore enemies of the people . . . You are to be sent to another part of our great and mighty country . . . " With these words a Russian soldier in June of 1941 brought to a harsh end "my lovely world," writes Esther Hautzig as she begins this vivid and moving account of her disrupted, unforgettable childhood.

When she was 10, Esther and her family, Polish Jews of wealth and prestige, were torn from their home in Vilna, herded into a cattle car and transported to a frontier village in Siberia. There were countless things—heat, ver-

min, hard work, near-starvation—to daunt the strongest spirit at the gypsum mine where the father drove and loaded carts, the mother dynamited, the grandmother shoveled gypsum, the child dug in the fields.

There were miserable living conditions—in wooden barracks, in crowded dung huts. There was, in winter, the lack of warm clothing, of fuel, of small comforts once taken for granted, always of food. There was grief for a grandfather reported dead in another labor camp, for a father ordered away to work in a labor brigade near the front lines. And there was the steppe, scorched by summer sun, swept by winter storms, feared at first but later loved by Esther for its endless space.

Also, for Esther, there came to be the excitement of haggling at the Sunday market, of discovering she was a born trader, of earning a few rubles by knitting and sewing. There was the thrill of seeing a Deanna Durbin film four times, of acquiring a best friend, of eventually having a home to themselves—"the hut was heaven." Best of all was going to school, of discovering the Russian classics, of learning Russian, of becoming editor of the school paper. Young Esther was indefatigable. There was nothing she would not try, no effort was too great to make. And when the five long years of exile were ended, she left some of her heart behind in Siberia.

This is a magnificent book. Amazingly free of bitterness and hate, it radiates the optimism, the resilience of the human spirit as typified in its vital young author. To share the trials and hardships she and her family suffered and the remarkable way they faced them together is a rewarding experience for any age.

> *Polly Goodwin, in a review of "The Endless Steppe: Growing Up in Siberia," in* Book World—Chicago Tribune, *May 5, 1968, p. 5.*

These are stunning events. Had I heard Mrs. Hautzig over a cup of coffee, in a New York city living room, tell how her grandmother and an old Vilna neighbor sat on a wooden cot in the one-room hut they shared with a Siberian peasant couple, discussing their Vilna servants, and the idiosyncrasies, in regard to food, of their respective husbands, I would have suggested that Mrs. Hautzig write a book about it. I would have been wrong. It isn't that Mrs. Hautzig is a bad writer. Mrs. Hautzig isn't a *writer.* No blame attaches.

Virginia Woolf describes how the young Orlando, who was going to be a poet, sat near a window writing a love poem with a lot of nature in it, when he happened to look out and saw a tree. He closed his notebook and gave up being a poet.

Writers are persons who habitually look out of windows, are appalled at the impossibility of translating what they see into words, and keep doing it. Non-writers do not look, are not appalled, and have no difficulty in calling upon the arsenal of words which the past has built up to deal with any occasion. Readers who are in the habit of looking at words know the difference.

If Mrs. Hautzig had looked back at herself stealing potatoes she would not have described herself as imagining, "the brutal arm of the law thrashing my fragile back." And I don't believe that she had, as a little girl, stroked the family album farewell. She is nudging us to care because, like a person telling a joke without being sure it's funny, she does not trust her words. She speaks in schoolgirl exclamations: "[The winter] came during the night . . . and scared me out of my wits . . . I thought all the wolves in Siberia had gathered to devour us." And in case she still has not reached us she tries a little joke: "This gypsum mine was not a cheerful place!"

I think it is only the writing down of these things that undid Mrs. Hautzig. I have an idea that over her coffee cup she would never have spoken so falsely. Judging from the decent, brave, intelligent little girl in her book, she must be a splendid person and she has a good story to tell. Give the book to your 12-year-old. She will probably enjoy it. I trust young digestions to deal with this kind of pale half truth as well as with the really nasty junk—so long as we keep feeding them their ration of what has been truly seen and written by *writers*.

> *Lore Segal, " 'A Tiny Bit Beautiful',*" in The New York Times Book Review, *May 5, 1968, p. 2.*

The account of the exiles' endurance is a great human document of individuals sharply etched with love and affection and humor, of the minutiae of their existence remembered with clear sensitivity, and of their deepest and most poignant emotions. The story of their bitter struggles for the barest essentials, the sharing of tiny quarters with others, reveals bravery and, remarkably, even festivity. For the family could celebrate their only child's twelfth birthday in a dung hut, and they could laugh and be "happy over an apple and a piece of meat. . . ." Their temporary privacy in this humble dwelling they cherished: "The hut was heaven. We ate when we wanted to, slept when we wanted to, at night we would sit outside and gaze at the Siberian sky where there was always something to see; we would sit there quietly, quietly."

Countless other detailed recollections are unforgettable, among them Dickens read as a revelation of the evils of capitalism; the teen-age rapture over a Deanna Durbin film seen four times and its songs memorized; the panic of a declamation contest—without shoes; the "worst day of my whole life," when Father, in whom "not even Siberia" had been able to extinguish a love of life, was sent off to a labor brigade on the front lines.

The one place where Esther forgot the cold was the library: "It was there that I was to become acquainted with the works of Dumas, Pasternak's translations of Shakespeare, the novels of Mark Twain, Jack London, and of course the Russians. It was in that log cabin that I escaped from Siberia—either reading there or taking the books home. It was between that library and two extraordinary teachers [in Rubtsovsk] that I developed a lifelong passion for the great Russian novelists and poets. It was there that I learned to line up patiently for my turn to sit at a table and read, to wait—sometimes months—for a book. It was there that I learned that reading was not only a great delight, but a *privilege*."

A rare, affecting, and deepening reading experience, the book will take its place with Anne Frank's diary. (p. 312)

> *Virginia Haviland, in a review of "The Endless Steppe: Growing Up in Siberia,"* in The Horn·

Book Magazine, *Vol. 44, June, 1968, pp. 311-12.*

Esther Hautzig's *The Endless Steppe* is one of those books which make all the appropriate words of commendation seem suddenly outworn and hackneyed. Moving . . . uplifting . . . a great human document . . . yes, it is all these but much more, it is *true*. This first-hand account of the experiences of a Jewish girl from the quiet city of Vilna in east Poland transported with her parents to Siberia by the Russians in 1941 is told with a regard for emotional as well as literal truth which makes it more telling than many more tragic and harrowing tales which have come out of the last war. . . .

Mrs. Hautzig writes well—one of the good things she has to say about Rubtsovsk is the excellence of the education she received there, due, in its later stages, to the presence of some very fine teachers driven from European Russia by the war—and she tells her story without a trace of self-pity. The pity she has she keeps for those who need it most: her mother, fated always to have hard, manual jobs (beginning with dynamiting in the mine); her grandmother, violently separated from her husband and later hearing of his death only at second hand; and for the many others whose lives were harder than her own. The things she celebrates are courage and humour, kindness which she finds in many unexpected places, and the sheer ability to survive. Her book is often very funny and her memories, in the way of those who survive such experiences in a moral as well as a physical sense, tend to have a happy turn.

Describing her second summer in Siberia she mentions typhus. She knew that people were dying in droves and she was terrified but, in the next breath, adds that it was also the summer she saw Deanna Durbin in *100 Men and a Girl* four times at the village cinema. Never, through all the real dangers and privations, does this cease to be the story of a child growing to girlhood in an alien but not wholly inimical environment. It is a timely reminder to the sentimentalists of childhood that in many respects the young are tougher and more resilient than their elders and can take much more in their stride. The one thing without which childhood dies Esther Hautzig had and abundantly thanks heaven for: she was always loved and had people to love and work for in return. . . .

This is a magnificent and heartening book. Mrs. Hautzig is a born writer and life has given her a subject of more power than any novel.

> *"Facing Life—and Death,"* in The Times Literary Supplement, *No. 3501, April 3, 1969, p. 349.*

The endless steppe is a first-person narrative, told by a girl who is ten years old at the beginning of the story and fifteen at the end. More important than this, the story is firmly rooted in a pattern and tradition of writing that has belonged to the world of children for centuries. The theme of human beings stripped of the luxuries and trappings of civilisation, forced to rely on improvisation and their own resources to survive, has always been popular, as far back as when *Robinson Crusoe* was wrested by the young from adult literature. There is a strong tradition of tales of this kind in the nineteenth century too. *The Swiss Family Robinson, Coral Island, Treasure Island* come immediately to mind. In the twentieth century there are other obvious ex-

An identification picture of Hautzig as a young girl in Siberia.

amples: Ivan Southall's adventure stories. A. Rutgers van der Loeff's *Children on the Oregon Trail;* and William Golding's *Lord of the flies* gives further evidence of children borrowing from the adult novel. The Second World War provided fresh material for the genre—Anne Holm's *I am David* and Ian Serraillier's *The silver sword.* But the outstanding example, a book so gripping and well told that it makes all similar war stories pale in comparison, is *The endless steppe.*

This book's authenticity of detail and background, its utterly convincing sense of deprivation and disorientation make *The silver sword,* which is exciting, competently written, and still widely read, seem like any second-rate children's adventure story dressed up for this occasion in Second World War costume with some nasty Germans and a not very well individualised mid-European landscape. Some of the good characters are in danger for most of the time—which is why the reader turns the pages eagerly—but they are usually rescued before anything too dreadful occurs. There is no sense of appalling hardship, of hunger, of suffering as in Esther Hautzig's book; no genuine feeling at any point that all will not come right in the end; no real dilemmas in which hope and despair are equally balanced. In *The endless steppe* these things are the very fabric of the novel, and therein lies its superiority.

The endless steppe is thinly-disguised autobiography. It

actually happened to Esther Hautzig, and that, in part, is the reason for the book's strength. No feat of the creative mind could even now adequately describe the plight of European Jews in the 1940s: the mass migrations of people, the deportations, the killings, the struggle to survive. It is still too awesome and too extraordinary to be assimilated and rendered as fiction by someone who did not live through it; unlike, say, the material of *Robinson Crusoe,* which can be brought alive without first-hand experience, because it is the common property of the human imagination—though it needs, of course, the writing genius of Defoe to turn it into a great novel. (pp. 350-51)

[In *The endless steppe*] it is attention to detail, the minutiae of existence, which more than anything else makes the emotional impact of the book so forceful. Release follows when Germany invades Russia. It is impossible, of course, to return to Vilna; so the family stays on in Siberia for the duration of the war, living in a hut in a small unfriendly town, fighting starvation, freezing cold, petty officialdom, disease. Like the narrator in Byron's *The prisoner of Chillon,* Esther grows to accept it, even to love some of it: it has become her world. Freedom, in 1945, she views with distress; she doesn't want to go back to Poland, much to her mother's uncomprehending astonishment. They do return, of course, and discover that all the other members of their family—aunts, uncles, cousins—have been murdered by the Germans.

I have said that the autobiographical nature of the book is partly why *The endless steppe* is so vivid and memorable. It isn't—it couldn't be—the sole reason. Other people have suffered similar experiences, but they haven't written books of comparable stature. This is where Esther Hautzig the creative artist succeeds better than some others: not only to endure the distress of reliving that period of her life, but to select and reject event and detail, to impose shape and pattern, to see, if possible, underlying meaning, and above all to write the whole thing in memorable English (for her, a foreign language). This is what conveys to the reader the authenticity of the almost unimaginable. (pp. 351-52)

How did [Esther and her family] survive, mentally and emotionally? Their physical survival was, to some extent, pure chance, the fortunes of war; but why didn't they crack up under the strain? Many tiny details point to reasons like inner toughness, dignity, even *joie-de-vivre* and optimism in the face of overwhelming odds: Grandmother wearing a chic Garbo hat and carrying a silver-handled umbrella all that time in the cattle-truck; Mrs. Rudomin, unable to bath or wash properly for six weeks, using a bottle of *L'Heure Bleu* scent. . . . There is also the closeness that perhaps only a Jewish family has, the refusal of any of them to indulge in useless recrimination or loss of temper, and an iron will to live. They have a belief that never wavers that they *will* survive.

Turning to *Hey, Dollface!,* written by Esther Hautzig's daughter, Deborah, is at first sight like observing something from a different planet. Linguistically they have little in common. The English of *The endless steppe,* a very British English, . . . has been replaced by something much more contemporary and American. . . . (pp. 352-53)

The story is about an intense friendship between two fifteen-year-old girls [Val and Chloe] that has strong lesbian overtones; in fact it is hinted that after the book has finished, when the girls are older, it may develop into a deeper, perhaps sexual, relationship. Such a theme isn't unique in teenage literature, but it is so unusual that a novel like *Hey, Dollface!* was long overdue when it appeared. There is no subject on which the educated public is more profoundly ignorant or has more absurd prejudices than homosexuality, and the needs of young people who are growing up gay, with the hostility and worries that heterosexual adolescents don't have to face, have for far too long been ignored. If only for this reason *Hey, Dollface!* would be worth reading, but Deborah Hautzig's merits as a writer are not to be dismissed, and when one realises that Esther of *The endless steppe* is Val's mother in *Hey, Dollface!* the book becomes particularly interesting. (pp. 353-54)

[Despite] the obvious differences between the two novels, they have several features in common. In both books the characterisation of the women is very strong, particularly the central characters. Esther and Val have a similar sparkle, a curiosity about life, an intellectual restlessness that questions, continues to question in the face of stiff adult opposition, and usually wins in the end. Both books are almost straight autobiography, childhood and adolescence not so much remembered by an adult as lived through a second time. And the Jewish upbringing: the ghetto closeness of a persecuted minority in the one becomes an accepted, scarcely-to-be-commented-on, fact of existence in the other, because in New York such things are unremarkable. It is almost a history of the American dream: the down-trodden European minority in *The endless steppe* transformed into the democratic free citizens of *Hey, Dollface!*, and living in a society where even an unusual sexual orientation is, if not totally acceptable, not regarded as a major wickedness. Both novels are inspired by a tremendous belief in freedom—from political oppression in the one, from pressures to conform in the other. (p. 354)

But the experiences of mother and daughter are so obviously unalike that freedom, when it comes, is not only of a quite different nature for Val, but much easier to accept and cope with than it is for Esther. Esther is scarred in a way that Val could never be. For Val, freedom is a normal step on the road to adulthood, a simple matter of maturity and choice. . . . For Esther it is much more difficult. She can say 'But we're alive. Our exile had saved our lives. Now we felt ourselves to be supremely lucky to have been deported to Siberia. Hunger, cold, and misery were nothing; life had been granted us', but sense, beneath that, another more complex set of emotions:

> All my feelings and all my thoughts were a tangle of confusion. I was like some little animal that had been in the trap too long for freedom. I was like the people who had stayed behind in the mine to freeze to death. I was desperately, terribly afraid of change. Perhaps the thought of going back to a world no longer inhabited by people I loved had something to do with it.

The inconclusive nature of the ending of both books is another similarity. In *The endless steppe,* Esther and her mother are re-united with 'Tata' at the railway station in Lodz, but the reader may ask, what happened then? The house in Vilna has become the headquarters of the local

NKVD; and Vilna, in any case, is now no longer in Poland. How did the family fare in post-war Poland? How long did they stay there? Why, and when, did they leave? Interesting though the answers to these questions are, they are not relevant to the novel. The last sentence—'The years out there on the steppe had come to an end; our exile was over'—is entirely appropriate. *Hey, Dollface!* ends with neither of the girls 'coming out' as gay, even to themselves. Whether they are likely to prefer their own sex for good is a question left in mid-air. Some critics have complained that this is a 'cop-out', an evasion of issues. It isn't. It's much more likely that fifteen-year-olds who are homosexual (even those who are one hundred per cent homosexual—and Val and Chloe are to some extent attracted to boys) would find difficulty in admitting to themselves that they are so inclined. And not just because of social pressures. To find out and accept that one's sexual orientation is different from the norm is not necessarily a blinding flash of insight, a once-and-for-all realisation; it can be a slow and gradual process that may take years. If Chloe and Val had been seventeen or eighteen, one might possibly say that the ending of *Hey, Dollface!* is evasive. But at fifteen the inconclusiveness seems right: fifteen is a very inconclusive age.

Beneath the surface of *Hey, Dollface!* the tragic circumstances of Esther Hautzig's early life are hinted at. It would be impossible for her daughter to escape the family's extraordinary past, but it is all to Deborah Hautzig's credit that she is not overawed by this terrible legacy. She doesn't limp along in her mother's shadow. She has said that she hopes that one day she, too, will write her version of those appalling years of European history, from the distant viewpoint of the second-generation American immigrant. This should prove very interesting indeed.

Taken separately, these two books are absorbing. Both are firmly in the centre of certain traditions of writing for the young: the one, the adventure story in which the child faces overwhelming odds; the other, the realistic teenage novel that shows the adolescent grappling with his or her first adult problems. Taken together, they become something more: a portrait of a certain section of European Jewry facing the darkest hour of its history, and what happened, years afterwards, to some of its survivors and their descendants. (pp. 355-56)

David Rees, "From Russia with Love? Esther and Deborah Hautzig," in The School Librarian, *Vol. 28, No. 4, December, 1980, pp. 350-56.*

In the Park: An Excursion in Four Languages (1968)

A multilingual picture book describes in four languages and in brightly colored pictures some of the pleasures of a day in the park, be it in New York, Paris, Moscow, or Madrid. The page layout is cluttered and confusing with text running both horizontally and vertically and with collage pictures [by Ezra Jack Keats] everywhere; nevertheless the book comprises an effective introduction to other languages because it presents the foreign words—French, Russian, and Spanish—within the framework of a universal childhood experience and places them together with the English. Some additional words are appended and phonetic equivalents are given for all foreign words in the book. (p. 1142)

> *A review of "In the Park: An Excursion in Four Languages," in* The Booklist and Subscription Books Bulletin, *Vol. 64, No. 19, June 1, 1968, pp. 1140, 1142.*

Very simple, very functional, very attractive. Parks are fun to visit, the text states, in New York—or Paris—or Moscow—or Madrid. Following this pattern, the names of familiar things are given in each of the four appropriate languages, with pronunciation below each word. The pictures are gay, the word-comparison can be fun, and the universality of children's interests is an implicit additional message. . . . [This] does not attempt to tell a story, so that it need not bear the label of a picture-book to discourage independent readers. A list of additional words and a pronunciation guide to the Russian alphabet are appended.

> *Zena Sutherland, in a review of "In the Park: An Excursion in Four Languages," in* Bulletin of the Center for Children's Books, *Vol. 22, No. 2, October, 1968, p. 28.*

Children today learn foreign languages through conversation and the learning of phrases, not by individual words which is the method used in this book. The book will prove more popular as a charming picture book for the very young rather than a language book for older children for whom it is obviously intended.

> *A review of "In the Park," in* The Junior Bookshelf, *Vol. 34, No. 2, April, 1970, p. 80.*

At Home: A Visit in Four Languages   (1968)

At Home follows *In the Park* in plan and purpose, and if the illustrations [by Aliki] are more homely and detailed, so's the setting. Again, the words for familiar objects, activities and individuals are given in English, French, Spanish, and Russian while families (in Chicago, Marseille, Barcelona and Leningrad this time) go through the motions of preparing and serving a company dinner and socializing afterward, as the children spend a rainy day doing what children do everywhere. (The cuisine and coiffures are more national-characteristic.) Additional words, also with phonetic equivalents, and a Russian alphabet are appended. Where *In the Park* was well-received, *At Home* will also be at home.

> *A review of "At Home: A Visit in Four Languages," in* Kirkus Service, *Vol. XXXVI, No. 19, October 1, 1968, p. 1106.*

How pleasant it is to be in one's own home in Chicago or Marseilles, Barcelona or Leningrad, to be spending a typical day doing sundry chores or preparing for the arrival of guests, enjoying a festive meal with them or engaging in various indoor pursuits in inclement weather. These subjects are cogently illustrated by the large, bold, colorful pictures in this attractive book but, unfortunately, are only ineffectually explained. Six explanatory statements in English introduce the presentation of objects and persons in the various homes in four languages, with pronunciations given. The verbs describing the actions of the charac-

ters are similarly presented. A list of 13 additional words and the Russian alphabet are included at the back of the book. This multilingual book does not take advantage of children's natural propensity for absorbing languages in the form of coherent sentences. The isolated words given can't be put together into sentences and indeed, for the mere purpose of memorization, are not even in their dictionary form—for example, the plurals but not singulars of olive, book, and pillow are given. The attractive format and illustrations can neither redeem the content nor justify the book's price. (pp. 65, 67)

> *Daisy Kouzel, in a review of "At Home: A Visit in Four Languages," in* School Library Journal, *Vol. 15, No. 6, February, 1969, pp. 65, 67.*

In School: Learning in Four Languages   (1969)

At Home, In the Park, In School—the child's world around the world is virtually completed by this volume. Again the key words are given in English, French, Spanish and Russian (with additional terms and a Russian alphabet at the back) while the text and pictures record a typical school day. But what is typical is hardly characteristic of "San Francisco or San Sebastian, Cherbourg or Odessa" and the UNifying moral is put forth at the expense of a geography lesson. (Although some indications of provenance creep into the pictures—as per the different desks and hair-dos—by and large they're dis-located.) (pp. 849-50)

> *A review of "In School: Learning in Four Languages," in* Kirkus Reviews, *Vol. XXXVII, No. 16, August 15, 1969, pp. 849-50.*

The author talks about typical school experiences and introduces relevant words (desk, notebooks, subtraction, blackboard) in four languages: English, Spanish, French, and Russian. A phonetic spelling for each word is given in parentheses. The Russian alphabet is printed at the end of the book together with a glossary of additional words. The book lacks the spontaneity of the author's earlier four-language titles (*In the Park* and *At Home*). The text is stilted and dull; but the pictures [by illustrator Nonny Hogrogian] are bright and lively, full of humor and mischief, and have universal appeal. The pictures, plus the continuing interest in languages, promise to make the book popular. (pp. 669-70)

> *Diane Farrell, in a review of "In School: Learning in Four Languages," in* The Horn Book Magazine, *Vol. XLV, No. 6, December, 1969, pp. 669-70.*

Esther Hautzig's four-language series meets the demand of most children's libraries for simple foreign-language phrase books. *In School* follows her established format: a simple story is told in English; words from the story are listed in English, Spanish, French, and Russian; and the story is followed up by a four-language list of additional school-related words, as well as a Russian alphabet. And, just as Ezra Jack Keats's clear, brilliant pictures for Hautzig's *In the Park* conveyed the universal joys of a Sunday outing, so do Nonny Hogrogian's more subdued, gently amusing drawings set the appropriate tone for a story about a pleasant day at school. While these books won't make multi-linguists of first-graders, they will foster a delight in words and languages and a natural identification with children everywhere.

> Sada Fretz, in a review of "In School: Learning in Four Languages," in School Library Journal, *Vol. 16, No. 4, December, 1969, p. 41.*

Cool Cooking: Sixteen Recipes without a Stove   (1973)

Though you might question whether following these sixteen recipes can properly be called cooking, they do have the advantage of safety, specificity and ultimate simplicity. Hautzig takes nothing for granted (instead of a mere "drain the strawberries" she specifies "Open the package of frozen strawberries. Put them in a strainer. Hold the strainer over the sink and let all of the juice drain off the berries. Shake the strainer a few times to help the juice drain . . . ") and her solicitous detail extends even to the arrangement of the goodies on individual plates for maximum eye appeal. Purists might object to the occasional Kool Whip, store-bought pound cake and other prepared ingredients, but Hautzig has come up with a number of respectable salads (tuna, three-bean and ham pineapple among them) and some reasonably nutritious fruit-based snacks that will appeal to kids without upsetting parents' stomachs or kitchens.

> A review of "Cool Cooking: Sixteen Recipes without a Stove," in Kirkus Reviews, *Vol. XLI, No. 11, June 1, 1973, p. 602.*

Simple kitchen tools (no stove is required) and easily available ingredients will produce no-fail, fun-to-make dishes for budding gourmets in the elementary grades. Instructions for the 16 recipes—ranging from "Grapefruit Cups" to "Strawberry Mint Julep"—are simple to follow, and even second graders can prepare anything from an appetizer to a dessert. *Cool Cooking* does not have the scope of *Betty Crocker's New Boys and Girls Cook Book* (Golden Pr., 1965), but it is a good additional cooking book with a different viewpoint . . . and a lively format. (pp. 38-9)

> Johanna Paras, in a review of "Cool Cooking: 16 Recipes without a Stove," in School Library Journal, *Vol. 20, No. 3, November, 1973, pp. 38-9.*

Moderately useful as a summer or snack cookbook for the child who wants to do some simple food preparation. . . . There is no table of contents or index; the sixteen recipes are arranged in serving order, from a fruit juice cocktail through salads and desserts to drinks. There isn't too much variety here, but the instructions are clear, most of the recipes have sweet ingredients that appeal to children, and the general instructions are useful for any kind of cooking, as well as for off-the-stove cooking like this. (pp. 95-6)

> Zena Sutherland, in a review of "Cool Cooking: 16 Recipes without a Stove," in Bulletin of the Center for Children's Books, *Vol. 27, No. 6, February, 1974, pp. 95-6.*

Let's Make More Presents: Easy and Inexpensive Gifts for Every Occasion   (1973)

Hautzig has had ten years since **Let's Make Presents** to collect more usable ideas and this assortment of 70 items shows that she has applied some thought and discrimination to the sequel. One can imagine "personal gifts" like her hair curler bag, shoe tote, pony tail holder (two buttons and a rubber band), tie-dyed T-shirt, and chef's apron actually being used, and maybe even such "gifts for the home" as a felt phone book cover, decoratively framed wall mirror, and the workshop shelf with lids of screwtop jars glued to the bottom. In addition Hautzig provides a ten-page reprint of her original sewing instructions, hints for novel and ecologically virtuous gift wrapping, some sensible procedural pointers (always "spread newspapers on the working surface" and "although neatness is not necessarily one of the great virtues of the world, it is just easier to make a nice-looking present if you use materials like glue, paint or shellac carefully and painstakingly".)—*and,* for one of the best homemade gifts of all, ten tempting candy recipes that another author might try to parlay into a separate book.

> A review of "Let's Make More Presents: Easy and Inexpensive Gifts for Every Occasion," in Kirkus Reviews, *Vol. XLI, No. 19, October 1, 1973, p. 1105.*

This book is a fine antidote to the Christmas List panics— the feeling that arises this time of year with a look at the calendar and the sudden realization that Christmas is practically around the corner and your children have no presents to give their special friends, let alone to Aunt Marion. With its comforting subtitle (and you'd do well always to note the subtitles on how-to books), Mrs. Hautzig as good as says, "Relax. I'll help you cope." And she does, with sensible and easy-to-follow instructions for making handsome and useful gifts of materials that usually cost less than a dollar. All the reader needs is the material, time—and a little love.

> Lavinia Russ, "How to Make Almost Everything," in The New York Times Book Review, *November 4, 1973, p. 62.*

A companion volume to the author's **Let's Make Presents** comprises personal gifts, house presents, gifts for holidays, and recipes, with both adult and juvenile recipients in mind. The book begins with sensible general advice about economy, carefulness, procedures, and safety; it concludes with suggestions for innovative and inexpensive wrappings, and it suggests that the reader feel free to adapt and improvise. The projects are varied, the diagrams clear, the style of writing informal. Few projects are difficult in this useful book. A relative index is appended.

> Zena Sutherland, in a review of "Let's Make More Presents: Easy and Inexpensive Gifts for Every Occasion," in Bulletin of the Center for Children's Books, *Vol. 27, No. 10, June, 1974, p. 157.*

Life with Working Parents: Practical Hints for Everyday Situations   (1976)

With fewer and fewer families able to afford a full-time

housewife, Hautzig's idea seems promising. But she begins with a lot of cautionary advice that applies whether parents work or not and that most kids have heard often: Never cross on a red light, never accept candy or rides from strangers, be sure your bike has brakes, call if you're not coming home after school, hang up your coat and towel, etc. Other matters she goes into, such as the use of household appliances and leaving a set of keys with a neighbor, are probably best left to each family to work out. Beyond this Hautzig throws in some first aid (but advises a handbook), a week's menu's (recipes run to canned soups and canned fruits, sometimes mixed together), and some time-killing crafts ideas—both for your own amusement or for babysitting a younger child, though the difference between the two categories is minimal. And those who don't know what to do together when the chores are done won't find much stimulation in her "find a hobby that the whole family can participate in." Flabby. (pp. 1171-72)

> *A review of "Life with Working Parents," in* Kirkus Reviews, *Vol. XLIV, No. 21, November 1, 1976, pp. 1171-72.*

Filled with incongruities, this guide has youngsters at home alone doing artsy-craftsy things with razor blades in chapter one, while in chapter two they are warned to look both ways while crossing the street. It also has children taking over responsibility for shopping and cooking, from clipping newspaper coupons to preparing four-course meals, as well as planning family outings and vacations. Covering the same territory as advice-for-the-new-bride books, kids who can adopt the program laid out here probably don't need parents at all.

> *Joan Scherer Brewer, in a review of "Life with Working Parents: Practical Hints for Everyday Situations," in* School Library Journal, *Vol. 23, No. 6, February, 1977, p. 65.*

Dealing in the first chapter with "General Suggestions and Hints," Hautzig briefly discusses planning and organizing but stresses leisure time projects; the second chapter discusses safety measures and rules in and out of the home, most of which pertain equally to children whose parents are at home: what to do if you have your keys stolen, do's and don'ts for bicycling, etc. Other chapters give advice on doing chores, on saving money or handling household appliances, on caring for pets or younger siblings, or on preparing meals. The advice is sensible and useful, but some of it is not really geared to children who are home alone as compared to those who have a parent or parents at home, and there is a rather noticeable emphasis on crafts and projects. A divided bibliography and an index are appended.

> *Zena Sutherland, in a review of "Life with Working Parents: Practical Hints for Everyday Situations," in* Bulletin of the Center for Children's Books, *Vol. 30, No. 8, April, 1977, p. 126.*

A Gift for Mama (1981)

On all special occasions, from birthdays to Hanuka. Sara has to make a gift. But this year Sara is determined to be very grown up and *buy* her mother a gift for Mother's Day. She's seen the perfect present in a shop window, a pair of black satin slippers.

But Sara has no money. She doesn't receive an allowance. Nor will her parents give her money unless they know how she is going to spend it.

While eating dinner with her Aunt Margola, Sara gets an idea. She can mend the tattered clothes belonging to her Aunt's college friends. Sara mends one scarf, one sweater, two pair of silk stockings, six socks, and turns seven shirt collars before she earns the nine zlotys for the slippers. When Sara's mama receives the present her first reaction is one of disappointment. But when she learns how Sara earned the money for the gift, her reaction pleases Sara very much.

Esther Hautzig's style is gentle and warm, reflecting the love, gaiety, and affection in Sara's family. The depth of characterization reveals Sara as an enterprising child whose upbringing has helped her become an independent, yet loving child. The beautiful black and white illustrations [by Donna Diamond] capture the gentleness and tenderness expressed throughout the book.

> *Lisa Lane, "Colorful Picture Books and Storybooks, a Summer Reading Roundup," in* The Christian Science Monitor, *July 1, 1981, p. 18.*

Set in Vilna, Poland, during the 1930s, the narrative is a gentle, uncomplicated tribute to family solidarity as well as a loving evocation of an era—drawn, like *The Endless Steppe*, from the author's reminiscences of her childhood. The accompanying black-and-white monoprint illustrations are vigorous and expressive. Less romantic than the artist's more familiar style, they capture the luminous charm of the book without becoming sentimental. (p. 424)

> *Mary M. Burns, in a review of "A Gift for Mama," in* The Horn Book Magazine, *Vol. LVII, No. 4, August, 1981, pp. 423-24.*

Although written in a simple low-key style, this book conveys sensitive insights into a child's struggle to maintain her growing sense of self amidst conflicting family traditions and expectations. . . .

The book is set in Poland, the author's homeland, and the reader learns much about Jewish customs and Polish lifestyle. . . .

The characters are compassionate and believable. Sara is a determined, loving child who cherishes her growing up. Mama is a sensitive woman who is caring enough to admit her mistakes. Papa, too, is warm and supportive. The story provides an alternative perspective through its Jewish characters and extended family setting.

This book is not for readers who need instant excitement, but its message is far more touching and gratifying than many of the popular adventure stories I've seen.

> *Jan M. Goodman, in a review of "A Gift for Mama," in* Interracial Books for Children Bulletin, *Vol. 13, No. 1, 1982, p. 20.*

Holiday Treats (1983)

Having written several books for children on culinary arts and handicrafts, the author now offers a generous collection of recipes for sixteen festive days observed throughout the United States. Each holiday is introduced by a brief succinct account of its history and of the customs associated with it; Christian, Jewish, secular, and patriotic celebrations are included. Pointing out that "holiday treats are, and always have been, sweets of one kind or another," the author presents traditional delicacies for some special days, such as Irish soda bread for St. Patrick's Day and *hamantaschen* for Purim, along with "timely treats," such as almond drop cookies for Christmas and two luscious Father's Day cakes—"favorites of fathers I know." General hints and instructions as well as specific directions are set forth in clear, nonpatronizing terms—thus fostering independence in young cooks—while sensible tips on kitchen cleanliness and safety are discreetly offered along the way.

> *Ethel L. Heins, in a review of "Holiday Treats," in* The Horn Book Magazine, *Vol. LX, No. 1, February, 1984, p. 74.*

While many of the recipes can be found in other cookbooks (and are not necessarily connected with any specific holiday), it is helpful to have these in one collection. Although intended for beginning cooks, it would be advisable for adults to help younger children. The directions, while clear, can become quite involved. In addition, often the ingredients are listed on one page and the instructions on another, which is inconvenient even for experienced cooks. Line drawings [by Yaroslava] are decorative rather than helpful. Overall, a very tempting (and delicious!) collection of treats.

> *Margaret Bauer, in a review of "Holiday Treats," in* School Library Journal, *Vol. 30, No. 6, February, 1984, p. 72.*

Although the author asserts that most offerings can be prepared without adult assistance, it will take a fairly self-assured chef to attempt such delectable confections as hamantaschen, cheese blintzes, and Emerald Isle pie. Necessary ingredients and utensils are helpfully listed in separate columns, recipe instructions are ordered in numbered steps, and basic techniques are outlined in the preface. Hautzig's brief remarks about each holiday are both interesting and thoughtful, as when she properly cautions that Passover treats should be "made in a way that will be acceptable to those who will eat them."

> *Karen Stang Hanley, in a review of "Holiday Treats," in* Booklist, *Vol. 80, No. 13, March 1, 1984, p. 967.*

Make It Special: Cards, Decorations, and Party Favors for Holidays and other Celebrations (1986)

Make It Special is a book for older children, due to the reading level and type size. Some of the more creative suggestions are for greeting cards and house decorations that are truly unique and would be lots of fun to try; other ideas, though, are for unimaginative projects, such as place cards and napkin holders. Fine-line ink drawings [by Martha Weston] provide the needed extra to make constructions of the many original ideas possible by even the least artistically inclined. The absence of an index will be sorely missed for quick access to the many nifty projects included. This book helps, but does not totally solve, the need for more quality material on holiday craft projects.

> *Anne Wirkala, in a review of "Make It Special: Cards, Decorations, and Party Favors for Holidays and other Celebrations," in* School Library Journal, *Vol. 33, No. 6, February, 1987, p. 80.*

Hautzig, author of *Holiday Treats,* gives ideas and instructions for designing holiday and greeting cards, decorating the house and table for special events, and making party favors and gifts. Although the decoration sections may be low-interest areas to children, many of the projects will be appealing if introduced by a parent, teacher, or scout leader. Clear line drawings accompany each project. Most of the craft ideas are fairly simple, explained and illustrated in a single page. Pressed flower cards, wreaths, mobiles, vases, candle holders, place mats, napkin rings, paperweights, clipboards, and pomander balls are among the ideas suggested. While the generalized special occasion theme makes this a less attractive selection for any single holiday, the book is undeniably an adaptable choice that could serve as a crafts resource for many celebrations.

> *Carolyn Phelan, in a review of "Make It Special: Cards, Decorations, and Party Favors for Holidays and other Celebrations," in* Booklist, *Vol. 83, No. 11, February 1, 1987, p. 843.*

Most of the projects suggested in this how-to book require materials that are easily obtainable and that are free or inexpensive. Hautzig's premise is that home-made decorations are festive and provide enjoyment for hosts and guests. The author gives a list of tools and materials needed for each project; she adds general suggestions to those specific to each, and reminds readers that they can adapt and invent, as well as follow instructions. The material is adequately organized, with chapters on such subjects as table decorations or party favors. The illustrations are useful for the most part, although on some pages there are step-by-step diagrams that are cluttered. (pp. 125-26)

> *Zena Sutherland, in a review of "Make It Special: Cards, Decorations, and Party Favors for Holidays and other Celebrations," in* Bulletin of the Center for Children's Books, *Vol. 40, No. 7, March, 1987, pp. 125-26.*

Carolyn Haywood

1898-1990

American author and illustrator of fiction and nonfiction.

One of the most prolific and popular authors of books for younger children, Haywood is applauded for creating realistic stories which characteristically describe the adventures and concerns of youngsters in the early grades with warmth and humor. During a career in which she wrote and illustrated fifty books in fifty years, she became considered among the most successful writers of works directed to readers in the primary and middle grades, an author whose books are acknowledged for capturing the essence of childhood and for reflecting her respect for children. Haywood's stories depict natural, active boys and girls, both urban and suburban, at school and at play. Her works, several of which feature the beloved characters Betsy and Little Eddie, describe the joys and near-calamities of early childhood in language noted for the accuracy of its dialogue and in black-and-white illustrations praised for their liveliness and clarity. Set against backgrounds of happy middle-class family life and characterized by their wholesomeness and innocence, the stories are acknowledged for being among the first to represent the everyday activities of childhood as both funny and exciting. Haywood structured her works as episodic chapters which are noted as ideal for early readers to read to themselves; her works are often praised for inspiring a love of reading in children.

Haywood began her career with *"B" Is for Betsy* (1939), a story often considered her best known book which describes six-year-old Betsy's first year in public school in a small American city and her vacation on her grandfather's farm. Haywood wrote a number of additional works about Betsy and her family and friends; several of these book feature Betsy's younger sister, Star. A character acknowledged as especially delightful and endearing, Eddie Wilson, is the protagonist of another of Haywood's most popular series. A small boy who lives in Betsy's neighborhood and is good friends with her, he is fond of animals and of collecting items considered junk by most people. Eddie hatches well-meaning yet amusing schemes, such as cooking giant hamburgers and attempting to become the town dog catcher, which often involve his pets and his collection. Haywood follows her characters in both the Betsy and the Eddie series as they advance in age and grade level; for example, Betsy is ten years old when her sister is introduced in *Betsy's Little Star* (1950). In the 1970s and 1980s, Haywood created several works, most frequently using the holidays as their theme, which combine episodes from earlier Betsy and Eddie books with new chapters. Other notable books from Haywood's career include a trio of realistic stories about red-haired Penny, an adopted boy; a group of fantasies about Santa Claus; *Primrose Day* (1942), the story of an English child's adjustment to her new American home; and *Make a Joyful Noise!* (1984), a selection of Bible verses presented in thematic sections with original homilies and reminiscences. Haywood received several awards from the state of Pennsylvania, in-

cluding being named an Outstanding Pennsylvania Author in 1979; she also received many child-selected awards for her works. (See also *Something about the Author,* Vols. 1, 29; *Contemporary Authors New Revision Series,* Vol. 5; and *Contemporary Authors,* Vols. 5-8, rev. ed.)

GENERAL COMMENTARY

May Hill Arbuthnot

Probably few adults will ever wholly share young children's enthusiasm for the chronicles of Betsy and her friends. Here is the [Lucy Sprague] Mitchell formula of giving back to the child himself, his family, his friends, their activities—and little more. But the stories are written with warmth and honest directness that immediately win young readers. Whether it is *"B" Is for Betsy* or *Betsy and Billy,* or *Betsy and the Boys,* there is always a background of happy family life, with lively children and understanding adults taking their ups and downs with good nature and a nice sense of fun.

These stories serve an important end by introducing the preschool child to the intricacies of school life or by interpreting that life for the children who are living it. Children read these books avidly, over and over, and demand more of them. Children identify themselves with Billy and Betsy and are absorbed by their activities. These books also satisfy the child's need to belong to a family, a neighborhood, and a school. They are happy, friendly little tales and have grown progressively better each year. *Peter and Penny* concerns two adopted boys and has been particularly welcome to families with adopted children. All the books are wholesome, but captious adults may wonder if, even at five and six, life might not be permitted just a touch of wildness. (p. 368)

The Carolyn Haywood *Betsy* books are full of sound social meanings for young children. Perhaps their chief value is their happy interpretation of home and school relationships. The children love them as stories, but they value them too because Betsy's school is so much like their school and Betsy's friends like their friends.

Such stories, rich in social meanings but primarily good stories, are few and far between. (p. 517)

> *May Hill Arbuthnot, "Of Many Things," in her* Children and Books, *Scott, Foresman and Company, 1947, pp. 502-31.*

Grace Shakin

To the younger children, [Carolyn Haywood's works] are "marvelous books," "neat and terrific books," for they are books which they can comprehend. Here are books about familiar situations at home and at school. Here are books that meet their need for a sense of life, a richness of vicarious experience. They supply younger children with clues to a clearer understanding of themselves and other people. Children are trying to tell us all this when they say to us, "That book was *just* right."

Such whole-hearted, enthusiastic comments of children indicate too that Miss Haywood's books are written in a style that is both readable and appropriate for them. The vocabulary is simple but not rigidly controlled. There is no writing down to children. The format is also pleasing to young readers. As Eric, a fourth grader said, "I don't like books that are just words, words, words—without any pictures." Miss Haywood's books are well illustrated. The thirty or more pictures which she has drawn for each book help to make the characters very real. Her black and white sketches fit in smoothly with the text and add to the attractiveness of the book.

Carolyn Haywood's stories have wide appeal. The accelerated reader of six and seven; the average reader of eight and nine; and the retarded reader of ten and eleven—all pronounce them good books. Several of them—*Back to School with Betsy, Betsy and the Boys,* and *Little Eddie*—have been read to groups of emotionally disturbed children with marked success.

The Little Eddie books are also "sure-fire" for reading aloud to seven-year-olds. Eddie's experiences make sense. They understand his fondness for animals. . . . Children appreciate Eddie's interest in junk of all kinds. "Of course, Eddie didn't call it junk. He called it his valuable property. He had old radio parts, ear phones, old tubes, and dials." They share his triumph when Eddie, the youngest of the four Wilson boys, brings home the most wood, a telegraph pole, and so gets Grandad's desk.

Through such reading aloud, many children first discover that not all books include the same necessarily limited material with which they are learning to read. Here are books with information for their growing experience, fun, adventure. Here are books that children *want* to read. Moreover, the fluent, effortless reading of the adult makes reading seem so easy!

Repeatedly it is one of Carolyn Haywood's stories which proves to be the right book for the right child at the right time. The result is a satisfying reading experience. From many such happy and satisfying experiences with books and reading will surely come a love of reading, one of the greatest gifts which home and school can give to children. With a love of reading and permanent interests in reading a child has one of the important tools of education. Reading is at the heart of learning. Carolyn Haywood's books have helped many children to go beyond the mastery of the mechanics of reading to a feeling for books and a love of reading. (pp. 3-5)

Carolyn Haywood's books present modern children and their everyday experiences at school and play. That first loose tooth; Eddie's attempts at cooking giant hamburgers; the second graders' preparation for an all-school bazaar—these are events familiar to all children. It delights them, from their wisdom as boys and girls, to be able to anticipate the outcome. (p. 5)

Warm family relationships are included in all of the Haywood books. Children take keen pleasure in meeting Betsy's or Eddie's family, so very much like their own, or as they would have their families be. The everyday happiness and enjoyment of simple things are relished by child readers. They are amused by the mild difficulties of Betsy, Eddie, Peter, or Penny. Children understand and appreciate Eddie's efforts to convince his father that a goat is a necessary and desirable addition to the Wilson houshold. They see the wisdom in the friendly policeman's explanation, "But you made a big mistake in not talking to him about it first. You should have told him all the nice things about the goat and got him interested. You should have smoothed the way. That's what you call diplomacy. If you take that goat home now, your father will probably throw it out."

But Eddie's persistence—and diplomacy—triumph. Gardenia, the goat, is added to the Wilson family. The era of Gardenia trouble then begins, "for Gardenia was only happy when she was eating something or had climbed on top of something. Gardenia managed to be happy most of the time." (pp. 7-8)

The humor in Carolyn Haywood's books is true to life and the kind younger children can understand and enjoy. The pancake batter, spilled on linoleum, that causes Betsy and Billy to slide all the way across the floor and right out the back door; the problem of trying to sell twenty-four cakes of Surething Flea Soap, soap with the worst smell in forty-eight states; and the contrariness of Eddie's parrot, Louella, whose one comment is "Texas is better"—these are hilariously funny incidents to young children. The humor is rooted in their own experience. . . .

Since 1939 when *B is for Betsy* was first published, parents, teachers, and librarians have been grateful to Carolyn Haywood. Hers is a significant contribution to the literature for younger children and for learning-to-reads in grades four, five, and six. Simply written, these books reveal Miss Haywood's sincere respect for young readers. Her choice of familiar, everyday happenings in home and school reveal her understanding of young children, their interests and needs. . . .

Miss Haywood's books will continue to help many children along the way to becoming real readers and true lovers of books. Through her books, younger children everywhere can continue to make the joyous discovery that reading is fun. (p. 8)

> *Grace Shakin, "Our Debt to Carolyn Haywood," in* Elementary English, *Vol. 32, No. 1, January, 1955, pp. 3-8.*

Paul C. Burns and Ruth Hines

The publication of Carolyn Haywood's *B is for Betsy* in 1939 was a significant event in the children's book world. The heroine is the kind of little girl one might find in any first grade class in the United States. The things that happen to her might happen to any child, but Miss Haywood makes the everyday activities of Betsy and her friends both exciting and funny. This was a new idea in literature for children. Since that time Miss Haywood has continued to write realistic stories about children at home and school that are entertaining and easy to read. (p. 172)

Miss Haywood began her career as a portrait painter, specializing in work with children. From the pupils of Howard Pyle she had learned much about writing and illustrating children's books, and after a time, decided to try it herself. She planned a picture book with little text, but she met an editor who suggested that she write about American boys and girls and the things they like to do. From this suggestion came *B is for Betsy* and all the other delightful stories that have followed since 1939.

B is for Betsy describes Betsy's experiences during her first year of school and her vacation on her grandfather's farm. . . . *Betsy and Billy* continues the adventures of Betsy and her friends in the second grade. Billy finds it difficult to stay out of trouble. *Back to School with Betsy* and *Betsy and the Boys* take the same characters through the third and fourth grades. (pp. 172-73)

The Betsy stories find an enthusiastic audience among young readers because they are close to their own experiences and interests. Children are interested in the events described and problems presented. The characters are not, however, as clearly defined as in the author's "Eddie" stories.

In *Little Eddie* Carolyn Haywood has created a real boy whose delightful personality endears him to children and adults alike. . . . Miss Haywood is often asked if the children in her books are real. Most of them are not, but just after she finished the story *Little Eddie* she met a small boy who was actually called Little Eddie and who might have been the Eddie of the story. Miss Haywood and this Little Eddie spent three days together while he posed for the illustrations for the book. After this, Eddie Wilson was a little something more than make-believe. (p. 173)

In *Eddie's Pay Dirt,* Eddie returns from Texas resplendent in a Mexican costume and brings along the strangest collection of "valuable property" yet. Eddie must make an important moral decision when his "pay dirt", given to

him by his friend Manuel, turns out to be truly valuable. Eddie knows Manuel did not realize the value of his gift. Should he give it back or keep it to buy the horse he has always wanted? Eddie's parents offer guidance but leave the decision to Eddie. (p. 174)

Eddie and His Big Deals is one of the best of the Eddie series. Eddie finds himself in competition with another collector who turns out to be, of all things, a girl! Eddie engages in a complicated series of exchanges—big deals—in order to obtain a printing press from his rival. Eddie's experiences with the school orchestra and a gardening project are the subjects of other books by Miss Haywood.

In addition to her "Betsy" and "Eddie" books, Carolyn Haywood has written several books about adopted children, Penny and Peter. These books can help children to understand the relationships of parents to adopted children. She has also written a number of other books not related to any of the series, but full of humorous situations in which children become involved—on the farm, twin "mixups", and riding the school bus. On one occasion when asked about her writing, Miss Haywood said, "Of all the delightful features about make-believe children, the most convenient one is that their author can control not only their growing up but their growing down. The world of books is indeed an 'Alice in Wonderland' world where there are bottles marked 'Drink me' and cakes marked 'Eat me' with the inevitable Alice results."

Carolyn Haywood ranks high among the favorite authors of children between the ages of seven and ten. Her stories are good for reading aloud to young children for, in many cases, each chapter is a complete story, though related to other chapters of the book. Good readers in the second grade and most third graders can read the books for themselves. They satisfy the need of beginning readers for a "fat" book—one that looks like a "grown-up" book instead of a picture book. The "Eddie" stories are enjoyed by older children and are especially appreciated by the slower or more reluctant reader in the middle or upper grades.

Children find more than entertainment in Miss Haywood's books. Her characters have their problems as well as their fun. They receive their share of scoldings from adults, have their disappointments, and some of their good ideas don't turn out well at all. However, they learn to accept their failures and begin new projects and explore new fields. Their relationships with parents and other adults are warm and friendly. Books such as these help children to grow in understanding of themselves and others. They help them to see that some frustration is a natural part of growing up and give them subtle encouragement in their own endeavors. (pp. 174-75)

> *Paul C. Burns and Ruth Hines, "Carolyn Haywood," in* Elementary English, *Vol. 47, No. 2, February, 1970, pp. 172-75.*

Sam Leaton Sebesta and William J. Iverson

Children's literature of the past reveals a middle childhood full of excitement, joy, and important but nonthreatening incidents. Perhaps this was characteristic of middle childhood in several past generations of Western culture. Children of this age seem to have been free to operate happily and with safe independence, suffering neither the insecurities of early childhood nor the pangs of adolescence. Some of the best of this literature is almost idyllic; troubles and problems are transient and easily overcome. Some stories present deeper concerns, but the pervading tone is optimistic.

The family, viewed through the eyes and actions of an intermediate-level child, forms the basis of many of these stories. In other instances, the adults are moved farther offstage, leaving the child protagonist to deal with his peers, as if this age group existed in a world of its own.

The world of Tom Sawyer and Huckleberry Finn is such a world as this, and so is the world in Booth Tarkington's books about Penrod and Sam. In the late thirties and forties Carolyn Haywood produced two dozen lively books about the neighborhood adventures of Betsy, Eddie, and Penny. In *"B" Is for Betsy* early, happy school days are recorded, a teacher, Miss Grey, demonstrates how lively early childhood education can be, and parents and peers ease Betsy along the way through her school experience. The hero of *Little Eddie* is more enterprising. He brings home a whole telephone pole for firewood, manages to redistribute the neighborhood cats, and runs for election as dog catcher. There's never any doubt in these books that

From "B" Is for Betsy, written and illustrated by Carolyn Haywood.

the audience is children. Haywood imparts genuine happiness, never resorting to contrived plots. (p. 251)

> Sam Leaton Sebesta and William J. Iverson, "Realistic Fiction," in their Literature for Thursday's Child, *Science Research Associates, Inc., 1975, pp. 243-306.*

Sheila A. Egoff

For the child, the pattern of a secure world is set by the microcosm of the family. And family stories [form a major group that has] survived into the modern age. Frequently a child makes the transition from picture books to "real" books via the light, even slapstick *Henry Huggins* (1950) by Beverly Cleary, and Carolyn Haywood's **"Betsy"** books (1940s and 1950s). These books are not "classics" in the old sense. Their characters are jauntily rather than finely drawn; but while they contain little depth in their portrayal of child life, they do offer fun and the secure family situation that makes such simple fun possible. (p. 25)

> Sheila A. Egoff, "Survival of the Fittest: Selection from the Golden Ages of Children's Literature," in her Thursday's Child: Trends and Patterns in Contemporary Children's Literature, *American Library Association, 1981, pp. 18-30.*

"B" Is for Betsy (1939)

I cannot too often repeat that whatever stories little American children are given to read, those that come home to them most closely and that they will read with the most interest and profit are such as show them other little American children in circumstances like their own, or like those they wish were their own. It would be hard, for example, to find a subject closer to the personal interests of a little girl in the first grade of a public school than life in the first grade of a pleasant public school. Betsy is just six when this story of life in the first grade begins. To a little girl not quite old enough to go to school, her adventures will have the charm of a golden future. To one who is living through that epoch-making year, it brings the joy of recognition, one of the greatest incentives to reading when you are young, and one of the lasting pleasures of reading, however old you may be.

Betsy's emotions were mixed at the prospect of going to school at all. According to the old man out at the farm, school in his day had been something you were glad to get away from. Indeed, pleasant as her young teacher was that first day, sunny the room and friendly the other children, there was a sick sort of all-gone feeling in Betsy's interior as she sat there, lonesome as only a first day at school can make a child much loved at home. But when she opened her school-bag, there was Koala Bear: father had foreseen he might be needed. She had that sort of parents, and this was a school where place was made for comfortable plush bears and even, temporarily, for large live dogs that would follow small boys to class. That very first day Betsy has the ever-memorable experience of finding a best friend. Later, she learns to go to school alone, to take her part in collective activities. There is a birthday party, a Thanksgiving secret, a puppy for a present, a circus given by the children, and an arrangement, creditable to all concerned, with the old lady whose violets Betsy has picked. Every day little events, told in very large, well leaded type, with pictures about everything, these daily doings are those of little children anywhere that good public schools flourish in little American cities.

> *May Lamberton Becker, in a review of " 'B' Is for Betsy," in* New York Herald Tribune Books, *April 9, 1939, p. 6.*

Finding a new author, and especially one who knows how to write the kind of book and also knows how to draw the kind of pictures that small boys and girls enjoy is like finding an understanding friend, and we all know what that means.

We feel just this way about Carolyn Haywood, whose first book for children, *"B" Is for Betsy,* appears among the new spring books. . . .

In this delightful story you will find out how Betsy learned to love school, and how each day brought interesting new experiences and new friends into her life. Especially nice is her friendship with Ellen, the little girl with whom she shared her jelly sandwiches, on that first day. This was a friendship that grew and grew through all the happy events of the school year. . . .

> *Florence Bethune Sloan, in a review of " 'B' Is for Betsy," in* The Christian Science Monitor, *April 24, 1939, p. 10.*

Two and Two Are Four   (1940)

Carolyn Haywood has already proved that she knows how to write for little children. *Two and Two Are Four* can be read to still younger children than her *B Is for Betsy,* but like *B Is for Betsy* its simple sentences and large print will make it useful for beginners in reading.

Teddy and Babs, 6 and 4 respectively, are living in a city apartment when we make their acquaintance in the first chapter. Soon, however, they move to a farm, where puppies, two playmates of their own age, Fourth of July picnics, haying, the circus, an adventure with a skunk and with the little pigs who jump the wall when Betsy visits them wearing her new hat, and a pony for a crowning glory, fill the days full to running over with interest and delight.

While the story deals with simple, everyday things, it does so with zest and imagination. Teddy and Babs are real, even to the spirit of mischief that now and then takes possession of them. The author knows and enjoys children and writes of them with humor and understanding. Pictures which have the simplicity and action which children enjoy illustrate the incidents of the story.

> *Anne T. Eaton, in a review of "Two and Two Are Four," in* The New York Times Book Review, *May 19, 1940, p. 21.*

Betsy and Billy   (1941)

Betsy, Carolyn Haywood's small heroine of *"B" Is for Betsy* and *Two and Two Are Four,* has now been graduated from the first grade. This easily read, simply told story mirrors the delights of second grade, pretty teachers, and school-day friendships. Home life too comes in for its fair share of attention—Father and Mother, Thumpy the cocker spaniel, and, of course, the new baby for Christmas. Boys and girls just starting school might find the classroom pleasanter, or at least more familiar, if before opening day they read—or have read to them—the "Betsy" stories. And third graders, proud of their ability to master a "thick book" (*Betsy and Billy* is not in picture book format) will most certainly have a wave of nostalgia for beginning days.

> *Siddie Joe Johnson, in a review of "Betsy and Billy," in* Library Journal, *Vol. 66, No. 14, August, 1941, p. 678.*

This third story about Betsy, the little heroine of *B Is for Betsy* and *Two and Two Are Four,* is even better than its predecessors. To write a story of a child's everyday life simple enough for beginners in reading, gay and spontaneous and dramatic on a little child's level, but never overdrawn nor overcolored, is a real achievement. *Betsy and Billy* fills a need for boys and girls from 7 to 9, for as they follow Betsy and her friends through the school year they will recognize children like themselves, concerned with the same things—dressing up at home and at school costume parties; Christmas and Valentine and May Day celebrations; bicycles and baby sisters and a pet that was lost and found.

Miss Haywood knows children and her touch is sure and light. The chapter "Bread and Molasses," showing what resulted from the combination of two children (whose intentions were the best in the world), an impetuous puppy and a jar of molasses, is a little masterpiece and incidentally gives us a glimpse of parents with wisdom and a sense of humor.

The type is large and clear and the lively drawings admirably illustrate each incident in the tale.

> *Anne T. Eaton, "Daily Living," in* The New York Times Book Review, *September 28, 1941, p. 12.*

Primrose Day   (1942)

Carolyn Haywood's stories of school life in suburban America, in which little girls can read about other little girls who might be next-door neighbors, have established themselves as aids to easy reading. Not only by large type, many pictures and a lifelike atmosphere but by a mild yet steady plot interest these books not only make it easy for a little girl to read but make her want to do so. This offering, more ambitious, is quite as successful.

Merry's middle name was Primrose: she was an English child, in America for the duration, not through any evacuation scheme but as guest of devoted Aunt Helen and Uncle Bill, not far from Philadelphia. An excitement about getting off disposes of tears, and once arrived, the little girl's experiences at school are like those of any newcomer. The other children find it ridiculous that she should call examples sums and speak of a truck as a lorry and a street car as a tram. Aunt Helen says they don't mean to be rude, but I think she's wrong. Normal children like to be rude sometimes. Happily, their memories are short, and Merry is getting along nicely when she learns that in America primroses do not grow wild.

This is a serious matter. In honor of her name she has always had a picnic on her birthday, which comes when yellow primroses are thick in the meadows: last year she made a chain of them for Mother. This one thing, that to an older person might seem a very little thing, strikes home the fact that she is far from home. But on a neighboring Pennsylvania estate primroses do grow in the grass—not wild, to be sure, but the English gardener is happy to have the picnic there and the chain made. The pleasant year goes on. Merry knits a scarf for Mother's Christmas present and would have sent one to Father had not her Scottie raveled it out. Something that makes this unimportant brings the tale to a happy close. It is as affectionate and unsentimental as Alice Dalgliesh's *Three from Greenways*. . . .

> *May Lamberton Becker, in a review of "Primrose Day," in* New York Herald Tribune Books, *March 8, 1942, p. 8.*

Little girls who like to read about children of their own age will follow Merry's journey from her English home to her American one with sympathy. Her courage on separation from her father and mother, her special feeling about primroses, as well as her surprises over strange American ways, show a natural child of today adapting herself to the changed conditions of war years. Miss Haywood knows how to write simply and understandingly of children's interests and, as well, how to draw them in happy, characteristic action.

> *Alice M. Jordan, in a review of "Primrose Day," in* The Horn Book Magazine, *Vol. XVIII, No. 2, March-April, 1942, p. 106.*

Back to School with Betsy (1943)

Those who made the acquaintance of Betsy in the author's first book, *B Is for Betsy,* and in the two succeeding volumes, *Two and Two Are Four* and *Betsy and Billy,* have followed the adventures of this very human and engaging little girl from her first day at school through the second grade and a summer vacation. Now Betsy, together with Billy and her other playmates, is back at school in the third grade.

The school year is full of activities and interests which child readers will recognize with pleasure as similar to their own. There is the making of the big Mexican picture to which all the children contribute; there is Daisy the pet chick who turns out in the end to be the wrong kind of chicken to lay the eggs the class is confidently expecting. There are happenings, too, outside the schoolroom, adventures in the empty house next door that is being made ready for a new occupant; the wedding of Miss Grey, Betsy's much-loved teacher, and the important matter of a wedding present for which Betsy, Billy and Ellen earned the money and which they selected all by themselves. . . .

The author writes with a sure touch. She knows children well and enjoys them; thus Betsy and her friends ring true in every particular. Miss Haywood is fortunate, too, in her ability to illustrate her own stories, for her drawings have

the same genuinely childlike quality and the same humor and liveliness as the text. The large type and well-leaded pages help to make this an inviting book to the inexperienced reader.

> *Anne T. Eaton, "Third-Grade High Jinks," in* The New York Times Book Review, *September 26, 1943, p. 24.*

Betsy, who goes to public school in a small American city—or it might be in any good American public school—is now making her third appearance in print large enough for inexperienced readers, whose confidence she gains at once by talking just as they do about things in which they are interested. You might think all this needed was to listen to children's talk and write it down. This simple plan rarely comes out; in Miss Haywood's case it does. Reading her stories is like overhearing everyday playground talk in the lower grades of a pleasant co-educational school.

> *May Lamberton Becker, in a review of "Back to School with Betsy," in* New York Herald Tribune Weekly Book Review, *October 24, 1943, p. 8.*

Here's a Penny (1944)

"Penny," so called because his red face and red-gold curls made him look like a brand new copper penny, is 6 years old in the story. Next door lives Patsy, also 6, and Miss Haywood tells in easy, spontaneous fashion of their doings at home and in school. How Penny got his two kittens and why he decided to name them Really and Truly; what happened when Patsy dressed Really and Truly in her doll's clothes and took them for a walk; a Hallowe'en party at which Penny and Patsy wore identical costumes; the result, for Penny, of choosing the top of a barrel of pitch as a seat on a hot day; and finally how Penny's dream of having a brother old enough to play with came true, make a story packed full of interest and entertainment for 5 to 7 year olds.

Once again Caroline Haywood, whose . . . Betsy stories have established a firm popularity among the younger boys and girls, has given us a friendly human book, in which she writes of children with quiet humor and thorough understanding. The many drawings by the author have a lively action and a clarity very satisfying to child readers. *Here's a Penny* is a book that reads aloud well and one that will be useful with beginners in reading.

> *Anne T. Eaton, "Happy Red-Head," in* The New York Times Book Review, *September 17, 1944, p. 21.*

When Miss Haywood's stories for very first readers began to appear, with *B is for Betsy* introducing its heroine to other first-graders, the large size of type was a special reason for the popularity they aroused. It was good to have stories, not in the least resembling school books but keeping within the little world of school, that used the large type on which eyes unaccustomed to the printed page had been trained. It is still a good idea; I am glad that this is used to tell of six-year-old William—given his nickname because at first sight of his red face and hair his father cried, "He looks like a brand-new copper penny!" But there is more in these tales than legibility. Miss Haywood, writing of everyday life, can express the brave new way in which little children look at their everyday world.

This story, however, starts with a situation not altogether every day. "Anyway," says a little girl next door, "I'm my mommy's and daddy's real little girl." "I know I'm 'dopted," says Penny. "My mother told me so. But I'm her real little boy." "Not really and truly," insists the tactless neighbor. The words sink into Penny's heart. He has always brought troubles to Mother; he brings this, and in no time at all that matter is done away with. Her method may be gathered from Penny's rejoinder. "That's the way I'm going to 'dopt my kitten; I'm going to wait till I find a black one with a white nose and white paws. And I'll love him so much that he'll be my really truly kitten."

Indeed, when he gets two kittens he names one Really and the other Truly, and they take part in the tale.

> *May Lamberton Becker, in a review of "Here's a Penny," in* New York Herald Tribune Weekly Book Review, *October 1, 1944, p. 6.*

Betsy and the Boys   (1945)

We confess to thinking this is a rather sissy book, but these *Betsy* books have built up a following. Betsy and her loyal pal, Billy, are in fourth grade now and make life lively for their mothers. They slide in the pancake batter and slither through a pink-satin bow tie; there are birthday parties, a Christmas play, a bad, cruel Valentine joke which almost ruins a friendship, and a lot of football combine to create reader interest for both small boys and girls. But everybody in the story over 13 is too good to be true, and the gang is a little too clean about the ears for authentic realism. The illustrations are very successful—good merchandise.

> *A review of "Betsy and the Boys," in* Virginia Kirkus' Bookshop Service, *Vol. XIII, No. 13, July 1, 1945, p. 297.*

Do you wonder what little boys and girls are really like—nice ones with good homes and amusing parents, who go to public school, but live, like all little children, in a private world of their own? You have perhaps forgotten what that world was like. Carolyn Haywood has not; reading her Betsy books, you think how true they are and possibly feel just a little sorry you had to grow up.

The first episode in this, her fourth, shows how little a born story-teller need worry lest material for stories be used up. Here is something that could happen in any kitchen in which a small boy and girl are permitted, in Mother's absence, to make pancakes for their own lunch. . . .

Adventures of Betsy with the boys begin just as her friend Billy is finding their society more engrossing than hers. She gets on the football team only by deviously producing a football. Valentine's Day comes with its elaborate system of letting others think they've surprised you, and of equally elaborate detective work to prevent being surprised. In this mystification Betsy forgets it's so unlike Billy to send fish-heads instead of a Valentine that he probably didn't, and stops speaking to him. When she

finds he really didn't, she realizes how silly it was "to forget what I really know about Billy."

These are little children who mean to be good and are encouraged to be so by their parents, not by the methods of the Fairchild Family, but in the good-natured, contemporary manner. Children can practice in these simple stories not only reading but living.

> *May Lamberton Becker, in a review of "Betsy and the Boys," in* New York Herald Tribune Weekly Book Review, *July 29, 1945, p. 5.*

Penny and Peter   (1946)

A sequel to the popular *Here's a Penny* (story of a little adopted boy)—and in this one Penny's parents decide to adopt Peter, too. This is a story of their subsequent adventures when Patsy forms the twosome into a trio. The two boys are irrepressible children, infallibly getting into trouble when they try to help. The crabs they bring from the seashore spill out of the basket on the train; the Christmas tree takes a tumble after the ornaments have been put on—and between these incidents lots of other things happen, simple, good-natured, might-be-true adventures.

> *A review of "Penny and Peter," in* Virginia Kirkus' Bookshop Service, *Vol. XIV, No. 19, October 1, 1946, p. 491.*

Penny and Peter, [is] illustrated with the author's own drawings, unassuming but appealing.

These adventures of two small boys have just the sort of humor and reality children most enjoy, simple bits of everyday living . . . all told with a most delightful quality of family affection. Peter and Penny are both adopted children, and their joy in belonging and in being "really truly brothers for ever and ever" gives this book a special underlying tenderness.

> *Frances C. Darling, "Stories with Lots of Pictures," in* The Christian Science Monitor, *January 14, 1947, p. 11.*

Little Eddie   (1947)

Carolyn Haywood's audience of children under ten has been rapidly rolling up since *B is for Betsy* introduced them to a little girl and her friends on the first step of the school ladder. Their number has grown in successive volumes, their ages gradually gaining, but this time a newcomer takes the center of the stage away from Betsy, Peter or Penny. This is the youngest of the four Wilson boys, Little Eddie, who is seven and, not unnaturally, rather put upon by the nine-year-old twins and Rudy, who is twelve.

That doesn't discourage Eddie. Nothing could, and the funny thing is that he isn't a pest by being so persistent. He has the strength of the weak, rather like Br'er Rabbit, only kinder. Eddie would like to be compared to that hero: he loves all animals. Cats follow him home; one of his characteristic triumphs is, when forced to clear the house of all his cats, that he emerges from the experience with a $25 reward and spends it on a white kitten. He collects everything: junk is his specialty, and what he can do with junk! There was the time he decided to run for dog catcher and paraded with a sign "Vote for Me," and the climax is when his friend Al starts for Hollywood—to hear him tell it—and all the children in the class think if he can succeed as fast as that, so can they, and hold that sweet thought—till Al gets back to school. He had been having the mumps.

These episodes, making a continuous story, are each the right length for reading aloud. They have qualities that will make them called for more than once—till, in all probability, the habit of ready reading will be well started.

> *A review of "Little Eddie," in* New York Herald Tribune Weekly Book Review, *November 16, 1947, p. 12.*

In *Little Eddie,* Carolyn Haywood has created a fine figure of a seven-year-old—astonishing, unpredictable, and entirely recognizable. Eddie's adventures are always peculiar and always plausible, at least from his point of view, and they are told with the dead-pan attention to detail which is necessary to bring really funny stories to life.

> *Jane Cobb and Helen Dore Boylston, in a review of "Little Eddie," in* The Atlantic Monthly, *Vol. 180, No. 6, December, 1947, p. 144.*

Penny Goes to Camp   (1948)

The third in a series about two adopted boys, Peter who is now 10 and Penny who is 8. After a rather unfortunate start, when camp is viewed as an unhappy necessity, forced on the boys (who want another summer at the seashore) because the parents are going to Europe, this develops into a rather commonplace story about minor adventures and misadventures at the camp. There is place for a good first camping book, but this doesn't measure up to expectations. The boys were convinced—camp turned out to be lots of fun—but neither the constructive aspects nor the psychological ones seem very convincing to this reader. And a good chance was missed to strengthen the boys' sense of security in giving them a voice in the decision.

> *A review of "Penny Goes to Camp," in* Virginia Kirkus' Bookshop Service, *Vol. XVI, No. 9, May 1, 1948, p. 214.*

Eddie and the Fire Engine   (1949)

The author of the popular *B is for Betsy* series with her second book for boys—and again about little Eddie. This time he gets himself involved with an old fire engine which the fire department is retiring, and an understanding father buys it for his birthday at the auction. (We wonder how Mother felt about it!) Children adore the absurdity of ridiculous might-be-true situations, and will laugh themselves silly over Eddie's unusual Christmas card, Anna Patricia's two front teeth and how they got lost at school, and how Gardenia, Eddie's goat, robbed a pie wagon. Boys and girls too will love it. Eddie and his friends are so real and such fun that they should be here to stay. The writer has the unusual gift of recognizing sure-fire situations that will appeal to small readers, and

telling the stories in the sort of language they accept as their own.

> *A review of "Eddie and the Fire Engine," in* Virginia Kirkus' Bookshop Service, *Vol. XVII, No. 12, June 15, 1949, p. 300.*

Betsy's Little Star   (1950)

The popularity of the hilarious story, **Eddie and the Fire Engine,** of last year, must have increased the already large audience of this writer for children just beginning to read. Her new book, in the familiar big type, with her own engaging sketches, is for little girls. Betsy is ten, her sister Star is four. Little girls will read it to themselves and also read it aloud to their own sisters of Star's age. It offers a good prelude to a four-year-old's first days at kindergarten. Star longed to go to school, and found many funny ways to manage it. Even her Koala Bear got to kindergarten in a wonderful way. Her adventures, funny or a bit sad, with new shoes, with her dog Thumpy, with the milkman and mailman, all ring true.

At the end comes a Santa Claus parade, and a family Christmas. Then Star is five, ready to go properly to kindergarten at last. The author knows her small children inside out. She writes a modern, everyday story that has quality because of its underlying spirit, a kind of humor and clarity that are happy and healthy for first readers.

From Little Eddie, *written and illustrated by Carolyn Haywood.*

Louise S. Bechtel, in a review of "Betsy's Little Star," in New York Herald Tribune Book Review, *August 13, 1950, p. 6.*

The joys and disappointments in a four-year-old girl's everyday life, centering around her yearning to join her playmates in kindergarten and the visits that, uninvited, she manages to pay to it. Though simple enough for second-graders to read themselves, it is written with a humorous understanding that makes the children described seem sufficiently well-rounded to step right out of the pages.

A review of "Betsy's Little Star," in The New Yorker, *Vol. XXVI, No. 41, December 2, 1950, p. 178.*

Eddie and Gardenia (1951)

Young Eddie, sturdy protagonist of **Eddie and the Fire Engine** and **Little Eddie,** has that dream adventure when he visits some Texas relatives who have a ranch and horses and cowboys and all such television wonders. Accompanying Eddie on his trip is the goat, Gardenia, relegated to enforced exile by Eddie's father who had had just about enough of Gardenia's indiscriminate appetite. But Gardenia's appetite does not diminish and her antics cause Eddie some difficulty until Gardenia is forced to live in a goat pasture with the masses. In the meantime Eddie—and the reader—are having a super-duper time what with the pony riding, exploring the new country, being cowboy-courageous, and even rescuing Gardenia from death, which exploit wins him his spurs. Not a word's breadth out of the young reader's ken—very real, full of giggles, whoops and chuckles. Illustrations—just right—by the author.

A review of "Eddie and Gardenia," in Virginia Kirkus' Bookshop Service, *Vol. XIX, No. 12, June 15, 1951, p. 292.*

Any 8 year old boy is sure to identify himself with the likable Eddie. He will chuckle over his funny adventures, respond eagerly to his devotion to his pet and his love for the ranch, and admire the pluck and self-reliance which finally won him his spurs. Eddie is beginning to grow up.

Polly Goodwin, in a review of "Eddie and Gardenia," in Chicago Sunday Tribune Magazine of Books, *September 2, 1951, p. 6.*

The Mixed-Up Twins (1952)

As a switch from her wonderful **Eddie** series, this is an equally successful twin story full of warmly expressed minutiae of daily living. Twins Ronald and Donald are visiting their grandmother in a small town. From the start, when a lovably mixed-up Vickie bumps into Donald, hunting for a lost kitten and so intent on his search that he ignores her repeated requests for his name, the incidents get progressively funnier. When Ronald enters the picture, Vickie is so confused she has to call her new friends the "Onalds". After a summer of painting pictures and swimming and a winter of losing mittens and building snowmen, Vickie gets straightened out when the Onalds' hair is cut and Ronald's grows in curly. Exhibitive of the writer's knowledge of how four-year-olds think, act and

orient themselves, and set down in their own language, this is a gem on the juvenile list. Her illustrations pleasantly round out the characterizations of the puzzled, joking threesome.

A review of "The Mixed-Up Twins," in Virginia Kirkus' Bookshop Service, *Vol. XX, No. 11, June 1, 1952, p. 323.*

Carolyn Haywood has created two characters, Betsy and Eddie, who have become so real to the younger boys and girls that everything that they do or say is of interest. Her story, last year, of Eddie and his goat, Gardenia, met with universal approval. In this new tale she introduces a four-year-old girl, Vickie, and two four-year-old twins, Ronald and Donald. There is also the usual quota of mothers and two very kind and obliging policemen. It is, perhaps, not as funny as the Betsy and Eddie books; but it is a very good story with attractive illustrations. (p. 39)

Harriet Simpson Arnot, "Realism and Imagination," in The Saturday Review, *New York, Vol. XXXV, No. 33, August 16, 1952, pp. 38-40.*

Eddie's Pay Dirt (1953)

We last saw that bouncy eight-year-old, Eddie Wilson, on his uncle's ranch. Now, with his whole school class, we wait at the station for him to return from the West. He steps off the train in the costume of a Spaniard, carrying the parrot Louella, who is yelling "Texas is better!" And his bundles! . . . [Though] one box has rubber snakes, and one pocket holds the real snake Percy, the carton marked "Pay Dirt" really makes good. It also poses a moral problem which the author solves in a very realistic, small-boy way.

We cannot say we found this up to the other Eddie books. The situations, right from the start, seem forced. But Eddie is still Eddie, and that will be enough for all his followers. Even six-year-olds will want his new one read aloud, and for early readers, the big type and many pictures are excellent.

Louise S. Bechtel, in a review of "Eddie's Pay Dirt," in New York Herald Tribune Book Review, *September 13, 1953, p. 12.*

Things began to happen the minute Eddie and his new parrot, Louella, came off the train. The box marked "Snakes," the aptness of Louella's vocabulary, Eddie's small-boy arithmetic and the great hamburger fiasco all help make this latest Eddie story as genuinely funny as the three which have gone before.

Parents as well as their children will be especially moved by Eddie's problem with the bucket of "pay dirt" that his Mexican friend gave him. The wisdom and restraint of the boy's father in pointing the way yet leaving the real decision to Eddie is so admirable that the grown-up reader may wonder if he himself could be as sensible.

Sarah Chokla Gross, "Home from Texas," in The New York Times Book Review, *September 13, 1953, p. 30.*

Children, and there will be thousands of them, who remember Eddie Wilson's trip to his uncle's ranch in Texas, accompanied by his goat Gardenia, last year will be delighted to see that this book welcomes Eddie home after his long sojourn. . . .

The . . . scene when both the snakes and the parrot join enthusiastically in the welcome to Eddie is one of the funniest that Miss Haywood has ever written. Of course, the pay dirt turns out to be really valuable, Eddie becomes more of a hero than ever, and in the end is so endearing in his independent decision about its value that he proves again to be the most popular of small boy heroes.

> *A review of "Eddie's Pay Dirt," in* The Saturday Review, *New York, Vol. XXXVI, No. 46, November 14, 1953, p. 64.*

Betsy and the Circus   (1954)

This homey, easy-to-read tale takes Betsy, her little sister, and their friends through another series of everyday adventures. In her characteristic, straight-faced manner, the author weaves humor into a number of near-calamities— the fate of Policeman Kilpatrick's birthday cake, Billy's chagrin when his prized Easter egg backfires, and Betsy's efforts to earn enough money for a coveted Mother's Day gift. A plot develops when Betsy and Billy meet the twin children of two circus performers, and their classmates refuse to believe that these twins really exist unless Billy produces them.

Miss Haywood obviously knows the heartaches that so often result from children's expanding friendships. When Betsy slights Ellen, her best friend, for one of the twins, the "three-is-a-crowd" issue is solved by a clear-cut, satisfying analogy. Many a little girl will see her own problem reflected here and find comfort in the story.

> *Rose Friedman, "Old Friends and New," in* The New York Times Book Review, *September 12, 1954, p. 32.*

Characteristically, Carolyn Haywood in this newest of the Betsy books uses for her material familiar episodes: a surprise birthday party for a favorite policeman, the overnight visit of Ellen and her small sister Linda, coloring of Easter eggs, and the coming of the circus. Equally characteristically, the possible overfamiliarity of each incident is offset by a twist of event or by a touch of humor. This faculty of tingeing everyday experiences with the unexpected and the humorous lends originality and interest to what otherwise might be mere literalness. For the eight- to ten-year-olds **Betsy and the Circus** will be a happy, wholesome reading experience.

> *Elizabeth Nesbitt, in a review of "Betsy and the Circus," in* The Saturday Review, *New York, Vol. XXXVII, No. 46, November 13, 1954, p. 78.*

Another story of Betsy and her friends at school. As in the earlier books, Betsy's adventures are those of any normal youngster her age and they are told with a light touch. The last few chapters, in which Betsy and Ellen have a temporary falling-out over Betsy's friendship with a new girl, will give youngsters a better understanding of some of their own problems in age-mate relations. Both the style

and the content make this a book for older readers than the age that usually reads the Betsy books, and there is not the spontaneity of the earlier stories.

> *A review of "Betsy and the Circus," in* Bulletin of the Children's Book Center, *Vol. 8, No. 4, December, 1954, p. 32.*

Eddie and His Big Deals   (1955)

Although not the best of the stories about Eddie Wilson, collector of "valuable property," this is entertaining and easy reading for grades two to four. Eddie's current trouble is with girls: first he discovers to his horror that the promising new boy and fellow collector next door is a girl, and then becomes involved in one of the most complicated and delicate negotiations of his collecting career in trying to make a deal for a coveted hand printing press—owned by a girl.

> *A review of "Eddie and His Big Deals," in* The Booklist, *Vol. 52, No. 1, September 1, 1955, p. 20.*

Betsy's Busy Summer   (1956)

Summertime for Miss Haywood's heroine includes an expected round of activities—playing in the summer house, receiving the kind offer of someone else's swimming pool, selling *Razburyaide,* and suffering such minor disasters as her little sister's friend's immersion in the fish pond. But through it all there are the unexpected turns of humor that come from this author's "perfect pitch" for the talk and feelings of children that goes far in telling what childhood is really like. Easy drawings by the author add to a narrative that is fun reading aloud too.

> *A review of "Betsy's Busy Summer," in* Virginia Kirkus' Service, *Vol. XXIV, No. 11, June 1, 1956, p. 355.*

From the time school closed in June until its reopening in September, Betsy was busy. There was the new summerhouse her father built, where they gave a watermelon party for the whole neighborhood; there was her and Billy's lemonade stand, which ended with "razburyaide" and a profit of twenty-five cents; there was the time Ellen hit the jackpot on a peanut machine, and much more excitement. Each chapter tells a complete story of good-humored people in interesting, credible situations. Miss Haywood's books are among the best of easily read, realistic stories; little girls will welcome this one.

> *Heloise P. Mailloux, in a review of "Betsy's Busy Summer," in* The Horn Book Magazine, *Vol. XXXII, No. 5, October, 1956, p. 348.*

Children always look forward with anticipation to a new Betsy book, knowing they'll find boys and girls very like themselves having the sort of everyday adventures and youthful problems which are familiar to them all. And, of course, lots of funny incidents to chuckle over. So, now, with Betsy and her friends that "busy summer" they can make Razburyaide, try to fry an egg on the hot sidewalk, count seeds at a watermelon party, and swim in the neighbors' new pool. Another of the author's highly satisfactory stories for 8 to 12s, in which, among the good times, are tucked several nicely handled lessons in good behavior.

> *Polly Goodwin, in a review of "Betsy's Busy Summer," in* Chicago Sunday Tribune Magazine of Books, *November 4, 1956, p. 10.*

Eddie Makes Music (1957)

The young-fry in grades two to four will welcome this new story of Eddie Wilson and his gang. Miss Haywood has a way of making even the simplest incident dramatic so that the reader identifies himself with the hero. This time Eddie is lured into learning to play a musical instrument so he can be in the school orchestra and appear with it on television. Complications set in, of course, but Eddie never lets his fans down. Nor does Miss Haywood.

> *Mary Peacock Douglas, in a review of "Eddie Makes Music," in* The Saturday Review, *New York, Vol. XL, No. 42, October 19, 1957, p. 56.*

This book is written in elementary English for grammar school age. Children who have been enthusiastic followers of Eddie's "doings" in Miss Haywood's previous volumes, will welcome his adventures into the baffling (to him) world of music. Those to whom this book serves as an introduction to Eddie will discover lovable youngsters in him and his little pal-neighbors Sidney, Spike, and the rest of them. There will be plenty of reader-identification for those youngsters who are struggling with music lessons. The humor is easily understood.

> *H. B., in a review of "Eddie Makes Music," in* The Christian Science Monitor, *November 7, 1957, p. 20.*

Betsy's Winterhouse (1958)

Another book about Betsy and her friends, ***Betsy's Winterhouse*** is full of those crises which have made Carolyn Haywood a favorite among children's authors. A cellar playhouse, a lost cat, a cake-stealing dog, and a birthday tree are just some of the ingredients that go into this easy-going story of the life of a good American family from November to May. The author's gift lies in her ability to find humor and excitement in the most credible details of ordinary domestic life.

> *A review of "Betsy's Winterhouse," in* Virginia Kirkus' Service, *Vol. XXVI, No. 14, July 15, 1958, p. 502.*

Popular Betsy and her friends appear again in this story, which is as fresh and entertaining as the earlier ones. Eight- to ten-year-olds find these stories simple enough to read readily, and the characters and their activities amusing, realistic, and absorbing. Adults will recognize this author's ability to interpret young children with humor and warm understanding.

> *Ruth Hewitt Hamilton, in a review of "Betsy's Winterhouse," in* Saturday Review, *Vol. XLI, No. 51, December 20, 1958, p. 29.*

Much of the fun in the latest of the ever popular Betsy-and-Star books comes from special words and names. For instance, because Betsy and her friends Billy Porter and Ellen have hugely enjoyed the summerhouse, Betsy induces her father to make a "winterhouse" in the basement. From November through May, the children have parties and a puppet theatre—all in the winterhouse. Clues to more of the amusing incidents are tucked into numbers of family catchwords like "the birthday tree"—originated so that little Star, always confused about loot on her Christmas-birthday, could know which presents were which.

Boys and girls now first meeting Betsy and her circle will be starting with one of the very best Haywood books—easy to read, a mirror of comical but true experience.

> *Sarah Chokla Gross, "All Words Can Mean," in* The New York Times Book Review, *January 4, 1959, p. 26.*

Eddie and Louella (1959)

As his large and devoted audience well knows, Eddie Wilson, dedicated collector of valuable junk, is also drawn, as the bee to the flower, to animals. Of all the pets which he has collected in previous adventures, the only permanent one is Louella, a parrot of reasonably amiable disposition and speech. Now, in the space of two days, Eddie acquires a stray dog (a habit which has been strictly forbidden by his father), lends Louella to a charity ball and retrieves the wrong parrot—who addresses Eddie's mother as Sourpuss instead of Pretty Girl.

It would be pointless as well as impossible to summarize the ensuing complications—only Carolyn Haywood can do them justice and this she does in her most persuasive manner, making the most, but never too much, of the comedy and suspense of the situation. And only Eddie, intense, resourceful, canny, could have sailed through them with such aplomb. He is, rather remarkably, when one considers most series, just as boyish and as unconsciously funny as when we first met him seven books ago.

> *Ellen Lewis Buell, "The Wrong Parrot," in* The New York Times Book Review, *September 27, 1959, p. 48.*

Any small boys who have not yet met Eddie should hurry. This is the seventh book about him and he's as real and funny as ever. Louella is a parrot and the book's plot revolves around mistaken parrot identity. It's stupendous fun, and easy reading for most third and fourth graders.

> *J. B., in a review of "Eddie and Louella," in* Chicago Sunday Tribune Magazine of Books, *November 1, 1959, p. 20.*

Few sounds are more heart-warming than the sudden, spontaneous laugh of a child reading to himself, and few books have the magical power to evoke it. Miss Haywood's usually do, and this new Eddie book is no exception. Once again, Eddie is Eddie. . . . Louella, Eddie, and a stray Golden Retriever wildly whirling in a hotel's revolving door are representative of the wonderful predicaments Eddie churns up so naturally. Many authors try to walk the tightrope of contemporary dialogue, character, and incident; most fall off into the cheap wisecrack or the deadly inaccuracy. Miss Haywood never seems to lose her balance.

Margaret Warren Brown, in a review of "Eddie and Louella," in The Horn Book Magazine, *Vol. XXXV, No. 6, December, 1959, p. 475.*

Annie Pat and Eddie (1960)

Turnabout is only fair, and in Carolyn Haywood's latest book about the world of Eddie Wilson, Eddie himself gracefully takes second place to his longtime friend, Anna Patricia, whom he visits for one summer at the shore. That is the summer when Annie Pat decides to be an actress (she does a fine job as a statue), tries to dye her hair red, wants to be a ballet dancer and then an artist. All during these feminine goings-on Eddie is right there, too, arguing, challenging and discovering finally that, dizzy though she may seem, Annie Pat is a good person to be with because she sees all kinds of things. Less antic than some of the Eddie tales, this is still good fun in the authentic Haywood style; full of natural dialogue, comic situations, surprises and jokes right out of the middle years of childhood.

Ellen Lewis Buell, "Summer at the Shore," in The New York Times Book Review, *October 16, 1960, p. 40.*

Small doings, funny sayings are 10 times more heartwarming with Carolyn Haywood to make the 8-12's (and any adult who can borrow her books) feel a part of the family circle. This, her 22d book, is about the summer Eddie spent with Annie Pat's family on the seashore, with Annie Pat's role at least as important as Eddie's. Annie Pat tries to dye her hair, Eddie becomes a member of the Hose Committee, Annie Pat is bitten by modern art. Almost every chapter is complete in itself. Dialogue that comes trippingly to the tongue, falls ponderously from most pens, but Carolyn Haywood uses conversations so skillfully and abundantly that they give life and immediacy to her stories.

P. M., "Pirates, Beware!" in The Christian Science Monitor, *November 3, 1960, p. 3B.*

Anna Patricia upstages Eddie all thru this gay story of a seaside summer, but even the most dedicated Eddie fans will forgive her. Her delight in making believe and in making pictures out of improbable objects like buttons is catching.

Like the seven other books about Eddie and his adventures, this amusing book is great tonic for reluctant readers.

Jean Baron, in a review of "Annie Pat and Eddie," in Chicago Sunday Tribune Magazine of Books, *November 6, 1960, p. 24.*

Snowbound with Betsy (1962)

More about that favorite junior miss, nine year old Betsy, and her family when a blizzard, just before Christmas, isolates them. They take in orphans of the storm, Neddie and Susan Byrd and their mother, and rescue a cardinal (bird) from the roof; the electricity goes off, but they make popcorn in the fireplace, as well as a snowman outdoors; and chapter to chapter leads from one resourceful, homemade

activity to another which Carolyn Haywood's readers will again find cheerful. The story as well as the vocabulary is comfortable and there is no thaw in this market. (The black and white illustrations by the author are definite if somewhat prosaic.)

A review of "Snowbound with Betsy," in Virginia Kirkus' Service, *Vol. XXX, No. 13, July 1, 1962, p. 561.*

Another pleasant book about Betsy, written with simplicity of style and an easy good humor; the children are natural and the small incidents of their lives are realistic. Family relationships are good; the book adds the pleasures of the Christmas season to the perennial appeal of everyday life events with which readers can identify.

Zena Sutherland, in a review of "Snowbound with Betsy," in Bulletin of the Center for Children's Books, *Vol. XVI, No. 1, September, 1962, p. 8.*

Here Comes the Bus! (1963)

A highly respected author demonstrates clearly her understanding of exuberant six-year-olds—here in Maine and mostly on a school bus. The pages are *not* crowded with "I love yous", "Have a pleasant day, Mama's darlings" and tender goodnight kisses, which plague so many easy-reading books about children. Jonathan is lively; he is forgetful; he is imaginative. The kids tease and pick on one another, and then in a minute are boisterous friends again. The realistic, eventful journeys to and from school are packed with natural dialogue and comical events. Definitely manageable vocabulary and large print. A few superfluous illustrations.

A review of "Here Comes the Bus!" in Virginia Kirkus' Service, *Vol. XXXI, No. 14, July 15, 1963, p. 660.*

Carolyn Haywood, who has now written 24 books since **"B" Is for Betsy** appeared in 1939, consistently avoids repetition and dullness. Her latest amusing story introduces Jonathan Mason, new to rural living, to the first grade and to riding a school bus. Jonathan foresees the daily trip as a trial but instead it proves to be interesting and pleasurable because Mr. Riley is the driver. That indomitable man expertly copes with a bus load of timid and brash youngsters, their pets, lost shoes and birthday cakes. As full of natural incident, credible characters, and humor as its predecessors, Mrs. Haywood's new book matches her best.

Sarah Chokla Gross, in a review of "Here Comes the Bus!" in The New York Times Book Review, *September 29, 1963, p. 30.*

Imagine, if you will, a school bus which has a special warm seat and a friendly driver who searches for a lost birthday cake, takes the whole first grade into the woods for a Christmas tree, bears with good humor a pumpkin man whose feather stuffing erupts, and transports a menagerie of pets from goldfish to sheep on Pet Day at school—and you have the ingredients of gentle humor and obvious affection and understanding of small children which shine throughout the pages of this book like a lan-

From Primrose Day, *written and illustrated by Carolyn Haywood.*

tern carried along a friendly path. A new book by this distinguished author and illustrator of children's books is always welcomed, both by her fans among the children and their parents who seek good reading for them. This is her 25th book and, though it was a delightful first adventure for this reviewer, it was announced by her young son of 10 that this was his 6th by his favorite author. (He had discovered her on his own and had been reading her books since kindergarten). It is especially enjoyable for the 6-9-year age group for whom the school bus is one of life's real adventures.

> *Barbara McCauley, in a review of "Here Comes the Bus!" in* The Christian Science Monitor, *November 14, 1963, p. 3B.*

Eddie's Green Thumb (1964)

Armed with a green thumb, a package of seeds, and a lot of excess energy, 8-year-old Eddie and three friends set out to become gentleman farmers—category novice. They begin rather inauspiciously with more rabbits than carrots and more crows than turnips. But the young farmers make pets of the pests and the vegetables thrive through the long summer despite—or because of—the sensible nonsense of the youngsters' planting exploits.

Carolyn Haywood employs here the same kind of gentle humor that has popularized her entire "Eddie" series. In the small world of her goody-goody children, Eddie is involved in only the mildest kind of mischief, and the novel proceeds briskly through a checkerboard garden of spinach, beans and watermelon to the successful end of the Green Thumb Project.

> *Ellen H. Goodman, in a review of "Eddie's Green Thumb," in* The New York Times Book Review, *November 1, 1964, p. 38.*

Another book about Eddie by this master of story-telling will be greeted with joy and read with absorption and laughter by 8-12's. Eddie is real boy and gives us never a dull moment. His vegetable garden project turned into a lot of projects, including raising baby rabbits, getting the seed packets mixed up, running a road-side stand (briefly!), and buying second-hand garments to make a scarecrow. Amazingly Eddie's family got some home-grown vegetables to eat, too. Here is a swift story told almost completely by means of conversation—a method demanding high literary skill. The conversation furthermore reveals character, and a background of family relationships that is understanding, cooperative, and kindly, as well as deliciously humorous not only to a young reader but, for different reasons, to his parents!

> *M. J. T., "Parisian Dogs and Others," in* The Christian Science Monitor, *November 5, 1964, p. 5B.*

Despite interference from baby bunnies, strange seedlings, beetle bugs, and a crafty crow, Eddie and his friends cultivate vegetables for the school-sponsored Green Thumb Project. . . . Eddie goes on to win a special award—and so should Miss Haywood, because her twenty-fifth-anniversary book has all the spontaneous humor and vivacity of her previous stories: a noteworthy achievement.

> *Priscilla L. Moulton, in a review of "Eddie's Green Thumb," in* The Horn Book Magazine, *Vol. XLI, No. 1, February, 1965, p. 46.*

Robert Rows the River (1965)

Robert is a 9 year old boy whose house is situated on the banks of the Thames, which means that every school day he has to row across the river to be picked up for classes and on holidays he can paddle around in his rowboat all he wants. This is the circumstance which launches Robert on a series of adventures, many of them otherwise unconnected, like: picking up odds and ends from the water; bringing some friends across to his tree house; and once waking up to find himself adrift. More importantly, he cruises into a friendship with Aaron, a Gypsy boy who comes complete with a pet monkey. Robert is temporarily cast into troubled waters as he meets up with some local prejudice against "gyppos" much of which is dispelled by his initiative, at least among his classmates. The problem is given a soft sell as the story glides from incident to incident. It is an easygoing entertainment for 8 and 9 year olds by a favorite author for that group.

> *A review of "Robert Rows the River," in* Virginia Kirkus' Service, *Vol. XXXIII, No. 12, June 15, 1965, p. 576.*

The summer friendship of these very different little boys,

enlivened by the capers of [a] mischievous monkey, is described with humor and sensitivity. Adventure, an English flavor and the Haywood style add up to another delightful book from this popular author-illustrator.

> Beatrice M. Adam, in a review of "Robert Rows the River," in Library Journal, *Vol. 90, No. 18, October 15, 1965, p. 4615.*

Eddie the Dog Holder   (1966)

Eddie's one of the durable dependables for this age group and this time he is trying to make some money (for a baseball mitt—until he wants a puppy) by holding dogs still for his friend Annie Pat so she can paint them. And she literally does paint them—and Eddie. They have an encounter with the dogcatcher, and Eddie makes more money selling another picture to a junk dealer, and so it goes. . . . The illustrations by the author haven't changed much either—not enough to keep up with the way kids look (and dress) today, but they'll be so pleased to be able to read it to themselves they won't notice.

> A review of "Eddie the Dog Holder," in Virginia Kirkus' Service, *Vol. XXXIV, No. 13, July 1, 1966, p. 627.*

Eddie Wilson is indefatigable, and his penchant here for getting in and out of scrapes will undoubtedly satisfy Carolyn Haywood's readers as much as it always has. . . . The author has an ear for dialogue and a light, humorous style, so the children's ploys and projects seem perfectly natural.

> A review of "Eddie the Dog Holder," in Saturday Review, *Vol. XLIX, No. 46, November 12, 1966, p. 47.*

Betsy and Mr. Kilpatrick   (1967)

Youngsters who remember Mr. Kilpatrick from the first day of school (*"B" Is For Betsy*) will share Betsy's dismay—the friendly Irishman is going to be replaced by *a lady policeman.* She and her friends quickly form the Kilpatrick Club, then haggle over who is going to be president (each votes for himself) and are stymied over the choice of a present—Billy insists on a police dog. Ellen thinks (she's Chairman of the Think Committee) and Betsy offers (in writing) to adopt a Chinese orphan for the childless Kilpatricks. But the Kilpatricks are going to have children aplenty; six nieces and nephews from Ireland are coming to stay while their burned-down house is rebuilt. The children rally with toys (from Share the Toys Day) and a welcoming party at the airport where Betsy is momentarily dismayed by the arrival of a lone Chinese girl—can it be Ah Ping, whom she wrote to?—who is later joined by her parents. The Irish children are a lively lot, especially little Brian who carries a leprechaun in a bag ("I say let him have his leprechaun"). The Kilpatrick Club becomes the Leprechaun Club and Ah Ping is not forgotten: the children raise enough money at a Halloween Party to support her for a year. *And* the lady policeman turns out to be Mrs. Kilpatrick. Though at times the Irish mist-icism is as thick as the brogue, good feeling and funny talk more than compensate.

> A review of "Betsy and Mr. Kilpatrick," in Kirkus Service, *Vol. XXXV, No. 17, September 1, 1967, p. 1047.*

How the children of the town welcome the newcomers, share their toys and bring them into the activities of the school and the community, make a delightful story. All the usual Haywood ingredients—humor, surprises, near-calamities, gaiety and warm relationships—are present in full measure.

> Beatrice M. Adam, in a review of "Betsy and Mr. Kilpatrick," in Library Journal, *Vol. 92, No. 22, December 15, 1967, p. 4612.*

Ever-Ready Eddie   (1968)

May the best man win? Boodles, backed by Eddie, is running against Annie Pat, managed by Sidney, for the class presidency, and Annie Pat's removable false teeth—her 'bridth"—are hard to beat. So's her campaign, even after heart-shaped cookies ("Vote for Anna Patricia Wallace! You know she has a heart for you!") are banned as bribery. Eddie matches *SMILE* (showing teeth) buttons with bigger buttons saying *BE WARY, Vote for B. Cary,* and generally tries to bolster Boodles but his candidate plays dirty—steals ideas from a tape of Annie Pat's speech—and Eddie has to decide whom to vote for. Fast, funny politicking, ethics-coded and election-timed.

> A review of "Ever-Ready Eddie," in Kirkus Service, *Vol. XXXVI, No. 19, October 1, 1968, p. 1114.*

Miss Haywood's flair for writing simple, realistic stories with casual dialogue, amusing mishaps, and the small achievements of ordinary boys and girls is again demonstrated in another story about Eddie Wilson. Eddie's two best friends are competing for the office of class president, and he maintains a fine balance between acting as campaign manager for Boodles and keeping the friendship of Annie Pat. Some of the action seems irrelevant, but this is what gives the author's stories the homey quality that has made them so popular.

> Zena Sutherland, in a review of "Ever-Ready Eddie," in Bulletin of the Center for Children's Books, *Vol. 22, No. 7, March, 1969, p. 111.*

Taffy and Melissa Molasses   (1969)

"Nufin' ever happens," frets post-kindergartener Taffy, surveying the quiet farm at the start of summer, and his observation is accurate even if his pronunciation isn't: this is one of the least substantial of Mrs. Haywood's many stories. Neither Taffy nor slightly older sister Melissa nor their friend Jonathan has any individuality, and most of the happenings are either disengaged (like the unexpected, unattended birth of a pony), elaborately inconsequential (a raw egg getting in with a batch of hard-boiled eggs, the school bus driver having a twin), or simply unlikely (a screen door hooking itself, a pony unhooking another). Moreover, there's virtually no continuity besides healthy appetites and Taffy's baby talk. Starchy.

A review of "Taffy and Melissa Molasses," in Kirkus Reviews, *Vol. XXXVII, No. 13, July 1, 1969, p. 673.*

The style of country living is portrayed well enough for children with town or city backgrounds to settle into the mood of the story easily. As usual, Miss Haywood has faithfully captured the spirit of youngsters in her characters' conversation, humor and behavior; and her writing is so well suited to the reading level of her audience.

Linda L. Clark, in a review of "Taffy and Melissa Molasses," in School Library Journal, *Vol. 16, No. 2, January, 1970, p. 233.*

Merry Christmas from Betsy   (1970)

[Eight] holiday episodes from earlier Betsy books plus two new ones, forming an intelligible, generally non-repetitive sequence centering on little sister Star. Today adults may demur at, and children challenge, her providential arrival on Christmas Eve (at home, unattended by a doctor), just the present Betsy wanted from Santa; and anyone who's gone through the formalities of entering kindergarten might well boggle at Star's getting her Christmas wish the very day she turns five. But the innocence that's always been bliss for Betsy and her following has its charms— Father's story of Little Claus and the godmother whose daily present no matter how large or how small always fit in the sock (Betsy: "Oh, I know. They were stretch socks"); the birds' Christmas tree festooned with popcorn and apple parings and especially peanut butter in orange skins that Father calls the first Garbage tree. Presentable certainly, with new illustrations that particularly enhance Lillybell, and no more specious than what has cheered little girls right along.

A review of "Merry Christmas from Betsy," in Kirkus Reviews, *Vol. XXXVIII, No. 15, August 1, 1970, p. 799.*

As always, the simplicity and realism of Miss Haywood's writing are appealing. The stories have a homely humor, and the charm of the Christmas motif adds to the attraction of the book, which, particularly because of the discrete episodes, is admirably suited to reading aloud to younger children.

Zena Sutherland, in a review of "Merry Christmas from Betsy," in Bulletin of the Center for Children's Books, *Vol. 24, No. 3, November, 1970, p. 43.*

Eddie's Happenings   (1971)

When Eddie finds a calendar of celebrations, listing everything from Granddad's Day to National Pancake Month, life becomes one special occasion after another. First there's Bean Soup Day in the school cafeteria; later there's Almost Christmas Eve, when Eddie wins a department store prize and must line up for Santa with the toddlers to collect it. Spanning the holiday episodes is the problem of the new boy. Tewfik Tully (called Toothpick or Tookey) and his "upside down imagination." Tookey tells tales of glory about himself and his family until he is caught in a whopper, but finally gets his imagination right-

side-up and creates the original skit that wins his class the George Washington's Birthday prize. It's easy to identify with Eddie and sympathize with Tookey, and easier still to breeze through the nimble banter, as usual, Miss Haywood makes a lively story out of everyday *Happenings.*

A review of "Eddie's Happenings," in Kirkus Reviews, *Vol. XXXIX, No. 16, August 15, 1971, p. 874.*

Twenty-four years after the publication of **Little Eddie,** the hero hasn't changed a bit: he's still seven-years-old, says " 'Yepper,' " collects junk, minds his mother, and occupies the same very secure, middle-class world. . . . The format offers the usual large, easy-to-read type and the author's full-page pen-and-ink sketches, but Eddie's innocuous adventures are only mildly amusing.

Cherie Zarookian, in a review of "Eddie's Happenings," in School Library Journal, *Vol. 18, No. 20, November, 1971, p. 3892.*

A Christmas Fantasy   (1972)

A Christmas Fantasy does not involve a cool Claus; it's the story of how a ". . . little boy whose name was Claus" grows up to be called Santa Claus. The babe, having "dropped down the chimney" complete with red socks and jingle bells around his diaper, lives with his godmother in a house with gingerbread trim. She doesn't know where he came from but is so pleased with such a jolly godson that she decides to put a present in his red socks every night of the year. When Claus starts school, he is sad to learn that not everyone gets presents so often. Therefore, he decides to give away some of his own to "all the good children." And to make sure that everyone gets what he/she wants, he asks them to write him notes. "Soon everyone called Claus, Good Claus." Finally, Claus tells his godmother that when he grows up he wants " 'to be in the present business.' " He'll deliver his goodies once a year on Christmas Eve. To get him started, godmother gives him a sleigh and eight reindeer. "And because he was never cross, but always loving and kind, he lives forever and all the boys and girls love him. They call him SANTA CLAUS."

This is indeed a whimsical idea, but even as fantasy it's unbelievable, sentimental and precious. And, children will have no better idea of why Santa Claus is called that after reading it. (p. 127)

Alice Miller Bregman, in a review of "A Christmas Fantasy," in School Library Journal, *Vol. 19, No. 2, October, 1972, pp. 125-28.*

The sickliness of the writing in this book is mitigated by the frivolity and delicacy of its illustrations. The tale is American in origin and possesses that unhappy 'tweeness' characteristic of so much transatlantic writing for the youngest child.

The story is about the childhood of Santa Claus but, whereas another aspect of the private life of this traditional figure was recounted by Raymond Briggs with vigour and originality, here the style is too coy and contrived to merit much discussion.

Gabrielle Maunder, in a review of "A Christ-

mas Fantasy," in Children's Book Review, *Vol. IV, No. 1, Spring, 1974, p. 11.*

Away Went the Balloons (1973)

The first graders at Blue Bell school are excited about their annual Balloon Day, when the pupils send off gas-filled balloons carrying tags with their names and the request that finders send back messages. Haywood follows seven of the balloons into the lives of an orphan in the hospital, a lonely old lady, two young dog owners at a pet show, etc.—then returns to the waiting first graders as the notes start coming in. Finally one little girl, Lynette, is reunited with her own balloon when the class goes to visit the local art museum. Balloon Day is an institution that readers will probably want to inaugurate at their own schools, and as usual the small thoughts and everyday actions of Haywood's children are instantly recognizable. The far-flung balloons allow for a nice variety of characters and settings, and the pictures indicate some racial variety among the children as well. (pp. 114-15)

> *A review of "Away Went the Balloons," in* Kirkus Reviews, *Vol. XLI, No. 3, February 1, 1973, pp. 114-15.*

"C" Is for Cupcake (1974)

Haywood has cranked out another easy-to-read book that is bland and unrealistic. . . . Throughout all of [the] carefree activities, there's no mention of responsibility and no subtle warning of the dangers of indiscriminate breeding of animals. In short, this overly long, inaccurate, and misleading portrayal of school life is one Haywood formula that falls flat.

> *Cherie Zarookian, in a review of "C Is for Cupcake," in* School Library Journal, *Vol. 20, No. 9, May, 1974, p. 47.*

To pick up **C is for Cupcake** is to walk into the first-grade classroom of a Mrs. Wilkins, and gradually to get to know the whole class through a series of adventures spanning one school year.

Christie is the sturdy little girl who owns Cupcake, a white rabbit who comes to live in the classroom. Cupcake meets Cinnamon Bun (a Belgian rabbit) and has babies that utterly and hilariously disrupt a class breakfast for fathers. Chuckie owns Cinnamon Bun, an outsize appetite, and a heart of gold. Bruce's father gives the class an old oven that enables it to win the school cookie contest . . . and so on.

Carolyn Haywood's 35th book is written simply, in short, easy sentences. Her loving eye for dialogue and detail will fascinate the 6-10 set.

If the endless "he said" and "she said" of the conversations is somewhat repetitious for a parent reading out loud, our own six-year-old (and four-year-old) hung on every word. Miss Haywood is a professional. Her drawings are also winsome, though younger children might wish for more of them.

> *David K. Willis, "A Mini-Shelf of Happy Fan-*

tasies," in The Christian Science Monitor, *May 1, 1974, p. F3.*

As always, Carolyn Haywood writes about small events that have the appeal of the familiar; the style is simple, the print large and well-spaced, and each chapter is a separate episode, so that the book is easy for independent readers in the primary grades and also can be used for installment reading. The chapters are linked by the story of Cupcake, a pet rabbit that is brought to school and kept there; the depiction of the first grade classroom, especially of the teacher, should make the prospect of school attendance enticing to preschool children.

> *Zena Sutherland, in a review of " 'C' Is for Cupcake," in* Bulletin of the Center for Children's Books, *Vol. 27, No. 11, July-August, 1974, p. 178.*

Eddie's Valuable Property (1975)

Eddie's valuable property is his junk collection which Dad says he can't take along when the family moves 150 miles away. But some of the stuff turns out to be really valuable antique toys, and then Eddie isn't even moved into the new house before he discovers a cigar store Indian (and a new friend) in the barn. Eddie and Jimmy take the Indian for show-and-tell on Eddie's first day at the new school, and the class discovers that "Big Chief Termites-in-the-Tummy" would be a suitable name for it. Besides friends (who flock around) and curios, Eddie also collects dogs—purportedly to fill his going-away-gift dog house though all of them end up sleeping in his room. Naming his hairy sheepdog Hippy doesn't really counteract the datedness of Eddie's exclamations ("swell! . . . Hot dickity!"), and reading *Ramona the Brave* . . . in the same sitting makes Haywood's limitations all the more evident; but Eddie's blander sort of innocence is always good for a few smiles from the age group that enjoys, for example, the verbal absurdities of Eddie's moving into "an old new house" with his "young old English sheep dog."

> *A review of "Eddie's Valuable Property," in* Kirkus Reviews, *Vol. XLIII, No. 6, March 15, 1975, p. 307.*

Readers may well get annoyed at how easily and nobly Eddie adjusts to the trauma of a family move. The lesson is too obvious—you don't lose friends when you move, you just "get a new bunch"—and the hero is too perfect, breaking up cliques in his new school and transforming the class introvert. The dialogue is often dull and dated (not many children still say "nifty"), and the title is misleading since it is central only to the first of the serial-type chapters. Haywood focuses on a real problem but places it in an unrealistic, things-always-work-out-for-the-best context. (pp. 55-6)

> *Nancy C. Bennett, in a review of "Eddie's Valuable Property," in* School Library Journal, *Vol. 21, No. 9, May, 1975, pp. 55-6.*

Like other Haywood books, this is realistic in reflecting children at school and play; there are never serious problems: life is always sunny, and the emphasis is on small events. But they are events that may loom large to children, the concerns are familiar ones, and the style is unassuming and easy to read.

> *Zena Sutherland, in a review of "Eddie's Valuable Property," in* Bulletin of the Center for Children's Books, *Vol. 29, No. 2, October, 1975, p. 27.*

A Valentine Fantasy (1976)

In the tradition of her similarly spurious **Christmas Fantasy,** Haywood fashions a holiday myth to suit the season's lace and ribbons. Her Valentine is a boy who excels with the bow and arrow but only shoots targets as the birds are his friends. In time the king imprisons Valentine for refusing to bring him the golden heart of a wonderful bluebird, but the bird saves him by getting Valentine's uncle to make a copy from his golden arrow. From bird to boy to king to neighboring princess, who then consents to be queen—the golden heart becomes the prototype of all those exchanged by lovers to this day. The best we can say for the whole gratuitous production is that the [Glenys and Victor] Ambrus' razzle-dazzle, mock medieval pictures never take a word of it seriously.

> *A review of "A Valentine Fantasy," in* Kirkus Reviews, *Vol. XLIV, No. 6, March 15, 1976, p. 316.*

The author of the Betsy books here tells the story of St. Valentine. . . . How the bluebird saves Valentine from imprisonment in the king's dungeon and how the king woos and wins his fair princess without killing the bird make for a gentle but slight story. Not even the lush and imaginative splendor of the full-color wash illustrations can mask the dullness of this little tale. (pp. 60-1)

> *Margaret Maxwell, in a review of "A Valentine Fantasy," in* School Library Journal, *Vol. 22, No. 8, April, 1976, pp. 60-1.*

Betsy's Play School (1977)

Betsy's good idea—to earn money by running a summer play group for preschoolers—turns limp if not quite null in the execution. Put six tots together, mix in a few assorted pets—including an imaginary friend's imaginary dog—and some funny mixups are bound to occur. A real Thumpy who piddles is more trouble, for instance, than a make-believe Tinkie who, insists friendless Rodney, doesn't ("You can't say what Tinkie does. I say. Nobody says but me"). Also in the cards is a disaster and a constructive response. But the garden burial of Sammy's beloved chicken Mona—run over by a car—is so mechanical as to demean the occasion (the weak pictures at least show some feeling). More dubious still is the dispatch of Rodney's "Bobo" and "Tinkie" that brings the book to a thudding close. Through contorted circumstances, Rodney wins a real dog, and then he acquires a real, loudmouth friend (to wit: "Yippie, I'm glad I'm real"). A Bobo by another, less clownish name would have been harder to dislodge, we'll warrant. But small children really do have special tastes in peanut butter and jelly, kittens do get into cute scrapes, and—a passing thought—these books still give you a run for your money. (pp. 784-85)

> *A review of "Betsy's Play School," in* Kirkus Reviews, *Vol. XLV, No. 15, August 1, 1977, pp. 784-85.*

Haywood's latest Betsy adventure finds the young heroine providing a summer play school for young neighborhood children. . . . Haywood links her happy-ending episodes with warmth and humor and casts them in a style that's simple and appealing. Shaded line drawings [by illustrator James Griffin] catch the summer fun.

> *Barbara Elleman, in a review of "Betsy's Play School," in* Booklist, *Vol. 74, No. 3, October 1, 1977, p. 295.*

In this latest addition to Haywood's series, Betsy organizes a summer play school for younger children in her suburban neighborhood and must cope with such mini-crises as an expectant mouse in the refrigerator she salvaged for refreshments and runaway dogs at obedience school graduation. Griffin's pen-and-ink sketches include a purposeful sprinkling of multi-ethnic children, but, otherwise, this runs true to tired form. The predicaments are all as mild as their happy endings are predictable, and Betsy is so sweet-tempered that it cloys.

> *Judith S. Kronick, in a review of "Betsy's Play*

From Here's a Penny, *written and illustrated by Carolyn Haywood.*

School," in School Library Journal, *Vol. 24, No. 3, November, 1977, p. 48.*

Eddie's Menagerie (1978)

Two separate series of incidents, flimsily connected, and not one of Eddie's more auspicious appearances altogether. In the book's first and better half, his natural way with animals and refusal to be put down gain him an unpaid (because he's underage) part-time job in crusty, kindly Mr. Cornball's pet shop, where he foils one child shoplifter and suspects poor classmate Roland of being another—but resourcefully replaces the presumed-stolen goods rather than let on. The bridge to part two is a red, white, and blue hat just like Mr. Cornball's that he buys (for $5) at the County Fair from—it just happens—booth-keeper Mrs. Cornball. College baseball star Sandy Lowicki admires it at the annual Spring Fair and soon everyone in the fifth grade (except unfortunate Roland) is sporting one and they're Sandy Lowicki hats—admission, eventually, to a Sandy Lowicki ball game (Mr. C. lends Roland his). Finally, tacked on, there's a real ($200) horse for Eddie, whose early yearning we took for a true-to-life pipedream. Together, Eddie's overstocked larder and Roland's bare cupboard make this surplus property, as we see it, for kids. (pp. 950-51)

> *A review of "Eddie's Menagerie," in* Kirkus Reviews, *Vol. XLVI, No. 17, September 1, 1978, pp. 950-51.*

Eddie Wilson is a very uncomplicated character. He is consistently cheerful and never naughty. He is much too good to be believed, and his adventures are a bit silly. But, Eddie continues to be popular with middle graders. In this latest addition to Haywood's long running series, Eddie's harmless escapades (he becomes friendly with a pet shop owner, acquires a number of pets, and meets the local baseball hero) provide some small drama. The light-hearted fun and large print combine to make a pleasing easy-to-read story.

> *Anne M. Hanst, in a review of "Eddie's Menagerie," in* School Library Journal, *Vol. 25, No. 2, October, 1978, p. 132.*

The King's Monster (1980)

Light of logic, this fantasy . . . should appeal to primary graders. **The King's Monster** is a local byword and threat to bad children and, though none has ever seen it, all have theories about it. When the motherless heroine receives suitors, her monarch father stipulates that any candidate must wrestle the creature. All flee except the young prince the princess favors, and together ("whither thou goest I will go") they brave the monster's dungeon. But they find only a mouse—and the subjects now tell one another "I told you so." The story is mild, but . . . even small children enjoy monsters that don't exist.

> *Ruth M. McConnell, in a review of "The King's Monster," in* School Library Journal, *Vol. 26, No. 9, May, 1980, p. 58.*

An original fairy tale becomes an allegory about the fears perpetuated by people's imaginations. . . . The lesson the

story carries is all too evident at times, detracting from the rather light and whimsical nature of the storytelling. But on the whole the book provides a satisfying tale. . . .

> *Karen M. Klockner, in a review of "The King's Monster," in* The Horn Book Magazine, *Vol. LVI, No. 3, June, 1980, p. 287.*

[The] story is adequately told although the vocabulary seems sophisticated for the picture book audience for whom this original tale in the fairy tale tradition is told: "It was a day of revels and much buffoonery," or, "He was always the victor, always unseating his opponent." Haywood's hints that the monster is imaginary are plentiful, and therefore the discovery of the empty dungeon seems rather anticlimatic.

> *Zena Sutherland, in a review of "The King's Monster," in* Bulletin of the Center for Children's Books, *Vol. 34, No. 1, September, 1980, p. 11.*

Halloween Treats (1981)

A collection of nine short stories with Halloween at their heart. The characters have appeared in other Haywood writings, and in fact half of the tales have been published in earlier books. This might sow some confusion for uninitiated Haywood readers, who meet Eddie Wilson, for example, on more than one Halloween. Haywood's knack for capturing childlike behavior remains firm, and her story lines are down-to-earth, yet tight enough to keep pages turning. A sure-fire addition to Halloween collections, especially since fans probably won't mind the repeat performances entertwined with new material.

> *Denise M. Wilms, in a review of "Halloween Treats," in* Booklist, *Vol. 78, No. 2, September 15, 1981, p. 106.*

Twin genes proliferate (three pair turn up here) in this apple-pie neighborhood where the houses are described as standing "cheek to cheek" and Eddie's main concern, as the pennies-for-UNICEF collection draws near, is expressed, "Oh, Mom! I hope I have enough to be 'Halloween Boy of the Year.' " (He does, as one rare 1909 penny turns out to be worth five hundred dollars.) Haywood's stories are calculated to curl susceptible children's toes with delight in cute tricks and coincidences, and she will no doubt succeed—but the after-effects of too many Halloween sweets aren't all in the tummy. (pp. 1159-60)

> *A review of "Halloween Treats," in* Kirkus Reviews, *Vol. XLIX, No. 18, September 15, 1981, pp. 1159-60.*

The writing is typical Haywood: bland style, slightly stilted dialogue, characters drawn with more consistency than depth, and incidents that have a modest amount of suspense or action followed by a placidly happy ending. The everyday life level, the familiarity of the experiences, and the recurrent appearances of characters like Eddie and Anna Patricia have made Haywood's books popular for years; presumably this will, with its focus on a holiday important to children, be similarly popular.

> *Zena Sutherland, in a review of "Halloween Treats," in* Bulletin of the Center for Chil-

dren's Books, *Vol. 35, No. 2, October, 1981, p. 30.*

Santa Claus Forever! (1983)

The cheerful ebullience of [illustrators Glenys and Victor Ambrus'] paintings, the humor and sentiment of pictures and story, and the happy solution to a problem should make this Christmas tale a great favorite with the read-aloud audience. After all his hard work fulfilling last-minute requests in children's letters, Santa Claus has a grueling distribution experience: he's hit by a loose brick in one chimney, has his pants singed in another, has a runner bent on the sleigh, etc. When he announces that he plans to retire, a man shows up in Santa Claus dress and announces he's the (self-elected) replacement: after hearing the man's ideas on how he'd run the operation, Santa Claus decides that he'll forget retirement, much to the joy of children all over the world.

> *Zena Sutherland, in a review of "Santa Claus Forever!" in* Bulletin of the Center for Children's Books, *Vol. 37, No. 2, October, 1983, p. 29.*

The story is not imaginatively presented or resolved and Santa seems simply petulant and arbitrary in his problems and decisions. Raymond Brigg's *Father Christmas* (Coward, 1973) remains the funniest and best treatment of a non-stereotypical Santa and his problems.

> *Jean Hammond Zimmerman, in a review of "Santa Claus Forever!" in* School Library Journal, *Vol. 30, No. 2, October, 1983, p. 176.*

Make A Joyful Noise! (1984)

Haywood offers a personal selection of Bible verses. Short homilies or reminiscences introduce each of the 12 thematic sections (covering such concepts as love, help, fear and joy). Verses have been chosen from both testaments; nearly half are from the Psalms; all are King James Version, slightly modified. [Illustrator Lane] Yerkes' cross-hatched pen-and-ink illustrations and decorations engagingly help unify the smorgasbord text. *Make a Joyful Noise!* is unique in its emphasis on Biblical quotations clustered around devotional thoughts. Tasha Tudor's *Lord is My Shepherd* (Philomel, 1980) and Helen Sewell's *A First Bible* (Oxford, 1934; o.p.) are other presentations of Scripture, each accompanied by outstanding illustrations.

> *Katharine Bruner, in a review of "Make a Joyful Noise!" in* School Library Journal, *Vol. 31, No. 1, September, 1984, p. 118.*

"Words from the Bible help us to see beauty in everything and light our way through the year," says Haywood in an introduction to her collection of Bible verses for children. The verses are grouped into 12 topical categories, such as love and friendship, nature, praise, and consolation. The lightly paraphrased selections come from both the Old and New Testaments. . . . Many verses are comfortably familiar, the sources of often-heard phrases that young readers are likely to recognize. Certain passages lose subtle shades of meaning when taken out of context, but each

of Haywood's choices reflects her keen understanding of children and their concerns. Though a table of contents is provided, the book lacks an index, and its primary use would seem to be as a personal resource for children who already know the Bible as well as those who may be reading its words for the first time.

> *Karen Stang Hanley, in a review of "Make a Joyful Noise!" in* Booklist, *Vol. 81, No. 4, October 15, 1984, p. 307.*

Summer Fun (1986)

Each chapter in this collection is a separate entity, although there are some instances of reiteration. Each tells of some mild summer adventure: a watermelon contest, a camping story, a near-accident at the beach, et cetera. There are some new characters, but many indestructible Haywood protagonists are here: Betsy, Eddie, and Annie Pat, for example. This is all in Haywood's usual style, identifiable but not distinctive in its simplicity and blandness; the tone is low-keyed, the activities are ones most children share, and the appeal lies primarily in that familiarity and the direct, easy-to-read writing. (pp. 128-29)

> *A review of "Summer Fun," in* Bulletin of the Center for Children's Books, *Vol. 39, No. 7, March, 1986, pp. 128-29.*

Animals, including a hermit crab and a porcupine, add a bit of zest to some of the otherwise bland adventures. The writing style and dialogue are also bland, and endings are predictable. A mild sense of humor enlivens the book. The familiar middle-class children that so many young readers have come to know and love since Haywood's first book (*B Is for Betsy*) was published almost 50 years ago, have changed little, if at all, over the years. These gentle stories, although supposedly contemporary, seem to take place in a more settled time than today. The book is sure to be read with enjoyment by most transitional readers in the early grades, but it may disappoint those who already know that life is not so golden.

> *Virginia Golodetz, in a review of "Summer Fun," in* School Library Journal, *Vol. 32, No. 9, May, 1986, p. 75.*

How the Reindeer Saved Santa (1986)

Haywood, well-loved by generations of children, has a knack for writing comfortably funny stories about subjects near and dear to them, in this case, Santa Claus.

Looking over his geriatric reindeer and rusting old sleigh, Santa doesn't want to be an old fogey. He orders a helicopter, brightly painted with Christmas decorations, puts the reindeer out to pasture, and sends the sleigh to the children's museum. Santa takes off in a merry mood, but the slick helicopter slides off a steep rooftop; then he loses the key in the snow. Panic overcomes him, but the faithful reindeer come to his rescue and, of course, all the toys are delivered on time.

The plot is familiar, the outcome predictable, but that will neither dull the glow nor diminish the suspense.

A review of "How the Reindeer Saved Santa," in Kirkus Reviews, *Vol. LIV, No. 14, July 15, 1986, p. 1118.*

With the ever-increasing number of beautiful Christmas books for children, a new offering has to be very special to be chosen from the treasures already available. Unfortunately, this latest Carolyn Haywood is not special. The story is pedestrian, and the premise of Santa using an alternative to his sleigh (in this case, a helicopter) has been overdone. We can do without the references to the reindeers' interest in TV commercials.

> *Beverly Woods, in a review of "How the Reindeer Saved Santa," in* Children's Book Review Service, *Vol. 15, No. 2, October, 1986, p. 13.*

Merry Christmas from Eddie   (1986)

Haywood offers nine stories, five old favorites and four new ones, about seven-year-old Eddie Wilson. The tales are simple fare—Eddie has a special picture taken with a snow-covered stuffed Santa; in another, he helps fix some toys for needy children. Some of the stories are slight, but for young readers who like Haywood, or for those wanting an uncomplicated chapter book, this should fill the bill.

> *Ilene Cooper, in a review of "Merry Christmas from Eddie," in* Booklist, *Vol. 83, No. 2, September 15, 1986, p. 132.*

Not every Christmas present is what it seems. Done up in new trappings are five stories taken from earlier Haywood books (slightly adapted and updated), mixed with four new stories, and tied together with the theme of Christmas. All of the stories revolve around Eddie Wilson. Since the older stories are longer, the new sections make up approximately only one third of the text. The older stories in their original context have a development and cohesiveness that is lacking in this pieced-together product. A disappointing package.

> *Judith Gloyer, in a review of "Merry Christmas from Eddie," in* School Library Journal, *Vol. 33, No. 2, October, 1986, p. 112.*

Hello, Star   (1987)

Star, a Christmas baby, was named by her sister, Betsy, in Haywood's **Betsy's Little Star.** While Betsy is away at camp this summer (by now, Betsy is about 11 years old), 5-year-old Star stays with her grandparents, Grammy and Grampy. Her summer is filled with quiet daily adventures on the farm, many with her six-year-old cousin, Jerri. For breakfast each morning, Star collects an egg from the hen house. Jerri, who is like a big brother to Star, takes her hand to cross the street to see the beautiful swans. The "swannies" nest, the children and Grampy save a wayward egg, and they all wait for a cygnet to hatch. Other experiences include watching a friendly raccoon family and playing with Jerri's pet lamb. Characteristic of the author, Star's adventures in this new book are quiet, rather child-like, dear, idealized, comfortable, and quaint. Adults should be aware that the approach to animals, particularly the raccoons, may require a bit more clarification and caution. **Hello, Star** is particularly appropriate for young children who read well independently.

> *Maria B. Salvadore, in a review of "Hello, Star," in* School Library Journal, *Vol. 34, No. 2, October, 1987, p. 112.*

Haywood's characters never grow old, a testimony to her own zest for living and evidenced by her ability to capture the spirit of childhood. . . . Throughout their delightful summer Star and Jerri gain appreciation for the ways of nature. [Illustrator Julie] Durrell's portrayal of the duo on the dust jacket seems clumsy and awkward, though true Haywood fans will not be deterred.

> *Phillis Nelson, in a review of "Hello, Star," in* Booklist, *Vol. 84, No. 4, October 15, 1987, p. 395.*

This coy, cute, "new" adventure creaks. Star discovers brown eggs have yellow yokes just like white eggs; falls in love with the "swannies" that swim in the pond and wants them for pets; plays dress-up with cousin Jerri's pet lamb, Beauty, calling her "Bootie." "I know," said Star. "You call her 'Bootie' because she is bootiful!" She laughs when the "naughty little raccoons" get into the kitchen and make a mess in the flour. Unfortunately, the cover illustration by Durrell does nothing to breathe life into these cardboard children.

> *A review of "Hello, Star," in* Kirkus Reviews, *Vol. LV, No. 20, October 15, 1987, p. 1516.*

Mary Ann Hoberman

1930-

American poet and author of picture books.

Regarded as an observant and ingenious writer of poetry characterized by its freshness, creative wordplay, and relevance to the world of young children, Hoberman offers verse to preschoolers and primary grade readers which focuses on informational topics and the experiences and emotions of childhood. Her collections of verse address such subjects as animals, both familiar and unfamiliar, and their habits; insects; apparel such as clothing and shoes; and forms of transportation such as a tricycle and water skis in a style noted for blending playful humor with unobtrusive, accurate facts. Designing her verse to entertain children while introducing them to the delights of language, Hoberman includes a variety of poetic forms in her collections, such as alliteration, free verse, and the tongue twister; for example, in *A House Is a House for Me* (1978), she uses alternating lines of anapestic tetrameter with internal rhymes and rhymes at the end of lines to describe the homes of animals, humans, and objects. Several of Hoberman's works reflect her use of unusual typography to convey her images; in *A Book of Little Beasts* (1973), for example, her poem about a mole stretches across four pages to represent the length of the trail being burrowed by its subject. In addition, her works demonstrate Hoberman's distinctive approach to literary styles: in her work on transportation, *How Do I Go?* (1958), she combines verse with lively prose in a question and answer format. Hoberman is also the creator of several other works, including a counting book in which a young boy looks for his lost cat, an alphabet book in verse which provides a rhyme for each letter, and picture books, some of which are in prose. Her first four works were illustrated by her husband, Norman Hoberman. *A House Is a House for Me* won the American Book Award for picture book paperback in 1983.

(See also *Something about the Author,* Vol. 5 and *Contemporary Authors,* Vols. 41-44, rev. ed.)

GENERAL COMMENTARY

Allen Raymond

Together with four of her longtime women friends, [Mary Ann Hoberman] has formed an organization called "Women's Voices" which gives dramatic readings throughout southern Connecticut. Their program, presented through poetry written by women, discussed childhood, mother and child, private lives, public lives (war, for instance) and concludes with poems which help women understand each other. The program's content spans four centuries, the theme built around women speaking to each other across space and across time. It is abundantly evident Mary Ann Hoberman brings a dramatic talent and flair to the group.

One could speculate that no matter how serious the cause,

Mary Ann Hoberman could write a rollicking poem to alleviate the tension while proving her point. Her books of poetry, however, are not written to prove a point. "These poems are fun," she says. "There is no way I want them made into chores or into something heavier than what they are!"

Continuing, she says, "They were written out of joy and fun and my delight at word play. I resent it when teachers make them heavy, have the children look for some special meaning in the poems."

If any of her poems have a special meaning, and some certainly do, that meaning is not part of a crusade, nor is the meaning hard to find. Probably one of her best-known poems, about her brother, couldn't be clearer:

> Brother
>   I had a little brother
> And I brought him to my mother
> And I said I want another
>   Little brother for a change.
>
> But she said don't be a bother
>   So I took him to my father
> And I said this little bother
>   Of a brother's very strange.

But he said one little brother
Is exactly like another
And every little brother
Misbehaves a bit he said.

So I took the little bother
From my mother and my father
And I put the little bother
Of a brother back to bed.

"Was that poem about your real brother?" we asked.

"It is precisely my brother. Precisely! I didn't have to write it," she said. "It had been rattling around in my head for years, and it wrote itself. I love my brother now, we get along perfectly. I'm not sure I loved him then!"

Mary Ann Hoberman has written 14 books of poetry for children. It began with **All My Shoes Come In Two's.** Her latest, **The Cozy Book,** was published a little over two years ago. She has been an instructor on writing for children, she has lectured on children's literature, and she has been a poetry consultant and Poet-in-the-Schools. (pp. 23-4)

Mary Ann likes poetry that rhymes and has rhythm. "Children love it," she says, "Adult poetry tossed out rhyme and regular rhythm; that's old hat now. Limericks, light verse—no one does that anymore. If I want to write poetry that way, writing for children is the last bastion."

"You can see why I think Edward Lear is just one of the greatest poets who ever lived," she said with a wide smile. "Oh, yes, and Lewis Carroll, too!' "

She stresses that word play is so important to children, that they should be encouraged to play with words, to experiment with words. She hopes teachers will help children to be aware of language," she comments. "I want them to love their language."

Finally: "I encourage children to memorize poetry. I wish teachers would do that, too. Poetry is so enriching. How I wish I had learned—memorized—Shakespeare as a child!" (p. 24)

> *Allen Raymond, "Mary Ann Hoberman: Fun-loving Poet, Student of Literature . . . ," in* Early Years, *Vol. 15, No. 5, January, 1985, pp. 23-4.*

All My Shoes Comes in Twos (with Norman Hoberman, 1957)

As a picture book of verse about shoes (which children have been known to love enough to take to bed with them) this has a fine central idea but falls short of the mark in expression. Though there are some laughable spots—several pictures of father, identical except for the sports shoes, a youngster delighted with his sly sneakers etc.—the rhymes are a little too grammatically correct and the pictures (by Norman Hoberman) sometimes fail through distortion in their attempt to express an idea. Weak stitching.

> *A review of "All My Shoes Come in Twos," in* Virginia Kirkus' Service, *Vol. XXV, No. 2, January 15, 1957, p. 35.*

Boy or girl, you'll find your
      shoes
Inside this book and all in twos.

So begins a unique treatment of a subject fascinating to the small child to whom all things in his new world are worth exploring. In a happy combination of light verse and humorous, colorful pictures are described all types of footwear: sneakers, ballet shoes, cowboy boots, everything indeed, from "slippers with zippers to boots big and square." In delightful rhythm we are told how shoes are made; how they are cared for, of the different sounds they can make and of the pleasures of a visit to the shoe store.

The value of the book may be slight to a child reading it to himself, but its reading-aloud and group-play possibilities are unlimited. It should be the source of many pleasant experiences between the child and any parent or teacher who can still appreciate the author's charming last couplet:

But no matter what I wear,
It's most fun when my feet
      are bare.

> *C. Elta Van Norman "Slippers with Zippers," in* The New York Times Book Review, *May 26, 1957, p. 26.*

The rhymed text is quite uneven, with some awkward spots and an occasionally nice bit of rhythm. The illustrations are rather pleasing, but fail almost completely to emphasize the shoes that are described in the text. In fact, it is frequently difficult to find the shoes, much less distinguish between different kinds.

> *A review of "All My Shoes Come in Twos," in* Bulletin of the Children's Book Center, *Vol. X, No. 11, July-August, 1957, p. 135.*

How Do I Go? (with Norman Hoberman, 1958)

How do I go? Well, answer the authors, that depends on where you go: An airplane for going up in the air, not a bird or a crane; for going round and round, a merry-go-round is nice, for going up, an elevator; try a parachute for coming down; bridges to go across; and steamships for crossing oceans. In free drawings [by Norman Hoberman], suggestive of a rather sophisticated child's art work, and a casually rhymed text, the beginning reader is introduced to a variety of places to go and ways to get there. A sort of educational whoop-de-whoop, **How Do I Go?** adds zest to a child's early reading experience.

> *A review of "How Do I Go?" in* Virginia Kirkus' Service, *Vol. XXVI, No. 13, July 1, 1958, p. 452.*

How to get from here to there is a complex and fascinating subject in this day and age, what with atomic submarines, sputniks and such. The tricycle set will be grateful to Mary Ann and Norman Hoberman, author and illustrator of last year's delightful **All My Shoes Come in Twos,** for skillfully simplifying the vast field of transportation in this crisp new picture book. In a combination of verse and rhythmic prose the text moves along in a conversational way from the familiar tricycle to the less familiar airplane, steamship and train, winding up with more unusual forms of getting around—parachutes and water-skis, for instance.

This sounds like quite a book-full for the very young, but the material is presented with such careful selectivity, using a question and answer technique which couples nonsense with grave logic, that it is all very clear and entertaining. The bright pictures, bold, broad and childlike in feeling, make it an effective and well-designed book. And the ending, which returns to the everyday limits of a child's world, is just right.

> *Alice Low "Getting Around," in* The New York Times Book Review, *September 28, 1958, p. 48.*

Sharing these dazzling pages with a reliable 4-6 guide it is easy to see how thrilling the world is and how exciting to have so many different ways to go. With bold, sweeping strokes and a line or two of big rhyming print, the authors show how fine it is to cross the deep blue ocean not "in a pail" or "on top of a whale" but to "take the trip / In a big steamship," or to go up in the air by plane—not crane. . . . And there on the very last page of this exuberant story it is good to be reminded of the little red tricycle for "staying just about where you are."

> *Pamela Marsh, "A Long-Haired Elephant, Alligator Children, and a Touch of Poetry," in* The Christian Science Monitor, *November 6, 1958, p. 15.*

Hello and Good-by (1959)

This sheaf of very young verses by Mary Ann Hoberman, each accompanied by an amusing black and white sketch by Norman Hoberman, is a truly childlike and charming small book. The fancies are not forced, the rhymes are gay, smooth and natural, their simplicity, like that of all good light verse, the result of the author's musical ear and painstaking care. Some show the natural rhythm of a little child's speech, the rhyme seeming (but only seeming) to be unconscious; "look! look! out on the grass, a bumblebee on some sassafras!" or "I had a little brother / And I brought him to my mother / And I said I want another / Little brother for a change." Others are pure nonsense, the King of Umpalazzo and the little llama who said "O llamally mama I need a pajama," for instance; while still others amusingly offer some mind-stretching ideas, like "How far, how far, how far is today when tomorrow has come and it's yesterday?" or how much difference is there between "a snail on the tail of a whale" and "the tail with no snail at all?" We think these will be enjoyed for many a day.

> *Margaret Sherwood Libby, in a review of "Hello and Good-by," in* New York Herald Tribune Book Review, *November 1, 1959, p. 2.*

One obvious way of judging poems for children is to try them out on some real live children. In our household last weekend we had, with two visiting cousins, a juvenile audience of six, aged 1 to 16, with the usual varieties of sex, temperament and literacy. Once more we came to a familiar realization: that for the 5-to-8-year-old crowd, poetry can be a smash hit. . . . "I'm a tiger / Striped with fur

/ Don't come near / Or I might Grr"—this little passage, from Mary Ann Hoberman's *Hello and Good-by,* was endlessly and delightedly chanted by the younger children last weekend, but their older siblings, and their parents, came to feel finally that it could be taken or left alone. Mrs. Hoberman's themes and vocabulary are so carefully pruned and simplified that a second-grader can easily manage to read her verses by himself, memorize them and enjoy them. This is a real achievement, one of whose happy consequences is that the second-grader can be persuaded to go off somewhere and read, leaving the rest of the family alone. (p. 2)

> *Walker Gibson, "Some Like the Tinkle of the Rhyme, Some Can Leave It Alone," in* The New York Times Book Review, *November 1, 1959, pp. 2, 44.*

This is a most engaging little book of verses—amusing childlike concepts and delightful nonsense in good meter—that should be easy to memorize and certainly fun to chant. Reminiscent of Laura E. Richards—high praise indeed—are some of them, particularly one which begins, "I had a little brother / And I brought him to my mother / And I said I want another / Little brother for a change," and the longest poem, **"The Llama Who Had No Pajama."** The line drawings [by Norman Hoberman] are in complete harmony.

> *Ruth Hill Viguers, in a review of "Hello and Good-by," in* The Horn Book Magazine, *Vol. XXXVI, No. 2, April, 1960, p. 140.*

What Jim Knew (1963)

The Hobermans' combined efforts weigh heavy on the world of fantasy which a child builds. Jim's secret things—his tunnelled contact with China, his thoughts of pushing his finger through the sky, etc.—are depicted in stiff, half-alive cartoon-type drawings [by Norman Hoberman]. Jim's hasty jaunt through this imaginative realm will doubtless fail to evoke identification among conscientious castle-builders. The Hobermans worked on *How Do I Go?* which was much more satisfying than this.

> *A review of "What Jim Knew," in* Virginia Kirkus' Service, *Vol. XXXI, No. 11, June 1, 1963, p. 511.*

Not Enough Beds for the Babies (1965)

And there's a shortage of unbridled imagination too. In versified form, a little girl assisted by friends and dolls demonstrates the game of house, with variations on the basic theme. The verses are well written—short, smooth, convincingly childlike phrases flow naturally into rollicking rhymes. According to the jacket copy "this is a book full of playing-house ideas." All this "mother" does for amusement is to blithely imitate the most mundane housekeeping chores. The ideas most children naturally come by are much more fun than that. (pp. 232-33)

> *A review of "Not Enough Beds for the Babies," in* Virginia Kirkus' Service, *Vol. XXXIII, No. 5, March 1, 1965, pp. 232-33.*

A collection of poems intended to stimulate imaginative play; the writing is adequate in style and varied in form, and the selections are loosely united by the theme of playing house. Some selections are dialogue, some are narrative, some are pleasant musing; there is little imagery and little humor, most of the book having the brisk and competent mood of a small child who is busily coping with her pretend-problems.

> *Zena Sutherland, in a review of "Not Enough Beds for the Babies," in* Bulletin of the Center for Children's Books, *Vol. XVIII, No. 8, April, 1965, p. 118.*

A Little Book of Little Beasts   (1973)

Even though Peter Parnall's plants and animals are no longer new, his crisp, clean drawings are far too fresh and witty for Hoberman's "Squiggly wiggly wriggly jiggly ziggly higgly piggly worm," her "Dear little / Mere little / Merry little / Meadow mouse," and her skunk family with pitter patter feet, flitter flutter eyes, flippy floppy tails and ickle pickle smell. For visual variety she sometimes puts the whole poem on one line (Worm) or makes it vertical with just one word per line as in "Birdsong-singsong" which reads "birds / need / bird / seed / bird / seed / feeds / birds / birds / sing / bird / songs / songs / with / bird / words. . . . " Some of the rhymes are tongue twisting fun ("A rabbit / bit / A little bit / An itty bitty / Little bit of beet. / Then bit / By bit / He bit / Because he liked the taste of it . . . ") and some are smartly put together . . . but on balance these eighteen little rhymes are a bit too itsy bitsy.

> *A review of "A Little Book of Little Beasts," in* Kirkus Reviews, *Vol. XLI, No. 5, March 1, 1973, p. 251.*

A Little Book of Little Beasts has fine potential in Peter Parnall's line drawings of black and white with bits of color. But Mary Ann Hoberman's text doesn't always measure up. The language in this collection of poems about small beasts—frogs, ants, mice, chipmunks—is often too ponderous for its intended audience.

But the use of unusual typography conveys some of the images graphically: the poem about Worm slowly s-t-r-e-t-c-h-e-s across two pages. One about Mole has words which move over the lumps and bumps of four pages of his moletrail.

This book will introduce young readers to the different forms poetry may take, and the fantasies pictures can make. Did you ever see a rabbit use a toothpick with his paw?

> *Karen Luke, "Bed Table Books: Some Mysteries of the Night," in* The Christian Science Monitor, *May 2, 1973, p. B2.*

An attractive little (9″ × 6¼″) book which effectively brings a skunk, a mouse, an opossum, a frog, and other small animals and their habits to life in gently humorous rhyming verse: e.g., "Gray squirrel / Small beast, / Storing up a winter's feast, / Hides a hundred nuts at least." The poems about the mole and worm flow across two pages in an undulating line to suggest the burrowing ac-

tion of the former and the squiggling of the latter. The stylized double-page spreads, in ink with touches of earthy browns and greens, strengthen the appeal of this book, which can be used for independent reading or story hour and will serve as a springboard for discussion of animal life.

> *Daisy Kouzel, in a review of "A Little Book of Little Beasts," in* School Library Journal, *Vol. 20, No. 12, September, 1973, p. 112.*

The Looking Book   (1973)

"Of course you know it's not much fun / To lose a cat upon page ONE"—but that's what Ned does anyway to get this exercise in self-conscious artifice on the road. "He started looking on page TWO . . . Not a clue," and the search continues all the way to TWENTY-EIGHT where the cat has been waiting patiently in a box marked THE END. On page FOURTEEN Ned meets a queen, on TWENTY-TWO he's at the zoo, and [Jerry] Joyner's post-*Yellow Submarine* cartoons do their best to provide varied backgrounds for the large fingerprint-textured numbers that are worked into the pictures on every page. But as there is no progression in Ned's wanderings—instead of getting gradually warmer he just stumbles upon the cat in the end—and no relationship among his various false leads, it is tediously clear by page TWENTY-EIGHT that this is all just too clever by HALF. (pp. 809-10)

> *A review of "The Looking Book," in* Kirkus Reviews, *Vol. XLI, No. 15, August 1, 1973, pp. 809-10.*

A novel approach to counting books, this story in verse and cartoons features Ned who's looking for his lost cat, Pistachio. Pistachio disappears on page one and Ned travels through every page—enduring a series of zany trials and meeting exotic people—until he's about to give up. On page 27, sunset comes. "So now poor Ned could hardly see. / 'Pistachio! Where can you be?' . . . 'Pistachio! Why, this is great! / You're here, right here, on 28!' " To add to the nonsense graphically, the cat answers that Ned found him in the end, and Pistachio is shown sticking out of a box labeled "The End." As good a way to learn to count as *Sesame Street* and just as much fun. (pp. 53-4)

> *A review of "The Looking Book," in* Publishers Weekly, *Vol. 204, No. 10, September 3, 1973, pp. 53-4.*

The Raucous Auk: A Menagerie of Poems   (1973)

Perfectly combined, the verses and [Joseph Low's] pictures create a mood more quizzical than inquisitive. On a page or two apiece, familiar creatures (the giraffe, the camel, or the walrus) share the poet's attention along with not-so-familiar animals (the okapi, the panda, or the tapir); and the black line drawings—supplemented with brown or gray washes—are obviously responsive to the poet's musings. For the author's humorously speculative verses lead to Ogden Nash-like conclusions, which are beautfilly reflected on the faces of the animals skillfully positioned on the well-designed pages. "The ocelot's a clever cat. / She knowsalot of this and that. / She growsalot of spotted fur / which looks extremely well on her." (pp. 59-60)

Hoberman with students at Connecticut's Greenwich School.

Paul Heins, in a review of "The Raucous Auk: A Menagerie of Poems," in The Horn Book Magazine, *Vol. L, No. 1, February, 1974, pp. 59-60.*

Hoberman's humorous collection of poems about animals is marked by sharp observation, neat phrasing, straight-faced nonsense, and melodic turns and surprises. The bouncy, rhythmic verses, reminiscent of Laura E. Richards, are perfect for telling aloud (e.g. "I often wonder whether / The rhinoceros's leather / Is as bumpy on the inside / As it is upon the skinside." . . .) Joseph Low's simple black line drawings with sepia washes complement the poems with their wry expressiveness.

Della Thomas, in a review of "The Raucous Auk: A Menagerie of Poems," in School Library Journal, *Vol. 20, No. 6, February, 1974, p. 53.*

One of the most engaging collections of poems about animals to be published in a long time is illustrated with raff-ish drawings that echo the cheerful tone of the writing. Some of the poems are haiku-brief, some are free verse, some patterned, and almost all of them give information that is accurate and unobtrusive—but any lesson to be learned is ancillary; this is a book that's full of wit and humor, these are poems that are deft and memorable.

Zena Sutherland, in a review of "The Raucous Auk: A Menagerie of Poems," in Bulletin of the Center for Children's Books, *Vol. 27, No. 8, April, 1974, p. 130.*

Nuts to You and Nuts to Me: An Alphabet Book of Poems (1974)

Hoberman starts with ants and scatters a few through the pages for children to watch for, and she ends with zebra which "unlike this book" starts with Z and ends with A. G is for good morning, good night and good-bye, H for hello, Y for yes, and though you'd never guess from these simpler, straighter rhymes that the author had it in her to write **The Raucous Auk,** the mood all through is positive and bouncy, the rhythm smooth and free.

A review of "Nuts to You and Nuts to Me: An Alphabet Book of Poems," in Kirkus Reviews, *Vol. XLII, No. 12, June 15, 1974, p. 631.*

Short poems that have a lilting breeziness are illustrated by [Ronni Solbert's] lively pictures (unfortunately printed in rather flat colors) that capture the mood of the writing. Sample: "Balloons to blow / Balloons to burst / The blowing's best / The bursting's worst!" or "Pockets hold things / Pockets hide things / Special private dark inside things / Pockets save things / Pockets keep things / Secret silent way down deep things." Visually, there is no emphasis on the letters of the alphabet, but the reader-aloud can stress them, and the poems are child-centered, pleasant to read aloud, and eminently memorizable.

> *Zena Sutherland, in a review of "Nuts to You and Nuts to Me," in* Bulletin of the Center for Children's Books, *Vol. 28, No. 4, December, 1974, p. 64.*

The value of rhyme as a mnemonic device for introducing the letters of the alphabet is not a new discovery. Little New Englanders dutifully learned that "In Adam's fall / We sinned all." Far less somber is the latest alphabetic concoction—a blend of lilting rhythms, unforced rhymes, and freshly conceived, childlike imagery cast in a variety of poetic forms. Some of the poems are tongue twisters: "Sun suits suit / the sun sun sun! / Swim suits suit / the sea sea sea!"; others are just plain nonsense: "Lambs are full of curly wool; / If they combed it, it would pull. / How lucky mother sheep don't care / If their children comb their hair"; while still others offer an unexpected yet wondrously logical twist: "O's a ring / Made of gold / O's a moon / Half-way old." Ingenious, unpretentious, and appealing.

> *Mary M. Burns, in a review of "Nuts to You and Nuts to Me: An Alphabet Book of Poems," in* The Horn Book Magazine, *Vol. LI, No. 2, April, 1975, p. 162.*

I Like Old Clothes (1976)

If second-hand clothes make a more original subject for rhyme than the animals Hoberman did so well with in *The Raucous Auk,* they also have far fewer possibilities. So Hoberman, despite her way with silly rhyme, is reduced to stretching that initial idea about as far as the children here stretch their clothing dollars: "I like old clothes, / Hand-me-down clothes, / Worn outgrown clothes, / Not-my-own clothes. . . . Clothes with a history, / Clothes with a mystery, / Sweaters and shirts / That are brother-and-sistery. . . . Once-for-good clothes, / Now-for-play clothes. . . ." etc., etc. There is also some speculation about who might have worn the clothes before "I" acquired them, but that theme too is more recycled than developed. Ditto for [Jacqueline] Chwast's overpopulated pictures, which change color (within severe limits) and setting (wildly—from local playground to tropical island to ancient Egypt) with every double page but never introduce any imaginative variety in the disposition of the freakish cast. You might try it on the way to Aunt Sally's . . . and then pass it along.

> *A review of "I Like Old Clothes," in* Kirkus Reviews, *Vol. XLIV, No. 7, April 1, 1976, p. 385.*

This little poem has a point to make, especially to kids who may object to a hand-me-down wardrobe. But because the poem lacks structure and action and just kind of rambles on, children will not become very interested. The illustrations are humorous, detailed and full of action with each page presenting its own story in pictures. However, the pictures don't work with the text, nor are they strong enough to stand alone so the book as an entity falls short.

> *L. Lauren Wohl, in a review of "I Like Old Clothes," in* Children's Book Review Service, *Vol. 4, No. 10, May, 1976, p. 85.*

A playful hymn to hand-me-downs—"Clothes with a history, / Clothes with a mystery." . . . The singable verse should make this fun for story hour, and the concept should comfort fast-growing siblings who must spend their lives in cast-offs.

> *Helen Gregory, in a review of "I Like Old Clothes," in* School Library Journal, *Vol. 23, No. 1, September, 1976, p. 101.*

Bugs: Poems (1976)

It's increasingly, regrettably clear that Hoberman's infectious *Raucous Auk* was a fluke. These rhymes about insects and such are so flat and plodding it's sad to imagine a grown-up grinding them out. Most are simply obvious and undeveloped observations on salient traits—the praying mantis is really preying, the silverfish is neither silver nor a fish, locusts are harmless in one's, two's, three's, etc., but only make trouble in crowds; some tiny poems ("Fireflies at twilight / In search of one another / Twinkle off and on") aim perhaps for a Haiku-like flash but reveal nothing; and the attempts at word play are forced and tiresome—like the one about "A B bred / on B bread" or the 30-line **"Combinations"** that goes on and on in the vein of "A flea flew by a bee. The bee / To flee the flea flew by a fly. / The fly flew high to flee the bee / Who flew to flee the flea who flew / To flee the fly who now flew by." We'd squash it.

> *A review of "Bugs: Poems," in* Kirkus Reviews, *Vol. XLIV, No. 19, October 1, 1976, p. 1098.*

Another collection of creature rhymes by the author of *The Raucous Auk: A Menagerie of Poems,* this one portrays a swarm of insects in verses which are generally nimble and sometimes take wing. There are a couple of duds which read like prose or, worse, like a science lesson: "Metamorphis: Caterpillar, chrysalis, / Butterfly is born." Most of the time insect facts are cited in a more memorable manner, making these selections, illustrated with drawings [by Victoria Chess] of identifiable bugs with comic personalities, fun to read aloud or to add sparkle to the study of insects.

> *June Cater, in a review of "Bugs: Poems," in* School Library Journal, *Vol. 23, No. 5, January, 1977, p. 82.*

Bugs could certainly do much worse
Than this book's wry and witty verse.
In fact, the reader might feel kind
To insects, who are oft maligned,
After reading the facts and seeing
They aren't such despicable beings.
Wonderful pictures, weird and funny,
Of butterflies and bees that make honey,
Ladybugs, June bugs, Doodlebugs, too.
Who would ever think that you

Might like 'em?

A review of "Bugs: Poems," in West Coast Review of Books, *Vol. 3, No. 2, March, 1977, p. 48.*

A House is a House for Me   (1978)

In alternating lines of anapestic trimeter and tetrameter with lots of end and internal rhyme, Hoberman introduces names for animal and object abodes. The 45-page list is exploratory and enthusiastic. It includes spider webs, airplane hangars, corn husks, pickle barrels, pits in peaches, as well as a glove as house for a hand, a book for a story, a throat for a hum. The image of a special, physical container for each thing is clearly shaped, but from a book that teaches language usage, one expects more care in choosing words, less counting of syllables and pushing of rhyme, however exuberantly—a *bottle* is house for some jam? a *lake* for a snake? [Betty] Fraser packs each large, shiny page with busy illustrations, with alphabet book detail and real things to recognize. Except for one mass of panicked-looking rabbits in an over-crowded hutch, she interprets with humor, putting bugs in the duchess's bed and interspersing echoes from children's literature: Alice and the Mad Hatter drinking tea; Jack climbing the beanstalk seen through the window of a castle in which the king eats crackers from cartons. This is a rich book; kids will reach for the color and chorus the refrain. If Hoberman had played with the droning rhythm as Fraser did with the pictures, she might have won more volunteers for the umpteenth reading.

Sharon Elswit, in a review of "A House Is a House for Me," in School Library Journal, *Vol. 25, No. 2, October, 1978, p. 133.*

"A hill is a house for an ant, an ant. / A hive is a house for a bee. / A hole is a house for a mole or a mouse / And a house is a house for me." From animal houses Hoberman moves on to people's (igloo, tepee, etc.), returning frequently to that same fourth line while Fraser, for variety, pictures the "house for me" as a tree house, a packing carton, a snowpile, and so on. And when it seems that Hoberman has gone too long with houses for things (". . . Barrels are houses for pickles / And bottles are houses for jam . . . "), she disarms with agreement and a twist: "Perhaps I have started farfetching / Perhaps I am stretching things some. / A mirror's a house for reflections / A throat is a house for a hum. . . . " But that's not the end, and at last she does go on too long in the same jogtrot rhythm and listmaking vein. Small children, however, tolerate that sort of repetition, and this could work were the rhyme not overwhelmed by the packaging. Fraser's jarringly clear-cut and conspicuous pictures provide much to look at—but far too much, and in too many styles, to allow even the visual impressions to cohere. And Hoberman's modest ideas and grace notes are lost in the blare.

A review of "A House Is a House for Me," in Kirkus Reviews, *Vol. XLVI, No. 19, October 1, 1978, p. 1067.*

It is difficult to say whether the rhyme represents an inventive concept carried to childlike great lengths or merely too much of a good thing. Either way, children will get caught up, at least for a while, in listening to Hoberman's—and perhaps imagining their own—variety of "houses." The text is highly rhythmic and begs for reading aloud. . . . Full-color illustrations unfortunately fill each page to bursting; nice details get lost amid the artist's disunited festival of media. Still, the book is good reading and a clever springboard to creative game playing.

J. G., in a review of "A House Is a House for Me," in Booklist, *Vol. 75, No. 7, December 1, 1978, p. 616.*

In Mary Ann Hoberman's **A House Is A House For Me,** with illustrations by Betty Fraser, a brisk, even headlong rhyme plunges us into a swirling cluster of images. From "A hill is a house for an ant, an ant / A hive is a house for a bee" through dozens of rhymes to the final "Each creature that's known has a house of its own / And the earth is the house for us all," we are flooded with an overwhelming profusion of examples of houses. If the rhyme seems too pushy, the images positively stun you. With surreal precision and changes of scale and color, animals—big and small, wild and tame—are placed cheek by jowl with children and familiar objects, and all are gathered together with a kind of demented enthusiasm; the book is a manic cornucopia of images and ideas. I can't help but admire the frenzied intelligence and care of it all, and recommend it for parents and children patient enough to slow down and take it in bit by bit. It's an astonishing picture book, one of the best of the year. (pp. 73, 93)

Harold C. K. Rice, "Good Looking," in The New York Times Book Review, *December 10, 1978, pp. 72-3, 93.*

Inventive, unusual illustrations for a splendidly achieved text, one of my special choices of the year. The CIP note says it 'lists in rhyme the dwellings of various animals and things'. And so it does, but with wit, subtlety, a compassionate sensitivity that requires considerable skill with language and a genuinely innocent nature to capture. I like, as well, the pedigree the verses frequently acknowledge in the pictures (an admirable integration of words and illustrations). Above a treatment of Alice at the Mad Hatter's teaparty, for example, we get: 'A box is a house for a teabag. / A teapot's a house for some tea. / If you pour me a cup and I drink it all up, / Then the teahouse will turn into me!' (Behind and beyond which also stands, of course, de la Mare's 'Miss T'.) . . . A must, it seems to me, for every infant and junior school, and high on the list of books every child should get the chance to see.

Aidan Chambers, in a review of "A House Is a House for Me," in The Signal Review of Children's Books, 1, *1983, p. 35.*

Yellow Butter, Purple Jelly, Red Jam, Black Bread: Poems   (1981)

Inexorably cheerful and rhymed, these are just the kind of verses young children might mutter to themselves over and over as they go about the business of growing up. **"Applesauce"** has a 23-line preamble of alternatives to eating ("Shall I dig a hole? / Shall I make it deep? / Shall I slope the sides? / Shall I make them steep?")—a dining pattern with which any parent is familiar. There are few subtleties of form or content, but they will not be missed in the warm, playful tone of everyday activities such as climbing trees, walking doll buggies, watching snow collect in the yard, or suggesting a swap of baby brothers. Traditional brown pencil drawings [by Chaya Burnstein] pick up the soft jollity. For sharing aloud with children aged 5-8. (pp. 1447-48)

> *Betsy Hearne, in a review of "Yellow Butter, Purple Jelly, Red Jam, Black Bread: Poems," in* Booklist, *Vol. 77, Nos. 22/23, July 15/August, 1981, pp. 1447-48.*

Fifty-eight rhymes in a tall skinny (5″ × 10¼″) package, illustrated with bouncy but unoriginal black-and-white drawings and ranging from jog-trotting variations on well-worn subjects (birthdays, playing dress-up, comparing height as in the old-fashioned "John is the tallest, he's even so high . . . ") to the catchier wordplay and nonsense of **"Fish," "The Llama Who Had No Pajamas,"** or **"The King of Umpalazzo."** But as some of the catchiest—**"Ocelot," "Advice"** (on the armadillo), **"A Rabbit"**—have been recycled from previous Hoberman collections, this tall mass-market lookalike doesn't look like much of a buy.

> *A review of "Yellow Butter, Purple Jelly, Red Jam, Black Bread," in* Kirkus Reviews, *Vol. XLIX, No. 16, August 15, 1981, p. 1009.*

A tall, narrow book, illustrated with soft brown line drawings that are nicely incorporated into the page layouts, has bouncy, cheery poems about children and animals. The subjects, the rhyme, the rhythm and word play will appeal to the lap audience and some of the literary devices (alliteration, repetition) may unobtrusively strengthen pre-reading skills. There are brisk nonsense poems about zoo animals, poems about play, and some (fewer) quiet and thoughtful poems about emotions. In sum, a very nice new selection for young children, deftly written by a practiced hand. (pp. 10-11)

> *Zena Sutherland, in a review of "Yellow Butter, Purple Jelly, Red Jam, Black Bread," in* Bulletin of the Center for Children's Books, *Vol. 35, No. 1, September, 1981, pp. 10-11.*

The Cozy Book (1982)

Featuring a little girl of indeterminate age, this is a cheery, bouncy celebration of "the cozy doings of a very dozy day"—which expands out from the immediate and concrete ("Scrambled eggs stirred soft and sunny / Melted cheese that's nice and runny") to all-time sensations and emotions. Among cozy smells: "Roses blooming / Wood that's burning / Bread that's baking"; or, apropos of "Cozy people": "Laps to sit in, hands to hold / Arms to hug you when you're cold." If anything, it's a too-lengthy catalogue, and too diffuse, for preschoolers; but kindergartners will find some "cozy words" to mouthe (including, ingeniously, "Pachysandra / Sarsparilla / Tusk and smug and fog"), along with an implicit invitation to classify all kinds of experiences. Tony Chen's full-color pictures are more often bright and crisp than resonant or evocative; but as broadly-attuned image-making, they'll do.

> *A review of "The Cozy Book," in* Kirkus Reviews, *Vol. L, No. 15, August 1, 1982, p. 864.*

Just as Hoberman dealt with all types of shelter in **A House is a House for Me,** here, through rhyme, she stretches the definition of the word *cozy* to include food, people, feelings, sounds, smells and more. Stanzas are intermittently ended with "cozy, cozy, cozy, cozy," providing a good spot for cuddling when sharing the book one-on-one. The author's purpose might have been better served had she left something to the imagination rather than giving us such an exhaustive list of cozies. Tony Chen's illustrations with beautifully modulated colors are elegant studies and cover double-page spreads. His colorful compositions in many places remind one of Mitsumasa Anno. In their splendid color and detail they very nearly overpower the text and ultimately the book is more often a delight for the eye than the ear. (pp. 60-1)

> *Brenda Durrin Maloney, in a review of "The Cozy Book," in* School Library Journal, *Vol. 29, No. 5, January, 1983, pp. 60-1.*

Every child may not like every food or activity in the book, but all children will find some joys they share, and everyone can appreciate the lilt of the rhymes, the relish for words, and the pictures, busy but never cluttered.

> *Zena Sutherland, in a review of "The Cozy Book," in* Bulletin of the Center for Children's Books, *Vol. 36, No. 7, March, 1983, p. 128.*

Mr. and Mrs. Muddle (1988)

Amiable Mr. and Mrs. Muddle (horses) love each other dearly, but have one problem: he can't abide cars ("They smell . . . They make noise. They go too fast"), and she loves them ("They smell good . . . They make nice noises. And they go very fast"). Seeking a compromise, they try a canoe in their local puddle and—once they learn that both must paddle lest they go in circles and that they must meet each other halfway if they want to be together after a spill—both are happy.

Hoberman's deft use of language extends even to her chapter headings: "The Riddle," "The Middle," and "The Puddle." Her dialogue is full of warmth and wry humor, well matched by the wit and charming detail in [Catherine] O'Neill's delicious illustrations. From the first glimpse of the couple sleeping in blissful disarray in a lop-sided bed, this strong-minded but affectionate pair and their antics are entrancing. Mr. Muddle and a friendly duck share a newspaper (what headlines!—"Bad mouse reforms"; "Siamese twins reunited") in a bathtub; Mr. Muddle hugs his wife, saying, "Nobody is perfect, but it's nice to come close"; and there's a connubial kiss in the canoe, while paddling, that could only happen between two long-nosed horses. Delightful.

> *A review of "Mr. and Mrs. Muddle," in* Kirkus Reviews, *Vol. LVI, No. 22, November 15, 1988, p. 1675.*

In the hands of another writer this story, with its obvious theme of concession and accommodation, might have become overly didactic and heavy-handed. Hoberman delights in the sounds of words, and, through her exploration with language, she raises this tale from the mundane to the inspired. Children will wrap their tongues around the titles of the three short chapters, "The Riddle," "The Middle," and "The Puddle," and relish the silliness of these two horses. O'Neill's humorous watercolor illustrations bustle with the commotion of two beings discovering how to live with one another. Parents and teachers will welcome the lighthearted treatment of a recurring problem; children will ask for repeated readings of this cheerful and satisfying story. (p. 54)

> *Ellen Fader, in a review of "Mr. and Mrs. Muddle," in* The Horn Book Magazine, *Vol. LXV, No. 1, January-February, 1989, pp. 53-4.*

Some children will note that the couple still has not resolved the original conflict, and the canoe will take them neither to the store nor to Aunt Bessie's. The somewhat didactic tone of the book is lightened by cheery illustrations which show the couple living happily in the clutter of their home. O'Neill uses lively fine line drawings and luminous watercolor wash, and adds plenty of the humorous details that children love (Mrs. Muddle optimistically takes her car keys and lavender handbag everywhere, and a trio of busy ducks participate in every event). Mrs. Muddle is shown to be vigorous and active and Mr. Muddle to be sedentary. This is a fine example of the illustrator adding character definition and charm to an unexceptional text.

> *Eleanor K. MacDonald, in a review of "Mr. and Mrs. Muddle," in* School Library Journal, *Vol. 35, No. 6, February, 1989, p. 71.*

Lorus J(ohnson) Milne
19??-
Margery J(oan) Milne
19??-

Lorus—Canadian-born American author of nonfiction.

Margery—American author of nonfiction.

A husband and wife team, the Milnes are respected for creating authoritative, stimulating works which present information on natural history and ecology to readers from the middle grades through high school. The authors characteristically focus on the functioning of ecosystems and on the interdependence of various forms of animal and plant life in books which often draw on their personal experiences and observations and are noted for their immediacy, clarity, and lyricism. Professors of biology and teachers of natural history and nonfiction writing, the Milnes consider such subjects as ecology, evolution, radioactivity, the likenesses of animals, and the life found in both water and soil. Reflecting their respect for the earth and concern about its future, the authors depict the consequences that occur when humanity misuses its relationship with the environment as well as the steps that can be taken to maintain or improve the status of the natural world. The Milnes are also the authors of several works for adults which address topics similar to those of their juvenile literature; several of these books have been recommended for use in high schools. In addition, they have also provided black-and-white photographs to accompany the texts of such works as *Gift from the Sky* (1967), *Insect Worlds: A Guide for Man on Making the Most of His Environment* (1980), and *Nature's Clean-Up Crew: The Burying Beetles* (1982).

(See also *Something about the Author,* Vol. 5; *Contemporary Authors New Revision Series,* Vol. 14; and *Contemporary Authors,* Vols. 33-36, rev. ed.)

AUTHORS' COMMENTARY

Editors continually need science articles to update their readers' understanding of their ever-changing world. Satisfying this hunger for scientific information and what it means can be an exciting and profitable activity for the scientist or the writer interested in science. Each week seems to produce new material that can be translated into significant articles an editor will buy—if they are written with accuracy and clarity in a way that connects with a reader's world. . . .

You may have found a fresh topic or a new angle on an old one. Relate everything to your subject, enhancing and clarifying it in an exciting way for the lay reader.

As you become a science writer, you learn to prepare lists, sentences, paragraphs, even phrases you would like to work into your piece, in draft form. A sentence you admire, quoted from some classic author not too far back in time, might well find a useful place. The secrets of science turn up in many different guises, because anything worth telling can be told in dozens of different ways.

Focus on a variety of related topics and try to expand your information by on-site observation and detailed reading. It is essential to write about what you know, even if your knowledge is quite new. You should serve as a strainer through which fine details can disappear while basic principles remain. Your own enthusiasm grows as you teach yourself. You might well speculate a little as a step toward making your readers care and want more. Science is particularly good for this because it is so open-ended. Rarely is anything final. More awaits discovery.

Keep exploring your subject, reading until you feel you have exhausted all the resources. When you are confident that you have a grasp of the subject, try explaining it to others and get them excited, too. Talking about the material gets you listeners who can respond. If their attention wanders, your idea or presentation needs improvement. If they keep asking questions that suggest new vistas to explore, you have something good. (p. 11)

The spark you need for an article may come from anywhere, even a paragraph or a news item in the paper. Read all you can find on the subject, and talk to people who are engaged in research on some aspect of it. (p. 12)

You don't have to be a scientist to write science articles or even books. Your own curiosity should drive you to educate yourself until you become a self-taught expert. True dedication frees you from the need for college courses on the subject. By hunting up what we needed to know and without special training, we wrote *A Time To Be Born,* a 218-page book on animal courtship and parenting. Space limitations kept us from citing the 466 references on which we had relied.

You have the advantage of personal excitement in presenting details that are new to you. As long as you select subjects that lend themselves to rather simple research you can become a winner by getting your account of the topic published. You'll be astonished at the number of different outlets that turn up as you progress. While the topic ripens in your mind, your file folders fatten with notes. The real question is how much the topic intrigues you and keeps you alert to scientific work, as it appears in technical journals and newspapers.

In every scientific field, the volume of literature includes a greater range of discoveries and statements than almost anyone can recall unaided. On annotated file cards, record the articles and other references you find for your subject. Follow the format of bibliographies in some standard scientific journal. Alphabetize your list and have a copy ready under the heading "Sources." Unless you are writing about long-past events, as Stephen Jay Gould so often does, your references should mostly be from 1980 onward, only a minority from farther back. Recent work needs more publicity and gives a modern flavor to what you write.

The first challenge in any scientific field is simplicity, both of presentation and vocabulary. Are you becoming involved with some aspect of natural science such as biology or geology, or of a physical science like physics or chemistry? Anyone who enjoys reading about physics will know what fiber optics are. Anyone with an interest in chemistry will recognize the symbols for elements and feel comfortable with a few simple formulae. Similarly, a person in sympathy with nature need not be told the difference between plants and animals, or that DNA and RNA are components of the mechanism of genetics and inheritance. Your role is to provide exciting and refreshing facts your readers will want to understand or know more about.

Broad as science is, one area of expertise is all you can consider in one topic. Within that area, choose the special vocabulary (the "jargon") that permits analysis and communication to be precise without lengthy explanations. Readers might tolerate special words if you introduce them clearly, one at a time, and not more than one to a page. Keep others in mind for your own use in reading from journals. Spare your audience.

Contrast the following:

> A) From the light focused on the retina the photo-sensitive molecules in the receptor cells absorb energy a quantum (photon) at a time, a molecule at a time, and trigger the sensation of sight.

> B) The light energy focused on the sensitive cells in the eye is absorbed by special molecules. One molecule, excited by a single unit of energy, can trigger the sensation of sight.

A good basis for deciding which technical term(s) to include would be the frequency with which you find the word(s) in a national magazine or newspaper.

Readers on science topics may know the names of outstanding scientists and their accomplishments. These can be guideposts within your article or book, helping you relate other scientific information to make it meaningful. You might find an analogy in something Charles Darwin attempted. What happened in North America or Europe during the years while Darwin was traveling around the world on *H.M.S. Beagle?* Wherever your curiosity leads you, dig out the facts, and let your readers know.

The scene around you can provide delightful anecdotes that are completely relevant. Puddles following a good rain in early June may be outlined in bright yellow, reminding you that the white pines are shedding their golden pollen and additional clouds of these dust-sized particles will billow forth if a lively squirrel shakes the branches. Even while jogging, be aware of your environment. Practice using your senses: sight, sound, smell, taste, touch. Think about what they detect and let you appreciate. These senses are the only avenues from the outside world to the brain. But environment affects the way we use them. In a city, we want privacy, and shut out the smell of onions cooking down the hall, the sound of buses starting up, fire sirens and garbage trucks. The country person, after going to the city, reacts to these sounds and smells. The city person in the country finds no sensory signals intense enough to crash through the protective wall, and wonders: Where is everything? Why is nothing happening?

The environment continually supplies you with two real advantages: it invites you to make your own observations, upon which you can count without quoting any authority, and it tends to be timeless, letting you safely combine information gathered from several different years.

Control your impatience, even while you wait for an editor to decide on the first version of the article you submit. Your time need not be lost, for the subject will ripen, letting you rethink paragraphs you wrote. Reread them with a critical eye. Substitute a better word or rearrange the sentence. Move an early sentence farther back (or forward). Expand if you need to. Keep it simple and show why it is relevant. Is that really the clearest way to express what you intended? Must the account read

> We know that, apart from encouraging the spread of forests, almost every change humankind makes in land leaves it drier. We have no wish to see in America the ultimate stage—the nearly irreversible alteration of valuable land into useless desert. In Africa, desertification has diminished living space for humankind at a frightening pace.

You could make that "pace" more specific by adding,

> "expanding the Sahara Desert during the past fifty years by an area twice the size of Spain." (*Country Journal,* vol. 7)

Honest science writing earns recognition. Even a rejection

slip may point the way toward improvement, toward recognizing the needs of the market, or to the existence of other opportunities. Rewriting proves your P.Q. (Persistence Quotient), continually strengthening your science writing output and sharpening your reading and listening skills.

Science writing has its rewards. Our awareness of the world's limited supply of fresh water led us to write a book on **Water and Life.** It brought us an invitation to discuss fresh water resources worldwide for a television program produced by the California Academy of Science. Our interview was even dubbed into Cantonese for re-broadcast from Hong Kong. Still later the National Geographic Society sent us to North Africa, Israel, Kuwait and other places where water use must be limited because of their meager supply. Hoarding water was one of the unforgivable sins for an Egyptian pharaoh, equal in gravity to murder. Merely mentioning such a detail in your science article creates a sense of time and place.

Think of the editor who needs a new version of the science topic in which you have immersed yourself and made a central theme in the pages you have written. The time has come to test it out, to let one and perhaps thousands of people enjoy what you have found. (pp. 12-13, 42)

> *Lorus J. Milne and Margery Milne, "So You Want to Write about Science," in* The Writer, *Vol. 99, No. 11, November, 1986, pp. 11-13, 42.*

Famous Naturalists (1952)

This is a good selection of biographical essays on great naturalists from Leeuwenhoek to Barbour: Linnaeus, Agassiz, Darwin, Muir, etc. The book starts with a chapter on "In the Distant Past" and concludes with one on "The Paths of Modern Naturalists." The essays are factual and charming, stressing the naturalists' work and contributions. Aside from a gross error in the opening chapter, which states that Marco Polo returned from China in 1254, this little book is interesting and worthy in every way.

> *Nina S. Chasteen, in a review of "Famous Naturalists," in* Library Journal, *Vol. 77, No. 6, March 15, 1952, p. 541.*

Here is a useful book for high school students, suggesting by inference some fascinating and unusual careers. The title uses "naturalist" to cover fourteen men whose beginnings were as "nature students." But for each final fame came in far different careers which are not summarized very exactly in the single words used in the table of contents, as "teacher," "thinker," "traveler," "writer," "observer."

However, the reader of these brief biographies, each illustrated with one photograph, finds which of these men remained "naturalists" as well, that is, "observers" like Thoreau, Fabre, Gilbert White, whose writings have been important and which of them went on into further scientific work, such as Linnaeus and Darwin. Their work often crosses the definition of "botanist" and often describes the thrilling travels of such varied "explorers" as Audubon, Agassiz, Fairchild.

The introduction is quite inadequate: it only hints at the long history of plant and animal "observation" and does not define the scope of the book. And the appearance of the whole makes it more a library reference book than a gift book.

> *Louise S. Bechtel, in a review of "Famous Naturalists," in* New York Herald Tribune Book Review, *April 6, 1952, p. 8.*

Because of a Tree (1963)

A whole balance of nature exists around each kind of tree—the bark has insects which in turn feed the birds who are likely to nest in its branches and the nut bearing trees have trunk holes that will harbor squirrels and certain types of birds; other trees have whole communities living in and on its roots. Each chapter of this book employs the interesting approach of presenting a tree as the center of various flora and fauna; first a description of the tree and the region it is likeliest to be found in and then on to all the activity that goes on in, around and under it. The outstanding tree members of all sections of the country are represented here. The black and white illustrations by Kenneth Gosner have a grainy, woody texture and are well placed in a text that is smoothly and simply written by authors who are well known at the adult level and who have written extensively about nature.

> *A review of "Because of a Tree," in* Virginia Kirkus' Service, *Vol. XXXI, No. 12, June 15, 1963, p. 560.*

Another volume of fascinating nature facts has been attractively organized for upper elementary-school children and older by two professors who have earlier written many nature books for adults. An ecological study, this elaborates on the theme that "Each tree forms a center in the community of nature" by discussing in separate chapters the varying environmental lives of the apple tree, suger maple, Christmas spruce and fir, coconut and date palms, the bald swamp cypress, redwood, aspen, and saguaro cactus. It describes the relationship to each of the animals, birds, and insects who depend on it for sustenance, either directly or indirectly, and of humans who profit from it in a variety of ways. An excellent bibliography is included of books for additional reading and reference. (pp. 516-17)

> *Virginia Haviland, in a review of "Because of a Tree," in* The Horn Book Magazine, *Vol. XXXIX, No. 5, October, 1963, pp. 516-17.*

In their dedication of **Because of a Tree,** Lorus and Margery Milne quote Hal Borland's words: "A tree shades man and beast, harbors songbird and squirrel, feeds bee and looping worm. Aided only by sun, rain and earth itself, it lives with the seasons, heals its own wounds, and outlasts its human neighbors." The Milnes, elaborating on that theme, describe the symbiotic relationship of a specific tree with its surrounding flora and fauna. (p. 18)

With deft and flowing style, the Milnes explain how man cares for a tree, and tell what gifts man receives from that tree; human history, sociology and customs are smoothly interwoven with natural history. The sugar maple, for example, is related in context to Christopher Columbus, Indians, the sugar maple industry, sugaring-off parties, and to ecology, mammal and horticultural. Without suggesting overt action, the authors provide facts in so stimulating a manner that readers will want to dash outdoors for exciting exploration of the active life on and around a tree or lawn, forest or open desert. Provocative information is presented in a personal manner in this highly recommended book. (pp. 18, 22)

> *Kenneth L. Franklin, "Teen-Age Science," in* The New York Times Book Review, *November 10, 1963, pp. 18, 22.*

The Crab that Crawled Out of the Past (1965)

After a detailed, clear study of a live crab through the eyes of the fisherman examining one he has caught, its unusual habits, strong sense of direction and amusing mating procedure are interestingly described. Next, in a romantic but substantially accurate survey of pre-history, the Horseshoe Crab is shown to have resisted evolutionary change to such a remarkable degree, through its lack of ambition and simple needs, that its nervous system and resistance to disease are of great interest to modern medical research. We are made to feel the tragedy that this crab is now in danger of extinction through its use as animal food or fertiliser. The relating of this technical subject to the younger child's world is so expert—with the exception of a shockingly bogus seventeenth century conversation between Richard Grenville and his men!—that unfortunately it may limit the book's appeal, although the facts described would interest any age of reader. (pp. 125-26)

> *A review of "The Crab that Crawled Out of the Past," in* The Junior Bookshelf, *Vol. 31, No. 2, April, 1967, pp. 125-26.*

Although primarily about the horseshoe crab, this book gives a very good simplified recapitulation of the main evolutionary patterns of geologic periods. The authors discuss the horseshoe crab's life cycle, its structure and function, and its unique position of being an anachronistic hold-out in the shifting pattern of adaptive evolution. All the factual material is authoritative, and the creature itself is fascinating. The book is weakened, however, by a slow start (in which a fisherman contrivedly examines a specimen) and by an occasional awkward tying-in of material when the text has veered from the subject: for example, "All around the horseshoe crabs the kinds of life were changing. But it did not matter to the crabs that the soft-bodied sea worms that they are were of new kinds, or that . . . " (pp. 121-22)

> *Zena Sutherland, in a review of "The Crab that Crawled Out of the Past," in* Bulletin of the Center for Children's Books, *Vol. XVIII, No. 8, April, 1965, pp. 121-22.*

The horseshoe crab, whose dishpan-shaped shell is a common sight on summer beaches and souvenir stands, is a living link with the beginnings of life 500 million years ago. Its nearly identical ancestors left tracks in the famous limestone fossil deposits of Bavaria before disappearing from European shores, to be found again by the settlers of America. Today, scientists are learning much of value from it.

These and other interesting facts about this miscalled

"crab" are mostly found in the last chapters of the Milnes's book. Only the most dedicated junior scientists, though, will persevere through the anatomical and biological details which, despite an attempt to dramatize them, clog the first pages. A monotonous repetition of simple statements, some unexplained terms, and a sprinkling of clumsy sentences, help to make the text as bumpy as a rocky seashore.

> *Michele Caraher, in a review of "The Crab that Crawled Out of the Past," in* The New York Times Book Review, *May 23, 1965, p. 30.*

Gift from the Sky (1967)

Mr. and Mrs. Milne, known throughout as "the naturalist" and the "the naturalist's wife," describe the impact of a swan's surprise arrival in their cozy New Hampshire town. They name the great bird Alice, and her coming changes everybody's life, adding a bit of beauty to daily routines, inspiring a committee to protect her, grade school teachers to assign drawings of her, and high school profs to lecture on the swan in literature and music. Exiled royalty and the winter freeze threaten Alice, but the town won't let her go; they find her a house for the winter and a mate for the spring. The plot, slight but sufficient, imparts a lot of historical and biological fact in a graceful way. A nature-lover's quiet little nook.

> *A review of "Gift from the Sky," in* Kirkus Service, *Vol. XXXV, No. 14, July 15, 1967, p. 812.*

The natural history of mute swans is interwoven with a story concerning a community's action in adopting and caring for the swan. The information about swans does not go far beyond that found in standard children's references. Interesting light reading for bird fanciers. (p. 177)

> *Albert C. Haman, in a review of "Gift from the Sky" in* School Library Journal, *Vol. 14, No. 2, October, 1967, pp. 176-77.*

All episodes have as background the natural history of the local pond and stream. There is an interesting chapter on English swans and how they have fared under royal protection. The story illustrates how local interest in wildlife can be stimulated by the introduction of a swan or two into a local setting, and this has happened intermittently throughout the United States while in England mute swans have decorated streams, estuaries, millponds and castle moats for centuries. Lively photographs and a short reference list are included, but no index. (p. 244)

> *A review of "Gift from the Sky," in* Science Books, *Vol. 3, No. 3, December, 1967, pp. 243-44.*

The Phoenix Forest (1968)

Like the legendary bird, a forest can be reborn from its own ashes, especially if "spot burning" is enforced. Foresters find that controlled fires clear the ground of highly flammable dead wood (equated with the phoenix's pyrenest), providing more space for seedlings, improving the quality of the soil, and maintaining an ecological status

From Gift from the Sky, *written and illustrated by Lorus and Margery Milne.*

quo for wildlife. The Milnes primarily relate an account of an accidental fire in an unidentified forest: ground kindling accumulates for years, lightning strikes an old oak, the metal from a bander's ring holds heat. That oak and this idea may have their roots in the "Dead Tree" chapter of *Because of a Tree;* the characters on the scene are less obtrusive than those in *Gift from the Sky.* The Ranger and the president of the lumber company discuss the future of the forest, and if that dialogue has the casualness of a presidential address it does convey some information which is considerably amplified by the authors in the closing chapters. The characters detract from a fragile crisscross of image, incident and theorizing but generally the dramatization is not effusive. (pp. 982-83)

> *A review of "The Phoenix Forest," in* Kirkus Service, *Vol. XXXVI, No. 17, September 1, 1968, pp. 982-83.*

The regrowth of a forest from the ashes of a devastating fire is the subject of this well-written narrative. The authors make a case for the use of controlled fire to improve forest life by showing what happens during and after a natural, lightning-induced forest fire. The description of life destroyed and renewed is vividly realistic and absorbing. Only two faults mar the book's effect. For one, the illustrations [by Elinor Van Ingen] bear little or no relation to the narrative. Secondly, the few humans who appear in the story serve only to give voice to the authors' views, seeming less lifelike than the forest about which they are concerned. These are minor flaws, however, in view of the excellent presentation of thoughts well worth everyone's consideration. The book should serve well as collateral reading, but not as a reference source. A list of suggested further readings is appended.

> *A review of "The Phoenix Forest," in* Science Books, *Vol. 4, No. 3, December, 1968, p. 219.*

By deftly relating the growth, burning and rebirth of the forest to the myth of the Phoenix, the authors have used a master's touch in handling the controversial subject of the use of fire in forest and wildlife management. They have presented a well organized and convincing case while fully recognizing the limitations and potential dangers of such management. . . . The last three pages "For Further Reading" add to the value of the book as a reference.

> *Frances Sherburne, in a review of "The Phoenix Forest," in* Appraisal: Children's Science Books, *Vol. 2, No. 3, Fall, 1969, p. 20.*

The Nature of Animals　(1969)

Faithful to its tradition, the Milne team has done an excellent job of bringing together many facts of the animal kingdom to show the many ways in which all animals are alike and in what respects they differ. The authors begin with a comparison of size using the smallest animal, the malaris fever disease protozoa, in contrast to the blue whale, 109 feet in length. Both live in a water environment. Aquatic animals are treated separately from land animals before the discussions of the major attributes of animal life. Separate interesting chapters are devoted to how animals live, reproduce, inherit their characteristics, and the place of animals in the balance of nature. Mankind and animal life make up the last chapter. Here the authors present the problem of animals facing extinction. They give both sides of the problem without over-sentimentalizing the situation. The book ends on an upbeat tone indicating that plants and animals can find a way to live together if mankind uses his wisdom.

> *A review of "The Nature of Animals," in* Science Books, *Vol. 5, No. 2, September, 1969, p. 151.*

A wide-ranging consideration of the characteristics of numerous animals and their relationship to their surroundings, this will introduce readers with some prior knowledge of biology to new and fascinating aspects of the animal world. The authors use an interesting approach, as they relate the animals and their activities through various structural, functional and ecological characteristics rather than discuss each organism independently. However, with this type of coverage, certain topics receive sketchy treatment. The writing style is straightforward and understandable, but some knowledge of the animal kingdom is necessary. There are too few illustrations [by Thomas R. Funderburk] to adequately support the text, especially for novice readers.

> *Daryl B. Smith, in a review of "The Nature of*

Animals," in School Library Journal, *Vol. 16, No. 3, November, 1969, p. 133.*

It should be logical to start an article on books about ecology by discussing books about ecology. A few have come out in the last year or two with "ecology" in their titles, for young people of perhaps 12 and up. But it seems to me that these are not the place to start, either for young people or their teachers. In such books—and it takes a good reader to get through any of them—the writing is based to a great degree on generalizations stating the basics of ecology. The generalizations will not have much meaning to the reader until he has acquired a background of information about individual plants and animals, by reading and by observation in the open. Better by far to start with something that will build such a background.

To use in this way, I am wildly enthusiastic about *The Nature of Animals* . . . , for high school and junior high students and perhaps good readers in the middle grades—and for teachers. Here is wonderful coverage of animal life, with much interesting detail about individual species that does not appear in biology textbooks. Typical chapters are "How Animals Live," "Aquatic Animals," and "Land Animals." Teachers and librarians will profit by reading the book, and parts of it can be read or told to children younger than those who can read it for themselves. (Warning: Start it, and they'll never let you put it down—nor will you want to!)

Against such a background, the "ecology books" are far more meaningful, and find their proper role of crystallizing previous experience and developing the terminology to express it. (p. 2)

F. Dorothy Wood, "Books about Ecology," in Appraisal: Children's Science Books, *Vol. 4, No. 1, Winter, 1971, pp. 1-2.*

When the Tide Goes Far Out   (1970)

Disposing in one quick complex chapter on Newton's discoveries ("The Work of the Moon") of the how and why of tides, the ambiguously entitled book moves immediately to the what that can be seen on shores bared by the tide's ebb. It's no substitute, then, for Ruth Brindze's *Rise and Fall of the Seas* or for Elizabeth Clemons' photo-illustrated *Waves, Tides and Currents,* but rather an older analog to the latter's *Tide Pools and Beaches*—or a lackluster catalog compared to the Jean C. George or Rachel Carson books. Visual descriptions . . . uncover "The Realm of the Slippery Seaweeds," "A World of Attached Animals," and "The Move-Abouts That Stay Behind"; profiles range from jackknife clam to periwinkle in the fauna department, and the "Garden By the Edge of the Sea" roams through rich varieties of flora, including ribbon kelp, rockweed, and sea lettuce. An appreciative nod to "The Wealth of the Sea" ends the informed but fragmented marine bio-logging, whose guide-lines (pale next to Bernice Kohn's stimuli for younger beachcombers) are academic, imagistic, and oriented toward passive observation.

A review of "When the Tide Goes Far Out," in Kirkus Reviews, *Vol. XXXVIII, No. 15, August 1, 1970, p. 812.*

A rather acceptable description of "walking the tide out" is provided. It explores each habitat and simply explains what is there to see. A few words used will not be clear to readers who have not lived near the coast. For the most part however, all new terms are explained. The book will hold the readers' interest. The ideas and concepts are clear but rather elementary but in a few places the generalization is almost misleading. The last chapter is a good example of low-key approach to the problems of pollution. There are some excellent statements relating to conservation and the environment. At times, the authors' love for the sea breaks forth in poetry, "The tang of sea air is a taste. It is salt dust riding the onshore winds from over the breaking waves." This book will make an excellent addition to a classroom or school's natural history library. It will best be used by students in elementary and junior high school.

A review of "When the Tide Goes Far Out," in Science Books, *Vol. 6, No. 3, December, 1970, p. 226.*

The possibilities for a good book are here—reliable authors, clear illustrations [by Kenneth Gosner], technically correct information—but the results are disappointing. The mathematical explanation of gravity and tides in the first chapter will discourage most readers in the intended age group, yet the format may attract younger ones. The casual, descriptive narrative is not suitable for a science book. And, the information concerning plant and animal life at various tide levels is interesting but available elsewhere: e.g., *Sea and Shore* by Hylander (Macmillan, 1950), *Spring Comes to the Ocean* by George (Crowell. 1966), etc.

Jane Austin, in a review of "When the Tide Goes Far Out," in School Library Journal, *Vol. 17, No. 6, February, 1971, p. 68.*

The Nature of Plants   (1971)

A moderately imposing introduction to the plant kingdom, presupposing motivation and some familiarity with essential terminology. Beginning with a descriptive survey, from algae on, of different aquatic and land plants and their distribution, and concluding with a review of plant geography and history that emphasizes adaptation and diversity, the Milnes detail as well the biochemical processes involved in photosynthesis, the mechanisms of reproduction and the investigations of plant heredity from Mendel to the findings on DNA in the 1960's. The authors throughout are up to date in content and orientation, with a faithfully scientific respect for uncertainties and qualifications. This is neither the classified catalog of a traditional botany text nor the stimulating lore of a fond naturalist, but a solid, sometimes unnecessarily heavy-going, digest of knowledge to date. (pp. 957-58)

A review of "The Nature of Plants," in Kirkus Reviews, *Vol. XXXIX, No. 17, September 1, 1971, pp. 957-58.*

The Milnes have authored a number of works on natural history topics. As are the others, this is quite readable and scientifically accurate. It would be most suitable for collateral reading by students of biology or by interested adult laymen, but not so suitable for use as a teaching text. The plant kingdom is treated in ten survey chapters that include brief ones on plant physiology "How Plants Live" and genetics "How Plants Inherit"; several on taxonomy, anatomy, and morphology; and on plant evolution and economic botany. . . . There is an index, but unfortunately, there is no bibliography. This is a good introduction to botany, but the reader is left with no suggestions for further pursuit of the subject. The chapters on ecology "Plants in the Balance of Nature" and plant geography "The Spread of Plant Life" are particularly good introductions and thus, are particularly distressing in their lack of bibliography. On balance this would be a good book for a personal collection or for a general science collection in a public or school library and it is on that basis that the recommendation is made.

> *A review of "The Nature of Plants," in* Science Books, *Vol. 7, No. 3, December, 1971, p. 239.*

Intended for students with advanced botanical backgrounds, this is a well-organized survey of the basic principles of plant life and growth and their usefulness to man. . . . Though the Milnes' title is basically a sound study, *Plants* by Went (Time-Life, 1963) is more fully illustrated and requires less previous knowledge.

> *A. C. Haman, in a review of "The Nature of Plants," in* School Library Journal, *Vol. 18, No. 8, April, 1972, p. 148.*

The How and Why of Growing   (1972)

Scientifically, among the least-understood phenomena in biology are growth, differentiation, and senescence and yet they become apparent to children at a very early age. Few books treat the subject in a manner both satisfying and intelligible to the very young. The Milnes succeed through a highly descriptive . . . treatment of the subject as it relates to microbes, plants, and animals. In the final chapter they turn to populations and present a clear ecological message in their discussion.

> *A review of "The How and Why of Growing," in* Science Books, *Vol. 8, No. 1, May, 1972, p. 47.*

The lack of diagrams, charts, and graphs severely limits the usefulness of this exploration of the growth of people, animals, plants, microbes, and populations. For example, the chapter on "How Microbes Grow" contains only one illustration—that of a cow! While accurate and at times interesting, the information is not logically organized to give a clear understanding of the processes involved. The brief treatment of photosynthesis is non-technical, yet the authors assume reader knowledge of stamens and ovaries in a discussion of flowers. The index does not refer back to information on birth defects and evidences of aging in fish. Herbert Zim's *How Things Grow* (Morrow, 1960) includes an abundance of excellent illustrations and is far superior for the intended audience. *A Place in the Sun, Ecology and the Living World* by Lois and Louis Darling (Morrow, 1968), useful for grades 4 through 12, provides much better explanations of the ecological relationships of all growing things and the problems of population growth.

There are also many good books which discuss growth in only one form of life.

> *Mary Neel Rees, in a review of "The How and Why of Growing," in* School Library Journal, *Vol. 19, No. 1, September, 1972, p. 133.*

As is usually the case with books written by this husband and wife team, **The How and Why of Growing** is outstanding. They have written with clarity and logical development, from the beginning of a new life through birth and growth. Illustrations from human beings, animals, and plants make understandable this complex subject. The chapter "How Microbes Grow" is especially good. The thought of vast numbers of "germs" leads easily to population growth. An excellent section follows on wildlife population, particularly as related to man. The final chapter, "The Secret of a Long Life," should be read by everyone, both young and adult, for the warnings it contains and the hope it implies.

> *Pearl B. Care, in a review of "The How and Why of Growing," in* Appraisal: Children's Science Books, *Vol. 5, No. 3, Fall, 1972, p. 26.*

Because of a Flower   (1975)

The beauty of flowers, the symbiotic relationships between their parent plants and animal life, is set forth delightfully, with none of the sickly-sweet sentimentality of the old-time and, I hope, obsolete "nature lover." None of "Mother Nature's laws" are declaimed in this wonderful book. The fascinating development of mutually dependent plant and animal life is described in a way that will hold the interest of young and old from the first page to the last. And, like the true scientists they are, the Milnes have included a brief bibliography and an adequate index. (p. 32)

> *R. Gregory Belcher, in a review of "Because of a Flower," in* Appraisal: Children's Science Books, *Vol. 8, No. 2, Spring, 1975, pp. 31-2.*

This would have made a good nature film; the Milnes know their subject and are smooth narrators, but without the benefit of bold visual aids, readers may have little inclination to sit this essay presentation out. What it specifically offers is a cross-disciplinary perspective on the importance of flowers in the plant and animal world. The authors focus on groups of flowers—water lilies, orchids, cacti, and milkweed, among others—and explain how their growth and reproductive processes influence their surroundings. A literate, clearly designed book that includes an index and suggestions for further reading; hopefully it will not be as overlooked as the authors imply their subject is.

> *A review of "Because of a Flower," in* The Booklist, *Vol. 71, No. 15, April 1, 1975, p. 818.*

"You can easily walk into a clump of cacti on any sand ground." This bum advice and other eyebrow-raising observations pit a text made tedious by far too many details and not enough effort to interest young readers. Based on the interesting idea that animal communities depend on plants that grow, bloom, and fruit, chapters are concerned with communities from those around briar patches to those supported by thistles, burdock, and dandelions. Best is, "In The Blackberry Tangle"; "The Yucca and Its Partners" and "Cactus Flowers" vie for worst. . . .

> *George Gleason, in a review of "Because of a Flower," in* School Library Journal, *Vol. 22, No. 5, January, 1976, p. 55.*

Gadabouts and Stick-at-Homes: Wild Animals and Their Habitats (1980)

"Almost everything important to an animal relates in some way to its home." With this for a binder the Milnes tie together ten chapters on topics as diverse as the lobster's life cycle and the practice of banding birds. They describe the mother beaver's life within her fairly permanent lodge, the hermit crab's restless existence in an ever-changing series of snail shells, and the habits of two kinds of ants, "homebody" and "gypsy." Among the more interesting chapters are stories of investigation and discovery: A biologist bands a community of bats and follows their moves as his meddling drives them from one day's roost to another; a gift received by missionaries from a remote group of Peruvian Indians solves the mystery of the chimney swift's winter home. Altogether, this is looser and less rigorous than previous Milne nature books. . . .

> *A review of "Gadabouts and Stick-at-Homes: Wild Animals and Their Habitats," in* Kirkus Reviews, *Vol. XLVIII, No. 11, June 1, 1980, p. 715.*

"In ancient Greece the word for home was *oikos*. In modern times this word has reappeared in English as the root of 'ecology'—the study of the home life of animals and plants." The Milnes' 10 essays explore a broad variety of ideas about the relationship of creatures to their habitat. The writing is smooth and the format pleasing in design, but theme development is often oblique. For instance, a chapter entitled "The Greatest Traveler of All" describes the migration pattern of the arctic tern, but there are four pages of text about other birds before the tern is even mentioned. Bats and beavers, ants and chimney swifts, lobsters and hares are among the beasts discussed. It seems likely that children will have difficulty sustaining interest in the loosely focused text, and there are more clearly written sources of information on animal homes, ecological relationships, and the various species.

> *Margaret Bush, in a review of "Gadabouts and Stick-at-Homes: Animals and Their Habitats," in* School Library Journal, *Vol. 26, No. 10, August, 1980, p. 78.*

This is a very thorough book about the habitats of wild animals. The title may not be meaningful to children since "gadabout" is not an expression children commonly use. Nevertheless, the clarity of the writing and the content are such that intermediate elementary and junior high students would not find it too difficult to read and would enjoy it very much. Younger children would also enjoy the book if it is read to them by the teacher and supplemented by additional illustrations. . . . Many children enjoy skipping around in a book and they can with this book because each chapter is self-contained. A child might choose to read about animals of particular interest rather than read the book from beginning to end. I highly recommend

the book for its interesting facts and clarity of writing style.

> *Martha K. Piper, in a review of "Gadabouts and Stick-at-Homes: Animals and Their Habitats," in* Science Books & Films, *Vol. 16, No. 3, January-February, 1981, p. 158.*

Insect Worlds: A Guide for Man on Making the Most of the Environment (1980)

These well-known biologists have co-authored more than thirty excellent books. This latest engaging, informative book brings to life the intriguing hunting and eating habits of certain insects. These "marvels of miniaturization" have managed to survive many millions of years because of their fascinating adaptations. The text and many photographs will supply much ammunition for unusual conversations. Don't overlook this fine book.

> *George Barr, in a review of "Insect Worlds: A Guide for Man on Making the Most of the Environment," in* Children's Book Review Service, *Vol. 9, No. 5, January, 1981, p. 38.*

This popular account of insect life is written with an emphasis on behavior. From the great diversity of insects, the authors have chosen numerous examples of adaptations that have contributed to the success of these animals. They also draw on their own observations, experiences and photographs. While their accounts are usually accurate and entertaining, they are often oversimplified, with an overuse of superlatives and trite analogies. The book is also flawed by occasional errors of fact, presentation, or interpretation, and by a lack of references or suggested readings. Better treatments of this material can be found in Howard Evans' *Life on a Little-Known Planet* or Michael Tweedie's *Insect Life*.

> *Robert E. Silberglied, in a review of "Insect Worlds: A Guide for Man on Making the Most of the Environment," in* Library Journal, *Vol. 102, No. 2, January 15, 1981, p. 157.*

Readers who have enjoyed other literary works by these authors will not be disappointed with their latest effort. Insect survival strategies are described in simple terminology and with a great deal of imagination. The majority of the text consists of carefully selected examples illustrating all aspects of insect life, most of which are drawn from the authors' personal experiences. The first two chapters deal with the characteristics of insects and their remarkable success in adapting to all environments. Methods of obtaining food, resisting predators, finding mates and producing new generations are covered in succeeding chapters. The final chapter deals with the social insects. A considerable amount of information on the lives of insects is compacted into this small book. Whether one is being introduced to insects for the first time or is an experienced entomologist, the reader cannot help but be impressed with the marvelous manner in which insects adapt. The authors' theme—if insects can "make the most of their environment" without destroying it, perhaps humans can do the same—is subtly developed. (pp. 263-64)

> *Barbara E. Bowman, in a review of "Insect Worlds: A Guide for Man on Making the Most*

of the Environment," in Science Books & Films, *Vol. 16, No. 5, May-June, 1981, pp. 263-64.*

Dreams of a Perfect Earth   (1982)

This is a difficult book to review, for it is both important and generally unsuitable for younger readers. As so often occurs, the publisher, in an effort to increase the potential for sales, has rated the book much below its actual level of suitability. The authors, a highly-respected team of biologist-writers, have put together a unique and well-argued case for an environmental point of view of the future that takes into account the needs of both humankind and ecological systems. For the authors, "dreams of a perfect earth" are tempered by the need of modern human society to grow and prosper. Unfortunately, as well as the case is presented, it will be difficult for the younger reader because the writing is dense and at a relatively high level of sophistication. Only the brightest and most committed youngster will be able to handle the book, and it will be slow and hard going, at that. The message, however, is important in these days of highly polarized ecological viewpoints. For this reason, the book is recommended for junior and senior high libraries and the public library.

> *A. H. Drummond, in a review of "Dreams of a Perfect Earth," in* Appraisal: Science Books for Young People, *Vol. 15, No. 3, Fall, 1982, p. 32.*

Accompanied by eight decorative drawings [by Stephanie Fleischer] that offer attractive glimpses of nature, these poetic descriptions of forest, field, river, shoreline, plain, mountain, desert and city probe the delicate balances of nature. The Milnes hope that this insight will be the means to "rethink the values in our environment" and identify the features that need to be restored, maintained or improved—moving always toward the more perfect earth. The overall effect is one of inspiration rather than specific information. Unfortunately the florid descriptions are encumbered by two wordy introductory chapters that philosophize and proselytize beyond the patience of the upper elementary and junior high school audience at which the book is aimed. The descriptions and suggestions for activities should have stood alone to deliver the message. And even then, there is not enough substance to warrant the expenditure.

> *Susan I. Matisoff, in a review of "Dreams of a Perfect Earth," in* School Library Journal, *Vol. 29, No. 4, December, 1982, p. 73.*

The Milnes care both about the natural world and about sharing knowledge with people of all ages in an effort to create an appreciation for life and an enjoyment in learning about plants and animals. Forest, woodland, river and lake, grassland and desert, shoreline and mountain, and city and county are explored in this book in the search for a perfect earth. Young readers are invited to investigate everything from the uses of seaweed as food supply to the cost of a bicycle in terms of the amount of fresh water used in its manufacture. . . . The Milnes have written extensively on nature and the environment. We have used the Milnes' [adult book] ***Water and Life*** successfully with fifth- through ninth-grade students for more than ten

years. ***Dreams of a Perfect Earth*** and ***Water and Life*** could be used to complement each other. ***Dreams*** is less factual than ***Water,*** reflecting a current trend toward the use of simpler material that invites personal involvement and that is designed to develop readers' ecological understanding. This book is an appealing combination of observations on nature, man's activities, and ideas for the future. It concludes: "All of us share the responsibility for keeping the future free, for sustaining diversity, and for guiding the changes in directions most likely to lead to improvement and opportunity."

> *Betty A. Little, in a review of "Dreams of a Perfect Earth," in* Science Books & Films, *Vol. 18, No. 3, January-February, 1983, p. 144.*

Nature's Clean-Up Crew: The Burying Beetles   (1982)

The life and habits of an interesting insect, the burying or sexton beetle, is closely examined in this poorly written book. The *nicrophorus,* common throughout the world, moves and buries the corpses of small animals many times its own size and uses the decaying mass for feeding the young. Murky black-and-white photographs [by the Milnes] throughout show the beetles in the process of moving various dead animals. The few drawings [by Tom Prentiss] included are clear and informative, but the photographs, except for those on the dust jacket, are of the poorest quality. The authors are obviously interested in and knowledgeable about their topic, but the repetition and tortuous phrasing make for difficult reading. A good index, however, makes the information accessible to older elementary school students.

> *Eva Elizabeth Von Ancken, in a review of "Nature's Clean-Up Crew: The Burying Beetles," in* School Library Journal, *Vol. 29, No. 3, November, 1982, p. 88.*

In ***Nature's Clean-Up Crew,*** the Milnes present a fascinating life story of burying beetles—also called sexton beetles. Photographs and drawings illustrate the authors' explanation of how the beetles move and bury dead birds and mice. The reader constantly has the feeling of being at the scene of activity. The amazing feats, persistence, and pair cooperation of these insects are detailed without the Milnes' resorting to assigning the beetles human emotions. Ideas for observation and the testing of burying beetle behavior are nicely woven into the text. This well-written book, reflecting the authors' lifelong interest in these beetles, leaves me with empathy for nature's undertakers. (pp. 92-3)

> *George Hennings, in a review of "Nature's Clean-Up Crew: The Burying Beetles," in* Science Books & Films, *Vol. 18, No. 2, November-December, 1982, pp. 92-3.*

Nature's Clean-Up Crew . . . is an interesting book for a person who is interested in burying beetles, but a book that will appeal to a limited number of people. My reaction was that it was a doctorate thesis, written at a child's level. I think the opening sentence is significant: "All living things are special." I agree with and appreciate that statement and feel that it has some bearing on the subject. The authors have taken what is a very narrow subject and dealt with it well in some depth. My only question is how many children are interested in the subject. Those that are will find the book fascinating. . . . A good functional index is provided at the end.

> *Peter Stowe, in a review of "Nature's Clean-Up Crew: The Burying Beetles," in* Appraisal: Science Books for Young People, *Vol. 16, No. 1, Winter, 1983, p. 46.*

Nature's Great Carbon Cycle   (1983)

Carbon—its origin, its significance in the universe and to life on Earth, its effect on climate and its uses—are presented in a clear, detailed discussion. It is difficult to find such a concise, cogent explanation of this topic elsewhere. Unfortunately, it is difficult to tell for whom the book is intended. The chapter headings ("Making Things Disappear" or "Magic in the Compost Heap"), the device of little stories to introduce each topic and the style indicate a preteen audience. However, much of the scientific vocabulary is undefined in the text and many of the concepts, such as the carbon cycle or climatic changes, are difficult. Most of the sources in the bibliography are from *Science* and *Scientific American*.. . . . Though this book can be an excellent resource, it may have difficulty finding an audience.

> *Meryl Silverstein, in a review of "Nature's Great Carbon Cycle," in* School Library Journal, *Vol. 30, No. 7, March, 1984, p. 174.*

The Mystery of the Bog Forest   (1984)

A catchy title, but there's no "mystery" about the bog forest; the authors explain exactly how it forms, what stages it goes through as it matures, what plants and animals are the inhabitants. The text is lucid and comprehensive—in fact, its minor weakness is that it goes into so much detail about individual examples of flora and fauna that it be-

A male monarch with wings outstretched. From Insect Worlds: A Guide for Man on Making the Most of the Environment, *written and illustrated by Lorus and Margery Milne.*

comes almost tedious. The many photographs [by the Milnes and Fred Bavendam] are of varying quality but are adequately placed and captioned. There are occasional lapses of style or syntax, but for the most part the writing is as capable as it is authoritative. Separate lists of some of the plants and animals of American peat bogs precede the index.

> *Zena Sutherland, in a review of "The Mystery of the Bog Forest," in* Bulletin of the Center for Children's Books, *Vol. 38, No. 1, September, 1984, p. 11.*

A nice touch is that the plants and animals mentioned in the text are listed with their scientific names at the end of the book. Most general reading material on bogs includes information on insectivorous plants and some fascinating archeological finds. Here, the authors also include information on commercial uses of bogs. The writing is simple enough for seventh graders, but the content is fulsome and interesting enough for general readers. Science teachers will find the book useful as a reference or as supplemental reading for students.

> *Joan W. McIntosh, in a review of "The Mystery of the Bog Forest," in* Science Books & Films, *Vol. 20, No. 2, November-December, 1984, p. 83.*

The authors, naturalists who have travelled throughout Northern Europe and North America observing bogs, write with a simple, fluid style, describing common bog creatures such as muskrats, mink, frogs, bog turtles, bull moose, and water snakes. They also focus on bog plants ranging from exotic highly evolved orchids to carniverous plants like bladderworts, Venus flytraps, and pitcher plants. The interdependency of bog life is illustrated with the pitcher plant, which feeds on some insects while others feed on it.

Unlike the more general *Wetland: bogs, marshes, and swamps,* by L. Buck (c. 1974) and S. Cowings' *Our Wild Wetlands* (c. 1980), the Milnes' book is valuable for its in-depth focus on bogs alone. (p. 26)

> *Lee Jeffers, in a review of "The Mystery of the Bog Forest," in* Appraisal: Science Books for Young People, *Vol. 18, No. 1, Winter, 1985, pp. 25-6.*

A Shovelful of Earth   (1987)

An exploration of soil, its composition and properties, and the multitude of creatures that inhabit it, with a clear, vivid and exciting text, full of fascinating tidbits to intrigue the nature enthusiast. This should have wide appeal for school and public libraries.

The simple experiments here can be done with household supplies; most require only a trowel or small digging tool, a hand lens, and careful observation. The author pulls together Charles Darwin's studies estimating the number of earthworms in an acre with current studies analyzing abrasions on grains of sand to determine where they have been. Chapters are included on special biomes: forest, grasslands, desert, arctic and alpine; and on food webs, food chains, and recycling with solar power. Glossary, index and bibliography.

A welcome addition to the science and nature shelf.

> *A review of "A Shovelful of Earth," in* Kirkus Reviews, *Vol. LV, No. 7, April 1, 1987, p. 556.*

Although there have been several recent books on soils and their composition (notably *Earthworms, Dirt and Rotten Leaves: An Exploration in Ecology* by Molly McLaughlin), this is more comprehensive in treating both biological processes and variations of geographical environment. The first half of the book covers plant and animal life by ground layer, and the second touches on special adaptations in evergreen, tropic, desert, Arctic, and alpine regions. The writing is not always smooth (the preface begins with a misplaced modifier), but the text is straightforward and generally well organized by chapter and subsection, with an index for access to specific topics.

> *Betsy Hearne, in a review of "A Shovelful of Earth," in* Bulletin of the Center for Children's Books, *Vol. 40, No. 10, June, 1987, p. 192.*

Call it what you will, soil or dirt or ground covers most of the lands, only feet thick but continent-wide. Even the biologists somewhat neglect it; soil science is mostly a product of the 20th century. These two biologist-writers point out a domain open to fresh exploration at modest effort almost everywhere. . . .

The drawings [by Margaret La Farge] make this darkened life vivid, and the text tells of the ways of counting and collecting it. You will enjoy some finds, but not all the methods are easy enough for the amateur to use. Soils differ; there are brief chapters on what is found under the evergreen forest, under land on which rain falls every day, under dry deserts and under frozen ground. How a single sand grain could be shown to have a history as a distinct particle for a couple of hundred thousand years, in desert dune, glacial ice and tidal flat, is well explained; for the electron-microscopic images that were the signs of that past you would need to look up the reference given. This is a fresh and important 100-page contribution, a first-rate small book for grade school biologists (or older beginners). (p. 157)

> *Philip Morrison and Phylis Morrison, "A Vacation Trip for Young Readers around the World of Science," in* Scientific American, *Vol. 257, No. 6, December, 1987, pp. 148-57.*

Understanding Radioactivity (1989)

A brief description of radioactivity, its uses, and the problems caused by both natural and man-made varieties.

Radioactivity is the energy released when unstable elements decay or when atoms are either split asunder (fission) or smashed together (fusion). The energy source can be the sun or naturally occuring uranium decaying into radon; more and more often, its sources come from the enterprises and accidents of man, with far-reaching results. The meltdown of the nuclear reactor at Chernobyl, for instance, was detected thousands of miles from the site—some of the aftereffects threatened the Finnish Lapland-

ers' food chain. But even when great care is exercised, as at the Oak Ridge laboratory, unexpected contamination through the natural plant-animal food chain has occurred. We get too soon hot and too late smart.

With nearly 50 books to their credit, the Milnes are veterans at researching and packaging information. Though atomic structure gets short shrift here (and is described so compactly that even those with some background may blink), and though more graphics would have clarified some topics—e.g., the relationship between various levels of roentgens, rems, and curies—the information is so important, and the facts presented so well chosen, that this belongs in most collections. Glossary; bibliography; index.

> *A review of "Understanding Radioactivity," in* Kirkus Reviews, *Vol. LVII, No. 7, April 1, 1989, p. 551.*

The Milnes give clear if overly compressed accounts of basic atomic structure, nuclear decay, and background radiation. But at the end of each chapter on human uses of radioactivity, they seem to grasp at straws of continued research to minimize the dangers that they describe. They oversimplify certain problems, such as the conflict over mining on native American lands, by not mentioning the terrible economic pressures applied by the nuclear industry. This simplification would be acceptable in a book for younger readers, but the vocabulary level and density of facts in the text aim it at students who will demand more explanation. . . . In comparison, Laurence Pringle's *Radiation: Waves and Particles/Benefits and Risks* (Enslow, 1983) gives a more detailed picture with fuller explanations and more attractive illustrations, but it is not as up to date. The Milnes' book is recommended as supplementary reading for school and public libraries.

> *Jonathon Betz-Zall, in a review of "Understanding Radioactivity," in* School Library Journal, *Vol. 35, No. 9, May, 1989, p. 130.*

A solid introduction to radioactivity, the energy emitted by unstable atoms as they decay, this book takes students comfortably into a complex subject. . . . Such timely issues as the earth's natural background radiation, nuclear warfare and power, and the effects of the increased release of radiation into the environment are pondered seriously and thoroughly in this compact work. The lessons learned from the accidents at Three Mile Island and Chernobyl—the topics that may be of most interest to students—are well documented.

> *Beth Herbert, in a review of "Understanding Radioactivity," in* Booklist, *Vol. 85, No. 18, May 15, 1989, p. 1652.*

Despite excellent writing and fine black-and-white drawings, this book about radioactivity . . . is a disappointment.

The Milnes explain the basics of radioactivity clearly and without jargon, touching on the pioneering work of the Curies, the nature of unstable radioactive atoms, the difference between alpha, beta, and gamma rays, and "background radiation"—the fact that radioactivity occurs naturally throughout nature, even in our bodies, in small amounts.

The authors get into trouble, however, when they move

on to commercial nuclear energy and nuclear weapons production.

They don't explain, for instance, the fundamental difference between the water-cooled reactors used by the U.S., Japan, and Western Europe, and the Soviets' graphite reactor at Cherynobyl. They simplify the discussion of nuclear waste—a complex issue—to such an extent that it becomes inaccurate. They say, for instance, that the federal government "plans to store high-level nuclear wastes in sites in Nevada, Texas, and Washington," but that "no safe method of storage has yet been found." In fact, commercial nuclear wastes will be stored deep underground in only one of these sites, probably Nevada. And it would be a shock to many scientists to hear that no safe method of storage has yet been found. For many years, the French have successfully stored their high-level wastes by "virtrifying" them—binding them into glass, then encasing them in a series of thick metal containers before burying them.

The Milnes also report that 75% of all U.S. nuclear reactor waste is stored at a facility in Hanford, Washington. In fact, only defense-related waste is buried there.

The failure to differentiate between commercial and defense-related nuclear wastes is perhaps their most glaring distortion. Commercial waste management practices are closely monitored and strictly regulated by the federal Nuclear Regulatory Commission. Defense-related wastes, by contrast, have often been handled haphazardly and secretively, by the Department of Energy—as we all know from recent reports about radioactive contamination at weapons production plants in Colorado, Ohio, and elsewhere.

Excellent in its early sections, this book is seriously flawed in later sections by incomplete, often inaccurate information. The authors also skew their book with a not-so-subtle anti-nuclear energy bias which is particularly apparent in the books chosen for the bibliography—books with titles like *No Nukes: Everyone's Guide to Nuclear Power*, and *Cover Up: What You are Not Supposed to Know about Nuclear Power*.

For a more balanced view of nuclear energy—although not as comprehensive an overview of radioactivity—readers would do better to look to *Nuclear Power: The Inside Story*, by Nigel Hawkes, and *Nuclear Safety*, a post-Chernobyl look at nuclear energy by the same author. (pp. 41-2)

Lee Jeffers Brami, in a review of "Understanding Radioactivity," in Appraisal: Science Books for Young People, *Vol. 23, No. 1, Winter, 1990, pp. 41-2.*

Nicholasa Mohr

1935-

Hispanic American author and illustrator of fiction and short stories.

Considered a powerful and insightful writer of books on the Puerto Rican experience for young adults and readers in the early and middle grades, Mohr is recognized for accurately representing the hardships and struggles of her people in the El Barrio section of New York City while celebrating their resilience, solidarity, pride, and variety of life. Especially well regarded as a creator of character and setting, she characteristically addresses the themes of self-discovery and maturation in a society where poverty, crime, and discrimination are omnipresent. Mohr candidly incorporates elements of urban life into her works which some observers find unconventional, such as failed marriages, homosexuality, teenage pregnancy, illegitimacy, spiritualism, and drug use; she also writes about the barriers facing women as well as the role of institutions in creating and sustaining poverty. In addition, Mohr's straightforward writing style, into which she introduces Spanish words and phrases, includes several examples of slang and street language. However, Mohr chooses to emphasize the feelings, emotions, and eventual growth of her characters rather than the harshness of their environment, and she balances her works with humor, hopefulness, and a concentration on such elements as family love, friendship, and self-esteem.

Beginning her career as a visual artist, Mohr became well known as a painter and printmaker before honoring a request made by one of her collectors, the head of a publishing house, to write about growing up Puerto Rican and female. The result was her autobiographical novel *Nilda* (1973), the story of four years in the life of Nilda Ramirez, who learns about being Puerto Rican in America during the Second World War. Nilda, who is nine when the book begins, changes from being a self-centered child to a young woman who learns to accept both her mother's death and the split of her family. Illustrated by Mohr with expressionistic black-and-white drawings which combine representational art with words and symbols, *Nilda* is often celebrated as a classic of both young adult and ethnic literature. Mohr's next work, *El Bronx Remembered: A Novella and Stories* (1975), describes the tragicomic lives of the young people and adults who live in an outgrowth of Spanish Harlem on New York's Lower East Side; *In Nueva York* (1977) is a collection of interconnected short stories again set in a Puerto Rican neighborhood on the Lower East Side. With *Felita* (1979) and its sequel *Going Home* (1986), Mohr introduces Felita Maldonado, who narrates both stories in a lively, colloquial fashion. In the first book, eight-year-old Felita moves to a new neighborhood with her family, where they encounter prejudice before returning home, while the second work describes how eleven-year-old Felita successfully blends her heritage and her American background on a summer trip to Puerto Rico. Mohr has also written short stories, essays, plays, and a novella for adults. *Nilda* won the Best Book Award

from *School Library Journal* in 1973 as well as the Jane Addams Children's Book Award in 1974; the novel also received a citation of merit for its book jacket in 1974. *El Bronx Remembered* won the Best Book Award from *School Library Journal* in 1975 and was a National Book Award finalist in 1976, while *In Nueva York* won the *SLJ* Best Book Award in 1978.

(See also *Contemporary Literary Criticism*, Vol. 12; *Something about the Author*, Vol. 8; *Something about the Author Autobiography Series*, Vol. 8; *Contemporary Authors New Revision Series*, Vol. 1; and *Contemporary Authors*, Vols. 49-52.)

AUTHOR'S COMMENTARY

[The following excerpt is from an interview by Paul Janeczko.]

P.J. How did you get started writing?

N.M. I got started writing four years ago, and it was something that happened quite unexpectedly. All my life, I had made communication through visual vocabularies as I was a painter and a graphic artist for eighteen years. I studied very hard; first I did oil paintings, drawings, acrylics, and I used tempera; and then I was fascinated with printmaking. As a fine artist, I never did commercial art. I managed to learn the art of printmaking, which is very specific; and you need to know a lot of technical steps to do an etching, because you work on metal, you work on stone. I did etching, embossing, lithography; and I did silk screening. I got very involved in that kind of work and I was not doing badly. . . . I was with an art agent who discovered that one of my collectors was a publisher—not Harper and Row, another publisher. They said they had heard me speak and I had a lot of graffiti—long before graffiti became so popular in certain areas, especially New York. They said, "Nicholasa, why don't you write about your experiences because you are from a particular group of American—Puerto Ricans—and there is so little written about them." My experiences were developed in my work. You could see them in my figurative work and the way I use colors. Sometimes I told a story through the visual interpretation and, hopefully, evoked feelings from the viewer. So this particular publisher who had collected my work said, "Have Nicholasa write fifty pages." I really wasn't interested; I was not a writer. I always liked to write; I had never had any difficulty writing. Some people play the piano. I can't, but I can write. So they continued bringing the subject up. Once I had a little bit of time, and I decided, well, why not? I'll sit down and write fifty pages. So, in the first person, I wrote about fifty pages, or a little less, in vignette form: what it was like to grow up as a young American Puerto Rican in the United States, in relationship to other Americans around you, and to be so economically deprived as I was as a youngster, and yet to have such a strong culture. My publisher liked it very much, but she didn't feel that it was quite what she wanted. I think what she expected was something much more sensational, the sort of stereotypical ghetto person. So I told her that much to my embarrassment I had never stolen anything, taken hard drugs, been raped or mugged. So I guess she thought my life was uneventful. I took back my vignettes and said, "Later." I went back to my art. Then I got a call from Harper and Row asking if I were interested in doing a cover for one of their books. While I was really not interested in commercial art, I came with my vignettes, and Ellen Rudin, who was my editor then, encouraged me to write and make these vignettes into a novel. I took out the first person form because it was too much of a confessional when you write I, I, I, and decided if I took it into the third person, I could take my experiences and base my plot and feeling on that. Then I could go further because I could narrate, I could step outside for character. Then I got a contract, and I wrote the first book, *Nilda,* which was put out by Harper. So that is how it happened. Then I fell very much in love with writing. At first, I was a little bit nervous; it was like getting a divorce. I did the coverjacket for the hardback and I did eight illustrations, because I just couldn't accept the transition that I could write so easily after all those years. I found that I could do certain things in writing and there was a crying need for what I had to say as a Puerto Rican, as someone living here, and as a woman.

P.J. For instance? (pp. 75-7)

[**N.M.**] What I could do with writing is be very specific; I could tell a story, really tell a story, and I could make people laugh. I could make people aware of what it was

like for myself at the time. It was almost like a catharsis, the first book. I was even thinking of going into sculpture, but all of a sudden I found a medium where I was really comfortable. I could draw a picture with words, and it was extremely stimulating and eye-opening to realize what one could do with words. I see fiction as an art form which I don't see myself as leaving. Everything I have done as an artist is transferable to a new craft. I don't consider myself a novice, but I do consider myself someone who is learning a new craft.

P.J. What is the essence of good writing?

N.M. Well, for me, I don't write for young people, per se. I write for people. Some of them are young and some of them are old. I don't like this division that young people sort of have a place; they're people. There's a certain freshness when they see the world, so that a young person reading my work can identify, and an old person can go back into an odyssey of time. Good writing is when it affects everybody. I feel that my books can be read by everyone. They're not from nine to twelve, or eleven to whatever. I feel you have to learn to read and write. Once you learn to read, you can read my books; I write very, very simply, no matter how complex my message may be. I like a simple vocabulary that anyone can read, and I have had older people reading my work. I'm very excited that younger people read my work and like it, because I feel that's part of life, that's part of being alive. But good writing is writing that someone picks up and says, "Okay, I want to go on with this, not because it's for a teenager or adolescent, but because the writer is saying something that I want to get involved with."

P.J. What do you owe your readers?

N.M. I owe my readers the same thing I owed the people who looked at my graphics; that is, I owe them first, a certain amount of honesty towards the product that I am trying to finish. If I finish a product, it's got to be totally honest, devoid of banality, and it's got to be something that I can live with, and something that I feel they can get into. If they can't, they can't. Not everyone can love you. But it's as honest and straight as possible. If I say I'm starting a subject, no matter how difficult that subject might be, I have to see it through. I have to come to some sort of conclusion and commit myself. And it is a total commitment, whether it's a book or canvas or print; and the viewer can feel that. If the viewer wants to reject it, that's okay; but the commitment is there. That's what I feel, basically, I owe anyone who is looking at my work or reading my work.

P.J. Is theme a conscious effort on your part, or do you start by telling a good story, and theme fits into that?

N.M. I think they are related; you almost cannot separate them. There are times when the theme is important, and sometimes when it's unimportant; but I don't think it's terribly conscious with me. I feel that the story line or the theme is only an aspect of the writing. It's how the characters begin to breathe and how real they are. People are very important to me in my stories. (pp. 77-8)

Nicholasa Mohr and Paul Janeczko, in an interview in From Writers to Students: The Pleasures and Pains of Writing, *edited by M.*

Jerry Weiss, International Reading Association, 1979, pp. 75-8.

Nilda (1973)

[*Nilda* is a] sad and beautiful book. . . . (p. 27)

What does it feel like being poor and belonging to a despised minority? Over the past 10 years many children's books have been written, exploring these very questions. Few come up to *Nilda* in describing the crushing humiliations of poverty and in peeling off the ethnic wrappings so that we can see the human child underneath.

Nilda is nearly 10 when the book begins in July, 1941, and 13½ when it ends in May, 1945. The Second World War is there in the background, important only in its unimportance to a family whose daily struggles to survive are so overwhelming. This is a very personal book. We see life in the Puerto Rican ghetto of New York City through a child's vision—baffled, resigned, angry and frequently joyful. Nilda is no idealized slum child. She punctuates her speech with four-letter words, and like all children, places her own private griefs ahead of larger, adult sorrows. "Mama, I gotta tell you something, Ma!" Nilda cries, eager to tell her weeping, grieving mother whose husband is dying how Sophie played a mean trick on her.

The main story line concerns Mama's efforts to take care of her large family—five children, sick husband, crazy aunt, and pregnant girl friend of one son. But what makes the book remarkable is the richness of detail and the aching sense of a child's feelings. When Nilda is sent to a Catholic charity camp and forced along with other girls to take nightly doses of milk of magnesia by a terrifying, smiling nun, it is hard not to feel her humiliation. It is equally hard not to rejoice with Nilda and her friends when they get their revenge on Miss Reilly, a language teacher who is trying to teach Castilian Spanish to her class of Puerto Rican students.

Nicholasa Mohr's harsh, distinctive drawings emphasize the nightmare of poverty, but her book goes far beyond being just another tale from the ghetto. Sad, funny, fascinating and honest, it will appeal to adults as well as children. (pp. 27-8)

Marilyn Sachs in a review of "Nilda," in The New York Times Book Review, November 4, 1973, pp. 27-8.

[*Nilda*] describes the life of Nilda Ramirez from her tenth to her fourteenth year as she grows up in Spanish Harlem. The author's view is an insider's view and is to be distinguished from views which might not be so intimately informed about the subtle meanings of the experiences narrated. But more importantly the author has such a good grasp of the social dynamics involved in her tale that it tells not only a story which in many ways typifies the life of the poor in Spanish Harlem, but it describes as well the plight of the urban poor everywhere. It recognizes the role institutions play in sustaining poverty, and it shows the extraordinary difficulty of breaking out, even for the strongest, most sensitive, and most intelligent. There is no pity here, for the author is too much aware of the humanity of her characters and of the other implications of pity to be in any way condescending. There is insider's humor, gentle, and in no way degrading. . . . All in all *Nilda* is what I would call a significant book, a touchstone by which others may be judged. (p. 231)

Donald B. Gibson, "Fiction, Fantasy, and Ethnic Realities," in Children's Literature: Annual of the Modern Language Association Seminar on Children's Literature and The Children's Literature Association, Vol. 3, 1974, pp. 230-34.

One of the finest books about the Puerto Rican experience is *Nilda*, a poignant story of ten-year-old Nilda Ramirez, living in Spanish Harlem during the 1940s. Nicholasa Mohr has written a powerful story of the hardships of being Puerto Rican and of the barriers facing women. For example, at a Catholic summer camp, Nilda is given equal doses of discipline, anti-Semitism, and laxatives (to purify her when she greets God). The welfare system also comes under attack. . . . Vivid accounts of police prejudice against Puerto Ricans, Puerto Rican prejudice against blacks, spiritualism, and superstition are also presented in *Nilda*. The story is enhanced by a series of powerful and surrealistic illustrations. The illustrations, language, and strong antiestablishment themes combine to make *Nilda* a moving statement about the Puerto Rican experience in America. (p. 219)

Myra Pollack Sadker and David Miller Sadker, "Other Selected Minority Groups as Portrayed in Children's Books," in their Now Upon a Time: A Contemporary View of Children's Literature, Harper & Row, Publishers, 1977, pp. 210-30.

Nilda is the story of a Puerto Rican family living in New York. It is narrated from the point of view of a young girl; Nilda is ten years old at the outset of the story which covers a four year period, from 1941 to 1945. I presume the author chose this time period because it coincided with her own childhood and early adolescence. There is no evidence in the novel that there was any other reason. The author was not striving to capture the flavor of the forties. The biggest event of the time, World War II, is incidental to the story. (p. 6)

The accumulation of details without dramatic purpose results in overwhelming boredom. This, I suppose, is more a failure of technique than of intention. The portrait of life in El Barrio is fair enough but the author seems to be depending on the inherent drama of poverty to carry the book. That drama never materializes. The characters have no depth. Though none of their actions strikes a false note, the reader is hard pressed to feel for them. Rarely is the book able to arouse any sympathy, pathos, or humor.

Two incidents in the book are exceptions. One occurs when Nilda goes to camp. The other girls in her bunk persecute a girl who did not have a suitcase—she had brought her clothes in a paper box. To compensate for her poverty she habitually bragged about make-believe luxuries, thus arousing the animosity of the other girls, who retaliate by vandalizing her cardboard box. This incident is handled sensitively and come across convincingly. The other scene of note involves Jimmy's girlfriend's going back home, after her baby is born. The outraged mother will not open the door to the suppliant daughter. The mother refuses even to acknowledge that it is her daughter on the other side of the locked door. This scene stands out for its dramatic force. Two good scenes however are not enough to make an interesting novel.

Surprisingly, the author creates then, throws away, an opportunity to make incisive political observations. She makes one of the characters, the step-father, a socialist, but proceeds to treat this fact as an aberration in his personality. If one knew nothing at all about socialism one might conclude from this book that all it entails is an irrational hatred of religion. None of the disruption caused by the war is even hinted at. The recent depression, which to this day is on the lips of people who lived through it, is never mentioned by anyone in the book. Spanish Harlem was not so isolated from the rest of New York as to have been so totally unaffected by the larger events of the day. If it had been, that in itself would be something to write about. The dynamics of the Welfare Department go unexplored, though going on public assistance is a traumatic event in the life of the family. Neither is the older brother's experience in prison utilized as social commentary. In fact, we get no hint at all of what personal circumstances and feelings drove him down the path of crime.

Assuming that the author did not digress into any of the above areas in order to concentrate on Nilda's experience, we would have the right to expect a psychological portrait of Nilda. We do not get it; cause and effect are here negated. She seems to be living through events which have no effect on her. (pp. 7-8)

> *Miguel A. Ortiz, "The Politics of Poverty in Young Adult Literature," in* The Lion and the Unicorn, *Vol. 2, No. 2, Fall, 1978, pp. 6-15.*

El Bronx Remembered: A Novella and Stories (1975)

"Qué fenomenal!" says Little Ray the Tiny Tim of Nicholasa Mohr's new book. Eleven short stories and a novella describe " . . . Puerto Rican migrants and their everyday struggle for survival, during that decade of the promised future 1946 through 1956, in New York City's 'El Bronx.' "

Ten years earlier, when I lived there, it was the struggle of poor whites—Jews, Armenians, Italians, Irish inhabiting the identical turf and sharing the same dreams. One of which was to move—east, north or west—any direction rather than stay in the South Bronx, where all of these stories are set.

While visions of elegant apartment houses on Grand Concourse or the bucolic life around Yonkers danced in the heads of our parents we children roamed the streets, experiencing its varieties and mysteries. Nicholasa Mohr's great skill as a writer is her ability to show how much has changed in ten years, and yet how little.

Little Ray, in **"A New Window Display,"** is a newcomer from Puerto Rico who marvels at all the wonders in El Bronx: to every new experience, he says, *"Qué fenomenal!"* His friends have told him about the snow, and he is particularly eager to see it. But he never does. He dies before it comes, and his friends mourn for him in the best possible way—by playing in it themselves, shouting, sliding, turning and crying out for him at its beauty, *"Qué fenomenal!"*

From Nilda, *written and illustrated by Nicholasa Mohr.*

If there is any message at all in these stories, any underlying theme, it is that life goes on. But Nicholasa Mohr is more interested in people than in messages. Essentially, she is an old-fashioned writer, a meat-and-potatoes writer, whose stories stick to your ribs. No complicated symbolism here, no trendy obscurity of meaning, no hopeless despair or militant ethnicity. Her people endure because they are people. Some of them suffer, some of them die, a few of them fail, but most of the time they endure, or others like them endure.

Most brilliant and tender, perhaps, of all these brilliant and tender stories, is **"Mr. Mendelsohn,"** the story of a lonely old Jewish man who is befriended by a Puerto Rican family. Even though Mr. Mendelsohn dies finally, it is no tragedy because his last years have been enriched by kindness and love. . . .

A couple of the stories are tragic, but most of Nicholasa Mohr's characters are too sturdy and resilient for defeat. Yvette and Mildred, the two friends in **"The Wrong Lunch Line,"** are humiliated by teachers when they try to eat their lunch together in school. Friendship, however, is not such a fragile thing, and the two girls, though hurt and confused, can laugh scornfully at the foolishness of adults.

And Hannibal, Joey, Ramona, Maria and Casilda, who

grow up in the course of three of the stories, can laugh too—and survive death, betrayal and religious conversion, as they bounce off the pages in the final story on their way to a dance at St. Anselm's and to a future that will always hold for Nicholasa Mohr's characters some promise, some hope.

In her earlier outstanding novel **Nilda,** it was apparent that if any author could make you hear pulses beating from the pages, Nicholasa Mohr was the one. In **El Bronx Remembered,** she has done it again.

Qué fenomenal!

> *Marilyn Sachs in a review of "El Bronx Remembered," in* The New York Times Book Review, *November 16, 1975, p. 30.*

A tree once grew in Brooklyn. Now, a complete garden blooms in El Bronx, the setting of Nicholasa Mohr's collection of a novella and stories. In all respects, it is a worthy sequel to her first ghetto novel, **Nilda.** . . .

Geographically, El Bronx is located on Manhattan's Lower East Side, an outgrowth of Spanish Harlem. Physically, its turf is over-populated, dingy, and poverty laden. Ethnically, it is comprised almost totally of Puerto Ricans who are strangers to the big city life and the American jargon that surround them. Only love, loyalty and understanding help them cling to one another.

Much has been written about Spanish-speaking communities, but it is rare to find such delicate insight combined with such deliberate detail. Miss Mohr has the ability to describe quite commonplace situations, dissect them, relate them to the reader, and then allow her interpretations to be savored. All the Papis and Mamis hit home to both the teenage and adult reader. The parent figures are aggressive, persuasive, and sometimes bewildered. The children are aggressive and persuasive but not at all bewildered, whether they are facing birth, death, or new shoes.

In contrast to the universality of the short stories, the subject matter of the novella, **Herman and Alice,** is somewhat more marginal and problematic for the younger reader and his conservative parents. It deals with a fifteen-year-old's pregnancy, an older man's homosexuality, their ensuing platonic marriage, the inevitable divorce, and her return to adolescent love-searching. It's potent, real, and subtle. Perhaps, it's too advanced for the younger crowd. But Miss Mohr tells it like it is for anyone who wants to learn that life still flourishes on Manhattan Island.

> *Anne M. Flynn in a review of "El Bronx Remembered," in* Best Sellers, *Vol. 35, No. 9, December, 1975, p. 266.*

Can a Puerto Rican be racist? How much sexist and racist ideology have we internalized? How can Puerto Rican writers accurately depict our present and help to create our future at the same time? What do we tell our children about ourselves, and what would we like them to be as adults? Does a Puerto Rican writer automatically possess a more relevant perspective?

El Bronx Remembered consists of eleven short stories and a novella describing the anxieties, fears, loves, hates, pride, despair, nostalgia and hopes of several Puerto Ricans in the barrio, El Bronx, from 1946 to 1956. The subjects of these well-written and descriptive tales want to escape to suburbia, or into the arms of men, or to be accepted and assimilated into a materialistic society which rejects and exploits them. But despite some truths and sharp insights, these are not stories of change, struggle or love. Rather, they are negative stories which reinforce stereotypes.

One incredibly racist story is about Jasmine, a gypsy, who wins the acceptance of her classmates by reading palms and telling stories. The description of Jasmine's appearance reads like a catalog of prejudices and, as in most of the stories in this book, sexism is prevalent as well.

The novella (a sick soap opera) tells of Alice, a pregnant fifteen-year-old who finds temporary comfort and happiness in the home of a mature, understanding homosexual. A conversation between Alice and her mother about the pregnancy reeks of puritanism—"I know you are sorry. I am too, Alice, but it's too late now. Because, now you see, you can be sorry for the rest of your life."—as does Alice's description of her sexual life: "The first time it was painful and she had cried; the second time it was almost as bad, except she had felt numb." To top it off, Alice forgets all the agony of her labor pains as soon as she gazes upon her new-born *son.*

In addition to having internalized myths about females, the novella's characters have also taken to heart certain myths about Puerto Ricans. Herman says of his own people, "Honestly, these people, a bunch of ignorantes, and they just keep making babies and more babies and being more miserable." Alice's mother buys her new clothes to go out with the "respectable" homosexual, so that he will not think their family is a bunch of "jíbaros" (peasants).

Although it is unusual to portray a gay person in a book for young people, no new ground is broken here in developing understanding of sexual differences. Alice marries Herman to escape from her critical mother. For Herman, the marriage serves to pacify his old parents in Puerto Rico who want him to be a husband and father. The characters are neither honest with themselves nor with each other.

Regarding the questions raised at the beginning of this review, **El Bronx Remembered** is evidence that oppressed people (in this case, Puerto Ricans or women) do not necessarily understand the mechanism of oppression. Unless we look critically at our lives, our family relations, our institutions, the positive and negative aspects of our culture, we will not develop the will to resist and to change things. Without that critical approach, our observations are but one small part of the truth and continue to reinforce negative stereotypes about ourselves and reflect the dominant society's negative values. (pp. 251-52)

> *A review of "El Bronx Remembered," in* Human—and Anti-Human—Values in Children's Books: A Content Rating Instrument for Educators and Concerned Parents, *edited by the Council on Interracial Books for Children, Inc., Racism and Sexism Resource Center for Educators, 1976, pp. 251-52.*

In Nueva York (1977)

These moving, interconnected stories—which can almost

be read as a loosely structured novel—mix humor and pathos in depicting the lives of Puerto Rican-Americans on New York's poverty stricken Lower East Side. Mohr's characters are warm and believable, and she succeeds admirably in involving readers in what happens to them. . . . Although the stories will have special relevance to teens in urban Spanish communities—Mohr sprinkles in Spanish phrases and, in one story, appropriate street language is used extensively—the superb characterizations will draw many others.

> *Jack Forman in a review of "In Nueva York,"*
> *in* School Library Journal, *Vol. 23, No. 8,*
> *April, 1977, p. 79.*

[This] stronger, tighter collection than **El Bronx Remembered** gradually zeros in on a few principals and ends more like an episodic novel. At center stage are beer-guzzling Old Mary (in her fifties) and her long-lost son from Puerto Rico, who turns out to be a dwarf; hard-working, hard-nosed Rudi at the luncheonette, unremorseful when he kills a teenaged "animal" who's tried to rob him; and Rudi's much younger bride, imported from the island and miserable here until Rudi breaks a leg and Old Mary's other, footloose son shows up to take care of Rudi's business. Others, less integrated as to plot but just as sharply observed, include a young homosexual, his partner, his lesbian bride, and the "Perfect Little Flower Girl" who participates in their bizarre wedding. (Though the story goes nowhere, the Arbus-like scene is enough.) In truth, it might be negative qualities that make this a juvenile—it's being neither demanding nor really disturbing. But that is not to deny the clarity, wry humor, genuine sympathy, and considerable success with which Mohr brings her neighborhood to life.

> *A review of "In Nueva York," in* Kirkus Re-
> views, *Vol. XLV, No. 7, April 1, 1977, p. 360.*

[**In Nueva York**] is composed of short interlocking episodes or stories. Undoubtedly the most ambitious of the three books [Laurence Yep's *Child of the Owl,* Brenda Wilkinson's *Ludell and Willie,* and Mohr's book] in literary terms, it seems, however, too obviously intended as slice-of-life fiction with the result that the characters are busier being Puerto Rican-Americans than being people. Several of the stories present intriguing situations but end inconclusively. An old woman's long lost son turns out to be a dwarf. A gay male marries a gay female. **"The English Lesson"** embarrassingly recalls H*Y*M*A*N K*A*P*L*A*N without laughs. Happily, sometimes better shows itself in the last few stories. In **"The Robbery"** and **"Coming to Terms"** a store owner kills a 15-year-old thief during a holdup and is publicly badgered by the dead youth's mother with demands that the storeowner pay for a headstone. In the end the man comes to terms, not with the mother ("This woman is stark raving nuts"), but with the battered alley cat whose life he has been threatening for years. There should have been more of this. All in all, it's Sociologists 8, Readers 4.

> *Georgess McHargue in a review of "In Nueva*
> *York," in* The New York Times Book Re-
> view, *May 22, 1977, p. 29.*

In a series of interrelated short stories set in a Puerto Rican neighborhood of Manhattan, Mohr creates a remarkably vivid tapestry of community life as well as of individual characters. Lali, the young bride of Rudi, who is twice her age and who has brought her to New York to help him run his luncheonette, goes to night school English classes with the dwarf William, who secretly adores her. William has just come from home to see Old Mary, who had not seen her illegitimate child since his infancy. The self-reliant Raquel, who works at times for Rudi, is independent enough to make her children feel comfortable attending the wedding of a gay friend, Johnny, who for a practical reason marries a lesbian. Jennie and Angie, who have a reunion at the luncheonette, are former schoolmates, one of whom is going on to college, the other trying to achieve a normal life after being a prostitute and drug addict. Tough, candid, and perceptive, the book has memorable characters, resilient and responsive, in a sharply-etched milieu.

> *Zena Sutherland in a review of "In Nueva*
> *York," in* Bulletin of the Center for Children's
> Books, *Vol. 30, No. 11, July-August, 1977, p.*
> *178.*

[**In Nueva York**] is a collection of stories tied together by their setting. A number of the characters appear in more than one story and the effect is an intimate look into the most interesting parts of several people's lives without the artificial strain of having them all squeezed into a single plot. For people who like to approach books from the social issues viewpoint, this is an excellent book to help people see beyond the stereotypes. The reader meets several individuals who share a common neighborhood and many common problems, yet each is unique and intriguing. The fact that readers come away with a knowledge of each character's individuality and an empathy for their feelings is due to Mohr's skill as a writer. There is really no way of evaluating a book from the viewpoint of its social effect without also judging its literary effect. On either score, **In Nueva York** ranks very high.

> *Aileen Pace Nilsen, in a review of "In Nueva*
> *York," in* English Journal, *Vol. 67, No. 2, Feb-*
> *ruary, 1978, p. 100.*

Felita (1979)

The move Felita and her family make to a new, "better" neighborhood is ill fated: Felita misses her friends, and residents spurn them. After several harassment episodes, the family returns to its old neighborhood. Felita is happy there despite the cramped quarters of their third and smallest apartment. She sorts out her anger over recent events with her beloved Abuelita and settles in anew with friends, school, and most of all, family. This is Mohr's first book for younger audiences, and it's moderately successful. The episodic story is usually engaging, and Felita's presence is lively and strong. Unfortunately, the first part of the story stands too much apart from the rest; moreover, a key scene rings false—it is not convincing that girls so friendly to Felita would turn on her in an instant as they do here. Despite its breaks, though, the story has spark enough to keep its audience involved.

> *Denise M. Wilms in a review of "Felita," in*
> Booklist, *Vol. 76, No. 7, December 1, 1979, p.*
> *559.*

Family relationships and schoolgirl friendships are the basis of an episodic, plotless story. Without remarkable literary attributes the book, nevertheless, has strong characters and is significant for its honest, realistic view of an important aspect of contemporary American life.

Virginia Haviland in a review of "Felita," in The Horn Book Magazine, *Vol. LVI, No. 1, February, 1980, p. 56.*

This begins with the Maldonado family preparing to move despite Felita's and her brothers' reluctance to leave their friends. The parents want the new, "better" neighborhood and public school for their kids, but before long the family has moved back, driven out by taunts, a beating, and harassment from the new neighbors who don't want any "spicks" moving in. Felita's first contact with the new girls, who accept her until their mothers call them home and abruptly turn them round, is too heavily handled, though readers are bound to feel for Felita; and the comments of her mother and her grandmother later on are simply models of the right thing to say. (Basically, the message is "Don't hate them, love yourself.") Realistically, if anticlimactically, the incident is left behind: the children are happy back on their old block, the parents more or less decide that the kids will be okay as long as they're looked after, and Mohr moves on to more reinforcing experiences. A casualty-free middle-of-the-night fire casts a glow of neighborly togetherness; a school play occasions a temporary rift between Felita and her best friend—and a talk from Grandmother on the value of friendship and the wisdom of making up; and her grandmother's death in the end brings out the note of family love and continuity. For the same reasons that Mohr seems to have written this, libraries will want it; but it hasn't the vitality of Mohr's earlier, older fiction.

A review of "Felita," in Kirkus Reviews, *Vol. XLVIII, No. 3, February 1, 1980, p. 127.*

Going Home (1986)

A charming sequel to the author's *Felita*. . . . Now 11, Felita is ecstatic over her upcoming trip to Puerto Rico, as well as her first boyfriend, shy Vinnie from Colombia.

While the upbeat tone never really darkens, there are conflicts: Mami's new strictness with Felita, her bossy brother Tito, the jealousies of other girls. When Felita gets to Puerto Rico she discovers homesickness and meets discrimination from some of the other kids, who call her "Nuyorican" and "Gringita." But justice is dealt, and Felita is surprised to find that she will miss the island and her new friends when she returns to New York. Felita's narration is colloquial and exuberant, and Mohr has a particularly sharp eye for the friendships (as well as the downright meanness) of pre-teen girls. And that Vinnie's a charmer.

Zena Sutherland in a review of "Going Home," in Bulletin of the Center for Children's Books, *Vol. 39, No. 9, May, 1986, p. 175.*

Felita's first-person narrative is bright and honest, and the story line is well developed through Felita's relationships—both positive and negative. There are few stories of Puerto Rican children, and this is deftly written and lively—an enjoyable story for any reader.

Denise M. Wilms in a review of "Going Home," in Booklist, *Vol. 82, No. 21, July, 1986, p. 1615.*

The story is told in Felita's vital, colloquial voice and breaks naturally into two parts: the period before her journey which describes her neighborhood, friendships and her growing relationship with a Colombian boy; and the summer in Puerto Rico. A bit melodramatic in the telling, the style accurately reflects Felita's strong, emotional responses to life, and the casual, occasionally earthy language brings a liveliness and veracity to her pictures of life in New York City and Puerto Rico. Felita is a vivid, memorable character, well realized and well developed. It is a pleasure to welcome her back.

Christine Behrmann, in a review of "Going Home," in School Library Journal, *Vol. 32, No. 10, August, 1986, p. 105.*

Helen Oxenbury

1938-

English author and illustrator of picture books and reteller.

Oxenbury is recognized as a gifted writer and artist of picture books for infants and early elementary graders. She has been praised for her understanding of and affection for children, and for depicting the everyday experiences of the young with accuracy, humor, and insight. A pioneer in the development of board books, works directed to babies and small children, Oxenbury is often considered the most successful contributor to the form. Considered an author and artist who brings new approaches to traditional concepts, Oxenbury arranges her works in a variety of formats which range widely in size and shape. She is also acclaimed for her illustrations, characteristically line drawings and watercolors noted for their vibrancy, design, and economy of line.

Oxenbury's first work, *Numbers of Things* (1968), an informational book that teaches preschoolers to count to fifty through the lively actions of human and animal characters, established her as an especially innovative picture book creator. Her next book, *Helen Oxenbury's ABC of Things* (1971), teaches the alphabet through letters, each of which represents several items depicted on the page. Especially well known for her two series of wordless and nearly wordless board books that trace the growth of the central character, a round-faced baby, Oxenbury introduces infants both to simple concepts, such as playing and getting dressed, and to more active concepts, such as helping with the dishes and imitating animals at the zoo, which parallel the baby's emerging mobility. Oxenbury is also the author and illustrator of a group of board books that focus on the senses, a series of board books in rhyming verse that feature multiethnic children engaged in lively pursuits, and a group of concept books featuring drawings of people and animals that can be rearranged to form a variety of figures. She has written and illustrated two collections of picture books for preschoolers which address experiences such as attending a birthday party and going to the doctor as well as two series of books for the same audience about Tom, a small boy, and Pippo, the stuffed monkey that serves as his alter ego. In addition, Oxenbury has contributed several picture books to the fantasy genre and is the reteller of ten folktales in *Helen Oxenbury's Nursery Story Book* (1985), a work which received mixed critical reactions for her editing of the stories. As an illustrator, Oxenbury provided award-winning pictures for Edward Lear's *The Quangle Wangle's Hat* (1969) and Margaret Mahy's *The Dragon of an Ordinary Family* (1969); she has also illustrated works by such authors as Lewis Carroll, Alexei Tolstoy, and Ivor Cutler. Oxenbury's illustrations also grace the poems selected by Brian Alderson for *Helen Oxenbury's Nursery Rhyme Book* (1986), a collection taken from his *Cakes and Custard: Children's Rhymes* (1974), which she also illustrated. Oxenbury received the Kate Greenaway Medal in 1969 for *The Dragon of an Ordinary Family* and *The Quangle Wangle's Hat,* and *The*

Helen Oxenbury Nursery Story Book was a runner-up for the Kurt Maschler Award in 1985.

(See also *Something about the Author,* Vol. 3 and *Contemporary Authors,* Vols. 25-28.)

AUTHOR'S COMMENTARY

It is difficult to say what makes me want to illustrate certain children's stories. I only know the attraction is instant and lasts till the endpapers.

I felt this very strongly with Edward Lear's **The Quangle-Wangle's Hat,** and I know here what the attraction was. I loved the strangeness and quiet sad humour. Fortunately I believe children like it too, and it has the added pleasure of rhythmic verse and dotty names that children delight in repeating over and over.

The Hunting of the Snark by Lewis Carroll was my next choice and I think for the same reasons as I chose the Edward Lear—the marvellous mixture of weird people in dreamlike situations surprising one by doing and saying quite ordinary and down-to-earth things one minute, and absurd, outrageous things the next.

I am now working on a book called **Meal One** by Ivor Cutler, whom I consider to be the nearest thing to a present-day Lear or Carroll.

Mediocrity and boredom come quickly with books for which I have not felt this instant sympathy, and yet have talked myself into for reasons such as children will love it. The only answer then is to abandon the whole idea, as I can be sure if the characters left me cold at the beginning of the story, by the end I would be feeling murderous towards them.

I believe children to be very canny people who immediately sense if adults talk, write or illustrate down to them, hence the unpopularity of self-conscious, child-like drawings that appear in some children's books. The illustrator is misguidedly thinking the child will be able to identify more easily with drawings similar to his own, while probably he is disgusted that adults cannot do better.

Similarly, I think most children appreciate, and more frighteningly recognise, honesty. I know this is true of my two. They are for instance unmoved by pictures of neat Mums in neat kitchens, cooking neat meals. They know very well it isn't like that, nor do farmers' wives any longer scatter corn for chickens and farmers use unromantic modern machinery. This doesn't mean that the old books that have started these clichés aren't still loved dearly. It just seems a little pointless to be continually rehashing them.

I find with my two children that they will look with the same eagerness at good and bad illustrations, and listen rapt to both good and bad stories. This is why I think it is important to expose them as much as possible to the best, for I'm sure that how they see things when their young minds are like sponges lives with them all their lives. (pp. 199-201)

> Helen Oxenbury, *"Drawing for Children,"* in *The Junior Bookshelf, Vol. 34, No. 4, August, 1970, pp. 199-201.*

GENERAL COMMENTARY

Jean Russell

It must be every child's dream to be like Rosie Randall, in Helen Oxenbury's new book, who answers the telephone and finds the Queen at the other end asking her over to her house to play. "Oh Rosie" said a worried voice "it's only the Queen. Can you come over and help me? I've got into one of my muddles, and I don't know what to do."

The muddle concerns the entertaining of the "difficult" King of Wottermazzy, but Rosie Randall is one of those liberated ladies who is the equal of any situation and soon has it firmly under control; with Patridge the butler being knocked down by the King's crown, Elsie the maid falling off the rope swing into a bed of nettles, the Queen ruining her new dress whilst hiding in the hen house and the ambassador catching his death of cold falling in the lily pond.

The Queen and Rosie Randall is a superb book, a frolic from end to end, and so full of subtle and not so subtle humour that every member of the family will find something in it to admire. Helen Oxenbury is at her best here, for the pages have scale and balance, warmth and a lovely blend

From Number of Things, *written and illustrated by Helen Oxenbury.*

of colour, and a fine attention to detail which is reflected in the tiny line drawing at the head of alternative pages of text . . .

Helen Oxenbury started off her picture book career by illustrating a counting book, **Numbers of Things** which immediately established her as a major children's book artist, for its shape, originality and use of colour.

Although trained at art school Helen Oxenbury specialised in theatre design, and the influence of perspective is often seen in her books, readers may remember the birds eye view of Helbert and his Mother playing football in Ivor Cutler's story **Meal One** and here in Rosie Randall we look down to see the admiring crowd as we swing with the King and Rosie Randall on the top of the rope. . . .

All Helen's pictures have a vibrant wit and delicacy which is so vital in stimulating the imaginative child. In her illustrations to Brian Alderson's collection of verses and rhymes **Cakes and Custards** she highlights the detail with a swift brush stroke. In this bumper collection Brian Alderson has found rhymes old and 'nearly new', poignant and rollicking, simple and puzzling.

> *Jean Russell, "Cover Artist: Helen Oxenbury,"*

in Books for Your Children, *Vol. 13, No. 4, Autumn, 1978, p. 3.*

Zena Sutherland and May Hill Arbuthnot

The increased awareness of the importance of language and books for the very young child has produced some excellent wordless books for infants. Helen Oxenbury's series of board books (*Family, Friends, Dressing,* etc.) has captions on the pages, but no text, and each book focuses on one familiar concept, with deft and comic pictures that can be used for delighted identification. A second series (*Mother's Helper; Good Night, Good Morning*) is just right for the more sophisticated three-year-old. (p. 102)

> *Zena Sutherland and May Hill Arbuthnot, "Books for the Very Young," in their* Children and Books, *seventh edition, Scott, Foresman and Company, 1986, pp. 80-105.*

Books for Keeps

[*Numbers of Things* and *Helen Oxenbury's ABC of Things* are two] tall, thin picture books first published in the sixties, and real bargains in their new paperback format; full of decorative and entertaining illustrations with plenty of surprises. Count to ten with a variety of creatures and characters to help, all of them drawn with both cosiness and humour, lots of balloons, fish, penguins, ladybirds to help with the bigger numbers . . . and finally to infinity and 'how many stars?'

ABCs may be thought of in some circles as old-fashioned but one glance at this one should reassure. An apprehensive yet appealing hippo looks out from his hospital bed; there's a vulture playing a violin and a weasel marrying a wolf! Just right for the Nursery as a talkabout book or in primary school for playing with sounds.

> *M. S., in a review of "Numbers of Things" and "Helen Oxenbury's ABC of Things," in* Books for Keeps, *No. 46, September, 1987, p. 17.*

Numbers of Things   (1968)

A gay counting book for the three-year-old. The examples chosen are, in the main, from the young child's familiar world—bicycles, balloons, cars, cats. Amusing pictures encourage him to count up to ten, and then, by tens, to fifty. The very appearance of the pages with their twenty balloons and fifty ladybirds, will help the child to comprehend the difference in quantity between these numbers. Too often he chants numbers with little idea of what they stand for.

The decorative title page, the clear colours, the detail in the cheerful pictures, will absorb children.

> *A review of "Numbers of Things," in* The Junior Bookshelf, *Vol. 3, No. 2, April, 1968, p. 97.*

[A] picture book that's delightful to share with small ones—another good candidate for your lap books collection. Wild and antic animals, children and people illustrate the sequence of numbers—from an absurd lion for *one,* to, with a few leaps of numbers in between, 50 lady-bugs going around in circles. But a fiddle-dee-dee on its instructional aspect! A hurrah instead for the fun of it all!

> *A review of "Numbers of Things," in* Publishers Weekly, *Vol. 193, No. 15, April 8, 1968, p. 51.*

Numbers of Things to count: 1 ONE one lion, two cars, six acrobats, ten animals, twenty balloons, fifty ladybugs which indicates the numerical range, the spread of subjects, doesn't suggest the variety achieved in fourteen tall, skinny illustrations. Miss Oxenbury is the wife of John Burningham and these have some of his bravado, some of Erik Blegvad's whimsy. Children will have to stay alert to count the separate objects; they're not neatly lined up but this would do handsomely as, say, a second counting book.

> *A review of "Numbers of Things," in* Kirkus Service, *Vol. XXXVI, No. 11, June 1, 1968, p. 549.*

The Dragon of an Ordinary Family   (1969)

[The Dragon of an Ordinary Family *was written by Margaret Mahy.*]

It is easy . . . to be lured into rash predictions by a book like *The Dragon of an Ordinary Family* which has illustrations crammed with detail, marvellously colored and tremendously imaginative, rising up out of every page. The artist, Helen Oxenbury, makes a giant of a dragon, for example, larger than book-size, and a family around a cluttered breakfast table all fit themselves between the covers of this exciting book. And the story, unusually long, is as fascinating and as witty as the illustrations. By her unexpected nonending, New Zealander Margaret Mahy manages to keep the story still going on in our imaginations.

> *P. M., "Dragons and Other Sights," in* The Christian Science Monitor, *November 6, 1969, p. B2.*

The Belsakis are a very ordinary British family, until one day Mr. Belsaki, rankled at being called a fuddy-duddy, brings son Gaylord a small, inexpensive dragon in a shoe box. The violet-eyed creature grows to inordinate size until the mayor finally orders the Belsakis to get rid of him. By this time, the family is quite attached to their pet, and only too happy to accept his invitation for Christmas on the Isles of Magic where they spend wondrous days meeting princesses, fairy people, witches and the like. The dragon, electing to stay, sends them home on a flying carpet with a kitten as a farewell gift. Wistfully the family wonders if such adventures can ever happen to them again. It immediately appears possible! The Isles of Magic episode, the only weak part in this extraordinary tale, is not well-developed and is too crowded with sketchy adventures; attempts at rhyme here are unsuccessful. But the illustrations throughout are excellent and full of delightful detail. The animals are droll, especially the dragon, a splendiferous fellow who fills double-page spreads superbly and who is surely a distant, more self-assured relative of *The Reluctant . . . !*

> *Marianne Hough, in a review of "The Dragon*

of an Ordinary Family," in School Library Journal, *Vol. 17, No. 1, September, 1970, p. 94.*

The Quangle Wangle's Hat   (1969)

[The Quangle Wangle's Hat *was written by Edward Lear.*]

Helen Oxenbury has an attractive version of *The Quangle Wangle's Hat.* All her beasts have amiable, slightly balmy and dubious faces and her Dong with the luminous nose is done in something approximating a cross between paisley and psychedelic dayglo. Since the text is minimal, it is unfortunate that there should be two typographical slips. (p. 65)

> *Nora L. Magid, "Clear the Stage for a Repeat Performance," in* The New York Times Book Review, *November 9, 1969, pp. 64-5.*

In this delectable picture book the humor of Lear's nonsense verse about the Quangle Wangle who let all manner of strange creatures build their homes in his 102-foot-wide beaver hat is happily matched by Oxenbury's highly imaginative page-filling colored illustrations.

> *A review of "The Quangle Wangle's Hat," in* The Booklist, *Vol. 66, No. 9, January 1, 1970, p. 566.*

This is an attractively illustrated version of Lear's nonsense poem . . . The artist's softly colored, whimsically droll, full- and double-page drawings greatly enliven the text, and make this fun for both read-alouds and independent reading.

> *Eleanor Glaser, in a review of "The Quangle Wangle's Hat," in* School Library Journal, *Vol. 16, No. 6, February, 1970, p. 72.*

Helen Oxenbury has all the ludicrous Lear ribbons, bibbons, loops and lace for her Quangle Wangle. Her Crumpetty Tree's tortured unearthly trunk and crumpet leaves are magnificent; her landscape is wide and magical, neither inviting nor repelling, but inexplicable—surely right for a Lear setting. I'm not happy with the characters who come to inhabit it, though. The Quangle Wangle itself is safe because you (rightly) never see his face; but the artist has got overexcited when confronted with unimaginables like the Fimble Fowl and the Attery Squash. I feel confused by the elaboration and decoration. Her Dong is a big mistake, a strange aardvark-like creature with a quasi-trunk. Lear meant the Dong to be humanised; he illustrated it as such. A detail within this particular poem, but a symptom of the excessive licence which Helen Oxenbury takes; perhaps she felt it was necessary to lay things on a bit thick for children. I don't agree with her. (p. 199)

> *Crispin Fisher, "A Load of Old Nonsense, Edward Lear Resurrected by Four Publishers," in* Children and Literature: Views and Reviews, *edited by Virginia Haviland, Scott, Foresman and Company, 1973, pp. 198-201.*

Helen Oxenbury's ABC of Things   (1971; also published as *ABC of Things*)

It is no bad thing if the book the small child pores over is one that gives him a gentle push in the direction of reading for himself. Helen Oxenbury's *ABC of Things* offers great imaginative rewards for the study of every picture and gives in large, clear print the name of each item depicted—more helpful to the non-reader than the rather desperate rhymes with which ABCs sometimes seek to unite objects with the same initial letter. Here, the work of unification is beautifully done in the pictures; the most incongruous associations are made in a perfectly matter-of-fact way, setting the mind off in pursuit of the stories that must lie behind them. Ant and Apple are easy to bring together in one picture, but what about Jam, Jelly and Juggler, Hare, Hippopotamus and Hospital, or Vulture, Violin and Volcano? Not all the pictures show such bizarre collections, but all are marked by Helen Oxenbury's splendid imagination and by her careful draughtsmanship, a Holbeinesque combination of scrupulous attention to surface textures and constant awareness of underlying form. (p. 1514)

> *"Good Enough to Keep," in* The Times Literary Supplement, *No. 3640, December 3, 1971, pp. 1514-15.*

As a companion volume to her counting book *Numbers of Things,* Helen Oxenbury has produced another nursery favourite, an 'ABC', its muted pastel shades contrasting sharply with the gay colours of the former, but once more showing her superb draughtsmanship to advantage. It is an object 'ABC' with most of the letters representing more than one item on each page. The objects are not arranged in splendid isolation, but are brought together to form composite pictures which are gently humorous and which can be used, according to the blurb, as a starting point for building a story. Most of the 'things' are animals, and it is here that the author is, perhaps, at her most perceptive and amusing. Two words which may prove confusing to the young child are more abstract than the others: 'hospital', which is suggested by hare and hippopotamus seen in two white beds, with a fever chart upon the wall, and 'wedding', represented by weasel wearing a lacy cloth springing from a tiara, carrying a bouquet of roses and walking arm in arm with wolf. The 'X' has the usual 'xylophone', but the xylophonist is away in a musical world of his own, his foot raised, his expression rapt and bemused. A charming and useful addition to school and nursery shelves.

> *Pat Garrett, in a review of "ABC of Things," in* Children's Book Review, *Vol. II, No. 2, April, 1972, p. 38.*

Pictures that are imaginative and humorous as well as handsome make this a far better than average ABC book. The verso page gives the letter, in big bold type, in upper and lower case; at the bottom of the page the object or objects on the facing page are identified. What adds zest to learning (or helping to learn) the alphabet are the engaging characters in the illustrations and the often-ludicrous combinations. "B" for example: baby, baker, bear, bird, and badger are entwined in affectionate embrace, although the baker looks somewhat bleary-eyed; there's nothing odd about a leopard and a lion in the same tree—except for the jaded expressions of infinite boredom on their faces. Occasionally a word may need explanation ("wedding" of the wolf and weasel) but there isn't enough of this to be a burden.

> *Zena Sutherland, in a review of "Helen Oxenbury's ABC of Things," in* Bulletin of the Center for Children's Books, *Vol. 26, No. 6, February, 1973, p. 96.*

Pig Tale (1973)

[Another] reminder that the simple life is where it's at and animals should definitely not wear clothing. Oxenbury's two pigs, bored and discontented though "they had plenty to eat, / a warm sty with a thatch, / An orchard to play in / and trees for a scratch," find a buried treasure and jubilantly convert it to clothes, a car and a house complete with swimming pool. But all the appliances and motors give them so much trouble that after one bad day they chuck it all and return to their orchard and mud, flinging off clothing with rapturous abandon as they go—for now "To be careless and free and to romp and to play / Was all that they wanted to do every day." Oxenbury's fleshy pigs are pictured with a free-and-easy flair; her rhymed text has some bright touches too, although it tends to become monotonous toward the end as it bounces along in the service of the overly familiar concept. (pp. 1259-60)

> *A review of "Pig Tale," in* Kirkus Reviews, *Vol. XLI, No. 22, November 15, 1973, pp. 1259-60.*

Helen Oxenbury's **Pig Tale,** the first story that this artist has both written and illustrated, is another fable, though it takes, refreshingly, a less rigid moral stance than [Bernadette Watts's *The Proud Crow* and Brian Wildsmith's *The Lazy Bear*]. The uncommitted approach is an advantage, freeing the reader to put any one of a number of valid interpretations on this story of a pair of bored pigs who find buried treasure and opt for a middle-class human way of life, only to be driven back to their formal pastoral ways by the intolerable responsibility of ownership and the intractability of their gadgets and machines. And if you don't like moral-hunting you can simply take pleasure in a good story enlivened by Helen Oxenbury's fluent verse and her exceedingly funny pictures. Her Bertha and Briggs are immutably porcine, but when they are dressed in human clothes, sitting in front of the telly or striving to master the labour-saving devices that accompany their new status, their appearance is enough to make you wonder whether similar transformations are not taking place every day unnoticed.

> *"Talking to the Animals," in* The Times Literary Supplement, *No. 3742, November 23, 1973, p. 1440.*

'This is the story of two bored pigs.' So the **Pig Tale** starts and what gorgeous, chubby pigs they are . . . Helen Oxenbury's considerable powers of illustrating animals both fabulous and factual are once again to the fore in this moralistic story of her own creation. There are fifty-three separate colour illustrations, some of them double-page spreads, in her delightfully humorous account of the rags to riches and back again story of two very endearing pigs.

Helen Oxenbury has proved once again that she can write as well as illustrate superbly well.

> *Edward Hudson, in a review of "Pig Tale," in* Children's Book Review, *Vol. III, No. 6, December, 1973, p. 172.*

Cakes and Custard: Children's Rhymes (1974)

[Cakes and Custard *was edited by Brian Alderson.*]

Is there any good reason to publish yet another compilation of nursery rhymes? In this instance, two very good reasons: editor and illustrator. Brian Alderson, who is children's book editor of the London Times, has brought together Mother Goose, jump-rope and counting-out rhymes worn smooth and renewed by children over the centuries, and for good measure, a few contemporary verses by James Reeves and Robert Graves to show, as Alderson stresses, the continuance of the nursery rhyme tradition. . . .

Alderson's plan of blending the known and the new has been complemented with felicity by Helen Oxenbury. Her background includes theater and film design, and these seem to have been rich sources for her. A good many of the costumes and settings in her drawings look classically timeless, others are eminently Victorian, some are quite à la mode, such as Elsie Marley "grown so fine / She won't get up to serve the swine." Elsie is portrayed with hair curlers, a maribou capelet, and a manicure tray atop the coverlet of her bed; she is putting on nail polish, and instead of concentrating, she is shown gazing off dreamily into the distance: her entire being conveys an air of slovenliness and daintiness at the same time.

In "Eight o'clock is striking, / Mother, may I go out?" Mother sits mesmerized in front of the TV set. It is part of the illustrator's gift that these modern props do not seem glaringly anachronistic. My favorite of the contemporary-minded illustrations is for "Needles and pins, needles and pins, / When a man marries his trouble begins." This brief couplet is given a double-page color spread and deserves it: a grand Freudian feast—the more one goes back to look, the more psychological nuances show up.

Oxenbury's pallet is less robust than that of Raymond Briggs; she inclines to the pastel, but this does not limit her humor or range. When she's good, she's very, very good, and when she is less so, she's borrowed: echoes of Burne-Jones, Kate Greenaway, even a touch of John Gruelle in one. But more often than not, her ideas are magically suitable, as in The Old Woman Who Lived in a Shoe: they are all Lilliputians, and the shoe is set down in a grassy sward. The shapes of the drawings vary from page to page, making for constant surprises; Tommy Tittlemouse's fishing line extends out of the oblong picture frame and fish dangle across the page; sometimes there is a circle within a circle, there are diamonds, ovals, squares, tiny postage stamp drawings, borders of letters and numbers, flowered end papers with appropriate verses set in.

The title rhyme states "When Jacky's a very good boy, / He shall have cakes and custard; / When he does nothing but cry, / He shall have nothing but mustard." For Oxenbury and Alderson, high tea with a lavish round of cakes and custard.

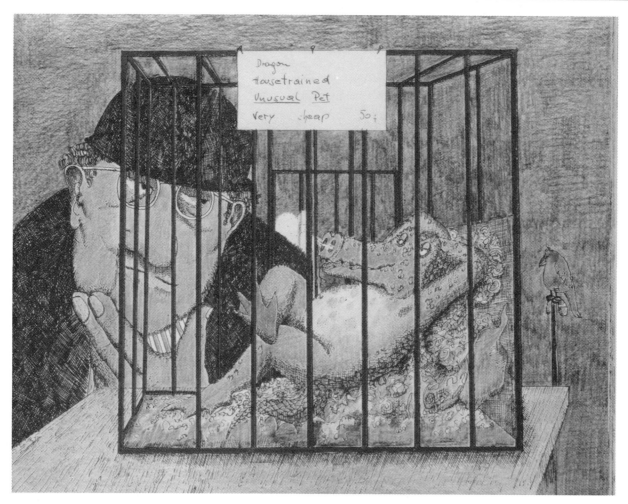

From The Dragon of an Ordinary Family, *written by Margaret Mahy. Illustrated by Helen Oxenbury.*

Eve Merriam, "Cakes and Custard: Children's Rhymes," in The New York Times Book Review, *November 16, 1975, p. 33.*

The best rhymes for young children are those that say something about pleasure and pain, vice and virtue, birth, love, death and all the other experiences that make up the human condition. Brian Alderson has dropped his bucket deep into the well and landed a motley collection of attractive vibrant rhymes, some old, some relatively new. And Helen Oxenbury, at her best when free to depict quirks in human nature, has excelled herself in page after inventive page of colour or sepia pictures, some round, some square, some spilling over their self-imposed borders in sheer exuberance. Sufficiently traditional to be instantly recognizable, these illustrations nevertheless have the unique Oxenbury wit, verve and magic. *Cakes and Custard* will surely be a long-lasting feast.

Elaine Moss, in a review of "Cakes and Custard: Children's Rhymes," in her Children's Books of the Year: 1974, *Hamish Hamilton, 1975, p. 83.*

The English critic of children's literature has gathered together an unusually generous, delightfully unorthodox collection. . . . Original and dynamic in layout and de-

sign, the book is illustrated by a masterful artist who has already been awarded one Kate Greenaway Medal and probably deserves another. Emphasizing the agelessness of the rhymes, she has dealt with time settings eclectically, making some of the characters look unexpectedly contemporary. A superb colorist and draftswoman, she has created a compendium of artistic possibilities and moods—from tiny vignettes to vigorous full-page pictures, from reticent lyricism to earthy, sardonic, even grotesque humor. (pp. 59-60)

Ethel L. Heins, in a review of "Cakes and Custard: Children's Rhymes," in The Horn Book Magazine, *Vol. LII, No. 1, February, 1976, pp. 59-60.*

The Queen and Rosie Randall   (1979)

The best of this is the original idea (which was provided by Jill Buttfield-Campbell). When the Queen runs into difficulties she rings up Rosie Randall, a scruffy but fun-loving little girl, and she cycles round to the palace to help her out. In this adventure Rosie entertains the King of Wottermazzy, most successfully although the ambassadors and even the Queen are less amused. Miss Oxenbury's grotesquerie is kept well within bounds, and there is a nice homeliness about this concept of royalty at play. But everyone might have been made just a little more likable.

> *M. Crouch, in a review of "The Queen and Rosie Randall," in* The Junior Bookshelf, *Vol. 43, No. 2, April, 1979, p. 109.*

Oxenbury's sunny illustrations make the best of a mediocre story which plays on the child's fantasy of being in command while the adults make fools of themselves. . . . Although the story is contrived and distinctly British, the busy illustrations offer disheveled appeal and humor, and the turnabout fantasy will appeal to many children. (pp. 46-7)

> *Jane Bickel, in a review of "The Queen and Rosie Randall," in* School Library Journal, *Vol. 25, No. 8, April, 1979, pp. 46-7.*

Pages of print with lively vignettes in black and white alternate with full-page watercolor paintings in a picture storybook that transforms ludicrous improbability into humorous delight. The restrained tonalities of the drawings and the paintings act as a foil for the comic characterizations which derive their effect from pantomimic expressiveness rather than from caricaturing. (p. 298)

> *Paul Heins, in a review of "The Queen and Rosie Randall," in* The Horn Book Magazine, *Vol. LV, No. 3, June, 1979, pp. 297-98.*

---

729 Animal Allsorts (U. S. edition as *729 Merry Mix-Ups*); *729 Curious Creatures; 729 Puzzle People* (1980)

These three books are part of a series that have heavy pasteboard pages split in thirds for the character's head, torso and legs to be scrambled with those of other characters on other split pages. This is not a particularly unusual concept, having been used before in such books as Alan Benjamin's *1000 Monsters* (Four Winds: Scholastic, 1979) and Peter Lippman's *Mix or Match Storybook* (Random, 1974). The difference here is a decidedly British cast. In *729 Merry Mix-Ups,* animals' heads, torsos and legs are shown, all standing upright. On each third is also part of the animal's name (in one case "dromedary" is given for what American children would recognize as a camel), so that the mixing of the body parts also mixes up names for the new character created. *729 Puzzle People* gives one third of a sentence caption with each body part so that the caption changes to become more silly with the new character created. *729 Curious Creatures* mixes animals with people, including one or two stereotypical British Types—Boris Bore complete with umbrella and bowler hat and Sarah Scrubup, a cigarette-smoking, run-in-her-stockings charwoman. Although the format would intrigue children, the books' spiral bindings will not stand up to repeated circulations and are therefore better for home libraries.

> *Patricia Homer, in a review of "729 Curious Creatures," "729 Merry Mix-Ups" and "729 Puzzle People," in* School Library Journal, *Vol. 27, No. 7, March, 1981, p. 135.*

Dressing; Family; Friends; Playing; Working (1981)

When *Pat the Bunny* has been patted, gouged, gnawed and torn, when that first baby book has been digested, one way or another, you might find, as I have, that there are very few other books simple and sturdy enough for a year-old child that also have appeal for the adult who helps the baby "read" them. These five board books, published first in England and now in this country, succeed admirably in this difficult and almost uninhabited territory of children's books.

Each volume introduces the child to seven words, all nouns that represent familiar subjects of a baby's experience. In *Family,* the words are mother, father, sister, brother, grandmother, grandfather and baby. *Friends* presents seven familiar animals, *Dressing* presents articles of clothing, *Playing* toys, and *Working,* by far the most amusing of the five books, presents the words highchair, potty, carriage, bowl, bathtub, bottle and crib. It is refreshing to think of these objects, as a small child must, as instruments of labor.

Each word has a two-page spread, with the word (given not for the child to read, but for the adult to say) written on the left-hand page. On the same page is an illustration of the word; on the facing page is an illustration of a baby with whatever the word represents. These pictures are obviously crucial to the success of a book in which the text is so, shall we say, modest. The pictures themselves are simple—line drawings either pencil colored or washed in color. The baby's head, for example, is little more than a circle, its eyes dots. Yet everywhere in the drawings there is subtle humor: the baby's head held just a bit tightly by an aggressively maternal older sister; the baby's hand held out tentatively with its crumbs of toast for a mallard; the special way a child lifts his feet when he is wearing new red shoes; the learned look he has while reading a children's book upside down. And in all these attitudes the baby strikes, there is a keenness of observation on the artist's part, a familiarity with the ways of the baby.

Organization, wit, keenness—all these appeal to the parent, or to the adult who buys and presents books to children of this age. The cynic says this adult is the only person children's books are written for anyway. But what about the child? In my survey of one—my son, 13 months old—I observed a passing interest in the Oxenbury books, an interest passing in about 45 seconds, when he was unfairly distracted. But I'll bet that under better conditions he'll like the books as much as I do, although for different reasons.

With the exception of a few of the animals (and, I confess, the potty), these are words we already are teaching him. The sound of the word and the picture accompanying the word "box" (found in *Playing*) will give him the pleasure of recognition, and he'll have the further pleasure of seeing the baby sitting in the box, as he himself is wont to do. Perhaps he will even pick up the humor of the situation. At least he will share the pleasure I get from the humor, and feign a hearty appreciation. And the next time he sees the picture his mirth will be real.

Pat the Bunny makes an admirable attempt to show the child how that which is on the page corresponds with something the child has experienced—how art imitates life, you might say. The child scratches the rough paper and scratches the father's rough beard. Do babies enjoy this book so much because they recognize these correspondences, as we hope they do, or simply because of the sensual pleasure of touching rough paper, or of seeing the shiny mirror. The Oxenbury books, which are for children older than six months, depend on these correspondences between word, image and object. Because they do not have the sensual gimmicks of *Pat* these books may answer more conclusively whether your child is making such connections.

The Oxenbury books, which are about 5½ inches square, are a nice size for a small child's hands. The corners of the pages are rounded, making them safe for eyes, and, according to the publisher, the pages (which have a shiny finish) can be wiped clean and are nontoxic. The pages are stiff cardboard, and the binding looks strong, so the books seem likely to last about as long as one of those leathery chew-bones lasts around a dog.

The only book in the series that troubles me somewhat is **Family,** because it tends to stereotype. Father is wearing a tie and a coat with an upturned collar; he obviously is just coming or going someplace in his active, busy life. Grandfather, on the other hand, wears a collarless shirt and a cardigan; he looks like he hasn't done anything useful in days. And all the faces are a nice scrubbed British pink; this would be an anomaly, happily, in melting-pot America's children's books. But on the whole, these books weathered their transatlantic crossing better than do many children's picture books published in England. (pp. 10-11)

> *Robert Wilson, "Please Don't Eat the Pages,"* in Book World—The Washington Post, *March 8, 1981, pp. 10-11.*

The closest thing we've had to this quality board book is Rosemary Wells' Max series, which aims at an older toddler audience. Oxenbury's five are really baby books, accurately portraying and perfectly in tune with the interests of the teething population, and at the same time executed with wit and the artistic awareness that at this age less is more. Of each double-page spread, the first pictures a single object, the second a baby using it. The objects are basic—diaper, crib, pot, cat, mother, bottle, etc.—the nontoxic pages completely uncluttered. Yet each picture manages to be extremely funny to an adult while just as warmly interesting to a child. Line, space, color, and content blend here for Everybaby appeal, and librarians will find these a most satisfying and successful recommendation for new parents. Chewable and viewable.

> *Betsy Hearne, in a review of "Dressing" and others, in* Booklist, *Vol. 77, No. 17, May 1, 1981, p. 1198.*

Board books alive and alert with humour and with an affectionate observation of small children conveyed in a demurely idiosyncratic style. 'Working' in infant terms means coping with high chair, pot and bath; the Friends (dog, rabbit, guinea-pig, sparrow and hen) all look dismayed at their role; 'Dressing' involves some highly typical contortions. A set of domestic portraits reflecting the snags of childhood with brilliant economy of line and colour and with a blithe and sympathetic sense of comedy.

> *Margery Fisher, in a review of "Friends" and*

others, in Growing Point, *Vol. 20, No. 2, July, 1981, p. 3919.*

Helen Oxenbury has chosen a delightfully lump-faced baby as the subject of her set of five books, **Dressing, Playing, Family, Friends** and **Working** (incidents in everyday life). He (I say "he" but one cannot tell) is seen enthralled by a real book (held upside down), and fast asleep on a long-suffering marmalade cat, bemused on the pot, and tucking fistfully into a bowl of green sludge. Each item, person or animal is shown on the left-hand page alone and on the right-hand page in association with the hero. With a glint in her eye, Helen Oxenbury has captured masterfully the expressions and postures of early childhood. This is certainly the series most likely to appeal to adults, but I am not sure that the infant reader will find enough in them to hold his attention for long. Once past the stage at which any picture is merely a set of abstract shapes and colours, children like pictures in which there is a lot going on, and here there is not.

> *Lucy Micklethwait, "The Indestructible Word," in* The Times Literary Supplement, *No. 4086, July 24, 1981, p. 840.*

Pictured are objects, persons and situations made familiar to infants by their daily routines. Each board double spread shows an item on the left, and that same item in use (or in interaction) on the facing page. Unfortunately, all the faces are pink, with indeterminate features. The eyes, for example, are pencil dots, and often the point of the drawing is lost in the vagueness of execution. Cute for adults who like things cute, and formless blobs to babies. The least successful of the five is **Working,** which relates to activities such as eating and using the potty and includes a number of pictures difficult to interpret. Since infants of a year or less are likely to mouth as well as read their books, sanitary as well as literary factors should be carefully considered by libraries contemplating purchase.

> *Joan W. Blos, in a review of "Dressing" and others, in* School Library Journal, *Vol. 28, No. 2, October, 1981, p. 133.*

Bill and Stanley (1981)

This new series, the 'Little Library', should make an immediate appeal for its compact octavo shape and for the vivacious approach of artists and authors to the well-worn pattern of infant days. Here is the Burningham-Oxenbury dog (Stanley) taking on the role of playmate to bored Bill; small children turning the pages and enjoying the mannered, exquisitely comic coloured pictures, should have no difficulty in believing that dog and small boy did in fact make mud pies together and act out the roles of soldiers or pirates. A very imaginative series for the young to carry about with them.

> *Margery Fisher, in a review of "Bill and Stanley," in* Growing Point, *Vol. 20, No. 4, November, 1981, p. 3983.*

Bill and Stanley . . . [has a] simple text about a boy who spends a happy afternoon playing with a dog, the twist being that the dog is mostly not acting like a dog at all but like another little child. He helps with the mud pies and appears in battle dress to join in the army game, and only

But his face you could not see,

On account of his Beaver Hat.

For his Hat was a hundred and two feet wide,

With ribbons and bibbons on every side,

And bells, and buttons, and loops, and lace,

So that nobody ever could see the face

Of the Quangle Wangle Quee.

From The Quangle Wangle's Hat, *written by Edward Lear. Illustrated by Helen Oxenbury.*

lapses into doggery in a moment of weakness when left alone with a bag of chocolate drops. Again there is plenty of detail in the pictures which are gentle and delicate as well as funny. My only hesitation is over the first page; "Bill ate his cabbage to please his mum. 'Now she will have to play with me,' he thought." There is something sad behind that lighthearted tease of mothers and their moral tangles at which I can't laugh. But it does not spoil what follows.

> *Ruth Hawthorn, "Intriguing Episodes," in* The Times Literary Supplement, *No. 4103, November 20, 1981, p. 1359.*

A very successful story about a little boy whose mother is too busy to play with him but who finds a companion in an untidy dog called Stanley. Stanley is the ideal friend; occasionally annoying, (he eats the sweets that are supposed to be for a game of Hunt the Sweet) but joining in every idea (for playing pirates or rolling about in the grass), with a truly child-like enthusiasm. Mum's comment at the end of the day, however, reveals the hidden depth of this simple tale. 'You *can* play by yourself,' she says. Does she know about Stanley? Is he Bill's dog or just a passing stray? *Does he exist at all?*

These questions opened up a long discussion on reality among my children. . . .

> *Liz Waterland, in a review of "Bill and Stan-*

ley," in Books for Keeps, *No. 46, September, 1987, p. 17.*

Beach Day; Good Night, Good Morning; Monkey See, Monkey Do; Mother's Helper; Shopping Trip (1982)

Oxenbury is a gifted author-illustrator whose picture books are as popular in this country as they are in her native England. She has added her delightful little wordless books to the Dial Very First line, stories told without words. These are among the adventures for parents to share with the tiniest "readers," who will respond to the colors, humor, action and familiar scenes. [In *Good Night, Good Morning*] a one-year-old bundle of raw energy keeps his poor daddy hopping through a day while he enjoys a bath, rides horseback (Father the horse, of course), watches Father shave and shoots the shaving cream on his own face and altogether exhausts himself as well as his parent.

> *A review of "Good Night, Good Morning," in* Publishers Weekly, *Vol. 221, No. 11, March 12, 1982, p. 84.*

Helen Oxenbury knows babies. For instance, she knows that as soon as you tuck a sleeping baby into his crib and leave the room, he bounces up like a jack-in-the-box, tosses teddy and blankie on the floor, and then whines. She knows that a toddler's idea of feeding the dog is to join him over his dish on the floor.

Her latest collection of books for babies and about babies has page after page of such scenes that will delight parents and entertain infants with images of themselves.

Alice Digilio, in a review of "Beach Day" and others, in Book World—The Washington Post, *March 14, 1982, p. 6.*

The first five books in this engaging set of board books for very young children . . . showed an infant too young to be very mobile. In the next set of five, of which [*Shopping Trip*] is one, the round-faced baby is not only capable of independent action, but manages to achieve a good bit of independent investigation and some damage, all of which leaves Mama limp by the ending of a shopping trip. A foray into a clothes rack, a broken packet of what looks like sugar, a raid on Mama's purse in a fitting booth followed by a sociable pulling back of its curtain, revealing Mama just emerging from the garment she's been trying on. Like the first books, this has no words and needs none; it is drawn with simplicity, humor, and flair. Other titles are *Beach Day; Good Night, Good Morning; Monkey See, Monkey Do;* and *Mother's Helper.* Fun, but more than that: these are geared to the toddler's interests and experiences. (pp. 155-56)

Zena Sutherland, in a review of "Shopping Trip," in Bulletin of the Center for Children's Books, *Vol. 35, No. 8, April, 1982, pp. 155-56.*

Where her phenomenally successful first set of board books—*Dressing, Family, Friends, Playing,* and *Working*—centered on babies from 6 to 24 months, this new series moves on to toddler activities. The basics of bottle and blocks have given way to "helping" with the dishes, trying on new shoes, climbing into bed with mom and dad, splashing in the ocean, and imitating animals at the zoo. This last example reveals the only failing of the books: they sometimes seem to look *at* the child from an adult standpoint rather than look at the world from a child's view. On the whole, however, youngsters will enjoy the familiar details Oxenbury depicts so humorously without a word. Her clean lines, warm colors, and simple scenes lend themselves to parent-child picture reading. (pp. 1258, 1260)

Betsy Hearne, in a review of "Beach Day" and others, in Booklist, *Vol. 78, No. 18, May 15, 1982, pp. 1258, 1260.*

Many familiar situations are featured in these small wordless board books. . . . Some scenes hold more humor for adults: Mother exhausted at the end of *Shopping Trip.* Some parents may find the child climbing into the parents' bed at the end of *Good Night, Good Morning* objectionable. Also objectionable may be the child on a stool at the sink washing a teetering stack of dishes (*Mother's Helper*). Father is pictured in only two of these (*Good Night, Good Morning* and *Beach Day*); Mother is featured very domestically in all: cleaning, cooking, shopping. The least appealing of the group for the very young is *Monkey See, Monkey Do,* which requires inferences about animal behavior and human imitations of it; the animals may not be familiar to toddlers. No adults appear in this entry, which reflects the everyday life of a toddler only slightly.

Ellen Fader, in a review of "Beach Day" and others, in School Library Journal, *Vol. 28, No. 10, August, 1982, p. 104.*

The Birthday Party; The Dancing Class; Eating Out (1983)

A new miniseries of books for the small child who's too sophisticated for Oxenbury's books for the very, very young like *Family* and *Dressing.* There are real plots here, but the same affectionate humor and the same clean, clear, bright illustration. In *Birthday Party,* a child chooses a present but hates to give it away, is miffed at the casual way the gift is received, has a splendidly messy time, and walks home triumphantly, enjoying the souvenir balloon all the more because it's clear that the birthday child didn't want to give it up. In *Dancing Class,* there's a minor disaster when the pudgy, engaging dancers collide, but the enthusiastic neophyte enjoys it all, and insists on doing the gallop all the way home, clinging to the hand of a frazzled Mum. *Eating Out* also has the disaster humor small children enjoy, with an irritated waiter and spilled food leading to a hasty exit and a bowl of cereal at home. These are just right, in the tone, length, and simplicity of the stories, for the preschool child, and they should bring a recognition reflex from the audience and some smiles from those who read the books to them.

Zena Sutherland, in a review of "The Birthday Party," "The Dancing Class" and "Eating Out," in Bulletin of the Center for Children's Books, *Vol. 36, No. 9, May, 1983, p. 174.*

Oxenbury once again has very accurately identified the foibles of youth but has missed the mark slightly because much of the humor comes from the children's funny antics—funny, that is, from an adult's point of view. Grownups may think it's amusing that a child won't hand over a birthday present; the child considers it perfectly logical behavior. Nevertheless, kids will enjoy the familiar situations, and Oxenbury's incredibly expressive drawing will continue to delight.

Ilene Cooper, in a review of "The Birthday Party," "The Dancing Class" and "Eating Out," in Booklist, *Vol. 79, No. 20, June 15, 1983, p. 1341.*

The 'memorable moments of childhood' in these hilarious miniatures will be familiar to parents and children alike, though in somewhat different ways. The shaggy-haired small girl who fidgets in the restaurant and trips over the laces of her dancing shoes crashes through the various scenes unforgettably, delineated with cosy exaggeration and blithe colour and a wonderfully uninhibited eye for the postures and agonised expressions the occasions demand.

Margery Fisher, in a review of "The Dancing Class," "The Birthday Party" and "Eating Out," in Growing Point, *Vol. 22, No. 2, July, 1983, p. 4110.*

This series has enchanted me. I like *The dancing class* best. Every parent who knows the classic trials of bringing up a child with a natural propensity for accidents will get as much pleasure from these witty pictures as the young reader will. Look at the narrator (about two and a half?) in the restaurant loo; it's a piece of social commentary. Back home to cornflakes. It's the postures of the characters that tell the hidden tale. Ask the children to read it to you.

> *Margaret Meek, in a review of "Eating Out," in* The School Librarian, *Vol. 32, No. 1, March, 1984, p. 41.*

The Drive (U. S. edition as *The Car Trip*); **The Checkup;** **Playschool** (U. S. edition as *First Day of School*)   (1983)

The children of Oxenbury's earlier board books are growing and with them is this author-artist's list of childhood-experience books. Her deft line-and-wash drawings play out such episodes as a car trip complete with inopportune potty stops and getting carsick; a first day of nursery school that's helped along somewhat by an enthusiastic teacher; and a visit to the doctor that leaves the doctor more frazzled than the child. Comedy is always central to Oxenbury's vignettes, and this trio of books is no exception. The author's knack for apt faces and wry detail is in full force; both children and parents will recognize themselves in these affectionate mirror views of their own foibles.

> *Denise M. Wilms, in a review of "The Car Trip," "The Checkup" and "First Day of School," in* Booklist, *Vol. 80, No. 1, September 1, 1983, p. 89.*

These three compact books are attractive in appearance and easy to read. Each deals with common experiences which the young child may be experiencing for the first time. Unfortunately, the negative aspects of each are emphasized (with the intent of dispelling any fears), and as a result, doubts may be suggested where they might not have previously existed.

> *Ellen J. Brooks, in a review of "The Car Trip," "The Checkup" and "First Day of School," in* Children's Book Review Service, *Vol. 12, No. 3, November, 1983, p. 25.*

Hail the three new books in Oxenbury's Out-and-About series, designed to entertain very small children but more likely to reduce their parents to helpless laughter. The minimal text [in **The Checkup**] is a perfectly straightforward account by a tad whose mother takes him to the doctor for a checkup. The pictures, in spiffy colors, are hilarious. Oxenbury has the singular talent for showing frazzled grownups and annoying kids as they are in real life. (pp. 65-6)

> *A review of "The Checkup," in* Publishers Weekly, *Vol. 224, No. 19, November 4, 1983, pp. 65-6.*

The hapless family in **The Car Trip** experiences every mishap imaginable. . . . The young rider sums up by telling his friends, "Today was the best car trip ever!" The contrast between the child's sense of adventure and adult's desire for no surprises couldn't be greater. The bright, exuberant drawings catch each moment at the most emotional peak of each incident. A happy romp sure to prompt discussions about whether delight and disaster are relative

terms. In **First Day of School** a little girl's mother is cheerfully reassuring in the slightly unrealistic, optimistic way that mothers of small children have—"Don't worry, you'll make lots of new friends." Everything is simplified when it is discovered that our heroine and Nora have the same kind of new shoes. Their comradery allows them to play, sing, listen to a story and share raisins. Four year olds, or children just getting "out and about" and needing reassurance about their emerging independent status, will love these books—and their parents will experience life from a four year old's viewpoint.

> *Dana Whitney Pinizzotto, in a review of "The Car Trip" and "First Day of School," in* School Library Journal, *Vol. 30, No. 5, January, 1984, p. 67.*

Gran and Grandpa (U. S. edition as *Grandma and Grandpa*); **Our Dog; The Visitor** (U. S. edition as *The Important Visitor*)   (1984)

Designed for toddlers just beginning to appreciate a world beyond the immediate household, three comfortably sized books concentrate on typical family activities—visiting grandparents, entertaining Mother's visitor, and coping with a lovable but obstreperous pet. Two of the stories feature girls; one features a boy. All three are first-person narratives accompanied by expressive soft-colored illustrations. Background details are minimal, emphasizing interaction among the characters through stance and situation. It is obvious that the author-illustrator not only knows how children move but also how they think, for the text is written in the matter-of-fact reportorial style used by young children. "Grandma and Grandpa let me do anything to them," boasts an insouciant charmer as she busily employs towels and napkins to bandage two prone figures whose heads are comfortably resting on pillows. Having been cautioned to behave properly while her mother discusses business with a visitor, another child remarks, "I let them talk for a long time. Then I turned on the radio and danced a little." And a tousled-haired boy struggles with his boots while a large, tail-wagging dog, waiting to go for a walk, is restrained by the mother. The characters in all three books are appealing without being prettified; each one is given a distinct personality. Comedy arises naturally, and the trilogy provides exemplary models of realism in books for the very young. (pp. 752-53)

> *Mary M. Burns, in a review of "Grandma and Grandpa," "The Important Visitor" and "Our Dog," in* The Horn Book Magazine, *Vol. LX, No. 6, November-December, 1984, pp. 752-53.*

Oxenbury has a keen eye for the comic situation, though her perspective sometimes has more in common with adult rather than childlike perceptions. These three slim picture books exploit some familiar family life occurrences for a great round of belly laughs. **Grandma and Grandpa** is perhaps most in tune with children in its depiction of a young girl who visits her grandparents and wears them out. Its situations—playing with Grandma's jewelry, playing doctor ("Grandma and Grandpa let me do anything to them"), or watching TV—are on target with real-life developments. **The Important Visitor** is more adult oriented in its slapstick display of how a child's insistent pres-

From Friends, *written and illustrated by Helen Oxenbury.*

ence can cause Mom's business meeting to go totally awry. . . . Vital to the vignettes are Oxenbury's deft illustrations. Her light lines have a beguiling trueness that's especially appealing in the **Grandma and Grandpa** and **Our Dog** books. (p. 722)

> *Denise M. Wilms, in a review of "Grandma and Grandpa," "The Important Visitor" and "Our Dog," in* Booklist, *Vol. 81, No. 10, January 15, 1985, pp. 721-22.*

As in her earlier books in this series, the main characters are young children involved in a family situation. Each book is an original story based on a simple idea. . . . Oxenbury's clever and colorful watercolor and ink illustrations add to the subtle humor of the texts. The white backgrounds and the clear black type emphasize the close parallel of the story line and the illustrations. Where Martha Alexander's books are popular, the Out-and-About Books should be too, so most school and public libraries should welcome these well-written family stories.

> *Amanda J. Williams, in a review of "Grandma and Grandpa," "The Important Visitor" and "Our Dog," in* School Library Journal, *Vol. 31, No. 6, February, 1985, p. 68.*

The Helen Oxenbury Nursery Story Book   (1985)

If you are looking for traditions, Helen Oxenbury is one of the few illustrators who clearly belongs to the Leslie

Brooke tradition. This is brought home most forcibly in this book which includes so many of the stories used by Brooke in the early years of the century. He had the advantage of a really good text. Helen Oxenbury's is no more than adequate, but she brings to the familiar tales—The Three Bears, The Three Little Pigs, Henny-Penny, and seven others equally well-known and loved—a generous measure of Brooke's warmth and keen observation. Her drawings really do add another dimension to each tale, and answer some of the questions that spring to a child's mind. How, for example, did the wolf put on Red Riding Hood's grandmother's nightie? We know now just how it was done. Miss Oxenbury is good at investing a figure with character with the minimum of details. Her Goldilocks is just the sort of prying child who would poke her snub nose into the affairs of harmless bears. She is as successful in adding human expressions to animals without violating their essential animalness. And although she doesn't, as Brooke did, fill every corner of the picture with funny detail, she puts each tale into its proper—and exquisitely drawn—environment. Altogether a joyous book, from jacket and enchanting endpapers to a final portrait of domestic harmony in the happy ending of The Little Red Hen. . . . [A] book designed to last for several generations and certain to bring delight to each.

> *M. Crouch, in a review of "The Helen Oxenbury Nursery Story Book," in* The Junior Bookshelf, *Vol. 49, No. 5, October, 1985, p. 220.*

An inviting collection of ten familiar nursery tales that will find a place in most libraries. All of the stories are available individually, but Rojankovsky's *The Tall Book of Nursery Tales* (Harper, 1944) and Rockwell's *Three Bears and Fifteen Other Stories* (Crowell, 1975) are the only two anthologies that contain many of them. These retellings have more explanations than other versions of the same tales, but since these stories were not originally intended for the nursery school audience, this consoling tone seems appropriate. (The three bears were kind and would not have hurt Goldilocks; the people who pulled up **"The Turnip"** "weren't hurt a bit" when they fell.) However, the omission of the "trip-traps" from **"The Three Billy Goats Gruff "** is almost heretical! The full-page, full-color illustrations of dot-eyed human and animal characters convey a cheerful witlessness. Oxenbury's visual style is extraordinarily comfortable and will be enthusiastically welcomed by young listeners. (p. 80)

> *Dana Whitney Pinizzotto, in a review of "The Helen Oxenbury Nursery Story Book," in* School Library Journal, *Vol. 32, No. 4, December, 1985, pp. 79-80.*

Folk tales enlarge and illuminate human situations through magic details incorporated in a universal theme. This universality of situation requires anonymous characters—a prince, a woodcutter, a cunning fox—while atmosphere and locality can mark one tale from another and make it memorable. Words do this, in good texts; illustrations most often make the first impression on the young. Whether small children hear the familiar tales for the first or the twentieth time, it is the pictures in *The Helen Oxenbury Nursery Story Book* which give them a special, strongly personal and essentially youthful feeling. One of the ten tales she has chosen, 'The Gingerbread Boy', shows her talents particularly well; not only has she made the edible boy a spanking personality but without departing from the fact that he is made of dough she has placed his limbs in a way that suggests movement and so conveys the glorious dramatic rush of this favourite story. Her clear colours and subtle shading suit animals especially well and there is a fine mixture of excitement and humour in her interpretation of 'The Three Pigs' and 'The Three Bears'. The ring of dancing animals with a child guest on the cover emphasize the contrast of happy oddity and quiet safety in a book that should be snatched up by any parent ready to introduce a small child to the tales told briefly and vivaciously here.

> *Margery Fisher, in a review of "The Helen Oxenbury Nursery Story Book," in* Growing Point, *Vol. 24, No. 5, January, 1986, p. 4548.*

Oxenbury offers a nice mix in her selection of 10 tales. There are old favorites, **"Goldilocks and the Three Bears," "Little Red Riding Hood,"** and **"The Three Billy Goats Gruff "** as well as lesser-known stories such as **"The Turnip".** The retellings are compact and just the right length for young listeners; but that also results in a tradeoff—brevity for flavor. Oxenbury's attractive watercolors highlight the fun. Although more pictures would have been nice, there is at least one drawing on every other page, some of which are full size. When the action warrants it, there are two-page spreads—for instance, a sprightly man, woman, cow, and horse all bearing down on the gingerbread boy. A good choice for parents starting to read aloud to their children. (pp. 759-60)

> *Ilene Cooper, in a review of "The Helen Oxenbury Nursery Story Book," in* Booklist, *Vol. 82, No. 10, January 15, 1986, pp. 759-60.*

A collection of simple folk tales may not be unique, but an extraordinarily attractive one for early independent reading surely is. Ten favorite stories derived from the European tradition are presented. . . . Two of the tales are a bit abbreviated or truncated: in **"The Three Billy Goats Gruff "** one misses the percussive hoof beats—"trip-trap, trip-trap"—as well as the characteristic couplet that rounds out the tale; and in **"The Three Little Pigs"** the ingenious episodes of the turnips, the apples, and the butter churn are omitted. At every turning of the page an illustration delights the eye. Emphasizing the universality and the timelessness of the stories, the artist has given some of the human characters a vaguely contemporary appearance. Her line is firm; her instinct for color superb; and from the smaller pictures to the full-page ones the artwork exudes vigor, movement, and an ebullient humor that manages to be both naive and sly. At several points the visual splendor reaches a climax in dramatically placed double-page spreads; with its eager, pink-nightgowned wolf providing a hilarious reminder of the famous Doré painting—a favorite of Freudians—the spacious illustration for **"Little Red Riding Hood"** is almost worth the price of the book. (pp. 65-6)

> *Ethel L. Heins, in a review of "The Helen Oxenbury Nursery Story Book," in* The Horn Book Magazine, *Vol. LXII, No. 1, January-February, 1986, pp. 65-6.*

I Can; I Hear; I See; I Touch   (1986)

Irresistible might be the best word for these new board books from Oxenbury. In *I See*, a toddler gets a close-up look at a butterfly and a squint at a distant airplane. In *I Touch*, there's the chance to compare Daddy's coarse beard with a slimy worm. In *I Hear*, a child listens to his Grandpa's wrist-watch and his baby sister's yelp. And in *I Can*, there is quiet joy on a baby's face as he stretches his arms over his head and bends over to touch his toes. The "I" in the title of each book says it all; the toddler is at the center of his or her cozy universe. Oxenbury's rosy babies are characteristically winsome. A child's world is pure perception, and the artist has captured that world with simplicity and charm.

> *A review of "I See" and others, in* Publishers Weekly, *Vol. 229, No. 17, April 25, 1986, p. 75.*

Many a board book has come down the pike since Oxenbury's first series in 1981. She's still one of the best in terms of maintaining simple concepts, lively art, and action generated from object. In *I Touch,* for instance, a picture of a ball is followed by a toddler rolling on it in characteristic play; the tattered blanket blowing dry on the wash line is followed by the pajama-clad child holding it, sucking a thumb with eyes closed in a bliss of softness. *I Hear* has a child clapping hands over ears beside a furiously barking dog, listening to grandfather's watch, and soothing a screaming baby sibling. *I Can* demonstrates typical movements, including stamping, falling, and stretching; and *I See* gently reminds little ones that flowers can be gazed on at ground level without being uprooted, and that a frog and a friend are wondrous sights. Good pickings for parent-sharing with the youngest.

> *A review of "I Can" and others, in* Bulletin of the Center for Children's Books, *Vol. 39, No. 10, June, 1986, p. 193.*

From the author of eight previous board books for babies and toddlers comes yet another quartet with a familiar look and sound. But in Oxenbury's case, familiarity breeds not contempt, but admiration. Using everyday concepts, simple drawings, and minimal color, she gives a child's view of ordinary things, creating books that are fresh, original, and appealing to both parents and children. As in the earlier titles, line drawings on white backgrounds are tinted with clear, harmonious watercolors. In *I Can* a toddler demonstrates twelve verbs such as *sit, jump, dance,* and *wave.* In *I See* a word such as *frog* or *moon* is illustrated in isolation on the left side of the page, while on the right a little boy observes or interacts with the object. *I Touch* and *I Hear* use the same format with a pleasing variety of subjects while never straying beyond the limits of a young child's experience. For instance, *I Touch* includes a child who picks up an earthworm with the polite, detached interest of a scientist, then later cuddles up to a blanket with the total absorption of a baby. A pleasure for readers and viewers of all ages, these deceptively simple picture books have that "just right" quality that is never accidental. (pp. 1462-63)

Carolyn Phelan, in a review of "I Can" and others, in Booklist, *Vol. 82, No. 19, June 1, 1986, pp. 1462-63.*

Oxenbury's sparingly drawn infants and toddlers—who are apt to be viewed literally by young children and more humorously by adults—experience everyday sounds, sights, and actions. The books on hearing, seeing, and touching effectively show and name a subject on the left-hand page—the rain, a telephone, a younger baby—and then show the child responding to the item in a larger context on the facing page. Although the stated themes of each volume seem less important than the various single events portrayed, adults may link these vignettes in talking through a book with a child to develop early observations on the senses or, in the case of *I Can,* with simple verbs. This series is especially apt to appeal to day-care providers for its teaching value. (pp. 578-79)

Margaret A. Bush, in a review of "I Can" and others, in The Horn Book Magazine, *Vol. LXII, No. 5, September-October, 1986, pp. 578-79.*

The Helen Oxenbury Nursery Rhyme Book   (1986)

[The Helen Oxenbury Nursery Rhyme Book *was edited by Brian Alderson.*]

A judicious mixture of familiar and obscure ('I had a young man He was double-jointed' and 'Trip upon trenchers and dance upon dishes' seldom appear in nursery-rhyme collections) makes this a book many will want to add to their shelves, particularly with the artist's blithe and varied crayon and line illustrations, which lean towards knockabout humour but offer also reminiscences of Victorian gift-books (in 'Rockabye Baby'), grotesquerie (in 'Desperate Dan') and even a Pre-Raphaelite romanticism in a scene where a fair maid bathes in the dew on May Day. Subtle colour and a variety of artistic techniques in a well planned and diverting selection.

Margery Fisher, in a review of "The Helen Oxenbury Nursery Rhyme Book," in Growing Point, *Vol. 25, No. 6, March, 1987, p. 4774.*

About half the length of the 156-page *Cakes and Custards* from which these verses are drawn, this book is even more exciting visually than the original. The page size is larger; the images are given more space and their reproduction sharpened. In some cases the drawings themselves have been revised, and in general the format is cleaner. Those who missed the first book will be delighted at the full range of color, textural contrast, expression, and variation of page design here. There's refreshing wit in depictions of the humorous verse. The hungry cow considering the piper's song about corn rigs is memorable, as is the "Don't Care" child being squashed into a pot by a ring of outraged adults, or the married man whose troubles begin with two glaring mothers-in-law ("Needles and Pins"), or Good King Arthur's bleary-eyed wife tottering out in her robe to fry last night's pudding. On the other hand, "I Am a Little Beggar Girl" is accompanied by a haunting, full-page portrait of a ragged child gazing through the window with her whole heart in her face. Illustrations appear variously framed and in shapes contrasting from circular to

rectangular but always coordinated for a smooth transition from page to page. The drawing is structurally sound and the coloration subtle but vivid. Alderson's selection and editing bring out the best in Mother Goose, street rhymes, and childhood chants, with a blend of popular and lesser-known choices. A prime pick. (pp. 201-02)

Betsy Hearne, in a review of "The Helen Oxenbury Nursery Rhyme Book," in Bulletin of the Center for Children's Books, *Vol. 40, No. 11, July-August, 1987, pp. 201-02.*

Some 60 nursery rhymes selected from this pair's *Cakes and Custard* are included in this companion volume to *Helen Oxenbury's Nursery Story Book* by Oxenbury. While almost all of the illustrations appeared in the earlier collection, a few are redrawn. The present volume's slightly larger size allows for bigger pictures, the framed watercolor and colored pencil drawings seem brighter, and the resultant look is sunny and spacious. Traditional and well-known Mother Goose rhymes keep company with less familiar ones, and while there are many illustrations and rhymes with childhood at the center, some selections will appeal to older readers as well. A little beggar girl looks poignantly out a window; a lascivious dish runs after an annoyed spoon; Elsie Marley is a floozy doing her nails in bed; and a drunken grenadier leans woozily on the barman's counter. For libraries that missed *Cakes and Custard* the first time around or whose patrons wish for a little less than the overwhelmingly complete and recent Mother Goose collections selected and illustrated by Arnold Lobel (Random, 1986) or by Tomie de Paola (Putnam, 1985), this makes a welcome addition.

Susan Hepler, in a review of "The Helen Oxenbury Nursery Rhyme Book," in School Library Journal, *Vol. 33, No. 11, August, 1987, p. 63.*

All Fall Down; Clap Hands; Say Goodnight; Tickle, Tickle (1987)

These delightful, action-filled "Big Board Books" show toddlers—black, white and Oriental—interacting with each other and care-givers of both sexes. A single line of rhyming text is just right for explaining the action. The text of *All Fall Down* goes: "Singing all together, running round and round, bouncy, bouncy, on the bed, all fall down." Oxenbury's illustrations in soft colors sweep across the double page. Her round and sturdy toddlers are expressive and individual. Toddlers will enjoy the little visual dramas: which dancing baby may lose his pants, which toddler is trying to take the cookie from his neighbor's tray, which baby is trying to comb her own hair, which baby sucks his thumb.

Sturdy, glossy, these 8½″ square board books open flat for easy viewing. Excellent choices for independent browsing and reading aloud.

A review of "All Fall Down" and others, in Kirkus Reviews, *Vol. LV, No. 13, July 15, 1987, p. 1074.*

Each of these board books consists of four double-page illustrations with a brief rhyming action verse. Chubby little toddlers engaged in a variety of activities spill off the pages in lively arrangements. Close-up views show multi-ethnic babies playing, bathing, eating, swinging, sleeping, etc. The watercolors, in bright pastels with pencil outline, are clear and appealing on a white background. The primary disadvantage of this set is the oversize format (8½" square). Tots will find these books hard to hold in their hands, and turning the pages will be frustrating. Older preschoolers who could manipulate the pages will find little story or plot to hold their interest. However, with an adult or older child turning the pages, these books will be enjoyed by the intended audience. (p. 168)

> *Nancy Kewish, in a review of "All Fall Down"*
> *and others, in* School Library Journal, *Vol. 34,*
> *No. 1, September, 1987, pp. 167-68.*

It's a jolly group of babies that populates these four large board books that have at their heart an appreciation of a baby's never-ending efforts to master the environment. In each of these titles babies of diverse ethnic origin engage in all sorts of action; the title activity may start things off, but it's by no means the only thing that's going on. In *All Fall Down,* for example, the tykes are singing, running around, bouncing on the bed, and *then* falling down. In *Clap Hands* the babies dance and spin, eat a snack, bang on pots, and wave to their parents. The books' size is large by board-book standards, and the pictures are equally large scale. The babies are simply drawn with a minimum of lines, so the compositions are easy to see—yet, as in the author's smaller board books, there is no lack of wit or grace. These are good choices for exposing the youngest children to the enjoyment of books.

> *Denise M. Wilms, in a review of "All Fall*

From Tom and Pippo in the Garden, *written and illustrated by Helen Oxenbury.*

Down" and others, in Booklist, *Vol. 84, No. 2, September 15, 1987, p. 152.*

One of the first—and still one of the best—creators of board books, Oxenbury here goes to a larger size format filled to overflowing with babies of similar plump shape but several colors of skin. The texts lend themselves to rhythmic play with wiggly listeners: "Clap hands, dance and spin, open wide and pop it in, blow a trumpet, bang a drum, wave to Daddy, wave to Mom." The sportive infants are doing just what's described, with funny flourishes: while two obediently "pop it in," the third grabs something from another's plate and the fourth pours his juice over his neighbor's head. There's great general appeal in this series. *Say Goodnight* shows babies being lifted and tossed ("Up, down, up in the sky"), pushed ("swing low, swing high"), bounced ("bumpity, bumpity, hold on tight"), and bedded down ("hush, little babies, say goodnight"). Buoyant action and vital colors against open white space will keep these moving from hand to mouth and back again.

> *Betsy Hearne, in a review of "All Fall Down"*
> *and others, in* Bulletin of the Center for Children's Books, *Vol. 41, No. 3, November, 1987,*
> *p. 54.*

Tom and Pippo and the Washing Machine; Tom and Pippo Go for a Walk; Tom and Pippo Make a Mess; Tom and Pippo Read a Story (1988)

With characteristic warmth and humor, Oxenbury captures a child's passion for a specific toy and the family's respectful response to the attachment. In this series of thick-paged books (ideal for recent board book graduates) Pippo, a stuffed monkey, is toddler Tom's constant companion. He tumbles with him into a puddle during a winter walk, reads with him when Tom's father is too tired for the job and silently takes the blame for the mess Tom makes when he "helps" his father paint the house. Children will identify all too well with Tom's anxious moments as Pippo faces a spin in the washing machine; Mom provides plenty of sympathetic reassurance. Black-and-white line drawings alternate with uncluttered full-color illustrations; in most pictures there is an expressiveness in Pippo's face worth watching, whether he is frowning as he is stuffed into the washing machine or reaching down longingly from the clothesline towards Tom's outstretched arm. The stories occasionally strain for a resolution—which is forgivable, given the brevity of each book—but they are right on target for this age level and sure to captivate their intended audience.

> *A review of "Tom and Pippo Go for a Walk"*
> *and others, in* Publishers Weekly, *Vol. 234,*
> *No. 5, July 29, 1988, p. 230.*

From one of the finest practitioners of the art of the picture book for the youngest children, four disarming vignettes about a toddler and his toy monkey. . . . In each book, busy little Tom is happy to learn by doing, imagining Pippo as his surrogate.

Oxenbury uses simple language, though her text is lengthy enough to extend listeners' verbal ability and to contain some subtle nuances in these healthy relationships. Her clear, admirably drawn illustrations are full of amusing detail, including expressions on faces—Pippo's comically show emotion despite his limp, long-suffering form. Pages are very sturdy but flexible—fine alternative to board books for tiny fingers learning to turn pages. Wonderful.

> *A review of "Tom and Pippo and the Washing Machine" and others, in* Kirkus Reviews, *Vol. LVI, No. 20, October 15, 1988, p. 1532.*

Four brief books for the very young, each one focused on a different situation in a toddler's daily life, feature a small boy and his alter ego—a toy monkey. In a context of uncomplicated familial and domestic serenity, Tom and his ever-present Pippo experience a series of miniature adventures. . . . Line drawings and uncluttered bright-colored pictures efficiently convey the progress of the stories while portraying the sturdy, busy toddler and the sometimes amiable, sometimes long-suffering monkey; and the terse, straightforward texts add details as well as some understated, childlike commentary.

> *Ethel L. Heins, in a review of "Tom and Pippo and the Washing Machine" and others, in* The Horn Book Magazine, *Vol. LXV, No. 1, January-February, 1989, p. 56.*

Four delightful books with single concepts developed through the simple texts. . . . Brightly washed illustrations show the two friends realistically drawn. These are comfortable books for lap reading to young audiences, and the large, clear typeface is well chosen for children who are just beginning to read. They will surely want to hear the stories again and again (and to tell the stories themselves). These are well designed and appealing books. (p. 89)

> *Sharron McElmeel, in a review of "Tom and Pippo and the Washing Machine" and others, in* School Library Journal, *Vol. 35, No. 8, April, 1989, pp. 88-9.*

Tom and Pippo Go Shopping; Tom and Pippo in the Garden; Tom and Pippo See the Moon; Tom and Pippo's Day (1989)

A gifted British author-illustrator continues the saga of a cheerful toddler and his toy monkey, first met in four titles in 1988.

When they go shopping, Tom keeps asking for things for Pippo to eat (a bit of cheese, a plum), but then eats it all himself while poor Pippo's face alternately registers hope and resignation. In the garden, Tom's care for Pippo parallels his mother's for him. When—on the night of a full moon—Dad tells Tom about rockets, he imagines going to the moon with Dad and Pippo (this will make a fine prequel to Barton's *I Want to Be an Astronaut*). And on a day when Daddy goes to work, Tom is also so busy that he forgets where Pippo is; fortunately, he finds him again, because "when it's time to go to sleep, I need to be with Pippo."

Tom is lucky to live in the nurturing family Oxenbury depicts with such warmth; his creative play with his beloved friend reflects his own security and capacity for healthy growth. The illustrations here are masterpieces of simplic-

ity: a few soft lines convey nuances of character and feelings, composition combines lively action with stable designs reinforcing the sense of Tom's security, and there is a good variety of details, well chosen to interest the toddler audience. Eight of these charming little books is not too many!

> *A review of "Tom and Pippo Go Shopping" and others, in* Kirkus Reviews, *Vol. LVII, No. 1, January 1, 1989, p. 52.*

Oxenbury serves up four more stories about the toddler, Tom, and his toy monkey, Pippo, to captivate the very young. As the duo participate in commonplace activities that to them seem like adventures, Pippo suffers the indignities of beloved stuffed animals everywhere. Not only is he fed dirt and blamed for his owner's mistakes, but he also loses his snacks to Tom and is callously tossed aside in favor of Daddy. Yet Tom cannot fall asleep without his beloved monkey, an attachment that many children will readily understand. Oxenbury's graphics are, as always, charming; amply executed in soft colors, they take up the entire right hand page. The left side is devoted to an enticing mix of text and pen-and-ink drawings, integral to the stories. Printed on extra-sturdy paper, these winning books will help ease the transition from board books to longer stories. (p. 1303)

> *Beth Herbert, in a review of "Tom and Pippo Go Shopping" and others, in* Booklist, *Vol. 85, No. 14, March 15, 1989, pp. 1302-03.*

Very young children are lucky, indeed, as Helen Oxenbury continues, in a second quartet of books, the adventures of Tom and his stuffed toy monkey Pippo. Identical in format to the previous four titles, the books offer brief but insightful glimpses into events of a small boy's life. In the limited experience of a toddler these incidents are the equivalent of full-blown adventures. . . . The books have an open feeling, with a smaller line drawing on one side facing a full-page, brightly-colored picture on the opposite. Amusing visual details abound: in *Tom and Pippo See the Moon* Tom flies Pippo through the air like a rocket; Tom, Pippo, and Daddy wear space suits for their trip; and a painting of a cow jumping over the moon hangs over Tom's bed. On paper heavier than usual but not quite as sturdy as that used in the author's board books for younger children, these volumes have been designed with children in mind. Oxenbury understands her audience; young people as well as adults will find pleasure in repeated readings of these unassuming gems, and no one will be able to resist the facial expressions and postures of the long-suffering Pippo. (p. 362)

> *Ellen Fader, in a review of "Tom and Pippo Go Shopping" and others, in* The Horn Book Magazine, *Vol. LXV, No. 3, May-June, 1989, pp. 361-62.*

Four more delightful glimpses of a preschooler's life. Tom himself tells these stories of days spent with his stuffed toy monkey, Pippo. . . . Tom, a handsome blond child, is bright, sweet, and personable. Black-and-white sketches on the narrative page contrast nicely with larger, full-color watercolors on the facing page. There is lots to observe, talk about, and enjoy for toddlers and adults, all noted with grace and simplicity. (pp. 129-30)

Anna Biagioni Hart, in a review of "Tom and Pippo Go Shopping" and others, in School Library Journal, *Vol. 35, No. 12, August, 1989, pp. 129-30.*

These are a beguiling sample from a series of eight titles.

The text, narrated by Tom, is simple and direct. It is presented in large, clear typeface with a few lines to each opening, which features a pen and ink sketch and the text on the left, and a full page in soft, clear colour on the right. Oxenbury has refined her style to a telling simplicity which is most appealing. Economy of line is used with striking effect to express the innocent world of the young child. It also makes for ease of presentation to groups of children.

Pippo's facial expressions and bodily attitudes are just priceless in demonstrating the ups and downs of his existence. These are just some of the many amusing little visual asides that reward the browsing reader.

Tom and Pippo are bound to appeal strongly to any child with a beloved soft toy. . . . Highly recommended.

Joan Zahnleiter, in a review of "Tom and Pippo Go Shopping," "Tom and Pippo's Day" and "Tom and Pippo in the Garden," in Magpies, *Vol. 4, No. 4, September, 1989, p. 25.*

Pippo Gets Lost; Tom and Pippo and the Dog; Tom and Pippo in the Snow; Tom and Pippo Make a Friend (1989)

Four new adventures in growing up occupy young Tom and his stuffed monkey, Pippo, as Oxenbury continues her successful series. In **Pippo Gets Lost** Tom misplaces his favorite friend and then finds him; Pippo is nearly carried away by a frolicking pup in **Tom and Pippo and the Dog;** the young boy gets up enough nerve to sled down a hill by himself in **Tom and Pippo in the Snow;** and, in **Tom and Pippo Make a Friend,** Tom finally brings himself to share Pippo with a little girl. Oxenbury manages to keep these books unforced and childlike, and her lines capture children's antics in a refreshing way. Add these where the toddler and his stuffed toy have a following.

Denise Wilms, in a review of "Pippo Gets Lost" and others, in Booklist, *Vol. 86, No. 4, October 15, 1989, p. 462.*

Toddler Tom and his stuffed monkey will once again delight readers in their four newest adventures, all of which offer children a view of Tom's world, a true microcosm of the toddler experience. Oxenbury has the uncanny ability to know exactly how young children spend their time, and she zeroes in precisely on their concerns and fears. **Pippo Gets Lost** in the first volume, but, with Tom's mother's help, he is found under the living room bookcase. In **Tom and Pippo and the Dog,** Oxenbury emphasizes Tom's love for Pippo and the fear he experiences when Pippo is threatened by a friend's dog. In **Tom and Pippo in the Snow,** Tom argues with his father that Pippo wants to sled down the hill first because Tom is frightened of tackling the hill alone. In **Tom and Pippo Make a Friend,** Tom experiences the trials and tribulations of sharing Pippo with a little girl in the park. Oxenbury's creative technique of backing black-and-white illustration on a page with the simple text opposite brightly colored full-page watercolors adds depth of artistry and variety. Prime choices for picture book collections and for toddler story programs.

Leslie Barban, in a review of "Pippo Gets Lost" and others, in School Library Journal, *Vol. 36, No. 1, January, 1990, p. 88.*

Peggy Parish
1927-1988

(Born Margaret Cecile Parish) American author of fiction, nonfiction, and picture books.

A prolific and popular author of comic fiction, informational and concept books, and picture books about both realistic and fantastic subjects, Parish is best known as the creator of one of the most beloved characters in children's literature, Amelia Bedelia, a scatterbrained maid who gets into a variety of mishaps by taking directions too literally and misinterpreting words with double meanings. In a series of twelve humorous books, the addled housekeeper encounters such predicaments as dusting the furniture with dusting powder, helping her employer throw a bridal shower by using the garden hose, and playing baseball by actually stealing the bases; however, Amelia is always forgiven despite the havoc her foolishness wreaks. The Amelia Bedelia books are credited with providing primary grade readers with a gently satiric view of the idiosyncracies of the English language while reassuring them that we can be loved despite our mistakes. In addition to the Amelia Bedelia series, Parish wrote several other works about eccentric yet lovable characters. In the three books for primary graders about Granny Guntry, for example, Parish introduces an absentminded yet independent elderly colonial woman who has a strong desire to have her own way; blithely taking on Indians, desperadoes, and wolves, she becomes involved in exciting adventures which conclude with her resolving these situations to her liking.

Parish is also the author of a series of mysteries for middle graders about two brothers and a sister who solve their cases by deciphering cryptic clues and coded messages in both word and picture; as with the Amelia Bedelia stories, these works are acknowledged for using language creatively to teach and entertain young readers. Parish received a mixed reception, however, for her stories about native Americans which initially featured nameless characters; regarded as lightly humorous, the works are also criticized for their lack of relevance to the Indian experience. In addition to her fiction, Parish wrote several well received nonfiction books on such subjects as grain, dinosaurs, manners, and the lives of early settlers. She is also the author of seven craft books which provide directions for making such items as costumes, holiday decorations, and mobiles as well as four concept books describing activities which relate to the growing competency levels of children from infancy through the early toddler stage. Parish is also the creator of several picture books for younger readers on such themes as sibling rivalry and the responsibilities in taking care of a pet as well as humorous fantasies which feature children and monsters in an easy reading format. Parish has received several child-selected awards for her works.

(See also *Something about the Author,* Vol. 17; *Contemporary Authors New Revision Series,* Vol. 18; and *Contemporary Authors,* Vols. 73-76, 127 [obituary].)

GENERAL COMMENTARY

Richard I. Ammon

Children are convinced that Amelia Bedelia is real. For those of you who are not familiar with this well-loved noodlehead, she's the eccentric housekeeper who takes directions much too literally in the book titles of the same name by Peggy Parish. . . .

Living and breathing, Amelia Bedelia may not be. But there's more than some basis in fact for her personality in Parish. I first saw her at a party given by a publisher where there were a number of other authors and people interested in children's books. Although I couldn't pinpoint what made me feel so certain that the woman across the room was Peggy Parish, I just knew—like those readers who believe Amelia Bedelia has to exist—that no one else there could have possibly written those funny books. (p. 41)

[When I told Parish, she] chuckled and said, "I can believe that. Do you know that I never met Fritz Siebel, the first illustrator of Amelia Bedelia? Yet, when I saw his pictures I had to admit that there is a similarity between Amelia Bedelia and the way I look! I guess that loving mischief as much as Amelia Bedelia and I do shows. I simply enjoy laughing at life."

The reasons why youngsters are so charmed by Amelia Bedelia are less inscrutable. Parish suggests that "perhaps in Amelia Bedelia children have the opportunity to laugh at adults." Also, she says her works are family books. "Mothers and fathers, sisters and brothers, grandmothers and grandfathers and teachers all enjoy sharing Amelia Bedelia with boys and girls."

But maybe the most important source of Amelia Bedelia's popularity with youngsters rests in the blunders she commits. The adult way of looking at things doesn't always make sense to kids, so they draw comfort from Amelia Bedelia's experiences and cheer her on. For example, Parish told me what one little boy said to his teacher after he had read one of the Amelia Bedelia stories: "Now I know it's all right to make mistakes!" And a group of older children once asked Parish, "Why does she do things wrong?"

"Wouldn't you like to do things Amelia Bedelia's way sometimes?" Parish asked.

"Yeah!" they giggled.

Like many of her books (she's authored 22 other fiction and nonfiction titles in addition to the *Amelia Bedelia* series), Parish's idea for the zany maid developed from her third-grade teaching experiences at the Dalton School, a private school in New York City. "These children were really pretty sophisticated. When I would say something like, 'Let's call the roll' (*Teach Us, Amelia Bedelia*), they would quickly respond, 'Do you really mean to say that?'"

Parish had a hard time summoning up enough courage to submit the first Amelia Bedelia manuscript to a publisher. She wasn't sure that her work was novel enough to attract attention. But she did, and it was. Harper & Row purchased the story immediately. However, achieving fame in her own backyard was a little more difficult. When the book finally appeared, one of her third graders said, "Oh, Miss Parish, you're not doing a thing but writing about yourself!"

Every experience of writing about her character involves a long incubation period in Parish's head. "I must get the story worked out in my mind before I can bring it to paper. I often lie in bed for hours at a time, staring at the ceiling, working very hard on a book."

Frequently, her involvement takes a more active turn. "The things I have Amelia Bedelia do must be plausible. When I was writing *Good Work, Amelia Bedelia* I thought of having her make a sponge cake in her own inimitable way. So, I spent one afternoon in the kitchen snipping pieces of a sponge into a cake batter. I didn't know whether it would get gooey, burn up or do what I hoped— stay like a sponge. Fortunately, the sponge stayed like a sponge and that's the way it is in the book."

As a teacher and a children's book author, Parish is as concerned about teaching literature and reading as she is about making Amelia Bedelia's antics credible. She strongly supports the idea that the goal of a reading/literature program should be to develop lifelong readers. To accomplish this, she believes that children must have the opportunity to make their own selections.

"Children's rights are taken away from them when they enter school. I won't read a book I don't like, so why should children be forced to do so?

"All the skills needed to read can be taught outside of textbooks. If schools taught children to read through the books they are interested in, then we would not have nonreaders. Children will only become lifelong readers by discovering the joy in books."

A big part of that joy is humor, as typified by the comic plays on words that Amelia Bedelia executes. These amusing manipulations of language present a wonderful teaching opportunity, as Parish once observed.

"A first-grade teacher said to her students, 'If someone asked you to plant a bulb, how do you think you would do that?' After the children offered their suggestions, the teacher said, 'Let's see how Amelia Bedelia would do that.' She read aloud the scene from *Teach Us, Amelia Bedelia* in which electric lights are tenderly buried, thus providing her students with their first lesson in double meanings."

After talking to Parish and thinking about the books, it occurred to me that they could offer a host of other learning possibilities. I tracked down a few teachers who made the same discoveries and thought of a few myself. There's just one caution. If you work with primary-grade children, you may find, at first, that they don't see Amelia Bedelia as funny. But once you explain the twists in meaning, you'll probably hear them guffaw and rush to tell others about this great form of silliness.

To further explore the meanings of homographs, ask children what the difference is when Amelia Bedelia is asked to dust furniture (*Amelia Bedelia*) and to dust the bugs (*Amelia Bedelia Helps Out*). Or, you could ask them for another meaning for "trim." Amelia Bedelia interprets the word by affixing fancy ribbons and lace to a cut of meat. But your students might think of the word as "cutting back a bush" or "decorating a Christmas tree" or the "woodwork around a wall."

In other instances, the books can provide good examples of homonyms. In *Amelia Bedelia Helps Out,* she is asked to stake/steak the beans and to sow/sew the grass seed. In *Thank You, Amelia Bedelia,* she is supposed to pare/pair the vegetables. Why not have your children draw up their own list of words that sound alike but have different meanings and spellings, and describe the ways in which Amelia Bedelia would confuse them?

Directly drawing from the books for classroom activities is not limited to language arts. A math-oriented discussion on units of measure and measuring instruments might begin by reading how Amelia Bedelia measures two cups of rice in *Amelia Bedelia.* She simply takes out her tape measure, calculates the lengths of the rice-filled cups and pours the grains back into the box.

Once students get the hang of thinking like Amelia Bedelia, it won't be difficult to encourage them to see her point of view in other projects. For example, consider asking them to hunt for newspaper headlines with more than one meaning. Parish remarked that she once saw "Committee to Call Nixon, Ford" and couldn't imagine why anyone would want to rename Mr. Nixon. Another day, she read, "Letter Jackets Arrive."

"I couldn't help wondering why letters needed jackets until I read the article and discovered that the high school team had received their basketball jackets with school letters on them!"

A thoroughly enjoyable art lesson I observed is to illustrate the plays on words. The teacher read aloud *Play Ball, Amelia Bedelia* and then had the students list baseball terms not mentioned in the book and draw pictures a la Amelia Bedelia. A "fly ball" became a ball with wings; a "screwball," a pitcher throwing screws; "on deck," a batter standing on a ship's deck, and "relief pitcher," a pitcher of lemonade selling aspirin.

As a culminating touch to a study of Amelia Bedelia, students can dramatize their favorite episodes. Sections of *Play Ball, Amelia Bedelia* and *Teach Us, Amelia Bedelia* are well-suited for dramatic interpretation because most children are very familiar with a school setting and know something about baseball. Plus, the anecdotes are easy to act out. Choose a different actor for the star role in each vignette. After all, the essence of Amelia Bedelia is individual "interpretation."

It's interesting to note that while Parish has often been mistaken for her character and admits that the two of them have a similar outlook on life, she has also undergone a role reversal of a kind. One first grader, upon meeting the author for the first time, asked incredulously, "Are you the real, live Peggy Parish?" (pp. 41-3)

> *Richard I. Ammon, "Amelia Bedelia: Sense Stuff and Nonsense," in* Teacher, *Vol. 97, No. 8, May-June, 1980, pp. 41-3.*

Good Hunting, Little Indian   (1962; revised edition as Good Hunting, Blue Sky)

Little Indian tries in vain to be a huntsman and succeeds in a most unorthodox manner as animal charges hunter who in turn comes riding in on the back of his prey. The instinct to jump and the luck to land straight save Little Indian from the horns of a wild hog and supply the tribe with enough meat for a feast. "But next time you go out hunting", warns Papa Indian, "*you* bring home the meat", instead of vice versa. The original and unpredictable outcome adds that special note to a story made especially appealing by Leonard Weisgard's artful pictures. . . .

> *A review of "Good Hunting, Little Indian," in* Virginia Kirkus' Service, *Vol. XXX, No. 4, February 15, 1962, p. 175.*

[*The following excerpt is from a review of* Good Hunting, Blue Sky.]

A revised edition of *Good Hunting, Little Indian.* The original version depicted a boy dressed as a contemporary Navajo who dwells in a tipi instead of a hogan, and who goes hunting for game with bow and arrow in a forest setting. [James] Watts' new illustrations correct these errors. The boy is now dressed as a member of the Algonquian group. His parents and other tribespeople are clothed and housed authentically for their Eastern woodland forest. Other present-day sensitivities are also addressed. The

word "Indian" is completely deleted; the child is now known as Blue Sky. The mother is now featured as prominently as the father, a slight raising of her status. The illustrations are in pleasing full-color rather than the predominant yellows and browns of the 1962 edition. However, Parish's text has also been altered to fit the "I Can Read" formula. For example, "There was a terrible crashing all around him," has now become, "The noise was all around him." This sort of thing has been called "dumbing down," and there is no good reason for it in this instance.

> *Ruth Semrau, in a review of "Good Hunting, Blue Sky," in* School Library Journal, *Vol. 35, No. 7, March, 1989, p. 68.*

Let's Be Indians   (1962)

Illustrated with gay drawings and diagrams [by Arnold Lobel], a book of instructions for making Indian costumes and accessories, models of Indian articles from puppets to villages, and explanations of some Indian games. The instructions are clear, the materials used are easily available and cost little or nothing. The child who can read and understand the directions is perhaps a bit too old for playing Indian, but the book will appeal to many because it is a stimulus for creativity, and it will certainly be suitable for adult use in guiding younger children. (pp. 46-7)

> *Zena Sutherland, in a review of "Let's Be Indians," in* Bulletin of the Center for Children's Books, *Vol. XVI, No. 3, November, 1962, pp. 46-7.*

Amelia Bedelia   (1963)

Amelia Bedelia has a very literal mind; when her directions say to "dress the chicken," she puts clothes on it. In this way she proceeds to follow all her other instructions during her first day at work. The development of a plot based upon double meanings of words can result in a hilarious book, but here the humor is lost in superfluous text and short choppy sentences. It is too hard for beginning readers and too poor to read aloud. The result is just another story with entertaining illustrations [by Fritz Siebel].

> *Harriet B. Quimby, in a review of "Amelia Bedelia," in* School Library Journal, *Vol. 10, No. 1, September, 1963, p. 106.*

Amelia Bedelia, the new maid, slightly suggests the famous Mary Poppins, but she makes her entry discreetly through the doorway, on her two feet, instead of blowing in on the wind. This is purely a "silly" book, with no lesson to impart, but it will seem hilarious to young children. Amelia Bedelia is given a list of things to do while the family is out, and how she does them is the zenith of foolishness. Fortunately, the family is long-suffering—and Amelia makes such wonderful lemon-chiffon pie that they can forgive her for everything else.

> *A review of "Amelia Bedelia," in* Saturday Review, *Vol. XLVI, No. 38, September 21, 1963, p. 42.*

Making fun of the vagaries of the English language offers

pleasure to many, from the Oxford philosophical semanticist to the smallest child who giggles at simple puns. Miss Parish provides several giggles for primary children over the way Mrs. Rogers' new helper, Amelia Bedelia, misinterprets the note of instruction she leaves for her when she is called away on the very first day. Amelia Bedelia must have Peterkin blood (and no Lady from Philadelphia to straighten her out). "These folk do want me to do funny things," she said, as she took a tape measure to "measure" two cups of rice, piled one upon another, "trimmed" the fat on the steak with lace and "dressed" the chicken in overalls. . . .

Children will certainly wish for more of her errors, especially if they are shown in such comical sketches as these of Mr. Siebel.

> *Margaret Sherwood Libby, in a review of "Amelia Bedelia," in* Book Week—New York Herald Tribune, *November 3, 1963, p. 22.*

Willy Is My Brother   (1963)

A candid approach to sibling relationships is made in a picture book with realistic illustrations [by Shirley Hughes]. Willy's little sister describes their squabbles and their shared pleasures in a text that is without storyline but is convincing both in being childlike and in being psychologically sound. Willy defends the sister he has been calling a pest when his chum says the same thing; a few moments later he is himself dismissing his sister as a pest. When another little girl comes along to play, Willy's sister promptly assumes the dominant attitude.

> *Zena Sutherland, in a review of "Willy Is My Brother," in* Bulletin of the Center for Children's Books, *Vol. XVII, No. 7, March, 1964, p. 114.*

[Willy Is My Brother *was published with new illustrations in 1989.*]

Parish's story of mild sibling conflict related through the limited vocabulary of the easy reader, first published in 1963, is back with new illustrations [by Jacqueline Rogers]. The plot is a series of typical squabbles in which Willy and his younger sister engage. Young readers will enjoy the off-hand humor generated by the description of events and the child-like dialogue. There is nothing overwhelmingly new here; the relationship between siblings is a perennially popular subject and has been treated with ironic humor and ingenuity by Judy Blume (*The Pain & the Great One* [Bradbury, 1984]), Patricia Lakin (*Don't Touch My Room* [Little, 1985]), and Martha Alexander in a variety of picture books and easy readers. Roger's black-and-white line drawings are well-integrated with the text, and the children's facial expressions give a pictorial dimension to the mood changes precipitated by the different events. It is obvious that Parish's sentiments are heart-felt; the theme of a loving and caring family permeates the text.

> *Martha Rosen, in a review of "Willy Is My Brother," in* School Library Journal, *Vol. 35, No. 10, June, 1989, p. 91.*

Thank You, Amelia Bedelia   (1964)

Amelia Bedelia, the literal-minded maid of all work is back again and she hasn't changed a bit. When told to remove spots from a dress, she carefully cuts them out; when told to string the beans and pare the vegetables, the first is made into a skinny garland and the tomato is paired up with a carrot etc.—good looking couples all. Perhaps the best comes when A. B. attempts to follow orders to make a jelly roll. Nevertheless, one of her perfect pies saves her employers' social standing. The illustrations [by Fritz Siebel] show the be-hatted Amelia Bedelia going about her balmy business with sober determination while quietly wrecking our impossibly imprecise language. A. B. fills a real need—there are so few books that test punning-readiness.

> *A review of "Thank You, Amelia Bedelia," in* Virginia Kirkus' Service, *Vol. XXXII, No. 19, October 1, 1964, p. 1007.*

An American reviewer compared Amelia Bedelia to Mary Poppins. Well, they are related through a common ancestry with Eve, but that is about all. Amelia is perhaps a distant cousin of Epaminondas. She certainly hasn't the sense she was born with, but she has a nicely literal sense. . . . I am not sure whether English children will quite get the point of stripping sheets and checking shirts, but the results are painfully clear. With a neat brief text and with Amelia Bedelia rendered most convincingly in pictures by Fritz Siebel, this is a little book which many children will greet with delight. (pp. 279-80)

> *A review of "Thank You, Amelia Bedelia," in* The Junior Bookshelf, *Vol. 29, No. 5, October, 1965, pp. 279-80.*

Almost 20 years old, this romp in Parish's popular series is still fresh fun, its spirit matched by Siebel's jaunty drawings, washed with shades of rose. Mrs. Rogers, the maid Amelia Bedelia,'s employer, insists that everything must go well on an important day. . . . [Amelia] strips the bed sheets, scatters roses, removes spots from Mrs. Rogers's dress and strings beans. The sheets are now ribbons; roses cover the floor; the dots have been cut from Mrs. Rogers's best gown; the kitchen is festooned with beans hanging from strings. But everything turns out all right, as always for flaky Amelia, because the Rogerses love her as just as much as Parish's readers always have.

> *A review of "Thank You, Amelia Bedelia," in* Publishers Weekly, *Vol. 223, No. 18, May 6, 1983, p. 99.*

The Story of Grains: Wheat, Corn, and Rice   (with William W. Crowder, 1965)

Intended as a supplementary reader for social studies in elementary school, this interesting history of agriculture limited to food grains is a welcome addition to children's literature. Local food customs, ancient lore, the advances in agricultural methods, and other interesting facets are woven into the fabric of the story.

> *A review of "The Story of Grains: Wheat, Corn, and Rice," in* Science Books: A Quar-

terly Review, *Vol. 2, No. 2, September, 1966, p. 147.*

Key to the Treasure   (1966)

More of a game than a story, the simple mystery follows Jed, Bill and Liza Roberts as they track down the clues to a collection of Indian artifacts Great-great-grandfather hid away just before he went off to the Civil War. He had been killed, and the first clue had been inadvertently destroyed, but the three children manage by chance to discover the second one. The book is very easy to read, and although it doesn't have the humor and energy of the author's *Amelia Bedelia* books, children will enjoy playing along with the word puzzles which the clues introduce and find it a pleasant first story of detection.

> *A review of "Key to the Treasure," in* Virginia Kirkus' Service, *Vol. XXXIV, No. 13, July 1, 1966, p. 626.*

Children beg for mystery stories at an ever-younger age, but many of the simpler ones are lifeless and commonplace. For newly independent readers, the author has written a cleverly detailed story of three children who track down a collection of long-lost treasures. . . . Young readers will be immediately involved when the children accidentally stumble upon the first of the coded clues, and can share the fun and excitement of unscrambling the codes and deciphering the cryptic instructions.

> *Ethel L. Heins, in a review of "Key to the Treasure," in* The Horn Book Magazine, *Vol. XLII, No. 6, December, 1966, p. 706.*

Amelia Bedelia and the Surprise Shower   (1966)

Paying the price of popularity is Amelia Bedelia, the maid who always does *exactly* what she is told, to the dismay of her mistress and the delight of growing numbers of youngsters: now she is easy-to-read-about. But, alas, the limited vocabulary has limited Amelia's powers of misconception. She *prunes* the hedge with dried fruit, *ices* the fish with frosting, and *showers* the party guests with water. (The guests may be surprised but readers are long forewarned.) Amelia can do better—or worse—than that; she doesn't even look her helter-skelter best in bright colors. Amelia Bedelia should be redrawn and returned—*un*limited!

> *A review of "Amelia Bedelia and the Surprise Shower," in* Virginia Kirkus' Service, *Vol. XXXIV, No. 18, September 15, 1966, p. 975.*

Amelia Bedelia and the Surprise Shower . . . is sure to be liked. Though Amelia comes off much better in full-length version, there is something captivating about her unfailing ability to do the wrong thing. The humor may be slapstick, but it gets large-size laughs from small-size people.

> *"Do-It-Yourself Readers," in* The Christian Science Monitor, *November 3, 1966, p. B5.*

Let's Be Early Settlers with Daniel Boone   (1967)

Not another let's-read-and-find-out-all-about-book-to-begin-on—but a follow-up for **Let's Be Indians.** As in the previous volume, there are simple instructions for a variety of simple projects, some large enough to use, some models; the former includes clothing, weapons and furnishings, the latter is aimed at assembling dioramas; general instructions (knots, braids, salt clay, flour paste) precede. Text supplemented by [Arnold Lobel's] illustrations tells all a third-or-fourth grader needs to know, making the book a boon for busy teachers and den mothers.

> *A review of "Let's Be Early Settlers with Daniel Boone," in* Kirkus Service, *Vol. XXXV, No. 17, September 1, 1967, p. 1051.*

Clear instructions amplified by detailed, intriguing illustrations lead the child to construct the necessities of pioneer life large enough to use or as models and dioramas. Among the many craft books available, none are comparable to this for a pioneer unit at this level. More explanation will be needed to clear up a few misconceptions, e.g., the mock-up spinning wheel with no thread and straws being glued to cardboard walls instead of being used directly to construct the walls of a log cabin. This book will be equally fascinating and educational to both boys and girls.

> *Flossie Perkins, in a review of "Let's Be Early Settlers with Daniel Boone," in* School Library Journal, *Vol. 14, No. 2, October, 1967, p. 177.*

Do you know how to make a coonskin out of cardboard and cotton? A braided rug for a doll's house out of a piece of cloth? A toy covered wagon from a matchbox?

These and nearly 50 other simple costumes and models are described in Peggy Parish's **Let's Be Early Settlers with Daniel Boone.** Following her earlier book on how to do things the Indians did, this new book for 6-10's by Miss Parish is entertaining and useful. It can be a big help to both children and their parents in making costumes, dioramas, models, and other items for school and other children's activities. Arnold Lobel's drawings are explicit. While they leave finishing touches to the costumes and models to one's own imagination, the basic directions are clearly spelled out. Parents who have struggled to help their children make these things will be particularly pleased with this delightful book.

> *James Nelson Goodsell, "Know-How—Daniel Boone Style," in* The Christian Science Monitor, *November 2, 1967, p. B4.*

Clues in the Woods   (1968)

After finding **The Key to the Treasure** at Grandpa's house, Jed and Liza and Bill start after the missing kitchen scraps: Grandma puts them out for the neighboring children each evening and during the night they disappear. So does new puppy Jelly Bean . . . and Liza's red sweater . . . and some of the best blackberries. A newspaper story about runaway stepchildren convinces the quick-sympathy threesome that they are the prowlers, especially after finding a trail into the woods, and they set out some solid food. The explanation is less maudlin if no more probable, but it hardly matters: the kids scrap convincingly among themselves, they're always on the go, and there are enough *clues in the woods* and narrow scrapes in the kitchen to keep readers rushing along. (One warning: they do twist words to get around their grandmother.)

> *A review of "Clues in the Woods," in* Kirkus Service, *Vol. XXXVI, No. 13, July 1, 1968, p. 691.*

Liza, Bill and Jed, first introduced in Miss Parish's **Key to the Treasure,** are sleuths again, this time solving the mystery of stolen garbage and a missing puppy. Believable characters, surroundings and situations and an action-filled plot which thickens steadily and surely to a logical solution make a book sure to win Miss Parish even more young fans.

> *Jeraline Nerney, in a review of "Clues in the Woods," in* School Library Journal, *Vol. 15, No. 3, November, 1968, p. 88.*

Little Indian   (1968)

A pleasant, easy-to-read text complemented by [John E. Johnson's] good-natured pen and ink drawings results in an appealing package for very young readers. When Little Indian asks his father why he doesn't have a real name, he is told that an Indian must make his own name for himself. Little Indian sets out to do just that, and in humorous misadventures tries unsuccessfully to catch birds for their feathers (thereby to become Bright Feather), snatch porcupine quills (to win the title of Quill Picker), capture a turtle, and so on. All ends well when the snapping turtle, unknown to Little Indian, attaches himself to the seat of the boy's pants, thus entitling Little Indian to the name of Snapping Turtle. This light-hearted book is good for both read-alouds and independent reading.

> *Eleanor Glaser, in a review of "Little Indian," in* School Library Journal, *Vol. 15, No. 5, January, 1969, p. 61.*

This is the fantasy story of a little Indian boy (tribe unspecified) who is searching for a name. He finally chooses Snapping Turtle when one catches on to his trousers and hitches a ride home. Needless to say, the story has little to do with the traditions of any tribe regarding naming customs. However, the book was probably never intended as a serious treatise on American Indian naming practices and rituals. Nevertheless, it is just such unconscious practices on the part of authors and illustrators (in this case John E. Johnson, who has provided typical "bow, arrow, and feather" fantasies in color) to which many Native American groups object. Parish and Johnson both demonstrate plenty of talent; a little research would make their efforts more fruitful. Poor.

> *Mary Jo Lass-Woodfin and others, in a review of "Little Indian," in* Books on American Indians and Eskimos: A Selection Guide for Children and Young Adults, *edited by Mary Jo Lass-Woodfin, American Library Association, 1978, p. 176.*

Granny and the Indians   (1969)

Top-notch juvenile editors are also top-notch marriage brokers. They find the right illustrator for the right author and presto, they've created a happy book. Peggy Parrish, who's long been known for taking the "How!" out of Indian stories, and Brinton Turkle, whose *Obadiah the Bold* established him as an artist with a gently humorous pen, have been brought together to tell and illustrate a story about a grandmother and some Indians who shared a common characteristic—neither had any use for nonsense.

> *A review of "Granny and the Indians," in* Publishers Weekly, *Vol. 195, No. 16, April 21, 1969, p. 65.*

Spunky Granny Guntry was driving the intrepid Indians frantic. Instead of being frightened by them, she appropriated the rabbits from their traps, picked up the wild turkeys their arrows had felled; and when her little house burned down, she calmly moved in with the chief. Thus it was that the desperate Indians built her a brand-new cabin and then bribed her to stay in it. An original, truly funny story, printed in large type to reassure children just beginning to read.

> *Ethel L. Heins, in a review of "Granny and the Indians," in* The Horn Book Magazine, *Vol. XLV, No. 4, August, 1969, p. 404.*

A light-hearted story for young independent readers, the illustrations echoing the humor of the text but lacking the polish of most Turkle pictures. . . . The role-reversal is amusing, but the artful touch that makes the tale most enjoyable is the fact that Granny never realizes how the Indians feel about her. (pp. 164-65)

> *Zena Sutherland, in a review of "Granny and the Indians," in* Bulletin of the Center for Children's Books, *Vol. 23, No. 10, June, 1970, pp. 164-65.*

A Beastly Circus   (1969)

A Beastly Circus provides plenty of fun in Peggy Parish's alliterative text and Peter Parnall's intensely alive animal drawings— . . . for those above the usual picturebook age. The verbal gaiety in an alphabet arrangement of animal acts is doubled by the detailed pictorial giddiness, and together these might well stimulate a child to try making up such lines as "Enormous elephants eagerly entertain elegant ermines" and "Rugged rangy rabbits rope rearing roaring rhinos." (p. 7)

> *Virginia Haviland, "Catching Essences with Pictures and Words," in* Book World— Chicago Tribune, *May 4, 1969, pp. 6-7.*

I was the last child in my class to learn to read. I stayed after school every day. I wept, the teacher wept, and, resolute late bloomer that I was, I was a long time in seeing what was on that blackboard. If I were in that position today and exposed to **A Beastly Circus,** I might take a vow of illiteracy. It is difficult to ascertain the purpose served by this forcedly antic alphabet book by Peggy Parish. No one can possibly want to hear lines like "Xanthic xeruses xylograph xylophones," and, while it must have been a

challenge for Peter Parnall to provide appropriate drawings, under the circumstances they smack of desperation.
(p. 54)

*Nora L. Magid, in a review of "A Beastly Cir-
cus," in* The New York Times Book Review,
May 4, 1969, pp. 52-4.

The author of the popular Amelia Bedelia stories has concocted an animal alphabet that was probably more fun to
write than it will be for beginners to read, although there
is no question that the book has tongue-twister appeal.
More contrived and demanding than Warburg's *From
Ambledee to Zumbledee* (Houghton, 1968), Parish presents real animals engaged in silly activities for each letter
of the alphabet—"Greedy gorillas gleefully grab great
green grapes." Some of the notions are potentially amusing; with others, such as "Xanthic xeruses xylograph xylophones," the alliterative technique is too strained, and the
text goes beyond the reach of the ABC crowd or beginning
readers, though eight-to-10-year-olds might enjoy the
book's tongue-twisting qualities if they are not put off by
the picture-book format. Parnall's witty, appealing line
drawings, similar in style and quality to his illustrations
for Griffen's *A Dog's Book of Bugs* (Atheneum, 1967), are
also quite sophisticated, and must be studied to be really
appreciated. All in all, a well-made luxury item for those
avid collectors of the ABC genre.

*Sada Fretz, in a review of "A Beastly Circus,"
in* School Library Journal, *Vol. 15, No. 10,
May, 1969, p. 2106.*

Jumper Goes to School (1969)

The peccadillos of a near-sighted truant officer and the
chimpanzee he deposits blindly in school—a slapstick that
overplays for laughs (previously Mr. Botts has hauled in
his own grandmother) and relies on hoary gags (Mr.
Botts: "If there is a chimpanzee in this room—then—
then—my face is red"—whereupon Jumper, the chimp,
splashes him with red paint). Bare knuckle-headed.

A review of "Jumper Goes to School," in
Kirkus Reviews, *Vol. XXXVII, No. 15, August 1, 1969, p. 773.*

A nonsensical story which appears to owe a great deal to
H. A. Rey, this is enlivened by cheerfully colored pictures
which show Jumper to be a cuddlesome beastie; *Curious
George* fans will probably take him to their hearts, with
giggles of delight.

*Susanne Gilles, in a review of "Jumper Goes to
School," in* School Library Journal, *Vol. 16,
No. 7, March, 1970, p. 132.*

Costumes to Make (1970)

With the nimbleness that became **Let's Be Indians,** Peggy
Parish lays out "Fifty easy-to-make costumes for parties,
plays and Halloween." Preliminaries are minimal (two
terms defined, a few practical tips) and so is the skill required, while costs may be kept down by making the basic
store-bought patterns of inexpensive materials. Miss Parish explains how to adapt these and provides step-by-step

instructions, with illustrations [by Lynn Sweat], for the
distinguishing accessories and decoration. History comes
in the comfortable guise—and comfortable garb—of
"Other Days, Other People," the aim being not to make
a replica but to create an effect; thus, the Ancient Greek
Boy wears a short tunic (adapted from a pajama pattern)
and a belt (plus, in the picture, a headband and high-laced
sandals), while the Ancient Greek Girl is decked simply
in a long, loose-fitting gown (her hair done up in the appropriate fashion, her hand holding a leafy branch). The
'historical' figures are staples—Indian, Puritan, Frontier,
Old-Fashioned children, Pirate, Cowboy and -girl
—with the timely addition of a Spanish pair, but there are
no wooden Dutch or *gemutlich* Tyroleans; there's no
cheapening of children either: the Hawaiian girl wears a
bodice not a bra. Among the "Holidays," Christmas is
particularly well served—by a Virgin Mary, a Joseph, a
Shepherd, an Angel in addition to Santa and a Choir Boy.
But it's "Storybook Characters" who are most fully and
refreshingly represented, from Mother Goose to the off-
spring of Perrault and Grimm to Peter Pan, Pinocchio,
Alice in Wonderland to the assortment of Animals from
a one-piece suit. And two tiny delights that take the measure of Miss Parish's talent: a dwarf in tights, wide belt
and peaked cap and an elf in hooded cap and coveralls.
Ideas for the enterprising teacher, aid for the frantic parent, fun for a mother-and-daughter team—or perhaps for
a ten-year-old with an adult on tap: in any case the results
encourage the effort.

A review of "Costumes to Make," in Kirkus
Reviews, *Vol. XXXVIII, No. 13, July 1, 1970,
p. 685.*

Any parent or librarian who has heard the plaintive cry,
"I wanna be a pirate," etc., and searched for simple pictures and directions will be glad to see this wonderfully
practical book. Someone in the family will need to be able
to sew and follow directions, but most of the instructions
call for ready-made patterns of ordinary dresses and pajamas which those who sew may already have. To these are
added hats, fringes, ruffles and imagination where needed.
The directions are neither so brief that important information is left out or assumed to be known, nor so complex
that heads spin and arms flail in exasperation. The 50 costumes are childlike—Indian boys and girls, cowboys, an-
gels and a long list of storybook characters starting with
Mother Goose and ending with animals of different kinds.
The drawings are appealing to the browser and illuminating to the seamstress. Unlike the inferior *101 Costumes for
All Ages, All Occasions* by Cummings (McKay, 1970), this
is a title that will wear well and enjoy a long welcome in
all libraries.

*Mary I. Purucker, in a review of "Costumes to
Make," in* School Library Journal, *Vol. 17,
No. 1, September, 1970, p. 106.*

Ootah's Lucky Day (1970)

When Ootah awakes he is alone and desolate "Oh, why
didn't the hunters take me with them!" in an Eskimo village that looks to be lifeless: upon his return with his walrus kill ("My people are hungry"), women and children
pour out of the igloos: the framework is askew, but then
so are the components. If Ootah's the seven or so he ap-

pears to be, what of the father who left him without fuel or food? and has he no mother? How explain his 'putting' water in the new harpoon-hole in the ice? where would he get it? wouldn't the hole just fill up? Then there's the walrus he harpoons: apparently it lays on the ice, actually (and one must look back to verify this) it's not altogether out of the hole. And consequently it's popped right out onto Ootah's sled by a second walrus surfacing behind it— providentially after Ootah's been unable to budge it. Time to stop seeking logic or plausibility: this is a snow job.

> *A review of "Ootah's Lucky Day," in* Kirkus Reviews, *Vol. XXXVIII, No. 15, August 1, 1970, p. 798.*

A neat "I can read" tale about a small Eskimo boy left behind in an Alaskan village in time of famine when the men go hunting. Flattering to all small boys, for Ootah, sneaking off, harpoons a walrus and manages to get it back on his sledge after defending it from a marauding polar bear; to his delight, the men have only brought back a few small fish. The illustrations [by Mamoru Funai] in blue and grey-black are full of humour and energy; the sentences are crisp, alert and clearly laid out.

> *Margery Fisher, in a review of "Ootah's Lucky Day," in* Growing Point, *Vol. 11, No. 2, May, 1972, p. 1952.*

Granny and the Desperadoes   (1970)

Innocent guile and a gun put the pie thieves in Granny's power until, too late, they learn that the gun doesn't shoot. The spectacle of the big bad desperadoes picking berries, sweeping the floor, catching ducks and fixing the roof for this "helpless old lady" pales, however, beside her effect on the Indians and altogether this is more conventional and less clever than its predecessor. But there'll always be takers for this kind of put-on.

> *A review of "Granny and the Desperadoes," in* Kirkus Reviews, *Vol. XXXVIII, No. 18, September 15, 1970, p. 1034.*

Granny captures two wanted men by holding her unloaded gun on them. Just as they have finished all of her household chores and odd jobs, the sheriff drops in and takes them away. Charming illustrations [by Steven Kellogg] add to a story that's completely implausible but packed with fast-moving action and rollicking humor.

> *A review of "Granny and the Desperadoes," in* School Library Journal, *Vol. 17, No. 4, December, 1970, p. 69.*

Haunted House   (1971)

Those eager beagles of **Key to the Treasure** and **Clues in the Woods,** Jed, Bill and Liza Roberts, are moving (for no particular reason) and the new house is reputed to be haunted—a situation that only Liza takes to heart. (She's an all-around *girl,* afraid of bugs too.) But though the one ghost that materializes is a joke (the boys') on her, there are daily messages in code that keep them all guessing. These, and the wanted tree house they lead to, are the work of two old friends and their uncle, new neighbor Dan

Coleman, whose ruse long ago started the rumor of a ghost. Tame to put it mildly, and the kids are interchangeable ciphers; not so the codes, so that if you've succeeded with the others you'll want a crack at this too.

> *A review of "Haunted House," in* Kirkus Reviews, *Vol. XXXIX, No. 2, January 15, 1971, p. 52.*

The Roberts family has just moved to an old house that is reputed to be haunted. When the children wake up after their first night there, they find a note on the window screen, possibly written by the ghost, which says "Welcome to your new home. Follow the clues to a treasure." Then come a series of messages, each in a different code, which will keep all cipher lovers guessing. It is too bad that characterization and plot are so much weaker than the codes.

> *A review of "Haunted House," in* School Library Journal, *Vol. 17, No. 9, May, 1971, p. 83.*

Sheet Magic: Games, Toys and Gifts from Old Sheets (1971)

This won't fill a crying need like the author's **Costumes to Make,** but there's something in it for just about everyone involved with day camps, Brownies, or the like. Most of the games are old ones sack race, tug of war (with a braided sheet), pin the nose on the clown—but in some the use of a sheet adds a new twist—indoor hopscotch, for example. Toys to make include flags, stuffed animals, dolls and doll dresses, mobiles, and bean bags. Gifts like shopping bags and pocket aprons that call for sewing are simple and safe enough for beginners. As in many books of this type, the unifying gimmick is sometimes forced: a sheet is not the best material for a blindfold, shield, jump rope or flowers. The book's value is in the simplicity of its projects; it will supplement staples like the Razzi craft books, as needed.

> *A review of "Sheet Magic: Games, Toys, and Gifts from Old Sheets," in* Kirkus Reviews, *Vol. XXXIX, No. 14, July 15, 1971, p. 743.*

A collection of 48 varied, though not original, children's projects utilizing discarded sheets. Included are games (blindman's bluff, hopscotch), toys (dolls, masks), and gifts (aprons, placemats). By using sheets in all the projects, the author stretches the point. For example, discarded sheets are not usually durable enough for making shopping bags or for use in sack races. Also, some of the games could be made more easily with other materials—e.g., a more effective ball in a cone is made from a juice can and a button. Parish further presupposes that children have some sewing experience and have at their disposal sheets, paints, crayons, needles and thread. While many of the projects could be enjoyed by primary grade children and while [Lynn Sweat's] black-and-white ink drawings are also designed for this age group, the text could not be read independently by most children before fourth grade. Similar projects are already available in *McCall's Golden Do-It Book* (Golden Pr, 1960); however, as a source of ideas, this title would have some use for parents and teachers.

> *Margaret M. Bauman, in a review of "Sheet*

Magic: Games, Toys, and Gifts from Old Sheets," in School Library Journal, *Vol. 18, No. 2, October, 1971, p. 106.*

[A] warning about **Sheet Magic** by Peggy Parish. Here are lots of things to make from old sheets: but my domestic adviser tells me you can't easily paint on a sheet, especially a superannuated one, and that the result of using the book incautiously might be a houseful of vandalised bed linen and hideously inflamed children. (p. 762)

Edward Blishen, "Pelted with Oranges," in New Statesman, *Vol. 83, No. 2150, June 2, 1972, pp. 761-62.*

Come Back, Amelia Bedelia   (1971)

The literal-minded housemaid has lost about 20 years and as many pounds at the hands of this new illustrator [Wallace Tripp]; unfortunately her talent for turning everyday English phrases inside out has also diminished. Fired for putting breakfast food in the cup when Mrs. Rogers asks for cereal with her coffee, Amelia tries working at a beauty shop (where she "pins up" a lady's hair with safety pins), a dress shop (where she "shortens" the skirts with scissors), an office (where she "files" the papers with a nail file), and a medical center (where she "puts the doctor's gloves on" herself). If the maid's previous escapades gave a child-pleasing boost to the lowest form of humor, her return is a dismal let-down. Will the real Amelia Bedelia please come back?

Parish holding an Amelia Bedelia doll.

A review of "Come Back, Amelia Bedelia," in Kirkus Reviews, *Vol. XXXIX, No. 20, October 15, 1971, p. 1118.*

None of the subsequent Amelia Bedelias has ever quite achieved the piquancy of her first misadventures which revolved around the consequences of literally interpreting idiomatic phrases. The sequels like . . . **Come Back Amelia Bedelia,** work too hard for idiomatic parallels. For example, "Cereal with coffee" doesn't inspire the same humorous confusion as "Dust the furniture." And, unfortunately, the perky pen-and-ink drawings with swatches of color can't make amusing bungles out of the overextended idioms.

Eleanor C. Trimble, in a review of "Come Back, Amelia Bedelia," in School Library Journal, *Vol. 18, No. 4, December, 1971, p. 69.*

Play Ball, Amelia Bedelia   (1972)

The literal-minded housemaid is now substituting for a sick boy in a baseball game, and we don't have to tell you how she responds to her teammates' shouted instructions to "tag Jack," "put Dick out," and "run home." But her final score breaks a tie and saves the game for her team, the Grizzlies, and when she returns the home plate (which she had "stolen" as directed) heaped with cookies, the Grizzlies cheer her even though they don't plan to make her a regular. This time Amelia has really **Come Back,** and the combination of bad puns and baseball setting should keep her hitting streak alive.

A review of "Play Ball, Amelia Bedelia," in Kirkus Reviews, *Vol. XL, No. 10, June 1, 1972, p. 622.*

Baseball terminology affords the literal mind of Amelia Bedelia a superb opportunity for misunderstanding. . . . Like other books about the amiable maid with the apparently irremovable daisy hat, this is broad comedy of the sort that appeals to younger children, and the setting will undoubtedly add to the enjoyment of beginning independent readers. Brief and humorous, the book is also a good choice for reading aloud to preschool and kindergarten children.

Zena Sutherland, in a review of "Play Ball, Amelia Bedelia," in Bulletin of the Center for Children's Books, *Vol. 26, No. 1, September, 1972, p. 13.*

Readers who know something about baseball can guess what mistakes Amelia will make, but this is light, entertaining reading for first and second graders. Amelia's followers will enjoy her new malapropisms, but libraries on limited budgets can get along with only the original **Amelia Bedelia** which offered more imaginative opportunities for errors.

A review of "Play Ball, Amelia Bedelia," in School Library Journal, *Vol. 19, No. 4, December, 1972, p. 72.*

Granny, the Baby, and the Big Gray Thing (1972)

Bearing as much resemblance to Mr. Magoo as to the differently muddled Amelia Bedelia, Peggy Parish's pioneer Granny takes a walk in the woods, bringing home a wolf she mistakes for a dog and a baby she finds hanging from a tree ("Thank goodness those Indians didn't find you" says Granny, though the pictures leave no doubt that the baby is an Indian papoose). There's a little misunderstanding when the Indians see her preparing to wash the baby and conclude that she is going to feed it to the wolf, but when the wolf does attack the baby, Granny whomps it with her gun, winning the Indians' cheers and restoring harmony on the frontier. There are funnier mix-ups on daily TV, but not so many in easy readers that children won't welcome the comic relief. (pp. 722-23)

> *A review of "Granny, the Baby, and the Big Gray Thing," in* Kirkus Reviews, *Vol. XL, No. 13, July 1, 1972, pp. 722-23.*

Another story about Granny, the staunch but naive old woman of colonial times, whose blithe disregard for the logical is always amusing if not convincing. . . . Not substantial, but it's an amusing bit of nonsense, illustrated [by Lynn Sweat] in an appropriately light style, and the familiar character will appeal to beginning readers who are already Granny's fans.

> *Zena Sutherland, in a review of "Granny, the Baby, and the Big Gray Thing," in* Bulletin of the Center for Children's Books, *Vol. 26, No. 3, November, 1972, p. 47.*

Indians are treated in a condescending manner in Peggy Parish's **Granny, the Baby, and the Big Gray Thing.** Nearsighted Granny finds a papoose hanging in a cradleboard, assumes it is lost and adopts it. " 'Thank goodness those Indians didn't find you,' " she says. The big gray thing is a wolf whom Granny thinks is a dog. But everything comes right in the end: the Indians rescue the baby and take the wolf back to the woods. This attempt at humor is in fact ridicule as neither Granny nor the Indians get their fair share of intelligence. Kids are too smart to bother with it.

> *A review of "Granny, the Baby, and the Big Gray Thing," in* School Library Journal, *Vol. 19, No. 4, December, 1972, p. 71.*

Dinosaur Time (1974)

Dinosaur Time, an Early I Can Read Book, is nicely packaged but impoverished. Peggy Parish's brief, large-type text gives so few facts on each animal that it is not very informative, even for a beginner. We learn just two things about Stegosaurus, for instance, that he had sharp, bony plates sticking up along his back and tail and that he ate plants. A beginning reader might question what the prickly plates were for and be intrigued to learn that they made it tough for this dinosaur's enemies to eat him. As for 8-year-olds: the many who are fascinated by these ancient beasts probably already know that Stegosaurus had a second "brain" in his tail to help warn of danger.

> *Barbara Madison Karlen, in a review of "Di-*

nosaur Time," in The New York Times Book Review, *July 7, 1974, p. 8.*

Shouts of welcome from besieged librarians as well as from fledgling readers will greet this new addition to the Early I Can Read series. Those who work with young children are aware that while neophytes may struggle over common monosyllables, they may well be on speaking terms with such sesquipedalians as *brachiosaurus* or *pentaceratops.* The plain-speaking text tells—with phonetic syllables—how to pronounce the name of each creature and gives a few facts about its appearance and habits; and there is an impressive illustration [by Arnold Lobel] of each one.

> *Ethel L. Heins, in a review of "Dinosaur Time," in* The Horn Book Magazine, *Vol. L, No. 4, August, 1974, p. 369.*

Too Many Rabbits (1974)

Simple drawings [by Leonard Kessler], simple style, lightweight plot, and an appealing subject are combined in a story for beginning independent readers, a story that emphasizes kindness to animals without belaboring the point. When elderly Miss Molly finds a rabbit on her doorstep, she takes it in just for the night. But next morning there are baby rabbits, too young to turn out; then the babies have babies, and the house is filled with them. Miss Molly arranges just the right home for them, happily cleans house, and decides to take in a cat. She's always wanted a cat—but the next morning, there is a litter of kittens, too young to turn out.

> *Zena Sutherland, in a review of "Too Many Rabbits," in* Bulletin of the Center for Children's Books, *Vol. 28, No. 1, September, 1974, p. 15.*

Pirate Island Adventure (1975)

Liza, Bill and Jed who found the **Key to the Treasure** and followed the **Clues in the Woods** are up to their well-scrubbed pink ears in another old family puzzle, this time engaging in a treasure hunt set up two generations ago by Grandpa's older brother John, now dead. In their efforts to turn up the hidden summer projects that Grandpa and Aunt Mary (also dead) never did find, the children follow Uncle John's sketched directions from blossoming bush to hickory tree to cave to a secret attic room, unchanged after some 60 years. The end result of all their bouncy, bubbly poking about is that Jed gets Uncle John's shell collection, Liza inherits Aunt Mary's needlework bag, Grandpa's ship model goes to Bill, and—with Grandma and Grandpa on hand for the unwrapping—all feel "very close to each other." An easy, innocent filler for summer readers, especially those who are aiming for a high count.

> *A review of "Pirate Island Adventure," in* Kirkus Reviews, *Vol. XLIII, No. 13, July 1, 1975, p. 713.*

Three pseudo-energetic children, far too good to be true, uttering words like "Wow!" and "Gee!", take off through a summer treasure hunt adventure story rather like Dick and Jane trying to find Puff and Spot on an awkward day.

The grandparents, parents, and plot are ordinary and trite. It tries to be simple but winds up being simple-minded.

> *Ardis Kemsey, in a review of "Pirate Island Adventure," in* Children's Book Review Service, *Vol. 4, No. 1, September, 1975, p. 4.*

December Decorations: A Holiday How-To Book (1975)

The end results in [**December Decorations**] won't take any prizes (moth-eaten looking snowflake, Betty Boopish angel), but the directions are businesslike, the diagrams textbookish but intelligible, the projects failproof. Best on nonsectarian items (clay covered dixie cup bell, sponge print wrapping paper), the text falls short in not explaining the significance of the Chanukah menorah and Star of David. Still, this is more than serviceable where simplicity is the first consideration. (p. 80)

> *Pamela D. Pollack, "Claus-trophobia: Closing in on Christmas '75," in* School Library Journal, *Vol. 22, No. 2, October, 1975, pp. 78-81.*

Each of 30 holiday-season decorations is explained separately and simply for the youngest readers. Primary-grade children can manage the project alone in many cases, and materials are easily obtained. Macaroni wreaths and gumdrop trees may not be original or automatically inspiring; however, the book's most rewarding benefit will be the reader's satisfaction in having read and followed instructions well enough to produce a pretty item. Illustrations [by Barbara Wolff] in green and black do a good job of explaining steps.

> *Judith Goldberger, in a review of "December Decorations: A Holiday How-To Book," in* The Booklist, *Vol. 72, No. 8, December 15, 1975, p. 582.*

Good Work, Amelia Bedelia (1976)

Few of us are at our best in the morning, and as the familiar literal-minded housemaid's day begins it seems that her creator is no wider awake than Amelia. Even a six-year-old would groan at the predictability of Amelia's response to Mr. Roger's "Go fly a kite"—and this after she has served him a raw egg for breakfast, because "you didn't say to cook it." However, she soon hits her accustomed bulldozing stride, "potting" the plants in all of Mrs. Rogers' cooking pots, hoisting the bread to help it "rise," cutting up a sponge for guess what kind of cake, and at last serving the master and mistress dried corn because "you said chicken dinner. That's what chickens have for dinner." Amelia's latest incarnation by Lynn Sweat has the appearance of an eager *au pair,* and though it's increasingly obvious that the maid's best work was done way back when (as Fritz Siebel's frump), there are others besides the Rogers who find reasons to keep putting up with her.

> *A review of "Good Work, Amelia Bedelia," in* Kirkus Reviews, *Vol. XLIV, No. 4, February 15, 1976, p. 198.*

There are two constants in the Amelia Bedelia books: the busy housemaid always wears her hat, indoors as well as

out, and she takes things literally. The former hasn't changed through several illustrators; here the pictures are not quite up to earlier standards, and the text is a bit less substantial. Amelia Bedelia makes one silly error after another, which will amuse children as it always has . . . , but there's no story line, simply a series of gaffes.

> *A review of "Good Work, Amelia Bedelia," in* Bulletin of the Center for Children's Books, *Vol. 29, No. 11, July-August, 1976, p. 181.*

Now in the Read-alone series with a new illustrator, the literal-minded housemaid Amelia Bedelia is her same old amusing self, depicted with spirit, carrying out faithfully, if foolishly, the commands of her mistress and master. . . . But her employers say, " 'One minute we're hopping mad at you . . . And the next, we know we can't do without you.' "

> *Virginia Haviland in a review of "Good Work, Amelia Bedelia," in* The Horn Book Magazine, *Vol. LIV, No. 4, August, 1978, p. 422.*

Let's Celebrate: Holiday Decorations You Can Make (1976)

Parish's holiday projects have the advantage of simplicity, but unless your demand for such material is endless (and it might be) they're redundant, considering the over-familiarity of an ersatz Lincoln log cabin or a Santa Maria model (both of paper) or the pointlessness of heads of Lincoln, Washington, Santa, pilgrims and Indians made from blown eggs or covered balloons. Too, the prospect of whole classes trotting home on February 14th with paper heart "mobiles" is dismaying—and why a straw and paper menorah when the smallest child's biggest Hanukkah thrill is lighting real candles?

> *A review of "Let's Celebrate: Holiday Decorations You Can Make," in* Kirkus Reviews, *Vol. XLIV, No. 17, September 1, 1976, p. 978.*

The decorations described here are very simple, most of them made of paper. General instructions precede the individual projects, so that the reader must refer back to "How to Cover a Balloon" when making a Santa Claus head. A brief list of "Things to Remember" gives seven points on procedure and materials, and the projects themselves are arranged chronologically by national, festive, and religious holidays, both Jewish and Christian. The instructions are clear, but they do not always give comparative sizes: "draw the shape shown" for figures A and B may not provide a young child with enough guidance to have A and B (two parts of a log cabin) be in proportion. (pp. 63-4)

> *Zena Sutherland, in a review of "Let's Celebrate: Holiday Decorations You Can Make," in* Bulletin of the Center for Children's Books, *Vol. 30, No. 4, December, 1976, pp. 63-4.*

Although many of the projects may be found elsewhere, the directions (for blowing eggs, making maché dough, etc.) are all easy enough for beginning readers to handle. Parish also includes both Jewish and Christian holidays. Step-by-step illustrations by Lynn Sweat show the projects at each stage of development and serve to clarify the simple text. Perfect for small craftspersons who haven't quite mastered small print reading.

> *Alice Ehlert, in a review of "Let's Celebrate: Holiday Decorations You Can Make," in* School Library Journal, *Vol. 23, No. 4, December, 1976, p. 66.*

Teach Us, Amelia Bedelia (1977)

If Amelia Bedelia was running out of ways to muck up the Rogers' household, she has a whole new forum here when the principal mistakes her for the new teacher and puts her in charge of a class. Following the lesson plan, she begins by calling the roll ("hey, roll!"); later the class plants light bulbs for science, practices their play (jump rope and other play), and, when the reading book says "run run run," they do—for Amelia Bedelia, whose books are cook books, the idea is to follow their instructions. The kids love it, especially when arithmetic turns into a free-for-all in the Rogers' backyard orchard ("Ginny has four apples, Paul takes two away") and ends with taffy apples all round. Up to grade.

> *A review of "Teach Us, Amelia Bedelia," in* Kirkus Reviews, *Vol. XLV, No. 6, March 15, 1977, p. 283.*

Amelia Bedelia in this Read-Alone book is a white, happy, uniformed maid. She even wears a bonnet. Aside from that her outstanding characteristic is that she interprets words literally. In this adventure she spends the day teaching school. . . . We all know about that high whistle that only dogs can hear. Certain children's books must give out a similar signal. One that only children respond to. (pp. 24-5)

> *Karla Kuskin, in a review of "Teach Us, Amelia Bedelia," in* The New York Times Book Review, *April 3, 1977, pp. 24-5.*

Never quite believable, but always amusing to beginning independent readers, this Amelia Bedelia tale is, like its predecessors, an exploitation of a one-gag situation, but it is—in addition to being mildly funny—good for the young reader's awareness of the pitfalls of our Own Dear Language.

> *Zena Sutherland, in a review of "Teach Us, Amelia Bedelia," in* Bulletin of the Center for Children's Books, *Vol. 31, No. 3, November, 1977, p. 51.*

Hermit Dan (1977)

Fresh from their last **Pirate Island Adventure**, Jed, Liza, and Bill Roberts are still visiting Gran and Grandpa and are ready for another easy mystery. This time they're out to prove the pirate origins of the island, taking on the reclusive Hermit Dan, whose forebears are rumored to have been the island's original buccaneers. Dan's kept up a gruff exterior to folks since arson destroyed his parents' home years ago, but the Roberts kids thaw him out with relentless cheerfulness, good manners, and amazing ease. Extras like two surprise birthday parties, the children's yapping pup, Jelly Bean, and a fistfight that earns Liza her

first shiner make this upbeat, undemanding summer reading.

> *A review of "Hermit Dan," in* Kirkus Reviews, *Vol. XLV, No. 17, September 1, 1977, p. 933.*

Taking an interest in the local eccentric, **Hermit Dan,** Liza, Bill, and Jed manage in short order to unravel his mysterious past and gain his friendship. Though everything works out too neatly for the children, it's easy to get caught up in the uncomplicated plot and the amiability of it all. (p. 62)

> *Andrew K. Stevenson, in a review of "Hermit Dan," in* School Library Journal, *Vol. 24, No. 4, December, 1977, pp. 61-2.*

Mind Your Manners! (1978)

"What can be the use of [manners]? . . . They make you a nice person to know." On that simple note, Parish begins a levelheaded catalog of graces for a variety of common situations, from meeting people and answering the telephone to giving a party or even just chewing gum. The tone is quite matter-of-fact but is lightened by [Marylin Hafner's] amusing illustrations. Best suited for classroom discussion or parent-child reading.

> *Judith Goldberger, in a review of "Mind Your Manners!" in* Booklist, *Vol. 75, No. 26, November 15, 1978, p. 552.*

No tongue-in-cheek *"What Do You Say, Dear?"* but a straight, simple lesson in the uses of *please, thank you,* and *may I be excused.* Except for telling kids to give their names when they answer the phone, it's all perfectly harmless, generally acceptable advice, such as "Chew with your mouth closed," "When eating at a friend's house, offer to help with clean-up," and "Don't touch [the merchandise] in stores." And no one could quarrel with Parish's tips on getting along with peers: "Wait your turn at games," "don't interrupt," and "don't whisper in front of others" all jibe with her reasonable observation that "Good manners make you a nicer person to know." Of course we all know that you don't acquire them this way, but there will probably always be parents who hope it will work. For their kids, Hafner at least makes it look nice and easy.

> *A review of "Mind Your Manners!" in* Kirkus Reviews, *Vol. XLVI, No. 22, November 15, 1978, p. 1245.*

Mind Your Manners! would be unbearably preachy without the irony of the illustrations by Marylin Hafner. Even so, the cumulative effect of the text seems to politely beat children over the head. After 55 pages of do's and don'ts, one longs for a more subtle story format, or the humor of Amelia Bedelia. "Use your best manners" seems a vague direction, at best; and the prescribed usage of Mr. or Mrs. for every adult may be a bit confusing for modern children taught to use first names for their parents' friends and even their teachers. At this age level [grades one to three], manners are learned more from actions at home than from etiquette books.

> *Kathy Coffey, in a review of "Mind Your Man-*

ners!" in School Library Journal, *Vol. 25, No. 4, December, 1978, p. 67.*

Be Ready at Eight (1979)

A neatly structured approach to the nicest of surprises—absent-minded Miss Molly is giving herself a party! This cheerful oldster awakens with a string on her finger, a reminder that "something special is happening today"; but her queries to neighbor Mr. Block cutting roses (". . . for the flower show?"), minister Dr. Wade ("I wanted to ask about the church supper"), and everyone else in this closely-acquainted small town net her only the information that they all expect to see her at eight . . . though the alert youngster might suspect what's up as soon as Mr. Block says evasively that the roses "are for something very special." But the best fun, and the nicest lesson in living loose, is Miss Molly's dawning realization that, for some reason or other, she's giving a party—so she'd better bake a cake and get herself ready. "I do love surprises," she says; and the door opens to a throng shouting "HAPPY BIRTHDAY!" Now, the cake served, Miss Molly can take off the string. It's a welcome return for the heroine of *Too Many Rabbits* and still another demonstration of Peggy Parish's ability to make us smile kindly at fuzzy-mindedness: Miss Molly, after all, is not unique. (pp. 516-17)

> *A review of "Be Ready at Eight," in* Kirkus Reviews, *Vol. XLVII, No. 9, May 1, 1979, pp. 516-17.*

Absent-minded Miss Molly wakes to find a string on her finger and can't remember what it's for; she finds the date in the morning paper, checks her calendar and sees she's written a note that tells her to be ready at eight. Ready for what? . . . [Readers will suspect] that Miss Molly has forgotten her own birthday, but will they, birthday-minded as they are, believe it? There's always pleasure in being a step ahead of the characters in a story, but that pleasure may be lessened by disbelief. Otherwise, the book is lightly humorous, appropriately simple, a bit over-extended as Miss Molly meets neighbor after neighbor who thwarts her efforts to learn what's going on. . . .

> *Zena Sutherland, in a review of "Be Ready at Eight," in* Bulletin of the Center for Children's Books, *Vol. 33, No. 1, September, 1979, p. 15.*

Amelia Bedelia Helps Out (1979)

The maid like no other has a visitor, her fond niece Effie Lou, who lends a hand as Amelia Bedelia goes about literally obeying her mistress, Miss Emma, once more. Amelia Bedelia and Effie Lou set to with a will, weeding the garden as instructed. They plant the biggest weeds around to shade the vegetables. They cut up the dinner steak to stake the beans. They dust the bugs with talcum powder; throw scraps (of quilting fabric) to the hens and, finally, make tea cake with tea leaves. Parish's jolly story and [Lynn] Sweat's witty color pictures unite in the latest story of everybody's favorite nut, to induce gales of happy laughter. (pp. 159-60)

> *A review of "Amelia Bedelia Helps Out," in*

Publishers Weekly, *Vol. 216, No. 4, July 23, 1979, pp. 159-60.*

With her characteristic confidence and well-known flair for the unintended pun, the cheerful maid astonishes [her] employer. . . . Her sunny disposition, her baking skills, and the good nature of her bosses as usual save the day. For some reason, the sameness of Amelia Bedelia's stories (last seen in *Good Work, Amelia Bedelia*), does little to lessen their funniness or appeal to children.

> *Judith Goldberger, in a review of "Amelia Bedelia Helps Out," in* Booklist, *Vol. 76, No. 2, September 15, 1979, p. 128.*

This time Amelia is on loan from the Rogers to "grand," good-natured Miss Emma, and she brings along her own niece Effie Lou to help. Effie, who consistently accepts her aunt's interpretations of the orders, doesn't add much to the proceedings and the change of scene is only that; but Amelia Bedelia's fans will no doubt enjoy this latest round of misconstructions as much as any.

> *A review of "Amelia Bedelia Helps Out," in* Kirkus Reviews, *Vol. XLVII, No. 21, November 1, 1979, p. 1260.*

Zed and the Monsters (1979)

Zed and the Monsters uses folklore themes, recasting them into the tale of a country boy who defeats four gross monsters. Except for an unfortunate tendency to make chapters that interrupt the flow and the strange choice of a governor as the gold-giver, Peggy Parish's story is a happy find. Paul Galdone's truly ugly monsters are zesty. My favorite wears a bone dangling from one pierced ear. (p. 55)

> *Jane Yolen, "Easy and Early," in* The New York Times Book Review, *November 11, 1979, pp. 55, 60.*

Zed, a boy who lived "a long time ago," was lazy but mercenary; only when he had empty pockets did he bestir himself and look for work. Greeting a man he encountered (who proved to be the Governor) Zed learned that there were four monsters at large. He filled his sack with grapes and noodles and, in a series of encounters with the monsters, outwitted them and claimed the gold the Governor had promised as a reward. Then Zed headed for home, anxious to sit in his rocking chair and be lazy again. Galdone's illustrations are lively, and there's some humor in the combination of bland style and derring-do events, but the writing—albeit simple—has a staccato quality. As fodder for beginning readers with a predilection for monster stories, however, it will serve.

> *Zena Sutherland, in a review of "Zed and the Monsters," in* Bulletin of the Center for Children's Books, *Vol. 33, No. 4, December, 1979, p. 78.*

Unfortunately the framework for *Zed and the Monsters* is better than the eye-gouging action itself. Despite the limitations of beginning reader vocabulary, Peggy Parish creates a country rhythm in her prose. Paul Galdone captures the character of Zed—lazy, but under the brim of his oversized hat, clever. One expects more fun from Zed than what follows. His encounter with monsters is riddled with clichés (e.g., substituting noodles for brains) and leaves little to the imagination. The hero becomes more interesting when he has polished off his adventure.

> *Kathy Caffey, in a review of "Zed and the Monsters," in* School Library Journal, *Vol. 26, No. 4, December, 1979, p. 96.*

Beginning Mobiles (1979)

The best thing about this do-it-yourself craft book is the author's presentation of basic forms: a simple, cardboard-and-string hanging frame and an "egg form" made from two egg holders cut out of a carton and glued together to make a sphere. With these structures Parish builds a multitude of mobiles, all appealing and designed to come out looking fine even in less well-coordinated hands. Many of the 26 mobiles have holiday themes; materials are readily available at home or from art stores. Though perhaps not challenging to adventurous minds, this book is very useful.

> *Judith Goldberger, in a review of "Beginning Mobiles," in* Booklist, *Vol. 76, No. 8, December 15, 1979, p. 619.*

A project book for readers in the primary grades is simple, explicit, and nicely illustrated [by Lynn Sweat] with the diagrams in a step-by-step format. General instructions precede the examples, all of which use the same base, a circle of oak tag or cardboard; none of the materials required is expensive or difficult to get: pipe cleaners, construction paper, staples and glue, scissors, egg cartons, etc. The print is large and is set off by ample space; the projects include mobiles that can be used for holidays and that may, as the author suggests, prompt children to try their own ideas.

> *Zena Sutherland, in a review of "Beginning Mobiles," in* Bulletin of the Center for Children's Books, *Vol. 33, No. 6, February, 1980, p. 114.*

I Can—Can You? (1980)

Eminently salable, the item introduced here consists of four small, soft books in a clear plastic carrying case with a red handle to fit toddlers' hands. The well-known author and illustrator teamed up to design the set for parents to share with babies, helping the children to respond, listen, learn while playing. Parish's minimal text and [Marylin] Hafner's frisky color cartoons explore the contests between babies Rebecca and Jason in Level 1; they try catching their toes, wiggling their fingers, etc. In Level 2, Sam and Jenny (a smitch older) roll balls, dig in the sand and have a good time, leading to Levels 3 and 4 when the quartet (black children and white friends) have advanced to the proud status of carrying out grown-up chores.

> *A review of "I Can—Can You?" in* Publishers Weekly, *Vol. 217, No. 25, June 27, 1980, p. 88.*

Four little books, each a bit more difficult in concepts and vocabulary, come in a plastic bag; the sturdy pages are almost indestructible and have bright pictures with plenty of white space to set them off. In the first book the focus

is on activities, and the format for the pages is exemplified by "Rebecca can clap her hands," picture, "Can you clap your hands." In the second book, Jenny swings and Sam can rock his doll and eat with a spoon. By level three, Sam can jump and play hide and seek, and by level 4, Jenny can ride a tricycle and Jason has learned how to share. In each book, the children are a bit older and have acquired new knowledge and physical skills. The books are attractive, and they are useful both for the progress they record (and the child's satisfaction, when listening, at achievement of similar progress) and for the fact that they can illuminate, for small children, concepts of growth and change.

> *Zena Sutherland, in a review of "I Can—Can You?" in* Bulletin of the Center for Children's Books, *Vol. 34, No. 3, November, 1980, p. 60.*

This 1980 series is worth locating. They show toddlers Jason and Rebecca (a white boy and girl) and Jenny and Sam (a Black girl and boy), who can do many things that other toddlers can imitate. (Volume One, for instance, begins with simple actions such as wiggling fingers.) It's nice to see human toddlers (instead of bunnies or frogs with human characteristics) and the toddlers' accomplishments in these books: Sam enjoys rocking his baby; Jenny likes to swing and ride her trike; Jason helps to bathe himself and Rebecca washes her hands. When we meet the children's parents in Volume Four, both mothers and fathers are shown caring for the children.

The books are printed on heavy cardboard to withstand the punishment little hands can dish out. They have simple, clear, appealing pictures. I heartily recommend them for any toddler.

> *Karen Plattes, in a review of "I Can—Can You?" in* Interracial Books for Children Bulletin, *Vol. 16, No. 1, 1985, p. 7.*

Amelia Bedelia and the Baby (1981)

Up to her old, unintentional tricks, Amelia Bedelia proves that communication gaps can be greater between parents and baby-sitters than between sitters and babies. Amelia lets infant Missy do a lot of the work she herself doesn't understand, which leads to a very messy, very happy baby. Missy gets to mash her own banana (skin and all) and feed herself (without benefit of utensils or bib) while Amelia plays with the toys and balks at instructions like "naptime," deciding to make strawberry tarts instead. If some bits of the pun-based fun are forced, using a baby as a comic vehicle counterbalances them as far as readers' enjoyment goes.

> *Judith Goldberger, in a review of, "Amelia Bedelia and the Baby," in* Booklist, *Vol. 77, No. 14, March 15, 1981, p. 1037.*

One might approach the prospect of Amelia Bedelia baby-sitting with apprehensive relish, but the misunderstandings in this session are mild ones and the verbal play almost nil. Amelia doesn't know what a baby bottle is until a neighbor drops in and fixes one for little Missy; meanwhile she gives the crying baby cans and boxes because they don't break as bottles do. She interprets the mother's written directions—"Use the baby powder," "nap time," and "play time"—as applying to her, not the baby, and gives Missy the specified "mashed bananas" by mashing the fruit whole in its skin. (Missy loves it and eats it anyway.) In her usual manner, Amelia Bedelia wins over the returning parents with the strawberry tarts she decided to bake instead of taking a "nap time." But her response to "Put Missy in her stroller and take her out for a while" (Amelia takes her out of the stroller, not outdoors) is about the only reminder of Amelia Bedelia's old, endearing literal-mindedness.

> *A review of "Amelia Bedelia and the Baby," in* Kirkus Reviews, *Vol. XLIX, No. 6, March 15, 1981, p. 355.*

No More Monsters for Me! (1981)

No More Monsters for Me! decides Minneapolis Simpkin after she brings home a baby monster who grows larger while she eats her dinner. Trying to hide the creature from her mother while he is growing to gargantuan proportions, Minn finally breaks down, tells the truth and returns the monster to his hill home, getting a *real* pet in the bargain. Marc Simont's monster, in green and orange, is the lumpish, hairy star here, even though he never speaks. The artist does an equally good job with Minneapolis, Peggy Parish's spunky, funny narrator who takes care of herself; Minn and her single-parent-mother make nice, noisy foils for each other.

> *Nancy Palmer, in a review of "No More Monsters for Me!" in* School Library Journal, *Vol. 28, No. 4, December, 1981, p. 74.*

There is a definite, beguiling character to Parish's tackling of the age-old pet conflict between parent and child. Much of the charm derives from the deft handling of an element of fantasy—a little lost monster whom the protagonist shelters nearly under the nose of her pet-hating mother. . . . Luckily, what Minn and readers know Mother does not; she even imagines her daughter's confession of guilt to be part of a desperate wish-fulfillment fantasy. The resolution: if things are that bad, thinks Mom, perhaps a pet *is* in order. Balance the neatly turned invention with realistic circumstances, personalities, and feelings and it all comes out resoundingly true.

> *Judith Goldberger, in a review of "No More Monsters for Me!" in* Booklist, *Vol. 78, No. 8, December 15, 1981, p. 554.*

Simont never draws any more than is necessary, so the cheerful pink and green tints of his monster and his two human characters have only enough background detail to complement the story, simply told in first person by Minn (Minneapolis Simpkins). . . . Brisk, funny, easy to read, with the appeal of wish-fulfillment and the satisfaction of being able to identify with a child who knows something an adult doesn't. (pp. 112-13)

> *Zena Sutherland, in a review of "No More Monsters for Me!" in* Bulletin of the Center for Children's Books, *Vol. 35, No. 6, February, 1982, pp. 112-13.*

Mr. Adams's Mistake (1982)

Instead of Amelia Bedelia misinterpreting directions, the mixup here derives from Mr. Adams' poor eyesight. Thus, in going about his "special job" which is hauling truant children back to school, Mr. Adams drags the newsstand man's chimpanzee helper Corky off to the classroom. Though the teacher and children know that Corky is not a boy, as Mr. Adams insists, they have to put up with him. But that becomes increasingly difficult as he throws his book, dumps the fish into the turtle bowl, and paints the children instead of the paper. Finally the newsstand man, Mr. Adams, and a policeman burst into the classroom—and, as Mr. Adams shouts "Show me a chimpanzee! If there is one in this class, my face is red," Corky splashes his paint and "Mr. Adams was red all over." That moment will get a laugh, but until then the classroom chaos has been uninspired and the pictures [by Gail Owens] flat and predictable.

> *A review of "Mr. Adams's Mistake," in* Kirkus Reviews, *Vol. L, No. 8, April 15, 1982, p. 488.*

Peggy Parish's story rolls right along, with the exception of the awkwardly contrived dialogue attending the story's climax and the out-of-synch illustration of that same scene. The chimp-at-school theme will click immediately, and the colorful cartoons by Gail Owens, aping Corky's antics, will guarantee the giggling.

> *Nancy Palmer, in a review of "Mr. Adams's Mistake," in* School Library Journal, *Vol. 28, No. 9, May, 1982, p. 80.*

The question that springs to mind upon reading Parish's Ready-to-Read is: where is the vivacity and originality that sparks the author's acclaimed stories about Amelia Bedelia? The prose is wooden, unhappily recalling the old Dick/Jane/Spot duds, not apt to interest beginners in Mr. Adams or the situations his near-sightedness creates. . . . [At the end of the book] Mr. Adams apologizes and promises to get eyeglasses as the story peters out. Owens's color cartoons don't add luster to the nonsense, but then, perhaps nothing could.

> *A review of "Mr. Adams's Mistake," in* Publishers Weekly, *Vol. 221, No. 23, June 4, 1982, p. 68.*

The Cats' Burglar (1983)

Everyone thinks Aunt Emma has about eight cats too many—she has nine. But Aunt Emma loves cats, and one evening when a burglar invades the apartment, the cats prove their worth. The burglar's allergy to cats alerts Aunt Emma, and then the cats pounce on him as though he were a piece of catnip, holding him hostage for the police. Now everyone agrees Aunt Emma has just the right amount of cats. The three-color artwork [by Lynn Sweat] features cats everywhere and has a real bounce to it. Parish sustains her sure touch for easy-to-reads. (pp. 974-75)

> *A review of "The Cats' Burglar," in* Booklist, *Vol. 79, No. 14, March 15, 1983, pp. 974-75.*

Literal beginning readers may query the fact that the opening of the story describes three visitors but the illustrations, line and wash, show only two. The vocabulary and sentence length are appropriate for the intended audience, but the pace is slow, with repetition that flattens the writing style. (pp. 174-75)

> *Zena Sutherland, in a review of "The Cats' Burglar," in* Bulletin of the Center for Children's Books, *Vol. 36, No. 9, May, 1983, pp. 174-75.*

Amelia Bedelia Goes Camping (1985)

Parish's Amelia Bedelia returns to send kids into gales of laughter in a dandy Read-Alone for beginners. [Lynn] Sweat's color pictures illustrate exuberantly the gaffes by the likable housemaid on a camping weekend with her patient employers, Mr. and Mrs. Rogers. "Time to hit the road," Mr. Rogers says, as they get into the car, so Amelia does; she gives the road a sharp rap with a stick. At the campsite, she's supposed to start a fire on the grill with pine cones and also "put coffee on." Dutifully, Amelia obeys, but neither the cones nor the coffee grounds creates a flame. She's waiting for the Rogerses to return from a walk when two boys pass by and she gets them to help pitch the tent—into a thicket. Although Mr. and Mrs. Rogers lose their cool, they quickly regain it when Amelia produces a gourmet meal, with a luscious birthday cake, a surprise for Mr. R., and the outing is a success.

> *A review of "Amelia Bedelia Goes Camping," in* Publishers Weekly, *Vol. 227, No. 9, March 1, 1985, p. 80.*

From her first appearance more than 20 years ago, Amelia has been doing everything right but getting everything wrong. Dust the furniture? She digs up some lovely Dusting Powder and dusts like mad. ("At my house we undust the furniture. But each to his own way.") Weed the garden? No problem: nice big weeds are planted row on row.

No child can resist Amelia and her literal trips through the minefield of the English language—and no adult can fail to notice that she's usually right when she's wrong. Both parents and children can learn, as well, from Amelia's kind employers. Mr. and Mrs. Rogers always come to understand Amelia's confusion and to admit that the language, not the user, is the culprit.

There is a good reason for their forgiving ways, though. Much as another beloved children's hero, Curious George (always in scrapes because of his curiosity), often saves the day because of his special monkey talents—so Amelia redeems herself through her special talent. She can cook. Just when things are at their darkest, or dustiest, or weediest, Amelia pulls out "a little this and a pinch of that" and comes up with the best meal in town. Like George, Amelia is forgiven because of her special gifts. Certainly a child could wish for no less.

In Amelia's new foray, the 10th in the series, the Rogers take her camping. The big question is whether Amelia can be as funny in the wilderness as she is in the living room. Of course she can. How will she "catch" a fish or "pitch" a tent? When asked to bring "sleeping bags," what will she bring? And what, oh what, is making her chocolate-chip cookies so crunchy? The answers are just what they ought to be and never what we expect, as Miss Parish gently brings her reader along the linguistic path from the literal to the colloquial.

The Amelia Bedelia books are part of the Greenwillow Read-alone series, and they are, in fact, accessible to a competent young reader. But how many adults want to give up the shared pleasure of bedtime with Amelia Bedelia? It's not as much fun to stand outside the bedroom door and listen to the cackles under the quilt.

> *Cynthia Samuels, in a review of "Amelia Bedelia Goes Camping," in* The New York Times Book Review, *March 10, 1985, p. 29.*

Amelia Bedelia is a model of well-intentioned mishap. The word play here is at just the right level; children will understand most of the phrases that confuse Amelia Bedelia (not always the case in some of the other titles), and they'll get their usual charge out of her misguided but determined cheerfulness. Amelia Bedelia has become such an institution and a welcome splash of comedy on the easy-reading shelf that one forgives the slightly patronizing domestic set-up. The line drawings in yellows, greens and browns help to put the joke across and are refreshing in their inclusion of some non-white faces. Go for it.

> *Nancy Palmer, in a review of "Amelia Bedelia Goes Camping," in* School Library Journal, *Vol. 31, No. 9, May, 1985, p. 107.*

Amelia Bedelia's fans will doubtless be satisfied; those for whom this is a first encounter may find this amusing because of the humor of a protagonist who takes everything literally. . . . As in earlier books, A. B. is perpetually clad in her maid's uniform plus an incongrous large-brimmed, flower-trimmed hat. Some readers may feel that A. B. lacks intelligence or is being typecast; others may accept her as matter-of-fact and comic. At any rate, just at the point when her employers, who have taken her along, are getting irritated at the way the expedition has been spoiled by A. B. (instead of sleeping bags and tent stakes, she's packed grocery bags and steak) the maid produces a picnic so lavish that all is forgiven. Funny, but a bit of a put-down.

> *Zena Sutherland, in a review of "Amelia Bedelia Goes Camping," in* Bulletin of the Center for Children's Books, *Vol. 38, No. 11, July-August, 1985, p. 213.*

Merry Christmas, Amelia Bedelia (1986)

Amelia Bedelia, possessor of the state of the art in literal minds, is back, this time "helping" Mr. and Mrs. Rogers prepare for Christmas.

Amelia bakes a date cake with dates from the calendar. She "trims" the Christmas tree with scissors and stuffs the stockings with homemade turkey stuffing. When asked to hang the balls on the tree, she does: basketballs, footballs, tennis balls. Though she rallies, she seems, at first, to have only a hazy memory of Santa Claus—hard to believe even for Amelia Bedelia. The illustrations [by Lynn Sweat] are adequate, but rather listless compared to the perky text. (Exceptions: the drawing of Mrs. Roberts sputtering and of tough Aunt Myra, who prefers things Amelia Bedelia's way, beaming in her sensible shoes.)

A funny and comforting story about a person who does things wrong a lot of the time, yet is enormously lovable. Not for children who will be distressed that Santa Claus is Mr. Rogers dressed up.

> *A review of "Merry Christmas, Amelia Bedelia," in* Kirkus Reviews, *Vol. LIV, No. 14, July 15, 1986, p. 1123.*

Christmas here is merely an excuse for Amelia Bedelia's usual misunderstandings; however, children will love her endless antics. Ultimately, she manages to please Mrs. Rogers with fresh popcorn balls and Mr. Rogers with hot spice cake. Is there room for another book about the literal-minded maid? There's *always* room for another book about Amelia Bedelia—she hasn't lost her touch.

> *A review of "Merry Christmas, Amelia Bedelia," in* Publishers Weekly, *Vol. 230, No. 13, September 26, 1986, p. 75.*

Children familiar with Parish's good-natured ding-a-ling will immediately guess that in this book she she will "trim the tree" in her own inimitable way. Like the previous stories about this literal-minded maid, this one is not so much a Christmas book as a further examination of the peculiarities of the English language. Young children struggling to master odd usages will find enormous pleasure in Amelia Bedelia's misinterpretations. The cartoon-like pictures ably serve to illustrate her mistakes. Not great art—just great fun for all of Amelia Bedelia's many fans.

> *Judith Gloyer, in a review of "Merry Christmas, Amelia Bedelia," in* School Library Journal, *Vol. 33, No. 2, October, 1986, p. 111.*

The Ghosts of Cougar Island (1986)

One of the more believable, and yet exciting, juvenile mysteries available. Liza, Bill, and Jed, characters from five previous mysteries by Parish, notice flickering lights on uninhabited Cougar Island, which, according to legend, is haunted. Following other mysterious incidents, the three siblings set forth in their boat to investigate. Parish includes many of the elements that young readers love—ghosts, animals, orphans, and, best of all, a happy ending. Liza and her brothers are realistic, occasionally squabbling siblings, but their grandparents are surely every child's dream: trusting enough to let the children set forth on their adventure, yet always concerned and loving. The short chapters help keep the pace moving nicely, and the few sketchy but well-done black-and-white illustrations [by Deborah Chebrian] will help sustain the interest of reluctant readers. The vocabulary is fairly easy, and the text relies heavily on convincing dialogue. Given the popularity of juvenile mysteries, this mystery-adventure should be a worthwhile addition to school and public libraries.

> *Ruth Reutter, in a review of "The Ghosts of Cougar Island," in* School Library Journal, *Vol. 33, No. 2, October, 1986, p. 180.*

Scruffy (1988)

By a veteran children's author, a heartwarming story that not only includes a message but is also probably the first easy reader to use the term "neuter."

Todd bounces up on his birthday because he's sure he's going to find a longed-for cat. The feline paraphernalia he unwraps confirm his hopes, but for the ultimate gift he and his parents must go to the animal shelter. There, Todd is introduced to a few facts on pet care and the many available kittens, and makes an unlikely choice: a standoffish (but lovable) older kitten with a crooked tail who, Todd says, "needs me . . . And I need him."

Parish introduces several ideas in the context of this simple story: why animals are given away, what happens to them if they are not adopted ("Often we have to put the animals to sleep"), and the importance of neutering both male and female pets. But though their story is written to a purpose, Todd and Scruffy have enough charm to make the medicine go down smoothly.

> *A review of "Scruffy," in* Kirkus Reviews, *Vol. LVI, No. 1, January 1, 1988, p. 58.*

In a modest way, this is an exemplary story for the beginning independent reader: vocabulary controlled (but not rigidly), story line sturdy, plot not taxing, subject appealing, print large, and pages uncluttered. It also gives some information about getting and caring for a pet, it advocates consideration for animals, and it tells the story of a child who gets just what he's wanted for his birthday, a kitten.

> *Zena Sutherland, in a review of "Scruffy," in* Bulletin of the Center for Children's Books, *Vol. 41, No. 6, February, 1988, p. 122.*

Put a kid with a pet and you have interesting story possibilities. Add to that Parish's writing skills plus illustrations [by Kelly Oechsli] which complement the text and give context clues for word meaning, and you have a winner of an "I-Can-Read-Book." Children will be able to identify with Todd's desire for a pet and his anguish over selecting just the right one from so many at the Animal Shelter. Gentle lessons are given about why animals are in the Shelter, what happens to them, and how important it is to have a pet neutered. This is a book with a message, and children will no doubt become emotionally involved with the drama of the discarded animals who are being cared for at the Shelter. However, the book is not didactic. It is a well-written story with a controlled vocabulary that young readers can enjoy.

> *Lee Bock, in a review of "Scruffy," in* School Library Journal, *Vol. 35, No. 9, June-July, 1988, p. 94.*

Amelia Bedelia's Family Album (1988)

There can probably never be too many books about Amelia Bedelia for her loyal fans. She has been around for 25 years; and although she doesn't *look* any older, her employers are planning a party to celebrate the fact that she's been with them "a long time." Amelia Bedelia, encouraged to invite her family, produces her family album, full of people like Uncle Alf, a garbage collector—whose neighbors have had to move away because of the smell; and poor Cousin Chester, a printer—because "We could never teach him proper writing." The puns are not outrageously clever; and after considering 17 of them, an adult might crave a change of pace. Still, there's no denying Amelia Bedelia's perennial popularity or her ability to make beginning readers chuckle and think twice about the meaning of language.

> *A review of "Amelia Bedelia's Family Album,"* in Kirkus Reviews, *Vol. LVI, No. 15, August 1, 1988, p. 1154.*

In a larger format than others in this series, Amelia Bedelia's latest seems designed more for the picture book audience than for beginning readers. . . . The same set-up is used for all seventeen relatives, and it does grow repetitive. Because the punch lines are (somewhat laboriously) provided in the text, rather than in the illustrations, [Lynn] Sweat has less real work to do here, but the bigger page size and less-constricted design allow him room for some funny portraits. (p. 16)

> *Roger Sutton, in a review of "Amelia Bedelia's Family Album,"* in Bulletin of the Center for Children's Books, *Vol. 42, No. 1, September, 1988, pp. 15-16.*

While this is not as clever or funny as some of the other Amelia Bedelia books, and some of the jokes will fall flat, the exploration of the nonsense and absurdity to be found in learning the English language probably will continue its appeal for early readers. Sweat's cheerful cartoon watercolors faithfully interpret Parish's text, and add the necessary information for understanding Amelia's descriptions.

> *Leda Schubert, in a review of "Amelia Bedelia's Family Album,"* in School Library Journal, *Vol. 35, No. 2, October, 1988, p. 126.*

Howard Pyle

1853-1911

American author and illustrator of fiction and reteller.

The following entry emphasizes general criticism of Pyle's career. It also includes a selection of reviews to supplement the general criticism.

Celebrated as both a writer and an artist, Pyle is regarded as one of the most important American contributors to the field of children's literature. Considered a pioneer for uniting text, illustration, and design in works for the middle grades through high school which reflect superior literary style and artistic beauty, he is regarded as an especially gifted creator of fairy tales, both original and retold; retellings of English legends; and historical fiction set in medieval times or in the eighteenth century. Pyle is credited with introducing a new attitude into the creation of books for the young: in contrast to the characteristic formality of the period, his works, several of which are considered classics in their respective genres, are noted for their vigor, wholesomeness, and quintessentially American quality. Called "the father of American illustration," Pyle is credited with making illustration the chief artistic mode of the time through the success of his art, which is often lauded for its imagination and technical skill, and the strength of his theories. The founder of what has now come to be known as the Brandywine School, he instructed such illustrators as N. C. Wyeth, Maxfield Parrish, Jessie Willcox Smith, Frank Schoonover, and Violet Oakley, and is considered a brilliant teacher whose philosophy of illustration, which emphasizes the artist's imagination and the feeling conveyed by the author of the work rather than reliance on models and on European artistic methods, is especially innovative. Praised for introducing what many observers consider the Golden Age of American Illustration, Pyle provided an influence on American art which is still active. He is also noted as a historian; his knowledge of the Middle Ages and the American Colonial and Revolutionary periods is especially well respected, and he is often acknowledged for creating the modern conception of pirates. As a writer, Pyle ranges stylistically from straightforward narratives to complex language in which he attempts to recreate the essence of archaic English; several of his books also contain original verse. As an illustrator, Pyle characteristically integrates black and white line drawings into his books which often include decorative panels and head and tailpieces; halfway through his career, he began using halftone oil paintings, but returned to pen drawings for his final works.

In many of his books for children, Pyle blends legend and history to create works which focus on chivalry and chivalric behavior; although they include evil and violence, a fact which critics question in the light of Pyle's Quaker background, these books stress such positive values as courage, humility, compassion, and responsibility. He is perhaps best known for his first work, *The Merry Adventures of Robin Hood of Great Reknown, in Nottinghamshire* (1883), which is often regarded as his best illustrated book as well as the best book on its subject. Basing his

story on old ballads about the outlaw, Pyle is credited with creating an accurate introduction to medieval England as well as an especially successful example of total book design. His next books, *Pepper and Salt; or, Seasoning for Young Folk* (1885) and *The Wonder Clock; or, Four and Twenty Marvellous Tales, Being One for Each Hour of the Day* (1888), are literary fairy tales often placed among Pyle's most well-received works; in these books, he transforms traditional folktales into humorous, modern stories and creates original tales in a folklike style. Pyle's first novel for young readers, *Otto of the Silver Hand* (1888), is usually regarded as the finest example of his historical fiction as well as one of the first historical novels to be written by an American. The story of the young son of a robber baron who loses his hand through his father's treachery, the work presents young readers with a grim picture of German twelfth-century life and the evils of chivalry while portraying its main character with sympathy. In Pyle's last works, four volumes in which he retells the Arthurian legends for young adults, he draws from both Celtic and Christian sources to describe the life and death of King Arthur and the adventures of the Knights of the Round Table. In these books, Pyle focuses on the grandeur, nobility, and romance of chivalry; considered his most mature work, the volumes are often regarded as the best prose retellings of the Arthuriad. Other outstanding titles for children include *Men of Iron* (1892), the adventure story of a young English squire during the time of Henry IV which is one of Pyle's most popular books, and *The Garden Behind the Moon: A Real Story of the Moon Angel* (1895), an allegorical fantasy written after the death of his young son which presents Pyle's views on life and death. Pyle also wrote and illustrated several adult novels and provided pictures for works by such authors as Tennyson, James Baldwin, Woodrow Wilson, and Henry Cabot Lodge. *Otto of the Silver Hand* received the Lewis Carroll Shelf Award in 1970.

(See also *Something about the Author,* Vol. 16; *Contemporary Authors,* Vol. 109; and *Dictionary of Literary Biography,* Vol. 42.)

AUTHOR'S COMMENTARY

[*The following excerpt is from an essay originally published in the April, 1912 issue of* The Woman's Home Companion.]

Usually success comes to a man just as other things of his life come to him. As year follows year, he becomes ever a little better known, perhaps, or a little more wealthy, or a little more influential—until, say at the end of fifty years, he finds himself possessed of fame, or success, or influence just as he has become possessed of gray hairs, and children, and taxable property, and responsibilities, and all those things that go to make up the life of any other respectable American citizen who is fifty years old.

Just when and how fame and success come to a man he cannot tell. Every day, from Monday morning, say, to Saturday at noon, he does his week's work just as well as he is able. His mind may be set on some great yet distant purpose, but he does not immediately bother himself about that. That which most concerns him, is that he shall do the work of today, and shall make that work the best that he is able to make it; and whilst he is busy about that, he does not stop to wonder whether what he is doing is going to make him great, or famous, or powerful. He just works along day by day until, after a while, he suddenly finds that people outside of his own town are talking about what he is doing.

And that is fame—to have people outside of your own town talk about the work that you are doing.

Between you and me in strict confidence, I may tell you that I have been quite lucky with my own work. I have been making pictures and writing stories for over thirty years, and now I find that quite a number of people outside of my town are talking about what I have been trying to do. Yet, if you should ask me when, or where, or how in those thirty years my good luck began, I could not tell you. It grew as I grew, and all I know is that men are now talking about the pictures I make, and are saying that they like them—which is a great satisfaction.

But everything must have a beginning, and I often think that my beginning must have begun in a very bright and happy childhood. First of all there was my mother—the best mother, I believe, that any boy ever had, unless it is the mother of my own boys. My mother loved good books and such pictures as were thought to be good in those

days. Not only did she like such things herself, but she took care that I should like them, too.

We children of forty-five years ago did not have so many books as children have nowadays; but many that we had were very good. Long before I could read myself, I had heard the story of *Robinson Crusoe,* and *Gulliver Among the Pygmies and Giants.* I knew the *Tanglewood Tales* and *Wonder Book* very well, and *A Midsummer Night's Dream* and *Ivanhoe* had been read aloud to me. I was acquainted with *Pilgrim's Progress,* and knew the best of Grimm's German Fairy Tales almost by heart. *Slovenly Peter* I loved, and likewise the *Original Poems* and the *Arabian Nights.* All these things we had when I was a little boy, and, after all, there is not much better literature to be found even nowadays than these and others I could name; such my mind was fed upon in those early days.

As I have said, my mother was very fond of pictures; but especially was she fond of pictures in books. A number of prints hung on the walls of our house: there were engravings of Landseer and Holman Hunt's pictures and there was a colored engraving of Murillo's Madonna standing balanced on the crescent moon, and there was pretty smiling Beatrice Cenci, and several others that were thought to be good pictures in those days. But we—my mother and I—liked the pictures in books the best of all. I may say to you in confidence that even to this very day I still like the pictures you find in books better than wall pictures.

As for our picture-books: not only did we have the old illustrated Thackeray and Dickens novels, and Bewick's Fables, and Darley's outline drawings to Washington Irving's stories, and others of that sort, but the *London Punch* (and there were very great artists who drew pictures for the *London Punch* in those days) and the *Illustrated London News* came into our house every week. I can remember many and many an hour in which I lay stretched out before the fire upon the rug in the snug warm little library, whilst the hickory logs snapped and crackled in the fireplace, and the firelight twinkled on the andirons, and the snow, maybe, was softly falling outside, covering all the far-away fields with a blanket of white,—many and many an hour do I remember lying thus, turning over leaf after leaf of those English papers, or of that dear old volume of *The Newcomes* (the one with the fables on the title-page), or of *The Old Curiosity Shop* where you may see the picture of Master Humphrey with the dream people flying about his head. So looking at the pictures, my mother, busy with the work in her lap, would tell me the story that belonged to each.

Thus it was that my mother taught me to like books and pictures, and I cannot remember the time when I did not like them; so that time, perhaps, was the beginning of that taste that led me to do the work I am now doing.

Then the house I lived in in those early days was the quaintest, dearest old place you can imagine. It was built of stone, and there were really three houses joined together. There was an old part built about 1740, I think. Standing against that was another part built about 1780, and then my father built an addition that stood against the 1780 part of the house, so when you went from one of these parts to another, you had to go up one step and down another.

In front of the house was a grassy lawn with a terraced

bank (I used to roll over and over down that bank in the soft warm grass on a summer's day), and there was a little grove, or park of trees, to one side, and beyond you could see the turnpike road. (pp. 6-9)

On the other side of the house to a little distance was a garden of old, old-fashioned roses and sweet shrubs that filled the air with fragrance when they were abloom. And there were beds of tulips and daffodillies, and there were graveled walks edged with box, and a greenhouse of shining glass at the lower end of the garden. And there was a wooden summer-house at the end of one of the graveled walks, and altogether it was such a garden as you would hardly find anywhere outside of a storybook. It seems to me that when I think of that garden I cannot remember anything but bloom and beauty, air filled with the odor of growing things, and birds singing in the shady trees in such a fashion as they do not sing nowadays.

When you take into consideration such a mother as I had, and such a home as I lived in in those early years of my childhood life, you may easily imagine that my mind was always very full of the thought of making pictures and of writing books.

I cannot remember the time when I was not trying to draw pictures.

At the time of the beginning of the Civil War we were all very loyal in our family. For many years I had an original picture, drawn by myself and tinted with water-color (I was eight years old when I made it), representing a bandy-legged zouave waving a flag and brandishing a sword as he threatened a wretched Confederate with annihilation. There was lots of smoke and bombshells in the picture, and a blazing cannon and an array of muskets and bayonets passing behind a hill, so that you would not have to draw all the soldiers who carried them. Accompanying this picture was a legend telling how the cannon-thunder roars, how the sword flashes in the air and falls upon the enemy of the nation. The text, I remember, concluded with the words, "Ded! Ded! Ded is the cesioner!" (Secessionist! I was never a good hand at spelling.)

And as for writing—I must tell you a story about myself. There was a great rock by the garden wall where there were ferns and ivy. I remember one time—I think it was springtime, and I know that the afternoon sun was very bright and warm—I was inspired to write a poem. My mother gave me some gilt-edged paper and a lead pencil, and I went out to this rock where I might be alone with my inspiration and purpose. It was not until I had wet my pencil point in my mouth, and was ready to begin my composition, that I realized that I was not able to read or write. I shall never forget how helpless and impotent I felt.

I must have been a very, very little boy at that time, for in those days a boy was sent to school almost as soon as he was old enough to wear trousers.

Such was my early childhood.

Maybe that was the beginning of such success as has since come to me, now that I am more than fifty years old. I cannot fix my sight on any other beginning.

After those few bright early years there came a sad time when we had to quit our beautiful home, never to return to it again. Then there succeeded other life pictures: there

From The Merry Adventures of Robin Hood of Great Reknown, in Nottinghamshire, *written and illustrated by Howard Pyle.*

was the house in the country; there were long years of school, where I was not very good with my studies, but where I filled my slate and my Caesar full of pictures; there was another weary time when my parents tried, I believe, to prepare me for college, and when they finally had to surrender to my disinclination to study and send me to an art school.

After that there follows the memory of a struggle in New York, in New York where the rushing and turbulent life was like a strong and powerful torrent and one had, like a young swimmer, to struggle with might and main to make head against the sweeping current, all full of other swimmers.

All these images pass before my memory, but nowhere do I find a single place (except it be in those early childhood days) whereupon I may set my finger, and say, "Here my fortunes began." Those fortunes, they grew as I grew, and came I know not how—like gray hairs, as I said, and gathering years. So if there really was a beginning of such success as has come to me, it must have been in those bygone days of forty-five years ago, and more.

But though success comes thus, one knows not whence nor how, yet you must not think that it ever comes to him who sits with his hands in his lap, waiting for its arrival in the course of time. It only comes to him who strives from day to day to do the best he can with the work that lies immediately before him to accomplish.

Yet in that striving, he who would succeed must arm himself with three vital and most necessary weapons. First, he must have ceaseless industry; second, he must have limitless ambition of purpose; third, he must possess unquenchable enthusiasm, coupled with a determination to succeed. Given these three, and something else beside—the gift of imagination—and it matters not, I believe, whether the life of a man begins in a cobbler's shop or a grocery store, or whether it begins in such an illuminating joyfulness in beautiful things as that which brightened my early childhood. With any beginning, success will, of a surety, be his who makes himself truly deserving of it. (pp. 9-12)

> Howard Pyle, "When I Was a Little Boy," in Something Shared: Children and Books, *edited by Phyllis Fenner, The John Day Company, 1959, pp. 6-12.*

The Critic, New York

Mr. Howard Pyle has never been in a better business than in preparing for American boys and girls *The Merry Adventures of Robin Hood.* These famous yarns are as much a boy's classic as *Robinson Crusoe* or *The Arabian Nights.* They are here re-told in modern antique English, quaint without objectionable affectation. In all particulars the book is creditable to author and publisher. It shows painstaking, and painstaking to good purpose. Mr. Pyle's drawings are in some respects the best he has ever made, and they have surprised even those who have long appreciated his cleverness as a draughtsman. There are many full-page illustrations in the style of the early German wood-engravers, some of which are particularly distinguished by spirited draughtsmanship. In the decorative work Mr. Pyle has been particularly happy, reminding us pleasantly of Walter Crane. Grown folks will admire the literary and artistic ability displayed in this handsome volume, while young folks will welcome it for the sake of the story told in text and illustrations.

> A review of "The Merry Adventures of Robin Hood," in The Critic, *New York, Vol. III, No. 90, November 10, 1883, p. 452.*

The Literary World

Out of [all the old materials on Robin Hood,] Mr. Howard Pyle, who shows himself as skillful with his pen as with his pencil, has deftly woven a new story of his *Merry Adventures,* illustrating it with a series of pictures which preserve the quaintness of old English wood-cuts with remarkable success. The title-page is an exact reproduction of the style of a book of the olden times, and the likeness of the past is carried along throughout the volume with most happy effect. Mr. Pyle has caught the old style of story-telling, too, and you might think his pages were torn outright from some choice black-letter tome in the Bodleian Library or the British Museum. . . . We cannot say that [the story] is the most profitable reading, but it is curious and entertaining, and is a good picture of traditionary life in England half a dozen centuries ago. Churchman and courtier, peasant and priest, stand before you in de-

lightful naturalness. In external attractions this book has few rivals the present season.

> A review of "The Merry Adventures of Robin Hood," in The Literary World, *Vol. XIV, No. 25, December 15, 1883, p. 447.*

Harper's Weekly

The earnestness with which Mr. Howard Pyle is devoting his facile pen and pencil to the entertainment of children, and to giving a wholesome direction to their fancy and imagination, should earn for him the gratitude of our young folk. A few years ago he lent himself to the task of preparing a superbly illustrated version of *The Merry Adventures of Robin Hood,* in which he collated and brought together in a continuous narrative all the legends and traditions relating to that popular outlaw and his "merry men," to the infinite contentment and delight of numberless boys and girls in their "teens." And now he has completed [*Pepper and Salt,*] another charming volume of legends, apologues, wonder stories, and fairy tales, in prose and verse, and addressed to the taste of the wee folk of the nursery. All these are rich in the marvels that appeal to the child's fancy, and are profusely embellished with antique outline drawings illustrative of characters or incidents described in the text, whose quaintly literal or as quaintly humorous designs are of the kind that are fullest of piqnant suggestiveness to very young people.

> A review of "Pepper and Salt," in Harper's Weekly, *Vol. XXIX, No. 1510, November 28, 1885, p. 786.*

The Bookmart

No one who has read Mr. Pyle's Fairy Tales, last Christmas, will let any other book of his escape him. [*Otto of the Silver Hand*] is a lovely and absorbing romance, nobly illustrated: a better gift for a girl or boy, on this Christian Anniversary, could not be chosen. And it will be found as delightful by men and women as by children: for it is given to few to achieve in both literature and art a success so brilliant and so well deserved as that of Howard Pyle.

> An excerpt from The Bookmart, *Vol. VI, No. 67, December, 1888, p. 296.*

W. J. Henderson

The Garden behind the Moon, a Real Story of the Moon Angel . . . is one of the handsomest as well as one of the best books of the holiday season. Mr. Pyle has a deep and sympathetic comprehension of child nature, and his imagination teems with beautiful ideas that are precisely suited to its demands. Every child has gazed at the soft, luminous face of the moon and wondered what mysteries thrived behind that one glowing eye of the summer night. Mr. Pyle has discovered that by walking along the golden path of the moonlight ripples on the sea one can reach the moon and so penetrate to the wonderful garden which lies behind it. David and Phyllis, the hero and heroine of this charming tale, meet with surprising adventures; but aided by the Black Winged-Horse, David rescues Phyllis from that most terrible of giants, the Iron Man, and of course, like a good Princess, she is married to him and they live happily ever afterward. This story is warm and lovely in conception and delightfully delicate in treatment. The pictures are genuine works of art, strong in conception and vigorous in execution. (p. 715)

> *W. J. Henderson, "Holiday Books for Young People," in* The Book Buyer, *Vol. XII, No. 10, December, 1895, pp. 703-24.*

Walter Crane

[*One of the most popular nineteenth-century English illustrators of children's books, Crane is considered, with Randolph Caldecott and Kate Greenaway, part of the triumverate of illustrators called the "Academicians of the Nursery." In his survey* Of the Decorative Illustration of Books Old and New, *he considers only two American artists—Pyle and Will Bradley.*]

Mr. Howard Pyle distinguished himself as a decorative artist in book designs, which showed, among other more modern influences, a considerable study of the method of Albert Dürer. (p. 273)

Of late in his drawings in the magazines, Mr. Pyle has adopted the modern wash method, or painting in black and white, in which, however able in its own way, it is distinctly at a considerable loss of individuality and decorative interest. (pp. 273-74)

> *Walter Crane, "Of Recent Development of Decorative Book Illustration, and the Modern Revival of Printing as an Art," in his* Of the Decorative Illustration of Books Old and New, *third edition, George Bell and Sons, 1905, pp. 185-279.*

Henry Mills Alden

[*The following excerpt is taken from an essay originally published in the January, 1912 issue of* Harper's Magazine *and is written by one of its editors.*]

Howard Pyle was distinguished by marked individual peculiarities from all the other artists of his time. Indeed, for any so peculiar type of genius we must revert to William Blake. Pyle was most like Blake in this—that in the representation of life and things he caught native aspects and meanings. He had no interest in the institutional fabric of our civilization, or of any other. Of Quaker parentage and an enthusiastic disciple of Swedenborg, it was natural that he should listen to the inner voice and reject the traditions of men and the authority of the schools—also that he should seek the inward and spiritual meanings of all things. Yet, without being at all picaresque, he often chose to portray the elemental passions of our human nature.

It was not with Pyle the love of the tragedy which grows out of evil passions that prompted him. He reverted to the elements of tragedy rather than to its scheme, allured by what was native in it, haunting, and antique. Comedy has always been concerned with the contemporaneous. Pyle, in his quaint and antique humor, would have nothing of this contemporaneity, and he was quite as averse from contemporary adventure. The boldly rough aspects of our pioneer Western life did not tempt him. His saunterings were confined to the Atlantic seaboard and the West Indies, in search of old romance, of peculiar people, and of the haunts of pirates. Europe, whether in the Cromwellian

era or in the remoter period of chivalry, was sufficiently disclosed to him and for his purpose in the annals of history. His imagination filled out the scene and supplied the temper and atmosphere of the story. For it was always the story he demanded, in all its spiritual meanings as interpreted in the terms of our fallible but heroically striving human nature—but yet the story in its concrete and clearly projected embodiment.

We are glad that at the last, and after he had disclosed the possibilities of his peculiar genius, he had sixteen months of Europe, and that he had this aftermath of his life in Italy. But, for the kind of work which gave him a distinction wholly his own, he had no need of the actual European scene. (pp. vi-vii)

[Pyle] was first of all and always an illustrator. Because he was transcendently that, he was something more than that, especially in his sense and handling of color and in the spirit which animated and informed his creations. He never failed to give his meaning in the picture itself, whether illustration or mural painting; but he delighted in correlating his meanings by means of the written story, which was always virile, significant, and charmingly antique and idiomatic.

His work as author and artist was, for us all, and a good part of it especially for youth, a fresh revival of the Romantic. But, though it occupied the field of wonder, it had no Rossetti-like transfiguration and exaltation, no vagueness. Without any loss of the wonder, his meanings were plain. We shall not see his like again. (p. vii)

> *Henry Mills Alden, "A Tribute," in* Howard Pyle: A Record of His Illustrations and Writings, *edited by Willard S. Morse and Gertrude Brinckle, The Wilmington Society of the Fine Arts, 1921, pp. vi-vii.*

Frank E. Schoonover

[*Schoonover, who studied with Pyle both at Philadelphia's Drexel Institute and at Chadd's Ford, Pennsylvania was considered one of Pyle's most outstanding pupils. An illustrator, painter, and teacher who traveled widely in order to represent his subjects authentically, he is well known for his works on the North American frontier and pirates.*]

Howard Pyle was practically a self-taught artist. Apart from a short time spent in New York and at Chadds Ford, Pennsylvania, about all of his work was done in Wilmington, Del. There he built himself a studio and later in 1900, upon the same plot of ground, a second building wherein he conducted a school for a number of years. His earlier work, from the first published drawing, about the year 1876, to 1894 (when he became the Director of Illustration at Drexel Institute) was produced without the use of full color. During that time he achieved for himself the lasting name of one of the greatest, if not the greatest illustrator in black and white the world has ever seen.

But even at that time a strong sense of color pervaded his work. There was a fine distinction of tone value and suggestion of absolute color as had not been produced before by means of such a limited palette. There was a difference between the green coat and the red vest. The vivid heat of a tropical sun and the cool of the shadow were all faithfully translated, and the reader has but to refer to the reproductions accompanying the article to more fully understand what might seem to the average observer to be quite impossible—that is, to produce color effects with the use of no color at all.

It was not entirely a sense of color and a knowledge of drawing that made his illustrations what they were: there was a "something" infinitely greater in them—an actual living in his creations that lifted them, even in the early efforts, from the commonplace. (pp. 431-32)

Up to the time of his Drexel experience and his establishing a summer-school at Chadds Ford, Howard Pyle had not accustomed himself to the use of a full palette. But when the duties of an instructor devolved upon him, it became necessary to instruct in color. And it is from that time his professional life was very closely interwoven with that of the pupil. He developed his own art even as he brought out the art of those under him. He often said he secured much more from the pupil than he gave. That may have been true, but it is absolutely certain that to those pupils who studied with him and whose work appears nowadays in the various periodicals and upon the walls of various institutions, there was given a practical foundation in art such as could be secured in no other school. Certainly a sense of eternal obligation should be theirs, for he saved them at least five to ten years of laborious efforts to "arrive." And not one penny for instruction was charged for all the many hours he gave to his school in Wilmington.

Surely no man without a soul possessed of unbounded love for his fellow creatures and withal as honest of purpose would have given so freely of his precious time to his students. I mention this because it may give to the reader a somewhat better understanding of Howard Pyle's own character and of why it was so much of the charm of life and that same love of humanity appears in his paintings.

It was his great desire to instill in the minds of the students his ideas and methods so that they would be carried on after his death. This, he felt, could be better done in a school of his own rather than in a single department of a large institution. And so there came about, while the summer school was in progress at Chadds Ford, the inception of what eventually proved to be his school of illustration in Wilmington. Here it was, by means principally of a class in composition, that he endeavored to make the pupil think for himself. He strove to stimulate and help the imagination with the ultimate idea always to make the picture *practical and of some use in the world*. And to this end there was always the physical example of his own productions. We were called, now and then, to come within his own work-shop, there to see the pictures that might be under way. Very often, then, he would talk to us about art, and it seemed to me then and even stronger now in memory, that the great artist was, at such times, very close to the great truths of art. He would caution the young student not to be led astray by fancies and trickery, but to hold up always the mirror of nature as a supreme guide. (p. 432)

[The] appreciation of the basic truths of nature, with its fragmentary groups of human beings, was divided and subdivided by Mr. Pyle into the most minute detail. Nothing seemed to be too small for careful consideration. In working upon his own pictures, after the broad lay-in, he would complete part with a loving care, that to use his own phraseology "was the projecting of one's mind into the picture and the elimination of one's self." "It was not sufficient," he would state, "to say here we will have a field with perhaps a man ploughing. Such a statement means nothing more to the observer than the usual observation that 'this is a fine day.' But when that self-same field is divided into its gentle slopes and rises, with its growth of grasses and flowering things; with the play of sunlight and the shadow of the soaring hawk; when the ploughman becomes a real personality and when the flock of crows follows the freshly turned furrow—then, and only then does the artist lift the man and the field from the commonplace into the realm of true art."

When such a picture is painted the layman is interested and the artist wonders why he never thought of it in just that way.

That careful consideration of detail and thought of the subject as has just been mentioned, was one of the lessons Mr. Pyle endeavored to teach his pupils. He had mastered it himself. By a quarter of a century of work; in the production of thousands of drawings, he had worked out what he called "The Theory of Mental Projection." This theory being the "something" in his art that was mentioned earlier in the article.

What is meant by the theory of mental projection?

It is more than obvious from the bare statement that it has to do with projecting one's mind into the subject in hand, whether it be, as in Howard Pyle's case, painting or writing. But that is not sufficient. The product of the mind plus one's idividuality very often accompany one another in this matter of mental projection. The product then becomes a mannerism and not a masterpiece. But when the soul of the mind evolves a thought, first in its entirety and then in its most minute detail and the picture is painted with all of its color upon that curtain that covers the soul of the mind: then if the artist has the power to reproduce that on canvas without any interference of his own preconceived idea, then indeed has he mastered that truth Mr. Pyle so aptly called "Mental Projection."

Let us for a moment see wherein Howard Pyle's pictures exemplify this theory. His paintings of American colonial life and those of the Buccaneer are known throughout the world. It is not that they are well composed and well drawn; they are, to be sure. But they breathe forth such a veritable atmosphere of truth that they seem to be contemporary and not a product of the present day. It mattered not if it was the struggling continental or the swaggering buccaneer; within the four walls of the Wilmington studio there lived for the time Blackbeard and Kidd with the flaming tropical sky and the treasure of the dead. And then by way of contrast to such pictures, the great Washington; the suffering men at Valley Forge; and the many dramatic incidents pertaining to the saving of a nation, are visualized upon the canvas. How difficult and yet how simple when one has mastered the problem of mental projection.

When Howard Pyle was painting "The Battle of Bunker Hill," he told the writer he could actually smell the smoke of the conflict and if his fellow workers in New York called him "The Bloody Quaker" it was only because he so lived in his work he actually seemed to have that element existent in his physical being. As a matter of fact Howard Pyle was always a gentle man, kind, loving and generous—generous to a fault. But it was the ability to live in the picture that, for the moment, transformed him to the character he was painting. (pp. 435-38)

> Frank E. Schoonover, "Howard Pyle," in Art and Progress, *Vol. VI, No. 12, October, 1915, pp. 431-38.*

Joseph Pennell

The most superficial comparison of Pyle's composition and handling with Dürer's proves what a careful student the nineteenth-century American was of the sixteenth-century German—too careful sometimes. And intelligent study of old work is absolutely necessary. That Pyle should do this in telling and illustrating a mediæval tale merely proves his desire to saturate himself with the spirit of the age in which the scenes are laid, and to give his work the color and character of the biggest man of that age. The figure of Time, in the drawing from the **Wonder Clock,** is Düreresque. But the figure of the small boy piping, although the lines of shadow are drawn in the manner of the old Germans, is not German at all but nineteenth-century American; and this is true of the tree in blossom and the stony foreground, though it, too, is founded on Dürer. They are better than anything in Dürer for us to study from, for the simple reason that we know more about landscape than the Germans of Dürer's time—in a way. This fashion of adapting the methods of an earlier generation to our own requirements is exactly what the old men did, and it is only by so doing art advances. It is so easy to invent out of one's head—so difficult to draw from nature. Pyle has preserved much that was good in the old work, and yet kept pace with modern technical and mechanical developments.

Among the books by Howard Pyle, which every student should know, are **Robin Hood, Pepper and Salt, Otto of the Silver Hand,** and the **Wonder Clock.** Many of the drawings are wanting to a certain extent in local color, a want due to the fact that Pyle never visited Europe till just before his death. But in technique they are better than anything that has been done in America. They are carried out with a thoroughness and completeness which give them originality, even though they preserve all the feeling of the old work. They are as good as decoration as Abbey and Parsons' realistic revivals, and would be better had Pyle known Europe as well. Near his death he made a pathetic confession that if he had only seen and drawn as Abbey did, some of the things he got from books, prints and photographs, without understanding, his work would have been far better. Some of his pupils have scarce his honesty, little of his ability, but have absorbed much of his tricks and faking and cribbing. He could disguise this in his work. The machinery and the ghosts loom large in that of his followers. (pp. 286-88)

> Joseph Pennell, "Of Pen Drawing in America," *in his* Pen Drawing and Pen Draughtsmen: Their Work and Their Methods, *The Macmillan Company, 1920, pp. 271-327.*

N. C. Wyeth

[*The following excerpt is from an essay by the painter and illustrator who is usually regarded as the greatest of Pyle's pupils and the one who most successfully carried on the Brandywine Tradition. The father of painter Andrew Wyeth, Wyeth is best known in the field of children's literature as the illustrator of many of the volumes in the Scribner's Illustrated Classics series, which includes works by such authors as Jules Verne, Robert Louis Stevenson, James Fenimore Cooper, and Marjorie Kinnan Rawlings.*]

As the privilege of writing a foreword to the record of Howard Pyle's work has come to one of his pupils, the point of view cannot be other than that of student to master. Perhaps, after all, his great appeal as a man can be better revealed from this exceptional and intimate relationship; and, as an artist must be greater than his works, so, it seems to me, the humblest efforts to tell of the man are to some purpose.

I am hardly the one to write of the tremendous impulse Howard Pyle gave to the improvement of magazine and book illustration, or of his intense earnestness and enormous success in emerging from the slackwater period in art which came at the end of the Victorian era—a period singularly stagnant in the field of graphic expression. With what energy and courage he pushed forward, almost alone, pouring into his hundreds of illustrations such sincerity and enthusiasm, such dramatic force, that the world of cultivation paused to look upon and applaud his efforts.

Meanwhile, his astonishing fertility of imagination and unequaled energy were producing written story after story for young readers, books which have since become juvenile classics: **The Wonder Clock, Pepper and Salt,** several rich volumes dealing with King Arthur and his knights, and his now famous **Merry Adventures of Robin Hood,** recognized in England today as the supreme modern interpretation in words and pictures of their beloved legend—these and many other volumes, of adventures with pirates, of excursions into the mystic land of souls and symbols, and even the daring, realistic fantasy dealing with the return of Christ in modern times. Within the covers of certain of these books are preserved Pyle's most important contributions to the world of art. I refer particularly to the pen drawings which adorn the pages of the Arthurian legends.

One wonders at and delights in his tone drawings and paintings in color, especially those depicting Colonial life. One marvels at the felicitous display of intimate knowledge of that remote period, and one is thrilled again and again by the masterfully dramatic presentation of incidents. All this is true, but for abstract beauty, character, and the compelling force of decorative craftsmanship (three enduring virtues in art) Howard Pyle's pen drawings represent his highest artistic achievement. They stand with the greatest works of all time done in this medium.

But Howard Pyle the man towers above his best efforts, and it is of the man that I feel more competent to speak.

A great stick of hickory is smoldering and gleaming in the fireplace before me. Its pungent fragrance scents the room. My pulse quickens to the magic aroma and my thought flies back to a day in October, eighteen years ago, when I first saw Howard Pyle. He was standing, tall, broad, and impressive, legs apart, hands clasped behind him, backed against another such open fire in his studio. The smell of burning hickory was in the air.

I had come to him, as many had before me, for his help and guidance, and his first words to me will forever ring in my ears as an unceasing appeal to my conscience: "My boy, you have come here for help. Then you must live your best, and work hard!" His broad, kindly face looked solemn as he spoke those words, and from that moment I knew that he meant infinitely more to me than a mere teacher of illustration. It was this commanding spirit of earnestness and of love that made his leadership distinctive, and which has perpetuated in the hearts of all his pupils a deep affection akin to that which one holds toward his own parents. (pp. xiii-xv)

There are many in this world who radiate the feeling of love and earnestness of purpose, but who have not the faculty or power to impart the rudiments of accomplishment. There is nothing in this world that will inspire the purpose of youth like the combined strength of spirituality and practical assistance. It gives the young student a definite clew, as it were, to the usefulness of being upright and earnest. Howard Pyle abounded in this power and lavished it upon all who were serious . . .

Howard Pyle's extraordinary ability as a teacher lay primarily in his penetration. He could read beneath the crude lines on paper the true purpose, detect therein our real inclinations and impulses; in short, unlock our personalities. This power was in no wise a superficial method handed out to those who would receive. We received in proportion to that which was fundamentally within us. (p. xvi)

It was the time spent with him in [the remote Pennsylvania village of Chadds Ford] that brings the fondest memories to most of us. . . . Many jolly evenings did we spend before his crackling log fires, eating nuts, telling stories, or, best of all, listening to his reminiscences, or stories from his full store of knowledge of history and of people. His intimacy with Colonial history and his sympathetic and authentic translations of those times into pictures are known and loved the world over.

Thus to know Howard Pyle—in this country of all countries, where Washington had fought, where from the spacious veranda we looked across the meadows upon Rocky Hill, the very location of the deciding conflict that sent Washington and his men to their memorable winter at Valley Forge—to know Howard Pyle here was a profound privilege. His accurate knowledge of the Battle of the Brandywine; his vivid word pictures of marches and countermarches, skirmishes and retreats; his anecdotes of the very families who had seen the running fight; the tales told him by his great-grandmother, who distinctly remembered the retreating Continentals, trailing their muskets over the dry fields of September, their shoeless bleeding feet wrapped in gunny-sack—these, and a thousand other things. Enthusiastic, generous, with a marvelous knowledge of events and a rich and versatile imagination, can you wonder that we loved him?

How can I tell in words the life of the thirty or more who lived in these historic, picturesque, rolling hills, working in the spacious and grain-scented rooms of an old gristmill? To recall the unceasing, soft rush of the water as it flowed over the huge, silent wheel beneath us thrills me through. I loved it. And here the teacher kept his class intact for five glorious summers. Who of us does not count those as golden days?

As we are slowly maturing into the various and independent ways of arriving at the solution of our personal viewpoint in art, we may feel at times a little impatient that we are not more individual, and that we have inherited a little too much from Howard Pyle that does not by right belong to us. But even so, it is likely that he awakened in many of us ennobling visions which without his golden touch might have always slept. (pp. xvii-xix)

> *N. C. Wyeth, in an introduction to* Howard Pyle: A Chronicle *by Charles D. Abbott, Harper & Brothers Publishers, 1925, pp. xiii-xix.*

Charles D. Abbott

[Howard Pyle: A Chronicle *is the first full-length biography of its subject. Written with the approval and assistance of Pyle's widow, it is usually considered the preeminent source on Pyle's life and work.*]

[Howard Pyle] discovered that the greatest charm of his literary work lay in the deftness of its appeal to children. At first nearly all that he did was in the form of animal fables, many of which Mary Mapes Dodge accepted for *St. Nicholas,* and in which she undoubtedly recognized evidences of ability that would probably develop into a real power of writing for young people, for she encouraged him in fostering this talent, encouraged him perhaps a little too much, for, as the diary letters show, he was almost tempted to devote himself exclusively to letters and allow his art

From Pepper and Salt, or Seasoning for Young Folk, *written and illustrated by Howard Pyle.*

to deteriorate. From this he was fortunately saved by the salutary influence of [some of his] early comrades, but the fact that he could write for children with a charm that was possessed by few men was always present in his mind. As time went by this ability increased, and with it he developed the power of drawing pictures to illustrate his children's pieces, pictures that were as full of appeal to the young mind as were the stories themselves. Equipped with this double ability, he could always claim the attention of the children; all he needed was something to write about.

Fairy tales had always fascinated him when he was a child. His mother had read to him all that could be found and he was saturated with their spirit. Now, when he in turn was about to provide amusement for children he harked back to his own childhood and remembered the great allurement which the land of faery had held. He delved into old, musty sources, he explored the mystery of the folk tale, and in this treasury of fanciful plots he found enough material to provide great quantities of entertainment, as well as considerable instruction which he never failed to make palatable. (pp. 92-3)

Naturally, when [fairy stories] were so delightful to him, he turned to them for the materials of some of his first work. In April, 1877, the story of **"Hans Gottenlieb, the Fiddler . . . "** was published in *St. Nicholas,* and with it began the long period of the writing of fairy tales. There followed for nine or ten years an almost never broken series of them, first in *St. Nicholas,* then in *Harper's Young People,* and finally in book form. Although he turned his attention to many other kinds of work in the meantime, still the fairy stories continued to pour forth. At first they were, like **"Hans Gottenlieb,"** mere retellings of old legends; they were the old plots put into slightly more modern form. Gradually, however, he built up a technique of story telling; from the skeleton of an old folk tale he would develop a story, so replete with details, and so changed to suit his own ideals, that one could scarcely recognize the framework of the original tale. Then, finally, after so much experience in the school of adaptation, he launched out for himself, inventing his own plots. A fairy tale to him meant more than an impossible story, the scene of which was laid in a fanciful country where grotesque figures and fantastic deeds were the order of the day; all the old machinery of fairyland he used, to be sure, but with it he always combined a touch of the moral, never heavy and nearly always artistic. Such beautiful opportunities were offered in his world of make-believe for the propounding of useful, everyday bits of common sense, that he could not keep himself from including them. They came as naturally as "flies in the summer time," as he humorously observes in regard to something else. (pp. 97-8)

The pictures that he drew for his fairy stories were beyond comparison. (p. 102)

These were pictures that defied analysis; they were crowded with haunting glimpses of glorious old castles, with jolly peasants whose faces shone with good humor, with princesses superbly beautiful and with quaint little gnomes and trolls, fascinatingly garbed in picturesque clothes. They were enough of themselves to endear him to the hearts of all the children who saw them. It was no wonder that his name became almost a household word with the younger generation.

About the middle of 1883 he conceived the idea of writing humorous verses, printing them out by hand and decorating them with pen-and-ink drawings on the same page. In a letter to his wife he first mentions his scheme: " . . . I wrote a verse for *Harper's Young People* which I propose making into a full page. If Harpers should take to it, as I hope they will, I propose writing a number of similar bits (say fifty) and turning them into a child's gift book next Christmas a year, first publishing them in *Young People.* . . . " Harpers did like it; in fact they considered it an excellent scheme. But it was a scheme fraught with difficulties for the artist; it was tedious and trying work. . . . Finally, in spite of all [the] little difficulties both of composition—for Howard Pyle always found the verse medium unwieldy—and of the manual strain of printing, twenty-four of the little verses were finished. They had appeared regularly in the magazine and had been uniformly successful with its readers. When the time came for gathering them into a book, it was concluded that a number of stories of the typically humorous, fantastic sort should be combined with them, and they were to appear under the title of **Pepper and Salt, or Seasoning for Young Folk.** (pp. 102-03)

The book was published in 1886, the first of the author's collections of fairy stories. Unfortunately, it was not very successful with the general public, perhaps because it was too costly, but it was, nevertheless, a genuine work of art, well arranged, bristling with good pictures, and sparkling with a quaint, kindly humor. Its main purpose was to provide entertainment pure and simple; the morals added to the tales and verses increased rather than diminished the broad appeal. (p. 104)

The style in which the stories are written is deserving of a word of praise. It is loose and rambling; there are no long and involved sentences, almost never a subordinate clause. It flows steadily along with no difficult decorations, no attempt to make the phrases tell a story in themselves. The narrative is slowly unfolded; simply and without turnings one event leads up to another with such clearness that the most immature mind can easily follow. Yet every word tells, every word is chosen with the precision that only a mind well acquainted with children, a mind initiated into the secrets of child life, could have. The author never nods to his grown-up readers as if to say "See how cleverly I do this. . . . " It would not be too high praise, when all these points are taken into consideration, to say that for its purpose the style is perfect.

Pepper and Salt had not even made its appearance before there began to be talk of another fairy book. (pp. 105-06)

A book was accordingly planned, but was not published until 1888. Again it was a collection of fairy tales, entitled **The Wonder Clock,** and was embellished with a series of twenty-four delightful little verses by the author's sister, Miss Katherine Pyle. The stories were of the same general character as those which had made up **Pepper and Salt,** but the workmanship was, if anything, better. There was even more charm, even more polish, and a much greater variety in subject. According to the plan of the book, every hour brought forth a new tale from the dilapidated old Wonder Clock which stood in Time's garret. Here again princesses and kings lived in the land of make-believe, the great Red Fox and Grandfather Mole talked with truly human sagacity. This book was an immediate success; its total lack of affectation made it an instant favorite. Howard Pyle himself always considered it his best book of fairy tales. It is interesting to note that the book has continued to grow in popularity through the years rather than to diminish. (pp. 107-08)

After the publication of the **Wonder Clock** there followed a period when the other phases of Howard Pyle's genius kept him from turning his attention to the realms of faery. It was not until 1895 that the third and last book of this nature, **Twilight Land,** appeared. Although in many ways it was an excellent collection of tales, it seemed to lack the inspiration of the two preceding volumes. Laurence Hutton claimed that one of the stories, **"The Talisman of Solomon,"** was one of the best that the author had ever written, but this could hardly be said of the rest of the book. The old fairy-tale zest which had been the distinguishing feature of **The Wonder Clock** and **Pepper and Salt** had to a certain extent passed away; Howard Pyle's mind was more occupied with other things. Still, this is not a book to be considered slightingly; it is, as has been said, a charming series of stories; it merely suffers because both **The Wonder Clock** and **Pepper and Salt** made their appearance before.

Though Howard Pyle's contribution to the literature of fairies came to an end with **Twilight Land,** the **Garden Behind the Moon,** which was published in the same year is, to be sure, in reality a fairy tale. It is something more, however. It is an allegory, and it is the allegorical side of it that is striking, that completely eclipses the fairy-tale element. With his three books of fanciful tales, however, Howard Pyle established himself as a master of the form. His tales were written and illustrated with a perfection that can only be marveled at; the duality of his genius placed him head and shoulders above his contemporary rivals. And throughout all of his tales there are no crudities, no useless cruelties, no inharmonious or evilly suggestive scenes such as are to be found in so many purely mythical stories. As one grateful parent wrote him, "we never have to skip a word." (pp. 108-09)

There is an appreciable link between Howard Pyle's stories of fairyland and his work in the period of the Middle Ages, by which term is not meant necessarily the definite historical era which goes by that name, but a somewhat imaginary time when knights and ladies experienced unusual adventures, when chivalry was an undeniable fact of society, when kings and princes found occasion to hobnob with less high-born individuals. The general spirit is very similar to that which finds its expression in **The Wonder Clock;** there is the same good humor, the same briskness and buoyancy, and the same keen interest in fanciful plots. But to these characteristics are added others: real historical personages figure actively, and the stories are based, at least partly, on materials which have been handed down from the Middle Ages themselves, on the great tradition of medievalism. Perhaps the nearest approach to similarity, however, lies in the pictures which accompany each venture into the field. In them appear the same resplendent ladies, and knights in gorgeous armor, looking as if each has been transported from some fairy isle. (p. 111)

[The **Robin Hood**] appeared in 1883 and was enthusiastically received by artists and writers on both sides of the Atlantic. . . . In it you can almost breathe the air of a romantic Sherwood; you feel irresistibly that the life portrayed, while not precisely real, is so crowded with human incidents that as an imaginary state of things it was quite possible in early England, and absorbingly pleasant to read about. Robin Hood, Little John, Friar Tuck, Will Scarlet, all are intensely human personages, yet all move in an atmosphere that is brimming with fanciful notions.

The basis of the book lies in two collections of old ballads . . .—Percy's *Reliques of Ancient English Poetry,* and Ritson's *Robin Hood.* Howard Pyle took the old ballads, read and re-read them, became thoroughly conversant with every detail of plot and character that could be drawn from them. Then he set about the writing of his own book, bringing into harmonious play all the many sides of his own genius. Every character was humanized, the settings were made vivid and natural, new details of plot were added to bring the various episodes into clear relation with one another. The style is a very successful adaptation of archaic English, not so complex as to be hard to read, but sufficiently antique to lend the charm of age to the narrative. The descriptions of the countryside are superb. . . . The most striking feature of the text, however, is the never-failing action; one exciting incident after another is related, each with an eye to the dramatic. It is a banquet of adventure that never palls on any child and in which grown-ups secretly find a great pleasure when they read it aloud to their children.

But perhaps the greatest charm of the book lies in its pictures. The large, full-page plates tell in full the story of Robin Hood, while delightful vignettes and highly decorative initial letters add glowing details. They were all done in pen and ink with consummate mastery. They are spirited and intimate; they illustrate the narrative without anywhere introducing a false note; they add to the text and never for a moment distract the attention. Yet the text would be incomplete without them. The only adverse criticism is perhaps that of Joseph Pennell in the statement, "Howard Pyle has given . . . in **Robin Hood** some beautiful ideas of a country he does not know." Be that as it may, a country was created which not only made a suitable setting for the story, but which seems today to be the ideal one for just that kind of imaginative literature. It is the very lack of realism that lends the proper tone of enchantment.

The ballads and songs which figure pleasingly throughout **Robin Hood** are largely Howard Pyle's own, although in a number of cases they are taken from Percy. He never looked back on these or on any other of his verse productions with any degree of satisfaction. The verse-medium, he thought, did not suit him. Yet some of them are graceful and light, with here and there a really lyric note . . . (pp. 113-15)

Many years later in replying to one of the many letters from the host of his child admirers, . . . Howard Pyle said that in looking back on his past work he felt that the **Robin Hood** was probably the only book of his which could in any sense be called a classic. There is no doubt today that **Robin Hood** deserves the rank he gives it; the only question is whether or not there are others which might be equally worthy of such opinions. Although the book was not immediately popular with the reading public at large, it gradually, slowly for a year or two and then very rapidly, grew to be one of the best sellers for children. By 1902, it was so well known and so appreciated, that the publishers—Charles Scribner's Sons—brought out a curtailed edition for schools, which has been used with great success throughout the country.

Otto of the Silver Hand, which was published in 1888, the same year which saw the birth of ***The Wonder Clock,*** is the second story of the Middle Ages. This time, however, the locale is changed; medieval Germany is the scene of the action. It is the story of the adventures of a brave little fellow, living in the strenuous times of the baronial robbers who made the Rhineland a place of terror. Little Otto suffers nobly from the effects of the warfare between his father and a neighboring baron. Through it all he is unspoiled, he remains sweet and kindly. As a character, he is drawn with a precision of touch that cannot be equaled even in ***Robin Hood;*** he is a real child and one that unfailingly attracts the sympathy of other children. (pp. 116-17)

[The book] shows, perhaps, more insight into a child's life, more sympathy with and more understanding of the trials of childhood, and at the same time it is a piece of work more serious in tone than the ***Robin Hood*** or the fairy books. It does not have the same playful humor and the light fantasy, but succeeds altogether on account of the unerring truth of its character portrayal and the poignant feeling of pathos which is never for a moment allowed to grow commonplace.

The next book to be grouped with these is ***Men of Iron,*** a stirring tale of England in the troublous times of Henry IV. It is pure adventure, full of resounding arms, of tournaments, and knightly feats. Here there is little fancy; it is a romantic tale, which none the less gives a nearly accurate picture of the period. Myles Falworth, the son of a former supporter of the deposed Richard, regains through his own valor and nobility a position equal to that of his father, who had suffered as an adherent to the old order after the insurrection against Henry. It is a story to make any boy's ambition surge; true worth is the only criterion by which judgments are made; Myles makes his way solely through his own merits. Howard Pyle has shown his sense of fitness by making of it a straightforward story, vigorous and manly. The "strenuous life" of America is carried back to medieval England. Although it lacks the subtle artistry of ***The Wonder Clock,*** of the ***Robin Hood,*** or of ***Otto,*** it has, since its publication in 1892, been among the most popular of its author's productions. This is probably due to the fact that it is a racing, adventurous tale, and that it appeals to a greater number of people than do the more exquisite perfections of the fanciful books.

The illustrations to ***Men of Iron*** mark a great change. The pen-and-ink work which had been so successfully used in each of the preceding books was abandoned, and black-and-white oil reproduced by photographic process was used in its stead. They were very suitable pictures for the book. With this new medium Howard Pyle was able to get a more solid, a more realistic effect than could have been obtained with pen-and-ink, for the delicate lines of ***Pepper and Salt*** would have been out of place in this story of combat and bloodshed. (pp. 119-21)

With these pictures of the Middle Ages, especially those for ***Men of Iron,*** which so admirably interpreted the spirit of the period, Howard Pyle gained a nation-wide reputation as a medievalist. So far-reaching was this fame, in fact, that he was desired on all sides to illustrate articles

and tales which would give him an opportunity of using this talent. (p. 122)

As a new form of the Arthurian legend [Pyle's] books have been signally popular. They give in a complete way a very straightforward and easy account of most of the adventures of the different knights. There are everywhere present in them the marks of good taste which were always characteristic of Howard Pyle. The pictures were all done in pen-and-ink and many of them, especially those in the first two volumes, are superb in their stateliness and grandeur. One needs only to see such pictures as **"Two Knights do battle before Camilard"** and **"King Arthur findeth ye old woman in ye hut"** to catch the delightful spirit of ancient romance that colors the whole Arthurian narrative; and the portrait pictures of the important characters are nearly always vigorous, strong, and full of meaning, as, for example, the one of Merlin. But as a whole, the books lack something of the compelling power of the earlier stories. They do not have the warmth and fire of ***Robin Hood*** and ***Men of Iron.***

All these books, from the ***Robin Hood*** to the last of the Arthur stories, constitute a collection of medieval story which has been a growing delight to children for the past four decades, and which is a princely heritage for the children of the future. As an expression of Howard Pyle's own feeling in regard to these productions and the importance which they held in comparison with the other fields of his endeavor, a paragraph from a letter to Merle Johnson is eminently fitting:

"My ambition in days gone by was to write a really notable adult book, but now I am glad that I have made literary friends of the children rather than older folk. In one's mature years, one forgets the books that one reads, but the stories of childhood leave an indelible impression, and their author always has a niche in the temple of memory from which the image is never cast out to be thrown into the rubbish-heap of things that are outgrown and outlived." (pp. 130-31)

Howard Pyle's interest in buccaneers and marooners was a gradual growth; it had in it something akin to the fascination which historical research held for him, but it was animated by a more romantic feeling, by an emotional impetus, as it were. Pirates and their adventurous lives held a strange attraction for him; he was never more content than when he had found some half-forgotten account of a notorious buccaneer, and had plenty of time to spend in an examination of it. (p. 132)

[His library] came to include almost every book which could shed any light upon the lives and deeds of Morgan, or Kidd, or Teach, or any of the notorious freebooters of a former age. . . . He was steeped in pirate lore, his own vivid imagination decorating the narratives from the books with romantic lights and shadows. (p. 139)

The absorption in pirates was so strong that when Howard Pyle came to write a boy's novel of life in Colonial Virginia, a buccaneer, Captain Edward Teach, better known as Blackbeard, figured as one of the most important characters. This book, ***Jack Ballister's Fortunes,*** was a faithful study of Colonial customs and conditions. Jack Ballister, the hero, is kidnapped and sold into the service of a Virginia planter whose daughter is captured by the famous pirate captain and finally rescued by the hero himself. The plot is well knit, the action moves smoothly and rapidly. There is never a dull moment. It is huge in its possibilities for boys, who cannot fail to revel in the mass of adventure so thrillingly chronicled. When it was first published serially in *St. Nicholas* with pictures in black-and-white, Mr. W. F. Clarke, one of the editors, called it "a noble story and an admirable picture of the time with which it deals." In 1895 it was published in book form. (pp. 146-47)

In February, 1889, both Mr. and Mrs. Pyle went to Jamaica for a short trip, leaving their only son in Wilmington with Mrs. Pyle's mother. During their absence he was taken sick and died before the parents could be reached. It was to both Mr. and Mrs. Pyle a terrific and staggering blow, the effects of which could not easily be softened, but the father found some outlet for his grief in the writing of [*The Garden Behind the Moon*]. There is more poetry, more beauty in it than in any other of his productions, and it is movingly sad. It sets forth in an allegorical way the very mystical theory of life and death at which the author had arrived after years of questioning.

The only explanation we have from the author as to the meaning of the allegory is in the following letter to Miss Phoebe Griffith:

" . . . There is indeed an intended inner meaning to *The Garden Behind the Moon,* but to explain it would require a long dissertation at the end of which that certain indefinable mystery with which I intended to surround the story would be altogether dissipated.

"I may tell you so much as this, although you probably have guessed it for yourself, that the Moon Angel represents the Angel of Death, and the Garden means that place in the other life to which little children go after they live the life of the world and before their minds and faculties are yet developed; that the Iron Man means not only the temptations, but the knowledges which belong to this world from which higher endeavor and diviner purpose must be rescued ere it can develop into full freedom of life; that the boy represents a certain spiritual purpose by means of which we overcome the temptations and knowledges of the world.

"There are many other things intended in the story, chief of which is the marriage between the inner and divine life and the spiritual purpose of manhood, which, however, I can hardly make clear to you in a letter. . . . " (pp. 198-99)

[At the time of his death, Howard Pyle had accomplished] his greatest mission in life: he had been instrumental, along with Abbey, Frost, and others of his early comrades, in raising the illustrative art in America to a level which had been hitherto unknown. He had by the consummate artistry of his own creative work and by the energy of his teaching helped to lift it from the tawdry commonplaceness in which he had found it in 1876 to the flowering beauty in which he left it in 1911. But in another field he had done more, and perhaps without so much conscious effort. Any child whose early years have been colored by the *Robin Hood* or *The Wonder Clock* or *Men of Iron* will not soon forget the pleasure which Howard Pyle has afforded him. The name of the author of *Robin Hood* should be written high upon the roll of those whom children love. (p. 248)

Charles D. Abbott, in his Howard Pyle: A Chronicle, *Harper & Brothers, 1925, 249 p.*

Grace Irwin

America's first great illustrator of children's books [was] Howard Pyle. . . . Throughout his long, busy years of working to make American illustrations finer and worthy to stand beside those of Europe, no man had more influence than he. He was a pioneer, giving to America and American children something new, something of their very own. Although the illustrators of today are not working in the same manner and style as Howard Pyle, we must give him all credit and honor and glory for being the first American artist to devote his talents and his labors to making children's books beautiful. . . . He inspired other artists and authors to give the best they had in them to children's books. He made people respect illustrators as they never had before. . . . (pp. 216-17)

Grace Irwin, "Howard Pyle and Some Others: Famous Illustrators of Children's Books," in her Trail-Blazers of American Art, *Harper & Brothers, Publishers, 1930, pp. 208-26.*

Anne Thaxter Eaton

Howard Pyle, whose books for children are real literature, is a striking example of a joy in the writing which is carried over to the reader. Anyone who has roamed the glades of Sherwood Forest with Robin Hood and his band, who has approached King Arthur's Castle of Tintagel under Howard Pyle's guidance and watched the pigeons wheel about the towers that stand out black against the sunset sky, or who has smiled at the salty humor, the fancy, and the human nature of the tales in *The Wonder Clock* and *Pepper and Salt,* realizes that he and the author are partners in pleasure. (p. 76)

Howard Pyle's stories in *The Wonder Clock* and *Pepper and Salt,* which are built on folklore sources and are so close in spirit to the actual folk tales that they may be mentioned with them, should be familiar to every child. (p. 143)

Howard Pyle put into his adaptations of the King Arthur stories so much atmosphere and idealism and so much of the spirit of chivalry that the child who makes the acquaintance of these four brown volumes between the ages of nine and thirteen lives enchanted days with the Round Table Knights as companions at arms. (p. 143)

Anne Thaxter Eaton, in her Reading with Children, *The Viking Press, 1940, 354 p.*

Robert Lawson

[*An American author and illustrator who was awarded both the Newbery and Caldecott Medals, Lawson is best known as the creator of such works as* They Were Strong and Good *(1940) and* Rabbit Hill *(1944) and as the illustrator of* The Story of Ferdinand *(1936) by Munro Leaf.*]

Howard Pyle was to become more than a great illustrator; he was to become an American institution. He was to stand as a symbol of all that is fine and honest and good in the art of illustration. He was a one-man movement which would exert an incalculable influence on the whole course of illustration in this country.

He has been dead for thirty-five years now, but his spirit shines in much of the best illustration of today, not only in the work of his pupils and their pupils, but in the work of all those who have felt and admired (and who has not?) his high integrity of purpose, his tremendous knowledge and skill. No illustrator worthy of the name can look on the work of Howard Pyle and then do careless or insincere work himself without feeling a sense of personal reproach, a sense of shame that he has failed this good and honest master. His presence is in every decent studio; inspiring, encouraging, helpful, corrective or justly wrathful.

And in the minds and hearts of innumerable others there are still dreams and visions of color and romance, glimpses of another world of beauty and chivalry, planted there long ago by the incomparable work of this simple, sincere craftsman. (pp. 105-06)

The clean-cut, healthy, joyous work of Howard Pyle came to the children of the late seventies like a fresh breeze flooding a fetid sickroom.

Here was "Picturesque Europe" indeed, but how different! Here were castles, not moss-hung but lived in, spacious, clean; deep-embrasured mullioned windows, massive furniture, rich hangings, moats and drawbridges that worked. Here were towers, not buried in ivy and watery moonlight, but soaring breathlessly into clear and sparkling skies; battered stout balconies and belfries, tilted roofs where pigeons strutted joyfully in the sun.

Here stone-paved courtyards were clean swept, filled with activity. Dogs rollicked, scullions chatted, men-at-arms furbished their weapons. In the surrounding gardens straw beehives stood in orderly rows beneath stout oak shelters. Trees were all about—and such trees! No dreary weeping willows these, nor moss-hung churchyard relics. These trees were vigorous, alive, clad in clean-cut leaves, gay with blossoms or laden with buxom apples or pears.

The villages too were quaint and picturesque, but not with the gloomy picturesqueness of mold and decay. Their crooked tile roofs glittered in the sun. Gay curtains and blossoming plants brightened the windows, smoke rose from the chimneys, people bustled in the streets. You could pick out the house you'd like to live in, not die in (at an early age). And always on the hill near the village were the white towers and walls of the great castle, smiling down protectingly. (p. 109)

Here were massive, spirited war horses, smart, grinning foxes, mischievous jackdaws. Here gay hares skipped nimbly out of harm's way, birds sang and swirled about the belfries.

And the people! Here were no sanctimonious little prigs with their "wasting diseases"; these were stout, jolly, healthy people. The heroes were handsome muscular princes or clever peasant lads; their heroines golden-haired princesses or well-fed goosegirls. Kings and Queens were human—querulous, futile, or impressively regal. Gorgeously caparisoned knights battled in flower-spangled meadows.

Stiles there were aplenty, but never draped with dreary lovers; on these stiles minstrels sang gay roundelays, gooseherds conversed with rabbits or foxes. Even the Devil appeared frequently, but not as that amorphous

threatening menace that blighted the lives and reason of so many Victorian children. *This* Devil was a dapper, handsomely appareled gentleman, clever and unscrupulous yes, but easily outwitted and frustrated by the still cleverer ploughboy hero or his good wife. And the jolly, earthy Men of God; priests, abbots, friars and saints! Stout, jolly, bearded fellows, as handy with staff or cudgel as with the ale mug; ready to drub a villain or perform a miracle with equal good humor. How different from the thin-whiskered, pasty purveyors of gloom, vengeance, repentance and the-wrath-to-come to whom children were accustomed both in real life and in their literature.

No wonder that this land and these people of Howard Pyle's seemed like a childhood vision of the Promised Land come true. Small wonder that children welcomed him with joyous hearts and, as they grew and developed, followed with loving interest the growth and development of his remarkable talent. For young children who discovered these first drawings were privileged to grow up for the next thirty-odd years almost hand in hand with their most beloved illustrator. The maturing of his work kept pace with their broadening horizons.

From the jolly young beginnings of **Pepper and Salt** and **The Wonder Clock** he led them into the golden land of Arthurian legend, into the green fastnesses of Sherwood Forest, where Robin Hood and Friar Tuck and Little John hunted the King's deer and baffled the Sheriff of Nottingham. The mysteries and glories of mediæval knighthood he opened to them in **Men of Iron,** the life of the German robber barons in the beautiful **Otto of the Silver Hand.** Soon they had grown up and were reveling in the gloriously colorful pageant that Howard Pyle's now fully-blossomed genius spread before them.

Knights, pirates and Indians, patriots and redcoats, kings, beggars, presidents and tailors, galleons and prairie schooners, farmers and frontiersmen poured from his prodigal easel in a flood tide. All this these now grown-up children were to enjoy until they were well into middle age, and in their old age many of them now turn back to these rich masterpieces for a nostalgic glimpse of a great era in illustration.

Almost simultaneously with the advent of Howard Pyle there came, for some reason, a sudden upsurge in our illustration; a new vigor, a healthy exuberance, truly American. The day of the graveyard, the parting lovers and the withering flower was done. In its stead burst out the new and living art of a more honest generation. (pp. 109-11)

Joel Chandler Harris' *Uncle Remus* as illustrated by [A. B.] Frost is one of those rare cases of a book in which text and illustrations are both so delightful and so perfectly suited one to the other that it is impossible to consider either separately. Not only did Frost—who, by the way, was Howard Pyle's lifelong friend and best man at his wedding—manage to catch all the subtleties of the animals' varied personalities in his magnificently accurate drawings, but every background, no matter how slight, has the flavor of the locality to an amazing degree. (p. 111)

One odd, though perfectly understandable thing, about this close and long friendship of A. B. Frost and Howard Pyle, is their complete difference, as far as work was concerned, on the point of humor. Pyle's work never gives any indication that he possessed a vestige of a sense of humor;

From The Wonder Clock, *written and illustrated by Howard Pyle.*

Frost's work simply drips with it. . . . [It] seems surprising that Howard Pyle, lacking in the important element of humor, could have achieved the great triumphs of understanding that his work always exhibits. It is not inconceivable that his friendship with Frost helped to supply him with some of this most necessary ingredient to all thorough understanding. (pp. 111-12)

In his work, especially his earlier work for children, there is a delightful atmosphere of good-natured fun and whimsicality, of pleasantly paternal benevolence and good will. But the humor is always conscious. Even in his personal letters his humor is heavy-handed and conscientiously worked at; well-meant, kindly, pleasant—but ponderous. (p. 112)

Another friend whose influence seems to appear briefly in Howard Pyle's work was [Edwin Austin] Abbey. In *Pepper and Salt* there appear two or three drawings which have always puzzled me, they are so completely unlike Pyle's usual work. They are weak, thin, scratchy, scattered—in short, terrible. Then I read in some of H. P.'s letters to his mother of his great admiration, almost envy, of his friend Abbey's delicate and refined draughtsmanship.

This, of course, is pure and unimportant speculation, but it seems extremely possible that these two or three unexplainably bad drawings were an unfortunately enthusiastic

impulse on Pyle's part to emulate the "delicacy and refinement" of Abbey's work. If so, it was a most unhappy impulse and one which never appears again. (pp. 112-13)

Much of Howard Pyle's work was definitely intended for children, much was for grownups, yet how can any sharp line of separation be drawn between the two? Certainly James Branch Cabell's *Chivalry* and Woodrow Wilson's *History of the American People* were adult books, but children loved and admired the illustrations. What child was ever too young to thrill at the gorgeous pageantry of Pyle's mediæval paintings, the sparkling drama of his drawings for Oliver Wendell Holmes's *Bunker Hill Battle,* or those colorful pirates who have been the envy and despair of so many illustrators? No child, even one too young to read, can look through *The Salem Wolf* or *The Mysterious Chest* without delighted shivers at their moonlit terror.

What adult has ever reached an age so dull that he fails to derive complete satisfaction from the intricately simple drawings for *Otto of the Silver Hand* or *Robin Hood?* Children's books both, yet of the volumes which Theodore Roosevelt took along on his famous African hunting trip one was Howard Pyle's *Robin Hood.*

And, child or adult, what American has not felt his pulse quicken at the vivid and understanding portrayals of the ragged heroes of Valley Forge, of Kaskaskia, or Bunker Hill? It is impossible to conceive how many thousands of Americans have had their patriotism raised a few degrees, how many horizons have been broadened, how many minds have been wakened to new perceptions of color, design, and sheer beauty by the prodigal output of this one man.

The latter years of the past century and the opening years of this were the Golden Age of American illustration, and of all the many who contributed to its glory Howard Pyle towers like a great oak over the fine but lesser trees of a rich forest. (pp. 121-22)

> Robert Lawson, "Howard Pyle and His Times," in Illustrators of Children's Books, 1744-1945, Bertha E. Mahony, Louise Payson Latimer, Beulah Folmsbee, eds., The Horn Book, Inc., 1947, pp. 105-22.

Donald E. Cooke

For over seven hundred years the stories of Robin Hood have been told and retold.

Throughout the long history of this fascinating legend, no single version has stood out as a literary masterpiece, or even held a wide readership over a long period of time, with the possible exception of Howard Pyle's *The Merry Adventures of Robin Hood.* . . . Yet even Pyle's classic seems to win the distinction more by default than by qualities of universal appeal, for by today's standards it is ponderously heavy reading. Pyle the author does not compare with the greatest juvenile writers—or the writers of great books, such as Stevenson, Mark Twain, Dickens, and other literary giants.

Like so many classics, Pyle's *Robin Hood* is beloved by discerning students of literature in spite of its flaws, partly because it contains so many truly delightful passages and partly because of his superb illustrations (after all, he was first and foremost a great illustrator). Finally, his book has been read by boys and girls because they love Robin Hood legends as such, and Pyle's version has stood head and shoulders above some very poor editions.

Without question the book typifies a particular era of children's literature, but in the light of present-day standards it would appear that a new Robin Hood has been needed for this generation. In an effort to fulfill the need, I devoted two years to the writing of *The Silver Horn of Robin Hood.* . . .

Most of us who read Howard Pyle in childhood have not reread him recently. Thus our memories of his Robin Hood often are lent enchantment through a rosy film of nostalgia. In the course of doing research for *The Silver Horn,* I reread the Pyle version thoroughly. I was surprised to find this quite a chore. Granted it is the best of the established American editions, it is nonetheless extremely difficult to read through. . . .

Part of the difficulty facing writers of this story has been that the source was not a single history, but a series of separate ballads which were composed by different people and embroidered over a period of many years. The result is that the ballads themselves do not always agree, and in fact, some of them were undoubtedly written—or at least greatly revised—as late as the eighteenth century. . . . (p. 618)

No one—including Howard Pyle—had successfully woven the separate incidents into an integrated story. If this could have been done, a far more popular edition would have resulted.

True, Pyle did make his story more or less continuous in the sense that he followed a chronology of events; but he made no attempt to weave a plot involving a conflict of key characters from beginning to end. Motivations and climaxes occur only in the separate adventures. Even where one adventure leads naturally into another, there is seldom a plotted interrelationship of cause and effect. (p. 619)

> *Donald E. Cooke, "The Call of Sherwood," in* Wilson Library Bulletin, *Vol. 31, No. 8, April, 1957, pp. 618-20.*

Carolyn Horovitz

Howard Pyle's **Men of Iron** is vigorously and directly told. He brings a strong note of authenticity to his time and place, setting the plot squarely in the reign of Henry IV, using the king as a pivotal factor in his plot. Though the plot is one of vindication, it is clear that Pyle wished to show the training of a youth in medieval times. Thirty years after reading the novel I still had a vivid recollection of the trials of young Myles Falworth as he trained to become a knight. Rereading it these many years later, I was as engrossed as I remember myself to have been on the first reading. Such an old favorite is always in danger of being a disappointment on rereading. And when it proves to be more than worth its mettle, it is almost impossible to look at it with anything but the fondest approbation.

Pyle uses the intrusive author to tell whatever he thinks is necessary, yet—far from detracting from the story—he seems only to add to the flavor and character of the novel. He begins firmly, anchoring his story to historical happen-

ings in his introduction, building on such a solid background of time and place that his further intrusions into the story are justifiable buttressings of fact:

> A quaint old book treating of knighthood and chivalry gives a full and detailed account of all the circumstances of the ceremony of a creation of a Knight of the Bath. It tells us that the candidate was first placed . . .

And on he goes for several pages of exposition which is not only palatable but necessary to understand what Myles must undergo to become such a Knight.

Simply and effectively, this book gives a keen sense of medieval life, the kinds of men it produced, and the challenges they had to meet. It unrolls an exciting story, one integrated in all events with the time and place. But this novel achieves still more; it gives the pith and marrow, the essence of an age. Long after the plot is forgotten, long after the information concerning what constitutes a Knight of the Bath has receded into the background, the feeling Pyle has created for this period will glow, unextinguished. (pp. 261-62)

> *Carolyn Horovitz, "Dimensions in Time: A Critical View of Historical Fiction for Children," in* The Horn Book Magazine, *Vol. XXXVIII, No. 3, June, 1962, pp. 255-67.*

Elizabeth Nesbitt

There are three reasons for [Pyle's] own final preeminence as a person of immeasurable influence on American illustration. These are his theories of illustration, the impact of his illustrations in themselves, and the far reaching results of his teaching. (p. 29)

His central belief in regard to illustration was that the artist should illustrate the feeling the author conveys, rather than a precise incident or scene mentioned in the text. If the illustrator is confined to the mere depicting of an event, he is restricted and hampered. The two arts, writing and illustrating should, in Pyle's words, 'round the circle instead of advancing in parallel lines upon which it is almost impossible to keep them abreast.' Pictorial art should represent some point of view that carries over the whole significance of a situation. It should convey an image of the meaning of the text. Therefore, in illustrating a book, it is preferable to choose for an illustration, some point descriptive of the text, but not necessarily mentioned in the text.

Illustration is then something more than the skilful representation of a fact; it is rather an expression of an ideal. The expression of an ideal can be achieved only if pictures are creations of the imagination. Pyle did not minimise the need for mastery of technique, but he did place the development of the imagination first. He claimed that a man is not a creative artist because of clever technique or method. He is an artist only when he is able to sense the inner significance of things and to convey that significance to the minds of others. The quality of imagination cannot be given by one person to another; but where it exists, its development should be encouraged, rather than 'stifled by a hard incrustation of academic methods.' His strong feeling on this point led him to distrust the methods of art instruction in art schools at home and abroad. It also led him to disapprove a too slavish use of models. Indeed, he claimed, or seems to claim, that in some pictures, the artist must be dependent completely on his imagination, since it is impossible for a model to be posed in and to hold certain positions. The originality of these ideas must, of course, be determined in relation to the time in which Pyle lived, a time when accepted theory was the reverse of his, when technique was the major emphasis, when schools advocated the drawing from models, and when illustration was considered to be a stepchild of the fine arts, if indeed it belonged to the fine arts at all.

In his own work, as in his theories of illustration, Pyle was an originator, acknowledgedly the most outstanding illustrator of the late nineteenth and early twentieth centuries in America. His originality extended beyond illustration to his conception of total book design. He understood the importance of beauty and harmony in every detail of the make-up of a book, and in this respect, as in so many others, he set standards which have permanent value. (pp. 29-31)

Joseph Pennell, in his *Pen Drawing and Pen Draughtsmen,* says that among the books by Howard Pyle which every student of art should know are *Robin Hood, Pepper and Salt, The Wonder Clock,* and *Otto of the Silver Hand.* N. C. Wyeth would undoubtedly have added the four volumes of Arthurian romance, which he considered outstanding.

All these are illustrated with pen and ink drawings. Many art critics have pointed out the similarities between Pyle's work in this style and that of Dürer. Certainly the similarities are there, but there is also much that is uniquely Pyle. His line drawings are so exquisitely harmonious with the contents of the books, so interpretative of the spirits of the books, that they have always overshadowed the half tones which he used later to illustrate *Men of Iron, The Garden Behind the Moon,* and *The Story of Jack Ballister's Fortunes.* It would be hard to say that they overshadow the magnificent imaginative quality and the dramatic colour of his pirate pictures. The preference for his pen drawings, on the part of laymen as well as artists and critics, is in large part due to the fact that these pictures and the texts they illustrate are interdependent, each contributing to the completeness and perfection of the whole, and thereby conforming with fine exactitude, to Pyle's leading theory of illustration.

His first illustrations of this kind, accompanying the fables published in *St. Nicholas,* in the late 1870s, show qualities new in illustration for children, in spite of the fact that poor reproduction to some extent diminished these qualities; they had a freshness, a wholesomeness, a strength, and a gaiety so different from the vacuousness of most that had gone before that they must have been startling.

Implicitly present in his earliest published drawings, these characteristics and others were fully realised in the illustrations in the books he wrote later. The illustrations for *Pepper and Salt* and *The Wonder Clock* are so matchless in their realisation of the fairy tales in the books that it is impossible to think separately of the pictures and the stories. An adult, turning over the pages of these two books, finds with incredulous astonishment that the spell has worked again. Without conscious effort, he has become a child, at home in the world of the folk tale, soaked in its atmosphere, breathing its spirit. In Pyle's pictures, it is a

storied world. The pictures are alive with movement and action, full of detail which in itself has storytelling quality. They are peopled with folk tale characters who, by reason of Pyle's skilful and imaginative pen, are quickened into life, animate, breathing representations of their prototypes in folk tales; kings and queens, beautiful princesses and handsome princes, rotund, shrewd, and cheerful peasants, gentle maidens, the gooseherd surrounded by his curious geese, sly and wicked foxes, elves, gnomes, boggarts, all enchantingly true to character. There is in the pictures in these books, as there is even more strikingly in the later illustrations for the Arthurian books, a lovely, haunting atmosphere in the glimpses of castles, towers, and quaint villages. Head pieces, tail pieces, decorated initial letters, add immeasurably, to the total beauty of design and at the same time enhance Pyle's lovingly sympathetic and sincere recreation of the flavourful spirit of folk literature. Adequate appreciation of the fineness of the illustrations in *Pepper and Salt* and *The Wonder Clock* can be attained only by browsing through earlier printings. In later printings, the necessity for using worn plates has dimmed the original beauty of the drawings.

In his last collection of fairy tales, *Twilight Land,* he also used line drawings. These, however, do not have the forcefulness, the outstanding folk quality, the impressiveness of detail, which so distinguish the illustrations for *Pepper and Salt* and *The Wonder Clock.*

The Merry Adventures of Robin Hood is thought by many to be Pyle's most perfect book. . . . What N. C. Wyeth called the 'compelling force of decorative craftsmanship' is explicitly demonstrated in the line drawings and decorations in the *Robin Hood.* The full page pictures, the vignettes, the decorated initials seem to grow out of the printed page, print and decoration becoming integrated parts of the whole. The entire make-up of the book is fully consistent with Pyle's belief that the arts of writing and illustration should round the circle. Equally consistent with his theories is the manner in which the illustrations convey the spirit of England and of these ballad stories, their vital, joyous, zestful quality. . . . [Here] Pyle created beautiful pictures of a country he had never seen. It is probable that Pyle had no intention of depicting, realistically and accurately, English landscape. Indeed he implies as much in his introduction to the *Robin Hood.* His intent was rather to draw upon his imagination, to idealise the landscape in keeping with the spirit which breathes in the stories.

The pen and ink drawings for his volumes of Arthurian stories show a comprehension of the subtlety, of the complexities of character, mood, and emotion, of the depth of human passions characteristic of the medieval romances and very different from the straightforwardness, the simple objectivity of the folk tale, and the frank, uncomplicated joy of life of the *Robin Hood* stories. This interpretative power is particularly observable in the portraits of the characters, of Merlin and Vivien and of Arthur. These are splendid in their drawing and intensely meaningful in their character portrayal. The details of the pictures recreate the inner life of the period. They are saturated with the spirit of the age. Together with the exceptional illustrations for *Otto of the Silver Hand,* they established Pyle's reputation as the artist of his time who could best bring to life the medieval period. This in turn brought an overwhelming number of requests that he illustrate writings on the Middle Ages.

Otto of the Silver Hand is the best of his historical fiction, the one which fully reveals the extent of his knowledge of the Middle Ages, and the only one of Pyle's historical stories to be illustrated in pen and ink. It could not have been illustrated so effectively in any other way. It is a book made beautiful and significant by the delicate harmony, consistently maintained, between the action of the story and the full page illustrations, and between the underlying meanings of the story and the symbolism of the head and tail pieces. It is the book which most closely resembles the work of Dürer; but the illustrations are not so much derivative as they are proof of Pyle's ability to so absorb a period that every detail of a book, writing, decoration, and design, are of that period. Once known, the pictures in this book are unforgettable in their immensely detailed recreation of the life and spirit of the Middle Ages. And once again, they demonstrate that Pyle's theories of illustration are not merely theoretical, but are capable of being put into practice with telling and enriching effect. Excellence of technique is certainly present. But the something more that makes these pictures memorable is the conveyance of the image of the text, the element which he considered so necessary to illustration, if that illustration were to enhance the meaning of the story or content.

Men of Iron, a story of knighthood in England, and ***The Story of Jack Ballister's Fortunes,*** with its background of the colonial period in America and of piracy, are stories very different from ***Otto.*** The emphasis is upon action and adventure rather than upon the subtler nuances of the periods. It is a tribute to Pyle's understanding of the requirements of illustration that these books should be illustrated with half tones. The delicacy, intricacy, and refinement of implication of his line drawings would have been so inharmonious with the nature of these stories that mere mention of the fact seems superfluous. The only legitimate purpose in mentioning it is to sharpen the realisation that his tone paintings and his paintings in colour have high merit of their own, in spite of the apparent consensus that his pen drawings constitute his greatest contribution to the art of illustration. The half tones lend to ***Men of Iron*** and ***Jack Ballister*** a solid reality, together with an actuality of detail and background eminently suitable to the nature of these stories.

The reasons for the use of half tones in ***The Garden Behind the Moon,*** an allegory in fairy tale form, is on first thought, less immediately explicable. It cannot be ascribed to a similar desire to achieve reality, since this book is a fantasy. The time of its publication is a possible explanation. Except for the return to line drawings in the Arthurian stories, Pyle at this time was using the medium of painting, in black and white and in colour. However, a knowledge of the book makes it seem more than probable that, once more, his infallible sense of propriety in illustration was chiefly responsible. The allegorical symbolism of ***The Garden Behind the Moon*** has a note very different from that in his short fairy tales. This note would have been out of tune with the peculiar genius of Pyle's pen and ink illustrations, so much so that one cannot imagine this book illustrated in line. The half tones seem appropriate, even though the unity which distinguishes the earlier books and the later King Arthur volumes has been lost. In spite of

this loss, the illustrations in ***The Garden Behind the Moon*** have beauty of imagination and execution. This is particularly exemplified in two of them, 'He was standing by the open window', on page 69, and 'Fast flew the black winged horse', on page 153.

The volume, variety, and superiority of Pyle's illustrative work had incalculable influence during his lifetime and later. This influence was deepened and extended by the quality of his teaching. The tributes paid him by his students might seem fulsome, sentimental, and too suggestive of hero worship unless attention is directed to the greatest and most creative aspect of his teaching. Given personality, expert knowledge of a subject, fluency, ease, and enthusiasm in presentation on the part of a teacher, and strong interest and motivation on the part of a class, inspiration frequently becomes disturbingly easy and possibly momentary. The greatness of Pyle's teaching lay in the combination of inspiration and challenge—the challenge being provided by the rigorous standards of achievement to which he held his students and which he exemplified in his own work—and the fact that he helped his students to develop their own individuality. None of those who became famous shows a likeness to Pyle in his work. His teaching was intensive and practical, as well as stimulating and idealistic, and its keynote was hard work, and its theme was that there is no easy way to the attainment of the high purposes of creative art. He had also one of the greatest gifts a teacher may possess, that of seeing beneath the first stumbling efforts, the true potentialities of his students, and he spared neither himself nor the student in the development of these potentialities. The tributes which might seem overstated become movingly sincere in the attempt to acknowledge the immensity of the debt owed him not only by those whom he taught but also by future generations. The impressive thing is that the influence emanating from his theories, his work, and his teaching spread from generation to generation and still persists. Pyle's best writing for children is in the books in which he did his best illustration. These books are of three kinds, retellings of traditional material, short fairy tales deriving from folk tales, and fiction with an historical background.

His first published writing for children was in the form of brief fables and fairy tales appearing in magazines. His first and last published books for children were retellings of traditional material. . . . Pyle's temperamental and lifelong affinity with folk literature was in tune with the spirit of the time, which produced some classics in retellings of traditional material.

Among these is ***The Merry Adventures of Robin Hood.*** In this book, Pyle has exemplified in full degree the requirements necessary in a reteller and a retelling, if that retelling is to recreate, literally or freely, the spirit and quality of the original. He steeped himself in the original sources of the Robin Hood stories, the old ballads. He became thoroughly conversant with every detail of the story, with every character, with every setting. he was filled with the feeling of the stories, with their love of action and adventure, their jollity and wit, their zest for life, their robust pleasure in food and drink and the fellowship of good comrades, their settings of forest and countryside.

In his retelling, these innate qualities are made emphatic by a prose style so harmonious with the distinctive attributes of the stories as to seem the inevitable expression of their dominant characteristics. The slightly archaic flavour of the language is artless in its ease and spontaneity, utterly without the pretentious, synthetic quality so often present in adaptations of the manner of speech of an earlier era. The animation of the stories is in part due to this touch of the archaic, and is intensified by the sharply delineated physical descriptions and character portrayals of Robin Hood and his men, each of them strongly individualised, and all of them quickened into life by Pyle's lively interpretation of their basic characteristics. A host of other characters, knights and yeomen, noblemen and peasants, beggars, landlords of inns and taverns, priests and burghers, pass through the stories, giving them a sense of teeming life, and a vigorous recreation of the age in which the stories originated. The constant action and adventure take place against a backdrop of scene and setting made beautiful by Pyle's lovely gift of painting word pictures as striking and unforgettable as are his pictures created by pen or brush. The descriptions of forest and countryside, of roads and inns and taverns, of the seasons of the year are so integral a part of the stories that mood and action, all the eager spirit of the tales, seem to be inspired and motivated by setting and situation. It is a book filled with laughter and with merriment, and with youthful relish of the savour of life. (pp. 32-42)

The task he faced [in retelling the adventures of King Arthur and his Knights] was far more colossal than that presented by the retelling of the Robin Hood ballads. The material itself is complex, cycle upon cycle of story, intertwined with one another, and all converging upon the central cycle of Arthur himself. The sources are manifold. It is certain that Pyle knew Malory's *Morte d' Arthur.* The comprehensiveness of the four volumes of his retelling, the identities of the stories included, even the manner of retelling, indicated that he consulted other sources but it is not possible to ascertain what these sources were. In a letter to a friend, he speaks of 'the most universally accepted sources' of the King Arthur romances, with a clear implication that he has consulted them. In addition to the extensive initial work involved in familiarising himself with the original material, he was confronted with the necessity of organising the mass of romances so that the four volumes finally decided upon would represent at least an approach to a consecutive whole. Finally he was now dealing with a kind of traditional material as complex in its mood, emotion, and motivation as in its size and pattern. This last aspect of the medieval romance was a source of anxiety to Pyle, and reveals an attitude in him which establishes him as a link between the past and the future in writing for children. The influence of the didactic school in children's literature which dominated the late eighteenth and early nineteenth centuries was dying hard. Hawthorne's and Kingsley's retellings of the Greek myths show the lingering effects of this school of thought, and indeed, so do many books of later periods. Pyle was troubled by the conflict between his desire to present to children only that which is noble and good, and the fact that medieval romance recognises human weakness even in the noblest characters. In a letter to a friend he mentions this difficulty in specific reference to the character of Sir Gawaine. Pyle admits that violence and treachery and greed and hate were an historic side of the Middle Ages. He also admits his reluctance to present this aspect to children. In *Otto of the Silver Hand,* published fifteen years before the first of the King Arthur volumes, he had shown the uglier

side of the Middle Ages, and had done it in such a way as to lend distinction to *Otto.* One can only surmise that his interest in the King Arthur cycles was so entirely directed towards their idealism and spirituality that recognition of their less lofty characteristics was distasteful to him. It is also more than probable that his constant insistence on the need for faithfulness to fact in dealing with history took precedence over everything else in *Otto* since this book is realistic fiction based on history. In defence of his attitude in relation to the *King Arthur,* it should be pointed out that in retellings of epics and romances, faithfulness to the original in point of fact frequently necessitates adaptation in view of considerations exacted by recognition of the immaturity and inexperience of children.

Except for the praise given to the illustrations, the retellings of the Arthur stories received less unanimity of acclaim than had the *Robin Hood.* Some contemporary criticism complained that the strength, sincerity, and conviction of Malory was lost in the diffuseness of Pyle's style. There is an element of truth in this criticism. Pyle's style in these books is characterised by prolific use of words, and by a long, complex sentence structure which rings strangely in ears accustomed to the simple and unadorned grandeur of the *Morte d' Arthur.* In Pyle's style, and in his handling of these stories, there is a Celtic rather than an English touch. For him, the appeal of this literature lay in its mysticism, its symbolism, its aura of magic and enchantment, its apprehension of the mystery of life, its mingling of spiritual and physical adventures, its search for the mystery of human destiny. His instinctive response to these elements was part of his inheritance from his mother, herself a strong mystic. These qualities are precisely those with which the Celtic race imbued their great bardic literature. That his style also partakes of Celtic characteristics may have been a matter of instinct rather than intention, but the Celtic strain is unmistakably present. It is observable in the 'magicalising of nature', a phrase of Matthew Arnold's to describe a distinctively Celtic literary habit. It is present in the use of description of scene to induce mood. It is echoed in the beauty of word sounds, in the lilting cadence of long, balanced sentences, in the stateliness of the prose, in the picturesque phrases, like 'the slanting of the day', in the irresistible temptation to interrupt action to draw word pictures vividly beautiful in their details. The four volumes of Arthurian romance represent the most comprehensive retelling of this great body of literature. In interpretation, style, and illustration they have an harmonious beauty which is unique.

It is a temptation to claim that Pyle was as much at home in the world of the folk tale as were the folk peoples who originated this kind of story. His childhood interest in folk stories had been such as to make it natural that his first writing should have been of this genre. (pp. 42-6)

In 1883, he had the idea of writing little stories in verse form, the verse to be decorated by pen and ink sketches. These were published in various issues of *Harper's Young People,* and Pyle at first intended to collect them in a small book which would be a kind of gift book for children. It was decided, however, to combine them with eight of his folk stories which had been published in *Harper's Young People* and to call the book of combined verse and story *Pepper and Salt or Seasoning for Young Folks.* Two years after the publication of *Pepper and Salt* in 1886, the same idea was used in *The Wonder Clock or Four and Twenty Marvellous Tales, Being One for Each Hour of the Day*. . . . Seven years elapsed before the publication of his next and last collection of this kind, *Twilight Land.*

The first two of these collections are superior to the third. Those qualities of storytelling and writing which gave the first two books excellence and Pyle pre-eminence as a teller of the so-called modern fairy tale (an ambiguous term) are lacking or at least diminished in *Twilight Land.* The stories in the last book are less folklike and childlike, less representative of Pyle's masterly control of the structure and expression of the folk tale. It is difficult to decide to what extent the diminution of these traits may be due to the nature of the stories. Most of them seem to stem from Eastern rather than Western sources, which may account for their greater degree of subjectivity and maturity. One interesting feature of this book is the introduction, in which Pyle reveals his wide knowledge of folk-tale sources. The introduction also places the setting and situation in which the stories are told, and this in itself is a provocative, though not basically original, idea. A traveller in Twilight Land comes to an inn, where are gathered Aladdin, Ali Baba, Sindbad, Jack the Giant Killer, Bidpai, St. George, the Blacksmith who made Death sit in his apple tree, Boots, and many others of the characters in folk literature. Each one of them tells a story.

This criticism of *Twilight Land* should be taken relatively. The stories here are well told, but the stories in *Pepper and Salt* and *The Wonder Clock* are exceptionally told. These

From Otto of the Silver Hand, *written and illustrated by Howard Pyle.*

two books offer sufficient and convincing evidence that Pyle could, and did, identify himself with the folk tale. All the structural qualities which make this type of story an outstanding example of the short story form are here . . . the beginning which, in a few sentences, gives essentials of setting, situation, and character; the close-knit, clearly motivated plot; the complete and final resolution of the tale. These are objective qualities. More subjective and therefore less easy to recreate, less easy even to imitate, are the manner of speech, the peculiarities of style, the way of thought, the kind of shrewdness and wisdom, the quality of humour, the essence of the characters, in short, that whole flavour of the folk tale which sets it apart from any form of sophisticated literature. Few have been able to comprehend these things, and to reproduce them with Pyle's sincerity, ingenuousness, and thoroughly sympathetic understanding. It is as if he originated these elements, rather than adapted them to his own use. He did add original touches, in the way of picturesque phrase, and gentle admonitions, but these are never disharmonious. He is of his age in his inclination to point a lesson. But in these stories, he seems to yield to the temptation with amusement at his inability to resist. As a result, the morals are accepted by the reader with a similar sense of amusement. It is also true that their phrasing is ingratiating and their relevance to the spirit of the story such that they never seem to be superimposed on the story.

The Garden Behind the Moon is Pyle's only long fairy tale. The origin of the story was in the death of his son, which took place while Pyle and his wife were on vacation in Jamaica, and before they could return home. The theme of the book is the search for the meaning of life and death and of the spiritual nature of man. It is an allegory in which the Moon Angel represents the angel of death, and the garden the place in another life where little children go after death. Inevitably the book has a sad and serious note struck first in the Dedication . . . 'To the Little Boy in the Moon Garden this Book is Dedicated by his Father'. The sadness is restrained and moving, and there is a felt sincerity in the book. Again, the style is notable for the vivid word pictures, those of the garden being touched with nostalgic memories of the beloved garden of his childhood. Pyle's ability to paint a word picture reminds one of the comparable ability Kenneth Grahame shows in *The Wind in the Willows*. (pp. 46-9)

The Garden Behind the Moon has overtones of social consciousness. This is pointedly present in one of the scenes witnessed by the boy David from a window in the moon—a boatload of slaves, fastened together with ropes. David sees the deaths of two of the slaves, a young mother and her baby, and hears the exultant singing of thousands of voices which heralds the entry of mother and child into the garden. In respect of social consciousness, Pyle's fantasy is like some of the great fantasies written during his lifetime, notably Kingsley's *The Water Babies* and George MacDonald's books.

The origin of *The Garden Behind the Moon* which necessarily controls its nature makes comparison with other fantasies of the same period seem somewhat inappropriate. However, except for the reiterated use of certain devices, there is little similarity among the really great fantasies. At the same time, there are certain essentials which should be present in every fantasy. *The Garden Behind the*

Moon has a degree of beauty in expression and meaning, in conception and execution, it has a moving pathos and sincerity, but it does not attain the stature of the great fantasies of its time, especially those by English writers of the late nineteenth and early twentieth centuries. It does not have the lingering sense of enchantment of George MacDonald's stories, the charm and variety of mood and emotion of *The Wind in the Willows*, the extraordinary power of creative imagination of W. H. Hudson's *A Little Boy Lost*. It rises above the average, but it does not achieve greatness.

Pyle's three books of historical fiction for children reflect his interest in history and his astonishing grasp of the most minute details of the life of a period. He was particularly interested in the colonial period in America and in the Middle Ages in Europe, and his books with historical background grow out of his particular knowledge of these two periods.

The Story of Jack Ballister's Fortunes has a long subtitle which is representative of the romanticism of the age and of the book and which succeeds in being as good a summary of the content of the story as could be written, 'Being the narrative of the adventures of a young gentleman of good family, who was kidnapped in the year 1719 and carried to the plantations of the continent of Virginia, where he fell in with that famous pirate Captain Edward Teach, or Blackbeard; of his escape from the pirates and the rescue of a young lady from out of their hands.' The introduction to the book tells of the situation which gives rise to the story—the need of the Virginia planters for intelligent labour, the unsuccessful competition with the New England colonies for such labour, the resultant profit in the exportation of labour from England, and the consequent reprehensible habit of kidnapping men and women from England to meet the demand. This background, together with the introduction of one of Pyle's favourite pirates, Blackbeard, inevitably means that the emphasis in the story is on adventure. The assets of the book are its well constructed plot, the plentiful action, and the authentic portrayal of Colonial America. To the adult interested in Pyle as a person, there is also the charm of the reflection of Pyle's childhood in Jack Ballister's memory of his mother and in his recollection of the garden of his boyhood home. The description of the garden is reminiscent of the garden described in Pyle's autobiographical sketch in *The Woman's Home Companion*. The positive qualities of the story are somewhat mitigated by a few negative ones. The progress of the plot, which is essentially a good one, is hindered by the interruptions provoked by Pyle's inclination to use opportunities afforded by the story to point lessons. The morals here are digressions, superimposed on the text, not an inherent part of it as they are in the fairy tale collections, in *King Arthur*, and in *Otto*. Neither does the dialogue have the spontaneity characteristic of these other books.

Men of Iron, laid in England in the fifteenth century, suffers a little from the same faults. Nevertheless, it too has its good points. It is also a story of strong adventure in which the unifying thread is the character of the boy Myles Falworth, and the chief motivation Myles' intention to redeem his father's good name and estate in life, lost because of his support of Richard II. Myles is a lifelike boy in his love of physical exploit, in his impulsive-

ness, and in his rebellion against what is to him unjust authority. To children, one of the most appealing features of the book would be Pyle's capture of the delight boys take in secret hiding places. For children interested in the institution of chivalry there is also the fascination of the descriptions of the training necessary for knighthood. As a whole, *Men of Iron*, with its more single-minded concentration on a direct plot and its greater simplicity, is a more genuine children's book than *The Story of Jack Ballister's Fortunes*, which is closer to the interests of the adolescent.

Again, his first book in this field of writing, *Otto of the Silver Hand*, is superior. In its own and different way, it offers an interpretation of medieval Germany as live and sensitive as the interpretation of Shakespearian England in John Bennett's *Master Skylark*, published nine years after *Otto*. Here Pyle's scruples as to the susceptibilities of children did not prevent him from revealing some of the harshness of life in the Middle Ages, its ugliness as well as its beauty, and the result is a great book. It is also proof that children in their reading may be confronted with evil as well as good, so long as the presentation is made understandable by the quality of compassion which Pyle displays in *Otto*. The story in all its aspects, character, incident, and emotion, is constructed on the principle of contrast, good opposed to evil, savagery to gentleness, love to hate, greed to self-sacrifice, physical victory to spiritual victory. Through it moves the figure of Otto, seemingly a victim of the worst passions of the period, actually a symbol of hope for the future. It is a gentle, tender, moving story. It is fitting to re-emphasise the fact that the spirit of compassionate understanding which permeates the book is a rare quality in books for children or books for adults.

In children's book collections in the United States are three other books which are compilations of Pyle's writings and illustrations. *Stolen Treasure*, published in 1907, contains four pirate stories: *With the Buccaneers; Tom Chist and the Treasure Box; The Ghost of Captain Brand; The Devil at New Hope.* These were previously published in adult periodicals. *Howard Pyle's Book of Pirates*, published by Harper's in 1921, is a collection of his writings on pirates with a selection of his best pirate illustrations. The success of this compilation led the compiler, Merle Johnson, to collect from books and magazines a large number of Pyle's historical illustrations. This collection was published in 1923, also by Harper's, with the title *Howard Pyle's Book of the American Spirit.* The text is taken from original sources, with a large degree of editing by Francis J. Dowd. These two books are splendid examples of Pyle's illustrations of pirates and of historical subjects. (pp. 49-54)

In the slightly more than thirty years which constituted Howard Pyle's productive lifetime, he created a body of illustration and writing which made him pre-eminent in his time and for all time. By reason of his distinctive qualities as an illustrator, he was the outstanding figure in a group of artists who, with the coming of the twentieth century, had brought to the art of illustration a high degree of excellence. His distinctive qualities as an illustrator are so many and so meaningful that one hesitates to enumerate them, lest the enumeration bring the accusation of extravagance and exaggeration. Nevertheless a fair and adequate appraisal of his place and influence in illustration demands emphasis on those aspects of his genius which contributed most to the permanence of his work and the extent of his influence. His originality of conception and execution is rooted in strength of creative imagination, which led him always to concentrate on the inner meaning of whatever he was illustrating. His power of imagination and his search for significance inevitably produced a dislike of regimentation, a distrust of insistence upon prescribed techniques and styles. His understanding of what can be conveyed by a union of the written and pictorial arts was unique in his day, and not surpassed since his day. His sense of total book design is infallible, and he set an example in this respect which remains an inspiration. He was an idealist, unsatisfied with anything less than the attainment of excellence. He was at the same time a realist, but a creative realist, who could insist on the fundamental need for accuracy of detail, and at the same time avoid the pedantry and tyranny of meaningless detail. His versatility in subject and medium had no tinge of superficiality, something not in his nature. His understanding of and devotion to the art of illustration made him, in theory and performance, a prophet of the future. His influence on illustration is permanent, not only because of his own high achievement, but also because of the power of his teaching, which has been transmitted by those who studied under him to succeeding generations of artists.

The writing for which he is and will be remembered is in the field of children's books. This is as it should be, for he came to love best his writing for children, and none knew better than he that a book for a child, beloved by generations of children, is assured of eternal life, and that the author of such a book is one who has given to mankind a gift of lasting value. Books of beauty and excellence, of wholesomeness and sanity, of joy and humour and pathos, of imagination and constructive realism read in childhood leave an ineradicable impression. High praise is rightly given to him who has written a genuine classic for children, a classic in the sense of a book which conveys something worth conveying, which has appealed to enough children over enough time to ensure its universality. Among such classics are Howard Pyle's *The Merry Adventures of Robin Hood, Pepper and Salt, The Wonder Clock, Otto of the Silver Hand,* and the four books of the Arthurian cycles, books made beautiful by Pyle's two-fold genius as author-illustrator.

Skilled craftsman in the graphic and written arts, romanticist and realist, lover of a good story and devotee of truth, man of spirituality and integrity, inspired and challenging teacher, he is the first truly great American author and illustrator of children's books. (pp. 65-7)

Elizabeth Nesbitt, in her Howard Pyle, *Henry Z. Walck, Incorporated, 1966, 72 pp.*

Henry C. Pitz

[*A student of one of Pyle's pupils, Thornton Oakley, Pitz is well known both as a painter and illustrator whose works carry on the Pyle tradition and as a writer of books on Pyle and on the technique of illustration.*]

By about 1890 Pyle had made himself master of three fairly well defined pen-and-ink styles. The pen fascinated him and he experimented with all kinds, from the goose quill to the flexible steel-point Gillotts. The goose quill suited

his bold, rich-line, medieval-inspired drawings that owed so much to the study of Albrecht Dürer and the little German masters. Some hints were gathered from the more decorative British illustrators of the sixties, Leighton, Rossetti, Sandys and Burne-Jones. This was the style that embellished the *Robin Hood, The Wonder Clock, Otto of the Silver Hand* and the King Arthur set. Even within the confines of this style he played variations—no one of these large sets of pictures possesses exactly the same characteristics as another.

Differing widely from these was the style strongly influenced by Daniel Vierge, the Spanish master of the pen. Using a flexible thin steel point, this style was characterized by a nimble, lighthearted line. It was ideally suited to the delineation of sparkling light, outdoors or indoors— the shadows were open crosshatchings of fine line, and a minimum of line was used in the lights—the effect was lively and buoyant. A great many of his incidental drawings for historical subjects in *Harper's Monthly* were done in this manner, as were some for *Harper's Young People* such as "The Talisman of Solomon" and the book illustrations for *The One-Horse Shay.*

A third and less easily defined style was partly an amalgam of the preceding two, partly an influence of Adolf Menzel's powerful work in Kugler's *History of Frederick the Great* and partly the result of an admiring study of several of the freer draftsmen of the British school such as Charles Keene and Boyd Houghton. In this style the exaggerated contrast between light and shadow of the Vierge influence was diminished by more insistence upon detail and local color.

In practice none of these styles was precisely defined and there are a fair number of maverick pen drawings that conform to none of them. Technically, pen and ink was the medium in which he indulged his most far-ranging exploration and experimentation and in which some of his most characteristic work was done. Oil paint, the major medium of his later years, displays little of the same sense of search and discovery.

As Pyle's abundant output continued through the nineties, it is easy to see the effect of the rapidly changing technology of reproduction and printing upon the art of illustration. The time was not quite ripe for dependable and widespread color printing but the halftone had now largely replaced the wood engraving, although the uncertainties of the new process still required considerable handwork by the now diminishing company of wood engravers. Pyle was now painting his black-and-white tonal illustrations in oil and this practice was an echo of what was happening throughout the illustrative fields.

The change was controversial and even today, well over half a century later, critics still take sides. The artists of that day almost to a man were enthusiastic about the new inventions. The artist could now count upon a much more faithful reproduction of his drawing—be it tonal or linear, subtleties of tone were more easy to come by and illustration making had become more flexible. But there was considerable criticism of the general softness and mushiness of the new halftones and regrets at the passing of the crispness of wood engraving. The blandness of the halftones eroded the sense of page design and the book field suffered particularly.

One of Pyle's medieval tales, *Men of Iron,* published in 1892, when compared with his slightly earlier *Otto of the Silver Hand,* points up two contrasting conceptions of bookmaking. The illustrations for *Men of Iron* are excellent but they are tucked into the book and give the appearance of afterthoughts. The gray halftones are printed on glazed paper (an unsympathetic surface at variance with the text stock) and tipped in at suitable intervals. The book is an example of bookmaking by rote. *Otto of the Silver Hand,* on the contrary, is a fine example of integrated design; text and picture pages are in harmony with each other, the pen drawings have reach and power to stir the youthful mind—the book is a unified product. (pp. 84-6)

Henry C. Pitz, "Moving Toward Fame," in his The Brandywine Tradition, *Houghton Mifflin Company, 1969, pp. 70-88.*

Richard McLanathan

In Pyle's own work, his wide-ranging imagination combined with a hard-won technical versatility enabled him to give convincing form to many characters and episodes of history and fiction. This gift he shared with his most distinguished pupil, N. C. Wyeth. For several generations of Americans, the mention of the pirate Blackbeard, of Robin Hood, of the knights of the round table, of characters from *Treasure Island, Kidnapped,* and *The Black Arrow* brings to mind with vivid clarity the creations of Howard Pyle and N. C. Wyeth. This achievement certainly admits them to the highest echelon of illustrators. And, when one sees the originals of those familiar and compelling illustrations, whether in the knowingly controlled line in black and white, or in the painterly handling of oil, there can remain little doubt about their being genuine artists as well.

Both men were, and to a great extent still are, broadly popular artists, a quality they share with N. C.'s son Andrew and his grandson, James. All are closely identified with the Brandywine valley and Chadds Ford. (p. 8)

Because of his introspective nature, perhaps the result of Swedenborgian mysticism superimposed on a Quaker heritage, Howard Pyle lived an intense inner life which enabled him to realize with such completeness imaginative works like his *Robin Hood,* in which literary style, illustration, decoration, and typography are combined to produce a creative whole. On the other hand his practicality enabled him to adjust to the varying developments in reproductive techniques used by the publishers with whom he worked. Like Winslow Homer in his illustrations, Pyle had a sense for the large design which could be translated by the wood engravers with maximum effectiveness and minimum loss in the process. Yet his conscientiousness led him to carry out the originals as works of art in their own right. (pp. 9-10)

We know from the record that Pyle was aware of what was going on in the art world, both at home and abroad. His own reputation became widespread: Van Gogh mentioned him in a letter to his brother Theo. There is evidence in Pyle's work of his interest in the Pre-Raphaelites, and also, rather surprisingly, of the sinuous forms of l'Art Nouveau perhaps seen in reproductions or through the designs of Louis C. Tiffany, since Pyle did not go abroad until 1910 and died within the year in Italy. His range of imagination led him into some curiously effective works

with suggestions of the mysterious and the sinister, and his preoccupation with pirates, whose bloodthirsty proclivities he did little to minimize, has overtones of violence oddly at variance with his outward personality. (p. 10)

Pyle's lettering was excellent, and his sense of the combination of lettering and illustration, as on covers and titles, was highly developed. Though N. C. Wyeth must have learned something of this from Pyle, he has his own marked abilities in this field. . . . Where Pyle's compositions were often carefully architectural and tended to be linear in structure, Wyeth's seem spontaneous and organic, made up of large forms, curving outlines, and dramatic light and shade with rich color. His characters are more strongly individualized than Pyle's. They have an earthiness and often a touch of robust humor. They are full of life and gusto, and have none of the delicate fantasy which sometimes appears in Pyle. Yet they have invention and variety, and also, in their larger forms and dramatic use of dark shadow often have a touch of the sinister. Their mood is pervasive, their images powerful. Their range is from the brutal effectiveness of *Blind Pew* through the suspenseful, momentary silence of *The Vedette* to the sensitivity of *The Newborn Calf.* Pyle occasionally lapsed into sentiment, Wyeth never.

Pyle was eclectic in a positive, not a negative sense. He was also influenced by Holbein, Hogarth, and the early German masters, especially Dürer, as seen in his command of a decorative line which appears in his *Robin Hood,* Arthurian books, *The Wonder Clock,* and *Otto of the Silver Hand.* Yet it was his own line, controlled by his own sense of order. Wyeth also had a personal line in his black and white work, and a sense of the relation of drawing to the book, but, because of the changes of the times, he had less opportunity to show his individuality in this way. Instead, his distinctive artistic personality, reflecting Emersonian ideals no doubt acquired during his New England boyhood, led him into a more personal involvement with life in his art, resulting in a vividness of impact which was all his own. He lived the precepts which Pyle offered his pupils: "throw your heart into the picture then jump in after it . . . ; feel the wind and rain on your skin when you paint it . . . " . . . Where Pyle was scholarly in every detail of his historical compositions, and was factual to a degree, Wyeth felt them as well as accurately recreated them, and tended to identify the past with his own experience, using familiar sights, models and objects from his own environment in a way which anticipates the approach of his son Andrew. (pp. 11-12)

Andrew shares with his father and with Pyle a special sense of time, but in his own way; he does not paint the past, but rather the evidences of it. He also has an intense sense of place as well as of moment, based upon an analytical vision, increasingly selective and often almost microscopic. (p. 13)

In the work of Andrew and his father, Pyle's faith in illustration as "a ground to produce painters" has proven justified. Andrew's son James, thanks to his father's instruction and direction and to his own application, has more than adequately shown his command of that technical facility which Pyle took for granted as a necessary means. The brilliance of his precocious achievement gives promise that Pyle's belief will prove true in another generation as well. . . . It is good to know that the tradition continues. (pp. 14-15)

Richard McLanathan, in a forward to The Brandywine Heritage: Howard Pyle, N. C. Wyeth, Andrew Wyeth, James Wyeth, *The Brandywine River Museum, 1971, pp. 7-15.*

Percy Muir

The development of the half-tone process and its further ramifications into colour printing were the undoing of Pyle as a book illustrator, although they affected his immediate popularity only favourably. This will be found a harsh saying by many of Pyle's admirers, and perhaps its bluntness requires a little more critical sharpening. Pyle's facility in black and white came to a peak at a time when photography had almost completely replaced wood-engraving as a process medium. Pyle quickly grasped the potentialities of the new technique and thus was able to produce ideal material for the purpose, while at the same time using the new medium to produce results hitherto rarely, if ever, achieved. (p. 263)

[Pyle knew] what he could do best and that this was seldom possible unless he supplied his own texts. His writings for children are especially good, and above all they show a visual imagination abounding in opportunities for graphic depiction. It is in this sphere that he captured and has retained the affection and regard of his countrymen as a nonpareil among book illustrators. (p. 264)

Percy Muir, "America," in his Victorian Illustrated Books, *Praeger Publishers, 1971, pp. 250-69.*

Henry C. Pitz

With the publication of *The Merry Adventures of Robin Hood* in 1883, Howard Pyle established himself in the first rank of both writers and illustrators of children's books. . . .

The book had been germinating in his head for years. It came straight from his early childhood; it merely waited for the necessary dual talents to ripen. When he wrote from New York to his mother telling of his plan to write and illustrate the book and asking her to send him the old family copy of Percy's *Reliques,* he only needed it as a general guide. He knew it quite by heart. But the sight and feel of the book brought back childhood horizons and established the youthful tone of what he would write and draw. (p. 70)

Although he had had relatively little practice in writing for children, mostly short tales for *St. Nicholas,* the prose of the new book had a pace and flavor of its own that was very congenial to young minds. He inserted a few archaic terms from time to time to nudge the mind backward in time, but he didn't overdo it. It was a natural, easy-paced prose that carried one along with jolly anticipation. Although a long book, it was not formidable. It could be taken in small or big bites. The end of each episode left a promise for the next.

The reading public and the critics immediately perceived that the text was not a mere convenience upon which to hang pictures nor were the pictures a subordinate embellishment of excellent narration. Both sprang from the same conception and were inseparable. The illustrations rounded out the characters. Backgrounds, costumes, and accessories implied a medieval atmosphere, albeit not a pedantically documented one. It was not an historian's report but an ageless folk theme reenacted for modern eyes. The decorative panels framing the full-page pictures are a most curious medley of Renaissance, baroque, and early Art Nouveau motifs. They take their playful place in somehow maintaining a medievallike climate although the grim purist might raise an eyebrow. They may have been given their form by an artist's happy whim. Certainly the prose-picture combination was a reiteration that a theme imbedded in the racial memory needs a new dress from time to time.

The success of *Robin Hood* opened the way to other books. Some of the books that followed were novellike tales of adventure written largely for older boys, but there was a group that had a kinship with *Robin Hood* in format and potential audience. In 1886 appeared *Pepper & Salt, or Seasoning for Young Folk.* . . . Pyle had been writing a series of tales in verse form for *Harper's Young People* with the intention of collecting them into a little giftbook. He had also been writing some folk stories for the same publication, and it was decided to combine the two groups in a larger format. This might suggest a kind of scrapbook collection but it was actually a most happy and unified collection, the kind that children delighted to dip into and taste bit by bit. The book, prose, verse, and picture, had an ingratiating, naive, and wholesome air in contrast with the generally prevailing Victorian stiffness and formality.

Two years later, in 1888, appeared *The Wonder Clock.* This should be linked with the *Robin Hood* and *Pepper & Salt* as a triumvirate of masterpieces. The three books are bound together by strong common excellences—the dominant hand is always visible but each has a personality of its own. All three are the happy triumphs of a rich creative period. In each case text, picture, and format design are in delightful accord. And through each runs the easy and ingratiating prose and verse of Pyle's youngish maturity, when his own childhood was not yet remote and his own young family was in the making. (p. 71)

[Essentially] Pyle's folklore style needed only a little practice to become excellent of its kind. The simple, homely vocabulary, the blend of peasant shrewdness and racial wisdom, the ingenious styleless style, made their way easily into children's minds. It was such a readable style, prose for the lips as well as the eyes. Its foundations were laid in his very early years, when he was read to. A little later he was reading for himself and searching for new material. When he first began to think in terms of a writing career, folklore seemed the nearest reservoir of material and he read even more widely and delved into the history and background of this age-old subject. Folklore, particularly the European, was now in his blood. It had been assimilated, and it came from his pen, in prose and picture, as though from an original source.

Wonder Clock, with its subtitle *Four & Twenty Marvellous Tales, being one for each hour of the day,* was, like *Pepper & Salt,* a combination of prose and verse, but this time the verses with their pen decorations were the work of Howard's sister, Katharine Pyle. There was enough similarity of thought and execution between the two to make a book unified in appearance and literary flavor.

Stylistically, both in text and appearance, these three books stand together and some years later would be joined by another masterpiece group of books, the four-volume retelling of the King Arthur cycle. (pp. 71-6)

One other book of folklike tales, *Twilight Land,* was published in 1895, but it stands apart from the earlier triumvirate both in style and appearance. Using a lighter pen line, a more modern touch creeps into the drawings and a somewhat more sophisticated tone into the prose. There is a wider range of source material, a great deal coming from the Eastern world, with an introduction that reveals Pyle as scholar and researcher. It is another excellent book but missing some of the intimacy and enfolding quality of the earlier three.

In the same year *The Garden Behind the Moon* was published. Although it may be classified as a long fairy tale, it is very different from the other books. It is not the retelling of an ancient tale or an improvisation upon one. It is an allegory and a fantasy and because of the painful and saddening circumstances that prompted its creation there is no easy comparison of it with any other thing that Pyle wrote. The garden theme, welling up from Pyle's childhood memories of the home garden on the Kennett Pike, was a theme that he reiterated a goodly number of times in his pictures and here it became the background theme of an entire book. *The Garden Behind the Moon* became the dwelling place of children in the afterlife. Naturally sadness permeates the tale, a sadness restrained and misty. It could scarcely hope for a wide readership even though it contains some of Pyle's most moving word pictures.

When, almost two decades after the publication of *Robin Hood,* Pyle broached the idea to Scribner's of his interest in retelling and illustrating the story of the King Arthur legends, he compared it with the earlier book, suggesting a similar style with perhaps a more poetic and mature approach. Indeed, the project was the most taxing and monumental that he had ever attempted. (pp. 76-9)

Work on the text and drawings for this monumental cycle was fitted into the intervals between his steady magazine commitments, other book illustrations, and several large mural commissions. The illustrations, executed in heavy ink line, show their debt to the *Robin Hood, Pepper & Salt, Wonder Clock* triumvirate, but have greater depth and power and a richer execution. They rose to the level of their epic subject and included many of Pyle's finest pictorial conceptions. Only in some of the last drawings are there signs of faltering and less convincing characterization.

The text also traces its line back to the earlier three books but that, too, with a change. Pyle was obviously working toward a more monumental prose that would nevertheless continue to impart a sense of intimacy to youthful minds. He made no particular attempt to imitate the Sir Thomas Malory prose, although it was the Malory version he had known from childhood days that was his principal source. But through his adult years he had explored other versions and the critical literature on the subject of the folktale, legend, and epic. We have no list of his studies in this direction but let us suggest that certain changes had taken place in his reaction to the folktale and the epic as he moved from youth to middle age. As the mature scholar added layers of learned information, he lost some of that inno-

cence with which children view the world. It seems likely that the easy bounce of the *Robin Hood* prose was no longer natural to him and his investigation of sources other than Malory had given him new ideas of prose style.

There were some criticisms at the time of publication to the effect that he had not followed the simple and stately style of the Malory version. Some later criticisms pointed out that the Nordic influence of Malory seemed to have given way to a kind of Celtic mood and interpretation. Certainly the mood had changed, and stylistically, the sentences were longer and much more involved. An aura of mysticism, of magic behind the ordinary face of things, also crept in. More insistent are the word pictures used to induce mood while the cadence of words was more akin to a bardic rhythm, a cadence inducing a background of mystery and a link with a world behind the world of appearances. All this is Celtic.

We have no complete record of Pyle's sources but we have his own word that he had pored over "the most universally accepted sources." Almost certainly these must have led Pyle to the widespread roots of the Arthurian legend stretching through most of Europe, even south of the Alps. He must have encountered the varied accents of these sources as they passed through the German imagination of Wolfram von Eschenbach or appeared in the pages of *Perceval le Gallois.* And the Celtic traces discerned in his own version must have sprung from the *Mabinogion,* that collection of Welsh fables, five of which are concerned with Arthurian themes. Here was a glimpse into a remote

Pyle in his studio.

pre-Christian world strangely different from the more orderly world of Malory. And the language rhythms were strange, too, dark, disordered, and shot with poetry. (pp. 79-82)

The Arthurian cycles were infinitely more complex than anything disclosed by the family volume of Percy's *Reliques.* The strange provocative cadences of the *Mabinogion* revealed to him the opportunity to add his own harmonics to the Arthuriad, as so many had done before him. His labors in that direction were a triumph of prose and picture, attuned to a new, ripe twentieth-century audience.

It is scarcely possible to devise neat self-evident categories for Pyle's numerous and diversified books. The nine books here discussed can be placed under a myth-legend-fairy tale label for convenience. Eight of these books spring from the deeper roots of the race, the multiple tellings of ancient themes. The exception is *The Garden Behind the Moon.* Beyond these nine, the remaining books that may be classified as intended for children are fiction with an historical or adventure purpose.

The one fiction title that is closely allied to the eight legendary titles mentioned, both in writing and quality of illustration, is *Otto of the Silver Hand.* This story, laid in medieval Germany, is unique among all the other fiction titles. It is the first and best of three historical tales intended for children.

Like all Pyle's books in this category, it displays his wide and deep penetration into the intimate life of a period, an instinctive sense of its flavor, and a convincing grasp of the details of the time. The book, published in 1888, was a clean break with the still prevailing reluctance of writers to deal with brutality and evil in books for children. It was Pyle's first contribution to historical fiction for children, and it was a bold one. It appeared at a time when, with only the fewest exceptions, children's authors timidly circled away from the bitterness of life or threw a veil over it. Pyle's book was in no sense a defiant challenge to this convention. Against a background of medieval Germany, it straightforwardly and touchingly told a story of family hatred, of the mutilation of a young boy, Otto, and the consequences of this brutality. In no sense was it a tale from which a child would wince; it immediately enlisted deep interest and sympathy and its understanding compassion reached out to its new audience. The Middle Ages enfolds the characters into its bitterness and beauty. Pyle produced a deeply moving story without a hint of preachiness.

Illustrations completed the tone and effect of the story—in fact they initiated it. Almost inevitably a reader's first message from an illustrated book is a pictorial one. The strong, contrasting strokes of Pyle's pen, his network of dramatic darks, the simple, powerful, and yet poetic compositions, tend to prepare the reading eye and make it receptive to the prose. How well the pictures introduce the characters—they are already presences with a nature, a body, and a past history before we read a word. Dual talents such as Pyle's are scarce, and it is rarer still to find them so equal and balanced.

There are three remaining books that can be considered to be for youthful readers. Two are historical adventure tales of novel length and the other a collection of four

short stories. Physically these latter three do not resemble the others that have been discussed, largely because they are obviously intended for a somewhat older audience and are illustrated with tonal drawings instead of pen and ink. In fact, one of them might well appeal both to adolescent and adult. Each of the three takes place in a different spot geographically and in a different historical period. As might be expected, they coincide with Pyle's favorite geographical and historical areas—English medieval history, early American history, and the Spanish-American and pirate world of the Caribbean.

The earliest of the three, **Men of Iron,** published in 1892, is laid in fifteenth-century England. Its plot is simple and quite conventional: the development and final triumph of the boy Myles Falworth—his schooling into young manhood under the shadow of an injustice done to his family, and his heroic righting of an old wrong. The theme is an old one, but Pyle gave it new conviction with his evocation of the relentless schooling for knighthood. Pyle's historical sense was extensive and thorough, yet it never conveyed a sense of mere accumulated facts. The knowledge seems to have been relived in his imagination long before words were found. His detailed story of young Myle's grueling years as a squire and his sudden leap into knighthood conveys a strong image of late medieval life. That image, however, is not strengthened by Pyle's illustrations, largely because the method of reproduction had changed. The halftone method had now become a reliable and accepted process, and pen and ink was in diminishing demand. At any rate, the new process dictated different techniques of illustration, principally painting in oil or watercolor. The **Men of Iron** pictures were painted in oil and well painted but they lack the bite and power of the pen drawings for **Otto of the Silver Hand.** They are well composed, the forms are there, the figures characterized, but the method of reproduction has sapped the contrasts and encouraged the shapes to be factually accurate rather than imaginatively arresting. The eye travels over the gray panels without much temptation to linger and find long satisfactions.

Three years later, **The Story of Jack Ballister's Fortunes** appeared. In order to impart an early eighteenth-century flavor to the book, Pyle added a long explanatory subtitle to the title page: "Being the narrative of the adventures of a young gentleman of good family, who was kidnapped in the year 1719 and carried to the plantations of the continent of Virginia, where he fell in with that famous pirate Captain Edward Teach, or Blackbeard; of his escape from the pirates and the rescue of a young lady from out of their hands." That subtitle is, of course, a synopsis of the plot, again a fairly standard one, but Pyle brings it to life with constant action, good characterizations, and his always reliable power to evoke an authentic historical setting. The story has been criticized over the years for Pyle's propensity to pause and instruct or point a moral. Certainly such a galloping tale is scarcely a suitable vehicle for admonishing interludes, but they are easily skipped and ignored.

The last children's book, **Stolen Treasure,** was certainly an afterthought, made up of four pirate tales that had originally appeared in magazines about ten years before. This compilation appeared in 1907. . . . (pp. 82-5)

It is interesting to note that of the thirteen children's books discussed in this chapter, seven had earlier publication in various magazines and another was excerpted. It is also noteworthy that eleven of the thirteen had simultaneous publication in England. England accepted Howard Pyle, word and picture. (p. 85)

> *Henry C. Pitz, in his* Howard Pyle: Writer, Illustrator, Founder of the Brandywine School, *Clarkson N. Potter, Inc., 1975, 248 p.*

Judy L. Larson

Pyle's fairy tales differed from European tales in that there was none of the primeval terror, deep mysticism, passion, or spiritualism of the latter. In Pyle's stories, one theme appeared over and over—that happiness and success are available to anyone who is clever, honest, and determined enough to pursue his or her goal. It could be argued that this was, in fact, the dream of every American during the last two decades of the nineteenth century. Pyle's stories were written at a time when America was moving from an agrarian to an industrialized society. It seems that these fairy tales in their simplicity and straightforwardness were Pyle's conservative efforts to stop that evolution. The belief that science and education would change the world and end suffering and ignorance was strongly held by many people in the late nineteenth century. But changes were happening so rapidly and transformations were so radical, that many people became skeptical of new-fangled inventions and technology. In the story **"A Victim of Science,"** from *Pepper & Salt,* two scientists waste time arguing over a current procedure for a wounded bird, meanwhile losing their patient. In another story Pyle reminisces about a tulip bed which used to be home to the fairies "before the smoke of the factories and the rattling of steam cars had driven the fairy-folks away from this world into no man's land." (pp. 25-6)

> *Judy L. Larson, "Folklore and Fairy Tales," in her* Enchanted Images: American Children's Illustrations, 1850-1925, *Santa Barbara Museum of Art, 1980, pp. 23-30.*

Sheila A. Egoff

In terms of grandeur and affinity with the material, no modern writer has approached Howard Pyle's cycle of the Robin Hood or Arthurian tales. . . . (p. 214)

If legends are not the favorite reading of most children today, it may be due largely to the mediocrity and enervated spirit of much of the retelling. Their successful retelling demands love, insight, scholarship, and an empathy for the historical as well as the legendary past, qualities that can be present in a committed amateur's enthusiasm, rather than lifelong scholarship, as is evident in Howard Pyle's vital, artistic, and literary reworkings of *King Arthur* and *Robin Hood.* Unfortunately most contemporary retellers appear amateurish in comparison. (p. 216)

> *Sheila A. Egoff, "Folklore, Myth and Legend," in her* Thursday's Child: Trends and Patterns in Contemporary Children's Literature, *American Library Association, 1981, pp. 193-220.*

John Cech

This year is the one hundredth anniversary of the publication of Howard Pyle's *The Merry Adventures of Robin Hood of Great Renown, in Nottinghamshire.* During the century it has remained in print, Pyle's re-visioning of the Robin Hood stories (his first book and the first time this material had been shaped in such an imaginatively coherent way) has become an acknowledged classic. (p. 11)

The essence of *The Merry Adventures,* it seems to me, is in its complex weave of contrasts and complements. His Robin is not simply a dumb jock or a charming con artist. Pyle reveals him as sensitive, cultivated, witty—as perfectly capable of trading sophisticated puns as he is sword thrusts. Robin is an appreciator of beauty, whether it be that of a fine spring day or of a marvelous song; and he is himself a singer of ballads, a teller of stories, and a dispenser of wisdom to his followers. After hearing a tale Will Scarlet tells about King Arthur, Robin philosophizes to his merry men (and Pyle to his readers also): "it doth make a man better . . . to hear of those noble men that lived so long ago. When one doth list to such tales, his soul doth say, 'Put by thy poor little likings and seek to do likewise.' Truly, one may not do as nobly one's self, but in the striving one is better". He is deeply moved by the plights of the sorrowful knight, Sir Richard of the Lea, the minstrel Allan a Dale, Will Scarlet, and the widow of Doncaster, among others—and he helps them all unquestioningly. In fact, and like most tragically star-crossed heroes, Robin's strength is also his flaw: loyalty. Ironically, his devotion to his friends and followers does not jeopardize him to the same, mortal degree that his utter loyalty to the crown does. His trip to London, to shoot before the King and Queen, at the invitation of the Queen, very nearly costs him his life. Indeed, the chase that results from this archery match signals the symbolic if not the literal end of Robin's relatively secure freedom in Sherwood, for it is from this point in Pyle's sequencing of the stories that life begins to become very difficult for Robin in Sherwood—with posses ringing the woods and a vicious bounty hunter (Guy of Gisbourne) hired to track Robin down. In the end, Robin's loyalty to King Richard, leads him away from Sherwood, estranging him further from the forest and the people he is so attached to there. His leaving Sherwood, Pyle shows us, represents "the breaking up of things."

Yet one also feels that Robin would act again out of loyalty in the same way that he does here, paying again the same, bittersweet price. For there are few more poignant figures than the Robin who returns to Sherwood many years later after having "followed the King to the wars, and found his time so full that he had no chance to come back to Sherwood for even so much as a day". . . . (pp. 12-13)

In these ways, Pyle expands the humanity of the character he finds in the traditional ballads, drawing the reader much closer in emotional sympathy with him. In a similar way, Pyle handles the dangerous, violent aspect's of Robin's character. For Robin Hood *is* a dangerous figure, from the point of view of the defenders of law and order, civil, moral, and otherwise. Robin belongs to the dark, Dionysian side of things. While the perception of him as merely an impulsive destroyer is not in keeping with Pyle's treatment, Pyle's Robin is still dangerous, because he feels deeply, acts passionately out of moral conviction, and only kills when he is given no choice—never out of whim or pride. The Robin Hood of the ballads and Pyle's Robin become outlaws in essentially the same way. Each is bullied and taunted by the King's rangers first into shooting one of the King's deer and then, in self defense, into turning his bow on the rangers. But in the ballad, Robin does not stop with one. . . . Though his murder of the taunting forester is justified as an act of self-defense, Pyle does not soften the effect of what his Robin does. Still, Pyle's Robin does not act out of a distorted sort of pride. It is simple, retaliatory anger. . . . But then Pyle adds what is not included in the ballad: a moral recognition on Robin's part about what he has done. . . . When Robin must kill Guy of Gisbourne, late in the book, he rationalizes it in this way: "This is the first man I have slain since I shot the King's forester in the hot days of my youth. I ofttimes think bitterly even yet of that first life I took but of this, I am as glad as though I had slain a wild boar that lay waste a fair country". The stunning illustration that shows the aftermath of Robin's fight with Guy of Gisbourne supports the claim that this is a morally justified killing. Wiping the bloody blade of his sword on a handful of long grass, Robin does look like he has just relieved the world of a dangerous animal, the body of which is sprawled before us in the foreground.

But, Robin cannot fall back on the same moral argument when he finally kills the Sheriff of Nottingham; and Robin knows it. Too much has happened for Pyle to give Robin a reprieve: he has disobeyed the king by staying more than three days in Sherwood Forest; it hasn't taken him more than a few hours, it seems, to find his old band and fall into his old haunts and habits again. Rather than meet the force led by the Sheriff that the king has sent to Sherwood with his earlier tactics that "shun blood and battle," Robin is impatient, and engages in a direct confrontation in which he kills his old, arch-enemy. Robin wins, but he loses. This murder "lay heavily on his mind, so that he brooded over it until a fever seized upon him". And it is this fever, this soul-sickness, that leads Robin to his fateful and fatal appointment at the nunnery. One leaves Pyle's version with the feeling that Robin, rather than the Prioress, is the actual agent of his own undoing. Pyle again provides strong visual accompaniment for the vents, showing us a Robin on his deathbed, about to shoot his last arrow through the open casement, while above him, in one of Pyle's remarkable borders, Azrael, one of the mystical angel-guides of the dead, looks on. (p. 13)

It is certainly fitting that Pyle's first big leap into his own imagination was Robin Hood. Robin is, to use Carl Jung's term, the shadow. For Pyle, for each of us, the shadow is "all the elements of the natural personality that have been discarded and overcome as a result of training and in accordance with the demands of society." According to Jung, the shadow is the first archetypal figure of the unconscious that we meet when we begin the process of becoming conscious of ourselves. Robin is both personal and collective shadow; he is the law-breaker, the thief, the defier of accepted authority—all that we are taught not to be. It is no wonder that "proper" literature repressed him, since he represents a threat to prescribed order. But as one cannot achieve wholeness without being willing to take risks, to find one's shadow and to claim, on some level, his experience as our own. In *The Merry Adventures* Pyle takes the chance and, in the process, he transforms the Robin of the shadows, making him visible to us all.

Clearly, Pyle threw his heart into *The Merry Adventures.*

It is a richly textured work that still has the power to hold us today because of the many levels on which it reverberates with feeling, meaning, and energy. Unfortunately, it may become in future years (even more than it already is) one of those great, unread classics—especially if "recommenders" of books for children to parents, like Nancy Larrick, continue to withdraw their endorsement of Pyle's version of the Robin Hood stories. I suspect that contemporary authorities on such matters as current reading tastes and attention spans would reject Pyle's book on the grounds that it was stylistically antiquated (i.e. too difficult) for today's young readers. And they would probably be right. But then Pyle did not mean for his book to have that written-last-week quality to it; it was meant to be, even at the time it was written, an old-fashioned book about a world where certain things never change. It's worth the climb to get there—to Pyle's merry and noble and bittersweet and shadowy "land of Fancy." (p. 14)

John Cech, "Pyle's 'Robin Hood': Still Merry After All These Years," in Children's Literature Association Quarterly, *Vol. 8, No. 2, Summer, 1983, pp. 11-14.*

Patricia Dooley

[*Robin Hood*] is certainly among the best . . . of Pyle's illustrated books for children. It was followed in quick succession by *Pepper and Salt, or Seasoning for Young Folks* and *The Wonder Clock.* All three are still in print; so are three others: *Otto of the Silver Hand, The Story of King Arthur and His Knights,* and *The Story of the Champions of the Round Table.* These six books, all easily available in inexpensive editions, may be taken to represent Pyle's pen-and-ink illustrations for children. . . .

It should be said that the style of these six books was not the only style Pyle used. . . . Whatever the merits or defects of Pyle's other style (it has been called impressionistic), however, the distinctive approach in the books to be considered here is the one he almost always used in his work for children. [Henry C.] Pitz describes this style as "decorative," a term which we may accept for the first three books but not for the last three, and argues that it came out of Pyle's childhood and his early immersion in illustrated books.

In *The Merry Adventures of Robin Hood,* the decorative note is decisively sounded. Wide and elaborate borders demarcate each picture, and the elements of the border or partial frame are so articulated as to become subordinate pictures themselves. The predominantly floral motifs of these borders are not merely decorative, however; they frequently have an iconographic relation to the central illustration. Above a scene depicting King Henry II, for example, the border shows a five-petalled rose, long a royal emblem; accompanying Robin's ducking by Little John is a border depiction of a water-loving iris; Robin's near-escape from death is bordered by columbine, a symbol of innocence, and his climactic encounter with King Richard is marked by a trumpet lily, symbol of the resurrection (since Robin Hood is no longer under sentence of death). The final headpiece of the book, introducing the 'Epilogue' of the hero's untimely death, bears the legend "So Ye Great Reaper reapeth among the Flowers," as Death cuts down more lilies: it has a border of poppies.

These prominent bands of decoration usually edge at least

two sides of an illustration, occasionally three or even four sides. The borders not only frame the picture; one of them generally encloses the caption within it. These brief, hand-lettered captions are often further enclosed by being inscribed on a ribbon, scroll, or banner, which is incorporated into the design of the frame. The effect of all this enclosure, naturally, is to distance the illustration, to set it off both from the text (and since the major illustrations, apart from the occasional headpieces, occupy a full page, they do not share the space of the text), and from the reader, who is thus visually prevented from entering the picture.

The impression of distance is heightened by some peculiarities of Pyle's graphic style. The extreme clarity and definition of line, the evenness of light and the absence of shadow, the precision of costume and the tidy-but-picturesque bits of vernacular architecture in the background, place the scenes in the timelessness, unchanging weather of an imaginary past, a fictional "Merrie England." Composition further enforces this distance: the action, usually featuring two figures in conjunction, occurs along a plane in the foreground, with the background hung like a theatrical dropcloth behind. . . .

In the vignettes accompanying the tales in *Pepper and Salt* Pyle evolved another approach to the presentation of Romance in a realistic style. Gone are the borders (with the sole exception of the frontispiece, whose design is an exact 'crib' from *Robin Hood*); instead, one side of the picture space is defined by the caption, lettered on a scroll (which often curves around or unfurls its ends to enclose two more sides). The graphic importance of the caption, and the placement of the vignette in the middle of the page of print, both make for a closer relation between text and illustration. Some of these small scenes are still all foreground; but in others a curving recession of the picture plane leads the eye to a depth which is truly boundless, with not even a straight black line dividing it from the white surface of the page. The pen lines are lighter, too— but they are also even freer of shadow. Appropriately, Pyle's handling of the illustrations seems dictated to a large extent by the light-hearted nature of the text. As the tales are more "folk" than "fairy" they may seem closer to our real world and more accessible; but the curving scrolls, and the lack of shadow, are enough to remind us of Romance. (p. 17)

In *The Wonder Clock,* Pyle moved still further from isolating the caption, returned to a border—but no more than a narrow black line—around the picture, and confined the purely decorative elements to the headpieces and the pages marking the 'hours.' Once again the illustrations are nearly squared, with the "two-shot" focus on the immediate foreground; but the caption (still hand-lettered, this time in a modified Old English gothic) floats in white space above, and several pictures are less than a full page, so that they share some part of the page with the text. There are still virtually no shadows, and many of the compositions are shallow, or on only two planes. Occasionally one does come upon a picture with real depth, which tempts the viewer to enter into the illustration or to connect its space with *real* space. These are exceptions, however, and in general the pictures are firmly centered in the world of Romance, preserving its disjunction with our world by their spatial organization as much as by their subjects. As in *Robin Hood,* the landscapes of *The Won-*

der Clock are well-ordered, charming, and in perfect repair; the characters are costumed neatly and picturesquely, and even the occasional holes or patches are artistic. Pyle's admiration for the Northern Renaissance style is evidenced here by his use of abundant draperies, breaking in deep folds or billowing richly around his figures, blown by no earthly wind. The explicitness of the drawing, which tends to produce an impression of accuracy and objectivity, is still in the service of the artist's imagination, which controls both the matter and the composition. Although there are not so many barriers as in *Robin Hood,* the world depicted is still in the realm of the unapproachably marvelous.

Otto of the Silver Hand is remarkable as much for its departures from Pyle's previous practice as it is for its introduction of elements that would be important in the Arthurian books. The most striking difference from the earlier books lies in the relation of the illustration to the text and to the viewer. Although all the pictures are full-page, and so divorced from the printed page, Pyle for once abandoned the hand-lettered and/or elaborately framed caption. Captions are set in small type and occupy an unobtrusive single line at the foot of the page, beneath the picture. These full-length, rectangular illustrations, moreover, have hardly a trace of border: there is little more than would be left by the edge of the woodblock they imitate. No barrier separates the picture from the beholder: it comes before one's eye in all its immediacy. Instead of alerting the viewer to the idea that the world depicted is the remote world of Romance, it invites participation and acceptance as a glimpse of the real. Furthermore, these illustrations are highly dramatic. In contrast to the slightly static quality of many of *The Wonder Clock* illustrations, which have a posed or over-composed look to them, like *tableaux,* most of the pictures in *Otto* look or are meant to look as if something were happening, or had just happened, or would happen in the next second. A figure is coming through a door, scaling a wall, attacking another figure from behind. The drama may also lie in the composition, with a greater use of diagonals, or the placement of the main figure just off center. What is even more striking is that Pyle has abandoned the clear unvarying light of the earlier books and has allowed himself to make considerable use of shading for dramatic effect. Daylight glances off arms and armor; light from windows or fires falls upon faces, illuminating—or still more impressively, half-illuminating—them; many scenes are set at night, with figures in a pool of dramatic light from torches or the moon. In all these instances it is not the otherworldly light of Romance that falls on the scene, but the common light of reality, however theatrically disposed. This approach is suited to the quasi-historical nature of Pyle's tale, which has none of the magical or marvelous elements of his previous stories (even *Robin Hood,* in which the series of amazing escapes, disguises, and *deus ex machina* endings makes for a fairy tale atmosphere).

In a tale set in medieval Germany, among castles and a monastery, with figures in period costume, the impact of Dürer is at its strongest. It can be seen in the way some faces, far from being Romantically idealized, approach the grotesque, in the characters' more life-like clothing (which, for all its occasional folds, now drapes solidly-conceived bodies), and in the deliberately archaic headpieces; all this adds to the sense of reality. Similarly, the three small headpieces depicting the story's locales—the Barons' castles and the monastery—drawn without any border at all and with the white of the page for sky, reinforce the viewer's impression of history: of a particular place drawn from observation rather than imagination.

If Pyle meant the reader to be fully engaged as much by the dramatic illustrations as by the moving story of *Otto,* he must have felt that such involvement would not be appropriate or desirable for his retelling of the Arthurian legends. Yet he did not go all the way back to the complete distance of the earlier works, either. Pyle did return to the layout of *The Wonder Clock,* with its square pictures, thin black borders, and elaborate neo-Gothic lettering floating above. In place of the distancing frame, however, is an intrinsic quality of strangeness in the pictures. In some illustrations, for example, "How Arthur drew forth ye sword," Pyle filled every corner of his space with a busy, shallow, tapestry-like arrangement of textures and pattern that recalls a Pre-Raphaelite print like D. G. Rossetti's "St. Cecilia—The Palace of Art." More often, Pyle works large white spaces into the composition, producing an effect of white light bathing the figures in the drama. This is particularly evident in the portraits regularly spaced through the two books, in which most of the background has been eliminated, or reduced to a few distant objects, while the sitter bears a freight of decorative and symbolic designs on armor, clothing, or jewelry. The men are craggy-faced (Uther, Merlin), shifty-eyed (King Mark, Pellias, Gawaine, Lionel), or blank-but-resolute (Launcelot, Tristram, Lamorack, Percival). They all look slightly ill at ease, and all hold swords, lances, or helmets as if, without them, they would be at a loss about what to do with their hands. In the portraits of women there is more variation in the background or pose, but less in physiognomy. Guinevere, The Lady of the Lake, Morgan Le Fay, and Vivien the Enchantress are all very much alike. They have curiously narrow, elongated eyes (lacking an eyelid fold, and so appearing Oriental), pouting mouths, sloping shoulders, small round breasts and tiny waists (much in evidence, since they wear skin-fitting bodices of thin material). They are as much of a piece as the women of Cranach (whom they in fact resemble).

In *The Story of the Champions of the Round Table,* the three ladies portrayed (Belle Isoult, Yvette the Fair, and Blanchefleur) are more differentiated physically, but they have the same remote, melancholy look as the others, as if they were thinking of their own sad stories. In the otherwise empty backgrounds of all three portraits (as with those of Guinevere and Vivien), the turrets of a small, distant castle appear off to one side. Why have these ladies come out in the open air, several miles from home, their hair disturbed by no chance wind? The answer to this question, and the cause of their male counterparts' unease, is the same: Pyle has chosen to portray each character in an *uncharacteristic* moment. The women have been removed from their natural setting, the castle, scene of their loves and tragedies; the men have been taken from the field of battle or from quest, and made to stand still instead of engaging in heroic actions. In making them subjects of portraiture, Pyle invites us to look for an individuality and depth of character not usually found in Romances. Pyle must have realized that the neat and smiling world of Romance he had previously delineated could not contain the often untidy, turbulent passions and events of Arthurian

legend. He needed to expand his conception of Romance, to go beyond the vision of ye-olde-England found in *Robin Hood* and the fairy tale books, but with more idealism and less sheer brutality than in *Otto.* The portraits were an attempt to allow greater depth into this new realm.

Pyle made an analogous attempt to envision a new landscape. The "realistic" elements of shadow, depth-of-field, and livelier composition, and the absence of barrier borders, play a role in those illustrations that are *not* portraits. In many cases the background, while not entirely blank, is minimal: a hill, some trees, a bare wall. Pyle chose only to suggest, instead of providing the picturesque details of the earlier books. In contrast, the characters' costumes are elaborate in the extreme, so that the reader's attention is necessarily drawn to them. It is as if Pyle felt that in these books, Romance resided in the characters, their motives, passions, and actions, instead of in the world through which they moved. . . . In *Champions* there are some highly dramatic pictures: Tristram leaping from a tower into the sea, The Queen of Ireland flying at Tristram, brandishing a huge two-handed sword above her head. In these pictures the faces of the principal actors are hidden by their own gestures, but there is nothing to distract us from the significance of the action.

In these Arthurian pictures, then, Pyle attempted to some extent to reconcile the Romantic and the realistic, to make his confident draughtsmanship convince the viewer of the dramatic logic of the unlikely events or unworldly characters portrayed. In his earlier works Pyle distanced the viewer from the world he created, by eschewing atmospheric effects and by his extensive use of framing. In *Otto* he allowed the dark side of an only too real world to confront us, almost without any buffer. In the Arthurian legends, Pyle finally achieved a synthesis of distance and immediacy, using only minimal framing and some conventions of realism, but altering the focus from setting to the characters and their actions. (p. 19)

Patricia Dooley, "Romance and Realism: Pyle's Book Illustrations for Children," in Children's Literature Association Quarterly, *Vol. 8, No. 2, Summer, 1983, pp. 17-19.*

Jill P. May

According to himself, Howard Pyle's urge to write fantasy came from a childhood filled with stories, many of which were read to him long before he could read for himself. After his tales of Robin Hood were published in 1883 and were an immediate success, Pyle determined to continue writing, and returned to the storehouse of fantasy he remembered from childhood: European folktales. . . .

The stories of *Pepper and Salt* seem very much like folklore in their vernacular phrasing; but these first tales are very different from the early European tales. Instead of depicting heroes whose luck depends upon magic, they describe clever people who express the New World philosophy of the early Puritan forefathers. Furthermore, they abound with evil spirits who, much like the New England devil, spend their time punishing humans who strike bargains. In the end, however, it is the humans who win, and when they do, lengthy moral statements explain why. . . .

These first stories abound with descriptive detail. The ac-

From Men of Iron, *written and illustrated by Howard Pyle.*

tivities of the magic folk are either romantically explained or humorously described. There was no need for Pyle to illustrate many of the scenes, since they are etched in his vigorous prose. (p. 19)

There are only eight tales in *Pepper and Salt* but each is well developed and complete in itself, and the book as a whole is Pyle's most unified collection of fairy tales. Pyle carefully added poems and controlled the graphic design to create an overall picture of another time, another set of standards. Actually, Pyle had begun writing the numerous poems contained in *Pepper and Salt* in 1883, and had decorated them with pen and ink illustrations; but when they were placed in a book together with his short fantasies, they were entirely compatible in format and in mood.

Pyle's real understanding of and appreciation for classical children's literature, displayed throughout *Pepper and Salt,* far surpassed most of his contemporaries. Part of his ability to understand and depict another era stemmed from his vast store of knowledge. He was a devout consumer of books and information, and steeped himself in historic detail before creating either stories or illustrations. . . . His stories became a strange combination of America's past, European lore, and his own Swedenborg ideology. . . .

The same thing must have happened as he recreated aspects of the European past. By the time Pyle published *The Wonder Clock* in 1887, his writing had become more sophisticated. Pyle himself thought this book contained his best fairy tales. Certainly the storytelling style, the plots, and the morals of *The Wonder Clock* are more reminiscent of European folklore than are the stories of *Pepper and Salt.* Usually good prevails, with the aid of good luck. The heroes are not as clever as they were in *Pepper and Salt,* and they depend upon the advice of others. Also the stories of *The Wonder Clock* are longer, so that stylistically they seem less robust and less original; there is more detail about activities, but few scenes are described as vividly as was the fairy life in the story I mentioned earlier. The narrator also speaks more to the audience, in casual asides which create the effect of a tale being told aloud. . . . While Pyle still delivers sermons in this collection, his morals are more quickly laid down than they were in *Pepper and Salt.* At the end of **"Bearskin,"** for example, he says that "wise folk don't tell all they know," and at the end of **"How the Good Gifts Were Used by Two,"** Pyle writes, "even the blessed saints cannot give wisdom to those who will have none of it. . . . "

The Wonder Clock also reflects a much more sophisticated use of oral folklore. Within each tale are the remnants of several tales, all used to advantage in creating a new story. (p. 20)

Pyle readily borrowed elements for his tales from his readings. In 1876 he had written his mother that he was re-reading Thorp's *Northern Mythology*, "hoping that these dry grains may fall on ground rich enough to produce a full-grown fairy tale or two." But also found in this collection is something of the American Quaker who shirked away from violence and who never forgot the importance of the family. Thus, in **"The Stepmother,"** the witch escapes unharmed, the old father is forgiven and cared for by his daughter and son-in-law, and war is avoided.

A lesser author would have garbled his stolen elements; but Pyle always remembered his story. Concerning his perceptiveness Jessie Willcox Smith wrote, "with Howard Pyle . . . there was your story, and you knew your characters, and you imagined what they were doing. . . . It was simply that he was always projected into his subject."

All things considered, *The Wonder Clock* is more distinctly old fashioned, and the stories are closer in form, to the lengthier oral legends of tradition. At first glance this collection seems inferior to *Pepper and Salt*, less original. But on a second reading something about the female characters seems unusual; they work their way through the drama with singleminded determination, until the reader wonders what they are about.

It seems that Pyle was struggling in these tales between picturing the clever, independent woman who is capable of taking care both of herself and others, and the submissive female of many nineteenth century marriages.

In **"King Stork,"** the young princess is in no hurry to marry, and is willing to trick all the young men who seek her hand. When at last the drummer outwits the girl, he is warned that "the princess is just as wicked as ever she was before, and if you do not keep your eyes open she will trip you up after all." He is then advised to "hold tight to her and lay on the switch, no matter what happens, for that is the only way to save yourself and to save her." Pyle was trying to depict both an intelligent heroine and a heroine who would submit her life to the dominance of a male. Marriage, he seemed to be saying, was best when the relationship was controlled by the husband.

Twentieth century children's artist Trina S. Hyman understands Pyle's attitude. Concerning her own illustration for this tale she writes,

> I resisted on that one, because of its blatant (I still think) chauvinist-piggishness. . . . You must understand that it was because of its sexist leanings that I had so much fun with it and pushed it the other way 'round.

Probably Pyle would have cringed at the idea that his tales were sexist; certainly he accepted female students in his art classes, although he rarely encouraged them to study with him. But those of his female students who were successful remained single, and seemed to support Pyle's belief that "the average woman with ambitions loses them when she marries." (pp. 20-1)

While Pyle never truly came to grips with his paradoxical attitudes toward women, at the very end of *The Wonder Clock* he planted a moral on marriage for all to see. In

"The Best That Life Has to Give," Pyle's hero is a young blacksmith's son who has to create beautiful goods from little or nothing. All the goods are taken to the queen who rules the kingdom, until at last she will be happy only if the youth comes and lives with her. She pursues him at his smithy, and asks him to come to the castle. So far she seems quite progressively aggressive. But Pyle ends:

> So he stepped from behind the stove and took her by the hand, and they walked out of the house and up to her castle on the high hill, for that was where he belonged now. There they were married, and ruled the land far and near. . . . And did the queen really get the best in the world? Bless your heart, my dear, wait until you are as old as I am, and have been married as long, and you will be able to answer that question without the asking.

In *The Wonder Clock*, Pyle wrote more somber pieces with deeper meanings. His style had changed from lighthearted prose full of episodic adventures to involved stories which could be interpreted in several ways; he was heading away from his early interpretations of folklore, and into more archaic medieval tales of courtly doings, of magical objects, and of animal fables. Not surprisingly, the format of *The Wonder Clock* is standardized. Each story has the same number of illustrations, each illustration is contained in a heavily-lined square, and most of the titles are illustrated with a rectangular pose of the main characters, creating a tableau effect. The freshness of page and spontaneous humor found within the illustrations of *Pepper and Salt* has disappeared; it was not to reappear in the books which Pyle later wrote and illustrated for children.

Pyle's fairy tale books must be evaluated from two standpoints: his literary genius and his innovative attitude toward the graphic arts. Pyle created total books when he wrote for children. He wrote the text, drew (or painted) his own illustrations, and even created his own calligraphy to explain the text or introduce the chapters. Some years after his death a critic wrote that while he was the best American illustrator, his greatest fame and contribution lay in children's literature: the stories "retold in Pyle's vigorous prose and illustrated with his bold and beautifully executed pictures stand at the top of American juvenile literature." (p. 21)

> *Jill P. May, "Pyle's Fairy Tales: Folklore Remade," in* Children's Literature Association Quarterly, *Vol. 8, No. 2, Summer, 1983, pp. 19-21.*

Malcolm Usrey

Along with Mark Twain's *The Prince and the Pauper*, Howard Pyle's *Otto of the Silver Hand* is one of the first historical novels written for children by an American. It is also one of the most remarkable, and it set the standard for many novels written since. There are two kinds of historical novels: those using both actual and fictional historical events and people, and those that use a historical period with fictional people and events. With the exception of Rudolph I and King Ottocar of Bohemia, there are no actual historical people in *Otto of the Silver Hand;* but that *Otto* is more fiction than history does not lessen its significance. It has all the marks of a good historical novel: it has an exciting plot, with ample conflict and believable characters; it uses language and dialect appropriate to its setting and the characters; it has a significant, universal theme, and it presents the details of daily life in Germany of the thirteenth century accurately and unobtrusively, making the period real and alive.

The conflict between the feuding houses of Baron Conrad and Baron Henry and the conflict between good and evil represented by the church and by the robber barons, generate the action and suspense of the novel. It focuses on the boy Otto, the innocent victim of the feud and the hope of a brighter, less cruel world, a hope nurtured by Otto's early years with the monks at St. Michaelsburg. Steeped in the plots of traditional folktales, Howard Pyle had learned well how to construct a story that would keep readers, young or old, swiftly turning pages "to see what happens next." Pyle is especially effective in creating suspense in the episodes in which Baron Henry burns Drachenhausen, in which One-eyed Hans rescues Otto from Trutz-drachen, and in which Baron Henry cuts off Otto's hand.

The characterization of *Otto* also seems to be modeled on traditional folktales. Nearly all the characters are all good or all bad; only Baron Conrad and One-eyed Hans have both good and bad traits. Pyle has portrayed the problem of good and evil on a symbolic canvas, flattening most of the characters and aligning them on the side of good or evil.

One of the problems all historical novelists have is to create a reasonable facsimile of the language suitable to the time of their settings that will still be comprehensible to their readers. A writer cannot recreate the language of a specific period, certainly not that of thirteenth century Germany; but if he wants to convey the mood and flavor of a particular historical period, he cannot use completely contemporary language. On the other hand, too many "quotha's," "beset's," and "eldritch's" will destroy a period mood and flavor. Pyle seems to have struck a happy mean in *Otto of the Silver Hand;* the language is neither too contemporaneous or too archaic. (p. 25)

Ideally, themes of historical novels should reflect truths valid for both the time of the story and for the present time. The theme of *Otto of the Silver Hand* was as important to its time as it is for ours. When Drachenhausen is rebuilt, Otto places beneath the scutcheon over the great gate a new motto for the Vuelphs: "Better a hand of silver than a hand of iron." The novel deals majestically with the theme expressed in this last sentence. It might be reworded, "Better kindness than cruelty," though Pyle's version is more richly connotative and perhaps more reflective of the time and temper of the story. Throughout the story, Pyle has shown the results of both cruelty and kindness, particularly by the contrasts between the evil in the feud between Baron Conrad and Baron Henry and the goodness, kindness, and enlightenment of St. Michaelsburg. Most of all, the theme reflected in the character of Otto, whose right hand is literally and symbolically one of silver. Otto embodies the goodness and kindness he learns in his twelve years at the monastery, and he carries these virtues with him to the world of the robber barons and their feuds. With his silver hand, he brings peace and harmony to the world of the robber barons and finally unites the two feuding houses by marrying Pauline, the

daughter of Baron Henry, who cut off his real hand and killed his father.

Among the primary requisites of historical fiction is that it make the period of the setting real and alive for readers. Readers should come away from a historical novel knowing how people dressed, what they ate, how they ate, slept, and worked—all the myriad details of daily living that make the past alive. But the historical data are secondary and must be worked naturally into the story, for the function "of a historical story is not to present the facts of history in readable form, but in going beyond historical data," to help us see and understand the past. In *Otto of the Silver Hand,* Howard Pyle fulfills this requirement of good historical fiction. . . . Details from his great store of knowledge of the Middle Ages are so naturally a part of Otto that a reader is hardly aware of his or her absorption of them. When readers finish the novel they have seen and heard "in winter time the howling wolves cours[ing] their flying prey across the moonlit snow and under the net-work of black shadows from the naked boughs above". And they have witnessed the cruelty and savagery of medieval evil and the sweetness and light of medieval kindness and compassion. Pyle's intimate knowledge of the Middle Ages is broad enough to make Otto stand out as more than just a good historical novel.

The concrete realism of Pyle's depiction of medieval life is particularly impressive. (pp. 25-6)

Pyle's equally impressive descriptions of Castle Drachenhausen and of St. Michaelsburg reflect the most distinctive quality of the novel, the contrasts Pyle built it around. Pyle's language in describing the castle connotes darkness, hardness, massiveness, and coldness, and suggests a furtively evil isolation. His repetition of hard k's and g's reinforces his connotations. . . . Pyle's picture of St. Michaelsburg connotes light, peace, harmony, and suggests a kind of sunny openness. Pyle's repetition of soft s's helps to create the mood of quiet peace the passage suggests. . . .

In *From Primer to Pleasure in Reading,* Mary F. Thwaite suggests that Pyle "brought new renown to the craft of historical fiction for youth with . . . *Otto of the Silver Hand.*" Pitz says that in this book, Pyle turns "his back upon the cliches and sweetly doctored prose of the great bulk of late Victorian children's literature. The book marked a turn of taste and conception." Historical fiction is certainly richer because Howard Pyle wrote *Otto of the Silver Hand.* (p. 26)

> *Malcolm Usrey, "A Milestone of Historical Fiction for Children: 'Otto of the Silver Hand',"* in Children's Literature Association Quarterly, *Vol. 8, No. 2, Summer, 1983, pp. 25-7.*

Jon Stott

An apparent paradox in the literary career of Howard Pyle is the fact that a man raised in the Quaker faith wrote so many stories steeped in violence and bloodshed. . . . At first glance, it may seem strange that such a man as Pyle should choose such subjects as the violent clashes of Arthurian knights, the feuds of German robber barons, and the cruel exploits of eighteenth century pirates.

However, a closer look at Pyle's works reveals not so much a paradox as a coherently developed theory of human nature and history. In *Howard Pyle's Book of Pirates* is found a statement which succinctly states his theory:

> Such is that black chapter of history of the past— an evil chapter; lurid with cruelty and suffering, stained with blood and smoke. Yet it is a written chapter and it must be read. He who chooses may read between the lines of history this great truth: Evil itself is an instrument toward the shaping of good. Therefore the history of evil as well as the history of good should be read, considered, and digested.

Here then is a key to the resolution of the apparent paradox and a key to the understanding of Pyle's stories of high adventure. He was not, as was Herman Melville's Nantucket whaler, a Quaker with a vengeance; rather, he was a man whose vision of history recognized the existence of evil and saw it as a necessary element in the struggle toward Christian goodness. The wicked men and the violent actions called forth good men and noble actions which led to the defeat of evil and to greater peace. The blood and thunder of his books, their violent adventure, are not gratuitous, but purposive. (p. 27)

> *Jon Stott, "The Purposiveness of Evil: A Note on 'Otto of the Silver Hand'," in* Children's Literature Association Quarterly, *Vol. 8, No. 2, Summer, 1983, pp. 27-8.*

Susan E. Meyer

Pyle's creative output alone would have qualified him as a great American illustrator of children's literature. But his legacy was far greater than the hundreds of books and articles he wrote and illustrated at the turn of the century. He was a natural teacher, the major force in what later came to be known as the Brandywine School. A compelling and vital man, Pyle was possessed with the idea of training—both spiritually and artistically—a younger generation of artists to conquer new, unexplored frontiers. If any person could be called the Father of American Illustration, it would be Howard Pyle, for no other American artist has left such a personal and enduring influence on its development during the twentieth century. (p. 211)

> *Susan E. Meyer, "Howard Pyle," in her* A Treasury of The Great Children's Book Illustrators, *Harry N. Abrams, Inc., 1983, pp. 211-32.*

Walt Reed and Roger Reed

The illustrations of Howard Pyle, are as exciting now as they were over 80 years ago, while pictures by many of his contemporaries today look dated and mannered.

Several special qualities combined to make Pyle America's foremost illustrator. Pyle was interested in pictures, first of all, as drama. . . . In his illustrations, Pyle sought to dramatize themes with universal appeal. The pictures portrayed basic human emotions: the ruthlessness of pirate greed, raw grief in the break-up of Lee's army after Appomattox, smug pride, humble petition.

Pyle's concept of a picture was never trite. He deliberately looked for new ways to tell a story and involved himself in his subject so thoroughly that his picture makes the reader an eye-witness to a vivid experience.

Having evolved his basic pictorial idea, Pyle developed his compositions; his pictures are fascinating to analyze. No area of a picture is wasted; each makes its contribution, through placement, line, tone, or color, to the whole story. Through the details, the viewer's eye is purposefully led toward the focal center.

Pyle wrote, as well as illustrated, many books himself. He did original research on the obscure subject of the buccaneers in the New World. It is from his famous *Book of Pirates* that our present-day concept of pirates has come. School children still read his *Men of Iron, The Story of King Arthur and his Knights, The Merry Adventures of Robin Hood,* and many other tales. . . .

At a time when it was customary and fashionable to study in Europe, Pyle had a strong conviction that students should seek their training and inspiration in America. Many of Pyle's greatest pictures came from his intense and loyal interest in Americana. His renditions of the Revolutionary War period and of Civil War subjects have since become standard pictures in our history books. . . . (p. 39)

> *Walt Reed and Roger Reed, "The Decade: 1890-1900," in* The Illustrator in America, 1880-1980: A Century of Illustration, *edited by Walter Reed and Roger Reed, Madison Square Press, Inc., 1984, pp. 28-47.*

Harold Von Schmidt

[*A student of painter and illustrator Harvey Dunn, a former pupil of Pyle's whom critics Walt and Roger Reed describe as "[of] all Pyle's students, perhaps the one most deeply imbued with his philosophy," Von Schmidt was a popular illustrator best known for his depictions of the American West. He was elected to the Society of Illustrators Hall of Fame in 1959 and was awarded the first gold medal by the trustees of the National Cowboy Hall of Fame in 1968.*]

[Howard Pyle was] probably the greatest illustrator America has ever produced. . . .

As an artist, Pyle's greatest love and interest was in Americana. He eagerly sought all information available about early Colonial times and actually interviewed a survivor of the Revolutionary War. His illustrations, as a result, carry an authentic stamp not only because of the accuracy of detail, such as in buttons or ruffles, but also because of his ability to portray the spirit of a rough-hewn but forthright American pioneering period.

Pyle's influence, had it rested on his pictures alone, would have been great; as a teacher his talents were equally important and created an even more lasting influence. . . .

As part of his teaching, Pyle made his students fully aware of the practical use to which their pictures would be put. Through his contacts with publishers and art directors, he arranged that the students work on actual commissions or that finished pictures be shown to art directors for possible use. As he taught, "When you are making pictures to be reproduced in print, you are then given no favor and your pictures must be good as pictures or else they are of no possible use . . . " As he described it, " . . . my final aim in teaching will not be essentially the production of illustrators of books but rather the production of painters of pictures, for I believe that the painters of true American art are yet to be produced."

Pyle's high purposes were more than justified. His pupils have gone on to achieve eminent names in their own right and, in turn, have continued to pass Pyle's spirit on to a third and fourth generation of illustrators. The total influence of his personality on the whole field can never be measured; but it is a privilege for me to pay this small tribute to him. (p. 48)

> *Harold Von Schmidt, "The Decade: 1900-1910," in* The Illustrator in America, 1880-1980: A Century of Illustration, *edited by Walt Reed and Roger Reed, Madison Square Press, Inc., 1984, pp. 48-83.*

Zena Sutherland and May Hill Arbuthnot

[Howard Pyle's] heroic and romantic pictures for such books as *Robin Hood, Otto of the Silver Hand,* and *Men of Iron* are meticulous in their fidelity to the historical costumes and weapons of the period. Yet his elaborations of robes, courtly trappings, and tournament details are always subordinated to the interpretation of character or mood. The poignancy of young Otto's tragedy moves anyone who looks at those pictures, and, in contrast, the high good humor of Robin Hood is equally evident. Here was an author-artist with a gift for telling stories in words and pictures. (p. 141)

Children enjoy hearing some of the ballads of Robin Hood read aloud, but the prose version by Howard Pyle, with his spirited illustrations, is the text they should know. It is hard reading for most children, and if they can't read it for themselves, they should hear it. For the lucky superior readers, it remains for generation after generation of children one of the most exciting narratives in all literature. (pp. 216-17)

> *Zena Sutherland and May Hill Arbuthnot, "Artists and Children's Books" and "Fables, Myths and Epics," in their* Children and Books, *seventh edition, Scott, Foresman and Company, 1986, pp. 132-62, 204-24.*

Lucien L. Agosta

Howard Pyle produced his best illustrations for his children's works, and as a writer for children his reputation remains secure. A new climate in literary and pictorial taste in juvenile entertainments has, however, done much to diminish the popular demand for his children's works that he enjoyed during his lifetime. Complex and dense in verbal style and visual design, prone to didacticism and laden with deliberate archaisms, Pyle's works do not compete well with the instantaneous, often crudely immediate images and plots featured in contemporary comic books, many recent picture books, popular movies such as *Star Wars,* and Saturday morning cartoons. Nevertheless, his classic works for children continue to delight sophisticated child and adult readers alike and still claim an enthusiastic audience, however diminished. His works for children live and breathe even in our smoggy air because they evince a masterfully created idyllic realm, a golden time-

out-of-time, a pastoral oasis, the innocence and robust freshness of which still propel the contemporary reader through the borders of Arcadia. This "Land of Fancy," variously named "Wonderland," "Never-never-land," and "Twilight Land," this safe refuge of "jollity and mirth," is no saccharine commonwealth, sticky with sugarplums and cushioned with gumdrops. Nor is it a darkly romantic country rigged up with operatic stage sets, dreamy and vague, glimmering with watery moonlight and replete with moldering castles and crumbling towers, that overstuffed furniture crowding the works of so many nineteenth-century romantic imitators of Tennyson and the Rossettis. Instead, Pyle's Arcadia is sun-drenched, invigorating, and fragrant; its habitations airy, spacious, clean-swept, and lived-in; its citizens robust and exuberant, above all muscular and alive, endowed with a delight and youthful wonder at the ample proportions of the land they occupy and at the fullness of creation in general. Pyle's "Land of Fancy" is ultimately so endearing, however, because it is paradoxically so unstable, so fleeting, threatened on every side by death, disillusion, and the passage of time. These verities are heroically held in abeyance in Pyle's pastoral idyll, fended off for a hearteningly long period, but they cannot be dispelled forever. Thus Robin Hood, after sporting long in his greenwood "Land of Fancy," loses his idealism and declines toward death. Thus, too, the grassy oasis in *Pepper & Salt* dissolves to the quotidian duration of schoolwork and chores, and the Wonder Clock ceases its hypnotic ticking so that Father Time stirs from his revery to retrieve his scyth and hourglass. Twilight Land fades to darkness, the roses of the Moon-Garden blanche and wither, and Arthur, too, for so long resplendent in breezy Camelot, sinks to grief. Pyle's "Land of Fancy," then, is a land bordered by loss, a glorious golden fabric frayed at its edges. His achievement and the continuing vitality of his works for children lie in his ability to suspend momentarily the depredations of time, to prolong and heighten that marvelous interval wherein youthful wonder and mirth exist untarnished.

These works for juveniles are historically important in the evolution of American children's literature. Pyle was instrumental in the nineteenth-century revitalization of the folktale, the conventions of which are everywhere to be found in his works and culminate in a series of vivid and highly entertaining fairy tales. His folktale collections and his Robin Hood and Arthur series mark a significant break with Victorian stiffness and formality in their defense of merriment and lightheartedness over ponderous morality, starched primness, and grim utilitarianism. In preface after preface Pyle defends the "innocent jollity and mirth" to be found in the pages of his volumes, offering "a pinch of seasoning in this dull, heavy life of ours," a momentary respite for those who "plod amid serious things." These prefaces pointedly exclude from his audience such dour Victorians as *Pepper & Salt's* "sober wise man" and all those even now "who think that life hath nought to do with innocent laughter that can harm no one." In seeking to dispel the chilly rectitude and straitlaced priggishness found in too many children's books, however, Pyle avoided those stratagems resorted to by kindly but unskilled and essentially dishonest writers for children—sentimentality, artificial coziness, spurious charm, and deliberate sprightliness. Instead, Pyle, like Twain and Stevenson, never hesitated to show young readers a picture of life strenuous and hard, of a world where harsh reality is often masked by beguiling appearances, where duty, frequently unpleasant, leads to success, and unchanneled desire inevitably to catastrophe. Pyle's legendary heroes—Robin and Arthur, particularly—disport in Arcadia, but come eventually to admit death's universal sway even there. His folktale and historical heroes—Otto and Myles Falworth, to name only two—often must hack through the world's inhospitable thicket to a place of refuge, order, and control. Thus Pyle's balanced view of life led him to portray for children a world suffused with mirth and wonder though tainted with trial and hardship. His works for children manifest an ingratiating and infectious joyfulness tempered with refreshing candor, qualities innovative in the children's fiction of his day and still attractive in our own. (pp. 146-48)

Lucien L. Agosta, in his Howard Pyle, *Twayne Publishers, 1987, 162 p.*

Taimi M. Ranta

If Bennett A. Brockman correctly defines children's literature as "imaginative literature marketed to children and designed for their amusement as well as their edification," then *The Merry Adventures of Robin Hood* stands at the apex of children's literature. . . . It embodies all of the significant ingredients of a successful story, regardless of a reader's age. The language befitting the characters of twelfth century England, the pastoral setting, and the lyrical tone all elicit the involvement of a reader or listener. The theme of good triumphing over evil helps the story fuse into a memorable work of fiction. Moreover, Pyle's picturesque, detailed illustrations add special texture and fabric to the story. . . . (p. 213)

[Pyle's] work on *The Merry Adventures of Robin Hood* is his main gift to American Literature. Indeed, his Robin Hood is one of the all-time quixotic heroes, at once Sir Lancelot, Cyrano de Bergerac, Don Quixote, Huck Finn, Tom Sawyer—a Medieval English hero with surprising resemblances to the romantic outlaws of legendary America. (p. 214)

The Merry Adventures of Robin Hood is still significant reading for children. The prose is such that it would interest even young readers who may not be accustomed to such a florid style; and the simplicity, gaiety, and morality of the story make this an incomparable book for teachers who wish to introduce their students to a classic milestone of children's literature. *The Merry Adventures of Robin Hood* is tasty enough to be palatable in and of itself but also complex enough to be a steppingstone to many other great books in world literature.

Nevertheless, teachers may be bewildered by the number of collections of Robin Hood stories that are available, even editions of the Pyle version. . . . [The] Dover edition of *The Merry Adventures of Robin Hood* is the best choice, for it is an unabridged and unaltered republication of the work originally published by Charles Scribner's in 1883. It includes Pyle's delightful borders for large full-page plates, his pleasing vignettes, and his decorative initial letters, all of which are such an integral part of the total illustration, and all of which were removed in the multilated and still available 1946 edition. (p. 218)

Children should become aware of the living, changing nature of language instead of thinking of it as a static entity;

From The Story of King Arthur and His Knights, *written and illustrated by Howard Pyle.*

and teachers should use carefully selected pieces of choice literature to develop awareness of these changes. In my own teaching, Pyle's version of the Robin Hood stories has been a key example of such changes, specifically for the Middle English flavoring that Pyle sought to capture.

Yet students today are attuned to the greater dependence of our English upon word order for meaning than was the language of Robin Hood's day. So, Pyle's text may sound somewhat foreign to modern ears and be slower to read than recently published adventure fiction. But since the sometimes archaic language is part of the book's charm and authenticity, it lends itself to reading aloud, at least in part, by the teacher and by better readers in a fifth or sixth grade class. Many of the children will know Robin Hood as a hero, but usually only through screen renditions, lesser versions, or hearsay. Expressive oral reading will convey the spirit of the Pyle version and recreate some of the flavor of the original oral tradition from which the stories stem. I often follow my own presentation of Pyle's version to upper elementary or middle school children, and also to college students in children's literature classes, with a short presentation of ballads, first some that Pyle used as source material and then other folk and literary ballads, including some modern ones.

I often hear the lament, "Where have all our heroes

gone?" Robin Hood is the very definition of the hero for children. He embodies the basic characteristics of the epic hero, those of courage, justice, and control. A book recommended for teaching should always say something important to students at that phase of their lives, and not be assigned merely to prepare them for some future goal in literary experience. Pyle's *The Merry Adventures of Robin Hood* does both. It involves the students in the exploits of an ageless hero of the people and leads them into the study of the ageless heroes like King Arthur, Beowolf, and Odysseus. (pp. 218-19)

Children should be encouraged to follow the Piper when Pyle himself in his preface says, "And now I lift the curtain that hangs between here and No-man's-land. Will you come with me, sweet Reader? I thank you. Give me your hand." (p. 219)

> *Taimi M. Ranta, "Howard Pyle's 'The Merry Adventures of Robin Hood': The Quintessential Children's Story," in* Touchtones: Reflections on the Best of Children's Literature, Vol. 2, *Children's Literature Association, 1987, pp. 213-19.*

Jill P. May

My fascination with Howard Pyle's version of the King Arthur legends began only after I had become an adult, so I cannot claim that I can remember their childhood appeal, and that I am now returning for a look in terms of my adult response. And since Lloyd Alexander once confessed to me that he had *never* read the versions by Pyle, I cannot even say that Pyle has been a direct influence on all later authors of fantasy. Yet I think that Pyle's King Arthur series indirectly established a tradition, for it was the first of many multiple-volumed sequential fantasy tales based upon new interpretations of Arthurian materials. And I believe that modern children's versions of these materials do contain adventures and characters similar to those found in Pyle's story. In fact, Pyle's historically significant role in the continual process of reinterpretation makes the first volume of his series on King Arthur (as well as the following ones) archetypal in children's literature.

Pyle took a backwards look at the old tales and created a new version for his modern audience. He sought to write a tale of Arthur which would be acceptable to his contemporaries. Today I look backwards at Pyle, knowing something about his sources, his plans, and his Arthur, and realize that I am looking at his work as an adult just as the adult Pyle looked at his own source materials when he determined to re-create Arthur for children. Like Pyle, I remember other versions of Arthur, only mine are both older and newer than his.

Northrop Frye once wrote, "We cannot in practice study a literary work without remembering that we have encountered many similar ones previously. Hence after following a narrative through to the end, our critical response includes the establishment of its categories, which are chiefly its conventions and its genre. In this way the particular story is seen as a *projection* of the theme, as one of the infinite number of ways of getting to the theme." Thinking about that comment I am struck by its similarity to Pyle's own belief in what he was doing with the King Arthur legends, and to his recognition that he was *reshap-*

ing earlier mythic and historic legendary tales, transforming tales of chivalry not yet available to young readers of English either in North America or the British Isles into an American romance. (p. 221)

Earlier, Pyle had woven the remnants of Robin Hood legend into a continual hero story. That book was extremely popular from the day of its release, for heroic legend was in vogue with American audiences. Pyle lived among fanatic readers of Sir Walter Scott; the Waverly novels were popular with the young boys of the Wilmington area. . . . Aware of Scott's popularity and encouraged by publishers, Pyle began to rewrite the loosely joined Arthurian legends into an easily followed chronological narrative. The episodes he chose are still those most often found in more recent children's versions of the Arthurian tales, and usually, the characters' personalities in these newer fantasies resemble the people in Pyle's version; for these reasons, the books must be considered archetypal in characterization.

The Story of King Arthur and His Knights was the first in a set of four books by Pyle about King Arthur's court and his knights. It sets up all of the patterns now familiar in questing hero stories. As such, it is the groundwork for establishing the courtly intrigue and the final collapse of Arthur's rule which are the subjects of the later books.

Each time Arthur or his knights go to battle during this first book, Pyle describes the countryside and the scene in detail. He sets most of the major battles between knights in glens within a woods, which the knights reach on horseback. The physical battles are not held inside the court; while help is sought from the court, the actual fighting occurs outside of the "civilization" of Arthur's rule. A knight on quest must leave Arthur's rule, travel into the unknown, seek adventure in the name of honor, and return home after an honorable fight. The highest battles are those which are fought to preserve the courtly system, save a damsel from disgrace, or revenge unknightly conduct. The low battles unworthy of glory are those involving power struggles between two knights. A knight will not fight a foe of lesser strength, and he cannot turn down a virtuous maiden's plea for help. In order to keep the peace established after a battle, Arthur takes the favorite son of his conquered enemy with him "to serve in court" (*or* to serve as ransom). (pp. 222-23)

Today's fantasy stories based on Arthurian traditions and written for children still contain questing male heroes who are gentle, faithful, true; Pyle did not say that a masculine hero needed to be intelligent, and no demands of intelligence are placed on later male heroes either. Taran, Lloyd Alexander's hero in the Prydain series, begins his quest with no knowledge concerning his adventure, gains friends he would defend at all costs, and in the end says, "I ask no reward . . . I want no friend to repay me for what I did willingly, out of friendship and my own honor". Alexander's hero fits into the code as easily as Pyle's heroes.

But knights are not all alike in Pyle's *The Story of King Arthur and His Knights.* Heroes are clearly differentiated from one another in the Pyle books. Many of these heroic personalities were already defined in the earlier versions, but Pyle reformed them to fit his needs. Within the first volume, for instance, Pyle establishes his character portrayals of Merlin, Sir Pellias, and Sir Gawaine. Each has an unique personality which is based in the earlier legends and is itself the basis for characters found in renditions created after Pyle's series.

Gawaine represents the earthy, hot headed young knight who is at times vain and brutal. The early French romances depicted Gawaine as both knightly in battle skills and lascivious and cruel. Pyle realized that in his story of Gawaine, he must explain why so noble a hero would act in less than virtuous ways when dealing with others. He decided to "try to represent Gawaine as proud and passionate, quick to anger, but with a broad basis of generosity and nobility" and admitted that he would "modernize Sir Gawaine". Pyle lets his readers know that Gawaine is a proud young man full of high spirits by describing him as such, and by having the courtly action center on him during a balmy afternoon when he is the "most gayly clad" of the court and is busy entertaining the others with song. Suddenly the queen's favorite greyhound runs in, jumps up and soils Gawaine's clothes. Pyle writes: "At this Sir Gawaine was very wroth, wherefore he clinched his hand and smote the hound upon the head . . . " Thus, Gawaine's high spirits drive him away from the court when he displeases Guinevere. But even the queen does not break his will. . . . In the end it is a fay who tames Gawaine, with her devoted love. After Gawaine is wedded to duty, Pyle tells the reader, he is one of the most virtuous of knights. Nevertheless, the reader is likely to remember that Guinevere sent him away, and to hold some suspicions that the two are not true friends.

Sir Pellias, on the other hand, foreshadows two knights still to come: Launcelot and Galahad. Pyle calls Pellias "the gentle knight," and has him go questing for Queen Guinevere's sake. He is a noble young man who would hold that the queen's honor is sacred, yet, unlike Launcelot, he would not honor the queen above all womankind, and, unlike Galahad, he would not sacrifice his belief in the powers of the fay in honor of the Christian God. In Pellias, Pyle has established a prototype of the two noblest of knights, and he has given the reader a sense of what it means to be the greatest warrior of chivalry. In this first book, Pellias has fallen in love with a dishonorable maiden who has used magical powers to bewitch him; he is saved by a fay who gives him another magical element, the water of life. Once he receives it, Pellias declares, "Thou hast given life unto me again, now do I give that life unto thee forever". Sir Pellias travels with his companion to the land of Avalon, the self-same land where Arthur will go upon his death. Pellias is a representation of Pyle's own ambivalence concerning the Christian belief in eternity and the Celtic land of death—Avalon. Pyle's story continually brings the best of knights who express the old ideals of chivalry to Avalon. Pellias will be joined by Arthur; Gawaine is married to a fay who chooses to become human for his sake.

The other character who reflects Pyle's modern beliefs is Merlin. In Pyle's version, the magician decides to share his knowledge with Vivien, a decision which Pyle calls a misuse of his God-given powers. Part of this may be Pyle's own philosophy; he had earlier expressed a disinterest in training women artists and sought to separate his creative world into two parts, one in which masculine peers worked side by side as artists, and the other the intellectu-

al ambiance of the afternoon soirée attended by both sexes. Considering that, it is difficult when reading about Merlin's failing to decide whether Pyle objects to Merlin's sharing knowledge with Vivien because she is evil, or because she is female.

Pyle's attitude towards his heroines is always interesting; it is both a backwards look at earlier legends and a modernized Pyle interpretation of woman's role in society. His version of the quest valorizes the female as heroine at home or villain when traipsing about the countryside, the male as the quester in journey or the wise leader while at home, and magic as somehow amoral yet most appealing.

Pyle successfully weaves together the Celtic and the Christian tales, but he does it at the expense of his female characters. He chooses to ignore the fact that Arthur is the bastard younger brother of Morgana, and to separate the Lady of the Lake's powers from Morgana's by making the Lady and her fays' motives ambigious, Morgana's evil. Yet, he has Morgana rule Avalon, and says, "This island of Avalon was a very strange, wonderful land, such as was not to be seen anywhere else in all the world. For it was like a Paradise for beauty. . . . Avalon would float from place to place according to the will of Queen Morgana le Fay, so that sometimes it would be here, and sometimes it would be there, as that royal lady willed it to be". In the end, he has Morgana return for Arthur upon his death and take him away with her to Avalon, implying some kind of sibling tie of loyalty or love. In this first book, however, Pyle calls Morgana cunning, and gives her no real motive for her outbursts of jealousy other than that she wishes to have power over Arthur's kingdom and respect from Arthur. Since the reader has no real knowledge of Morgana's claim to Arthur's throne, she seems petty and mean. . . . What Pyle did was to represent "all that is noble and high and great" and omit "all that is cruel and mean and treacherous" in terms of male supremacy and the Christian masculine code of honor. And so, he depicted Morgana as the dark side of religious beliefs representing black magic, and placed the saving Christian graces in the male hero Galahad.

This interpretation is not new with Pyle, but it was solidified in children's literature by him. Pyle's tradition of a series which depicts an evil queen and a gentle but forceful male ruler is seen again in C. S. Lewis's Narnia series, and is also followed in Alexander's Prydain series. The pattern was not to be broken until women fantasy authors such as Cherry Wilder returned to the Celtic legends as source materials for their fantasy series.

Pyle's interpretations of women are never flattering. Even Guinevere is less than perfect. (pp. 223-26)

The women, then, are more ornamental or meddlesome than they are comforting. The only noble spirits in this first volume are the fay, and they are aloof for the most part.

Pyle's Arthurian cycle is firmly established in the first book. He has created a court for his king, has established the women as troublemakers within the court, and has repeatedly shown the conduct of a worthy knight in battle. His choice of ignoring the Celtic and Welsh ideals of women as leaders and spiritual guides, and of showing Arthur as a hero "as pure as snow," probably stemmed from his background reading. He had read Malory and Scott;

it is not certain that he read the *Mabinogian.* Even if he had, he knew that youngsters were reading Sir Walter Scott and his version of Robin Hood. His intended American audience, with its full blown optimism and its thirst for heroism, would have been more receptive to a manly version of the quest.

What Pyle established for future writers was a chronological adventure story which wove the various legends into a consistent story. Years later, English reading audiences would not only have newer versions in children's fantasy but also could see theatrical representations of the continuous story in *Camelot* and *Excalibur.* Pyle's books have inspired many young boys to play act knightly quests based, whether they knew it or not, upon his ritualistic pattern. Today's youth use these character types when they participate in Dungeons and Dragons.

Pyle's *The Story of King Arthur and His Knights* was greeted with high praise in his own time. It brought together old legends, and created a romantic adventure that captured the hearts of its readers. Full of jousts and courtly activity, it glorifies an aristocracy based on male honor and feminine beauty. Northrop Frye has called the medieval chivalric romance "a ritualized action expressing the ascendancy of a horse-riding aristocracy", one which "expresses that aristocracy's dreams of its own social function, and the idealized acts of protection and responsibility that it invokes to justify that function". Pyle's turn of the century volumes gave his youthful reading audience that tradition. The entire cycle was strongly conservative in its attitudes. It firmly supported the established code of ethics found within American society. Within his Arthurian cycle, Pyle was able to bring alive the old ideas of a code of honor, of the virtues in serving a worthy cause, and the glories of battle. He also sought to show male readers the pitfalls of putting trust in a woman's advice or becoming too infatuated with the woman you serve (unless she happens to be fay). And so, the questing hero was born in children's literature. (pp. 226-27)

As part of a literary tradition continuously being reinterpreted, Pyle's first children's version of Arthur is an essential beginning in our understanding of the Arthurian cycle and its significance in children's literature. (p. 227)

> *Jill P. May, "Howard Pyle's 'The Story of King Arthur and His Knights': A Backwards Look at Chivalry," in* Touchstones: Reflections on the Best in Children's Literature, Vol. 2, *Children's Literature Association, 1987, pp. 221-27.*

John Rowe Townsend

Pyle was his own illustrator, and was undoubtedly a designer of high ability; his books form individual and visually satisfying wholes. But I cannot share American enthusiasm for him as a writer. The reason is partly personal: I find conscious archaism uncongenial, and Pyle's work strikes me in the same way as imitation medieval or Tudor architecture; it does not properly belong either to its own time or to the one it imitates. This perhaps is an unduly puritanical attitude; it can be maintained that artists of all kinds are perfectly entitled to work in styles of the past if their talents so impel them. But there is more to it than that; for, as with pseudo-Tudor buildings, I feel that again and again the details are not quite right. In *The Merry Adventures of Robin Hood* the young Robin, aged eighteen, meets a party of foresters, of whom one accosts him:

> 'Hulloa, where goest thou, little lad, with thy one penny bow and thy farthing shafts?'
>
> Then Robin grew angry, for he was mightily proud of his skill at archery.
>
> 'Now,' quoth he, 'my bow and eke mine arrows are as good as thine; and I'll hold the best of you twenty marks that I hit the clout at three-score rods.'
>
> At this all laughed aloud, whereat Robin grew right mad. 'Hark ye,' said he; 'yonder, at the glade's end, I see a herd of deer, even more than three-score rods distant. I'll hold you twenty marks that I cause the best hart among them to die.'

With the best will in the world I cannot believe in this, or many other passages, as English dialogue of any period. Pyle's Arthurian books I find totally impenetrable. To my mind, his writing is at its best in his fantasy *The Garden Behind the Moon,* a sad and often moving allegory which is strongly reminiscent of George MacDonald. Unfortunately it does not have MacDonald's imaginative force and has not withstood the erosions of time. (pp. 90-2)

The outstanding late-nineteenth-century American figure is Howard Pyle. Illustrating his own books, Pyle took immense pains to integrate text and picture, often with much laborious hand-lettering and with deserved success. One has to admire his industry as illustrator no less than as writer. For me, the trouble with Pyle the artist is content rather than form. His work has been described by such adjectives as hearty, healthy, clean, cheery and honest; but I have to confess myself unconvinced by his depiction of those merry old times which I suspect to have been somewhat less merry, and a good deal less wholesome, than Pyle's drawings would imply. (pp. 129-30)

> *John Rowe Townsend, "The Never-Lands" and "Pictures That Tell a Story," in his* Written for Children: An Outline of English-Language Children's Literature, *third revised edition, J. B. Lippincott, 1987, pp. 84-93, 125-42.*

Allen Say

1937-

Japanese-born American author and illustrator of picture books and fiction and reteller.

Recognized for creating works which are notable for providing preschoolers, primary graders, and young adults with substantial messages in a gentle manner, Say focuses on such themes as the relationships between people or between people and nature in works which characteristically include Oriental characters and settings. Several of his books are autobiographical or semi-autobiographical in nature. For example, in his young adult novel *The Inn-Keeper's Apprentice* (1979), Say parallels his own life with the maturation of the student assistant of a famous Tokyo cartoonist in post-World War II Japan. Frankly describing the variety of experiences Kiyoi encounters in his thirteenth to fifteenth years which lead him to self-reliance, Say also shows the effects of the Western influence on Japan and its older Eastern traditions. Another well-received autobiographical work is *The Bicycle Man* (1982), a picture book based on an incident from Say's childhood. The story describes how a classroom of Japanese schoolchildren encounter American soldiers for the first time at a spring sports day in 1946; when one of the soldiers borrows the principal's bicycle and puts on a show, he wins the largest prize.

Among Say's most consistent themes are those relating to the preservation of nature and the relationships between boys and their male relatives. In the picture book *A River Dream* (1988), which describes the fishing trip young Mark imagines he shares with his uncle after receiving a box for trout flies from him, Say depicts the warmth shared by the boy and his uncle while underscoring his work with a powerful environmental message. In *The Lost Lake* (1989), a story for primary graders, Say portrays how a father and son try to find a special place from the man's youth and, in the process, find their own special place as well as a deeper understanding of each other. His other works include a retelling of a Japanese folktale about how greed is punished, a picture book which humorously offers a plea for nonviolence, and a story for young readers about the adventures of two brothers who leave their tiny Japanese fishing island for the wonders of the mainland. Considered a gifted illustrator who is often credited for his evocative renderings of the natural world, Say most often uses watercolors and pen-and-ink drawings to accompany his texts. He has also provided pictures for the works of other authors, with Dianne Snyder's *The Boy of the Three-Year Nap* and Ina R. Friedman's *How My Parents Learned to Eat* being especially well known titles.

(See also *Something about the Author,* Vol. 28 and *Contemporary Authors,* Vols. 29-32, rev. ed.)

Dr. Smith's Safari (1972)

Jaunty Dr. Smith's safari begins with sunny promise in a luxurance of fauna and foliage that recalls a spruced-up

Ungerer, but the outing ends with the sportsman destroying his gun in remorse after dining with a happy assortment of jungle animals and shooting at an unseen disturbance that turns out to be some odd little men throwing coconuts. The message is obvious but the delicately cross-hatched black-and-white pictures aren't. Though there are shades of the *Wild Things* in the jungle scenes and perhaps a distant relationship between Dr. Smith and Lobel's *Mister Muster,* Say's slyly amusing animals, flowered fields, and candlelit interiors have their own hospitable appeal.

A review of "Dr. Smith's Safari," in Kirkus Reviews, *Vol. XL, No. 5, March 1, 1972, p. 256.*

Allen Say's black-and-white illustrations humorously depict expressive jungle animals but, despite the plea for peace, the story is weakly constructed and the abrupt ending disappointingly flat.

Judith Kronick, in a review of "Dr. Smith's Safari," in School Library Journal, *Vol. 19, No. 1, September, 1972, p. 71.*

Once Under the Cherry Blossom Tree: An Old Japanese Tale (1974)

This classic Japanese joke tale concerns a mean, miserly landlord who swallows a cherry pit and sprouts a tree on top of his head. When he pulls it up, a hole that fills with water and then fish remains. While chasing children who're fishing in his cranial cavity, his body does a back flip into the hole and disappears, leaving in its place a lovely pond. Say's pen-and-ink sketches, which appear on right-hand pages, effectively develop the story's humor and also contain interesting details of traditional Japanese life. Attractive format, large print, and simple style make this suitable for second and third grade independent readers.

> Mary B. Mason "Once Under the Cherry Tree: An Old Japanese Tale," in School Library Journal, Vol. 20, No. 9, May, 1974, p. 51.

Allen Say handles his ancient Japanese "joke tale" with delicacy. In *Once Under the Cherry Blossom Tree* a miserly landlord swallows only a cherry pit, but wakes up next morning with a tree growing out of his head. Say illustrates the story with fine line drawings that make the absurdities precisely imaginable and the Japanese setting palpable, while reinforcing the mood of straight-faced lunacy.

> Sada Fretz, "Once Upon a Picture," in Book World—The Washington Post, May 19, 1974, p. 4.

The illustrations are lovely, appropriate in mood and fine in detail; the style of the adaptation is simple but lacks the cadence of the oral tradition; the story seems to indicate that selfishness and greed are punished, but the message is less effective than it would be if there were some contact between the old man and the villagers—save for the fishing incident, the relationship is described rather than demonstrated. (p. 164)

> Zena Sutherland, in a review of "Once Under the Cherry Tree: An Old Japanese Tale," in Bulletin of the Center for Children's Books, Vol. 27, No. 10, June, 1974, pp. 163-64.

The Feast of Lanterns (1976)

In a small, unorchestrated story that reads a bit like a memory, Bozu and Kozo leave their tiny fishing island of Kamome Jima to visit the mainland, which they call "the better place." Snitching Uncle Tojo's boat on the first day of the Feast of the Lanterns, they drift across to a cove and—alternately frightened, astonished, and very hungry, frequently scolded for smelling like fish and having no money—they roam the market, follow a troupe of clowns with a monkey onto a train, watch a fireworks display that turns into a town fire, and huddle for the night in a roadside shrine where a policeman finds them and takes them to their father. Say turns out to be less adept at realistic narrative and conversation than at the tall/folk tale, but somehow the very lack of polish to the prose adds to the credibility here. And even if children don't know where Kamome Jima is, they'll appreciate the chance to share the exploration of a different (if not better) place without being subjected to a geography lesson—or any other kind.

> A review of "The Feast of Lanterns," in Kirkus Reviews, Vol. XLIV, No. 19, October 1, 1976, p. 1095.

Flashes of affection push through the telling: the author is indulgent with his protagonists, which suggests autobiographical roots of some sort. This personal aspect vitalizes what is otherwise an unremarkable story. Observers who remember Say's graceful, articulate lines for *Once Under the Cherry Blossom Tree: An Old Japanese Tale, Retold* will be disappointed by the comparatively crude pen cartoons that provide illustration. (p. 612)

> Denise M. Wilson, in a review of "The Feast of Lanterns," in Booklist, Vol. 73, No. 8, December 15, 1976, pp. 611-12.

Many appealing full-page black-and-white drawings enhance the ordinary plot line. The people are all pictured wearing kimonos because it is a holiday, but this is not explained and thus will tend to perpetuate the notion in young children that Japanese always dress that way. It is also unfortunate that the author does not specify Japan as the locale, since some children might be confused by the setting and customs which are the unique features of the story.

> Cynthia T. Seybolt, in a review of "The Feast of Lanterns," in School Library Journal, Vol. 23, No. 5, January, 1977, p. 85.

The Inn-Keeper's Apprentice (1979)

Kiyoi is thrilled when the "great master," a famous cartoonist, takes him on as a student-assistant, and from that moment his life becomes rich and exciting. There are heady discussions, festive celebrations, and above all the honor of filling in the backgrounds for the master's published cartoons. There are life drawing classes, where the new student has trouble getting used to the nude models, and horizon-expanding outings—a Van Gogh show, a demonstration that turns into a riot—with his fellow apprentice, a somewhat older youth who seems disturbingly attracted to violence. There is also the pleasure of living alone in one shabby room, and the terror of discovering, when a neighbor there takes him out on the town, that the aggressive bar girls in the sinister, dim cafe are men. Say's autobiographical novel would be vibrant and affecting even if Kiyoi's were a typical art student's existence. As it is, two unusual circumstances heighten the interest: it occurs in post-World War II Japan, which gives the experience a special texture (bean cakes and kimonos and samurai tradition coexists with the Van Gogh show, Degas reproductions, and Hesse's novels); and, though it's hard to believe his grandmother's allowing him to live alone, Kiyou is only 13 when he begins his apprenticeship, 15 when he leaves to accompany his remarried father to America. A sparkling, touch-true portrait of a young person coming into his own.

> A review of "The Inn-Keeper's Apprentice," in Kirkus Reviews, Vol. XLVII, No. 5, March 1, 1979, p. 267.

Say relies on episodic development rather than plot to carry his autobiographical-sounding story along. Selected incidents perceptively illuminate personality nuances of

From A River Dream, *written and illustrated by Allen Say.*

Shinpei, Tokida, and several other peripheral characters, and Kiyoi's own mental turning points evolve smoothly. Post-World War II Tokyo is the setting, and Kiyoi is living on his own even while attending school. Such circumstances generate a rich mix of experience—some funny, some warm, some frightening and sobering—such as when a neighbor takes him to a transvestite bar. But Kiyoi's own emergent self is always centered, humane, and never out of sight of his art. He's a pleasure to watch.

> *Denise M. Wilms, a review of "The Inn-Keeper's Apprentice," in* Booklist, *Vol. 75, No. 18, May 15, 1979, p. 1443.*

A kind of cultural adjustment is required in reading the first-person account of a young Japanese teenager who lived alone in Tokyo. . . . Written in a frank but nonsensational style, the narrative juxtaposes the American and Western influences on modern Japanese living with the persisting ancient ways: Kiyoi was as familiar with Michelangelo's *David* and Van Gogh's paintings as he was with comic strips, and he referred to his growing awareness of sex and love without prurience. The dialogue is lively, the characters are sharply drawn, and the episodes of the loose, realistic narrative are significant events in the maturing of a self-reliant Japanese adolescent.

> *Paul Heins, in a review of "The Inn-Keeper's Apprentice," in* The Horn Book Magazine, *Vol. LV, No. 3, June, 1979, p. 312.*

The Bicycle Man (1982)

A delightful story, reportedly a memory from Say's childhood, of the children's first encounter with American soldiers at a 1946 spring sports day in a Japanese elementary school. Say shows us charming little figures, with just a whiff of resemblance to early Sendak tykes, rushing about in streaming red headbands: preparing the playground, then dashing around the track in the first-grader's race, and later racing piggy-back and pulling in the tug-of-war. Boxed prizes are awarded, and then we see the families picnicking on their mats, unloading spiced rice and fish cakes and other "good things to eat" from their layered lacquer boxes. It is during the grownups' three-legged race that the soldiers appear—one of them "with bright hair like fire," the other "black as the earth" and "the tallest man I had ever seen. And his clothes! Such sharp creases! And his shoes shone like polished metal!" Borrowing the principal's bicycle, the black American then puts on a show that leaves the crowd agape—from the first wheelie ("What an athlete!" exclaims the art teacher) to the flying finale. When the cheering stops, the principal leads the soldier to the platform and presents him with the largest box from the prize table. Handing it over, "He looked like the emperor awarding a great champion." And so, with an "Ari-ga-tow, ari-ga-tow" (thank you, thank you), the two soldiers go off down the mountain, "waving and laughing." Say makes no comments and none are needed. Savor it, share it, and let the Japanese traditions and the wonderful meetings speak for themselves.

> *A review of "The Bicycle Man," in* Kirkus Reviews, *Vol. L, No. 14, July 15, 1982, p. 796.*

The opening words transform a memory into a tale. "When I was a small boy I went to a school in the south island of Japan. The schoolhouse stood halfway up a tall green mountain. . . . When a strong wind blew, the trees made the sound of waves and the building creaked like an old sailing ship. From the playground we could see the town, the ships in the harbor, the shining sea."

As the Japanese author continues, his tone becomes somewhat more matter of fact. . . .

Although a demanding editor might have helped heighten the mood of the ending and smooth a few awkward phrases (" 'Oh, look!' we stirred."), Mr. Say, like the bicycle rider, is a master of his art. With a pen line as unerring as his eye, he details a schoolyard alive with wonderfully individual children and adults. Animated crowds are arranged in busy, charming groups. Backgrounds fade into distant landscapes colored as delicately as Japanese wood-cuts. Throughout, sweetness, humor and skill shine from the handsome pages.

> *Karla Kuskin, in a review of "The Bicycle Man," in* The New York Times Book Review, *October 24, 1982, p. 41.*

Allen Say returns with another memory of growing up in southern Japan. In this picture book, children competing in Sportsday activities are captivated by an American soldier's feats on a bicycle. The faces of the children—their determination in running the race, the joy as they watch the soldier perform and the joy of performing shown by the soldier is international. The mood of the writing and of the masterfully-drawn pen-and-ink with wash illustrations is simple and subtle; Say captures the time perfectly. Once again through a well-balanced and forceful but quiet tale, Allen Say teaches us what only those who have lived in two cultures can and must tell. It is not the differences between cultures that is so evident but their similarities.

> *W. A. Hardley, in a review of "The Bicycle Man," in* School Library Journal, *Vol. 29, No. 5, January, 1983, p. 66.*

A River Dream   (1988)

Mark has a high fever so Uncle Scott sends him a gift—a small metal box for trout flies. The container brings back memories of Mark's first fishing trip with his uncle when Mark hooked a huge rainbow trout that got away. A second chance to nab a fish appears when he opens the box and sets in motion a wonderful dream in which he and his uncle are once more fishing. Uncle Scott catches a fish straightaway, but to Mark's surprise, lets it go, telling the boy that he likes to leave the river the way he finds it. After Mark catches his fish, he too must decide whether the fun of fishing must go hand in hand with death. Say's message about the sanctity of life is well stated, but the details of the fishing expedition, especially the one set in a dream, may appeal most to readers who already love fishing. However, it is in those dreamy aspects of the story that the lovely, meticulous illustrations with their pure, clear colors work the best, carrying out the mood fully. A softly wrought story with significant content.

> *Ilene Cooper, in a review of "A River Dream," in* Booklist, *Vol. 85, No. 1, September 1, 1988, p. 84.*

The quiet text here is pleasant enough, but unexceptional; the message that "it's good to leave the river the way [you find] it" is flawed: the joy of the catch is well known, but it is surely cruel to the fish to hook it merely for sport. Nonetheless, Say's watercolor illustrations are outstanding: spare interiors rendered into elegant patterns by light shining through windows, the play of late afternoon shadow on trees bordering the river, mayflies dancing like stars, the warm link between the boy and his uncle (orientals, incidentally), the drama of the catch. Reason enough for purchase; and the story may prompt thought among would-be fisher-people.

> *A review of "A River Dream," in* Kirkus Reviews, *Vol. LVI, No. 19, October 1, 1988, p. 1475.*

Rainbow trout, rejoice, **A River Dream,** joins *Nathan's Fishing Trip* (Scholastic, 1988) in the genre of anti-killing-fish picture books. . . . The spacious, quiet, and peaceful full-page watercolors create a dream-like mood, with shimmering, watery reflections. The affectionate relationship between Mark and his pipe-smoking uncle is deftly portrayed. The book may contribute to some intense discussions about why people eat animals. (pp. 101-02)

> *Leda Schubert, in a review of "A River Dream," in* School Library Journal, *Vol. 35, No. 4, December, 1988, pp. 101-02.*

The Lost Lake   (1989)

The narrator Luke, a boy about 10, has come to live with his father, but Dad is busy, and there's not much communication between the two. When the boy starts cutting out pictures of mountains and people fishing, his father gets the message that his son would enjoy a camping trip. And Dad would like it, too. He is eager to re-create moments he shared with his own father at Lost Lake. However, when Luke and his father arrive, they quickly see that Lost Lake has been found by other campers; so they journey farther into the wild to find their own special place. Luke wearies as they go deeper into the woods, but once the duo discovers that elusive spot, he realizes that the harder road can be the most satisfying. Say deftly blends this message with several others: that relationships need work to flower and that the sanctity of the wilderness must be preserved. Obviously, it will take an older child to understand the story's subtleties, but younger children will respond to the pleasing artwork. Using colors as crisp and clean as the outdoors, Say effectively alternates between scenes where father and son are the focus and those where the landscape predominates. Both in story and art, a substantial piece.

> *Ilene Cooper, in a review of "The Lost Lake," in* Booklist, *Vol. 86, No. 3, October 1, 1989, p. 355.*

This is an absorbing story which takes readers on two journeys. The obvious trek is into the wilderness, but there is a parallel route which follows the boy and his father as they develop a deeper understanding of one another. The illustrations are meticulous, clean, and have an air of serenity. In the early scenes, readers sense the loneliness and isolation of the father's apartment, while the challenge, the mystery, and the wonder of being off the beaten track are captured in evocative woodland landscapes. The pictures of Luke and his father display a tenderness and warmth altogether different from the landscapes. In each, Say reveals his considerable talent which quietly and effectively draws readers into each of the scenes depicted. A wholly satisfying story.

> *Phyllis G. Sidorsky, in a review of "The Lost Lake," in* School Library Journal, *Vol. 35, No. 6, December, 1989, p. 88.*

This touching drama resonates with respect for the characters, who are struggling to forge new ways of being together in a difficult world of splintered families and visitation rights. But it is Say's watercolor paintings, embracing the many moods of the natural world—from the misty gray of rain and fog and the green of the deepest part of the forest to the blazing gold of an early morning sunrise—that really command attention. Readers will feel that they have been on their own journey of discovery.

> *Ellen Fader, in a review of "The Lost Lake,"*
> *in* The Horn Book Magazine, *Vol. LXVI, No.*
> *1, January-February, 1990, p. 56.*

Annie M. G. Schmidt

1911-

Dutch poet, author of fiction and picture books, and scriptwriter.

Called "the queen of Dutch children's and juvenile literature" by critic Toin Dujix, Schmidt is considered the premier children's writer of the Netherlands. The first Dutch author to win the Hans Christian Andersen Medal, she is a prolific and popular writer who has been addressing books to the preschool through high school audience for over forty years. Although she has published many books internationally, only a handful of her works have been published in English-language editions. Schmidt contributes to a variety of genres: she has written realistic and historical fiction, fantasy, musicals, and scripts for both radio and television. Many of these works, some of which are written for adults, are considered classics in the Netherlands, where she is a household name. However, she is perhaps best known for her poetry, light verse which characteristically contrasts the imaginative world of childhood with the logical, conservative world of adults. Credited as pivotal in the development of Dutch children's poetry, Schmidt's verse centers on both everyday life and fantastic subjects. Many of her poems, which are characterized by their lyricism, humor, liveliness, and happy endings, focus on the resistance of children to the regulations imposed on them by adults and the eventual triumph of youthful imagination and hope. Although twelve volumes of her poetry have never been out of print, the only book of Schmidt's verse to have appeared in English thus far is *Pink Lemonade: Poems for Children* (1981).

As with her poetry, Schmidt's fiction often blends reality and fantasy. Among her most popular works are *Abeltje* (1953; translation as *Little Abel*) and its sequel *De A van Abeltje* (1955; translation as *Abel's A*), the adventures of a stockboy who has humourous and suspenseful encounters with the fantastic. The award-winning *Wiplala* (1962) again contrasts familiar environments with imaginative occurences as it describes how the historian Mr. Blom and his two young friends deal with the world around them after they are made small by the tiny magician Wiplala. Schmidt is also well known for her realistic fiction, especially for the series of books about Jip and Janneke, known in English both as Mick and Mandy and Bob and Jilly. Short episodes about how the two five-year-old neighbors make friends, quarrel, slide down bannisters, find birds' nests, and have other adventures, the works were criticized in the 1970s for being antiquated and overly optimistic; however, they are most often acknowledged as charming and accurate observations of early childhood. Schmidt is also the creator of several works about Dusty, a small Dutch tomboy, and her puppy Smudge, who turn such premises as going to a wedding and getting a haircut into amusing situations. In 1964, Schmidt became the first author to receive the Staatsprijs voor kinder- en jeugdliteratuur, the Dutch State Prize for children's and juvenile literature. She won the Constantijin Huygens Award, the highest literary distinction in the Netherlands, in 1987, the

first time that this award was given to a writer known mainly for her children's literature. In 1988, Schmidt received the Hans Christian Andersen Medal for writing, an award for which she was a runner-up in 1968 for *Wiplala*. She has also received several other European awards for her works.

AUTHOR'S COMMENTARY

[The following excerpt is taken from a speech which was originally delivered in 1970.]

Having been a librarian in a children's reading-room myself, and being a writer now, I know that these two jobs have a lot in common, to the extent of being basically the same.

To me the essence of working in a library for young people was being able to say: "Dinner is ready, come in, there is a lot to eat, there are delicious things. Sausages and cheese, but also crisps and sweets. Try this and try that. You only want ice-cream? That's alright. There is white ice-cream and there is pink ice-cream. White is really better, there is real cream in it, but pink looks nicer. Just try them and you will find that the white ice-cream tastes better than the pink." That was what I felt to be the essence. It was the feeling: Share my food. Come and look at everything that's here.

Writing for children is essentially the same thing. Why does a person take up writing for children? I am talking about the *real* writers now, not about the false ones. The false ones think: "Well, writing for children is not difficult . . . let's see . . . children like adventure and suspense, I'll make something up." Other false writers think: "You must teach children something, morals, ethics and culture; I will place myself on this platform and from this height I will give them something to help them along their path of life."

The real writer does not go in for all this. He only does what the librarian does: Share my food, share my imagination . . . share my truth, come with me, I'll show you a great many things that have made a great impression on me, share my experience.

Share my imagination, share my truth. And by truth I don't mean reality, for *that* is something quite different. An absurd fairy-tale can contain more truth than a documentary.

In fact, fairy-tales have always contained more truth than everyday reality. By truth I don't mean *the* truth either, but the writer's own truth. When I have written a story, I read through it again to see whether it is *true.* Even when it is about a troll or a unicorn. For truth does not lie in the probability or the practical possibility, but there is an inner truth that has nothing to do with reality. It has to do with intuition, with inner logic, with a wholeness emanating from the creative process: making something that is a whole, a round totality. Writing is not only an act, it is also a process. There is an embryo that has to grow in warmth, like a babe unborn. But it is not simply a matter of sitting comfortably, waiting for the child to be born. You have to work at it, you have to shape the features of the face yourself, with your skills, with your judgment, with your technique.

What the writer wants is to share his world with the child. His world? The world of a grown-up? No, his child's world. The real writer of children's books has, in a way, remained a child. He still has his wings. He has never lost them. We know that little children can draw beautifully and make astonishing works of art. When they go to primary school two years later, they lose this artistic gift. They start copying, they become rationalistic, they adapt themselves to the reality of the grown-ups; they have lost something, their spontaneity, their intuition, their unconventional way of communication.

The artist, every artist is somebody who has not lost that faculty. The writer of children's books has also retained the child's way of looking at things; he can laugh at things children laugh at, cry about things children cry about and feel their suspense. All this he wants to share with them. That's why he sits down to write his story or his book. Not to make money, not to instruct or to moralize, not even to amuse. No, just to share.

You see that both jobs have this factor in common. But we have more in common than this. This for example: How can you make the good white ice-cream attractive when there is so much glaringly pink ice-cream around.

Pink ice-cream that looks more attractive at first sight, which makes children reach out for it first. You can't say: "Be careful, don't eat pink ice-cream, it's poisoned"— because it's not true. It is not poisoned. All you can say is: That pink ice-cream was made in the factory with a lot of chemicals and fake strawberries; mine is home-made, it tastes better.

And again, translated into the language of creativity: *That* book was made, it is a product. *This* book looks less attractive, it is also a bit more difficult; but it is better, for it was not made, it originated, it was born, it was created.

This problem has always existed as long as children's books have been written. But at present the problem is becoming more and more urgent, mainly because of the permissiveness of our society. That we live in a permissive society no one will deny. But the interesting thing is that the permissiveness comes from three sides, is three-fold.

One, from the commercial side. Children are consumers, there is a demand. The commerical dealers shout: Let those children read anything they want. Let them eat as much pink ice-cream as they want. Go ahead, let them consume. Second: The educational-psychological trend of the post-war years: Don't frustrate the children, don't thrust anything upon them, let them be free to choose. Don't force anything, it may be bad for their little souls. And third: the new anti-authority trend. The anti-paternalizing groups fighting for the alternatives in society. They go even further and should like to have the children not only choose, but also decide what's good for them.

How can we stand up against such odds? The only result is that we no longer even dare to say that white ice-cream may be better than pink ice-cream. And if we still dare to say it, we suddenly feel very old.

Language is a writer's instrument. The true writer works with simple language. No on purpose, but intuitively. He avoids abstractions, he remains concrete as much as possible, *and* he tries to handle his language in such a way that it comes across; he tries to make sentences that penetrate, that create a direct image. Directness and simplicity are characteristic of the true artist, not only in literature. The artist has already done this in the Cro-magnon caves by direct, intuitive communication of the message. But in the world we live in now the secret of the use of direct language has been discovered and adopted by the commercials, and has been cleverly imitated by them. (pp. 3-5)

A friend of mine, a composer of children's songs, told me that he was desperate because every time he invented a melody, he heard it as a tune for a commercial the next day. He complains that they have stolen all his tunes. Writers are in exactly the same position as concerns creative language. A writer knows: I have invented a story. This is my child, it has been conceived, it has grown inside me. Shaping its face is what I have to do next. In order to do this I must use language that is simple and gripping, communicative and penetrating. But it frightens him when he discovers that all simple language has been used up. All the magical language has become cliché. All the magical sentences have already been used . . . to make pink ice-cream. The commercial artist has acquired the know-how, he has learned the trick, not only on T. V., but in the headlines of papers, the magazines, the booklets, the slogans, the hundreds of messages that are poured out to stimulate consumption. And children are indifferent consumers, they gulp them down. They know what is a commercial and what is not. Just as they know the difference between a fairy-tale and reality. *That* is not the problem. They know the difference all right, but they don't *make* any difference, it *makes* no difference to them. They lap it all up. And they lose the faculty to distinguish between what is intrinsically true and what is intrinsically false. In my view this is one of the dangers threatening literature, for the children will grow up and they still won't know the difference between the truth and the fake.

We, you and I, we recognize the difference, because we have been trained to do so. We know that commercials only offer images, without a concept, and without any idea. The commercial images are completely empty, they are empty shells. . . . Most artists in the grown-up world have concluded: No more shells! That is why art has gone abstract. No pictures in painting, no melody in music, no story or anecdote in literature. In literature there is even a trend to break up the language itself. But when you write for children you can't break with conventions and traditions, with agreements. Children are conventional, they are conformists. An author who works for children has to bear his audience in mind, just like a playwright.

The next problem runs parallel with the former one:

All children like stories. What they like is the story in the first place. They don't read a book because of the characters, or because of the description of the scenery or because of the philosophical concepts or the beautiful psychological ideas. No, it's the story they want in the first place. And the story must have suspense. A story without suspense is not story. By suspense I don't just mean wild adventures—the threat from outside; it may be another kind of suspense, from the inside, a struggle against one's own weakness, one's own fear, one's own aggression. But there must always be some amount of suspense, however small or modest, something of danger and escape, something of battle and victory. This is a general human emotional need, and you simply can't ignore this when you are dealing with children. A good writer knows by intuition where to put the tension and where the relief. He uses danger and escape, tension and relief, as a skeleton, as a plot. But in the world of today exactly the same thing happens as stated in my former problem: The commercials have taken all the plots.

By commercials I don't mean only the advertising slogans, but the hundreds of plots you see on your screen, plus the hundreds and thousands of comic strips you can buy in the supermarket and in the bookshops. The T. V. serials, the western, thrillers, adventure stories, children are glutted with them, overwhelmed by them, stuffed up, sometimes three a night. As far as I know nobody has ever seriously studied the effects of all this tension and relief. What effect does all this have on children, on people, in the long run? Apart from the violence they get used to, just the effect of so much suspense and escape, three times a day, five times a day, it's like having too many coitions in one night, too many climaxes, one after the other.

Can they stand it? Oh, yes, they can. One right after the other, on and on. But they have become greedier and more impatient. An instalment of a T. V. serial must at present contain twice as much emotional material as ten years ago. I know this from experience. That doesn't mean that script and dialogue should be twice as long, forty minutes remain forty minutes; but the emotional material must be doubled, twice as many events. Less dialogue, more action, a quicker shift from one scene to the other, more and quicker! Everybody feels this when he sees a film from the 'fifties. People say: It's too slow, why don't they hurry up.

Such a vast number of plots is needed for all these T. V. stories that they have now become practically exhausted. It's impossible to invent a story that hasn't been used one way or another in a serial.

Not only the threat from outside has been used by the makers of television serials, but *also* the inner tension, the inner threats and problems. The questions of morals, ethics and conscience have all been dealt with and used and re-used, and now they lie around us, discarded, soiled and overworked, the refuse of "throw-away" art.

I know that for a writer neither the language nor the story is the most important thing. Most important are the warmth, the characters, life itself, the humour, the personality, the irreplaceable individuality. *That* is what matters. But he needs the story, he needs the thread, the skeleton. And all the threads, all the skeletons, all the plots have become dirty, used rags. He would rather not use them at all, but he has to, for he must take his audience into account. Children want a story and they do need their tension and relief, in whatever form. What is he to do?

It is impossible to invent an original plot. He knows that all he can do is give a variant of an existing plot. He knows that a thousand variants have been made for every existing plot. Some westerns are already made by computers, that means that before long millions of variants of existing plot-material can be made and will be made.

All a writer can do is sigh and say: Come on, I'll pick one, it doesn't matter which. I'll fill it up with my humour, my fantasy, my humanity, my vision. But it is not inspiring and it is not easy. It's least hard on the very young writers and the very old ones. The very young writers still think that what they invent is completely new and original. The very old ones act as if television didn't exist, they ignore it, never watch it, despise it and say: we don't have anything to do with it. Both groups fool themselves. Television *does* exist and it offers today's children a very easy way of experiencing emotions, at an ever-increasing pace.

The 12 to 14 year-olds have always been a great worry to everyone having anything to do with juvenile literature. There are no books for them, too few at any rate, too few good books. It has always been like that as long as I can remember. It seems to be a very difficult age in this respect.

"Children of that age have left the children's world behind them and take their first hesitant steps in society." When I read that, I thought: Thirty or forty years ago there *was* no society. Well, it was there, but you didn't have to enter it. Not when you were twelve and not when you were older. Society was an abstraction for sociologists, journalists and economists to bother about, but for ordinary people society did not exist. There was a world with people and animals and children. You had your own church. And you had your own country; you were only confronted with it on the queen's birthday and when war threatened, but there was not a society that stayed with you night and day. And there is now. That society doesn't belong to one country, it is not national, but international. Western Society. Not an abstraction any longer, food for sociologists and economists, but a daily reality as well.

And it is a fact that when children are ten or twelve they become members of the club and they are confronted, not with an idea, but with reality. . . . This world, the world of the adults in society, that concerns everybody, physically and directly, in which these children must take their first steps when they are twelve, is incredibly complicated, incredibly involved. In the past, in the pre-technological era, it was possible to translate the grown-ups' world for children. You could say: John's father is a baker, he bakes bread for people. That was simple. But John's father is not a baker anymore. He works for an advertising agency and invents slogans like: "Queen's bread. Keeps fresh longer", or he works at an office in a big building, and in order to explain exactly what John's father does and why, it would take a whole chapter. Authors of children's books notice this to their profound dismay. As soon as they want the children to experience their characters within society, they don't get anywhere. Far too complicated.

Family relations, school adventures, vacation stories, all right.

But those writers who want to handle the problems of our time are faced with great difficulties. They find their way obstructed by a complexity which is impossible to translate into simple language. More serious however for most of us is the ambivalent attitude we have towards today's society.

Juvenile literature must be positive. That is something everyone agrees upon, although the one may mean something else by positive than the other. But nobody will say: Now I'll write a really negative book for children. In general, being positive boils down to conforming. Conforming to the existing norms. Have your conflicts, we say—be they inner or outer—but conform to the ethical and social norms we have set up for you during all those centuries of our Christian-humanistic-thinking-world. They are good and they will be valid for ever.

And so we offer our children positive books until they are fourteen or fifteen. The message of these books is clear: In essence, man is good. All you have to do is follow your conscience and be nice to your fellow-people.

Then suddenly, when they are fifteen or sixteen, they are confronted with grown-up literature (*if* they are lucky enough to be confronted by literature at all).

What happens is this: A child that has been brought up with "Man is good" enters the world of Norman Mailer, Jean Paul Sartre, Samuel Becket, Arabal, or—in Holland—Jan Wolkers, van het Reve.

This is absurd.

It is like holding your children by the hand, blindfold, while you keep telling them: We are in a beautiful park with wonderful trees and ponds and flowers, everything is lovely. Suddenly you rip the bandage off their eyes and they are in a slaughterhouse, they see blood and revolting things and you cry: "Ha ha, I fooled you."

A lot of people say: You just can't tell children that they live in a slaughterhouse, you can't confront them with the horribleness of life in all its reality. They would lose their faith. They need some kind of protection. Other people say: This modern literature is corrupt and false; we prefer the nice old-fashioned novels about nice gentlemen and ladies. But we have to face the fact that modern world-literature absolutely lacks this positive element we would like to give to our children. Adult literature is negative in this sense that the authors say: Man is not good, he is bad and society now is rotten to the core.

Perhaps what they say is not *the* truth, but it is *their* truth, the authors'. We, the adults, may essentially agree with the message of modern literature, but we don't know how to pass it on to our children, or whether we should pass it on at all.

It is part of the nature of parent-child relations to say: Act like us. We'll teach you what to do. Just imitate us. What we are really saying is: Look, this is our world, our society, conform to that society. Be good. Be obedient, obey authority incorporated in the law, in the current norms, in the conventional opinion. Be nice.

In practice this facile "Be nice" boils down to "Be indifferent to all misery in the world, just as indifferent as we are. Look at the famine on television and don't do anything but give a shilling out of your piggy bank. Look at war and riots on T. V. and say just like we do, Why can't those people behave?"

"Be obedient" means in practice that you *may* become an Eichmann, who was *very* obedient. (pp. 5-10)

We know now that obedience may lead to Eichmann or My Lai. It need not, of course. But it *may*.

We know now that conforming to society may lead to the production and the use of nerve gas.

We, the adults, we know these *"mays"*. They frighten us. We don't dare passing them on to our young folks. *That* is why this gap exists between the positiveness of juvenile literature and the amorality of grown-up literature. This gap is part of the whole generation gap. There's the rub.

We see before our eyes all those young people who get stuck in subculture *or* become radicals *or* become well-adapted men working for a large company. Who dares answer the question whether those well-adapted people form the best part of our society? I don't.

What I would like to suggest is change the ethical starting point. Not the facile "Be good" or "Be obedient", but "Be critical. Learn to think for yourself. Learn to ask yourself: What am I *really* doing? Does it tally with what my parents taught me?"

At this critical junction nothing is more important than realizing what you are really doing and wanting. And why.

So, both writers and librarians should say to our young people not only: Share my experience. But: *Share my doubt!*

It needs courage. (p. 10)

Annie M. G. Schmidt, "Some Questions Fac-

ing the Author," in Bookbird, *Vol. IX, No. 3, September 15, 1971, pp. 3-10.*

GENERAL COMMENTARY

Henrietta Ten Harmsel

Windmills, tulips, canals, Rembrandt, Vermeer, Van Gogh: these are the words and names, all nonliterary, which many foreigners associate with Holland. For Dutchmen themselves there is another name that has become a household word: Annie M. G. Schmidt. Hollanders of all ages read, memorize, and sing the poems of this prolific and versatile prize-winning writer. Her twelve volumes of children's poetry are never out of print and continue—with her children's stories, other light verse, and recent long-running musicals—to captivate large audiences. Although Annie Schmidt has already been translated into German, French, Japanese, Swedish, Danish, and Finnish, her poems have only recently appeared in English (my own translations, in **Pink Lemonade**). (p. 135)

Although she wrote for her own amusement even as a child, Annie Schmidt's schooling, in the old, classical tradition, did very little to encourage her imaginative talents. Her love for books led her naturally to prepare for a library career, which gave her opportunities to work in various Dutch libraries, finally, for more than a decade, in the children's room of a library in Amsterdam. Since Dutch children's literature had been dominated by a highly didactic, moralistic tone, she was urged to use such literature—or at least highly "literary" materials—to edify the children who came to hear her read or tell stories on Wednesday afternoons. From this period Annie Schmidt reports an amusing incident which she says was much more instructive for her than for her young listeners.

One day when she was attempting to inspire them by reading something very "uplifting," they staged a noisy rebellion, demanded the return of the two cents apiece they had paid, and finally had to be dismissed by the concierge. When Annie Schmidt left the library that day, several children again accosted her for their two cents, for money was precious to them in that depression era. "They taught me a lesson I never forgot," she says. "After that I began to read and tell only stories and poems which would genuinely appeal to children, even including some of my own things, which I had then never considered publishing." Again Annie Schmidt's imaginative world was being formed: a genuine children's world containing no condescension but allowing plenty of room for stimulation, fantasy, and challenge. She learned that "something must happen" even in poems, which for her always contain narrative and dramatic as well as rhythmic and lyrical elements. She believes that any "edification" which occurs must be so subtle that it seems only to amuse and so natural that the poem could not exist without it. (pp. 135-36)

Extremely critical of her own writing and diffident about publishing it, Annie Schmidt was finally encouraged by friends to publish—first in newspapers and journals and later in the books of poetry that soon became best sellers. Her public career began late but led speedily from one success to another: many volumes of children's poems; children's stories; a radio series ("The Family Cross-Section"), which kept most Hollanders at home on the

nights it was broadcast; a popular television series; various outstanding prizes (including the first Dutch national award for children's literature and an Austrian national award); and, in recent years, several musicals that ran for two years in Amsterdam, and later all over Holland. Still Annie Schmidt agrees with the writer of this article that it is her writing for children, still constantly in progress, which will probably be her longest-lasting contribution. A few illustrations from the poems themselves may best show whether this is true.

Like all good children's poetry, Annie Schmidt's poems are full of fantasy. The Andersen influence is strong but appears in a uniquely Schmidtian form that always transcends mere imitation. In an elemental princess-in-a-tower poem, she presents the heroine as "the girl with nylon hair," who is rescued from her tower prison by a young fisherman only after her own tears cause the surrounding waters to ascend:

> Because so many big tears fell there,
> Up rose the water of Saint Koedelare.
> Up rose the boat to the window—fast!
> They were together at last.
>
> Off went the girl with the nylon hair,
> Off with the fisherman, with him to fare
> Over the waves and water, and then
> They never came back again.

The absurd bur realistic "nylon hair" demonstrates how Schmidt transforms old fantasy by giving it a current touch, but how she still maintains its authenticity in a new era. The "nylon" appeals to Dutch children, who often have dolls with nylon hair, but also suggests that even in our synthetic age the traditional fairy-tale motifs persist.

The setting for another of Annie Schmidt's imaginative romances is not a far-away tower but rather a cozy hearth, where she has the poker marry the tong, thus charmingly domesticating the old theme of love and marriage. Just as in Andersen's "The Steadfast Tin Soldier" the toys come to life, begin to play, receive guests, and enjoy parties, so in Schmidt's poem **"Miss Poker"** the poker and the tong come to life and merrily dance together "a sarabande by the fire". . . . (pp. 136-38)

The ending of the poem reveals Annie Schmidt's penchant for happy endings, which she considers important for the creation of a secure world for children. In bringing inanimate objects to life and having them marry, like the poker and clout in Andersen's "Little Sandman," the poem stands in a long fairy-tale tradition but seems also realistically and humorously to affirm the warmth, gaiety, and charm of "love in the kitchen."

Like Andersen's tales, Annie Schmidt's poems often contrast the rather stuffy, logical adult world with the highly imaginative world of the child. In "Little Ida's Flowers" Andersen dramatizes something of the complexity of bringing the two worlds together: the jolly student who encourages Ida's dream visions; the tiresome old counselor who calls them "silly rubbish"; the vivid beauty of the flowers who dance for Ida at night; and the resonant amalgam of sorrow and hope in the morning "burial" of the poor dead flowers. In Annie Schmidt's poems, often more literally connected with everyday life, the child's imaginative world usually triumphs, sometimes rather amusingly, over the adult world. In **"Henry John and Henry Joe,"**

Schmidt with the Hans Christian Andersen Award: a gold medal and a diploma.

ditional dream journey, much more realistic than those that Andersen's "Sandman" inspires, but still in the same tradition. In Schmidt's poem the little boy who goes for a long ride in his bed every night—through tunnels, down streets, past flashing traffic lights, and finally to New York—finds his mother very understanding the next morning:

> Then back to his room—quick as a leap—
> For Johnny is tired
> And wants to sleep.
> He says hello to the sheep on the wall
> And falls asleep curled up like a ball.
> Next morning Mom says, "Where have you been?"
> "The same," says John, "to New York again."

Although here the radiant visions of Andersen's dancing flowers are replaced by much more realistic street scenes growing out of Johnny's everyday aspirations to drive off in a car, and although the life-and-death imagery which brings "Little Ida's Flowers" to an almost mystical conclusion is missing, still the reader senses that childhood fantasy is beautifully affirmed in Schmidt's poem and that the amusing and enigmatic aplomb evidenced by both John and his mother establishes a rich and satisfying world which child and adult can inhabit together.

In **"The Time of Elves,"** one of Annie Schmidt's finest poems, the child-hero, whose dream visions take him to the fairy world every night, is confident and adamant in his affirmation of the "never-never land" about which his parents are trying to disillusion him. . . . (pp. 138-40)

Here Annie Schmidt's eclectic style comes to a resonant poetic climax. As always in her poems, there is a plot—something happens. Here the happening, drawn from the long tradition in which Andersen's "Sandman" is a leading example, becomes dreamlike in spite of its realistic dialogue; psychologically authentic in spite of the parents' unqualified disagreement with the child; and, although not evidencing Andersen's frequently religious symbols and overtones, almost mystical in the credo it states in the closing refrain of each stanza ["Pooh, pooh, fiddle dee doo, / nobody knows what's really true!"]. Here, too, the sharp conflict between the child and his parents centers on a world that is visionary—as, for instance, R. L. Stevenson's "The Little Land" charmingly affirms such a world—but it goes beyond mere charm to assert with dramatic power the inescapable conflict between the literal and the imaginative, concluding on the recklessly triumphant credo of the boy's indestructible dream vision.

Even in the detailed denials of the parents there lies a rich psychological affirmation of the very world they are trying to destroy. They admit that there once was (for them?) a "time of elves," since it has "gone away." The colorful clarity with which they detail that world—the darting of the elves, the park, the flowering bushes, the moonlit garden, and the highest dune—belies their disbelief and almost turns their protesting into bravado. At least the fast sleep which blinds the parents to the boy's imaginative flights may be more than literal, for it represents the adult darkness in which the vivid denizens of his dreamworld disappear. But the boy can still "see as a child" as he swoops from one exciting experience to another, finally even playing "hopscotch with the king himself," a delightfully absurd but triumphant climax. The complex credo of the closing couplet allows the reader to believe that for-

a poem with the comical tone of a Belloc or a Silverstein, the twin boys look so much alike that even their father can't tell them apart. Totally exasperated, he finally decides to clip one boy's head completely bald and force the other to wear braids. "All right, from now on I will know who's who," the father says. But with charming simplicity the boys' world still wins out:

> But look, the poor man still can't tell!
> I'll be! I still don't know!
> The bald one, is that Henry John,
> Or is it Henry Joe?
> And so the father still repeats—
> Just as he used to do—
> Now which is which, and what is what,
> And who is really who?

Although this situation is far removed from Andersen's dream visions, it coyly suggests the inability of some adults ever to comprehend or master the child's world.

In other Schmidt poems the gap between the child's world and the adult world is delightfully bridged. Sometimes her adults, like the student Andersen presents in "Little Ida's Flowers," naturally accept the child's dreams and fantasies. Such a merger occurs in one of Schmidt's dream poems, **"The Little Bed That Can Ride."** It contains a tra-

tunately neither the boy himself, nor the protesting parents, nor anyone who is human will ever be able to discover a neat world in which everyone knows "what's really true."

And so, with unending variety, the poems go on, not all equally good, of course. The title poem of the *Pink Lemonade* collection at first seems simply charming, lightly comical, and playfully proper. . . . (pp. 141-42)

Although the charming fairyland of "**Pink Lemonade**" might fit a collection of R. L. Stevenson's poems, here again there are hints of a more versatile and resonant vision supporting Schmidt's images. Delightfully comic touches give a desirable edge to the charm: sipping from the pond [full of pink lemonade] through the "very long, elegant straw" and licking the children who have flopped out of the boat. In fact, underneath the placid charm lies even a hint of fairy-tale horror, lightly suggested by the quick rescue of the children from the "terribly sticky and pink" pond on which they are so serenely sailing.

One concluding poem should serve to round off this introduction to Annie Schmidt and to encourage readers to get to know her better. "**Late at Night**" presents one of her imaginative, traditional visions of the dream world. In fact, it could be considered a direct descendant of Andersen's "The Little Sandman." However, Schmidt's poem takes on a more dreamlike tone, partly through the mesmeric quality of its music. It integrates the two stanzas into an organic psychological unity instead of presenting a dream for each night of the week, and it entirely omits Andersen's moralistic note that naughty children will receive no pleasant dreams.

> As soon as it gets dark out, and the moon begins to shine,
> The people in the houses draw their curtains and their blinds.
> And then the big fat carpenter and Mrs. Taylor, too,
> All go to sleep just like the cat and all her kittens do.
> And all the colts fall fast asleep, each one beside his mother,
> And all the little pigs, and Mr. Farmer and his brother.
> The little calves, the little lambs, and even the big dog,
> And all the little children lie there sleeping like a log.
> And when the hens are sleeping, and the fishes in the streams,
> A little man comes running with his basket full of dreams.
>
> As soon as they start dreaming, all the fishes think they're whales;
> The carpenter starts counting all his hammers and his nails.
> And Mrs. Taylor dreams that she is taking cooking courses,
> And all the little colts that they are finally big horses.
> The children dream of ice cream, and the hens about their eggs,
> And all the little calves that they have very sturdy legs.
> Yes, just at ten, when all the fish are sleeping in their streams,
> That little man comes running with his basket full of dreams.
> He has just one left over, made of yellow, pink, and blue,
> And when you fall asleep tonight, that dream will be for you.

The psychological connections between stanzas one and two demonstrate Schmidt's constant desire to bring the worlds of reality and imagination together. Although some of the dreams that come to Andersen's little boy connect naturally with his everyday life, most of them are pure fantasy—long sailing voyages through fairy worlds to far-off countries. Each of Schmidt's realistic situations in stanza one is soundly developed in the corresponding dream version of stanza two: Mrs. Taylor takes cooking courses, the colts finally become "big horses," and the little calves finally attain "very sturdy legs." Thus fantasy in the fairytale sense of the term is retained but also attains the realistic dimension of the everyday fantasies of life as they appear in "dreams come true."

In the poem's closing lines Schmidt demonstrates both comparisons and contrasts with Andersen's famous tale and his characteristic tendencies. Since her poems never convey an overtly Christian vision, she does not introduce death, the ultimate conveyor of beautiful or horrible dreams, as Andersen does at the end of "The Little Sandman." But, like him, she does step from the imaginative poem into real life as she ends with an invitation to the reader to enter the wide-awake world of her colorful imagination:

> He has just one left over, made of yellow, pink, and blue,
> And when you fall asleep tonight, that dream will be for you.

(pp. 143-44)

Henrietta Ten Harmsel, "Annie M. G. Schmidt: Dutch Children's Poet," in Children's Literature: An Annual of the Modern Language Association Seminar on Children's Literature and The Children's Literature Association, *Vol. 11, 1983, pp. 135-44.*

Toin Duijx

Within the past 40 years Annie M. G. Schmidt has produced a voluminous set of works covering many genres: poems for children and adults, cabaret texts, musicals, children's stories, newspaper columns, radio- and television programs and others. It is difficult to classify her works. Even the most superficial classification into works for children and works for adults is problematical, because there is no difference in tone and hardly any in her subject matter. All of her children's books are intended for readers aged five to 95 and her works for adults show the same open-minded outlook on the world as her children's books do. (pp. 3-4)

1950 saw the publication of her first volume of children's poems, *Het fluitketeltje en andere versjes.* . . (*The little teakettle and other rhymes*); for the next ten years Annie M. G. Schmidt published a volume of poems each year.

In 1960 Jip and Janneke (Mick and Mandy/Bob and Jilly) were born. Eight volumes about the adventures of these two neighbour children were published in all, with excellent illustrations by Fiep Westendrop. Since 1964 children's books by Annie M. G. Schmidt have appeared regularly, and they can all be considered highlights of Dutch children's and juvenile literature. . . .

Annie M. G. Schmidt also became famous in Holland for her poetry. Her volumes of children's poems have never gone out of print. Although her prose has been translated into many languages, only one anthology of her poetry has appeared in English (*Pink Lemonade*).

The poems of Annie M. G. Schmidt are full of fantasy. The influence of Andersen is strong! In one poem the classical princess-in-a-tower theme takes a remarkable turn when the princess' tears cause the surrounding waters to rise and a fisherman comes to rescue her in his boat. They row off on the waves, never to come back again.

Although we are not certain that this is a happy ending, we find many happy endings in the poetry of Annie M. G. Schmidt. This contributes to the creation of a secure world for children by giving them the hope that is necessary for growing old. Her poems are pedagogical, but not didactic or moralistic.

In much of her poetry the logical adult world is contrasted with the highly imaginative world of the child, which usually triumphs rather amazingly in the end. Sometimes her adults naturally accept the child's dreams and fantasies and turn out to be big children themselves rather than grown-ups who always know what's best for the child.

Annie M. G. Schmidt's poems always have some sort of plot—something happening, suspense building up. . . . The poems of Annie M. G. Schmidt represent a turning point in the history of Dutch children's poetry. Although they resemble the nursery rhyme in style, many of them deal with children's resistance to the rules and regulations established by grown-ups. Numerous other poems are on very ordinary, everyday subjects, however.

Generations of Dutch people have been brought up on Jip and Janneke. (p. 4)

250 adventures about Bob and Jilly came into existence, all depicting a cosy and secure world and told from the point of view of the two children. Although adults do play a part in the stories, it is not the common moralizing one. When the children get into mischief or make silly mistakes, an adult lends a hand, but the adults, too, often make blunders.

In the 1970s the Jip and Janneke books were severely criticized for their optimistic outlook on life. Their traditional cast and their failure to deal with social problems like divorce and aggression were considered reason enough to try to banish the series to a museum of antiquated children's books. The children didn't bother about this criticism, however. Librarians and teachers still made propaganda for our heroes and parents continued to read the stories to their children. As one children's book reviewer put it 25 years after the publication of the first edition: "We all know that there is enough trouble ahead of us, but just before bedtime things should be nice and cosy for at least ten minutes." The Jip and Janneke stories confine themselves to matters that are existential to the two children. The very lack of adult commentary and directiveness continues to make the stories attractive to the adult who ceaselessly has to read them aloud.

Abeltje (Little Abel) (1953) and *De A van Abeltje (Abel's A)* (1955) have been considered classics for a long time and jubilee editions of these books appeared in 1986 on the occasion of Schmidt's 75th birthday.

Abeltje is a liftboy at the "Knots" stores. Quite a dull living until one day . . .

> Alfy stretched out his hand and pressed the topmost button that wasn't meant for anything.

> The elevator trembled and shot up swift as an arrow. "Ohhh," Laura cried. She had a terrifying feeling in her stomach. Through the glass door they saw the first floor gliding by, then the second, the third, the fourth . . .

> Now we will arrive at some sort of a loft, Alfy thought. But the elevator didn't slow down. They heard a faint cracking, a ringing of glass. . . . It was as though they were breaking through a glass roof.

> Then the four of them looked through the glass door, paralyzed with terror. The elevator was flying through the skies. It had flown out of the building and was still going upward at a staggering speed.

> "Good heavens!" Alfy said. "Good heavens!"

By way of humor and suspense Annie M. G. Schmidt has succeeded in creating a very genuine juvenile book that captivates readers until the very last page.

In 1964 the volume of fairy-tales, *Heksen en zo (Witches and so on)* was published. A little princess turns herself into a thrush and flies away. A prince goes off to look for her, but "all the thrushes just sang their little tunes that never changed and there was nothing to tell a person which thrush was a princess." The prince nevertheless manages to find her. " 'You must be it,' the prince said. 'Only a princess can be more fond of pearls than of food.' So he threw the witches' net over the bird and all of a sudden a beautiful princess stood in front of him."

Another fairy tale is about a young man who inherits a matchbox into which all sorts of things can be conjured. Then there is the tale of the hairdresser who on his day off happens upon the empire of the frozen ladies, falls in love with one of them and in the end has to watch as she melts away from him. . . . The tales in *Heksen en Zo* repeatedly poke fun at educational ideals and convey contemporary ideas. Yet they have retained the fairy-tale atmosphere of the traditional "Once upon a time . . . "

The other books by Annie M. G. Schmidt, too, contain ironic observations next to sober statements of fact, all clearly described with apparent ease and simplicity. The ready flow of language almost leaves the reader unaware of the skillfulness behind the simplicity and vividness. It is through this skill that Schmidt has leveled the barrier between children's books and literature as a whole, between little rhymes and genuine poetry.

Merry anarchy reigns in her children's books. There is not the slightest trace of moralizing. While much of children's literature teems with know-alls explaining the children's world to them and with kindly aunties conjuring up a rosy atmosphere for them, the books of Annie M. G. Schmidt are real and don't tell lies. Her stories are situated in that enchanted land that comes before the one populated by adults. In this world every word still has meaning and the names still have a magic sound. There we encounter fascinating personalities, like the lady who would rather be a wildcat, revolt against rules invented by adults and an occupation with things that really matter—with a loose tooth, for instance.

Annie M. G. Schmidt is one of the most important writers

for children and adolescents. Perhaps she is even the most important. (pp. 5-6)

> *Toin Duijx, "Quite a Dull Living Until One Day . . . Mick and Mandy Met. Annie M. G. Schmidt, Winner of the Medal for Writing," in Bookbird, No. 3, September 15, 1988, pp. 3-6.*

Wiplala (1962)

Wiplala deserves a double welcome, first as the work of a great writer for children, then for its great intrinsic quality. For this is a very good book. Not many funny books are really consistently funny, and few books for children have a childlike humour. *Wiplala* is pure humour and pure children's book.

It is the story of Mr. Blom, a very serious historian, and his children John and Nelly Delly, and Wiplala. Wiplala is a very small man, the size of a smallish mouse, who has imperfect powers of pixilation. His inefficiency leads him and the Bloms into some unusual adventures, from which they are just able to emerge with safety. In the course of their adventures they meet some extraordinary, and terribly convincing, characters.

Nonsense stories which grow from an inner consistency are rare indeed, and *Wiplala* deserves a place alongside such miniature masterpieces as *Stuart Little* and *Pinky Pye*.

> *A review of "Wiplala," in The Junior Bookshelf, Vol. 26, No. 3, July, 1962, p. 144.*

Wiplala is a charming comic fantasy from the foremost of Dutch writers for children. Its theme is a familiar one, that of humans who are reduced to a height of a few inches, but the development is highly individual and full of genuinely imaginative invention. Designed with great skill and admirably illustrated [by Jenny Dalenoord], this is that rarest of books, a comedy whose humour is consistently on a child's plane but which is neither trivial nor vulgar. It should give a great deal of pleasure.

> *M. S. Crouch, in a review of "Wiplala," in The School Librarian and School Library Review, Vol. 11, No. 2, July, 1962, p. 213.*

Wiplala is infinitesimal—yet he is a man with a rare and irksome power. Capable of changing people and animal into strange creatures, he is not always able to whisk them back to their original form. In this gay fantasy, Wiplala befriends, Mr. Blom, Nelly Delly and Johannes. He "pixilates"—(a nice word from the realm of make-believe) all three to his miniature height at once but cannot remember how to pixilate them back again. Naturally the house is too big, the telephone too cumbersome, the tables, chairs and dishes too large. In the process of adjusting their size to this new world, the three friends are led into many exciting and funny adventures by their leader Wiplala. By the time they are transformed to their proper proportions, Mr. Blom, Nelly Delly and Johannes have little to regret. Their experiences in the world of Wiplala will delight the less earthbound audience.

> *A review of "Wiplala," in Virginia Kirkus'*

Service, *Vol. XXX, No. 15, August 1, 1962, p. 688.*

The basic gaiety and the excitement of the story result mostly from the contrast between the realistic environment and the fantastic happenings caused by Wiplala. The Bloms alone know about the secret of tinkling, but all three of them realize that no one would believe them. They have to play along therefore, whether they like it or not. This results in delightful scenes with people talking past each other and taking reality ad absurdum. (pp. 29-30)

> *A review of "Wiplala," in Bookbird, Vol. VII, No. 1, March 15, 1969, pp. 29-30.*

Bob and Jilly (1976)

The stories bunched together here are well suited to reading aloud to a four-year-old. There is nothing difficult or unusual about the small adventures which two children in adjoining houses enjoy—finding birds' nests, playing "lady and gentleman", making an aeroplane for doll and teddy bear, jumping in puddles and so on. Slightly arch, placidly authentic, the stories lack the verbal and psychological edge of, say, Leila Berg's Little Pete tales, but they have a slender charm of their own. (p. 3007)

> *Margery Fisher, in a review of "Bob and Jilly," in Growing Point, Vol. 15, No. 5, November, 1976, pp. 3005-07.*

Bob and Jilly live next door to each other. They are nice, small children and play every day doing the things small children do. They walk in puddles, eat the apples they are supposed to be delivering to Grandpa, fight when playing doctor and patient, play with toy trains and generally live normal lives. What is extraordinary though is that the writer has managed to compress each episode in the life of Bob and Jilly into two pages or less. This means that each is just the right length for a quick Read Aloud story or, if the child has started to read for himself, it is just the right length to enable him or her to read a complete story without becoming bored or tired. The vocabulary is simple, although not over-easy, and the illustrations [by Carolyn Dinan] bear out the fact that here are normal children who are more often dirty than clean, more often happy than sad. (pp. 331-32)

> *G. L. Hughes, in a review of "Bob and Jilly," in The Junior Bookshelf, Vol. 40, No. 6, December, 1976, pp. 331-32.*

Dusty and Smudge Spill the Paint (1977)

One of four lively tales about a little Dutch girl and her pup who share a talent for getting into mischief, whether with paint, hair-cutting, water or typewriter ribbon. The crisp, amusing texts have a nice touch of the unexpected about them and so have the illustrations [by Fiep Westendorp], with their mildly grotesque version of domestic mishaps.

> *Margery Fisher, in a review of "Dusty and Smudge Spill the Paint," in Growing Point, Vol. 16, No. 5, November, 1977, p. 321.*

The Island of Nose (1977)

Out of England via The Netherlands, this is a 15½" x 11" grotesquerie that alternates pages of senseless plot with [Jan Marinus's] skillfully drafted but over-colored and ham-handed cartoon portraiture. In response to an urgent call for help from his uncle, prime minister of the Island of Nose, big-eared, schoolboy Tom hitchhikes across Holland. A dragonmobile picks him up and speeds him to the estate of wicked Lord Cloverick where Tom and a small dragon are scheduled to provide the climax to an orgiastic costume party—the dragon is to be beheaded and Tom's big ears are to be lopped off. The nude statues at the estate whisper a jingle to Tom that saves him and the dragon from the axe. Lord C's spell is broken. The dragon turns into the daughter of the house and the statues return to life. Tom and the girl pick up a farmer and his wife (who has been transformed by Lord C. into a cow) and press on toward Nose. They embark with four freaks representing the seasons in a mechanized frog and are received by Tom's uncle, now king, who had hoped Tom would help return the seasons to Nose. The resident wizard changes the farmer's wife back to normal and all celebrate madly at Nostril Palace. Landscapes and cityscapes feature graphically drawn fauna and miscreated humans. The most arresting illustration is a group portrait of the costume party where the revelers include a man with three eyes, a woman with three breasts, and a man with three penises. It's not a successful picture book for adults or for children, despite its publisher's "all ages" approach to marketing it.

> *Lillian N. Gerhardt, in a review of "The Island of Nose," in* School Library Journal, *Vol. 24, No. 3, November, 1977, p. 63.*

In *huge* format, we get a tale of a boy who leaves home and has fantastic adventures among monsters, demons, and magicians. What color! What imagination! The book is too large for a library shelf, which may be just as well, for one picture in particular will bring out the raving censor in all but the most liberal librarians.

> *William Cole, in a review of "The Island of Nose," in* Saturday Review, *Vol. 5, No. 5, November 26, 1977, p. 41.*

Tom is unhappy because everybody calls him Big Ears. But he cheers up when he gets a letter from his Uncle Horace asking him to come to the Island of Nose to help the inhabitants. Tom hurries off even though the only thing he's sure about is that he must go to the sea to find the Island of Nose. His adventures along the way may be the surrealistic fantasy the publishers say it is, but the story is so disjointed, the reader gets lost more often than Tom does on his way to the Island of Nose. The illustrations live up to the surrealistic label.

> *Terry Dunnahoo, in a review of "The Island of Nose," in* West Coast Review of Books, *Vol. 4, No. 1, January, 1978, p. 66.*

Dusty and Smudge and the Bride (1977)

Dusty is one of those engaging tomboy girls who creates chaos wherever she goes aided and abetted by Smudge her dog. When the girl next door is getting married Dusty takes Smudge to see the wedding but as she cannot find his lead she resorts to pulling the ribbon out of the typewriter. The catastrophic result when the enthusiastic Smudge wraps himself excitedly around the bridal couple has to be seen to be believed. An engaging small picture book from Holland with witty pictures [by illustrator Fiep Westendorp] which will be much appreciated by four year old horrors.

> *J. Russell, in a review of "Dusty and Smudge and the Bride," in* The Junior Bookshelf, *Vol. 42, No. 1, February, 1978, p. 20.*

Dusty and Smudge Keep Cool (1977)

The weather is hot and Dusty has hair like a bird's nest so she is sent to have it cut. Together with her dog she goes the whole hog and emerges from the hairdresser shaved bald. At first her friends scoff but soon they see the advantages of shaven heads which they inscribe with the legend "We want ices". After a bit of correction on their spelling they get them. An economic tale, simple and to the point, one hopes it will not be copied by too many children or there will be some irate mums about.

The illustrations [by Fiep Westendorp] match the text, clear, amusing and uncluttered.

> *M. R. Hewitt, in a review of "Dusty and Smudge Keep Cool," in* The Junior Bookshelf, *Vol. 42, No. 1, February, 1978, p. 31.*

Bob and Jilly Are Friends (1977)

The familiarity created by a series of books is important to young readers as an aid to understanding. Annie M. G. Schmidt has exploited this in the **"Bob and Jilly"** books, which are translated from the Dutch. There are thirty-seven stories in *Bob and Jilly are Friends* which at one a day is over a month's reading. The stories are one or two pages long and each is an accurately observed and often funny incident. The length of the stories is related to the concentration span of an early-reader and a twist in the tail helps the enthusiastic reader on to the next.

> *Sarah Gray, "Tailor Made," in* The Times Literary Supplement, *No. 3966, April 7, 1978, p. 378.*

Living next door to one another gives Bob and Jilly plenty of opportunity for playing together. It is not clear whose garden the hedgehog appears in, or whether Sausage, the dog whose nose it pricks, is primarily the pet of Bob or Jilly. Although each child does possess two parents, the character known as mother is generally a composite figure on the edge of the children's affairs.

Together the two slide down the bannisters, play cops and robbers, scare the birds from the cherries, eat too much ice cream and buy balloons. The passing of the seasons imposes a vague pattern on their doings.

Thirty-seven tiny stories are told, each on two pages of print. They have a gentle charm and should please everyone except women's libbers, who are likely to be inflamed by the contrast between Bob's ambition to be a pilot and Jilly's wish to become a mother.

R. Baines, in a review of "Bob and Jilly Are Friends," in The Junior Bookshelf, *Vol. 42, No. 3, June, 1978, p. 145.*

Bob and Jilly in Trouble (1980)

[This] is the third collection of thirty very short stories about friends Bob and Jilly. Clear print, simple language, short sentences and repetition of words will bring the tales within the capacity of most beginner readers. (pp. 298-99)

Parents will recognise Bob and Jilly as normal five-year-olds, who quarrel and make friends, have tantrums, over-eat and get into mischief. They will not be so happy when they get away with kicking and biting. (p. 299)

A. Thatcher, in a review of "Bob and Jilly in Trouble," in The Junior Bookshelf, *Vol. 44, No. 6, December, 1980, pp. 298-99.*

Bob and Jilly get into thirty short and varied incidents in this book for pre-school children. Escapades vary from dropping the bread in the coal shed to painting themselves instead of the Easter eggs. The stories—anecdotes is perhaps more descriptive of these short episodes—are realistic to the extreme. Quite often the reader has to stop to think if anything in fact happened in the chapter. When Sausage the dog steals Jilly's slippers she declares when she retrieves them finally that she will never remove them again. When mother tells them how a butterfly will develop from the caterpillar they find, Bob and Jilly ask of every butterfly thereafter, "Is that the caterpillar?" Character development is not much more imaginative than the plot. Bob and Jilly are "nice" children. When Jilly shoves Bob off the stool when he is "shaving" they soon make up. When Bob seesaws too roughly and Jilly's doll falls off, he makes amends. Children might find these stories mildly interesting to listen to, but this is certainly not material that will fire young imaginations nor help to interpret incidents of life.

A review of "Bob and Jilly in Trouble," in Book Window, *Vol. 8, No. 2, Spring, 1981, p. 8.*

Pink Lemonade: Poems for Children (1981)

Most of the forty-two poems in [this] volume are long narratives, several unfortunately crammed onto a double-page spread, together with one or more drawings [by Linda Cares], resulting in some almost illegible pages. Nevertheless, this collection contains some very amusing and fanciful verses that succeed in conveying thoughtfulness and even in teaching something, with wit and charm. The collection is over-long: it might work more effectively with only the better poems included. But some of the poems included here will be enjoyed by both adults and children.

There is, for example, the tale of three imaginative mice and a very dull giraffe, who go for a walk together. When the mice see a wall or a hedge, they imagine all sorts of wonderful things on the other side, but the giraffe tells

them "there's nothing at all." The mice finally desert the giraffe, preferring their imagined images to the dull reality that the giraffe sees. . . . There is **"Weeping Willie,"** who drowns in his own tears; and Lily Jo, a Mexican fly who is very proud because she once bit a Spaniard in the arm, so now she has Spanish blood; and John, a boy who drives to New York every night in his bed. These stories are told at a galloping pace, which perfectly suits them.

In the best poems in this collection language is more than a means by which a story is conveyed; it is delightful for its own sake. When, for example, in **"The Ducks,"** the ducks on the pond decide to turn the tables and feed Johnny, one of them observes that "this is ducky to do." After shopping for, preparing, and feeding Johnny his breakfast, the ducks offhandedly "called out as they walked through the gate, / 'Tomorrow it's your turn; be sure you're not late.'"

In **"Doll Party,"** the queen of the dolls "plans the dolly follies" that all dolls attend one night a year, to dance the "boogie-woog" and drink "dolly pop." (pp. 188-89)

The translations are not perfect; occasionally [Henrietta] Ten Harmsel lapses into a phrase which is awkward or impossible in English. Of twin boys she tells us, "They were exactly even old"; when . . . thieves plan to take the moon from the sky they say, "We're off to rob the moon!" Three towers piled on top of each other are "higher than the highest dome." In spite of these lapses and a tendency to pad the line ("but yet she said she couldn't stop"), Henrietta Ten Harmsel has produced a collection of poems which, for the most part, seem as if they might have been written originally in English.

What emerges from the stronger poems in this collection is the sense that there is a poet who has written them. That poet has a twinkle in her eye, and she knows how to talk to children and to play games with them in a language that they can understand and appreciate. She tells them her fantasies, but she also speaks to them of their concerns, complaints, and dreams through imagery which transforms but does not distort its true subject. Nor is she afraid to be serious with them on occasion. In **"The Proud Little Light,"** an electric Christmas-tree light flies out the window and over the countryside, so that the people who see it believe it is a star. When it falls before the force of wind, sleet, and snow, the people wish on it:

> The people all felt very glad;
>   they all felt warm inside,
> And all of them began to work:
>   "We must work hard," they cried,
>
> "So that the peace for which we wished
>   will really come about."
> As for the star, he fell to earth,
>   and glowed, and faded out.

Perhaps no American adult writing today can risk the simple sentiment of these lines. Yet the electric light has become a symbol, the falling star is a childhood talisman, and the poem's straightforwardness makes it accessible and meaningful, while at the same time encouraging the child to understand it on more than the literal level. I'd like to have had ***Pink Lemonade*** to read when I was a child. (pp. 189-90)

Marilyn Nelson Waniek, "A Trio of Poetry

Books for Children," in Children's Literature: Annual of the Modern Language Association Seminar on Children's Literature and The Children's Literature Association, *Vol. 11, 1983, pp. 182-90.*

Kay Thompson

1912(?)-

American author of picture books.

Thompson is best known as the creator of a series of humorous picture books about Eloise, a spirited, impish six-year-old girl who lives in New York City's Plaza Hotel. A sophisticated and self-assured child whose curiosity and lack of inhibition leads her into a variety of scrapes and adventures, Eloise provides frank observations on the world of adults in stream-of-consciousness language which often includes colorful turns of phrase. Although her first appearance, *Eloise: A Book for Precocious Grown-Ups* (1955), was not intended for children, Eloise quickly became a favorite with young readers as well as with the adults and young adults who gave the book its best-seller status. Thompson has also written two books about the character, *Eloise in Paris* (1957) and *Eloise in Moscow* (1959), in which she provides young readers with tongue-in-cheek looks at French and Russian life, as well as *Eloise at Christmastime* (1958), a book in verse in which Eloise brings Yuletide cheer to the inhabitants of the Plaza. The works are illustrated with black-and-white line drawings by Hilary Knight, whose pictures are often credited with contributing greatly to the success of the books. A singer, arranger, pianist, composer, actress, choreographer, and creator of acts for nightclubs, radio, and television, Thompson developed the character of Eloise while on tour, entertaining her fellow performers with her impressions of a lively six-year-old with a beguiling personality. At the height of the popularity of her works, Thompson founded Eloise Ltd., a company which produced records, postcards, and other related items; the character of Eloise has also inspired dolls, hotel kits, a line of children's clothing, and a television special. Thompson has also been honored by the Plaza Hotel, where she lived and often performed: a portrait of Eloise by Hilary Knight was placed in its lobby and a room was named in honor of the character and furnished according to Knight's illustrations.

(See also *Something about the Author,* Vol. 16 and *Contemporary Authors,* Vols. 85-88.)

AUTHOR'S COMMENTARY

[The following excerpt is from an interview by Cynthia Lindsay.]

In show business the noun "genius" is as loosely used as the adjectives "great," "fabulous" and "sensational." In the case of Kay Thompson they have been applied endlessly and justifiably to her talents as a singer; arranger; pianist; composer; choreographer; actress; creator of nightclub acts, radio and television shows; and author. Her notices have been phenomenal. One critic on *Variety* simply gave up and said, "Miss Thompson is more than an act; she's an experience." Audiences, musicians and critics alike raised their hands and cried, "Hallelujah! Here at last is a *genuine* genius!" (p. 6)

Eloise was conceived, in proper theatrical tradition, while Kay was on a night-club tour. During rehearsals and between shows Kay entertained her fellow performers with the ingeniously mimicked, stream-of-consciousness prattle of a little girl. The little girl's name was Eloise and she became a running gag.

Everybody went along delightedly with the gag, and Kay says about her friends: "Bless them! They kept her alive; I didn't. They just wouldn't let loose of her. They'd call and say, 'Hello, Kay, I don't want to talk to you. I want to talk to Eloise.' Then I would go into the bit, and pretty soon it all became a habit."

Eloise herself was born at the Plaza. Kay was playing in the Persian Room and staying at the hotel. One Sunday a close friend called, started the "Let me talk to Eloise" line, then asked Eloise the answer to some of her own, rather serious, grownup problems. Eloise's wisdom in answering must have impressed the friend, because suddenly she said, "Look, Kay, Eloise is a book—and I've got just the person to illustrate it. His name is Hilary Knight. You come right over here."

"I went over," says Kay, "carrying my own ashtray. This girl doesn't smoke and hates dirt. When I arrived, my friend said, "I'll call Hilary from across the hall.' A Princetonian young man, shy, gentle and soft-spoken, came in. He seemed terribly impressed with me, which naturally impressed me terribly with him. I noticed his hands, which were slim and artistic, and thought that was a step in the right direction. So I wrote twelve lines on a piece of paper and handed it to him. 'I'm going to write this book,' I said. 'I'll leave this with you. If you're interested, get in touch with me.' Then I spoke a few words of Eloisiana and left.

"That Christmas I received a card from Knight. It was an interesting, beautifully executed and highly stylized picture of an angel and Santa Claus, streaking through the sky on a Christmas tree. On the end of the tree, grinning a lovely grin, her wild hair standing on end, was Eloise. It was immediate recognition on my part. There she was. In person. I knew at once Hilary Knight had to illustrate the book. I knew also that I'd have to write it first. So I took three months off and wrote it.

"I holed in at the Plaza and we went to work. I just knew I had to get this done. Eloise was trying to get out. I've never known such stimulation. This girl had complete control of me. Ideas came from everywhere. Hilary and I had immediate understanding. Eloise was a little girl who lived at the Plaza, and she was a very special kind of little girl. We wrote, edited, laughed, outlined, cut, pasted, laughed again, read out loud, laughed and suddenly we had a book. We took Eloise to Jack Goodman at Simon and Schuster and he recognized and understood Eloise immediately. We all became close friends, and the book went into print—only a thousand copies the first time, just to see how it went. It went. The avalanche started and hasn't stopped—we're in the sixth printing, with no sign of a letup." (p. 8)

Cynthia Lindsay, "McCall's Visits Kay Thompson," in McCall's, *Vol. LXXXIV, No. 4, January, 1957, pp. 6, 8, 10.*

Eloise: A Book for Precocious Grown-Ups (1955)

Eloise is likely to be the most controversial literary heroine of the year. She charms and terrifies like a snake. In a new book, *Eloise,* . . . she tells the story of her busy life at New York's staid and splendid Plaza Hotel where she runs down the halls "slomping" her feet, skitters in and out of elevators, haunts the lobby, plagues Room Service with orders for "one raisin" and surveys debutantes, dowagers and doormen with the frank and condescending eyes of a 6-year-old. Intended for grownups, the book may also be popular with children, who will envy Eloise's wicked life.

"The Stately Old Plaza Harbors a Hellcat," in Life *Magazine, Vol. 39, No. 24, December 12, 1955, p. 149.*

Eloise in Paris (1957)

Word must have filtered down even to the grassroots, by now, that Eloise of the Plaza and her entourage (Nanny, Weenie and Skipperdee) have taken themselves to Paris, and, while one's imagination immediately begins to run

riot at the implications of this meeting of two great Natural Forces, even the most riotous imaginings can hardly approach the facts as described by those successful collaborators, Kay Thompson and Hilary Knight. The whole project was the idea of Eloise's invisible but far from hypothetical mother, who visualizes it as a means of getting "roses in our cheeks" (surely a new approach), and by the time the safari gets under way from Fifty-Ninth Street, "everyone knew we were going but no one cried," as Eloise herself chose to put it.

What with Fouquet's, the Etoile, the Apollo Belvedere, champagne with peaches ("You cawn't cawn't cawn't get a good cup of tea"), foot-baths in cucumber milk, Maxim's, Longchamps, and the Flea Market, nobody had any reason to cry in Paris, either, except possibly from sheer exhaustion. "Il y a beaucoup de cobblestones in Paris and some of our feet are getting round." Besides, there was Koki at their disposal ("He is my mother's lawyer's chauffeur"), who weighed 137 pounds without his crest ring and hibernated in the winter in the south of France and possessed a number of invaluable talents, including playing the guitar.

As is always the case with Eloise, there is no paraphrasing her inimitable language and no substitute for the drawings detailing her Odyssey. A sequel rarely comes up to the level of its original impulse, but in Eloise's case, happily, Miss Thompson and Knight seem to have turned the trick.

Sylvia Stallings, "Et Encore la Petite Eloise! Quel Fun!" in New York Herald Tribune Book Review, *December 15, 1957, p. 5.*

Ballyhoo and attendant byproducts are all at work to make us Eloise-conscious and Eloise-resentful. Let us be fair to the author and to Hilary Knight, whose pictures are more telling and rather less knowing than the text. The first few pages will keep most people in stitches. But eventually laughter dies away. There is only one joke, which is Eloise, and she is far too long sustained. There is no story, only Eloise's reaction to Paris, France. Where all the girl's money comes from, why all the skivvies don't throw caution to the wind and strangle her, what she is going to do with all those terrible traumas when she grows up—well nobody really cares. As part of the ballyhoo, many personalities of show business testify to their love of Eloise on the back of the wrapper. Amongst them, Robert Morley says, 'I recommend Eloise' (he does not say what for). A cat may look at a king, and my own quote is that, like rather a lot of children especially fiction, Eloise is hell. (p. 779)

Robin Denniston, "Eloise and Ballyhoo," in The Spectator, *Vol. 201, No. 6805, November 28, 1958, pp. 778-79.*

Eloise at Christmastime (1958)

Eloise "jingles, skibbles, zaps and zimbers" in high fettle and so do the verses but the season is just a little too much for her—her bite isn't quite so sharp as it was—even though she is still very funny to watch in Hilary Knight's pictures.

Ellen Lewis Buell, in a review of "Eloise at

Christmas-Time," in The New York Times Book Review, *November 30, 1958, p. 66.*

[*The following excerpt is taken from a review of* Eloise at Christmastime *and* The Wonderful World of Aunt Tuddy *by Jeremy Gury. Both books are illustrated by Hilary Knight.*]

Aficionados, devotees, lovers of nonconformity,
Your champion's here . . . Eloise
Delicious in a new enormity.
Psychologists blanch at her life so abnormal,
But what matters here is really pictorial.
Eloise careening down the halls of the Plaza,
Christmas joy that is just the bazaza.
Eloise bestowing her Christmas cheer:
Carols and goodies, and for the doorman . . . a
    beer!
Not for our girl any melancholy,
Joyeux Noel, wassail,
Here comes the Plaza's folly.
And what do you suppose will become of Eloise?
We think she's got a relative, now if you please.
Not officially, but still they really are buddies,
Kay Thompson's terror and little Aunt Tuddy.
Bizarre, off beat, and just a wee bit fey.
Eloise and Tuddy, who is going quite gray.
Life for her was not wholly a round of pleasure
Until that gift certificate came in abundant mea-
    sure.
Then everything changed for Aunt Tuddy and
    friends,
Including her cats;
Changed in a twinkling
Just as quick as that!
What happened is fun
If not exactly unique
Because again Hilary Knight rescues
A story that on its own would sink.
Bless Hilary Knight, he's drawn two grand sto-
    ries.
He's created Eloise and Tuddy
And given them their glories.
No matter what the calendar says your age to be,
Eloise and Tuddy will please you
As they did me.

> *Anne Nicholson, "Here's the Plaza Pixie, Eloise, Again, in the Company of a Kindred Spirit," in* Chicago Sunday Tribune Magazine of Books, *December 7, 1958, p. 4.*

Eloise in Moscow (1959)

Kay Thompson's well-known imp pays a visit to Moscow in this new adventure, accomplished only by Nannie and Weenie. (Skipperdee developed a nervous cough and had to be returned to New York and the Plaza.) Eloise's escapades in the Soviet are somewhat slim—rather as if her creator, like Eloise, had spent only a few days there, cooped up in the National Hotel on Gorky St., and mak-

ing occasional sightseeing forays, escorted by Zhenka, the dogmatic guide. Zhenka's whirlwind tour is accompanied by such running comments as: "Is possible to see here So-viets-kaya Square Pleasure Garden with Statues. In for-mer days was Empty Lot. Is not possible to see here water works, gas house, power house, is reconstruction. Is not possible to see here reconstruction, is blizzard." As Eloise says, "Zhenka does absolutely nothing but talk."

Accompanied by Zhenka there are visits to the Moscow subway, the Bolshoi ballet, and the Circus. There is also a brief excursion to a winter resort, which leads to very lit-tle. And Eloise does a certain amount of snooping through hotel keyholes, a la Soviet. Unfortunately, Eloise's usually lively observations are few, and and the humor of most of them is pallid. Only Hilary Knight manages to extract the fullest delight from the onion-domed city, and his fur-hatted and coated heroine. His pictures reach a new height in ornate zaniness, which almost compensates for the sketchy nature of Eloise's latest journey.

> *Anne Brooks, "Crisis in Russia—Eloise Is There," in* New York Herald Tribune Book Review, *December 20, 1959, p. 8.*

Irrepressible as ever, Eloise, Nanny, and Weenie (in a por-cupine coat) visit Moscow, and it is a moot point as to who comes out best, Eloise or the Russians. In any case, it is a lot of fun for the reader as Eloise arrives at the National in a Rolls Royce, tries to cope with a Russian menu, shops in GUM, visits the marble subway, and attends the Bol-shoi. Eloise would not be Eloise, if she did not take a noc-turnal stroll through the hotel, and her keyhole comments on what is going on in the other rooms is one of the best parts of the book. Her digs at Russian life: "Everybody can see what everybody's doing in Moscow." "Is possible to see . . . " "Is not possible to see . . . " will be fully appreciated by young people. This is the best one since the first Eloise.

> *A review of "Eloise in Moscow," in* Junior Li-braries, *Vol. 6, No. 7, March, 1960, p. 152.*

Eloise in Moscow, at first glance a book both for children and about children, is actually neither, although they may well enjoy it as much as their parents. . . . It is very accu-rately aimed, like a good night club act, at a sophisticated adult audience, who live in the same grown-up world as Eloise without getting anything like the uninhibited fun out of it that she does. Children's books, after all, are not *bought* by children, and undoubtedly this is one good way of getting in on the market: write a book ostensibly for children with a strong, though subtle, adult appeal. As to the merits of this, the fourth, Eloise book, it would appear that the theme is virtually inexhaustible, although the mixture becomes slightly more diluted each time.

> *Rory McEwen, "Into Orbit," in* The Specta-tor, *Vol. 205, No. 6907, November 11, 1960, p. 752.*

CUMULATIVE INDEX TO AUTHORS

This index lists all author entries in *Children's Literature Review* and includes cross-references to them in other Gale sources. References in the index are identified as follows:

Author Index

Author Index

CUMULATIVE INDEX TO NATIONALITIES

Nationality Index

CUMULATIVE INDEX TO TITLES

Title Index

Title Index

Title Index

Title Index